the Antiques Collecting Directory

the Antiques Collecting Directory

compiled by Lorraine Johnson

Pan Books Ltd
London and Sydney

Conceived and produced by Johnson Editions Ltd
30 Ingham Road, London NW6 1DE

First published 1983 by Pan Books Ltd
Cavaye Place, London SW10 9PG

0 330 26970 4

CREDITS

Produced by: Imago Publishing Ltd
                    Filmset in Palatino

Phototypeset in Linotron 202 by
Graphicraft Typesetters Hong Kong

Contributor: Gabrielle Townsend
                    Museums and Collections

And with thanks to Kyle Cathie

Trade cut illustrations on pages 108, 168,
173, 177, 181, 199, 201, 205, 211, 255
from the HANDBOOK OF EARLY ADVERTISING ART
Dover Publications, Inc., New York

Antiquity illustrations on pages 10, 14, 27
from THE COMPLETE ENCYCLOPEDIA OF ILLUSTRATION
by P.G. Heck, Crown Publishers, New York

Illustrations of object on pages 25, 37, 61, 77, 91,
95, 120, 150, 180, 202, 230, 239, 240 from
EDWARDIAN SHOPPING by R.H. Langbridge,
David and Charles, Newton Abbot

Lacquer box illustrations on page 200 from
A TREATISE OF JAPANING AND VARNISHING 1688
by John Stalker and George Parker, Alec Tiranti, London

Printed by Gráficas Reunidas, S. A., Madrid, Spain

Attachment to the by-products of the past takes many forms and often presents its own unique dilemmas. You don't have to possess rooms of priceless objects to need a restorer, to want to view a certain collection, to need to contact a specialist dealer. Almost everyone under the spell of antiques, whether collector, dealer, museum buyer or occasional browser has these requirements at one time or another. The following pages are an attempt to make antique collecting easier and more enjoyable.

The first section is concerned with buying and selling antiques, the second with caring for them, and the third with viewing them. Each of these main sections has several divisions as explained below, and each of these is arranged geographically as shown on the opposite page. London, as the international art and antiques centre always appears first within each division, and a map of the capital's postal districts appears on page 61.

The first major section, devoted to buying and selling antiques, is divided into four parts: Specialist Dealers, Antique Markets, Antique Fairs and Auction Houses. These four categories contain all the outlets that our research

uncovered — if we have missed a venue or shop, we are very sorry. Please write to us with the details, care of the publishers, so we can include you in the next edition. In these pages, no attempt is made to advise on what or when to buy or sell. Instead we tell you where.

To protect the buyer and the vendor, there are two well-known trade associations in the U.K.: B.A.D.A. (British Antique Dealers' Association) and L.A.P.A.D.A. (London and Provincial Antique Dealers' Association). Both are non-profitmaking, but the latter is an international concern. Both also aim to establish and maintain confidence between member dealers and the public by annually reviewing the qualifications of each dealership under their aegis. For more information on these bodies, see page 254.

As a guideline to making a successful purchase, bear three things in mind — appearance, age and condition. In other words, always buy the best you can in the best possible condition. If you purchase a damaged piece, get it repaired immediately, or the damage will get worse. The second section of the book covers just this

subject — caring for antiques. It comprises specialist restorers, full and part-time courses and products related to restoration, maintenance and display.

Restorers are divided according to the type of material or kind of article they deal with. Advice on approaching and commissioning those vanishing craftspeople is given in the introduction to that section on page 168. The two pages given over to restoration courses covers those at amateur level and those leading to degree certification. Beginners with only a few hours' experience in restoration are strongly advised not to tackle valuable pieces or complex processes. However, if the task is simple or the only problem is finding the correct materials, the last division of this section will prove useful. On these pages you will find manufacturers of polishes, glasses, chemicals, tools, paints, etc.

The third major section of the book, covering museums and collections, is a distillation of the hundreds of such places now open to the public. For reasons of space, the relevant information has been reduced to the bare minimum. However, the most

NUMERICAL KEY TO COUNTIES ON THE MAP OF THE BRITISH ISLES

1. HIGHLAND	34. GWENT	67. LONDONDERRY
2. GRAMPIAN	35. HEREFORD & WORCESTER	68. ANTRIM
3. TAYSIDE	36. WEST MIDLANDS	69. TYRONE
4. CENTRAL	37. WARWICKSHIRE	70. FERMANAGH
5. FIFE	38. LEICESTERSHIRE	71. ARMAGH
6. STRATHCLYDE	39. SOUTH GLAMORGAN	72. DOWN
7. LOTHIAN	40. GLOUCESTERSHIRE	73. MAYO
8. BORDERS	41. NORTHAMPTONSHIRE	74. SLIGO
9. DUMFRIES & GALLOWAY	42. CAMBRIDGESHIRE	75. LEITRIM
10. CUMBRIA	43. NORFOLK	76. CAVAN
11. NORTHUMBERLAND	44. SUFFOLK	77. MONAGHAN
12. DURHAM	45. BEDFORDSHIRE	78. CONNEMARA
13. TYNE & WEAR	46. BUCKINGHAMSHIRE	79. GALWAY
14. CLEVELAND	47. OXFORDSHIRE	80. ROSCOMMON
15. NORTH YORKSHIRE	48. AVON	81. LONGFORD
16. LANCASHIRE	49. WILTSHIRE	82. MEATH
17. GREATER MANCHESTER	50. BERKSHIRE	83. LOUTH
18. WEST YORKSHIRE	51. HERTFORDSHIRE	84. CLARE
19. HUMBERSIDE	52. ESSEX	85. OFFALY
20. ISLE OF ANGLESEY	53. GREATER LONDON	86. WESTMEATH
21. GWYNEDD	54. KENT	87. DUBLIN
22. CLWYD	55. SURREY	88. KILDARE
23. CHESHIRE	56. HAMPSHIRE	89. KERRY
24. DERBYSHIRE	57. SOMERSET	90. LIMERICK
25. SOUTH YORKSHIRE	58. DEVON	91. TIPPERARY
26. DYFED	59. CORNWALL	92. WICKLOW
27. POWYS	60. DORSET	93. LAOIGHIS
28. SALOP	61. WEST SUSSEX	94. CORK
29. STAFFORDSHIRE	62. EAST SUSSEX	95. WATERFORD
30. NOTTINGHAMSHIRE	63. ISLE OF WIGHT	96. KILKENNY
31. LINCOLNSHIRE	64. ISLE OF MAN	97. CARLOW
32. WEST GLAMORGAN	65. MERSEYSIDE	98. WEXFORD
33. MID GLAMORGAN	66. DONEGAL	

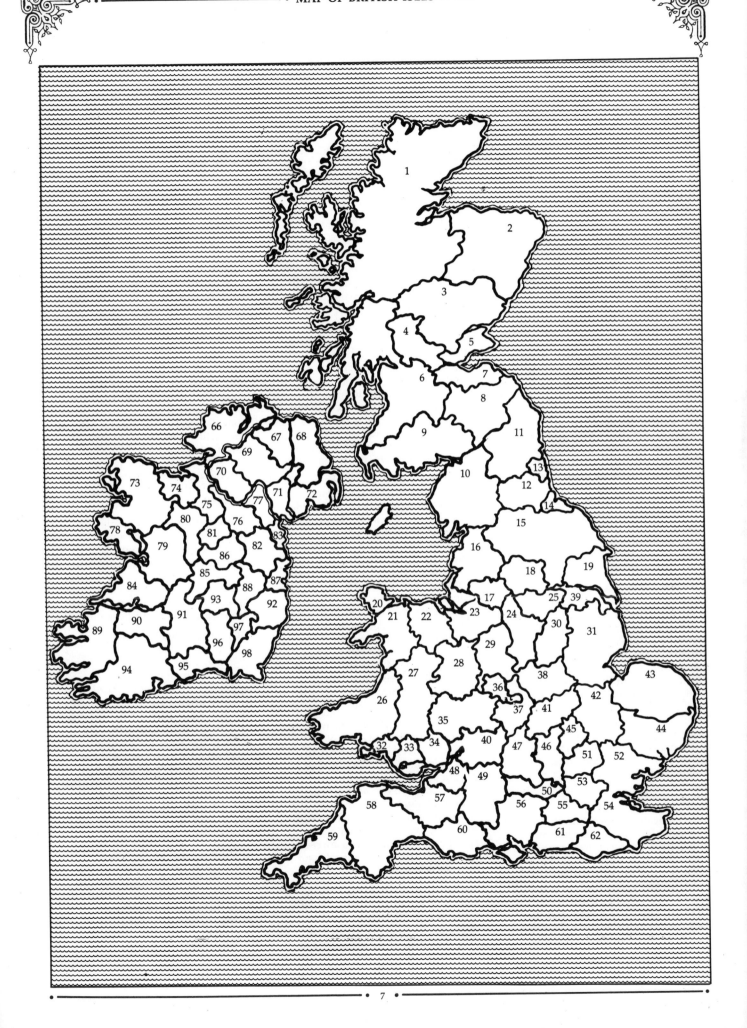

important and best-displayed collections are included and we hope the selection will prove of interest to antique lovers of all ages and means. Opening times are given throughout,

but because of recent national cuts in the arts budget, the times are subject to fluctuation. A phone call is advised before arranging a visit.

Finally, the last pages of the book are devoted to useful addresses including the specialist packers and shippers throughout the U.K.

BUYING AND SELLING ANTIQUES

This section is concerned with buying and selling antiques and comprises four parts: Specialist Dealers, Antique Markets, Antiques Fairs and Auction Houses and Salerooms. Each of these is an excellent place for buying, but is also a venue for selling any item you have tired of, or on which you want to realize a gain. When buying, markets and auctions are arguably the best sources of bargains, because there are only low dealer's overheads. On the other hand, in the excitement of the moment, it's easy to develop "auction or market fever" and make unwise purchases. Antiques fairs, for their part, are a very mixed bag – some deal only in the finest pieces, while others are totally eclectic. Again, a keen eye and calm nerves are an advantage. As for dealers in shops, they are the backbone of the trade and more often than not have a consistent quality of stock as well as a good knowledge of their field.

Of course, selling is always more difficult. If possible, sell to a friend or a private collector; if not, you could ask a dealer to place the item in his or her shop on a sale-or-return basis, for which you may be charged a small commission. Alternatively, put the item in an auction. Local auctions and salerooms will realize the money more quickly, but if the item is fairly valuable, you are advised to place it with one of the larger, more prestigious houses. See pages 160–167 for information on buying, selling and bidding, plus a list of auction houses and salerooms in the U.K.

As a guideline, there are three requisites for making a successful purchase. First, buy only what you really like. That way, your home or collection will develop a style of its own. Secondly, buy the best you can afford – if you need a chest of drawers, stretch your resources to buy the best possible piece. Thirdly, buy in perfect condition if possible,

and on no account buy an imperfect piece if you have no intention of getting it restored. If you never seem to get around to carrying out repairs, no matter how small, avoid imperfect pieces.

When considering purchasing an item which needs to be restored, it is advisable to seek the advice of a qualified restorer before making the purchase. In this way, the overall price of the piece including restoration can be calculated. In this instance the dealer may be able to recommend a suitable restorer. Alternatively, refer to the section on Specialist Restorers, pages 168–221.

In the following pages, we have included about 3,500 specialist dealers throughout the U.K. In order to qualify as a specialist, the dealer must fulfil at least one of the following four requirements – the articles he or she sells are made from a particular material, e.g. glass; may be in a category or from a manufacturer within that material, e.g. Lalique; may come from a specific period or date; or may be a certain object made from the material, e.g. paperweights. Thus, careful reading of each entry within the various sub-sections should facilitate your search.

Obviously, because of the nature of antiques, even those dealers who specialise will not always have precisely what you are looking for. However, once alerted to the object of your search, the dealer may suggest that you contact a colleague or offer to watch out for the item over the forthcoming weeks. (Obviously, never approach a dealer with a specific request unless you are ready to house the piece immediately and have sufficient funds.)

Antique markets and fairs provide additional hunting grounds, though are far less predictable in their offerings. Antique market stalls are ever-changing, so it's impossible to

give definite listings, although phone numbers and the number of units within each market are given, plus an idea of the type of goods sold. The market section is divided into geographical areas like the rest of the book. For a map of the British Isles, see page 7.

Antiques fairs are grouped under the months in which they occur, although this is by no means a complete listing. As with markets, the venues and sponsors change, so consult local newspapers for news of the smaller, more obscure fairs. The final part of this section, Auction Houses and Salerooms, is arranged first by county, and then alphabetically by town, on pages 160–167.

The above listings as complete as possible. However, the author would be grateful to know to any specialist dealers, fairs, markets or auctions which are unlisted. Letters can be sent care of the publisher, and apologies are extended to anyone who has inadvertently been omitted.

Acquiring antiques is a delightful, though sometimes frustrating pastime; it can also be a rewarding and educational pursuit, if approached intelligently. Lord Clark, the well-known art historian, makes the distinction between the acquirer and the collector, saying that the former buys without thought, responding to whim and without any intention of finding out about the object. The collector, on the other hand, learns about his field of interest, makes careful choices and has an over-all idea of what he wants his collection to be.

Perhaps most of us don't think of ourselves as serious collectors, but anyone with a selection of antiques surely has aspirations to be one. We hope this section will make the process of selecting easier and more enjoyable.

Above: St Charalambos, a Greek saint, within an arched and carved frame panel, circa 1690, courtesy of Maria Andipa Icon Gallery.

LONDON

MARIA ANDIPA ICON GALLERY
162 Walton Street
London SW3
Tel: (01) 589 2371
Greek, Russian, Byzantine, Coptic and Syrian icons, jewellery and embroideries.

IAN AULD
1 Gateway Arcade
Camden Passage
London N1
Tel: (01) 359 1440
African and Oceanic ethnographic items.

AXIA
43 Pembridge Villas
London W11
Tel: (01) 727 9724
Islamic and Byzantine ceramics.

CALL TO ARMS
79 Upper Street
London N1
Tel: (01) 359 0501
Red Indian artifacts, specialising in war items.

COBWEB
2 Englands Lane
London NW3
Tel: (01) 586 4605
Ancient European and Far Eastern pottery, bronze, and carvings.

CORK STREET FINE ARTS LTD
5–6 Cork Street
London W1
Tel: (01) 734 9179
Antiquities from 1400 B.C. on.

CHARLES EDE LTD
37 Brook Street
London W1Y 1AJ
Tel: (01) 493 4944
Greek, Roman, Egyptian and Near Eastern antiquities, dating from before 450 A.D., and including pottery, sculpture, glass, jewellery and documents. See overleaf for illustration.

PHILIP GOLDMAN
30 Cyprus Road
London N3
Tel: (01) 346 8413 (By appointment only)
Primitives from South East Asia and Oceanic.

ROBERT HALES ANTIQUES LTD
133 Kensington Church Street
London W8
Tel: (01) 229 3887
17th to 19th c. primitive Oceanic, African and American art.

HARRIS AND FRANK LTD
53 Holland Park
London W11 3RS
Tel:(01) 727 4769 (By appointment only)
Russian icons.

ERIC HUDES
142 Portobello Road
London W11
Tel: (0376) 83767 (Home)
Oriental ceramics from 900 A.D.

PETER KEMP
174a Kensington Church Street
London W8
Tel: (01) 229 2988
Chinese porcelain from the 10th c. and mediaeval bronzes.

MOMTAZ GALLERY LTD
42 Pembridge Road
London W11
Tel: (01) 229 5579
Islamic pottery from 9th to 14th c.

SYDNEY L. MOSS LTD
51 Brook Street
London W1
Tel: (01) 629 4670/493 7374
Chinese and Japanese ceramics from 1500 B.C.

NIHON TOKEN
23 Museum Street
London WC1A 1JT
Tel: (01) 580 6511
Japanese antiquities including ceramics, bronzes, lacquer, sculpture, paintings, furniture and arms.

JACK OGDEN
42 Duke Street
London SW1
Tel: (01) 930 3353
Antiquities including gold jewellery, marbles, bronzes and pottery. See entry under "Specialist Dealers, Jewellery" for illustration.

THE OLD DRURY
187 Drury Lane
London WC2
Tel: (01) 242 4939
Greek, Roman, Cypriot, Phoenician, Indian, African, Far Eastern, Egyptian, pre-Columbian, tribal and ethnic antiquities.

PHILLIPS AND PAGE LTD
50 Kensington Church Street
London W8
Tel: (01) 937 5839
Ethiopian crosses.

RABIRAFFI ANCIENT ART
36 Davies Street
London W1
Tel: (01) 499 9363/9384
9th to 13 to c. Islamic pottery and first to sixth c. Roman glass.

ANTIQUITIES

SHEPPARD AND COOPER LTD
5–6 Cork Street
London W1
Tel: (01) 734 9179
Glass from 1400 B.C.–1800 A.D.

JOHN SPARKS LTD
128 Mount Street
London W1
Tel: (01) 499 1932/2265
Chinese pottery and porcelain, B.C. to late 18th c.

SPINK AND SON LTD
5, 6 and 7 King Street
London SW1
Tel: (01) 930 7888
Ancient coins, sculpture and objets d'art. For illustrations, see entry under "Coins and Medals".

ROBIN SYMES LTD
3 Ormond Yard
Duke of York Street
London SW1
Tel: (01) 930 9856/7
Roman, Greek and Egyptian antiquities including bronzes, marbles, vases and jewellery.

TEMPLE GALLERY
4 Yeoman's Row
London SW3
Tel: (01) 589 6622
13th to 19th c. Russian and Greek icons.

VALE ANTIQUES
21 Tranquil Vale
London SE3 OBU
Tel: (01) 852 9817
Pottery, jewellery, seals and bronzes from 3000 B.C.–1500 A.D.

WANGCHUCK
Thondup Studio
The Clergy House
London EC2
Tel: (01) 729 4969
Pre-18th c. Chinese and pre-19th c. Tibetan, Japanese and Buddhist

SOUTH AND SOUTHEAST ENGLAND

ERIC HUDES
Paigles, Perry Green
Bradwell, Braintree, Essex CM7 8ES
Tel: (0376) 83767
Oriental ceramics from 900 A.D.

Below: 15th c. bronze French seal matrix inscribed for the villagers and officials of Fontainnes, courtesy of Vale Antiques.

MALDWYN ANTIQUES
12 and 12a Beynon Parade
Carshalton, Surrey
Tel: (01) 669 0793 and 393 4530 (Home)
Egyptian, Grecian and Roman pottery.

ODELL ANTIQUITIES
Millmead
Wonersh, Surrey GU5 OQL
Tel: (0483) 892375
Egyptian, Greek, Roman and Oriental icons and antiquities.

Below: Egyptian XXVIth dynasty head, courtesy of Odell Antiquities.

Above: Bell Krater pot, made in the Greek colonies in southern Italy in 4th c. B.C., courtesy of Charles Ede Ltd.

SOUTHWEST ENGLAND AND WALES

CAMPBELL AND MARSH
Old Barn
Perranarworthal
Truro, Cornwall TR3 7NY
Tel: (0872) 863831
Ethnographica, especially from West Africa.

Above: Jacobean-style oak panelling having carved strapwork pilasters and a lozenge frieze with dentil cornice above, reproduced from old timbers, courtesy of T. Crowther and Son Ltd.

LONDON

GEORGE AMOS AND SONS
Lion Works
New End Square
London NW3
Tel: (01) 435 0052/3
Architectural items including panelling, fireplaces and fittings.

THE ARCHITECTURAL ANTIQUE MARKET
4–8 Highgate High Street
London N6
Tel: (01) 341 3761/348 4846/340 8476/359 4330 and 830 5256
Architectural salvage items including fireplaces, stained glass, doors, tiles, and ironwork, 17th to 20th c.

BALCOMBE GALLERIES
7 Stanley Studios
Park Walk
London SW10
Tel: (01) 352 4353 and 352 9996 (Home)
Garden furniture and urns.

T.F. BUCKLE LTD
427 Kings Road
London SW10
Tel: (01) 352 0952
Architectural features such as columns, pilasters, architraves, doors, windows and spiral staircases.

CHAPMAN AND DAVIES ANTIQUES
10 Theberton Street
London N1 OQX
Tel: (01) 226 5565/348 4846/359 4330
Stained glass panels, especially those just before and after turn of the century.

T. CROWTHER AND SON LTD
282 North End Road
London SW6 1NH
Tel: (01) 385 1375/7
Oak and pine panelling plus panelling and fitments made to order from old timber. Also 18th c. carved wood and marble chimneypieces and garden statuary.

CSAKY'S ANTIQUES
133 Putney Bridge Road
London SW15
Tel: (01) 870 1525
Stripped pine doors.

CHRISTOPHER GIBBS LTD
118 New Bond Street
London W1
Tel: (01) 629 2008/9
Garden statuary.

HALLIDAYS CARVED PINE MANTELPIECES LTD
28 Beauchamp Place
London SW3
Tel: (01) 589 5534
Carved pine and marble mantlepieces, grates, corner cupboards, and panelling.

HASLAM AND WHITEWAY
105 Kensington Church Street
London W8
Tel: (01) 229 1145
Stained glass, from Victorian onwards.

LAMONT ANTIQUES
Newhams Row
175 Bermondsey Street
London SE1
Tel: (01) 403 0126
Architectural items including leaded light windows.

A. LANDAU
45 Mill Lane
London NW6
Tel: (01) 794 3028 and 452 3993 (Home)
Late Victorian and Edwardian stained glass including Art Nouveau.

THE LONDON ARCHITECTURAL SALVAGE AND SUPPLY COMPANY LTD
Mark Street (Off Paul Street)
London EC2A 4ER
Tel: (01) 739 0448/9
Architectural items such as doors, flooring, columns, railings, fireplaces, shop fittings, doors, shutters, windows, panelling, door furniture and secondhand timber.

MALLETT AT BOURDON HOUSE LTD
2 Davies Street
London W1Y 1LJ
Tel: (01) 629 2444/5
Garden statuary and ornaments. See overleaf for illustration.

JACK MARSHALL AND SUE WIGFIELD
228 Burrage Road
London SE18 7JU
Tel: (01) 894 4568
Antique and second-hand spiral staircases.

KEN NEGUS LTD
44 South Side
Clapham Common
London SW4 9BU
Tel: (01) 720 2938
Restoration of stonework brickwork, marble, terracotta, etc, both internally and externally.

PAGEANT ANTIQUES
122 Dawes Road
London SW6
Tel: (01) 385 7739
Architectural fittings, fireplaces, panelling, period architraves, doors, plus wrought and cast iron staircases.

Left: Italian 14th c. Istrian marble font, circa 1370, courtesy of Mallett and Son Ltd.

REYNOLDS ANTIQUES LTD
30 Aldermans Hill
London N13
Tel: (01) 886 0917/803 4413/886 6791
Architectural items including fireplaces, stained and leaded glass and bathroom fittings.

SCALLYWAG
Wren Road, Camberwell Green
London SE5
Tel: (01) 701 5353
Architectural items including doors, panelling, mouldings, church furnishings, staircases and fire surrounds.

TOTTERS
236 Fore Street
London N18
Tel: (01) 803 4413/886 0917/886 6791
Architectural items, including fireplaces, stained and leaded glass and bathroom fittings.

R. WEARN AND SON LTD
322 Kings Road
London SW3
Tel: (01) 352 3918
Garden ornaments.

Below: One of a pair of marble caryatids, formerly at Richmond Terrace, Whitehall, Westminster, courtesy of Pageant Antiques.

PENNY FARTHING ANTIQUES ARCADE
177 Bermondsey Street
London SE1
Tel: (01) 407 5171 and 777 1185 (Home)
Stained glass.

E.S. PHILLIPS AND SON
99 Portobello Road
London W11
Tel: (01) 229 2213
Stained glass windows, architectural fittings, panelling, flooring, and fireplaces.

THE PINE MINE
100 and 318 Wandsworth Bridge Road
London SW6
Tel: (01) 736 1092/5312
Chimneypieces, mantels, doors and fittings in pine.

POTTLES
6 Camden Walk, Camden Passage
London N1
Tel: (01) 226 9438
Old shop fittings.

PRINCEDALE ANTIQUES
56 Eden Grove
London N7
Tel: (01) 727 0868/609 4238
19th and early 20th c. architectural fittings.

PRINCEDALE ANTIQUES
70 Princedale Road, London W11
Tel: (01) 727 0868/609 4238
Architectural fittings.

BARRIE QUINN ANTIQUES
1, 3 and 4 Broxholme House
New Kings Road, London SW6
Tel: (01) 736 4747
Garden statues and furniture; specialising in Victorian jardinières and wire planters.

RAG AND BONE
109 Kirkdale Road, London SE26
Tel: (01) 699 1363 and 692 2845 (Home)
Stained glass.

RELIC ANTIQUES AT CAMDEN LOCK
248 Camden High Street
London NW1
Tel: (01) 485 8072/388 2691/586 7648
19th and early 20th c. shop, pub and marine items plus fair ground art and animals.

WHITEWAY AND WALDRON LTD
305 Munster Road
London SW6
Tel: (01) 381 3195
Architectural fittings including stained glass panels, panelling, doors, fire surrounds, ironwork from 1750 and carved church woodwork from 1850. See opposite for illustration.

SOUTH AND SOUTHEAST ENGLAND

BALCOMBE GALLERIES
Balcombe, Sussex
Tel: (044 483) 439
Spiral staircases and garden furniture.

CROWTHER OF SYON LODGE LTD
Busch Corner, London Road
Isleworth, Middx.
Tel: (01) 560 7978
Architectural decorations including panelling, chimney pieces, marble and bronze statues, wrought iron entrance gates and garden ornaments such as fountains and seating. See overleaf for illustration.

MARBLE HILL GALLERY
72 Richmond Road
Twickenham, Middx
Tel: (01) 892 1488
Pine and French marble mantels.

REDUNDANT CHURCH FURNISHINGS
The Warren, Church Road
Woldingham, Surrey
Tel: Woldingham 2366
Victorian ecclesiastical fixtures and fittings.

THE RICHMOND ANTIQUARY
28 Hill Rise, Richmond, Surrey
Tel: (01) 948 0583 and Egham 7229 (Home)
Architectural antiques including doors, mantelpieces and panelling.

SOUTHWEST ENGLAND AND WALES

ARCHITECTURAL HERITAGE OF CHELTENHAM
Boddington Manor, Boddington
Nr Cheltenham, Glos GL51 0TJ
Tel: (024 268) 741/(0242) 22191
17th to 19th c. panelled rooms, doors, stained glass, pub, shop and civic exteriors, garden statuary, gates and period flooring. Brochure sent upon request.

FROM DOOR TO DOOR
The Old Smithy
Cerrigydrudion, N Wales
Tel: (0490 82) 491
Architectural fittings including doors, spindles, newel posts, pews and fire surrounds.

RELIC ANTIQUES
Brillscott Farm
Lea, Nr Malmesbury, Wilts
Tel: (06662) 2332
Architectural antiques including fairground art and animals plus shop and pub fittings.

Above right: Part of a stained glass window by Sir Edward Burne-Jones, as restored by Whiteway and Waldron Ltd.

Right: "The Walnut Billiard Room" rescued from Little Aston Hall, courtesy of Architectural Heritage of Cheltenham.

Above: Two 18th c. figures from a set of four depicting the seasons in carved stone, courtesy of Crowther of Syon Lodge Ltd.

WALCOT RECLAMATION
108 Walcot Street
Bath, Avon BA1 5BG
Tel: (0225) 310182
Architectural ornaments including doors, railings, architraves, doors, shutters, stained glass panels, fire surrounds, spiral staircases, flooring, and bathroom antiques.

MIDLANDS AND EAST ANGLIA

USHER
South Hill
42 Southgate Street
Bury St Edmunds, Suffolk
Tel: (0284) 4838
Carved pine mantlepieces and garden ornaments.

NORTH OF ENGLAND AND SCOTLAND

ROBERT AAGAARD LTD
Frogmire House
Stockwell Road
Knaresborough, N Yorkshire
Tel: (0423) 864805
17th to 19th c. marble and pine interiors including panels and chimneypieces. See entry under "Fireplaces" for illustration.

H.H. CRAFTS
325 Abbeydale Road·
Sheffield, S Yorkshire ST15
Tel: (0742) 589872
Architectural conservationists with stained and etched glass, wood panelling, doors, carved woodwork, fire surrounds, and ornamental cast iron work. Will remove from site and deliver to clients.

**ANDY THORNTON
ARCHITECTURAL ANTIQUES LTD**
Ainleys Industrial Estate
Ellan, W Yorkshire HX5 9JP
Tel: (0422) 78125/6
Large-scale architectural fittings including pulpits, shop fronts, staircases, stained glass and doors.

LONDON

CALL TO ARMS
79 Upper Street
London N1
Tel: (01) 359 0501
World War I and II items, including Nazi militaria and also antique guns.

COLLECTOR'S CORNER
1 North Cross Road
East Dulwich
London SE22 9ET
Tel: (01) 693 6285
Worldwide military and parachute insignia, specialising in German items from 1923–1945, plus head wear and U.S. police badges and patches, but excluding firearms and edged weapons.

PETER DALE LTD
11/12 Royal Opera Arcade
London SW1
Tel: (01) 930 3695
16th to 19th c. firearms, 14th to 19th c. armour and edged weapons plus militaria and campaign medals.

Right: Interior view showing a selection of arms and armour, courtesy of Peter Dale Ltd.

Left: Early 18th c. Indian mogul dagger with jade handle which has been set with rubies in gold. Bottom chape in silver and steel blade with silver inlay, courtesy of Robert Hales Antiques Ltd.

ROBERT HALES ANTIQUES LTD
133 Kensington Church Street
London W8
Tel: (01) 229 3887
17th to 19th c. Oriental and Islamic arms and armour.

R. HOLT AND COMPANY LTD
98 Hatton Garden
London EC1
Tel: (01) 405 5286
Chinese swords.

NIHON TOKEN
23 Museum Street
London WC1
Tel: (01) 580 6511 and 444 6726 (Home)
Japanese swords, armour and related accessories.

PUG ANTIQUES
191/193 Hartfield Road
London SW19
Tel: (01) 542 3409 and Ashtead 77342 (Home)
Arms, armour, and militaria from 1750 on.

HOWARD RICKETTS LTD
180 New Bond Street
London W1
Tel: (01) 499 7357 and 409 1071
European and Oriental arms.

Right: 15th c. Lokinko sword guard with gold and silver inlay, showing temples and mountains around a beautiful lake, courtesy of Nihon Token.

TRADITION
5a and 5b Shepherd Street
London W1Y 7LD
Tel: (01) 493 7452
Hand-made military miniatures and all forms of militaria, including uniforms and arms.

VALE ANTIQUES
21 Tranquil Vale
London SE3 OBU
Tel: (01) 852 9817
British war medals and decorations.

DAVID YOUNG
104 Chepstow Road
London W2
Tel: (01) 229 0660
British militaria and weapons.

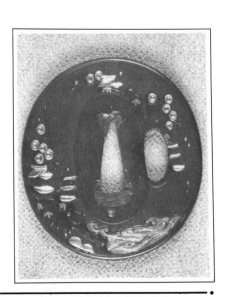

SOUTH AND SOUTHEAST ENGLAND

BRIGHTON ANTIQUES GALLERY
41 Meetinghouse Lane
Brighton, Sussex
Tel: (0273) 26693
Firearms, edged weapons, orders, decorations, medals, badges, and uniforms, and head-dresses specialising in Kaiser Reich and Third Reich periods. Catalogue available.

GREAT GROOMS ANTIQUES LTD
Parbrook
Billingshurst, Sussex
Tel: (040 381) 2263
19th and early 20th c. African swords.

MALDWYN ANTIQUES
12 and 12a Beynon Parade
Carshalton, Surrey
Tel: (01) 669 0793 and 393 4530 (Home)
Guns from 1600–1870.

DAVID PATTERSON
20 Queen Street
Lostwithiel, Cornwall
Tel: (0208) 872879
Guns from 1740–1800.

TRINITY ANTIQUES
7 Trinity Street
Colchester, Essex
Tel: (0206) 77775
Militaria from 1800 onwards.

WARNER'S MILITARY SPECIALISTS
2 The Apple Market
Eden Street
Kingston-upon-Thames, Surrey
(Mail order only)
16th to 19th c. arms and armour including Nazi and Imperial German regalia.

SOUTHWEST ENGLAND AND WALES

ANGHARAD'S ANTIQUES
106 Chester Road
Shotton, Clwyd, Wales
Tel: (0244) 812240
19th c. pistols and cannons.

PENYGROES ANTIQUES
19a Water Street
Penygroes, Gwynedd, Wales
Tel: (028 689) 332
18th and 19th c. swords and guns.

MIDLANDS AND EAST ANGLIA

J.C. RISEBOROUGH
Coltishall Antiques Centre
Norwich, Norfolk
Tel: (0603) 738306
Antique guns, pistols, swords, and bayonets.

WESTLEY RICHARDS AND COMPANY LTD
Grange Road
Birmingham B29 6AR
Tel: (021) 472 2953
Percussion pistols and guns, flint-lock pistols and guns, plus armour, swords, daggers, bows and arrows.

Right: Spanish rapier and maingauche, circa 1700, courtesy of Andrew Spencer.

NORTH OF ENGLAND AND SCOTLAND

ANTIQUE MODELS AND MILITARIA
38 Union Place
Dundee, Tayside Scotland
Tel: (0382) 86649
Badges, medals and weapons from 1850.

JEFFERY BATES AND ANDREW BOTTOMLEY
P.O. Box 4
Holmfirth, Yorkshire
Tel: (0484) 89 5234
Antique arms and armour.

NICHOLSON ANTIQUES
3 Cranston Street
and
297 Canongate
Edinburgh, Lothian, Scotland
Tel: (031) 225 5918
18th and 19th c. weapons.

ANDREW SPENCER
32 Rotcher Hill
Holmfirth, Yorkshire
Tel: (048 489) 5234
Arms and armour including Japanese sword fittings. For illustration of Japanese sword fittings see entry under "Oriental".

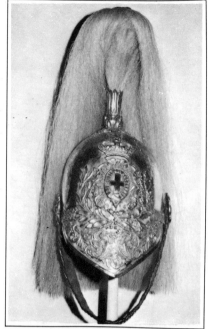

Above right: Household cavalry officer's helmet, courtesy of Warner's Military Specialists.

Right: Original oil painting on canvas depicting the Kaiser and Field-Marshall Von Hindenburg at the Front, signed and dated Berlin 1915 (background); a Prussian Garde-du-Korps Gala helmet of an officer in the Kaiser's personal bodyguard (left); an Imperial German reservist's Schnaps flask (below); an officer's dress sword of the Prussian Horse Artillery of The Guard (centre); and an Imperial German reservist's beer stein with military scenes (right), courtesy of the Brighton Antiques Gallery.

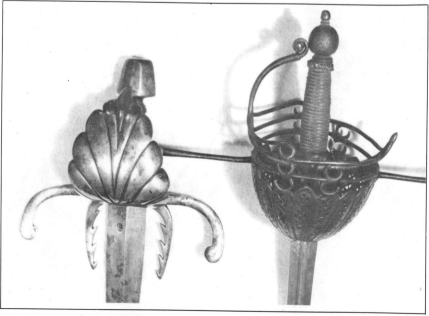

ART NOUVEAU AND ART DECO

Left: Dressing table covered in silverleaf with jade-coloured enamelling surrounding the contours, and glass ring handles attached with eau-de-Nil silk loops, standing on eight-sided ebony feet. It was exhibited at the Paris Exhibitions of 1925, made by W. Rowcliff for Sir Edward Mausse, courtesy of David Gill.

JUDY FOX
81 Portobello Road
London W11
Tel: (01) 229 8130
Late 19th to early 20th c. pottery, including Art Deco.

GALLERY 25
4 Halkin Arcade, Motcomb Street
London SW1
Tel: (01) 235 5178
Art glass and signed furniture from 1900–1930.

GALERIE 1900
267 Camden High Street
London NW1
Tel: (01) 485 1001 and 969 1803 (Home)
Art Nouveau and Art Deco glass, pottery metalware, lighting and furnishings.

DAVID GILL
25 Palace Gate
London W8
Tel: (01) 584 9184 (By appointment only)
Art Deco furniture, paintings and sculpture.

DAN KLEIN LTD
11 Halkin Arcade
Motcomb Street
London SW1
Tel: (01) 245 9868
Furniture, jewellery and decorative art from 1850–1960 including Art Deco and Art Nouveau items. See overleaf for illustration.

A. LANDAU
45 Mill Lane
London NW6
Tel: (01) 794 3028 and 452 3993 (Home)
Art Nouveau furniture, tiles and stained glass

Below: "The Oargirl" sporting figure by F. Preiss, in bronze and ivory on bronze and onyx base, circa 1930, courtesy of Catspa.

LONDON

ASTORIA
222 Munster Road
London SW6
Tel: (01) 385 9888
Art Deco furniture, ceramics, glass, lighting, statuary, cocktail and smoking accessories, specialising in jewellery and the visual arts. See entry under "Specialist Dealers, Jewellery"

BALCOMBE GALLERIES
7 Stanley Studios, Park Walk
London SW10
Tel: (01) 352 4353 and 352 9996 (Home)
Art Nouveau including pewter.

CATHERWOOD AND COMPANY
334 Wandsworth Bridge Road
London SW6
Tel: (01) 736 0542
Art Nouveau furniture.

CATSPA
Chenil Gallery
Kings Road
London SW6
Tel: (01) 883 3992 (By appointment only)
Art Nouveau and Art Deco bronze and ivory figures especially by Preiss, Chiparus and Lorenzyl.

CHAPMAN AND DAVIES ANTIQUES
10 Theberton Street
London N1 0QX
Tel: (01) 226 5565
Gothic Revival and Arts and Crafts furniture.

SHERIDAN COAKLEY ART DECO
12 Hollywood Road
London SW10
Tel: (01) 351 1771
Art Nouveau and Art Deco furniture.

COBRA AND BELLAMY
149 Sloane Street
London SW1
Tel: (01) 730 2823
Late 19th and early 20th c. furniture, silver, jewellery, glass, sculpture and paintings, including Decorative Arts and Art Deco.

JOAN COLLINS
Shepherds Arcade
153 Portobello Road, London W11
Tel: Not Available
Art Nouveau and Art Deco including silver.

THE FACADE
196 Westbourne Grove, London W11
Tel: (01) 727 2159
Art Deco light fixtures.

FOREST HILL ANTIQUES
7 Davids Road, London SE23
Tel: (01) 699 4061 and 693 5050 (Home)
Art Nouveau and Art Deco furniture, glass, china and clocks.

ART NOUVEAU AND ART DECO

LEINSTER FINE ART
9 Hereford Road
London W2 4AB
Tel: (01) 229 9985
Art Nouveau glass, lighting, prints and posters. For illustration, see entry under "Lighting".

NELLIE LENSON AND ROY SMITH
16 Pierrepont Row
London N1
Tel: (01) 226 2423
Vienna bronzes.

LIBERTY AND COMPANY LTD
Regent Street
London W1
Tel: (01) 734 1234
Art Nouveau pewter, silver, glass and furniture.

LORDS GALLERY
26 Wellington Road
London NW8
Tel: (01) 722 4444
19th and early 20th c. original posters including Kurt Schwitters and Friedrich Meckseper.

MARTINS-FORREST ANTIQUES
8 Halkin Arcade, Motcomb Street
London SW1
Tel: (01) 235 8353 and 341 0673 (Home)
Art Nouveau and Art Deco furniture, silver, glass, ceramics, jewellery, lighting and bronzes.

DEREK MOSS
33 Islington Green
Camden Passage
London N1
Tel: (01) 359 2328
Art Deco specialist.

PICCADILLY GALLERY
16 Cork Street
London W1
Tel: (01) 499 4632
Symbolist and Art Nouveau paintings, drawings, and watercolours.

MADELINE POPPER
Harris's Arcade
163 Portobello Road
London W11
Tel: (01) 727 6788 and 435 4864 (Home)
Antique, second-hand, and Art Deco jewellery, including cut steel and Berlin iron.

THE PURPLE SHOP
15 Flood Street
London SW3
Tel: (01) 352 1127
Art Nouveau and Art Deco jewellery, silver, glass and studio pattery.

BARRIE QUINN ANTIQUES
1, 3 and 4 Broxholm House
New Kings Road
London SW6
Tel: (01) 736 4747
Victorian jardinières, including Art Nouveau.

SMIFFS ANTIQUES
121 High Road
London N2
Tel: (01) 883 6121
Art Nouveau and Art Deco lighting and fireplace accessories.

P. AND L. WOOLMAN
351 Upper Street
London N1
Tel: (01) 359 7648 and 340 2468 (Home)
Art Nouveau and Art Deco glass including Gallé, silver, pottery, porcelain and clocks.

SOUTH AND SOUTHEAST ENGLAND

C. CLEALL ANTIQUES
16 Brewers Lane
Richmond, Surrey
Tel: (01) 940 8069
Art Nouveau and Art Deco furniture, pottery, porcelain, jewellery, silver and glass.

MOLLIE EVANS
84 Hill Rise
Richmond, Surrey
Tel: (01) 948 0182 and (01) 940 3720 (home)
Art Nouveau and Art Deco pottery, copper, brass and bronzes.

GALLERY 10
10 Richmond Hill
Richmond, Surrey
Tel: (01) 948 3314
Art Nouveau and Art Deco oil paintings.

PETER AND DEBBIE GOODAY
20 Richmond Hill
Richmond, Surrey
Tel: (01) 940 8652
Art Nouveau and Art Deco, especially pieces made by Liberty and Company.

J. RANGER
148 Nine Mile Ride
Finchampstead, Wokingham, Berks
Tel: (0734) 732754
Art pottery especially Branham and Art Deco pottery especially Clarice Cliff.

SOUTHWEST ENGLAND AND WALES

ASPIDISTRA ANTIQUES
46 St James Parade
Bath, Avon
Tel: (0225) 61948
Art Nouveau and Art Deco furniture, and prints.

Above: Pottery, silver and glass objects designed by Christopher Dresser, courtesy of Dan Klein Ltd.

NORTH OF ENGLAND AND SCOTLAND

JOSEPH H. BONNAR
60 Thistle Street
Edinburgh, Lothian, Scotland
Tel: (031) 556 9003
Art Nouveau and Art Deco jewellery.

DRAGON ANTIQUES
10 Dragon Road
Harrogate, N Yorkshire
Tel: (0423) 62037
Art Nouveau and Art Deco glass and pottery.

E.B. FORREST AND COMPANY ANTIQUES
2 and 3 Barclay Terrace
Edinburgh, Lothian, Scotland
Tel: (031) 229 3156
Art Nouveau and Art Deco jewellery, silver, glass and metalware.

GROSVENOR ANTIQUES
22 Watergate Street
Chester, Cheshire CH1 2LA
Tel: (0244) 315201
Small items in the Art Deco style, such as jewellery, silver, pottery and porcelain.

GREIG LINTON ANTIQUES
95 West Bow
Edinburgh, Lothian, Scotland
Tel: (031) 226 6946
Art Nouveau glass and bronzes.

THE RENDEZVOUS GALLERY
100 Forest Avenue
Aberdeen, Grampian, Scotland
Tel: (0224) 323247
Art Nouveau and Art Deco glass, jewellery, pottery, plus paintings and watercolours, especially of the Scottish school.

STEIGAL FINE ARTS
6 Northwest Circus Place
Edinburgh, Lothian, Scotland
Tel: (031) 226 4563
Decorative Arts period pottery and glass.

LONDON

ANTIQUE TOY CENTRE
51 Camden Passage
London N1
Tel: (01) 226 4255/607 0846
Late 19th to early 20th c. mechanical money boxes.

ARTIFACTS
9 Camden Passage
London N1
Tel: Not Available
18th and 19th c. mechanical instruments.

JACK DONOVAN
93 Portobello Road
London W11
Tel: (01) 727 1485
Automata and music boxes including mechanical singing birds.

VINCENT FREEMAN
8–10 Gateway Arcade
Camden Passage
London N1
Tel: (01) 226 6178
Music boxes.

GREENS ANTIQUE GALLERIES
117 Kensington Church Street
London W8
Tel: (01) 229 9618/9
19th c. Automata.

KEITH HARDING ANTIQUES
93 Hornsey Road
London N7
Tel: (01) 607 6181/2673
Music boxes.

THE LITTLE CURIOSITY SHOP
24 The Green, Winchmore Hill
London N21
Tel: (01) 886 0925
Victorian music boxes.

PENNY FARTHING ANTIQUES ARCADE
177 Bermondsey Street
London SE1
Tel: (01) 407 5171 and 777 1185 (Home)
Music boxes.

A.M. WEBB
93 Portobello Road
London W11
Tel: (01) 727 1485
19th c. Automata.

SOUTH AND SOUTHEAST ENGLAND

JOHN COWDEROY ANTIQUES
42 South Street
Eastbourne, Sussex
Tel: (0323) 20058
18th and 19th c. cylinder and disc music boxes.

Above: Swiss "24 Airs" music box, courtesy of John Cowderoy Antiques.

HADLOW ANTIQUES
No. 1, The Pantiles
Tunbridge Wells, Kent
Tel: (0892) 29858
Mechanical instruments.

NEALE ANTIQUES
21 and 21a Old Cross
Hertford, Herts SG14 1RE
Tel: Hertford 52561
Georgian to Edwardian disc and cylinder music boxes.

SOUTHWEST ENGLAND AND WALES

ARTHUR S. LEWIS
The Stables
Linkend House
Corselawn, Glos GH9 4LZ
Tel: (0452) 78 258
18th and 19th c. cylinder and disc music boxes.

MIDLANDS AND EAST ANGLIA

TURRET HOUSE
Middletown Street
Wymondham, Norfolk
Tel: (0953) 603462
Music boxes.

LONDON

ABINGTON BOOKS
Ground Floor
'F' Block, I.O.C.C. Complex
53/79 Highgate Road
London NW5
Tel: (01) 267 2701 and (0223) 891 645
(Home) (By appointment only)
*Books on Oriental rugs from 1877 and
volumes on classical tapestries from 1600.*

J.A. ALLEN AND COMPANY
1 Lower Grosvenor Place
London SW1
Tel: (01) 834 5606
Horse books from 1600.

ANGLEBOOKS LTD
2 Cecil Court
Charing Cross Road
London WC2
Tel: (01) 836 2922
Antiquarian books.

J. ASH RARE BOOKS
25 Royal Exchange
London EC3
Tel: (01) 626 2665
Books from 1550–1970.

M. AYRES
31 Museum Street
London WC2
Tel: (01) 636 2844
Antiquarian books.

BRIAN BALL
227 Ebury Street
London SW1
Tel: (01) 730 5000
Nursery books and games.

H. BARON
136 Chatsworth Road
London NW2
Tel: (01) 459 2035 (By appointment only)
*Antiquarian music, musical literature,
autograph music, and musical iconography.*

BELL BOOK AND RADMELL
80 Long Acre
London WC2
Tel: (01) 240 2161
*First editions of English and American
literature from 1880 to date, specialising in
detective and fantasy fiction.*

TONY BINGHAM
11 Pond Street
London NW3 2PN
Tel: (01) 794 1596
*Antiquarian and second-hand books on
musical instruments; catalogue available.*

ANDREW BLOCK
20 Barter Street
London WC1
Tel: (01) 405 9660 and 435 1350 (Home)
Antiquarian books.

LOUIS W. BONDY
16 Russell Street
London WC1
Tel: (01) 405 2733
Rare books.

JOANNA BOOTH
247 Kings Road
London SW3
Tel: (01) 352 8998
17th to 19th c. books.

CLIVE BURDEN LTD
13 Cecil Court
Charing Cross Road
London WC2
Tel: (01) 836 2177 (By appointment only)
Antiquarian books, pre-1870.

RICHARD BURNETT
3 Macaulay Road
London SW4
Tel: (01) 622 9393/4 (By appointment only)
Antiquarian music, manuscripts and books.

CHELSEA RARE BOOKS
313 Kings Road
London SW3
Tel: (01) 351 0950
Antiquarian books.

CINEMA BOOKSHOP
13–14 Great Russell Street
London WC1
Tel: (01) 637 0206
Books and magazines on the cinema.

J. CLARKE-HALL LTD
7 Bride Court
Off Fleet Street
London EC4
Tel: (01) 353 4116
*18th c. English literature, especially Dr
Samuel Johnson plus 19th c. illustrated books
and review copies.*

STANLEY CROWE LTD
5 Bloomsbury Street
London WC1
Tel: (01) 580 3976
*Books relating to topography of Great Britain
including Ireland.*

DAWSON RARE BOOKS
16 and 17 Pall Mall
London SW1
Tel: (01) 930 2515
*English literature, colour plate books, and
volumes on science, medicine, travel,
economics and music, all 1500–1900.*

DIVERTISSEMENT
19 Arlington Way
London EC1
Tel: (01) 837 9758
*Antiquarian books especially on music, ballet
and the theatre.*

ROBERT DOUWMA LTD
93 Great Russell Street
London WC1
Tel: (01) 636 4895
Atlases and illustrated books to late 19th c.

LEON DRUCKER
25 Dicey Avenue
London NW2
Tel: (01) 452 1581 (By appointment only)
*First editions and autograph material from
1850–1940.*

MADAME J. DUPONT ET FILS
68 Lincoln Road
London N2
Tel: (01) 883 7852 (By appointment only)
*Antiquarian books on travel, costume,
flowers, sports.*

EAST ASIA COMPANY
103 Camden High Street
London NW1
Tel: (01) 388 5783
*Oriental antiquarian books on history and
culture.*

**PETER EATON (BOOKSELLERS)
LTD**
80 Holland Park Avenue
London W11
Tel: (01) 727 5211
*Antiquarian and used books, with large
selection of books on antiques and the arts.*

J. FAUSTUS
94 Jermyn Street
London SW1
Tel: (01) 839 3388
Old and rare books.

FISHER AND SPERR
46 Highgate High Street
London N6
Tel: (01) 340 7244
Books, 15th c. on.

THE FLASK BOOKSHOP
6 Flask Walk
London NW3
Tel: (01) 435 2693
*Second-hand books and modern first editions
on literature and the arts.*

H.M. FLETCHER
27 Cecil Court
Charing Cross Road
London WC2
Tel: (01) 836 2865
Rare and antiquarian books.

W. FOSTER
83a Stamford Hill
London N16
Tel: (01) 800 3919
Bibliography and books about books.

W. AND G. FOYLE LTD
119–125 Charing Cross Road
London WC2
Tel: (01) 437 5660
Antiquarian books.

FROGNAL RARE BOOKS
18 Cecil Court
Charing Cross Road
London WC2
Tel: (01) 240 2815
*Antiquarian books on law, art, economics,
history, philosophy and literature in English,
French, German and Italian from 1500–1900.*

GAME ADVICE
1 Holmes Road
London NW5
Tel: (01) 485 2188 and 485 4226 (Home)
18th and 19th c. children's and cookery books.

**STANLEY GIBBONS ANTIQUARIAN
BOOKS, MAPS AND PLAYING
CARDS**
37 Southampton Street
London WC2
Tel: (01) 836 8444
Antique atlases.

DAVID GODFREY
37 Kinnerton Street
London SW1
Tel: (01) 235 7788 and 828 9467 (Home)
*Antiquarian newspapers from 1665–1865
with rare or special content.*

GOLFIANA MISCELLANEA LTD
84 Kingsway
London WC2
Tel: (01) 405 5323
Out-of-print books on golf.

BOOKS

ROBIN GREER
30 Sloane Court West
London SW3
Tel: (01) 736 5438/730 7392 (By appointment only)
Children's and illustrated books, especially on the subject of travel to Middle and Far East.

GREGORY, BOTTLEY AND LLOYD
8–12 Rickett Street
London SW6
Tel: (01) 381 5522
Old and antiquarian books on mineralogy.

OTTO HAAS
49 Belsize Gardens
London NW3
Tel: (01) 722 1488 (By apointment only)
Manuscripts, printed music and rare books on music.

JOHN HALL ANTIQUES AND PRINTS
17 Harrington Road
London SW7 3ES
Tel: (01) 584 1307
18th and 19th c. engraved and lithographed music.

KEITH HARDING ANTIQUES
93 Hornsey Road
London N7
Tel: (01) 607 6181/2672
Horological books.

HERALDENE LTD
33 Victoria Road
London E18
Tel: (01) 989 3286
Military books.

HERALDRY TODAY
10 Beauchamp Place
London SW3
Tel: (01) 584 1656 and Ramsbury 617 (Home)
Heraldic and genealogical books.

G. HEYWOOD HILL LTD
10 Curzon Street
London W1
Tel: (01) 629 0647
Victorian, illustrated children's and natural history books.

B. HIRSHLER
62 Portland Avenue
and
71 Dunsmore Road
London N16
Hebrew and Jewish books.
Tel: (01) 800 6395

THE HOLLAND PRESS LTD
37 Connaught Street
London W2 2AZ
Tel: (01) 262 6184
Antiquarian and second-hand books on gastronomy, cartography, travel, bibliography, fine and applied arts.

STEPHANIE HOPPEN LTD
37 Connaught Street
London W2
Tel: (01) 235 4859 (By appointment only)
Illustrated books from 1490–1700, plus atlases, especially of the Holy Land.

JAPANESE GALLERY
66d Kensington Church Street
London W8
Tel: (01) 229 2934 and 226 3347 (Home)
Japanese books.

E. JOSEPH
48a Charing Cross Road
London WC2
Tel: (01) 836 4111
Antiquarian and second-hand books.

KEW GARDENS BOOKSHOP
3 Station Approach
Kew, Surrey
Tel: (01) 940 7370
Antiquarian and second-hand books.

CLIFFORD E. KING
2 St John's Lodge
Harley Road
London NW3
Tel: (01) 722 8067 (By appointment only)
Continental antiquarian books on travel, medicine and science.

FOULK LEWIS COLLECTION
274 Fulham Road
London SW10
Tel: (01) 352 8950
Books from 1900–1939.

S. LINDEN
33 Craven Street
London WC2
Tel: (01) 930 3659
Antiquarian and second-hand books.

P.G. DE LOTZ
20 Downside Crescent
London NW3
Tel: (01) 794 5709
Antiquarian books on war history – naval, military and aviation.

PETER LOVEDAY PRINTS
46 Norland Square
London W11 4PZ
Tel: (01) 221 4479
Antiquarian and second-hand books on sport and sporting art.

MAGGS BROTHERS LTD
50 Berkeley Square
London W1
Tel: (01) 499 2051/2007
Rare books, manuscripts, atlases and autograph letters.

THE MAP HOUSE
54 Beauchamp Place
London SW3
Tel: (01) 589 4325/9821
Antique and rare atlases.

MARCHMONT BOOKSHOP
39 Burton Street
London WC1
Tel: (01) 387 7989
Books on literature, especially modern first editions.

MARLBOROUGH RARE BOOKS LTD
35 Old Bond Street
London W1X 4PT
Tel: (01) 493 6993
Rare and out-of-print books on the fine and applied arts, eg architecture, garden design, furniture, bibliography, calligraphy, and typography.

RICHARD MAUDE TOOLS
6 Malbrook Road
London SW15
Tel: (01) 788 2991 (By appointment only)
18th and 19th c. books and old trade catalogues related to the woodworking and carpentry trade.

MAY AND MAY
5 Hotham Road
London SW15
Tel: (01) 788 9730
Antiquarian music and music literature.

THE MOORLAND GALLERY
23 Cork Street
London W1
Tel: (01) 734 6961
Rare and antiquarian books on sport and wildlife.

W.A. MYERS LTD
Suite 52, Second Floor
91 St Martin's Lane
London WC2
Tel: (01) 836 1940
Autograph letters, documents, books, manuscripts and catalogues.

NIHON TOKEN
23 Museum Street
London WC1A 1JT
Tel: (01) 580 6511
Ancient and antique Japanese scrolls and books.

RAYMOND O'SHEA GALLERY
6 Ellis Street
(Off Sloane Street)
London SW1
Tel: (01) 730 0082
Cartographic specialist with atlases, celestial charts and illustrated books.

PHILIP AND RICHARD PARKER
98 Fulham Road
London SW3
Tel: (01) 589 7327 and 947 5569 (Home)
17th to late 19th c. books.

MICHAEL PHELPS ANTIQUARIAN BOOKS
203 Upper Richmond Road
London SW14
Tel: (01) 878 4699
16th to 20th c. books specialising in medicine, science and technolgoy.

PICCADILLY RARE BOOKS LTD
30 Sackville Street
London W1X 1DB
Tel: (01) 437 2135
Second-hand and rare books, specialising in travel, history, biography, cookery and wine. Amazingly, open seven days a week, from 10am to 6pm.

PICKERING AND CHATTO LTD
13 Brunswick Centre
London WC1
Tel: (01) 278 5146 (By appointment only)
17th to 19th c. English literature.

PLEASURES OF PAST TIMES
11 Cecil Court
Charing Cross Road
London WC2
Tel: (01) 836 1142
19th c. children's and theatre books.

JONATHAN POTTER LTD
1 Grafton Street
London W1
Tel: (01) 491 3520
16th to 19th c. atlases and travel books.

ARTHUR PROBSTHAIN
41 Great Russell Street
London WC1
Tel: (01) 636 1096
Oriental and African books.

BOOKS

QUADRILLE ANTIQUES
27 Craven Terrace
London W2
Tel: (01) 262 7824
*Music covers and unusual ephemera,
especially theatrical.*

QUEVEDO
25 Cecil Court, Charing Cross Road
London WC2
Tel: (01) 836 9132
15th to 19th c. rare and antiquarian books.

WILLIAM REEVES BOOKSELLER LTD
1a Norbury Crescent
London SW16
Tel: (01) 764 2108 (By appointment only)
Books about music from 1800–1970.

BERTRAM ROTA LTD
30/31 Long Acre
London WC2
Tel: (01) 836 0723
*Antiquarian and second-hand books especially
first editions, private press English literature
and literary autographs.*

ST GEORGE'S GALLERY BOOKS LTD
8 Duke Street
London SW1
Tel: (01) 930 0935
Second-hand books on art and antiques.

CHARLES J. SAWYER
1 Grafton Street
London W1X 3LB
Tel: (01) 493 3810
*18th and 19th c. English literature
specialising in sets and first editions plus fine
bindings, Churchilliana, Africana, private
press books, sporting books and coloured plate
books.*

B.A. SEABY LTD
Audley House
11 Margaret Street
London W1
Tel: (01) 580 3677
Numismatic and military books.

**STANLEY SMITH AND KEITH
FAWKES**
1–3 Flask Walk
London NW3
Tel: (01) 435 0614
Antiquarian books.

HENRY SOTHERAN LTD
2, 3, 4, and 5 Sackville Street
London W1X 2DP
Tel: (01) 734 1150
*Antiquarian and rare books covering English
literature, natural history, travel and
topography.*

SOUTHWOOD BOOKSHOP
355 Archway Road
London N6
Tel: (01) 340 6264
*Antiquarian books, especially on literature and
the arts.*

SPINK AND SON LTD
5, 6 and 7 King Street
London SW1
Tel: (01) 930 7888
Numismatic books.

SPREAD EAGLE ANTIQUES
23 Nelson Road
London SE10
Tel: (01) 692 1618/858 9713
19th c. books.

**ERIC AND JOAN STEVENS
BOOKSELLERS**
74 Fortune Green Road
London NW6
Tel: (01) 435 7545
19th and 20th c. books.

PETER STOCKHAM AT IMAGES
16 Cecil Court, Charing Cross Road
London WC2
Tel: (01) 836 8661
*Art and illustrated books including children's
books and fine printing.*

HAROLD T. STOREY
3 Cecil Court, Charing Cross Road
London WC2
Tel: (01) 836 3777
*16th to 20th c. antiquarian books and 19th c.
illustrated books.*

STRIKE ONE LTD
51 Camden Passage
London N1 8EA
Tel: (01) 226 9709
Horological books.

*Above: A Sangorski and Sutcliffe pictorial
binding with coloured morocco inlays on the
cover depicting the three central characters
from the novel "Evelina" by Fanny Burney.
Bound and finished in 1942, probably
produced as a "labour of love" by the bindery
in the slack and difficult war years, courtesy of
Charles J. Sawyer.*

ALAN G. THOMAS
c/o Westminster Bank
300 Kings Road
London SW3
Tel: (01) 352 5130 (By appointment only)
Manuscripts, bibles and early printed works.

THOMAS THORP
47 Holborn Viaduct
London EC1
Tel: (01) 353 8332
*Antiquarian and second hand books, including
very early printed books and specialising in
English law books, Charles Dickens, botany
and travel.*

BOOKS

R.V. TOOLEY LTD
33 Museum Street
London WC1
Tel: (01) 631 1632/1
Maps, atlases and autographs.

TRAVIS AND EMERY
17 Cecil Court
Charing Cross Road
London WC2
Tel: (01) 240 2129
Musical literature and music.

THE TRYON AND MOORLAND GALLERY
23–24 Cork Street
London W1
Tel: (01) 734 6961/2256
Sporting and natural history books.

ROGER TURNER BOOKS LTD
22 Nelson Road
London SE10
Tel: (01) 853 5271
Antiquarian books on the history of science, horology and linguistics.

UNDER TWO FLAGS
4 St Christopher's Place
London W1
Tel: (01) 935 6934
Books of military interest.

WALDEN BOOKS
38 Harmood Street
London NW1
Tel: (01) 267 8146
Second-hand books with small antiquarian selection.

G.W. WALFORD
186 Upper Street
London N1
Tel: (01) 226 5682
Antiquarian books.

WATKINS BOOKSHOP
19 and 21 Cecil Court
Charing Cross Road
London WC2
Tel: (01) 836 2182
Antiquarian books.

B. WEINREB ARCHITECTURAL BOOKS LTD
93 Great Russell Street
London WC1
Tel: (01) 636 4895
Architectural books.

F.E. WHITEHART RARE BOOKS
40 Priestfield Road
London SE23
Tel: (01) 699 3225 and Orpington 73560
Books on science, medicine and technology.

EDNA WHITESON LTD
343 Bowes Road
London N11
Tel: (01) 361 1105/449 8860 (Home)
Books from early 17th c. onwards.

WORLD OF BOOKS
30 Sackville Street
London W1
Tel: (01) 437 2135/734 6608
Second-hand and antiquarian books.

HARRIET WYNTER LTD
50 Redclyffe Road
London SW10
Tel: (01) 352 6494 (By appointment only)
16th to 19th c. scientific books.

ZENO BOOKSELLERS
6 Denmark Street
London WC2
Tel: (01) 836 2522
Antiquarian books.

A. ZWEMMER LTD
76–80 Charing Cross Road
London WC2
Tel: (01) 836 4710
Antiquarian and second-hand books on fine art.

SOUTH AND SOUTHEAST ENGLAND

THE ANTIQUARIAN BOOK SERVICE
Pates Manor
Belfont, Middx
Tel: (01) 890 2790 (Mail Order Only)
Antiquarian books on occultism, mysticism, astrology, magic, yoga, witchcraft, health and healing.

ASPIDISTRA
46 St James Parade
Bath, Avon
Tel: (0225) 61948
19th and early 20th c. books on anthropology and especially North America.

THOMAS BARNARD A.B.A.
11 Windsor Street
Uxbridge, Middx
Tel: Upminster 56963
Antiquarian books.

MARY BLAND
9 Mortlake Terrace
Kew, Richmond, Surrey TW9 3DT
Tel: (01) 940 2512
Old, rare and out-of-print books on botany, gardening and all other natural history subjects.

A. BURTON-GARBETT
35 The Green
Morden, Surrey
Tel: (01) 540 2367 (By appointment only)
16th to 20th c. books on travel, the arts, and antiquities of South and Central America, Mexico and the Caribbean.

C.P. FLOREY A.B.A.
18 Whitehorn Gardens
Shirley Park
Croydon, Surrey
Tel: (01) 654 4724
Antiquarian books.

THE GUILDHALL BOOKSHOP
Rear of 8 Victoria Road
Surbiton, Surrey
Tel: (01) 390 2552/892 0331
16th to 20th c. antiquarian and second-hand books.

THE GUILDHALL BOOKSHOP
25 York Street
Twickenham, Middx
Tel: (01) 892 0331/390 2552
Antiquarian and second-hand books, including foreign languages.

PETER HOWARD BOOKS
347 Brighton Road
Croydon, Surrey
Tel: (01) 688 6558 and 681 1627 (Home)
Antiquarian and second-hand books.

IVELET BOOKS LTD
18 Fairlawn Drive
Redhill, Surrey RH1 6JP
Tel: Redhill 64520
Old, rare and out-of-print books on early agriculture, botany and gardening.

MICHAEL KATANKA LTD
103 Stanmore Hill
Stanmore, Middx
Tel: (01) 954 0490
18th to 20th c. books.

ANDREW LEVERTON LTD
12 Walton Court
Lyonsdown Road
New Barnet, Herts
Tel: (01) 440 2279/886 6038
Books including atlases and early bibles.

D. LLOYD
4 Hillcrest Avenue
Chertsey, Surrey
KT16 9RD
Tel: Not Available
Catalogue only on gardening and botanical books.

NORTHWOOD MAPS LTD
17 Hallowell Road
Northwood, Middx
Tel: Northwood 21525 (By appointment only)
16th to early 20th c. atlases.

PERIWINKLE PRESS
Chequers Hill
Doddington
Sittingbourne, Kent ME9 OBN
Tel: (079 586) 246
Antiquarian books.

RUDGE BOOKS
Swanspool
Loudwater, Herts
Tel: Rickmansworth 74110
Second-hand and out-of-print books on natural history and gardening.

RITA SHETON
148 Percy Road
Twickenham, Middx
Tel: (01) 894 6888
Horological books, including some on bells and ornamental turning.

WARNER'S MILITARY SPECIALISTS
2 The Apple Market
Eden Street
Kingston-upon-Thames, Surrey
Tel: Not Available (Mail Order Only)
Books on militaria from 1900–1960.

SOUTHWEST ENGLAND AND WALES

GEORGE BAYNTUN
Manvers Street
Bath, Avon
Tel: (0225) 66000
First and fine editions of English literature, standard sets, illustrated and sporting books, poetry, biography, and travel and antiquarian books in original bindings.

BIBLIOTIQUE
2 Canton Place
London Road
Bath, Avon
Tel: (0225) 312932
Early children's and illustrated books.

CORRIDOR STAMP SHOP
7a The Corridor
Bath, Avon
Tel: (0225) 63368 and 316445 (Home)
Books related to philately.

HAYES BOOKSHOP
11 Hayes Bridge Road
Cardiff, S Glamorgan, Wales
Tel: (0222) 28495
Antiquarian and second hand books.

CHRISTOPHER HOLTOM
Esperanza
Aust, nr Bristol, Avon.
Tel: (045 45) 2557 (Evenings and week-
ends only) (Mail Order Only)
Pre-1900 children's books.

TOM LLOYD-ROBERTS
Old Court House
Caerwys, nr Mold, Clwyd, Wales
Tel: (035 282) 276
Antiquarian books.

J. PARKER
150 Penylan Road
Cardiff, S Glamorgan, Wales
Tel: (0222) 26678 (By appointment only)
Pre-1850 antiquarian books.

REGENT GALLERY
10 Montpelier Arcade
Cheltenham, Glos GL50 1SU
Tel: (0242) 512826
Antiquarian atlases.

W.G. POTTER AND SON
1 West Street
Axminster, Devon
Tel: (0297) 32063
Antique and second-hand books.

MIDLANDS AND EAST ANGLIA

THE ENCHANTED AVIARY
Long Melford
Sudbury, Suffolk
Tel: (0787) 78814
19th c. books on natural history.

G.K. HADFIELD
Black Brook Hill House
Ticklow Lane
Shepshed
Longborough, Leics
Tel: (050 95) 3014
*Antiquarian and second-hand books on all
aspects of horology.*

TURRET HOUSE
Middletown Street
Wymondham, Norfolk
Tel: (0953) 603462
Antiquarian books.

NORTH OF ENGLAND AND SCOTLAND

ABOYNE ANTIQUES OF ROYAL DEESIDE
Station Square
Aboyne, Aberdeen, Grampian, Scotland
Tel: (0339) 2231
19th c. books.

R. AND J. BALDING BOOKS LTD
81 Great King Street
Edinburgh, Lothian, Scotland
Tel: (031) 556 9003
*Antiquarian books, specialising in rare
volumes.*

JAMES BISSET LTD
Upperkirkgate
Aberdeen, Grampian, Scotland
Tel: (0224) 53528
Antiquarian books.

CROSBY BOOKS
P.O. Box 510
Edinburgh, Lothian, Scotland
Tel: (031) 447 8000
Books on Oriental rugs and glass collecting.

BERNARD EDWARDS
20 Dundas Street
Edinburgh, Lothian, Scotland
Tel: (031) 557 1903
Illustrated books.

THE MCEWAN GALLERY
Glengarden
Ballater, Aberdeen, Grampian, Scotland
Tel: (033 82) 429
Scottish and natural history books.

POTTERTON BOOKS
8 Montpelier Parade
Harrogate, N Yorkshire HG1 2TY
Tel: (0423) 521439 and (0532) 812973
(Home)
Antiquarian books.

ALAN RANKIN
72 Dundas Street
Edinburgh, Lothian, Scotland
Tel: (031) 556 3705
*Antiquarian books and scholarly books from
1850 on.*

JAMES THIN BOOKSELLERS
53–59 Southbridge
Edinburgh, Lothian, Scotland
Tel: (031) 556 6743
Antiquarian and second-hand books.

ADRIAN WALKER
160 Victoria Road
Scarborough, N Yorks YO11 1SX
Tel: (0723) 73029
Second-hand books.

BOXES

LONDON

*SEE ALSO ENTRIES UNDER
"SPECIALIST DEALERS,
SEMI-PRECIOUS MATERIALS".*

ASTLEYS
109 Jermyn Street
London SW1
Tel: (01) 930 1687
Cigar boxes.

PETER FRANCIS
26 Museum Street
London WC1
Tel: (01) 637 0165
*Boxes including tea caddies and those from
papier mâché and painted tôle.*

GREGORY, BOTTLEY AND LLOYD
8–12 Rickett Street
London SW6
Tel: (01) 381 5522
Spar boxes.

M. HAKIM
4 The Royal Arcade
Old Bond Street
London W1
Tel: (01) 629 2643
Snuff boxes.

HALCYON DAYS
14 Brook Street
London W1Y 1AA
Tel: (01) 629 8111
*18th c. English boxes including those in
enamel, tortoiseshell and papier mâché.*

THE HAY LOFT
332 Upper Richmond Road
London SW14
Tel: (01) 876 5020
Boxes and tea caddies from 1800–1910.

LESLEY HEPHERD ANTIQUES
47 Camden Passage
London N1
Tel: (01) 359 1755
Snuff boxes and card cases.

JILL LEWIS
Collector's Corner
138 Portobello Road
London W11
Tel: (040) 372 2357
Snuff boxes.

HUGH MOSS LTD
23 Bruton Lane
London W1
Tel: (01) 492 1835
Chinese snuff boxes.

PAT NYE
Collector's Corner
138 Portobello Road
London W11
Tel: (01) 948 4314
*18th and early 19th c. snuff boxes and pipe
tapers.*

PARK ANTIQUES
62 New Kings Road
London SW6 4LT
Tel: (01) 736 6222
*Painted, lacquered, papier mâché, horn and
tortoiseshell snuff boxes and card cases.*

S.J. PHILLIPS LTD
139 New Bond Street
London W1A 3DL
Tel: (01) 629 6261
*Early 19th c. boxes, including those in silver
and gold.*

A.J. REFFOLD AND PARTNERS LTD
28 Pimlico Road
London SW1
Tel: (01) 730 6788
Lacquer and papier mâché boxes.

ROGERS DE RIN ANTIQUES
76 Royal Hospital Road
London SW3
Tel: (01) 352 9007
Snuff boxes.

Above: Selection of enamel boxes and bonbonnières, courtesy of Halcyon Days.

RUTLAND STREET GALLERY
8 Rutland Street
London SW7
Tel: (01) 581 3761
Gold boxes.

EDWARD SALTI
43 Davies Street
London W1
Tel: (01) 629 2141 and 723 3662 (Home)
18th c. Battersea boxes

GERALD SATTIN LTD
25 Burlington Arcade
London W1
Tel: (01) 493 6557
Boxes in silver, tortoiseshell, enamels, especially unusual pieces.

C.W. SMITH AND G. ROBINSON
Portwine Market
175 Portobello Road
London W11
Tel: (01) 727 4681/998 8160 and 579 5620 (Home)
Mother-of-pearl boxes.

JOANNA WARRAND
99 Kensington Church Street
London W8
Tel: (01) 727 2333
18th and 19th c. boxes.

WARTSKI
14 Grafton Street
London W1
Tel: (01) 493 1141/2/3
Gold and gold-mounted snuff boxes, especially those in semi-precious materials. See "Specialist Dealers, Semi-precious Materials" for illustration.

SOUTH AND SOUTHEAST ENGLAND

HOUSE OF ANTIQUES
4 College Street
Petersfield, Hants
Tel: (0730) 2172
18th and 19th c. boxes, specialising in Tunbridgeware.

Right: Victorian Tunbridgeware tea chest, courtesy of The Hay Loft.

JOAN JARMAN ANTIQUES
81a High Street
Teddington, Middx TW11 8HG
Tel: (01) 977 4260
Tunbridgeware boxes and articles.

SOUTHWEST ENGLAND AND WALES

MORRIS TUCKER
Lower Town House
Chudleigh Knighton, Devon TQ13 OME
Tel: (0626) 852123
Specialist in maritime items with snuff boxes and workboxes.

MIDLANDS AND EAST ANGIA

MERIDIAN HOUSE ANTIQUES
Meridian House
Market Street
Stourbridge, W Midlands
Tel: (038 43) 5384
18th and 19th c. boxes.

NORTH OF ENGLAND AND SCOTLAND

EUREKA ANTIQUES
18 Northenden Road
Sale, Cheshire M33 3BR
Tel: (061) 962 5629
18th and 19th c. boxes, including tortoiseshell and papier mâché.

CHARLES HAY ANTIQUES
44 High Street
Coldstream, Borders, Scotland
Tel: (0890) 2552
18th and early 19th c. boxes, including papier mâché.

JANE POLLOCK ANTIQUES
4 Castlegate
Penrith, Cumbria
Tel: (0768) 67211 (By appointment only)
Georgian and Victorian wooden boxes.

WHEELWRIGHTS ANTIQUES
Pinfold Lane
Fishlake, Doncaster
S Yorkshire DN7 5LA
Tel: (0302) 841411
Wooden boxes.

BRONZES

LONDON

ANTIQUES AND FINE ARTS
152 Upper Richmond Road
London SW15
Tel: (01) 788 9123
19th c. bronzes.

BALCOMBE GALLERIES
7 Stanley Studios
Park Walk
London SW10
Tel: (01) 352 4353 and 352 9996 (Home)
18th and 19th c. bronzes.

BARHAM ANTIQUES
83 Portobello Road
London W11
Tel: (01) 727 3845
Victorian bronzes.

E.G. BRUSCHWEILER ANTIQUES LTD
3 Lonsdale Road
London W11
Tel: (01) 229 3106 and (062) 185 1252
(Home)
19th c. bronzes.

CATHAY ANTIQUES
12 Thackeray Street
London W8
Tel: (01) 937 6066
18th c. Chinese and Japanese bronzes.

CATSPA
116/118 Islington High Street
London N1
Tel: (01) 359 7616 and 883 3992
*Art Nouveau and Art Deco figures in bronze
and bronze and ivory.*

CHANCERY ANTIQUES LTD
357 Upper Street
London N1 OPD
Tel: (01) 359 9035
Chinese and Japanese bronzes.

CHANTICLEER ANTIQUES
105 Portobello Road
London W11
Tel: (01) 385 0919 (By appointment only)
Chinese and European bronzes.

J. CHRISTIE
26 Burlington Arcade
London W1
Tel: (01) 629 3070
18th and 19th c. animalier bronzes.

WILLIAM CLEVELAND
40 Queensdale Road
London W11
Tel: (01) 603 5050 and 727 1620 (Home)
18th and 19th c. large bronzes.

COBWEB
2 Englands Lane
London NW3
Tel: (01) 586 4605
*Ancient and antique European and Far
Eastern bronzes.*

COHEN AND PEARCE
84 Portobello Road
London W11
Tel: (01) 229 9458
Chinese bronzes.

JEREMY COOPER LTD
9 Galen Place
Bury Place
London WC1
Tel: (01) 242 5138/404 0336
English bronzes from 1830–1930.

*Above: Bronze figure of a disciple from Siam,
circa 1650, courtesy of Raymond Le Brun.*

D.J. FERRANT ANTIQUES
21a Camden Passage
and
39 Essex Road
London N1
Tel: (01) 359 2597/1639
Georgian bronzes.

ELAINE FREEDMAN ANTIQUES
Camden Passage
London N1
Tel: Not Available
18th and 19th c. bronzes.

VICTOR FRANSES GALLERY
57 Jermyn Street
London SW1
Tel: (01) 493 6284/629 1144
19th c. bronzes.

GAY ANTIQUES
1 Beauchamp Place
London SW3
Tel: (01) 584 9615
French bronzes.

ANTHONY JAMES AND SON LTD
253 New Kings Road
London SW6
Tel: (01) 731 3474
Bronzes, pre-1830.

MELVYN AND GARY JAY ANTIQUES
64a Kensington Church Street
London W8 4DB
Tel: (01) 937 6832
19th c. bronzes.

RICHARD LALLY LTD
152 Upper Richmond Road
London SW15
Tel: (01) 788 9123
18th and 19th c. bronzes.

RAYMOND LE BRUN
39 Ovington Street
London SW3 2JA
Tel: (01) 589 7945 (By appointment only)
17th to 19th c. bronzes.

NELLIE LENSON AND ROY SMITH
16 Pierrepont Row
London N1
Tel: (01) 226 2423
Vienna bronzes.

J. LIPITCH LTD
177 Westbourne Grove
London W11
Tel: (01) 229 0783
18th c. bronze and ormolu.

THE LITTLE CURIOSITY SHOP
24 The Green
Winchmore Hill
London N21
Tel: (01) 886 0925
Victorian bronzes.

L.P.J. ANTIQUES LTD
c/o Laurence Mitchell Antiques
27 Camden Passage
London N1
Tel: (01) 359 7579
Chinese bronzes.

LYONS GALLERY
47–49 Mill Lane
London NW6
Tel: (01) 794 3537
Art Nouveau bronzes.

**DAVID MARTIN-TAYLOR ANTIQUES
LTD**
592 Kings Road
London SW6
Tel: (01) 731 5054
Oriental bronzes.

MARTINS-FORREST ANTIQUES
8 Halkin Arcade
Motcomb Street
London SW1
Tel: (01) 235 8353 and 341 0673 (Home)
Art Nouveau and Art Deco bronzes.

THE MOORLAND GALLERY
23 Cork Street
London W1
Tel: (01) 734 6961
Sporting and wildlife bronzes.

MOMTAZ GALLERY
42 Pembridge Road
London W11
Tel: (01) 229 5579
Luristan bronzes.

NASH ANTIQUES
183 Westbourne Grove
London W11
Tel: (01) 727 3796
Oriental and Japanese bronzes.

NIHON TOKEN
23 Museum Street
London WC1A 1JT
Tel: (01) 580 6511
Ancient and antique Japanese bronzes.

**E.R. O'CONNOR AND
D. WALTER-ELLIS**
19 Crawford Street
London W1
Tel: (01) 935 1245
12th to 18th c. bronzes.

JACK OGDEN
42 Duke Street
London SW1
Tel: (01) 930 3353
Ancient bronzes.

ORMONDE ORIENTAL ANTIQUES
181 Westbourne Grove
London W11
and
Portwine Arcade
London W11
173 Portobello Road
Tel: (01) 221 4219
Indian, Tibetan, Chinese, Japanese, Burmese and Thai bronzes.

KEVIN A. PAGE ANTIQUES
5 Camden Passage
and
6 Gateway Arcade
Camden Passage
London N1
Tel: (01) 226 8559
19th c. Oriental bronzes.

WILLIAM REDFORD
9 Mount Street
London W1
Tel: (01) 629 1165
French bronzes.

THE SLADMORE GALLERY
32 Bruton Place
Berkeley Square
London W1
Tel: (01) 499 0365
Bronze animal sculpture.

GERALD SPYER AND SON LTD
18 Motcomb Street
Belgrave Square
London SW1X 8 LB
Tel: (01) 235 3348
18th c. and Regency bronze and ormalu ornaments.

ROBIN SYMES LTD
3 Ormond Yard
Duke of York Street
London SW1
Tel: (01) 930 9856/7
Roman, Greek and Egyptian bronzes.

TEMPUS ANTIQUES
43 Kensington Church Street
London W8
Tel: (01) 937 4359
Japanese bronzes.

TROVE
71 Pimlico Road
London SW1
Tel: (01) 730 6514
Bronzes from 1700–1850.

THE TRYON AND MOORLAND GALLERY
23–24 Cork Street
London W1
Tel: (01) 734 6961/2256
Sporting and natural history bronzes.

UNDER TWO FLAGS
4 St Christopher's Place
London W1
Tel: (01) 935 6934
Bronzes of military interest.

VALE STAMPS AND ANTIQUES
21 Tranquil Vale
London SE3
Tel: (01) 852 9817
Bronzes 3000 B.C.–500 A.D.

MARY WISE
27 Holland Street
London W8
Tel: (01) 937 8649
18th and 19th c. bronze and ormolu objects.

CHRISTOPHER WOOD GALLERY
15 Motcomb Street
London SW1
Tel: (01) 235 9141/2
Victorian bronzes.

DOUGLAS WRIGHT LTD
34 Curzon Street
London W1
Tel: (01) 629 9993
Japanese and Chinese bronzes.

SOUTH AND SOUTHEAST ENGLAND

ADRIAN ALAN LTD
4 Frederick Place
Brighton, Sussex BN1 4EA
Tel: (0273) 25277/25015
19th c. bronzes.

APOLLO GALLERIES
61, 65 and 67 South End
Croydon, Surrey
Tel: (01) 681 3727/680 1968
19th c. bronzes.

MOLLIE EVANS
84 Hill Rise
Richmond, Surrey
Tel: (01) 948 0182 and 940 3720 (Home)
Bronzes, including Art Nouveau and Art Deco.

GREAT GROOMS ANTIQUES LTD
Parbrook
Billingshurst, Sussex
Tel: (040 381) 2263
19th c. bronzes.

THE MAGPIE
25 Sandrock Hill Road
Wrecclesham, Farnham, Surrey
Tel: (025 13) 3129
Small bronzes, especially 20th c.

WALTON ANTIQUES
7 Duke Street
Richmond, Surrey
Tel: (01) 948 2258 and 940 6519 (Home)
17th to 19th c. Burmese bronzes.

SOUTHWEST ENGLAND AND WALES

ABOYNE ANTIQUES
13 York Street
Bath, Avon
Tel: (0225) 64850 and 319961 (Home)
18th and early 19th c. bronzes.

R. AND D. COOMBES
The Old Priest House
Aldbourne
Marlborough, Wilts
Tel: (0672) 40241
Pre-18th c. Oriental bronzes.

NORTH OF ENGLAND AND SCOTLAND

COLIN DAVIES ANTIQUES
15 Wolverhampton Road
Stafford, Staffs
Tel: (0785) 40545
French bronzes.

WILLIAM GOODFELLOW
The Green
Over Kellet
Carnforth, Lancs LA6 1BU
Tel: (0524) 733030
French and English bronzes, pre-1900. For illustration see entry under "Furniture".

GREIG LINTON ANTIQUES
95 West Bow
Edinburgh, Lothian, Scotland
Tel: (031) 226 6946
Art Nouveau bronaes.

PAUL M. PETERS
15 Bower Road
Harrogate, N Yorkshire
Tel: (0423) 60118
17th to 19th c. Chinese and Japanese bronzes.

CARPETS AND RUGS

LONDON

DAVID ADAM ORIENTAL CARPETS
118 Brompton Road
London SW3
Tel: (01) 584 6499
Oriental carpets and rugs.

ATLANTIC BAY CARPETS
739 Fulham Road
London SW6
Tel: (01) 736 8777
English, Oriental, Persian and Chinese carpets.

ROBERT BAILEY ORIENTAL CARPETS
51–53 Rivington Street
London EC2
Tel: (01) 729 4215 and 550 5435 (Home)
Late 19th c. Persian, Turkish and Russian carpets.

BENNISON
91 Pimlico Road
London SW1
Tel: (01) 730 8076
17th to 19th c. carpets.

BENARDOUT
31a Buckingham Palace Road
London SW1
Tel: (01) 834 8241 and 952 5565 (Home)
Oriental carpets and rugs, from 1800.

RAYMOND BENARDOUT
5 William Street
London SW1X 9HL
Tel: (01) 235 3360
15th to early 20th c. Oriental and tribal rugs and carpets.

DAVID BLACK ORIENTAL CARPETS
96 Portland Road
London W11 4LN
Tel: (01) 727 2566
Specialists in antique Near Eastern tribal rugs, kelims, soumas, dhurries and embroideries.

BOHUN AND BUSBRIDGE
c/o Celia Barker-Mill
24 Iverna Gardnes
London W8
Tel: (01) 937 9145
Mid-19th c. Turkish tribal rugs.

THE CARPET BAZAAR
220 Westbourne Grove
London W11 2RH
Tel: (01) 229 8907
Persian carpets, rugs and kelims, and Oriental carpets and rugs from all periods.

CARPET PALACE LTD
28–30 Knightsbridge
London SW1
Tel: (01) 235 7447/7997 and Radlett 7017 (Home)
Oriental rugs and carpets from Persia, Turkey and Pakistan.

ELICHAOFF BROTHERS LTD
76 Mountgrove Road
London N5
Tel: (01) 359 2180
Hand-knotted Oriental rugs and carpets.

ELKANS ANTIQUES LTD
137 Kensington Church Street
London W8
Tel: (01) 221 4026
19th and 20th c. Oriental carpets and rugs.

J. FAIRMAN LTD
218 Westbourne Grove
London W11
Tel: (01) 229 2262/3
Persian carpets, rugs and tapestries.

ROBERT FRANSES AND SON
5 Nugent Terrace
London NW8
Tel: (01) 286 6913
European and Oriental carpets, Turkish village rugs and early Chinese rugs.

S. FRANSES AND COMPANY LTD
71–73 Knightsbridge
London SW1
Tel: (01) 235 1888/3609
Oriental carpets and rugs.

VICTOR FRANSES GALLERY
57 Jermyn Street
London SW1
Tel: (01) 493 6284/629 1144
Oriental and European rugs and carpets.

HERAZ
25 Motcomb Street
London SW1
Tel: Not Available
19th and 20th c. Oriental carpets plus cushions made from early textiles and tapestries.

HESKIA
19 Mount Street
London W1
Tel: (01) 629 1483
Oriental carpets, rugs and tapestries.

ALEXANDER JURAN AND COMPANY
74 New Bond Street
London W1
Tel: (01) 629 2550/493 4484
Nomadic, tribal and Caucasian rugs, carpets and tapestries.

GALLERY KAMRANPOUR
121 Kensington Church Street
London W8
Tel: (01) 727 4703
Rare and decorative Oriental carpets and rugs.

Below: Large stellaform Isphahan rug, courtesy of Portman Carpets.

KENNEDY CARPETS AND KELIMS
9a Vigo Street
London W1
Tel: (01) 439 8873
Mid-19th and early 20th c. Oriental carpets and kelims.

THE LACQUER CHEST
75 Kensington Church Street
London W8
Tel: (01) 937 1306
Carpets from 1800–1900, specialising in the unusual.

JOSEPH LAVIAN
53–79 Highgate Road
London NW5
Tel: (01) 485 7955 and 346 3140 (Home)
18th and 19th c. carpets, rugs and kelims.

LOOT
76/78 Pimlico Road
London SW1
Tel: (01) 730 8097
18th and 19th c. Oriental carpets.

M. AND M. ORIENTAL GALLERY LTD
14 Hallswelle Parade
Finchley Road
Temple Fortune
London NW11 ODL
Tel: (01) 455 4392
Old and antique oriental carpets and rugs from the Caucasus, Persia, Central Asia, Anatolia and other tribal districts.

ALAN MARCUSON LTD
3 Warwick Place
London W9
Tel: (01) 286 7307/8
Central Asian rugs.

A. MAURICE AND COMPANY LTD
78 Wigmore Street
London W1
Tel: (01) 935 1774
16th to 19th c. Persian and Oriental, plus 18th c. European, rugs and carpets.

MAYFAIR CARPETS GALLERY
8 Old Bond Street
London W1
Tel: (01) 493 0126/0127
Antique Persian carpets and rugs.

MAYORCAS LTD
38 Jermyn Street
London SW1
Tel: (01) 629 4195
European carpets and rugs.

NEW STREET CARPET COMPANY LTD
F Block
53–79 Highgate Road
London NW5
Tel: (01) 485 2857
Oriental carpets.

LEON NORELL PERSIAN CARPETS
The International Oriental Carpet Centre
53–79 Highgate Road
London NW5
Tel: (01) 485 8384
Persian and Chinese carpets.

*Below: Mid-19th c. Modjur prayer rug,
courtesy of Zadah Persian Carpets Ltd.*

PARS CARPET COMPANY
137 New Bond Street
London W1
Tel: (01) 499 6952
Persian carpets.

PERSIAN AND ORIENTAL CARPET CENTRE
63 South Audley Street
London W1
Tel: (01) 629 9670
Oriental carpets and kelims from 1850 on.

PHOENIX ANTIQUES LTD
235 Westbourne Grove
London W11
Tel: (01) 221 7218
18th and 19th c. Oriental carpets.

PONTREMOLI LTD
11 Spring Street
London W2
Tel: (01) 723 6664/589 1308

PONTREMOLI LTD (CON'T)
*Carpets including needlework carpets and
Aubusson.*

PORTMAN CARPETS
7 Portman Square
London W1
Tel: (01) 486 3770/9314
*Specialists in traditional, handmade Persian
carpets and rugs.*

PORTMEIRION ANTIQUES
5 Pont Street
London SW1
Tel: (01) 235 7601
Rugs from 1700–1900.

RABIRAFFI ANCIENT ART
36 Davies Street
London W1
Tel: (01) 499 9363/9384
Persian carpets.

RARE CARPETS GALLERY
23 Old Bond Street
London W1
Tel: (01) 491 4315 and 455 4069 (Home)
*Persian, Turkish, Caucasian, Kashmir,
Pakistani and Beluch carpets and rugs.*

SHAIKH AND SON LTD
16 Brook Street
London W1
Tel: (01) 629 3430
Persian carpets and rugs.

VIGO CARPET GALLERY
6a Vigo Street
London W1
Tel: (01) 439 6971
Antique and old rugs, carpets and tapestries.

M.L. WAROUJIAN
110–112 Hammersmith Road
London W6
Tel: (01) 748 7509
Oriental and Persian carpets and rugs.

ZADAH PERSIAN CARPETS LTD
20 Dering Street
New Bond Street
London W1R 9AA
Tel: (01) 493 2622/2673
*Chinese, Tibetan, Turkoman, Caucasian, East
Turkistan, Qashgai, Beluch and Serapi
carpets.*

SOUTH AND SOUTHEAST ENGLAND

HERAZ
3 Market Place
Chalfont St Peter, Bucks
Tel: (02813) 83401
*Antique Oriental carpets plus cushions made
from early textiles and tapestries.*

SOUTHWEST ENGLAND AND WALES

ARTS OF LIVING
18 Green Street
Bath, Avon
Tel: (0225) 64270
*Persian, Afghan, Caucasian, Turkoman, and
old tribal rugs.*

BATH ORIENTAL CARPETS
5 London Street
Walcot
Bath, Avon
Tel: (0225) 60780
Oriental carpets and rugs.

CARPETS AND RUGS / COINS AND MEDALS

J.P.J. HOMER ORIENTAL RUGS
Stoneleigh
Parabola Road
Cheltenham, Glos GL.50 3BD
Tel: (0242) 34243
*Antique and second-hand Oriental carpets and
rugs, specialising in tribal articles.*

ERIC PRIDE ORIENTAL RUGS
8 Imperial Square
Cheltenham, Glos GL50 1QB
Tel: (0242) 580 822
*Old Persian, Central Asian and Caucasian
carpets, rugs and kelims.*

NORTH OF ENGLAND AND SCOTLAND

BEHAR CARPETS
11A Bath Street
Glasgow, Strathclyde, Scotland
Tel: (041) 332 5317
19th c. Oriental rugs and carpets.

A.S. CROSBY
P.O. Box 510
Edinburgh, Lothian, Scotland
Tel: (031) 447 8000
Turkoman carpets.

NORWOOD ANTIQUES
1 Norwood
Beverley, Humberside
Tel: (0482) 868851
18th to early 20th c. Oriental rugs.

WHYTOCK AND REID
Sunbury House
Belford Mews
Edinburgh, Lothian, Scotland EH4 3DN
Tel: (031) 226 4911
19th c. Eastern carpets and rugs.

COINS AND MEDALS

LONDON

A.H. BALDWIN AND SONS LTD
11 Adelphi Terrace
Robert Street, London WC2
Tel: (01) 930 6879/839 1310
*Coins from 600 B.C. to present day and
medals from 16th to 20th c.*

M. BORD
Gold Coin Exchange
16 Charing Cross Road, London WC2
Tel: (01) 836 0631/240 0479
*Roman to Elizabeth II gold, silver and copper
coins.*

COLLECTOR'S CORNER
1 North Cross Road
London SE22
Tel: (01) 693 6285
*American and German insignia, badges and
medals.*

DOLPHIN ANTIQUES
2b Englands Lane
London NW3
Tel: (01) 722 7003
*English and Continental gold and silver coins
from 100 B.C.*

E.H.W. AND COMPANY
12 Sicilian Avenue, Southampton Row
London WC1
Tel: (01) 405 5509
Milled coins and stamps.

STANLEY GIBBONS CURRENCY LTD
17 Piccadilly Arcade, Piccadilly
London SW1
Tel: (01) 493 5082
*British and foreign orders, decorations and
medals from late 18th c.*

HERALDVENE LTD
33 Victoria Road
London E18
Tel: (01) 989 3286
Medals.

KNIGHTSBRIDGE COINS
7 Thurloe Place
London SW7
Tel: (01) 584 7659 (By appointment only)
British, American and South African coins.

JAN LIS
Beaver Coin Room
57 Philbeach Gardens
London SW5 9ED
Tel: (01) 373 4553
*European coins from the Middle Ages to 1850
and commemorative medals from the 15th to
early 20th c.*

MICHAEL COINS
6 Hillgate Street
London W8
Tel: (01) 727 1518
*English and foreign coins, 1066 A.D. to date,
plus stamps and banknotes.*

B.A. SEABY LTD
Audley House
11 Margaret Street
London WC1N 8AT
Tel: (01) 580 3677
*Ancient, mediaeval and modern coins plus
commemorative and campaign medals.*

SICILIAN GALLERY
25 Sicilian Avenue
London WC1
Tel: (01) 458 9933 (Home)
*World coins from 250 B.C.–1900 A.D. and
historical medals from 1500–1900.*

SPINK AND SON LTD
5, 6 and 7 King Street
London SW1
Tel: (01) 930 7888
*Ancient, Mediaeval and modern coins,
banknotes and bullion plus orders and medals.*

VALE ANTIQUES
21 Tranquil Vale
London SE3 OBU
Tel: (01) 852 9817
*Ancient and mediaeval coins, plus British war
medals.*

V.C. VECCHI AND SONS
23 Great Smith Street
London SW1
Tel: (01) 222 4459
*Greek, Roman, Byzantine (post 500 A.D.),
mediaeval and modern coins.*

*Left: Silver medal of the Royal Family, George
II and Queen Caroline, struck in 1732 for
presentation to foreign dignitaries, (centre);
Maximilian I guldiner commemorating his
wedding, circa 1512, (left); and silver "Three
Emperors" thaler of Maximilian I, Charles V
and Ferdinand I, struck between 1612–19 in
Prague, (right), courtesy of B.A. Seaby Ltd.*

HOUSE OF ANTIQUES
4 College Street
Petersfield, Hants
Tel: (0730) 2172
18th and 19th c. medals.

MALDWYN ANTIQUES
12 and 12a Beynon Parade
Carshalton, Surrey
Tel: (01) 669 0793 and 393 4530 (Home)
Coins from 1600–1870.

WARNER'S MILITARY SPECIALISTS
2 The Apple Market
Eden Street
Kingston-upon-Thames, Surrey
Tel: Not Available (Mail Order Only)
Military coins.

SOUTHWEST ENGLAND AND WALES

BATH COIN SHOP
Pulteney Bridge
Bath, Avon
Tel: Not Available
Roman, hammered, early milled, gold, silver and copper coins.

NORTH OF ENGLAND AND SCOTLAND

STRATHEARN ANTIQUES
2 and 8 Comrie Street
Crieff, Tayside, Scotland
Tel: (0764) 4344
17th to 20th c. coins.

Above: Portrait medal (top row, front and back views) made by Hans Schwartz for King Zygmunt I of Poland in 1527, in cast and chased silver; and Trinity medal (bottom row, from and back views) made by Hans Reinhart to the order of Duke Moritz of Saxony in 1544, in cast and chased silver, courtesy of Jan Lis.

W.H. COLLECTABLES
2nd Floor
Westcombe House
56–58 Whitcombe Street
London WC2
Tel: (01) 930 3770
18th to 20th c. British shares plus 19th and 20th c. Russian and Chinese bonds.

STEWART WARD LTD
8 Blenheim Street
London W1
Tel: (01) 629 6166
Gold, English, hammered and milled silver coins, plus Roman and historical medallions and war medals.

SOUTH AND SOUTHEAST ENGLAND

J.D. GOLD
20 Prince Albert Street
Brighton, Sussex
Tel: (0273) 28813
Various numismatic collections.

Right: Order of the Garter, Breast Star (top left), Order of the Indian Empire, sash badge (top right), Order of St Michael and St George, breast star (centre), Order of the Indian Empire (bottom left) and Order of the Bath Military, breast star (bottom right), courtesy of Spink and Son Ltd.

LONDON

ARMOUR-WINSTON LTD
43 Burlington Arcade
London W1
Tel: (01) 493 8937
Specialists in carriage clocks.

ASPREY AND COMPANY LTD
165–169 New Bond Street
London W1Y OAR
Tel: (01) 493 6767
and
153 Fenchurch Street
London EC3
Tel: (01) 626 2160
18th and 19th c. bracket, longcase and carriage clocks.

WILLIAM BEDFORD ANTIQUES LTD
88 Fulham Road
London SW3
Tel: (01) 584 1120
and
327 Upper Street
Islington Green
London N1 2XQ
Tel: (01) 226 9648
18th and 19th c. clocks.

RONALD BENJAMIN ANTIQUES
25b Hatton Garden
(Entrance in Grenville Street)
London EC1
Tel: (01) 242 6188/9105
Clocks and watches from 1800–1920.

Below: A walnut miniature longcase clock with bronze mounts, circa 1890, courtesy of Chelsea Clocks.

BIG BEN
5 Broxholme House
New Kings Road
London SW6
Tel: (01) 736 1770
Antique clocks specialising in early English wall clocks and longcases, plus a selection of watches.

BONROSE ANTIQUES
172 Kensington Antiques
London W8
Tel: (01) 229 5486
French clocks.

F.G. BRUSCHWEILER ANTIQUES LTD
3 Lonsdale Road
London W11
Tel: (01) 229 3106
18th and 19th c. clocks.

BUSHES ANTIQUES
52/53 Camden Passage
London N1
Tel: (01) 226 7096/5972
English and Continental clocks.

BUTLER AND WILSON
189 Fulham Road
London SW3
Tel: (01) 352 3045
1920's and 1930's Rolex watches.

CAMERER CUSS AND COMPANY
54/56 New Oxford Street
London WC1
Tel: (01) 636 8968
Clocks from 1600–1900 and watches from 1600–1930.

CHELSEA CLOCKS
479 Fulham Road
London SW6
Tel: (01) 731 5704
19th to early 20th c. clocks.

JOHN CLAY
263 New Kings Road
London SW6
Tel: (01) 731 5677
18th and 19th c. clocks.

Below: English 8-day ebonized bracket clock by Thwaites and Reed, Clerkenwell, circa 1810, courtesy of Asprey and Company Ltd.

CLOCKS AND WATCHES

COUNTRY PINE LTD
13 Chalk Farm Road
London NW1
Tel: (01) 485 9687
*Pine clocks including longcase clocks from
1820–1920.*

DAEDALUS
43 The Village
Charlton
London SE7 8UG
Tel: (01) 858 2514
*16th and 17th c. European clocks, specialising
in English longcase and bracket clocks.*

DE HAVILLAND ANTIQUES LTD
48 Sloane Street
London SW1
Tel: (01) 235 3534
17th and 18th c. clocks.

DE VILLIERS ANTIQUES
311 Fulham Palace Road
London SW6
Tel: (01) 731 3859
18th and 19th c. clocks.

DOLPHIN ANTIQUES
2b Englands Lane
London NW3
Tel: (01) 722 7003
18th c. English clocks.

PHILIP AND BERNARD DOMBEY
174 Kensington Church Street
London W8
Tel: (01) 229 7100
French clocks.

*Below: Early 17th c. gold German
clock-watch, courtesy of Daedalus.*

JACK DONOVAN
93 Portobello Road
London W11
Tel: (01) 727 1485
Unusual clocks.

EALING ANTIQUES
34 St Mary's Road
London W5
Tel: (01) 567 6192
18th and 19th c. longcase and bracket clocks.

D.J. FERRANT ANTIQUES
21a Camden Passage
and
39 Essex Road
London N1
Tel: (01) 359 2597/1639
Georgian clocks.

FOREST HILL ANTIQUES
7 Davids Road
London SE23
Tel: (01) 699 4061 and 693 5050 (Home)
*18th to early 20th c. clocks, including Art
Nouveau and Art Deco.*

ELAINE FREEDMAN ANTIQUES
Camden Passage
London N1
Tel: Not Available
18th and 19th c. clocks.

VINCENT FREEMAN
8–10 Gateway Arcade
Camden Passage
London N1
Tel: (01) 226 6178
Clocks from 1750–1900.

GAY ANTIQUES
1 Beauchamp Place
London SW3
Tel: (01) 584 9615
French clocks and clock sets.

GREENWICH CHIMES
Nelson Road
London SE10
Tel: Not Available
18th and 19th c. longcase and wall clocks.

KEITH HARDING ANTIQUES
93 Hornsey Road
London N7
Tel: (01) 607 6181/2672
Musical clocks.

W.R. HARVEY AND COMPANY LTD
67/70 Chalk Farm Road
London NW1 8AN
Tel: (01) 485 1504/267 2767
Clocks from 1650–1830.

E. HOLLANDER
80 Fulham Road
London SW3
Tel: (01) 589 7239
*Longcase and English bracket clocks from
1750–1825.*

J.C. ANTIQUES
12 Warwick Terrace
London E17
Tel: (01) 539 4275 and 802 0582 (Home)
19th c. clocks.

ANTHONY JAMES AND SON LTD
253 New Kings Road
London SW6
Tel: (01) 731 3474
Clocks, pre-1830.

MELVYN AND GARY JAY ANTIQUES
64a Kensington Church Street
London W8 4DB
Tel: (01) 937 6832
19th c. clocks.

JULIAN ANTIQUES
67 Park Road
London NW1
Tel: (01) 723 0653
Extremely ornate French clocks and clock sets.

GERALD F. KAYE
60 Lymington Road
London NW6
Tel: (01) 794 1766
Clocks from all periods, specialising in wall clocks.

H. KNOWLES-BROWN LTD
27 Hampstead High Street
London NW3
Tel: (01) 435 4775
Clocks and watches from the Renaissance on.

RICHARD LALLY LTD
152 Upper Richmond Road
London SW15
Tel: (01) 788 9123
18th and 19th c. clocks.

THE LANTERN MAN
2 Beauchamp Road
London SE19
Tel: (01) 653 0930
17th c. longcase and bracket clocks plus Gothic iron clocks.

ERIC LINEHAM ANTIQUES
62 Kensington Church Street
London W8
Tel: (01) 937 8650
English and Continental clocks and clock sets.

THE LITTLE CURIOSITY SHOP
24 The Green
Winchmore Hill
London N21
Tel: (01) 886 0925
Victorian clocks.

LUCKY PARROT
2 Bellevue Parade
Bellevue Road
London SW17
Tel: (01) 672 7168
Longcase and wall clocks from 18th c.

M. AND W. ANTIQUES
2 Parsifal Road
London NW6
Tel: (01) 959 0753
Decorative French clocks and clock sets in ormolu, marble and bronze.

MALLETT AND SON LTD
40 New Bond Street
London W1Y OBS
Tel: (01) 499 7411
18th c. lacquer longcase clocks.

MARSHAL'S ANTIQUES
67 Chancery Lane
London WC2
Tel: (01) 405 4158
19th and 20th c. watches.

JONATHAN MCCREERY
315 Kings Road London SW3
Tel: (01) 352 5733 and (063 583) 680 (Home)
18th and 19th c. clocks.

Above: 19th c. marble and ormolu garniture de cheminée with original gilding, courtesy of Julian Antiques.

MORTLAKE ANTIQUES
69 Lower Richmond Road
London SW14
Tel: (01) 876 8715
Georgian, Victorian and Edwardian longcase and wall clocks.

NORTH LONDON CLOCK SHOP
72 Highbury Park
London N5
Tel: (01) 226 1609
18th and 19th c. longcase, bracket, carriage and skeleton clocks.

OLD TIMES FURNISHING COMPANY
135 Lower Richmond Road
London SW15
Tel: (01) 788 3551
18th and 19th c. clocks.

RAYMOND O'SHEA GALLERY
6 Ellis Street
(Off Sloane Street)
London SW1
Tel: (01) 730 0082
Cartographic clocks.

S.J. PHILLIPS LTD
139 New Bond Street
London W1A 3DL
Tel: (01) 629 6261
Early 19th c. watches.

PORTOBELLO ANTIQUE COMPANY
133 Portobello Road
London W11
Tel: (01) 221 0344
Victorian clocks, from 1860.

RAVEN ANTIQUES
256 Lee High Road
London SE13
Tel: (01) 852 5066
Clocks from 1760–1900.

SOUTH AUDLEY ART GALLERIES LTD
36 South Audley Street
London W1
Tel: (01) 499 3178/3195
19th c. English and French clocks.

STRIKE ONE LTD
51 Camden Passage
London N1
Tel: (01) 226 9709/359 7022/878 2769
Clocks to 1870, especially early English and Act of Parliament clocks, longcase clocks from 1675–1820. English bracket and lantern clocks, French carriage clocks, early Black-Forest clocks, and 18th and 19th c. watches.

IGOR TOCIAPSKI
39–41 Ledbury Road
London W11
Tel: (01) 229 8317
Clocks and watches from 1500–1900.

BRIAN R. VERRALL AND COMPANY
20 Tooting Bec Road
London SW17
Tel: (01) 672 1144
17th to 19th c. clocks.

VOLPONE
12 Wynatt Street
London EC1
Tel: (01) 837 5686
Rare, antique and early electrical clocks.

A.M. WEBB
93 Portobello Road
London W11
Tel: (01) 727 1485
Unusual clocks.

KENNETH WHITE
39 Church Road
London SW19
Tel: (01) 947 3222
18th and 19th c. French clock sets.

J. WOLFF AND SON LTD
1 Chester Court
Albany Street
London NW1
Tel: (01) 935 3636
18th and 19th c. English and French mantel clocks.

P. AND L. WOOLMAN
351 Upper Street
London N1
Tel: (01) 359 7648 and 340 2468 (Home)
Clocks, especially carriage clocks from 1800–1900.

Right: Act of Parliament clock by Daniel Cornwall of Billericay, circa 1795, courtesy of Strike One Ltd.

SOUTH AND SOUTHEAST ENGLAND

ADRIAN ALAN LTD
4 Frederick Place
Brighton, Sussex BN1 4EA
Tel: (0273) 25277/25015
18th and 19th c. clocks.

APOLLO GALLERIES
61, 65 and 67 South End
Croydon, Surrey
Tel: (01) 681 3727/680 1968
18th and 19th c. English and Continental clocks.

ARTBRY'S ANTIQUES
44 High Street
Orpington, Kent
Tel: (01) 868 0834 and 954 1840 (Home)
18th and 19th c. clocks.

CLOCK INVESTMENT
Orpington, Kent
Tel: Orpington 31431 (By appointment only)
English and French carriage, longcase, regulator, skeleton, bracket and wall clocks.

THE CLOCK SHOP
284 Wickham Road
Shirley, Surrey
Tel: (01) 656 2800
18th and 19th c. clocks.

JOHN COWDEROY ANTIQUES
42 South Street
Eastbourne, Sussex
Tel: (0323) 20058
18th and 19th c. clocks. See overleaf for illustration.

HADLOW ANTIQUES
No 1, The Pantiles
Tunbridge Wells, Kent
Tel: (0892) 29858
Clocks and watches. See overleaf for illustration.

HAMPTON WICK ANTIQUES
48 High Street
Hampton Wick, Surrey
Tel: (01) 977 3178
Clocks including longcase, Vienna regulators, bracket and French.

PETER HUNWICK
The Old Malthouse
Hungerford, Berks
Tel: (048 86) 2209
17th to 19th c. longcase, dial, and bracket clocks.

IMPERIAL ANTIQUES
1 Royal Parade
Chislehurst, Kent
Tel: (01) 467 8020
17th and 18th c. clocks.

JULIAN ANTIQUES
124 High Street
Hurstpierpoint, Sussex
Tel: (0273) 832145
Extremely ornate French clocks and clock sets. See entry under "London" for illustration.

KINGSTON ANTIQUES
138 London Road
Kingston-upon Thames, Surrey
Tel: (01) 546 2221
17th to 19th c. clocks.

KNAPHILL ANTIQUES
36–38 High Street
Knaphill, Surrey
Tel: (048 67) 3179
19th and early 20th c. longcase, bracket, wall and mantel clocks.

LE CENTRE ANTIQUES
20 King Street
The Green
Richmond, Surrey
Tel: (01) 948 1505
18th to early 20th c. clocks.

LINCOLN HOUSE GALLERIES
587 London Road
Westcliff-on-Sea, Essex
Tel: (0702) 339106
Pre-Edwardian clocks.

NADJ'S ANTIQUES
36 Crown Road
Twickenham, Middx
Tel: (01) 892 6965
Clocks from 18th c.

B.M. NEWLOVE
139–141 Ewell Road
Surbiton, Surrey
Tel: (01) 399 8857
Longcase clocks.

Right: Westminster chime clock with Nicole Frères music box in the base, dated 1857, courtesy of John Cowderoy Antiques.

NORTON ANTIQUES
56 London Road
Beaconsfield, Bucks HP9 2JH
Tel: (049 46) 3674
18th and 19th c. clocks.

ONSLOW CLOCKS
36 Church Street
Twickenham, Middx
Tel: (01) 892 7632
17th to early 19th c. longcase clocks, 17th to early 18th c. bracket clocks, plus 18th and 19th c. small bracket, carriage and Vienna regulator clocks.

PERIOD FURNITURE SHOWROOMS NO 49
London End
Beaconsfield, Bucks
Tel: (049 46) 4112
18th and 19th c. clocks.

W.A. PINN AND SONS
124 Swan Street
Sible Hedingham
Halstead, Essex
Tel: (0787) 61127
17th to early 19th c. clocks.

J.T. RUTHERFORD AND SON
55 Sandgate High Street
Folkestone, Kent
Tel: (0303) 39515
18th and 19th c. bracket and longcase clocks.

SURREY GALLERIES
295 High Street
Croydon, Surrey
Tel: (01) 681 0975 and 660 9294 (Home)
18th and 19th c. clocks.

TELLING TIME ANTIQUES
42 Park Street
Thame, Oxon
Tel: (0844) 21 3007
Clocks, including verge and fusée, and watches.

Below: 19th c. gold, hunting-cased, minute-repeating, perpetual calendar chronograph, courtesy of Hadlow Antiques.

S. WARRENDER AND COMPANY
4 Cheam Road
Sutton, Surrey
Tel: (01) 643 4381
Carriage clocks from 1860–1900.

WITHAM ANTIQUES
27a Bridge Street
Witham, Essex
Tel: (0376) 512407
Longcase clocks specialists.

YELLOW LANTERN ANTIQUES LTD
34/65b Holland Road
Hove, Sussex BU3 1JL
Tel: (0273) 771572
19th c. clocks specialising in ormolu.

SOUTHWEST ENGLAND AND WALES

ABOYNE ANTIQUES
13 York Street
Bath, Avon
Tel: (0225) 64850 and 319961 (Home)
18th c. clocks.

BELL PASSAGE ANTIQUES
38 High Street
Wickwar
Wotton-under-Edge, Glos GL12 8NP
Tel: (045 424) 251
18th and 19th c. clocks and barometers.

THE CLOCK SHOP
9 Walcot Street
Bath, Avon
Tel: (0225) 62756 and (027 588) 2279
Longcase clocks.

COUNTRY ANTIQUES
Castle Mill
The Bridge
Kidwelly, Dyfed, Wales
Tel: (0554) 890534
Pre-1900 clocks.

MICHAEL G. COX
Avon House
Tetbury, Glos
Tel: (0666) 52201
17th to early 19th c. English clocks.

JOHN CROFT ANTIQUES
3 George Street
Bath, Avon
Tel: (0225) 66211
17th to early 19th c. clocks.

GEORGE CURTIS
14 Suffolk Parade
Cheltenham, Glos
Tel: (0242) 513828
17th to 19th c. English and Continental clocks.

GASTRELL HOUSE
33 Long Street
Tetbury, Glos GL8 8AA
Tel: (0666) 52228
17th to early 19th c. clocks.

ARTHUR S. LEWIS
The Stables
Link End House
Corselawn, Glos
Tel: (0452) 78 258
18th and 19th c. clocks.

MIDLANDS AND EAST ANGLIA

COLIN DAVIES ANTIQUES
15 Wolverhampton Road
Stafford, Staffs
Tel: (0785) 40545
French clocks and watches, especially clock sets and carriage clocks.

FEARNS ANTIQUES
9 Coleshill Street
Fazeley, nr Tamworth, Staffs
Tel: (0827) 54233
18th to early 20th c. clocks.

LOCKES
The Buttercross
Ludlow, Shropshire
Tel: (0584) 2061
Clocks, watches and scientific instruments.

JOHN NOOTT FINE PAINTINGS
Picton House Gallery
Broadway, Worcs
Tel: (0386) 85287
19th and 20th c. clocks.

WHERRY HOUSE ANTIQUES
The Street
Sutton, Norfolk NR12 9RF
Tel: (0692) 81487 (By appointment only)
18th and 19th longcase, wall and mantel clocks.

NORTH OF ENGLAND AND SCOTLAND

ADAMS ANTIQUES
65 Waterloo Row
Chester, Cheshire CH1 2LE
Tel: (0244) 319421
18th and 19th c. clocks.

ANTIQUES
55 High Street
Biggar, Strathclyde, Scotland
Tel: (0899) 20371
19th c. longcase clocks.

BROWNS OF ARGYLE STREET LTD
1060 Argyle Street
Glasgow, Strathclyde, Scotland
Tel: (041) 248 6760
19th c. longcase, bracket and mantel clocks.

HAMISH M. EDWARD
50 Wellington Street
Glasgow, Strathclyde, Scotland
Tel: (041) 248 7723
18th and 19th c. clocks.

EUREKA ANTIQUES
18 Northenden Road
Sale, Cheshire M33 3BR
Tel: (061) 962 5629
18th and 19th c. clocks.

Below: Louis XVI ormolu and marble mantel clock, often known as a "Reading and Writing" clock, circa 1780, courtesy of W.A. Pinn and Sons.

HAREWOOD ANTIQUES
26–27 Harrogate Road
Harewood, Leeds, W Yorkshire LS17 9LH
Tel: (0532) 886327
Victorian clocks.

PITTENWEEM ANTIQUES
The Shaw House
Boreland, nr Lockerbie,
Dumfries and Galloway, Scotland
Tel: (057 66) 223 (By appointment only)
Clocks including 17th c. marquetry, longcase, musical, English carriage and bracket.

VICTORIANA ANTIQUES
70 Rosemount Viaduct
Aberdeen, Grampian, Scotland
Tel: (0224) 20219
18th c. to early 20th c. longcase clocks.

WHEELWRIGHTS ANTIQUES
Pinfold Lane
Fishlake, Doncaster, S Yorkshire DN7 5LA
Tel: (0302) 841411
Longcase clocks.

CHRISTOPHER WOOD
37 Colinton Road
Edinburgh, Lothian, Scotland
Tel: (031) 447 2381
17th to 19th longcase and bracket clocks.

NORTHERN IRELAND

THE ANTIQUE SHOP
Main Street
Templepatrick, Antrim, N Ireland
Tel: (084 94) 32645
18th c. clocks.

GREYABBEY TIMECRAFT LTD
18 Main Street
Greyabbey, Co Down, N Ireland
Tel: (024 774) 416
19th c. clocks and watches.

K. AND M. NESBITT
21 Tobermore Road
Magheraflet, Londonderry BT45 5HB
N Ireland
Tel: (0648) 32713
18th to 20th c. clocks and watches.

LONDON

ANNIE'S ANTIQUES AND CLOTHES
10 Camden Passage
London N1
Tel: (01) 359 0796
Period costume and accessories to 1950.

BOHUN AND BUSBRIDGE
8 Clarendon Road
London W11
Tel: (01) 229 7825
Kashmir, Paisley, and Norwich shawls, folk costumes, lace, and silks, all 16th to 19th c.

BUTLER AND WILSON
189 Fulham Road
London SW3
Tel: (01) 352 3045
Crocodile wallets.

THE BUTTON QUEEN
19 Marylebone Lane
London W1
Tel: (01) 935 1505
Old and antique buttons and buckles including those made from ivory, bone, horn, etc.

COLLECTOR'S CORNER
1 North Cross Road
London SE22
Tel: (01) 693 6285
American and German military items including uniforms, helmets, badges, and medals.

CORNUCOPIA
12 Upper Tachbrook Street
London SW1
Tel: (01) 828 5752
Clothes and accessories from 1910–1960.

GLAMOUR CITY
54 Battersea Bridge Road
London SW11
Tel: (01) 223 7436
Clothes and accessories from 1930–1960.

LUNN ANTIQUES
86 New Kings Road
London SW6
Tel: (01) 736 4638
Pre-war clothing and some early costume.

SPREAD EAGLE ANTIQUES
8 Nevada Street
London SE10
Tel: (01) 692 1618/858 9713
Costume, pre-1940.

THREE FIVE ONE
351 Lillie Road
London SW6
Tel: (01) 381 0724
Ladies' and mens' clothing from 1920–1950.

TRADITION MILITARY ANTIQUES
5a and 5b Shepherd Street
London W1
Tel: (01) 493 7452
Military uniforms.

SOUTH AND SOUTHEAST ENGLAND

THE LEOPARD
41 Gloucester Road
Brighton, Sussex
Tel: (0273) 507619
18th to early 20th c. clothes, specialising in lace-trimmed items.

Below: Edwardian lace-trimmed undergarment, courtesy of The Leopard.

Left: Linocut by Gerry Richards, the owner of Cornucopia, showing the type of clothing and accessories sold.

SOUTHWEST ENGLAND AND WALES

CORNER HOUSE ANTIQUES
31a Rivers Street
Bath, Avon
Tel: Not Available
18th to early 20th c. costume.

ORIENTAL ANTIQUES
4 Belvedere
Lansdown Road
Bath, Avon BA1 5ED
Tel: (0225) 315987
Oriental costume and embroidery.

RED BARN
Pontcanna Street
Cardiff, S Glamorgan
Tel: (0222) 513437
Period clothes from 1900–1950 including buttons.

NORTH OF ENGLAND AND SCOTLAND

HAND IN HAND
3 North West Circus Place
Edinburgh, Lothian, Scotland
Tel: (031) 556 8897
Victorian costume and shawls, including Paisley.

J. MASTERTON
93 West Bow
Edinburgh, Lothian, Scotland
Tel: (031) 225 5918
Military costumes, badges and medals.

NORWOOD ANTIQUES
1 Norwood
Beverley, Humberside
Tel: (0482) 868851
18th to early 20th c. costume.

NOSTALGIA
101 Spital
Aberdeen, Grampian, Scotland
Tel: (0224) 630469
Clothes from 1900–1940.

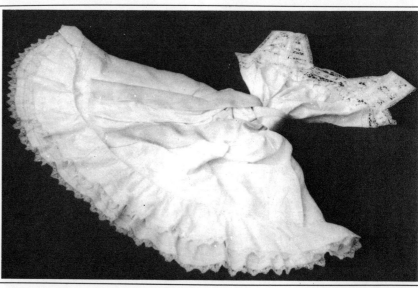

DOLLS AND DOLLS' HOUSES

Left: Armond Marseilles 390 doll with bisque face, composition body, circa 1900, courtesy of Anthea Knowles.

SOUTH AND SOUTHEAST OF ENGLAND

ARTS DE DIANE
7 Odeon Parade
London Road
Isleworth, Middx
Tel: (01) 560 2423
Victorian dolls.

CURIOSITY SHOP
72 Stafford Road, Wallington, Surrey
Tel: (01) 647 5267
19th and early 20th c. dolls.

HADLOW ANTIQUES
No. 1, The Pantiles
Tunbridge Wells, Kent
Tel: (0892) 29858
19th and early 20th c. dolls.

YESTERDAY CHILD
Woburn Abbey Antiques Centre
Woburn, Beds
Tel: (052 525) 350
Dolls from 1800–1925, including rare French Bébés, character dolls and dolly-faced dolls from babies to toddlers.

SOUTHWEST ENGLAND AND WALES

CHINA DOLL
31 Suffolk Parade
Cheltenham, Glos
Tel: (0242) 33164
Dolls with china or wax heads plus accessories, houses and furnishings.

COUNTRY ANTIQUES
Castle Mill, The Bridge
Kidwelly, Dyfed, Wales
Tel: (0554) 890534
Pre-1900 dolls.

STUDIO TWO ANTIQUES
11 Upper Clwyd Street
Ruthin, Clwyd, Wales
Tel: (082 42) 3814
Dolls and juvenalia.

TREWITHEN COTTAGE DOLLS
Trewithen Cottage
Fore Street
Grampound, Truro, Cornwall
Tel: (0726) 882692
China-headed dolls from 1870–1925.

WEST WALES ANTIQUES
18 Manselfield Road
Bishopston, Nr Swansea
W Glamorgan, Wales
Tel: (044 128) 4318
and
6a Corvus Terrace
St Clears, Dyfed, Wales
Tel: (0994) 230 576
Dolls from 1880–1920.

MIDLANDS AND EAST ANGLIA

MERIDIAN HOUSE ANTIQUES
Meridian House
Market Street
Stourbridge, W Midlands
Tel: (038 43) 5384
Victorian and Edwardian dolls.

LONDON

ANTIQUE TOY CENTRE
51 Camden Passage
London N1
Tel: (01) 226 4255 and 607 0846
Late 19th c. to early 20th c. dolls.

KAY DESMONDE
17 Kensington Church Walk
London W8
Tel: (01) 937 2602 (By appointment only)
Dolls, doll's houses and doll's house furniture.

THE DOLLS HOUSE TOYS LTD
29 The Market
Covent Garden
London WC2
Tel: (01) 379 7243
Doll's houses and miniature furniture.

THE DOLLS HOUSE TOYS LTD
116 Lisson Grove
London NW1
Tel: (01) 723 1418 and (0787) 75884 (Home)
Doll's houses and furniture.

GREENS ANTIQUE GALLERIES
117 Kensington Church Street
London W8
Tel: (01) 229 9618/9
19th and early 20th c. dolls.

ANTHEA KNOWLES
42 Barnsbury Street
London N1 (By appointment only)
Tel: (01) 607 0846
19th and early 20th c. dolls.

JILL LEWIS
Collector's Corner
138 Portobello Road
London W11
Tel: (040) 372 2357
Doll's house items.

THE SINGING TREE
69 New Kings Road
London SW6
Tel: (01) 736 4527
Victorian doll's houses and accessories.

TRAFALGAR ANTIQUES
117 Trafalgar Road
London SE10
Tel: (01) 858 3709
Dolls from 1750–1900.

YESTERDAY CHILD
24 The Mall
Camden Passage
London N1
Tel: (01) 354 1601 and (0908) 583403
Dolls from 1800–1925 including rare French Bébés and character dolls.

LONDON

ABBOTT AND HOLDER
73 Castlenau
London SW13
Tel: (01) 748 2416
18th to early 20th c. drawings under £500.

THOMAS AGNEW AND SONS LTD
43 Old Bond Street
London W1X 4BA
Tel: (01) 629 6176
Drawings by Old Masters of all schools.

ASTORIA
222 Munster Road
London SW6
Tel: (01) 385 9888
Art Deco drawings.

BALCOMBE GALLERIES
Stanley Studios
Park Walk
London SW10
Tel: (01) 352 4353
Drawings from 1830–1920.

BASKETT AND DAY
173 New Bond Street
London W1
Tel: (01) 629 2991
16th to 19th c. Old Master drawings, plus early English drawings.

JOANNA BOOTH
247 Kings Road
London SW3
Tel: (01) 352 8998
Old Master drawings.

BROD GALLERY
24 St James's Street
London SW1
Tel: (01) 839 3871/2
Flemish drawings.

THE BROTHERTON GALLERY LTD
77 Walton Street
London SW3 2HT
Tel: (01) 589 6848
19th and early 20th c. landscape and natural history drawings.

YVONNE TAN BUNZL
c/o Barclays Bank
19 Great Cumberland Place
London W1
Tel: (01) 229 7856 (By appointment only)
19th c. French and Italian Old Master drawings.

JOHN CASSAYD-SMITH
4 Royal Opera Parade
Pall Mall
London SW1
Tel: (01) 930 2571 and Watford 29932 (Home)
15th to 19th c. Old Master drawings.

CHAPMAN AND DAVIES ANTIQUES
10 Theberton Street
London N1
Tel: (01) 226 5565/348 4846/359 4330
17th to early 20th c. drawings.

CHAUCER AND VAN DAM GALLERIES
45 Pimlico Road
London SW1
Tel: (01) 235 8235
Old Master drawings.

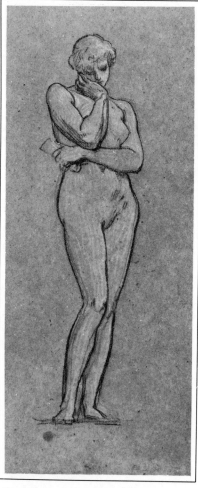

Above: Figure study in black chalk by Frederick, Lord Leighton (1830–1896), courtesy of Julian Hartnoll.

CLARGES GALLERY
158 Walton Street
London SW3
Tel: (01) 584 3022
19th and 20th c. British drawings.

COLNAGHI AND COMPANY
14 Old Bond Street
London W1
Tel: (01) 491 7408
Old Master drawings.

JEREMY COOPER LTD
9 Galen Place
Bury Place
London WC1A 2JR
Tel: (01) 242 5138/404 0336
Architectural drawings from 1830–1940.

JOHN DENHAM
The Gallery
50 Mill Lane
London NW6
Tel: (01) 794 2635
17th to 20th c. drawings.

DOUWES FINE ART
38 Duke Street
London SW1
Tel: (01) 839 5795
Old Master drawings.

EYRE AND HOBHOUSE LTD
39 Duke Street
London SW1
Tel: (01) 930 9308

EYRE AND HOBHOUSE LTD (CON'T)
19th c. drawings relating to subjects by European artists in India and the Far East.

FRY GALLERY
58 Jermyn Street
London SW1
Tel: (01) 493 4496
Old Master drawings, specialising in 18th and 19th c. English drawings.

GREEN AND HEWETT
188 Dartmouth Road
London SE26
Tel: (01) 699 5461
Early English drawings.

A. AND K. HART-DAVIS
10 Hampstead Way
London N11
Tel: (01) 455 6581/458 4000
18th and 19th c. drawings.

JULIAN HARTNOLL
Second Floor
14 Masons' Yard
Duke Street
London SW1
Tel: (01) 839 3842 (By appointment only)
19th c. British drawings, especially Victorian figure drawings.

HAZLITT, GOODEN AND FOX LTD
38 Bury Street
London SW1
Tel: (01) 930 6422/3
19th c. English and French drawings.

MILNE HENDERSON
99 Mount Street
London W1
Tel: (01) 499 2507
Chinese and Japanese drawings.

N.W. LOTT AND H.J. GERRISH LTD
14 Masons Yard
Duke Street
London SW1
Tel: (01) 930 1353
19th and early 20th c. drawings.

PETER LOVEDAY PRINTS
46 Norland Square
London W11
Tel: (01) 221 4479 (By appointment only)
Drawings, especially of British sporting life.

MAAS GALLERY
15a Clifford Street
London W1
Tel: (01) 734 2302
Victorian drawings.

MATHIESEN FINE ART LTD
7/8 Masons Yard
Duke Street
London SW1
Tel: (01) 930 2437
Old Master drawings.

JOHN MITCHELL AND SON
8 New Bond Street
First Floor
London W1
Tel: (01) 493 7567
17th c. Dutch, 18th c. English, and 19th c. French drawings.

MORTON MORRIS AND COMPANY
32 Bury Street
London SW1
Tel: (01) 930 2825
17th to 19th c. English drawings.

Above: "The Artist's Sister Rose", by Gerald Ososki a red chalk drawing from 1932, courtesy of C.J. Orson.

GERALD OSOSKI
7 Heath Hurst Road
London NW3
Tel: (01) 435 2959
16th to early 20th c. Old Master drawings.

MICHAEL PARKIN FINE ART LTD
11 Motcomb Street
London SW1
Tel: (01) 235 8144
British drawings from 1840–1940.

ANNABEL POPOVIC
11 Shafto Mews
Cadogan Square
London SW1
Tel: (01) 727 9705/1207 (By appointment only)
Old Master drawings.

SABIN GALLERIES LTD
4 Cork Street
London W1
Tel: (01) 734 6186
Georgian drawings.

CHARLES J. SAWYER
1 Grafton Street
London W1
Tel: (01) 493 3810
Antiquarian bookseller with drawings by book illustrators from 19th and early 20th c.

G.T. SIDEN
69 Compayne Gardens
London NW6
Tel: (01) 624 9045 (By appointment only)
16th to 19th c. drawings.

Right: "Montague's Harrier" a charcoal and wash drawing signed by the artist, Joseph Wolf, R.I. (1820–1899), courtesy of the Brotherton Gallery Ltd.

THE SLADMORE GALLERY
32 Bruton Place
Berkeley Square
London W1
Tel: (01) 499 0365
Wild life drawings.

ANDREW SMITHSON MASTER DRAWINGS
50 South Molton Street
London W1
Tel: (01) 629 4434
16th to 18th c. Dutch and Italian Old Master drawings.

CHARLES YOUNG LTD
Second Floor
Old Bond Street House
6/8 Old Bond Street
London W1
Tel: (01) 499 1117
19th c. English drawings.

LEIGH UNDERHILL GALLERY
100 Islington High Street
London N1
Tel: (01) 226 5673
British drawings from 1900–1940.

SOUTH AND SOUTHEAST ENGLAND

BALCOMBE GALLERIES
Balcombe, Sussex
Tel: (044 483) 439
Drawings from 1830–1920.

HAMPTON HILL GALLERY
203 and 205 High Street
Hampton Hill, Middx
Tel: (01) 977 1379/5273
18th to early 20th c. drawings.

SOUTHWEST ENGLAND AND WALES

C.J. ORSON
London House
Ruardean, Glos GL17 9UT
Tel: (0594) 542309
18th to 20th c. English drawings, specialising in works by Gerald Ososki RBA.

NORTH OF ENGLAND AND SCOTLAND

THE FINE ART SOCIETY LTD
12 Great King Street
Edinburgh, Lothian, Scotland
Tel: (031) 557 1903
British, especially Scottish, drawings from 1800 on.

Above: Guinness poster by Ron Gilroy, an artist famous for his Guinness posters, printed for Christmas 1958, courtesy of Dodo.

LONDON

BRIAN BALL
227 Ebury Street
London SW1
Tel: (01) 730 5000
Nursery games, postcards and other ephemera.

ANDREW BLOCK
20 Barter Street
London WC1
Tel: (01) 405 9660 and 435 1350 (Home)
Printed ephemera.

CINEMA BOOKSHOP
13–14 Great Russell Street
London WC1
Tel: (01) 637 0206
Cinema posters.

CLUNES AND FOSTER ANTIQUES
9 West Place
Wimbledon Common
London SW19
Tel: (01) 946 1643
Theatricalia.

DODO
185 Westbourne Grove
London W11
Tel: (01) 229 3132
Advertisements, posters, signs, tins, toys, shop display figures and fittings, English, French and American labels from fruit crates, wine, beer and scent bottles.

GAME ADVICE
1 Holmes Road
London NW5
Tel: (01) 485 2188 and 485 4226 (Home)
Games, puzzles, jigsaws, cards and other 18th and 19th c. ephemera.

STANLEY GIBBONS
391, 395 and 399 Strand
and
37 Southampton Street
London WC2
Tel: (01) 836 8444
Playing cards and postcards.

GLAMOUR CITY
54 Battersea Bridge Road
London SW11
Tel: (01) 223 7436
Original 1940's pin-up calendars and ephemera.

GOLFIANA MISCELLANEA LTD
84 Kingsway
London WC2
Tel: (01) 405 5323
Golfing memorabilia.

JOHN HALL ANTIQUES AND PRINTS
17 Harrington Road
London SW7 3ES
Tel: (01) 584 1307
Victorian greeting cards, postcards and ephemera relating to music and the theatre.

JUBILEE POSTCARDS
25 Arlington Way
Sadlers Wells
London EC1
Tel: Not Available
Ephemera, specialising in postcards.

LONDON POSTCARD CENTRE
21 Kensington Park Road
London W11
Tel: (01) 229 1888/727 0505
Postcards, photographs, posters and advertising ephemera.

THE MINERAL KINGDOM
3 Pierrepont Arcade
Camden Passage
London N1
Tel: Not Available
Pre-1914 postcards.

PLEASURES OF PAST TIMES
11 Cecil Court
Charing Cross Road
London WC2
Tel: (01) 836 1142
19th c. decorative ephemera including postcards, Valentine cards, posters and playbills.

HENRY SOTHERAN LTD
2, 3, 4, and 5 Sackville Street
London W.1X 2DP
Tel: (01) 734 1150
Antique documents and autograph letters.

SPREAD EAGLE ANTIQUES
8 Nevada Street
London SE10
Tel: (01) 692 1618/858 9713
Postcards, pre-1940.

PETER STOCKHAM AT IMAGES
16 Cecil Court
Charing Cross Road
London WC2
Tel: (01) 836 8661
Printed ephemera.

TAURUS GALLERY
637 Fulham Road
London SW6
Tel: (01) 736 1031
17th to 19th c. ephemera.

TAVERN TREASURES
7b Nelson Road
London SE10
Tel: (01) 853 5777 (By appointment only)
Wine and beer trade relics, including prints and posters.

Above: Large "La Raphaelle Liqueur Bonal" poster, printed in 1908, courtesy of Dodo.

VALE ANTIQUES
21 Tranquil Vale
London SE3 OBU
Tel: (01) 852 9817
Edwardian cigarette cards and postcards.

SOUTH AND SOUTHEAST ENGLAND

CURIOSITY SHOP
72 Stafford Road
Wallington, Surrey
Tel: (01) 647 5267
Early 20th c. postcards.

SOUTHWEST ENGLAND AND WALES

BIBLIOTIQUE
2 Canton Place
London Road
Bath, Avon
Tel: (0225) 312932
19th and early 20th c. ephemera.

CORRIDOR STAMP SHOP
7a The Corridor
Bath, Avon
Tel: (0225) 63368 and 316445
Picture postcards and cigarette cards from 1895–1940.

COUNTRY ANTIQUES
Castle Mill
The Bridge
Kidwelly, Dyfed, Wales
Tel: (0554) 890534
Pre-1900 postcards.

NORTH OF ENGLAND AND SCOTLAND

STRATHEARN ANTIQUES
2 and Comrie Street
Crieff, Tayside, Scotland
Tel: (0764) 4344
19th and early 20th c. postcards.

ADRIAN WALKER
160 Victoria Road
Scarbrough, N Yorks YO11 1SX
Tel: (0723) 73029
Postcards and ephemera.

FIREPLACES AND STOVES

Left: Antique German coal or solid fuel stove, manufactured by Gebr. Siegel in Mulhausen about 1910, courtesy of Infourneaux.

WILLIAM CLEVELAND
40 Queensdale Road
London W11
Tel: (01) 603 5050 and 727 1620 (Home)
18th and 19th c. marble mantelpieces.

T. CROWTHER AND SON LTD
282 North End Road
London SW6 1NH
Tel: (01) 385 1375/7
18th c. carved wood and marble chimneypieces and accessories.

A. CURD
221 Dawes Road
London W6
Tel: (01) 385 0484
Marble and wood mantelpieces, cast iron firepieces, plus fireplace equipment such as brass fenders and fire irons.

A. AND R. DOCKERILL LTD
78 Deodar Road
London SW15
Tel: (01) 874 2101
French and English marble and pine chimneypieces plus oak and pine panelling.

J. GOTTLIEB LTD
227–229 Westbourne Grove
London W11
Tel: (01) 874 7832
Old fireplace equipment.

J. GROTTY AND SON LTD
74 New Kings Road
London SW6
Tel: (01) 385 1789
18th and 19th c. fire grates and fenders plus marble and pine mantelpieces.

HALLIDAYS ANTIQUES
28 Beauchamp Place
London SW3 1NJ
Tel: (01) 589 5534
Original mantelpieces (and reproductions) plus all accessories for the period fireplace.

HEIRLOOM AND HOWARD LTD
1 Hay Hill
Berkeley Square
London W1
Tel: (01) 493 5868
Specialists in armorial antiques, ie those with coats-of-arms or crests on them, including fire-screens.

HOLLINGSHEAD AND COMPANY
783 Fulham Road
London SW6
Tel: (01) 385 8519
Marble and wood mantelpieces, grates, fenders and fire irons.

INFOURNEAUX
65 Mill Lane
London NW6 1NB
Tel: (01) 794 1511
Continental and British stoves, plus Victorian, Edwardian and Art Nouveau fireplaces and mantels.

JULIAN ANTIQUES
67 Park Road
London NW1
Tel: (01) 723 0653
16th to 18th c. French marble fireplaces, fenders and fire-screens.

Below: Late Victorian cast iron fire surround with tile panels, courtesy of Mr Wandle's Workshop.

SEE ALSO ENTRIES UNDER "SPECIALIST DEALERS – ARCHITECTURAL ITEMS".

LONDON

ACQUISITIONS LTD
269 Camden High Street
London NW1
Tel: (01) 485 4955
Victorian and Edwardian fireplaces and fireplace accessories.

ACTINO ANTIQUES
136 Lee High Road
London SE13
Tel: (01) 318 1273
19th and early 20th c. fireside accessories.

AMAZING GRATES
Phoenix House, 61–63 High Road
London N2
Tel: (01) 883 9590
Georgian, Victorian and Edwardian fireplaces and mantelpieces in marble or iron plus period ceramic tiles and fire irons.

THE ARCHITECTURAL ANTIQUE MARKET
4–8 Highgate High Street
London N6
Tel: (01) 341 3761/348 4846/340 8476/359 4330 and 830 5256
Architectural items including fire surrounds.

BLUE MANTLE
299 Old Kent Road
London SE1
Tel: (01) 237 3931
Victorian, Edwardian and Art Nouveau fireplaces.

Right: Cast iron, French enamelled stove, circa 1930 (left) and French wood-burning stove finished in coloured glass enamel with hot plate on top, circa 1910, (right), courtesy of the Stove Shop.

TOBY MITCHELL
17 Chalk Farm Road
London NW1
Tel: (01) 485 0831
Leather-topped fenders.

ODDIQUITIES
61 Waldram Park Road
and
20 Sunderland Road
London SE23
Tel: (01) 699 9574
Fireplace accessories from 1780–1920.

PAGEANT ANTIQUES
122 Dawes Road
London SW6
Tel: (01) 385 7739
Marble and wood fireplaces.

H.W. POULTER AND SON
279 Fulham Road
London SW10
Tel: (01) 352 7268
English and French marble chimneypieces, and hearths, plus grates, fenders, fire irons and brass accessories.

PRATT AND BURGESS LTD
7 Old Brompton Road
London SW7
Tel: (01) 589 8501
18th c. mantelpieces.

SMIFFS ANTIQUES
121 High Road
London N2
Tel: (01) 883 6121
Brass, copper and iron fenders, fire-screens and fireplace accessories.

STOVE SHOP
Camden Lock, Chalk Farm Road
London NW1
Tel: (01) 969 9531
19th and early 20th c. Scandinavian and French stoves and cooking ranges.

MR WANDLE'S WORKSHOP
200–202 Garratt Lane
London SW18 4ED
Tel: (01) 870 5873
Victorian and Edwardian fireplaces and surrounds, specialising in cast iron. See previous page for illustration.

WHITEWAY AND WALDRON LTD
305 Munster Road
London SW6
Tel: (01) 381 3195
Fire surrounds in wood and cast iron.

O.F. WILSON LTD
Queens Elm Parade
Old Church Street
London SW3
Tel: (01) 352 9554
English and French mantelpieces.

SOUTH AND SOUTHEAST ENGLAND

HALLIDAYS ANTIQUES
The Old College
Dorchester-on-Thames, Oxon OX9 8HL
Tel: (0865) 340028
Original mantelpieces and accessories.

MARBLE HILL GALLERY
72 Richmond Road
Twickenham, Middx
Tel: (01) 892 1488
Pine and French marble mantels.

BERTRAM NOLLER
14a London Road
Reigate, Surrey RH1 5RY
Tel: Reigate 42548
Specialists in brass fenders of all periods.

MIDLANDS AND EAST ANGLIA

R.N. USHER
42 Southgate Street
Bury St Edmunds, Suffolk
Tel: (0284) 4838
Pine and marble mantelpieces.

Above: Finely carved 18th c. chimneypiece, circa 1750, courtesy of Robert Aagaard Ltd.

NORTH OF ENGLAND AND SCOTLAND

ROBERT AAGAARD LTD
Frogmire House
Stockwell Road
Knaresborough, N Yorkshire
Tel: (0423) 864805
17th to 19th c. pine and marble chimneypieces, hob grates and fire irons.

H.H. CRAFTS
325 Abbeydale Road
Sheffield, S Yorkshire ST15
Tel: (0742) 589872
Wood and cast iron fire surrounds.

FURNITURE INTRODUCTION

Furniture is, by its very nature, the broadest category in which antique dealerships fall. In this section, you will find shops of two kinds – those which specialise in a certain object such as brass beds, and those which sell furniture from a specific period, such as Georgian. If you know a little about furniture styles, the entries in the latter category will give you an idea of the "look" of the furniture in the shop.

You will also occasionally come across dealers whose stock covers a relatively long period of time, such as those selling "18th and 19th c. furniture". This generally implies that the dealer has a very extensive range of furniture, usually occupying several hundred square feet. Of course, most furniture dealers, whatever their size, do carry a selection of furniture. It would not make economic sense for them to carry, say, just chairs, neither would it make geographic sense, as buyers would have to travel miles, darting from one shop to the other.

When looking for a particular piece, a few well-placed phone calls to similarly-described dealers in your locale, followed by a visit or two, should locate the piece you're after. If you cannot find the item, but like the stock of the dealer, do not hesitate to ask if he/she knows where you might locate the thing you are looking for. Most dealers will be more than happy to assist you. They may have another shop, or be able to recommend a colleague who carries similar things.

If time is short, it makes sense to visit one of the vast warehouses or markets listed on pages 153–155. Alternatively, frequent an area where there are clusters of individual antique shops. Competition is stiff in these areas, so business is brisk and stock changes quickly. However, don't expect to locate antique furniture the way you'd buy modern built-in pieces. Half the fun in visiting antique shops is finding just the right thing in an unexpected place, when you are not looking for it.

LONDON

ADAMS ANTIQUES
47 Chalk Farm Road
London NW1
Tel: (01) 267 9241
18th and 19th c. country furniture including mahogany and pine.

NORMAN ADAMS LTD
8–10 Hans Road
London SW3
Tel: (01) 589 5266
18th c. English furniture.

ALBANY ANTIQUES LTD
79 Albany Street
London NW1
Tel: (01) 387 3187
18th c. furniture.

DAVID ALEXANDER ANTIQUES
102 Waterford Road
London SW6
Tel: (01) 731 4644
16th to early 18th c. English and Continental furniture.

ALEXANDER AND BERENDT LTD
la Davies Street
London W1
Tel: (01) 499 4775
17th and 18th c. French furniture.

PETER ALLEN ANTIQUES LTD
17–17a Nunhead Green
London SE15
Tel: (01) 732 1968
and
111 Portobello Road
London W11
Tel: (01) 727 3397
Victorian furniture.

GEORGE AMOS AND SONS
Lion Works
New End Square
London NW3
Tel: (01) 435 0052/3
Georgian country and decorative furniture including pine and mahogany.

MARIA ANDIPA ICON GALLERY
162 Walton Street
London SW3
Tel: (01) 589 2371
Early country furniture.

AND SO TO BED LTD
96b Camden High Street
London NW1
Tel: (01) 388 0364/5
and
638–640 Kings Road
London SW6
Tel: (01) 731 3593/4/5
and
7 New Kings Road
London SW6
Tel: (01) 731 3593
Victorian four-posters, half-testers and headboards in brass, brass and wood, and iron and brass.

ANFORA LTD ANTIQUES
20 Motcomb Street
London SW1
Tel: (01) 235 6317 and 229 2342 (Home)
15th to 19th c. Continental furniture, specialising in Italian.

Below: Bow-fronted mahogany chest-of-drawers, circa 1800, courtesy of Anno Domini. See overleaf for entry.

ANNO DOMINI
66 Pimlico Road
London SW1
Tel: (01) 730 5496
18th and early 19th c. furniture. See previous page for illustration.

STEPHEN ANSON
25 Bassingham Road
London SW18
Tel: (01) 874 1529 (By appointment only)
English, oak and country furniture, from 1600–1800.

IRMA ANTICHITA
42–61 Ledbury Road
London W11
Tel: (01) 229 7942 and 373 8047 (Home)
Continental furniture.

THE ANTIQUE GALLERY
40 Peckham Rye
London SE15
Tel: (01) 732 7808
Victorian and Edwardian furniture, specialising in oak.

ANTIQUE AND DECORATIVE FURNISHINGS
60 Hoppers Road
Winchmore Hill
London N21
Tel: Not Available
19th c. English furniture.

THE ANTIQUE HOME
104a Kensington Church Street
London W8
Tel: (01) 229 5892
18th and 19th c. English furniture.

ANTIQUE PUSSY
965 Fulham Road
London SW6
Tel: (01) 731 2814
Furniture from 1650–1939.

ANTIQUE RESTORATIONS
211 Westbourne Park Road
London W11
Tel: (01) 727 0467
Painted furniture.

ANTIQUES
11 Lordship Lane
London SE22
Tel: (01) 693 9136 and 670 6428 (Home)
Furniture from 1750–1910.

ANTIQUES AND FINE ARTS
152 Upper Richmond Road
London SW15
Tel: (01) 788 9123
19th c. furniture.

ANTIQUES LTD
18 Parson Street
London NW4 1QB
Tel: (01) 203 1194
18th and 19th c. furniture.

THE ARK ANGEL
14 Camden Passage
London N1
Tel: (01) 226 1644
Lacquered and painted furniture.

ARTINTERIAS LTD
3 New Cavendish Street
London W1

Below left: Selection of antiques with two heavily inlaid chest of drawers from Vienna in foreground, circa 1840, courtesy of Antiques Ltd.

Above: English oak chest of joined and boarded construction, the top front rail carved with lunettes, each panel inlaid with a lozenge in holly and bog oak, from the latter quarter of the 17th c., courtesy of Stephen Anson.

ARTINTERIAS LTD (CON'T)
Tel: (01) 935 6912 or 459 0782 (Home)
Louis Philippe furniture.

ASHBY ANTIQUES
82 Wandsworth Bridge Road
London SW9
Tel: (01) 731 5008
Oak and mahogany furniture.

Below: Pair of George III mahogany armchairs in the French taste, the cartouche-shaped backs with moulded frames headed by flower and leaf carving, the cabriole legs also headed by leaf carving ending in scroll toes, circa 1765, courtesy of Asprey and Company Ltd.

Left: Pair of Sheraton period satinwood card tables supported on square, tapering legs, circa 1775, courtesy of William Bedford Antiques Ltd.

ASPREY AND COMPANY LTD
165–169 New Bond Street
London W1Y 0AR
Tel: (01) 493 6767-
17th to 19th c. furniture.

ASTORIA
222 Munster Road
London SW6
Tel: (01) 395 9888
Furniture from 1900–1940, specialising in Art Deco.

G. AUSTIN AND SONS
19 Peckham Rye
Tel: (01) 639 3163
and
39 Brayards Road
London SE15
Tel: (01) 639 0480
19th and early 20th c. furniture.

JOHN M. BAILEY
111 Barnsbury Street
London N1
Tel: (01) 607 4378
18th and 19th c. English pine and oak country furniture.

Below: Early oak chest with deeply carved front panels and side and foot details, courtesy of Balcombe Galleries.

SERGE BAILLACHE
189 Westbourne Grove
London W11
Tel: (01) 229 2270
18th and 19th c. English, Continental and decorative furniture.

BALCOMBE GALLERIES
7 Stanley Studios, Park Walk
London SW10
Tel: (01) 352 4353 and 352 9996 (Home)
Early oak, pine and country furniture.

JOHN BALL ANTIQUES
178a Westbourne Grove
London W11
Tel: (01) 727 3607 and 452 9049 (Home)
Decorative furniture.

PETER BARHAM
111 Portobello Road
London W11
Tel: (01) 727 3397
Victorian walnut furniture.

BARHAM ANTIQUES
83 Portobello Road
London W11
Tel: (01) 727 3845
Victorian walnut furniture.

ROBERT BARLEY ANTIQUES
48 Fulham Road
London SW6
Tel: (01) 736 4429
16th to early 19th c. English and European furniture.

BARLING OF MOUNT STREET LTD
112 Mount Street
London W1
Tel: (01) 499 2858
15th to 17th c. European furniture.

BARNES ANTIQUES
16 Lower Richmond Road
London SW15
Tel: (01) 789 3371
19th c. English, Continental and Oriental furniture.

BARNES ANTIQUES LTD
83 Church Road
London SW13
Tel: (01) 748 7752
18th c. Georgian and Regency furniture.

BARNET ANTIQUES AND FINE ART
1180 High Road
Whetstone
London N20
Tel: (01) 445 9695
18th c. Regency furniture.

G.P. BASTILLO AND SONS ANTIQUES
27 Battersea Rise
London SW11
Tel: (01) 223 5341 and 673 1792 (Home)
Victorian and Edwardian furniture.

J. AND R. BATEMAN ANTIQUES
92 Waterford Road
London SW6
Tel: (01) 736 4149 and 228 9654 (Home)
17th and 18th c. oak and country furniture.

H.C. BAXTER AND SONS
191–193 Fulham Road
London SW3
Tel: (01) 352 9826/0807
Furniture from 1730–1810.

WILLIAM BEDFORD ANTIQUES LTD
327 Upper Street
Islington Green
London N1 2XQ
Tel: (01) 226 9648
and
88 Fulham Road
London SW3
Tel: (01) 584 1120
Huge showroom of 17th to early 19th c. English furniture.

RAYMOND BENARDOUT
4 William Street
London SW1
Tel: (01) 235 3360
17th to mid-19th c. English and Continental furniture.

BENNISON
91 Pimlico Road
London SW1
Tel: (01) 730 8076
17th to 19th c. furniture.

Above: Mahogany Regency work-table on lyre-shaped supports, circa 1815, courtesy of James Billings.

PETER BENTLEY ANTIQUES
22 Connaught Street
London W2
Tel: (01) 723 9394
Georgian, Regency and Victorian furniture.

JAMES BILLINGS
352 Kings Road
London SW3 5UU
Tel: (01) 352 1393
18th c. English and Continental furniture including decorative country pieces.

H. BLAIRMAN AND SONS LTD
119 Mount Street
London W1
Tel: (01) 493 0444
18th and 19th c. English furniture and 18th c. French furniture.

R. BONNETT
582 Kings Road
London SW6
Tel: (01) 736 4593 and 788 2763 (Home)
18th and 19th c. furniture.

BONROSE ANTIQUES
172 Kensington Antiques
London W8
Tel: (01) 229 5486
French furniture.

JOANNA BOOTH
247 Kings Road
London SW3
Tel: (01) 352 8998
Oak furniture from 17th c. onwards.

CLAUDE BORNOFF
20 Chepstow Corner, Pembridge Villas
London W2
Tel: (01) 229 8947
17th and 18th. c. oak and mahogany furniture.

BOURCHIER GALLERIES
104 Islington High Street
London N1
Tel: (01) 359 0363
English oak furniture.

PHILIP BRADY
3 Blenheim Crescent
London W11
Tel: (01) 727 7536
18th and 19th c. small furniture.

BRAEMAR ANTIQUES
2a Bedford Gardens
London W8
Tel: (01) 727 4573
18th and 19th c. furniture.

A. BRANDT
9c Adam and Eve Mews
Kensington High Street
London W8
Tel: (01) 937 4016
17th and 18th oak furniture, plus Continental pieces including gentlemen's mahogany wardrobes.

WILLIAM BRAY
58 Fulham High Street
London SW6
Tel: (01) 731 1170
Georgian furniture.

BRISIGOTTI ANTIQUES
186 Westbourne Grove
London W11
Tel: (01) 727 3493
Continental furniture.

BEVERLEY BROOK ANTIQUES
22 High Street
London SW13
Tel: (01) 878 4899 and 878 5656 (Home)
Regency, Victorian and Edwardian small furniture.

DAVID BROWER ANTIQUES
113 Kensington Church Street
London W8
Tel: (01) 221 4155
French and Oriental furniture.

ARTHUR BROWN LTD
392–400 Fulham Road
London SW6
Tel: (01) 385 4218
18th and 19th c. painted and gilded furniture, specialising in four poster beds.

F.G. BRUSCHWEILER ANTIQUES LTD
3 Lonsdale Road
Westbourne Grove
London W11
Tel: (01) 229 3106 and (062) 185 1252 (Home)
18th and 19th c. furniture.

BUCK AND PAYNE ANTIQUES
5 and 6 The Lower Mall
Camden Passage
London N1
Tel: (01) 226 4326
17th to early 19th c. English and French country furniture.

C.W. BUCKINGHAM
301–303 Munster Road
London SW6
Tel: (01) 385 2657 and 385 8475 (Home)
Victorian furniture specialising in Windsor chairs and pine pieces.

TONY BUNZL AND ZAL DAVAR
344 Kings Road
London SW3
Tel: (01) 352 3697
17th and 18th c. English oak and French provincial furniture.

BURGUNDY ANTIQUES
95 Pimlico Road
London SW1
Tel: (01) 730 0044
18th and 19th c. English and Continental furniture.

RICHARD BURNETT
3 Macaulay Road
London SW4
Tel: (01) 622 9393/4 (By appointment only)
Musical furniture and accessories.

BUSHWOOD ANTIQUES
317 Upper Street
London N1
Tel: (01) 359 2095
Georgian and Victorian furniture.

BUTCHOFF ANTIQUES
48–56 Peckham Rye
London SE15
Tel: (01) 639 0736
18th to early 20th c. furniture.

BUTTONS ANTIQUES
1597 London Road
and
457–459 Streatham High Road
London SW16
Tel: (01) 764 0324/3399
Stripped pine furniture.

CANONBURY ANTIQUES
13 Canonbury Place
London N1
Tel: (01) 359 2246
Furniture, specialising in upholstered pieces.

LEWIS M. CAPLAN ASSOCIATES LTD
50 Fulham Road
London SW3
Tel: (01) 589 3108 and 584 6328
Art Nouveau and Art Deco furniture, from 1890–1945.

Below: 18th c. French fruitwood hanging shelves and 18th c. walnut French provincial commode, courtesy of Tony Bunzl and Zal Davar.

FURNITURE

MICHAEL CARLETON
77–81 Haverstock Hill
London NW3
Tel: (01) 722 2277/586 4458
Decorative furniture.

CARLTON HOBBS
533 Kings Road
London SW10
and
66 Ledbury Road
London W11
Tel: (01) 351 3870
English and Continental furniture.

CARSON BOOTH ANTIQUES
80–82 Pimlico Road
London SW1
Tel: (01) 730 7004/235 1512
Continental, English (especially walnut) and Oriental (including lacquer) furniture.

CATHERWOOD AND COMPANY
334 Wandsworth Bridge Road
London SW6
Tel: (01) 736 0542
Victorian, Edwardian and Art Nouveau furniture.

CATSPA
116–118 Islington High Street
London N1
Tel: (01) 359 7616/883 3992
Art Nouveau and Art Deco furniture, from 1845–1939.

ODILE CAVENDISH
14 Lowndes Street
London SW1
Tel: (01) 235 2491
Oriental furniture including screens.

CAWTHROW ANTIQUES LTD
16 Camden Passage
London N1
Tel: (01) 226 1850
Lacquer and inlaid furniture.

CHANCERY ANTIQUES LTD
22 Park Walk
London SW10
Tel: (01) 352 6016 (By appointment only)
Georgian and early Victorian furniture.

CHAPMAN AND DAVIES ANTIQUES
10 Theberton Street
London N1
Tel: (01) 226 5565/ 348 4846/ 359 4330
18th and 19th c. English furniture.

Below: Small ash and pine dresser base, circa 1820, courtesy of Simon Coleman Antiques.

CHATTELS
53 Chalk Farm Road
London NW
Tel: (01) 267 0877
18th and 19th c. country furniture.

CHELSEA BRIC-A-BRAC SHOP LTD
16 Hartfield Road
London SW19
Tel: (01) 946 6894 and 542 5509/8112 (Home)
Furniture including pine from 1800–1920.

CHELSEA CLOCKS AND ANTIQUES
479 Fulham Road
London SW6
Tel: (01) 731 5704
19th and early 20th c. small furniture.

CHISWICK FURNITURE CENTRE
160 Chiswick High Road
London W4
Tel: (01) 995 4166
Pine, oak and mahogany furniture.

CHRISTOPHER ANTIQUES
201 New Kings Road
London SW6
Tel: (01) 731 2147/8
Furniture, especially bamboo pieces.

CHURCH STREET GALLERIES LTD
77 Kensington Church Street
London W8 4BG
Tel: (01) 937 2461
Fine English furniture from William and Mary to Regency, specialising in walnut.

GERALD CLARK
1 High Street
London NW7
Tel: (01) 906 0342
18th and 19th c. small English furniture.

JOHN CLAY
263 New Kings Road, London SW6
Tel: (01) 731 5677
18th and 19th c. furniture.

JOHN CLYNE
3–10 Blenheim Crescent, London W11
Tel: (01) 727 7536
Victorian and Edwardian furniture.

SHERIDAN COAKLEY ART DECO
12 Hollywood Road, London SW10
Tel: (01) 351 1771
Art Nouveau and Art Deco furniture.

COBRA AND BELLAMY
149 Sloane Street
London SW1
Tel: (01) 730 2823
Late 19th and early 20th c. furniture.

COEXISTENCE
2 Conduit Buildings, Floral Street
London WC2
Tel: (01) 240 2746
16th to 18th c. country furniture.

AUBREY J. COLEMAN
14–15 Halkin Arcade
London SW1
Tel: (01) 235 9594
English and Continental furniture, from 1680–1800.

SIMON COLEMAN ANTIQUES
51 High Street
London SW13
Tel: (01) 878 5037
18th and 19th c. country furniture including pine and fruitwood pieces, specialising in English and French farmhouse tables.

Above: A walnut cabinet made by Crace to the designs of A.W.N. Pugin circa 1860, now in the Palace of Westminster, courtesy of Jeremy Cooper Ltd.

PHILIP COLLECK LTD
84 Fulham Road
London SW3
Tel: 584 8479
17th to early 19th c. English furniture.

THE COLLECTOR ON LAVENDER HILL
43 Lavender Hill
London SW11
Tel: (01) 223 8683
Victorian to Art Deco furniture.

FRANK COLLINS
233 Westbourne Grove
London W11
Tel: (01) 727 6572
Georgian and 17th c. oak furniture.

ISABELLE COLLINS
154 Wandsworth Bridge Road
London SW6
Tel: (01) 731 4695
Pine and country furniture.

PETER COLLINS
92 Waterford Road
London SW6
Tel: (01) 736 4149
Country furniture, specialising in period oak.

COLNAGHI AND CO
14 Old Bond Street
London W1
Tel: (01) 491 7408
15th to 18th c. furniture.

JEREMY COOPER LTD
9 Galen Place
Bury Place
London WC1A 2JR
Tel: (01) 242 5138/404 0336
Furniture from 1830–1940 including Decorative Arts period.

FURNITURE

THE CORNER CUPBOARD
28 Camden Passage
London N1
Tel: (01) 226 4539/(047 333) 206
Small furniture from 1790–1860.

COUNTRY PINE LTD
13 Chalk Farm Road
London NW1
Tel: (01) 485 9687
Pine furniture from 1820–1920.

RICHARD COURTNEY LTD
112–114 Fulham Road
London SW3
Tel: (01) 370 4020
18th c. English furniture.

JOHN CREED ANTIQUES LTD
3–5a Camden Passage
London N1
Tel: (01) 226 8867
Country furniture, specialising in stripped pine.

CREST ANTIQUES
313–315 and 287 Putney Bridge Road
London SW15
Tel: (01) 789 3165
18th c. oak and walnut furniture, plus Victorian and Edwardian inlaid furniture.

T. CROWTHER AND SON LTD
282 North End Road
London SW6 1NH
Tel: (01) 385 1375/7
18th c. furniture.

CSAKY'S ANTIQUES
133 Putney Bridge Road
London SW15
Tel: (01) 870 1525
Pine furniture.

CSAKY'S ANTIQUES
20 Pimlico Road
London SW1
Tel: (01) 730 2068
Early English and Continental oak furniture.

D.D. ANTIQUES
53 Northfield Road, London W13
Tel: (01) 567 3655
Victorian and Edwardian furniture.

JOHN DALE
87 Portobello Road
London W11
Tel: (01) 727 1304
Georgian furniture.

CLIVE DANIEL ANTIQUES
91a Heath Street
London NW3
Tel: (01) 435 4351
19th c. English furniture.

ARTHUR DAVIDSON LTD
78–79 Jermyn Street
London SW1
Tel: (01) 930 6687
16th to 18th c. oak furniture. For illustration, see entry under "Metalware".

TONY DAVIS INC
235–9 Lavender Hill, London SW11
Tel: (01) 228 1370/1 and 223 9532 (Home)
19th c. furniture, specialising in upholstered pieces.

MICHAEL DAVISON
52–54 Ledbury Road
London W11
Tel: (01) 229 6088
Regency furniture.

ZAL DAVAR
26a Munster Road
London SW6
Tel: (01) 736 2559/1405 (Trade and export only)
Victorian furniture.

DE HAVILLAND ANTIQUES LTD
48 Sloane Street
London SW1
Tel: (01) 235 3534
17th and 18th c. furniture.

DEN OF ANTIQUITY
96 Coombe Lane
London SW20
Tel: (01) 947 0850
Victorian and Edwardian furniture.

DE VILLIERS ANTIQUES
311 Fulham Palace Road
London SW6
Tel: (01) 731 3859
18th and 19th c. furniture.

ROBERT DICKSON ANTIQUES
819 Fulham Road
London SW6
Tel: (01) 731 5778 (Trade only)
18th and early 19th c. furniture.

DIGBY COUNTRY ANTIQUES
20 Park Walk
London SW10
Tel: (01) 352 6152
Pine furniture and Victoriana.

DIPPERVALE LTD
25 Chepstow Corner
Chepstow Place
London W2 4TY
Tel: (01) 229 8456
Specialists in papier mâché and lacquer furniture.

DODO
185 Westbourne Grove
London W11
Tel: (01) 229 3132
Point-of-sale and display furniture.

DOLPHIN ANTIQUES
2b Englands Lane
London NW3
Tel: (01) 722 7003
18th c. English furniture.

DOME ANTIQUES
75 Upper Street
London N1
Tel: (01) 359 7711 and 226 1070 (Home)
18th and 19th c. English furniture specialising in desks and library and dining tables.

DRAGONS OF WALTON STREET LTD
25 Walton Street
London SW3
Tel: (01) 589 3795 and (0323) 845081 (Home)
18th c. English and French furniture.

EALING ANTIQUES
34 St Mary's Road
London W5
Tel: (01) 567 6192
18th and 19th c. furniture.

MARY ELKINGTON
27 Holland Street
London W8
Tel: (01) 937 8647
18th c. English furniture.

ELDRIDGE AND ELDRIDGE LTD
Farringdon House
Farringdon Road
London EC1
Tel: (01) 278 8901
Huge warehouse of 18th and 19th c. furniture.

ESTER ANTIQUES
88 Highbury Park Road
London N5
Tel: (01) 359 1573
Victorian and Edwardian furniture.

EVANS ANTIQUES LTD
81 Kensington Church Street
London W8
Tel: (01) 937 3754
17th to 19th c. English and Continental furniture.

THE FACADE
196 Westbourne Grove
London W11
Tel: (01) 727 2159
Victorian and Edwardian furniture.

FARIDEH ANTIQUES
2a Englands Lane
London NW3
Tel: (01) 586 0798
Furniture from 1750–1850.

FAYME ANTIQUES
56 Elgin Crescent
London W11 2JJ
Tel: (01) 727 9526
Specialists in small pieces of rural furniture.

FELTON ANTIQUES
134 Peckham Rye
London SE22
Tel: (01) 299 1123
19th c. furniture.

FERNANDES AND MARCHE
23 Motcomb Street
London SW1
Tel: (01) 235 6773
18th c. English furniture, specialising in giltwood pieces such as consoles and mirrors.

D.J. FERRANT ANTIQUES
21a Camden Passage
and
39 Essex Road
London N1
Tel: (01) 359 2597/1639
Georgian furniture.

FIVE FIVE SIX ANTIQUES
556 Kings Road
London SW6
Tel: (01) 731 2016 and 624 5173 (Home)
Early and unusual furniture.

GEORGE FLOYD LTD
592 Fulham Road
London SW6
Tel: (01) 736 1649
18th and early 19th c. English furniture.

FOREST HILL ANTIQUES
7 Davids Road
London SE23
Tel: (01) 699 4061 and 693 5050 (Home)
18th to early 20th c. furniture, including Art Nouveau and Art Deco.

ANTHONY FORTESCUE
19 Walton Street
London SW3
Tel: (01) 584 7586
18th c. English furniture.

Above: Pair of Hepplewhite armchairs upholstered in silk, circa 1780, courtesy of Michael Foster.

MICHAEL FOSTER
118 Fulham Road
London SW3 6HU
Tel: (01) 373 3636
18th and early 19th c. English furniture.

FOULK LEWIS COLLECTION
274 Fulham Road
London SW10
Tel: (01) 352 8950
Decorative French and English furniture from 1900–1939.

A. AND J. FOWLE
542 Streatham High Road
London SW16
Tel: (01) 764 2896
Victorian and Edwardian furniture.

JUDY FOX
81 Portobello Road
London W11
Tel: (01) 229 8130
Edwardian inlaid furniture.

PETER FRANCIS
26 Museum Street
London WC1
Tel: (01) 637 0165
Furniture from 1760–1840.

APTER FREDERICKS LTD
265–267 Fulham Road
London SW3
Tel: (01) 352 2188
17th to early 19th c. English furniture.

C. FREDERICKS AND SON
92 Fulham Road
London SW3
Tel: (01) 589 5847
18th c. furniture.

ELAINE FREEDMAN ANTIQUES
Camden Passage
London N1
Tel: Not Available
18th and 19th c. furniture.

FURNITURE CAVE
533 Kings Road
London SW10
Tel: (01) 352 7013/5373
Country furniture especially pine, oak and Victoriana.

FURNITURE FAIR
22 Church Street
London NW8
Tel: (01) 262 1338
Victorian furniture specialising in chairs and chaises longues.

FURNITURE VAULT
50 Camden Passage
London N1
Tel: (01) 734 1047
19th and early 20th c. furniture.

ROBIN GAGE
50 Pimlico Road
London SW1
Tel: (01) 730 2878
English furniture from 1750–1850; Continental furniture from 1700–1850; 18th and 19th c. English and Chinese lacquer furniture and 19th c. nautical furniture, including sea chests.

GALERIE 1900
267 Camden High Street
London NW1
Tel: (01) 485 1001 and 969 1803 (Home)
Art Nouveau and Art Deco furniture.

GALLERY 25
4 Halkin Arcade, London SW1
Tel: (01) 235 5178
Signed furniture from 1900 to 1930.

GAY ANTIQUES
1 Beauchamp Place
London SW3
Tel: (01) 584 9615
French furniture.

GENERAL TRADING COMPANY
144 Sloane Street
London SW1
Tel: (01) 730 0411
18th and 19th c. English furniture.

GERANIUM
121 Upper Street
London N1
Tel: (01) 359 4281
Victorian pine furniture specialising in dressers, chests, tables, storage furniture and tables.

CHRISTOPHER GIBBS LTD
118 New Bond Street
London W1
Tel: (01) 629 2008/9
18th and 19th c. English and Continental furniture.

DAVID GILL
25 Palace Gate
London W8
Tel: (01) 584 9184 (By appointment only)
Furniture from 1900–1930. For illustration, see entry under "Specialist Dealers, Art Nouveau and Art Deco".

GLAISHER AND NASH LTD
Lowndes Lodge, Cadogan Place
London SW1
Tel: (01) 235 2285/6
18th c. furniture.

GODDARD AND FARMER
8 Thackeray Street
London W8
Tel: (01) 937 4917
Victorian furniture, including overstuffed pieces.

RICHARD GODSON ANTIQUES
310 Kings Road
London SW3
Tel: (01) 352 8509
18th and early 19th c. English furniture.

GORE AND PLAYER
49 Church Road
London SW13
Tel: (01) 748 8850 and 748 7644 (Home)
18th and 19th c. decorative furniture.

GOTHIC COTTAGE ANTIQUES
70 Station Road
London SW13
Tel: (01) 876 2026
Stripped pine furniture.

J. GOTTLIEB LTD
227–229 Westbourne Grove
London W11
Tel: (01) 874 7832
Victorian furniture.

GRACE ANTIQUES
28 Pembridge Villas
London W11
Tel: (01) 229 4415
18th and early 19th c. furniture.

IMOGEN GRAHAM
585 Kings Road
London SW6
Tel: (01) 736 2465
Furniture specialising in English oak, country pine, painted and bamboo pieces.

GRANDIDGE ANTIQUES
62 Barnes High Street
London SW13
Tel: (01) 878 4599
Late 17th to early 19th c. furniture.

MARION GRAY
33 Crouch Hill
London N4
Tel: (01) 272 0372
17th to 19th c. furniture.

GREAT EXPECTATIONS
62 Old Church Street
London SW3
Tel: (01) 352 9850
19th c. furniture.

JUDY GREENWOOD
657 Fulham Road
London SW6
Tel: (01) 736 6037
*Country furniture including pine and
Victoriana.*

GREGORY, BOTTLEY AND LLOYD
8–12 Rickett Street
London SW6
Tel: (01) 381 5522
*Collectors' cabinets, especially for fossils and
minerals.*

GORDON GRIDLEY
41 Camden Passage
London N1
Tel: (01) 226 0643/9033
*17th to 19th c. English and Continental
furniture.*

NICHOLAS GRINDLEY
37 Bury Street
London SW1
Tel: (01) 930 6670
Oriental furniture.

L. GUERRA ANTIQUES
82 Portobello Road
London W11
Tel: (01) 727 0374
Victorian furniture.

GUINEVERE ANTIQUES LTD
574–580 Kings Road
London SW6
Tel: (01) 736 2917
18th and 19th c. furniture.

GWYNETH ANTIQUES
56 Ebury Street
London SW1
Tel: (01) 730 2513
*Oriental and decorative furniture, including
lacquer pieces.*

CHARLES HAMMOND LTD
165 Sloane Street
London SW1
Tel: (01) 235 2151
*Decorators with a selection of painted
furniture.*

ANDREW HARRIS
813 Fulham Road, London SW6
Tel: (01) 731 2050
*Decorative furniture specialising in bamboo
and painted pieces.*

M. HARRIS AND SONS
44–52 New Oxford Street
London WC1
Tel: (01) 636 2121/2
*17th to early 19th c. English and French
furniture.*

W.R. HARVEY AND COMPANY LTD
67–70 Chalk Farm Road
London NW1 8AN
Tel: (01) 485 1504/267 2767
*Fine 17th, 18th and early 19th c. English
furniture.*

HASLAM AND WHITEWAY
105 Kensington Church Street
London W8
Tel: (01) 229 1145
British, Victorian and Edwardian furniture.

HAVERSTOCK
78 Haverstock Hill
London NW3
Tel: (01) 267 1627
*Georgian, Regency and Victorian furniture in
mahogany, elm, oak, pine, and rosewood.*

THE HAY LOFT
332 Upper Richmond Road
London SW14
Tel: (01) 876 5020
Small furniture from 1800–1930.

J.C. HEATHER
225a Camberwell New Road
London SE5
Tel: (01) 703 4130
Furniture from 1700–1890.

*Below: William and Mary period burr elm
escritoire, circa 1690, courtesy of W.R.
Harvey and Company Ltd.*

HEIRLOOM AND HOWARD LTD
1 Hay Hill
Berkeley Square
London W1
Tel: (01) 493 5868
*Amorial furniture, i.e. those with crests or
coats of arms on them, such as hall chairs.*

HELIUS ANTIQUES
487–493 Upper Richmond Road
London SW14
Tel: (01) 876 5721
*18th to early 20th c. pedestal desks, bureaux,
writing tables, secretaries and bookcases.*

MARTIN HENMAN ANTIQUES
218 High Road
London N2
Tel: (01) 444 5274
Furniture from 1710–1920.

FURNITURE

LESLEY HEPHERD ANTIQUES
47 Camden Passage
London N1
Tel: (01) 359 1755
18th c. English furniture.

HERMITAGE ANTIQUES
97 Pimlico Road
London SW1
Tel: (01) 730 1973 and 435 5993 (Home)
17th to 19th c. English and French provincial furniture.

FELIX HILTON
45 St John's Wood High Street
London NW8
Tel: (01) 722 7634
18th and 19th c. small furniture specialising in small tables.

HIRST ANTIQUES
59 Pembridge Road
London W11
Tel: (01) 727 9364
17th and 18th c. oak furniture.

HOLBEIN ANTIQUES LTD
8 Holbein Place
London SW1
Tel: (01) 730 1957
Decorative furniture.

HOLLYWOOD ROAD ANTIQUES
1a Hollywood Road
London SW10
Tel: (01) 352 5248
Country and decorative furniture.

HOOPER AND PURCHASE
303 Kings Road
London SW3
Tel: (01) 351 3985 and 352 1391 (Home)
17th to 19th c. English and Continental furniture.

HOTSPUR LTD
14 Lowndes Street
London SW1
Tel: (01) 235 1918
English furniture from 1690 to 1800.

Left: 18th c. French provincial armoire, from Normandy, courtesy of Hermitage Antiques.

THE HOUSE OF ANDOR
17a The Burroughs
London NW4
Tel: Not Available
18th and 19th c. furniture.

J.T. ANTIQUES
11 Webb's Road
London SW11
Tel: (01) 228 7171
18th to early 20th c. small furniture.

ANTHONY JAMES AND SON LTD
253 New Kent Road
London SW6
Tel: (01) 731 3474
18th and early 19th c. English and Continental furniture.

MELVYN AND GARY JAY ANTIQUES
64a Kensington Church Street
London W8 4DB
Tel: (01) 937 6832
19th c. English and Continental decorative furniture.

TOBIAS JELLINEK LTD
18 Chepstow Corner
Chepstow Villas
London W2
Tel: (01) 727 5980
17th c. English oak furniture.

JELLINEK AND SAMPSON ANTIQUES
156 Brompton Road
London SW3
Tel: (01) 589 5272
17th and 18th c. oak furniture.

JEREMY LTD
255 Kings Road
London SW3
Tel: (01) 352 3127/0644
18th c. English and French furniture.

JOAN OF ART LTD
48 Walton Street
London SW3
Tel: (01) 589 8840
18th and 19th c. English and Continental furniture.

WILLIAM JOB LTD
86–88 Pimlico Road
London SW1 8PL
Tel: (01) 730 7374
17th c. English oak furniture and 18th c. country furniture.

D. JORDAN AND SONS LTD
Acton Depository
628 Western Avenue
London W3
Georgian to Victorian furniture, for trade only or hire purposes.

JORGEN ANTIQUES
40 Lower Richmond Road
London SW15
Tel: (01) 789 7329
18th and early 19th c. English and Continental furniture.

JULIAN ANTIQUES
67 Park Road
London NW1
Tel: (01) 723 0653
French furniture.

JUST DESKS
20 Church Street
London NW8
Tel: (01) 723 7976
Victorian and Edwardian desks, writing tables, davenports, bureaux, filing cabinets and roll tops. For illustration, see entry under "Specialist Restorers, Furniture".

KEEBLE LTD
13 Walton Street
London SW3
Tel: (01) 581 3676
Late 18th c. furniture.

JOHN KEIL
154 Brompton Road
London SW3 1HX
Tel: (01) 589 6454
and
25 Mount Street
London W1
Tel: (01) 499 8220
18th c. English furniture. See entry under "Specialist Dealer, Furniture, Southwest England" for illustration.

KENSINGTON FURNITURE BAZAAR
214–216 Kensington High Street
London W8
Tel: (01) 937 4973
19th and early 20th c. furniture.

KENWAY ANTIQUES
70 Kenway Road
London SW5
Tel: (01) 373 1631
Victorian furniture.

THOMAS KERR ANTIQUES LTD
11 Theberton Street
London N1
Tel: (01) 226 0626
17th to 19th c. English and Continental furniture.

ERIC KING ANTIQUES
203 New Kings Road
London SW6
Tel: (01) 736 3162
Specialist in unusual furniture including French provincial, Chinese and Japanese screens, plus wicker and cane conservatory seating.

KING'S ANTIQUES
589 Kings Road
London SW6
Tel: (01) 736 0853
Country furniture.

DAN KLEIN LTD
11 Halkin Arcade
Motcomb Street
London SW1
Tel: (01) 245 9868
Furniture from 1850 to 1960 including Art Deco and Art Nouveau.

L.P.J. ANTIQUES LTD
c/o Laurence Mitchell Antiques
27 Camden Passage
London N1
Tel: (01) 359 7579
Chinese furniture.

THE LACQUER CHEST
75 Kensington Church Street
London W8
Tel: (01) 937 1306
Furniture from 1800–1900, specialising in the unusual.

RICHARD LALLY LTD
152 Upper Richmond Road
London SW15
Tel: (01) 788 9123
18th and 19th c. furniture.

LAMONT ANTIQUES LTD
Newhams Row, 175 Bermondsey Street
London SE1
Tel: (01) 403 0126
Victorian and Edwardian furniture including naval-style painted pieces.

A. LANDAU
45 Mill Lane
London NW6
Tel: (01) 794 3028 and 452 3993 (Home)
Late Victorian and Edwardian furniture including Arts and Crafts and Art Nouveau.

E. LASSOTA
596 Kings Road
London SW1
Tel: (01) 736 3932
Hepplewhite, Regency and Victorian furniture.

RAYMOND LE BRUN
39 Ovington Street
London SW3 2JA
Tel: (01) 589 7945 (By appointment only)
17th to 19th c. Continental and Oriental furniture.

LEDBURY ANTIQUES
48–50 Ledbury Road
London W11
Tel: (01) 229 3169
Continental furniture and English mahogany.

LEE AND STACY
5 Pond Street
London NW3
Tel: (01) 794 7904/452 0056
18th and 19th c. furniture.

LENNOX MONEY LTD
68 and 99 Pimlico Road
London SW1
Tel: (01) 730 2151/730 3070
Indian ebony and ivory furniture.

M.D. LEWIS
1 Lonsdale Road
and
172 Westbourne Grove
and
60 and 62 Ledbury Road
London W11
Tel: (01) 727 3908
Continental furniture, especially Victorian.

STEPHEN LEWIS
192 Westbourne Grove
London W11
Tel: (01) 229 8747
Victorian furniture from 1860.

LILLIE ANTIQUES
244–246 Lillie Road
London SW6
Tel: (01) 385 9852 and 385 2100 (Home)
17th to early 19th c. English furniture.

J. LIPITCH LTD
177 Westbourne Grove
London W11
Tel: (01) 229 0783
English and Continental furniture, from 18th c.

Right: Louis XV gilded bed, A la Turque, signed L. Delanois, circa 1750, courtesy of Raymond Le Brun.

MELVYN LIPITCH
120–124 Fulham Road
London SW3
Tel: (01) 373 3328
18th c. English furniture.

THE LITTLE CURIOSITY SHOP
24 The Green
Winchmore Hill
London N21
Tel: (01) 866 0925
Small Victorian furniture.

LOLITA'S ANTIQUES
179 Westbourne Grove
London W11
Tel: (01) 221 5781 and 997 1283 (Home)
English and Continental furniture.

STEPHEN LONG
348 Fulham Road
London SW10
Tel: (01) 352 8226
18th and early 19th c. painted furniture.

LOOT
76–78 Pimlico Road
London SW1
Tel: (01) 730 8097 and 352 0135 (Home)
Oriental and decorative furniture from 1650–1900.

LOTT 32
32 Camden Road
London NW1
Tel: (01) 267 5828
Stripped pine furniture.

LYONS GALLERY
47–49 Mill Lane
London NW6
Tel: (01) 794 3537
Art Nouveau and Art Deco furniture, including Arts and Crafts pieces.

IVAR MACKAY
5 Pitt Street, London W8
Tel: (01) 937 7367 (By appointment only)
Small pieces of country and cottage furniture, pre-1830.

Above: Louis XV semanier in amaranthe and rosewood, retaining its original brèche d'Aleppe marble top, complete with ormolu escutcheons and sabots, signed by Delorme (1691–1768), courtesy of Mallett at Bourdon Flouse Ltd.

C.H. MAJOR ANTIQUES LTD
154 Kensington Church Street
London W8
Tel: (01) 229 1162 and 997 9018 (Home)
English mahogany furniture from 1760 onwards.

MALDEN ANTIQUES
4 Malden Road, London NW5
Tel: (01) 267 4601
18th and early 19th c. furniture.

Left: A Regency elbow chair of simulated rosewood with simulated gilt decoration, similar to designs by Heinz Holland, courtesy of Michael Marriott Ltd.

Below: George I walnut bureau bookcase with many unusual features including a pull-out slide and opening doors enclosing the writing section, the exterior fitted with fine brass mouldings and key escutcheons; the interior's innermost compartments enclosed by small mirror doors, from the ex-collection of Admiral Lord Rodney (1718–1792), courtesy of Mallett and Son Ltd.

MALLETT AND SON LTD
40 New Bond Street
London W1Y 0BS
Tel: (01) 499 7411
English furniture from 1680–1850.

MALLETT AT BOURDON HOUSE LTD
2 Davies Street
London W1Y 1LJ
Tel: (01) 629 2444/5
18th to 19th c. English and Continental furniture.

G. AND M. MARDELLIS
109 Kensington Church Street
London W8
Tel: (01) 727 7413
Continental furniture.

MICHAEL MARRIOTT LTD
588 Fulham Road
London SW6
Tel: (01) 736 3110
18th and 19th c. English furniture including upholstered pieces.

A.V. MARSH AND SON
Vale House
Kingston Vale
London SW15
Tel: (01) 546 5996
18th and early 19th c. furniture.

DAVID MARTIN-TAYLOR ANTIQUES LTD
592 Kings Road
London SW6
Tel: (01) 731 5054
Oriental furniture.

MARTINS-FORREST ANTIQUES
8 Halkin Arcade
Motcomb Street
London SW10
Tel: (01) 235 8353 and 341 0673 (Home)
Art Nouveau and Art Deco furniture.

PAUL MASON GALLERY
149 Sloane Street
London SW1X 9BZ
Tel: (01) 730 3683
Specialist dealer in paintings and prints who also has antique portfolio stands, from 1830–1920.

MASSEY ANTIQUES
11 The Mall
Camden Passage
London N1
Tel: (01) 359 7966
19th c. furniture.

JONATHAN MCCREERY
315 Kings Road
London SW3
Tel: (01) 352 5733 and (063 583) 680 (Home)
18th and 19th c. furniture.

JOY MCDONALD
50 Station Road
London SW13
Tel: (01) 876 6184
18th and 19th c. furniture including pine pieces.

Below: Rosewood portfolio stand, circa 1845, courtesy of the Paul Mason Gallery.

FURNITURE

S. MESSIM
63a Ledbury Road, London W11
Tel: (01) 727 1706
18th and 19th c. English and Continental furniture.

TOBY MITCHELL
17 Chalk Farm Road, London NW1
Tel: (01) 485 0831
Leather-topped brass tables.

RICHARD MORRIS ANTIQUES
136–142 Wandsworth Bridge Road
London SW6
Tel: (01) 736 1448
Pine furniture from all periods.

TERENCE MORSE AND SON LTD
197 Westbourne Grove, London W11
Tel: (01) 229 9380
Georgian to early Victorian furniture.

MORTLAKE ANTIQUES
69 Lower Richmond Road
London SW14
Tel: (01) 876 8715
Victorian and Edwardian furniture, including stripped and unstripped pine.

STEPHEN MOSBACHER
210 Westbourne Grove
London W11
Tel: (01) 229 1063
Furniture especially pedestal and partners' desks.

HUGH MOSS LTD
23 Bruton Lane, London W1
Tel: (01) 492 1835
Oriental furniture.

MRS MUNRO ANTIQUES LTD
11 Montpelier Street, London SW7
Tel: (01) 589 0686/5052
18th and 19th c. furniture.

SYLVIA NAPIER LTD
32 Ledbury Road
London W11
Tel: (01) 229 9986/7
Decorative furniture, especially Oriental and French Provincial. For illustration, see entry under "Oriental".

NASH ANTIQUES
183 Westbourne Grove
London W11
Tel: (01) 727 3796
Oriental and Japanese furniture.

NING LTD
8 Symons Street, London SW3
Tel: (01) 730 9111
Decorative furniture, pre-1860 and period pine.

NORWOOD ANTIQUES
219 Whitehorse Lane
London SE25
Tel: (01) 771 9567
Victorian furniture.

CHARLES L. NYMAN AND COMPANY LTD
230–242 Camden High Street
London NW1
Tel: (01) 485 1907 (Trade only)
19th c. English and Continental furniture.

ODD SPOT
336 Footscray Road
London SE9
Tel: (01) 850 5940
Victorian furniture.

OLD PINE
571 Kings Road, London SW6
Tel: (01) 736 5999
Renovated 18th c. and Victorian pine furniture.

OLD TIMES FURNISHING COMPANY
135 Lower Richmond Road
London SW15
Tel: (01) 788 3551
18th and 19th c. furniture.

THE OLD TREASURE CHEST
Dunmow Hall
62–64 Station Road
London SW13
Tel: (01) 876 2666
Victorian and Georgian furniture.

OLD WORLD TRADING COMPANY
867–869 Fulham Road
and
565 Kings Road
London SW6
Tel: (01) 731 4708 and 736 6309
Period and Victorian furniture.

ONCE UPON A TIME
115 and 119 Lower Richmond Road
London SW15
Tel: (01) 788 5551
Wooden and brass beds.

OOLA BOOLA ANTIQUES
166 Tower Bridge Road
London SE1
Tel: (01) 403 0794 and 693 5050 (Home)
Victorian and Edwardian furniture, especially mahogany.

ALEC OSSOWSKI
83 Pimlico Road
London SW1
Tel: (01) 730 3256
Gilt furniture, especially 18th c.

SEE PAGE 61 FOR MAP OF LONDON'S POSTAL DISTRICTS

P.J. ANTIQUES LTD
12 Lower Richmond Road
London SW15
Tel: (01) 789 3198
18th to early 20th c. furniture.

PARAGON ANTIQUES
558 Kings Road
London SW6
Tel: (01) 736 6454
Victorian upholstered furniture.

MICHAEL AND MARGARET PARKER
24 Cheval Place
London SW7
Tel: (01) 589 0133
Italian and French provincial furniture plus early English lacquer.

JOHN PARKER ANTIQUES LTD
88 Fulham Road
London SW3
Tel: (01) 581 3696
17th and 18th c. English and Continental furniture.

PHILIP AND RICHARD PARKER
98 Fulham Road
London SW3
Tel: (01) 589 7327 and 947 5569 (Home)
17th to 19th c. furniture.

PARTRIDGE FINE ARTS LTD
144–146 New Bond Street
London W1
Tel: (01) 629 0834
English and French furniture.

PAST TIME ANTIQUES
94–96 Kirkdale Road
London SE26
Tel: (01) 699 9187 and 290 5207 (Home)
Furniture from 1800–1920.

Below: Mid-18th c. Northern Italian commode in fruitwood with inlay of villagescape on drawer fronts, courtesy of Michael and Margaret Parker.

FURNITURE

PECKHAM PINE ANTIQUES
80 Peckham Rye
London SE15
Tel: (01) 639 9723 and 732 6201 (Home)
*Furniture, specialising in pine, from
1750–1930.*

PEEL ANTIQUES
131d Kensington Church Street
London W8
Tel: (01) 727 8298
18th c. mahogany furniture.

DAVID PETTIFER LTD
269 Kings Road
London SW3
Tel: (01) 352 3088
18th c. English furniture.

PHILIP
59 Ledbury Road
London W11
Tel: (01) 727 7915
16th and 17th c. furniture.

PHILIPS AND HARRIS
54 Kensington Church Street
London W8
Tel: (01) 937 3133
English furniture from 18th c. on.

PINE AND DESIGN
28 Shelton Street
London WC2
Tel: (01) 836 1977/8
*19th c. English and Austrian stripped pine
furniture including dressers, wardrobes,
mirrors, and tables.*

PINECRAFT
132a Liverpool Road
London N1
Tel: (01) 609 2653
*Pine strippers who have a selection of pine
furniture.*

THE PINE MINE
100 and 318 Wandsworth Bridge Road
London SW6
Tel: (01) 736 1092/5312
*Period and Victorian pine tables, chests, and
dressers.*

THE PINE SHOP
12b Camden Passage
Charlton Place
London N1
Tel: (01) 226 2444
Pine furniture.

THE PINE WAREHOUSE
162 Wandsworth Bridge Road
London SW6
Tel: (01) 736 2753
Stripped pine furniture.

PETER PLACE
156 Walton Street
London SW3
Tel: (01) 584 2568
*17th and 18th c. country furniture, English
and Continental.*

PORTMEIRON ANTIQUES
5 Pont Street
London SW1
Tel: (01) 235 7601
*Mid to late 19th c. blondwood furniture
specialising in Austrian Biedermeier and
English maplewood pieces.*

POTTLES
6 Camden Walk
Camden Passage

POTTLES (CON'T)
London N1
Tel: (01) 226 9438
Bentwood and painted furniture.

PRATT AND BURGESS LTD
7 Old Brompton Road
London SW7
Tel: (01) 589 8501
18th c. furniture.

PRINCEDALE ANTIQUES
56 Eden Grove
London N7
and
70 Princedale Road
London W11
Tel: (01) 727 0868 and 609 4238
19th and early 20th c. stripped pine furniture.

BARRIE QUINN ANTIQUES
1, 3 and 4 Broxholme House
New Kings Road
London SW6
Tel: (01) 736 4747
Pine, oak and mahogany Victorian furniture.

RAG AND BONE
109 Kirkdale Road
London SE26
Tel: (01) 699 1363 and 692 2845 (Home)
Stripped pine and wicker furniture.

RANDALL'S ANTIQUES
46–52 Church Road
London SW13
Tel: (01) 748 1858
18th and 19th c. furniture.

J.S. RASMUSSEN FINE ARTS
5 Logan Mews, Logan Place
London W8
Tel: (01) 373 6527
18th c. European furniture.

WILLIAM REDFORD
9 Mount Street
London W1
Tel: (01) 629 1165
French furniture.

PAUL REEVES
102 Bennerley Road
London SW11
Tel: (01) 223 3399
*English furniture, including Arts and Crafts,
from 1880–1910.*

A.J. REFFOLD AND PARTNERS LTD
28 Pimlico Road
London SW1
Tel: (01) 730 6788
*18th and 19th c. English decorative furniture,
specialising in bamboo items.*

RELCY ANTIQUES
9 Nelson Road
London SE10
Tel: (01) 858 2812 and 858 7218 (Home)
*18th and 19th c. English furniture, especially
bureaux and bookcases.*

REMEMBER WHEN
7 Rocks Lane
London SW13
Tel: (01) 878 2817
Pine country furniture.

RENDLESHAM AND DARK
498 Kings Road
London SW10
Tel: (01) 351 1442
*Pre-18th c. English and Continental
furniture.*

PETER REYNOLDS
67 New Kings Road
London SW6
Tel: (01) 736 7797
*18th and 19th c. painted, lacquer and pine
furniture.*

A. ROCH AND SONS LTD
99 Crawford Street
London W1
Tel: (01) 724 0563
Georgian furniture.

ROCHEFORT ANTIQUES GALLERY
32–34 The Green
Winchmore Hill
London N21
Tel: (01) 886 4779
*18th and 19th c. English and Continental
decorative furniture.*

RODERIC ANTIQUES
237 Westbourne Grove
London W11
Tel: (01) 229 2912
Furniture, especially wooden four-poster beds.

GEOFFREY ROSE LTD
77 Pimlico Road
London SW1
Tel: (01) 730 3004
Late 18th and early 19th c. English furniture.

F.J. RUTTER AND A. FAGIANI
28–30 Wagner Street
London SE15
Tel: (01) 732 7188
Bookcases, military chests and pedestal desks.

BARRY SAINSBURY
145 Ebury Street
London SW1
Tel: (01) 730 3393
*Chinese and Japanese lacquer furniture. See
"Specialist Dealers, Lacquer" for illustration.*

EDWARD SALTI
43 Davies Street
London W1
Tel: (01) 629 2141
18th and 19th c. French furniture.

GERALD SATTIN LTD
25 Burlington Arcade
London W1
Tel: (01) 493 6557
English furniture from 1760–1860.

SAVILE PINE
560 Kings Road
London SW6
Tel: (01) 736 3625
Pine furniture.

SAXON ANTIQUES
163 Tower Bridge Road
London SE1
Tel: (01) 403 6833
Georgian and Victorian furniture.

SCALLYWAG
Wren Road
London SE5
Tel: (01) 701 5353
*18th and 19th pine and 19th c. mahogany
furniture.*

PETER SCHNICHT ANTIQUES
56 New Kings Road
London SW6
Tel: (01) 736 8474
18th and early 19th c. furniture.

G. SEGAL
566–567 Kings Road
London SW6
Tel: (01) 736 8443
Oak furniture.

SENSATION LTD
66 Fulham High Street
London SW6 3LQ
Tel: (01) 736 4135
18th and 19th c. furniture.

JEAN SEWELL ANTIQUES LTD
3 Camden Street
London W8
Tel: (01) 727 3122
19th c. furniture.

SYLVIA SHEPPARD
71 Kensington Church Street
London W8
Tel: (01) 937 0965
Georgian furniture.

GEORGE SHERLOCK
588 Kings Road
London SW6
Tel: (01) 736 3855
*Furniture from 1650–1900, including
lacquered pieces.*

SHIELD AND ALLEN
584–586 Kings Road
London SW6 2DX
Tel: (01) 736 7145
*17th to 19th c. decorative Continental
furniture.*

ROBIN SIMS
7 Camden Passage
London N1
Tel: (01) 226 2393
Victorian furniture.

KEITH SKEEL ANTIQUES
94 Islington High Street
London N1
Tel: (01) 359 9894
*Bamboo, lacquer and Continental decorative
furniture.*

T. GORDON SMITH
50–51 Crawford Street
London W1
Tel: (01) 262 7341
17th to early 19th c. furniture.

*Above: Gilded English console table in the
manner of Matthias Lock, circa 1745, courtesy
of Stair and Company Ltd.*

ARTHUR J. SNOWDON
Rear of 157 Mare Street
London E8
Tel: (01) 985 6757 and 539 4075
18th c. French and English furniture.

SOPHISTO-CAT
190–192 Wandsworth Bridge Road
London SW6
Tel: (01) 731 2221
Pine furniture from 1700–1900.

SOUTH AUDLEY ART GALLERIES
36 South Audley Street
London W1
Tel: (01) 499 3178/3195
19th c. French furniture.

SOUTHBANK PINE
258 Battersea Park Road
London SW11
Tel: (01) 223 8657
Pine furniture.

SUSAN SPITZ ANTIQUES
561 Kings Road
London SW6
Tel: (01) 736 0375
*Georgian to Victorian furniture, specialising
in music stands.*

SPREAD EAGLE ANTIQUES
22 and 23 Nelson Road
London SE10
Tel: (01) 858 9713/692 1618
18th and 19th c. furniture.

GERALD SPYER AND SON LTD
18 Motcomb Street
Belgrave Square
London SW1
Tel: (01) 235 3348
Pre-1830 furniture.

STAIR AND COMPANY LTD
120 Mount Street
London W1
Tel: (01) 499 1784/5
17th and 18th c. English furniture.

LOUIS STANTON
299 Westbourne Grove
London W11
Tel: (01) 727 9336
Early English and Continental oak furniture.

JOHN STARMER ANTIQUES
56 Ledbury Road
London W11
Tel: (01) 229 5991
English and Continental furniture.

*Left: Pair of mahogany side chairs in the
Chippendale style, circa 1760, and English
mahogany chest of drawers, circa 1750,
courtesy of T. Gordon Smith.*

Left: Interior view showing Adam satinwood bonheur, circa 1770, and pair of Adam giltwood torchères, circa 1770, courtesy of Gerald Spyer and Son Ltd.

WILLIAN TILLMAN
30 St James Street
London SW1
Tel: (01) 839 2500
18th to early 19th c. English furniture.

FERENC TOTH
598a Kings Road
London SW6
Tel: (01) 731 2063 and 602 1771 (Home)
19th c. furniture.

TOTTERS
236 Fore Street
London N18
Tel: (01) 803 4413 and 886 0917/6791
Stripped pine furniture.

TRAFALGAR ANTIQUES
117 Trafalgar Road
London SE10
Tel: (01) 858 3709
Decorative furniture from 1760–1900.

DAVID TREMAYNE LTD
320 Kings Road
London SW3
Tel: (01) 352 1194
Chinese hardwood furniture.

DAVID TRON ANTIQUES LTD
275 Kings Road
London SW3
Tel: (01) 352 5918
17th to 19th c. furniture.

TROVE
71 Pimlico Road
London SW1
Tel: (01) 730 6514
Furniture from the 17th c. on.

M. TURPIN LTD
21 Manson Mews
Queen's Gate
London SW7
Tel: (01) 373 8490 and 736 3417
18th c. English and Continental furniture.

VANE HOUSE ANTIQUES
15 Camden Passage
London N1
Tel: (01) 359 1343
18th and early 19th c. furniture.

VERMOUTIER AND BANKS
25a Holland Street
London W8 4NA
Tel: (01) 937 3262
18th c. English country furniture.

VILLAGE GREEN ANTIQUES
348 Upper Street
London N1
Tel: (01) 359 3942
18th and 19th c. furniture.

VILLIERS GALLERY LTD
114 Eaton Square
London SW1
Tel: (01) 235 7206
19th c. English and French furniture.

W. 13 ANTIQUES
10 The Avenue
London W13
Tel: (01) 998 0390
18th and 19th c. furniture.

STELWOOD LTD
192 Westbourne Grove
London W11
Tel: (01) 229 8748
Victorian and inexpensive oak furniture.

JACOB STODEL ANTIQUES
116 Kensington Church Street
London W8 4BH
Tel: (01) 221 2652
17th to 19th c. English and Continental furniture.

STRATTION ANTIQUES ETC
165 Thames Road
London W4
Tel: (01) 994 3140
18th and 19th c. country furniture.

PAMELA STREATHER
4 Studio Place
Kinnerton Street
London SW1
Tel: (01) 235 3450 (By appointment only)
16th and 17th c. furniture.

SUFFOLK FINE ARTS
c/o The Rowley Gallery
115 Kensington Church Street
Tel: (01) 727 6495
16th to 18th c. furniture especially oak, yew, walnut and fruitwoods.

DAVID SUMMERS ANTIQUES
18 Theberton Street
London N1
Tel: (01) 226 8402 and 249 7520 (Home)
18th and 19th c. mahogany furniture.

SUNDRIDGE ANTIQUES
564 Kings Road
London SW6
Tel: (01) 736 0828
Furniture from 1680–1910.

TERRACE ANTIQUES
3a The Terrace
London SW13
Tel: (01) 876 7550
Stripped pine country furniture and Victoriana.

TERRY ANTIQUES
175 Junction Road
London N19
Tel: (01) 263 1219 and 889 9781 (Home)
Mid-18th to mid-19th c. mahogany, rosewood and walnut furniture.

THIS AND THAT FURNITURE
50–51 Chalk Farm Road
London NW1
Tel: (01) 267 5433
Country furniture from 1880–1900 especially stripped pine. Also late Victorian and Edwardian polished oak and mahogany pieces.

WALBROOK
c/o Betty and Vera Vandekar
101b Kensington Church Street
London W8
Tel: (01) 727 2471
Oriental, English and Continental furniture.

W.E. WALKER
277–279 Camden High Street
London NW1
Tel: (01) 485 6210/4433
17th to 19th c. furniture.

WANDLE ANTIQUES
20 Bellevue Road
London SW17
Tel: (01) 672 7071
Country furniture including dressers.

**WATTS AND CHRISTENSEN
ANTIQUES**
54 Cambridge Street
London SW1
Tel: (01) 834 3554
Continental and Scandinavian decorative and painted furniture.

TRUDE WEAVER
71 Portobello Road
London W11
Tel: (01) 229 8738
17th to 19th c. European furniture.

RON WELDON
109 Regents Park Road
London NW1
Tel: (01) 485 6210/4433
18th c. oak, walnut, elm and fruitwood furniture, plus 19th c. mahogany and stripped oak furniture.

KENNETH WHITE
39 Church Road
London SW19
Tel: (01) 947 3222
18th and 19th c. furniture.

TEMPLE WILLIAMS LTD
3 Haunch of Venison Yard
Brook Street
London W1
Tel: (01) 629 1486
Regency furniture.

O.F. WILSON LTD
Queens Elm Parade
Old Church Street
London SW3
Tel: (01) 352 9554
17th to early 19th c. English and French furniture.

WIMBLEDON PINE COMPANY
7–8 Wimbledon Arcade
The Broadway
London SW19
Tel: (01) 542 2894
19th c. pine furniture.

THE WITCH BALL
206 Westbourne Grove
London W11
Tel: (01) 229 3908
Victorian furniture, specialising in deep-buttoned upholstered pieces.

J. WOLFF AND SON LTD
1 Chester Court
Albany Street
London NW1
Tel: (01) 935 3636
18th and 19th c. English and French furniture.

WOODWORKS
Camden Lock
Commercial Parade
London NW1
Tel: (01) 485 4457
Stripped pine furniture.

CLIFFORD WRIGHT
171 Dawes Road
London SW6
Tel: (01) 385 9175
Gilded furniture from 1685–1820 and polished furniture from 1740–1820.

ROBERT YOUNG ANTIQUES
68 Battersea Bridge Road
London SW11
Tel: (01) 228 7847
18th c. English country furniture.

ROBERT YUEN
105 Pimlico Road
London SW1
Tel: (01) 730 9257
17th to 19th c. furniture.

SOUTH AND SOUTHEAST ENGLAND

ABBEY ANTIQUES AND ARTS
97 High Street
Hemel Hempstead, Herts
Tel: (0442) 64667
17th to 19th c. furniture.

Below: Early oak chair with carved back and legs, courtesy of Balcombe Galleries.

ADRIAN ALAN LTD
4 Frederick Place
Brighton, Sussex BN1 4EA
Tel: (0273) 25277/25015
18th and 19th c. Continental and English furniture.

ANTIQUE MART
72–74 Hill Rise
Richmond, Surrey
Tel: (01) 940 6942
18th and 19th c. furniture.

APOLLO GALLERIES
61, 65 and 67 South End
Croydon, Surrey
Tel: (01) 681 3727/680 1968
18th and 19th c. English and Continental furniture.

ART AND MARINE
19 Lion Street
Rye, Sussex
Tel: (07973) 4200
Nautical antiques including campaign furniture.

ARTBRY ANTIQUES
44 High Street
Orpington, Kent
Tel: (01) 868 0834 and 954 1840 (Home)
18th and 19th c. furniture.

BALCOMBE GALLERIES
Balcombe, Sussex
Tel: (044 483) 439
Early oak, pine and country furniture, plus some garden furniture.

Right: Intricately brass-inlaid Regency writing table in rosewood, courtesy of Wilfred Bull.

PAUL BARKER LTD
906 London Road
Thornton Heath, Surrey
Tel: (01) 684 0907
Georgian to Victorian furniture.

BARNET ANTIQUES AND FINE ART
236 High Street
Barnet, Herts
Tel: (01) 440 3620/445 9695/440 9473
George III furniture.

MICHAEL BEAUMONT ANTIQUES
Hempstead Hall
Hempstead
Nr Saffron Walden, Essex CB10 2PR
Tel: (044 084) 239
17th to 19th c. furniture, specialising in oak and mahogany.

C. BELLINGER ANTIQUES
91 Wood Street
Barnet, Herts
Tel: (01) 449 3467
18th and 19th c. French and English furniture.

BIZZY LIZZY
6–8 Paved Court
Richmond, Surrey
Tel: (01) 940 1813
Small Victorian furniture.

N.A. BRAZIL ANTIQUES
145 Brighton Road
South Croydon, Surrey
Tel: (01) 680 2707
Victorian furniture.

WILFRED BULL
85 West Street
Coggeshall, Essex
Tel: (0376) 61385
18th c. English and Continental furniture.

CAROUSEL
12 Springfield Road
Harrow, Middx
Tel: (01) 863 9455
Stripped pine furniture.

CARSHALTON ANTIQUE GALLERIES
5 High Street
Carshalton, Surrey
Tel: (01) 647 5664
Victorian furniture.

CATHERINE OF ARAGON
c/o Royston Browne
Dogmerfield, nr Basingstoke, Hants
Tel: (025 14) 6585
Regency furniture.

CEDAR ANTIQUES
High Street
Hartley Wintney, Hants
Tel: (025 126) 3252
17th and 18th c. furniture, specialising in pieces made from fruitwood and yew.

CHISLEHURST ANTIQUES
7 Royal Parade
Chislehurst, Kent
Tel: (01) 467 1530
Furniture from 1760–1900.

ANNARELLA CLARK ANTIQUES
19 High Street
Ditchling, Sussex
Tel: (07918) 4033
English and Continental painted and country furniture.

C. CLEALL ANTIQUES
16 Brewers Lane
Richmond, Surrey
Tel: (01) 940 8069
Art Nouveau and Art Deco furniture.

COLLECTORS' CORNER
73 High Street
Teddington, Middx
Tel: (01) 977 1079 and 977 6450 (Home)
Georgian and Victorian furniture.

RODNEY COOK ANTIQUES
58 Richmond Road
Twickenham, Middx
Tel: (01) 892 6884
Furniture, pre-1900.

BELINDA COTTE ANTIQUES
63 High Street
Hartley Wintney, Hants
Tel: (025 126) 2213
18th and 19th c. country furniture.

COURT HOUSE ANTIQUES
19 Market Place
Brentford, Middx
Tel: (01) 560 7074
Victorian furniture.

THE CUPBOARD ANTIQUES
Woburn Abbey Antique Centre
Woburn, Beds
Tel: (01) 427 3505
Fine 18th and 19th c. furniture.

RICHARD DAVIDSON ANTIQUES
Lombard Street
Petworth, Sussex
Tel: (0798) 42508
17th to early 19th c. English furniture in mahogany, walnut and oak.

Below: Yew comb-back, cabriole leg Windsor chair, circa 1780, and cherrywood gate-leg table with bobbin-turned legs, circa 1670, both courtesy of Cedar Antiques.

Above: 18th c. yew and mahogany sideboard with applied brass mouldings, all in the Gothic manner, courtesy of Richard Davidson Antiques.

THE DESK SHOP
41 St Clements
Oxford, Oxon OX4 4AG
Tel: (0865) 45524
18th and 19th c. desks including partner's, roll-top, pedestal, cylinder top and davenport styles. Also desk-finding service.

DOLPHIN ANTIQUES
13 Holywell Hill
St Albans, Herts
Tel: St Albans 63080
Specialists in 19th c. decorative furniture.

EASDEN'S ANTIQUES
4 Royal Parade
Chislehurst, Kent
Tel: (01) 467 3352
18th c. furniture.

EDGWARE ANTIQUES
19 Whitchurch Lane
Edgware, Middx
Tel: (01) 952 1606
Victorian and Edwardian furniture.

MOLLIE EVANS
84 Hill Rise
Richmond, Surrey
Tel: (01) 948 0182 and 940 3720 (Home)
Early country furniture.

FARNBOROUGH ANTIQUES
20 Church Road
Farnborough, Kent
Tel: Farnborough 51834 and 54286
17th to 18th c. oak furniture.

HARVEY FERRY AND WILLIAM CLEGG
1 High Street
Nettlebed, Oxon RG9 5DA
Tel: (0491) 641533
18th c. furniture.

PAUL FEWINGS LTD
38 South Street
Titchfield, nr Fareham, Hants
Tel: (0329) 43952
Stripped pine furniture from 1750–1900. See overleaf for illustration.

THE GALLERY
18 Endwell Road
Bexhill-on-Sea, E Sussex
Tel: (0424) 212127
17th to late 19th c. furniture. See entry under "Specialist Dealers, Pottery and Porcelain" for illustration.

Below left: Victorian mahogany cylinder-top pedestal desk with retractable writing surface and satinwood interior, courtesy of The Desk Shop.

Below: Queen Anne burr walnut double dome bureau bookcase of small size, courtesy of Harvey Ferry and William Clegg.

Above: Lincolnshire pine chiffonier, circa 1860, courtesy of Paul Fewings Ltd.

GRAY ANTIQUES
6 Shirley Grove
Rusthall Tunbridge Wells, Kent
Tel: (0892) 20288
Georgian and early mahogany furniture.

GRAY ANTIQUES
Volunteer
Queen Street
Twyford, Hants
Tel: (0962) 712 866
Country furniture.

GREAT GROOMS ANTIQUES LTD
Parbrook
Billingshurst, Sussex
Tel: (040 381) 2263
17th to 19th c. furniture.

DEREK GREEN
Cedar Antiques
Hartley Wintney, Hants
Tel: (025 126) 3252
17th and 18th c. furniture with emphasis on yew, walnut, fruitwood and oak.

GREEN LANE ANTIQUES
1 Maxwell Road
Northwood, Middx
Tel: Northwood 22177
Victorian and Georgian furniture.

GUMBRELLA
3 Church Road
Farnborough Village, Kent BR6 7DB
Tel: Farnborough 56642
Small Victorian furniture.

RICHARD AND ANN HAGEN
Bakehouse Cottage, Northwood End
Haynes, Beds
Tel: (023 066) 424
Country furniture from 1690–1840.

HALLIDAYS ANTIQUES LTD
The Old College
Dorchester-on-Thames, Oxon OX9 8HL
Tel: (0865) 340028
Georgian, Regency and country furniture.

Right: Regency sofa table in figured rosewood, the brass inlaid folding surface above hinged, inlaid lopers and drawers, the pedestal of square section with carved gadrooning, the base on four swept legs with brass stringing and paw feet, circa 1820, courtesy of Hallidays Antiques.

S.K. HEDGES LTD
74 Green Lane
Northwood, Middx
Tel: Northwood 22044
18th and 19th c. furniture.

A. HENNING
48 Walton Street, Walton-on-the Hill
Tadworth, Surrey KT20 7RZ
Tel: Tadworth 3337
English mahogany furniture from 1740 to 1840.

HILL RISE ANTIQUES
26 Hill Rise
Richmond, Surrey
Tel: (01) 948 1140 and 876 4114 (Home)
Georgian to Victorian furniture.

HOUSE OF ANTIQUES
4 College Street
Petersfield, Hants
Tel: (0730) 2172
18th and 19th c. furniture.

HOUSE OF MALLETT
67–69 Brighton Road
Surbiton, Surrey
Tel: (01) 390 3796
Mahogany and pine furniture.

PETER HUNWICK
The Old Malthouse
Hungerford, Berks
Tel: (048 86) 2209
Late 17th, 18th and early 19th c. walnut and mahogany English furniture.

JOAN JARMAN ANTIQUES
81a High Street
Teddington, Middx TW11 8H6
Tel: (01) 977 4260
Furniture from 1760–1860.

PAUL JONES ANTIQUES
10 Market Place
Chalfont St Peter, Bucks SL9 9LA
Tel: Gerrards Cross 83367
19th c. furniture.

JULIAN ANTIQUES
124 High Street
Hurstpierpoint, Sussex
Tel: (0273) 832145
French furniture.

Above: Walnut davenport with small concealed pencil drawer, circa 1850, courtesy of Joan Jarman Antiques.

KELVEDON ANTIQUES
90 High Street
Kelvedon
Colchester, Essex
Tel: (0376) 70557
18th c. walnut and mahogany furniture, as well as country furniture in oak, elm and fruitwood.

JEAN KERSHAW
West Farm Antiques
High Street
Orwell, nr Royston, Herts
Tel: (022 020) 464
18th and 19th c. furniture especially country styles.

SHIRLEY KING
2 Johnston Road
Woodford Green, Essex
Tel: (01) 505 5774
Small 19th c. furniture.

Above: George III mahogany clothes press, circa 1785, courtesy of Kelvedon Antiques.

KNAPHILL ANTIQUES
36–38 High Street
Knaphill, Surrey
Tel: (048 67) 3179
Victorian and Edwardian furniture.

LAYTON ANTIQUES
1 Paved Court
The Green
Richmond, Surrey
Tel: (01) 940 2617
18th and 19th c. furniture, especially George III.

Below: A selection of pine furniture, courtesy of Ann Lingard, Rope Walk Antiques.

LE CENTRE ANTIQUES
20 King Street
The Green
Richmond, Surrey
Tel: (01) 948 1505
18th to early 20th c. furniture.

LENNARD ANTIQUES
6–8 Old Cross
Hertford, Herts
Tel: (0582) 552070 and 840220 (Home)
17th, 18th and early 19th c. furniture.

LINCOLN HOUSE GALLERIES
587 London Road
Westcliff-on-Sea, Essex
Tel: (0702) 339106
Victorian furniture.

Above: Two from a set of eight country chairs in oak, circa 1800, courtesy of Market Place Antiques.

ANN LINGARD
Rope Walk Antiques
Rye, Sussex
Tel: (079 73) 3486
18th and 19th c. pine furniture.

MICHAEL LIPITCH
60 Waggon Road
Hadley Wood, nr Barnet, Herts
Tel: (01) 440 7797 (By appointment only)
18th c. English and Continental furniture.

MALDWYN ANTIQUES
12–12a Beynon Parade
Carshalton, Surrey
Tel: (01) 669 0793 and 393 4530 (Home)
Staffordshire furniture.

KATHLEEN MANN ANTIQUES
49 High Street
Harrow, Middx
Tel: (01) 422 1892
17th to 19th c. furniture.

MANOR HOUSE ANTIQUES
The Green
Datchet, Berks
Tel: (0753) 42164/41460
18th and 19th c. mahogany, rosewood, and walnut furniture including bureau bookcases, set of chairs, mirrors, and pedestal desks.

JOHN MANUSSIS
321 Richmond Road
Kingston-upon-Thames, Surrey
Tel: (01) 546 0366
18th and 19th c. furniture.

MARBLE HILL GALLERY
72 Richmond Road
Twickenham, Middx
Tel: (01) 892 1488
Victorian furniture.

MARKET PLACE ANTIQUES
35 Market Place
Henley-on-Thames, Oxon
Tel: (04912) 2387
Country furniture, especially pine.

B. AND A. MARKS
London House
4 Market Square
Westerham, Kent
Tel: (0959) 64479
Georgian furniture.

MARGARET MCCLOY ANTIQUES
49 Surbiton Road
Kingston, Surrey
Tel: (01) 549 6423
Stripped pine furniture.

MILLERS ANTIQUES
46 High Street
Kelvedon, Essex
Tel: (0376) 70098
*17th, 18th and early 19th c. mahogany, oak
and walnut furniture.*

**MILLERS OF CHELSEA ANTIQUES
LTD**
Netherbrook House
Christchurch Road
Ringwood, Hants
Tel: (042 54) 2062
*French and English country furniture
including 19th c. mahogany.*

CHARLOTTE AND BETTE MORSE
Larks-in-the-Wood
Pentlow, Sudbury, Suffolk
Tel: (0787) 280377
17th and 18th c. oak furniture.

J. MOWATT
Southdown House Antiques
Easole Street
Nonington, nr Dover, Kent CT15 4HE
Tel: (0304) 840987
*Furniture, specialising in upholstered and
cabinet pieces.*

NADJ'S ANTIQUES
36 Crown Road
Twickenham, Middx
Tel: (01) 892 6965
18th c. to early 20th c. furniture.

B.M. NEWLOVE
139–141 Ewell Road
Surbiton, Surrey
Tel: (01) 399 8857
*17th to 19th c. furniture especially early oak
and Georgian mahogany.*

*Below: 17th c. carved oak chest, courtesy of
The Old Forge.*

NORTON ANTIQUES
56 London Road
Beaconsfield, Bucks HP9 2JH
Tel: (049 46) 3674
18th and 19th c. mahogany furniture.

THE OLD FORGE
Pilgrims Way
Hollingbourne, Kent MF17 1UW
Tel: (062 780) 360
Early oak furniture.

THE OLD HOUSE
15–17 High Street
Seaford, Sussex
Tel: (0323) 892091
18th to early 20th c. furniture.

ANGELA PAGE ANTIQUES
Sion House, 15 Mount Sion
Tunbridge Wells, Kent
Tel: (0892) 22217
*17th and 18th c. furniture, specialising in
English and North European.*

**DERMOT AND JILL PALMER
ANTIQUES**
7–8 Union Street
The Lanes
Brighton, Sussex
Tel: (0273) 28669
*Specialist in lacquer, pine and painted
furniture, including screens.*

PAMELA AND BARRY ANTIQUES
126 Sandridge Road
St Albans, Herts
Tel: St Albans 51109
18th and 19th c. furniture.

PENNY FARTHING ANTIQUES
71 High Street
Chobham, Surrey
Tel: (099 05) 7718
Country furniture.

**PERIOD FURNITURE
RESTORATIONS LTD**
186 Main Road
Gidea Park, nr Romford, Essex
Tel: (01) 550 9540
Victorian furniture.

*Below: Interior view showing a selection of
furniture, courtesy of Period Furniture
Showrooms No. 49.*

**PERIOD FURNITURE SHOWROOMS
NO 49**
London End
Beaconsfield, Bucks
Tel: (049 46) 4112
18th and 19th c. furniture.

PHELPS LTD
129–135 St Margaret's Road
Twickenham Middx
Tel: (01) 892 1778/7129
*Victorian and Edwardian furniture, including
Art Nouveau.*

W.A. PINN AND SONS
124 Swan Street
Sible Hedingham
Halstead, Essex
Tel: (0787) 61127
17th to early 19th c. furniture.

PRIESTS ANTIQUES AND FINE ARTS
56 North Street
Thame, Oxon
Tel: (084 421) 4461
17th to 19th c. English furniture.

RENDALL ANTIQUES
297 Sandycombe Road
Kew, Surrey
Tel: (01) 948 4876 and 948 4400 (Home)
*Georgian mahogany furniture from
1740–1830, plus Victorian and Edwardian
walnut and oak furniture.*

THE RICHMOND ANTIQUARY
28 Hill Rise
Richmond, Surrey
Tel: (01) 948 0583 and Egham 7229 (Home)
Late 18th and 19th c. furniture.

ROGERS ANTIQUES
22 Ewell Road
Cheam, Surrey
Tel: (01) 643 8466
*18th and 19th c. furniture, including
upholstered leather furniture.*

J.T. RUTHERFORD AND SON
55 Sandgate High Street
Folkestone, Kent
Tel: (0303) 39515
18th and 19th c. furniture.

*Below: Regency period rosewood work-table,
circa 1810, courtesy of W.A. Pinn and Sons.*

FURNITURE

R.G. SCOTT FURNITURE MART
Bath Place
and
Grotto Hill
Margate, Kent
Tel: (0843) 20653
Stripped pine furniture.

J.M. SELLORS ANTIQUES
28 St James Road
Croydon, Surrey
Tel: (01) 689 1004/647 1768
Small pine furniture.

SPENCER SWAFFER
30 High Street
Arundel, W Sussex
Tel: (0903) 882132
Pine and country furniture.

STANMORE HILL ANTIQUES
105 Stanmore Hill
Stanmore, Middx
Tel: (01) 954 0490
18th and 19th c. small furniture.

STEPPES HILL FARM ANTIQUES
Steppes Hill Farm, Stockbury
Sittingbourne, Kent
Tel: (0795) 842205
17th to 19th c. English furniture.

STOTFOLD ANTIQUES
21 High Street
Westerham, Kent
Tel: (0959) 63055
Victorian and Edwardian furniture including large stripped pine and gilt mirrors, and specialising in upholstered furniture.

SUNDRIDGE ANTIQUES
4 Sundridge Parade
Plaistow Lane
Bromley, Kent
Tel: (01) 460 8164
Furniture from 1680–1920.

SURREY GALLERIES
295 High Street
Croydon, Surrey
Tel: (01) 681 0975 and 660 9294 (Home)
18th and 19th c. furniture specialising in chaises longues and chairs.

TAURUS ANTIQUES LTD
145 Masons Hill
Bromley, Kent BR2 9HY
Tel: (01) 464 8746
Regency furniture.

THE TOKEN HOUSE
7 Market Parade
High Street
Ewell, Epsom, Surrey
Tel: (01) 393 9654
19th c. furniture.

TRENGROVE
46 South End
Croydon, Surrey
Tel: (01) 688 2155
Victorian furniture.

TRINITY ANTIQUES
7 Trinity Street
Colchester, Essex
Tel: (0206) 77775
Pine furniture.

TURPINS ANTIQUES
4 Stoney Lane
Thaxted, Essex
Tel: (0371) 830495
17th to 19th c. English furniture.

VALION ANTIQUES
42 Chancery Lane
Beckenham, Kent
Tel: (01) 658 6644
18th and 19th c. furniture.

VAN BROEK ANTIQUES
101 Station Road
Hampton, Middx
Tel: (01) 979 2089
Pine, Victorian and second-hand furniture.

VINE COTTAGE ANTIQUES
High Street
Streatley
Reading, Berks RG8 9JD
Tel: (0491) 872425
18th and 19th c. furniture.

WALTON ANTIQUES
7 Duke Street
Richmond, Surrey
Tel: (01) 948 2258 and 940 6519 (Home)
18th and 19th c. furniture.

JOHN WESTLEY
41–42 Windsor Street
Uxbridge, Middx
Tel: Uxbridge 34933
Victorian furniture.

WINSTON GALLERIES
68 High Street
Harrow, Middx
Tel: (01) 422 4470
18th and 19th c. furniture.

WITHAM ANTIQUES
27a Bridge Street
Witham, Essex
Tel: (0376) 512407
Georgian, Victorian and Edwardian furniture.

NORMAN WITHAM
2 High Street
Beckenham, Kent
Tel: (01) 650 4651
Small Victorian furniture.

YELLOW LANTERN ANTIQUES
36/65b Holland Road
Hove, Sussex BU3 1JL
Tel: (0273) 771572
Georgian to Victorian English furniture.

ZAFER
36 Church Street
Twickenham, Middx
Tel: (01) 891 3183
18th and 19th c. furniture.

SOUTHWEST ENGLAND

ABOYNE ANTIQUES
13 York Street
Bath, Avon
Tel: (0225) 64850 and 319961 (Home)
18th c. furniture.

ALDERSON AND ALDERSON
23 Brook Street
Bath, Avon
Tel: (0225) 21652
18th and 19th c. furniture.

ASPIDISTRA ANTIQUES
46 St James Parade
Bath, Avon
Tel: (0225) 61948
Victorian and Edwardian furniture including Art Nouveau and Art Deco.

BELL PASSAGE ANTIQUES
38 High Street
Wickwar
Wotton-under-Edge, Glos GL12 8NP
Tel: (045 424) 251
18th and 19th c. furniture.

BOX HOUSE ANTIQUES
35 Gay Street
Bath, Avon
Tel: (0225) 20337
17th to 19th c. furniture.

CAMPBELL AND MARSH
Old Barn
Perranarworthal
Truro, Cornwall TR3 7NY
Tel: (0872) 863831
18th to early 20th c. furniture.

KATHERINE CHRISTOPHERS
St Catherines Court
St Catherines
Bath, Avon
Tel: (0225) 858159
Medieval to early 18th c. oak and walnut furniture.

JOHN H. COLLINGS LTD
Prospect House
Knightcott
Banwell, Avon
Tel: (0934) 823181
Furniture from 1760–1850.

J. COLLINS AND SON
63 and 28 High Street
Bideford, North Devon
Tel: (023 72) 3103
18th and 19th c. furniture. See overleaf for illustration.

CORINIUM ANTIQUES
23 Gloucester Street
Cirencester, Glos
Tel: (0285) 2839
18th and 19th c. country furniture.

CORNER HOUSE ANTIQUES
31a Rivers Street
Bath, Avon
Tel: Not Available
18th to early 20th c. small furniture.

JOHN CROFT ANTIQUES
3 George Street
Bath, Avon
Tel: (0225) 66211
17th to early 19th c. furniture.

ANDREW DANDO
4 Wood Street
Queen Square
Bath, Avon
Tel: (0225) 22702
18th and early 19th c. furniture.

GERARD DEACON
2 Wood Street
Queen Square
Bath, Avon
Tel: (0225) 25907
18th and early 19th c. English furniture.

D.H. AND H.P. DENNISON
22 High Street
Lewes, Sussex BN7 2LN
Tel: (079 16) 3665
Mahogany and rosewood furniture from 1800–1825.

FOR MAP OF THE BRITISH ISLES, SEE PAGE 7.

Right: Set of early 18th c. comb-back Windsor arm-chairs, courtesy of J. Collins and Son.

FINE PINE LTD
Woodland Road
Harbertonford, Totnes, Devon
and
85 High Street
Totnes, Devon
Tel: (080 423) 465
Stripped pine and country furniture.

FRAMFAM LTD
High Street
Moreton-in-Marsh, Glos
Tel: (0608) 50648
18th and 19th c. British and country furniture.

GASTRELL HOUSE
33 Long Street
Tetbury, Glos GL8 8AA
Tel: (0666) 52228
English furniture from Queen Anne to Regency.

GLOUCESTER HOUSE ANTIQUES LTD
Market Place
Fairford, Glos
Tel: (0285) 712790
17th to early 19th c. English and French country furniture.

J.P.J. HOMER
Stoneleigh, Parabola Road
Cheltenham, Glos
Tel: (0242) 34243
17th c. oak furniture.

E.R. HYATT
Regency House
Old Fore Street
Sidmouth, Devon
Tel: (0395) 4284
19th c. furniture.

RUTH JOLY ANTIQUES
Petty France House
Petty France
Badminton, Avon
Tel: (045 423) 310
Furniture, pre-1870.

JOHNSONS OF SHERBORNE LTD
South Street
Sherborne, Dorset DT9 3NF
Tel: (093 581) 2585
18th and 19th c. furniture, specialising in satinwood and decorative pieces.

JOHN KEIL
10 Quiet Street
Bath, Avon
Tel: (0225) 63176
18th c. English furniture.

JOY KING-SMITH
High Street
Moreton-in-Marsh, Glos
Tel: (0608) 50917
Fine period furniture, specialising in mahogany, satinwood and marquetry pieces.

MINETY ANTIQUES
Malmesbury, Wilts
Tel: (066 640) 255 (By appointment only)
Country furniture.

EDWARD A. NOWELL
21–23 Market Place
Wells, Somerset BA5 2RF
Tel: (0749) 72415
18th and early 19th c. English furniture.

NORTH DEVON ANTIQUES
113 East Street
South Molton, N Devon
Tel: (076 95) 3184
English Georgian furniture.

OLD BARN ANTIQUES COMPANY
The Abbey Antique Shop
Half Moon Street
Sherborne, Dorset
Tel: (093581) 2068
18th and 19th c. furniture.

ORIENTAL ANTIQUES
4 Belvedere
Lansdown Road
Bath, Avon BA1 5ED
Tel: (0225) 315987
Decorative and Oriental furniture.

DAVID PATTERSON
20 Queen Street
Lostwithiel, Cornwall
Tel: (0208) 872879
Victorian pine furniture.

W.G. POTTER AND SON
1 West Street
Axminster, Devon
Tel: (0297) 32063
17th to 19th c. furniture.

Below: Sheration clothes press, in rosewood with satin-wood inlay, circa 1790, courtesy of Gastrell House.

Below: A selection of pine and country furniture, courtesy of Fine Pine Ltd.

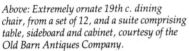

Above: Extremely ornate 19th c. dining chair, from a set of 12, and a suite comprising table, sideboard and cabinet, courtesy of the Old Barn Antiques Company.

Below: A fine George III Adam period mahogany sidetable, the serpentine top above a fluted frieze with carved corners, courtesy of John Keil.

Above: 18th c. mahogany sofa table with double crossbanding of satinwood and tulipwood, courtesy of Anthony Preston Antiques.

ANTHONY PRESTON ANTIQUES LTD
Sandywell Park
Whittington, Cheltenham,
Glos GL54 4HF
Tel: (024 282) 404
and
The Square
Stow-on-the Wold, Glos
Tel: (0451) 31586
18th and early 19th c. walnut and mahogany furniture.

PRIORY ANTIQUES
37 East Street
Blandford, Dorset
Tel: (0258) 53472
18th and 19th c. furniture.

GEOFFREY STEAD & ROBERT KIME
The Old Rectory
Dowdeswell, nr Cheltenham
Glos GL54 4LX
Tel: (024 282) 571
English and Continental furniture.

SUTTON AND SONS
15–33 Vicarage Street
Frome, Somerset BA11 1PX
Tel: (0373) 62062
18th and 19th c. English furniture.

TETBURY ANTIQUES
39a Long Street
Tetbury, Glos GL8 8AA
Tel: (0666) 52748
French provincial furniture.

WALES

ALICE LIGHTING AND ANTIQUES
3 Wellfield Road
Cardiff, S Glamorgan, Wales
Tel: (0222) 499156
Victorian furniture.

F.E. ANDERSON AND SON
5 High Street
Welshpool, Powys, Wales
Tel: (0938) 3340
17th and 18th c. furniture.

ANGHARAD'S ANTIQUES
106 Chester Road
Shotton, Clwyd, Wales
Tel: (0244) 812240
19th c. small furniture.

ARCHWAY ANTIQUES
Llandough Castle
East Wing
Cardiff, S Glamorgan, Wales
Tel: (0222) 2746
Oak, pine and country furniture.

BAYVIL HOUSE ANTIQUES
39 High Street
Cardigan, Dyfed, Wales
Tel: (0239) 2654
18th and 19th c. furniture, especially oak and mahogany.

BEAUFORT ANTIQUES
16 St Mary's Street
Chepstow, Gwent, Wales
Tel: (029 12) 5957
Mahogany and walnut furniture.

AUDREY BULL
15 Upper Frog Street
Tenby, Dyfed, Wales
Tel: (0834) 3114
Welsh country furniture.

JONATHAN AND JANE BULL ANTIQUES
The Strand
Saundersfoot, Dyfed, Wales
Tel: (0834) 812659
Furniture from 1650 on.

W.S. AND J.B. CAYLESS
Maesgwyn Farm
Trecastle, Powys, Wales
Tel: (087 482) 760 (By appointment only)
Pine furniture.

THE CELLAR ANTIQUES
17 High Street
Lampeter, Dyfed, Wales
Tel: (0570) 422531
Welsh furniture.

COUNTRY ANTIQUES
Castle Mill
The Bridge
Kidwelly, Dyfed, Wales
Tel: (0554) 890534
Pre-1900 furniture in oak, pine, walnut and mahogany.

CWMYNEIFON ANTIQUES
Cnwc Y Llwyn
Brechfa
Carmarthen, Dyfed, Wales
Tel: (026 789) 252
18th and 19th c. small furniture.

*Right: One of a set of four late 18th c.
Northern Italian chairs, carved in the
Neo-Classical style, courtesy of Peter Philp.*

DOLWEN ANTIQUES
430 Abergele Road
Old Colwyn
Colwyn Bay, Clwyd, Wales
Tel: (0492) 57823
Victorian and Edwardian small furniture.

GLADSTONE HOUSE ANTIQUES
Manod Old School
Blaenau Ffestiniog, Gwynedd, Wales
Tel: (076 689) 220
Pine furniture.

JONATHAN GLUCK
Maes Y Glydfa
Llanfair Caereinion
nr Welshpool, Powys, Wales
Tel: (0938) 810384
18th and 19th c. pine and oak furniture.

JOHN GODDARD ANTIQUES
18 High Street
and
The Arcade

JOHN GODDARD (CON'T)
Penllan Street
Pwllheli, Gwynedd, Wales
Tel: (0758) 2754
18th and 19th c. stripped pine furniture.

COLIN HUGHES
36 Penralit Street
Machynlleth, Powys SY20 8AJ, Wales
Tel: (0654) 2363
*18th c. oak, pine, mahogany and walnut
furniture.*

RON JONES
Pen Lon, Cross Inn, nr Llanon
Dyfed, Wales
Tel: (097 46) 607
Welsh oak furniture.

RICHARD LLOYD
Old Vicarage
Llangeler, nr Llandyssul
Dyfed, Wales
Tel: (0559) 370582
Country furniture.

Above: A selection of furniture, courtesy of Anvil Antiques.

MACLEAN ANTIQUES
3–3a Carmarthen Street
Llandeilo, Dyfed, Wales
Tel: (055 03) 509
18th and 19th c. country furniture, specialising in oak and pine.

MILES ANTIQUES
Albany Road
Cardiff, S Glamorgan, Wales
Tel: (0222) 31485
16th and 17th c. furniture specialising in Welsh oak.

GILBERT MORRIS AND SON
Old Village School
Northop, Clwyd CH7 6BD, Wales
Tel: (0352) 58758
18th and 19th c. furniture.

NASH ANTIQUES
17–17a Upper Church Street
Gilwern, nr Abergavenny
Gwent, Wales
Oak and mahogany furniture.

NORTHGATE ANTIQUES
6–10 Northgate Street
Pembroke, Dyfed, Wales
Tel: (064 63) 4416
18th and 19th c. oak and pine furniture.

GERALD OLIVER ANTIQUES
14 Albany Terrace
St Thomas Green
Haverfordwest, Dyfed, Wales
Tel: (0437) 2794
Pre-1870 furniture.

J. PENDER AND SONS
Tan-yr-Allt
Abergele, Clwyd, Wales
Tel: (0745) 30072
17th to 19th c. English and Welsh furniture.

PENYGROES ANTIQUES
19a Water Street
Penygroes, Gwynedd, Wales
Tel: (028 689) 332
Georgian and Victorian small furniture.

PETER PHILP
77 Kimberley Road
Cardiff, S Glamorgan CF2 5DP, Wales
Tel: (0222) 493826
17th to early 19th c. English, Welsh and Continental furniture.

RAGLAN ANTIQUES
High Street
Raglan, Gwent, Wales
Tel: (0291) 690327
17th and 18th c. furniture.

MARK RHYS
High Street
Caerleon, Gwent, Wales
Tel: (0633) 420535
17th and 18th c. Welsh oak furniture.

STUDIO ANTIQUES
11 Upper Clwyd Street
Ruthin, Clwyd, Wales
Tel: (082 42) 3814
19th c. small furniture.

THREE SALMONS ANTIQUES
Three Salmons Hotel Ltd
Usk, Gwent NP5 1BQ, Wales
Tel: (02913) 2133/4
Jacobean and early English furniture.

TIMES PAST ANTIQUES
Rossett Cottage
Rossett, nr Wrexham
Clwyd, Wales
Tel: (0978) 820792
19th and early 20th c. furniture.

JOHN TREFOR
Rhuallt Hall Farm
Rhuallt, nr St Asaph
Clwyd, Wales
Tel: (0745) 583604
18th and 19th c. oak and mahogany furniture, including Welsh dressers.

PAUL WANGER ANTIQUES
2d Wellfield Road
Cardiff, S Glamorgan, Wales
Tel: (0222) 35446
18th and 19th c. furniture.

WYE NOT ANTIQUES
49 Monnow Street
Monmouth, Gwent, Wales
Tel: (0600) 3854
18th and 19th c. oak and mahogany furniture.

MIDLANDS AND EAST ANGLIA

DAVID ABBOTT
9 Kings Avenue
Framlingham
Woodbridge, Suffolk
Tel: Not Available
Specialist in Victorian and Edwardian brass beds.

LIZ ALLPORT
Corner Antiques
Coltishall Antiques Centre
Coltishall, Norfolk
Tel: (0603) 737631
Small Victorian furniture.

ANGLIA ANTIQUE EXPORTERS
33 New Holt Street
Holt, Norfolk
Tel: (026 371) 3530
Victorian furniture.

ANTIQUES A.G.
Erwarton Hall
Shotley, Ipswich, Suffolk 1P9 1LQ
Tel: (0473) 34645
Early English oak and country furniture.

ANVIL ANTIQUES
The Old School, Alsop Street
Leek, Staffs
and
The Warehouse
Old Step Row
Leek, Staffs
Tel: (0538) 371657 or 385280
Stripped pine furniture in all conditions, specialising in Irish and Welsh pieces.

MRS A.G. BANNISTER
Abode
The Shrieve's House
40 Sheep Street
Stratford-upon-Avon, Warks
Tel: (0789) 68755
Stripped pine furniture, French furniture and some mahogany and oak pieces.

T.S. BARROWS AND SON
Hamlyn Lodge, Station Road
Ollerton
Newark, Notts
Tel: (0623) 823600
Furniture restorers who sell a selection of restored furniture.

BITS AND PIECES
34 High Street
Highham Ferrers, Northants
and
3a Church Street
Finedon, Northants
Tel: (0933) 680430
Country style (mainly pine) furniture.

BROCKDISH ANTIQUES
Commerce House
Brockdish, Diss, Norfolk
Tel: (037 975) 498
Antique and second-hand furniture.

I. AND J. BROWN
58 Commercial Road
Hereford, Heref & Worcs HR1 2BP
Tel: (0432) 58895
Enormous selection of country chairs, farmhouse tables and other country-style pieces such as dressers and lowboys. See overleaf for illustration.

BROWNHOUSE ANTIQUES
1 Ipswich Road
Claydon, Ipswich, Suffolk
Tel: (0473) 830130
Stripped pine furniture and Victoriana.

SIMON CARTER GALLERY
23 Market Hill
Woodbridge, Suffolk
Tel: (03943) 2242
English furniture from 1600 to 1830.

E.M. CHESHIRE
The Manor House
Market Place
Bingham, Notts
Tel: (0949) 38861
17th and 18th c. oak, mahogany and walnut furniture.

ANDREW CLOVER ANTIQUES
10, 12, and 25 St Peter's Street
Ipswich, Suffolk
Tel: (0473) 216563 and (0473) 88500 (Home)
17th and 18th c. English and Continental furniture.

THOMAN COULBORN AND SONS
Vesey Manor
64 Birmingham Road
Sutton Coldfield, W Midlands B72 1QF
Tel: (021 354) 3974 and 3139
18th c. English and Continental furniture, specialising in dining tables and sets of chairs.

RICHARD CRANMER
Rackheath Hall
Norwich, Norfolk
Tel: (0603) 720326
18th and 19th c. English and Continental furniture.

COLIN DAVIES ANTIQUES
15 Wolverhampton Road
Stafford, Staffs
Tel: (0785) 40545
Fine French furniture and objets d'art.

FEARNS ANTIQUES
9 Coleshill Street
Fazeley, nr Tamworth, Staffs
Tel: (0827) 54233
18th to early 20th c. furniture.

H.R. FOXALL
42a Underhill Street
Bridgnorth, Shropshire
Tel: (07462) 2437
Victorian and Edwardian furniture including mirrors.

DAVID GIBBINS ANTIQUES
21 Market Hill
Woodbridge, Suffolk
Tel: (03943) 3531
17th and 18th c. furniture.

Above: Adam period mahogany hall chair with contemporary crest of the Duke of St Albans on the radial back; George II mahogany Chippendale kettle stand shown with Louis XIV cast brass coffee pot; early 19th c. mahogany jardinière, all courtesy of David Gibbins Antiques.

Below: low-back Windsor chair with crinoline stretcher, courtesy of I. and J. Brown.

Below: Fruitwood dresser with cupboards, circa 1740, courtesy of E.M. Cheshire.

Below: Early 18th c. mulberry wood bureau cabinet, circa 1715, courtesy of Thomas Coulborn and Sons.

Above: Georgian twin pedestal dining table in mahogany, shown with a set of 18th c. chairs and a 18th c. mahogany bookcase, courtesy of Great Brampton House Antiques.

GREAT BRAMPTON HOUSE ANTIQUES
Madley, Hereford, Heref & Worcs
Tel: (0981) 250244
18th to early 20th c. English and Continental furniture.

JOYCE HARDY PINE AND COUNTRY FURNITURE
Hachestow
Woodbridge, Suffolk
Tel: (0728) 746485
Pine furniture specialising in chairs, tables and dressers.

DAVID HARFORD ANTIQUES
White Hall
Himley, nr. Dudley, W Midlands DY3 4LB
Tel: (0902) 894533
Fine quality 17th to 19th c. furniture.

THE HAY GALLERIES LTD
4 High Town
Hay-on-Wye, Heref & Worcs HR3 5AE
Tel: (0497) 820356
Period pine furniture.

PAUL HOPWELL ANTIQUES
30 High Street
West Haddon, Northants
Tel: (078 887) 636
17th and 18th c. oak, walnut, and mahogany furniture.

ANTHONY HURST ANTIQUES
Church Street
Woodbridge, Suffolk
Tel: Woodbridge 2500
18th and early 19th c. furniture.

JALNA ANTIQUES AND RESTORATION
Coley Lane
Little Haywood
Stafford, Staffs ST18 0UP
Tel: (0889) 881381
Victorian chairs and chaises longues.

H.W. KEIL LTD
Tudor House
Broadway, Heref & Worcs WR12 7DP
Tel: (0386) 85 2408
Specialists in 16th and 17th c. oak furniture and fine walnut pieces form 1690 to 1750, plus 18th c. mahogany.

KESTREL HOUSE
72 Gravelly Hill
North Erdington, Birmingham
W Midlands B23 6BB
Tel: (021) 373 2375
Victorian and Edwardian furniture.

Above: Pair of 18th c. urns on two mahogany-fitted pedestals, circa 1790, courtesy of H.W. Keil.

Below left: A selection of pine furniture, courtesy of Joyce Hardy.

Below right: A selection of period pine furniture, courtesy of Hay Galleries.

LOWE OF LOUGHBOROUGH ANTIQUES
37–39 Church Gate
Loughborough, Leics
Tel: (0509) 212554
17th to 19th c. country furniture including Windsor chairs, dressers and corner cupboards; Georgian and Regency furniture plus Victorian upholstered furniture including spoonback chairs and chesterfield sofas.

MERIDIAN HOUSE ANTIQUES
Meridian House, Market Street
Stourbridge, W Midlands
Tel: (038 43) 5384
18th and 19th c. small furniture.

NEPTUNE ANTIQUES
86–88 Fore Street
Ipswich, Suffolk
Tel: (0473) 51110
17th and 18th c. furniture.

NEVILL ANTIQUES
9–10 Milk Street
and
30–31 Princess Street
Shrewsbury, Shropshire
Tel: (0743) 51013
18th and 19th c. furniture.

PEPPERS PERIOD PIECES
29 Guildhall Street
Bury St Edmunds, Suffolk
Tel: (0284) 68786
17th c. to early 20th c. furniture.

MRS A.M. PONSONBY ANTIQUES
Upham House
Ashfield, nr Stowmarket, Suffolk
Tel: (072 882) 200
18th and 19th c. furniture up to Victoriana.

SERENDIPITY
Montague House
4 St Mary's Street
Ross-on-Wye, Heref & Worcs
Tel: (0989) 3836
18th and 19th c. furniture, specialising in Welsh dressers and pedestal desks.

SUFFOLK FINE ARTS
High Street
Ixworth, nr Bury St Edmunds, Suffolk
Tel: (0359) 31442
16th to 18th c. furniture especially oak, yew, walnut and fruitwoods.

R.N. USHER
42 Southgate Street
Bury St Edmunds, Suffolk
Tel: (0284) 4838
18th and early 19th c. mahogany furniture.

PERCY F. WALE LTD
32–34 Regent Street
Leamington Spa, Warks CV32 5EG
Tel: (0926) 21288
18th and 19th c. furniture specialising in George III mahogany, Victorian walnut and Edwardian mahogany pieces.

WESTLEY RICHARDS AND COMPANY LTD
Grange Road
Birmingham, W Midlands B29 6AR
Tel: (021) 472 2953
Marble furniture, specialising in Oriental pieces.

WHERRY HOUSE ANTIQUES
The Street
Sutton, Norfolk NR12 9RF
Tel: (0692) 81487 (By appointment only)
19th and early 20th c. small furniture.

Above: Mid-19th c. commode secretaire in mahogany oak-lined, with ormolu mounts and gallery and marble top, courtesy of Adams Antiques

NORTH OF ENGLAND AND SCOTLAND

ABERFORD ANTIQUES LTD
Hicklam House
Aberford, nr Leeds, W Yorkshire
Tel: (0532) 813209
Stripped pine furniture.

ADAMS ANTIQUES
65 Waterloo Row
Chester, Cheshire CH1 2LE
Tel: (0244) 319421
18th and 19th c. furniture.

ALEXANDER ADAMSON
48 St Stephan Street
Edinburgh, Lothian, Scotland
Tel: (031) 255 7310
and
Hawthornden Castle
Lasswade, Lothian, Scotland
Tel: (031) 440 2180
18th and 19th c. English furniture.

ALADIN
114–116 Strathmartine Road
Dundee, Scotland
Tel: (0382) 86649
19th c. furniture especially couches.

ALDGATE ANTIQUES LTD
13 High Street
Perth, Tayside, Scotland
Tel: (0738) 20107
18th and 19th c. furniture.

ANDERSON AND SLATER ANTIQUES
8 King Street
Knutsford, Cheshire WA16 6DL
Tel: (0565) 2917
18th and 19th c. furniture.

AND SO TO BED LTD
133 Deangate
Bolton, Lancs
Tel: (0204) 392386
and
65 Whitley Road
Whitley Bay
Tyne & Wear
Tel: (0632) 524611
and
60 West Street Sowerby Bridge
Halifax, W Yorkshire
Tel: (0422) 39759
Victorian four-posters, half testers and headboards in brass, brass and iron and brass and wood.

THE ANTIQUE SHOP
12 Castle Terrace
Bridge of Weir, Strathclyde, Scotland
Tel: (0505) 612670
Victorian and Edwardian furniture.

Left: Regency fold-over tea table of unusually large size, in mahogany with original patination, circa 1820, courtesy of Wm Goodfellow Antiques.

ATHOLL ANTIQUES
322 Great Western Road
Aberdeen, Grampian, Scotland
Tel: (0224) 53547
Victorian Scottish furniture.

ATTICA ANTIQUES
62 Candlemaker Row
Edinburgh, Lothian, Scotland
Tel: (031) 225 9400
18th and 19th c. furniture.

BANKFOOT ANTIQUES
Main Street
Bankfoot, Tayside, Scotland
Tel: (073 887) 333
17th to early 19th c. furniture.

WALTER S. BEATON
75 Kinnoull Street
Perth, Tayside PH1 5EZ, Scotland
Tel: (0738) 28127
18th and early 19th c. furniture.

JOHN BELL OF ABERDEEN LTD
56–58 Bridge Street
Aberdeen, Grampian, Scotland
Tel: (0224) 24828
18th c. furniture.

BIELDSIDE ANTIQUES
85 North Deeside Road
Bieldside, Aberdeen, Scotland
Tel: (033 82) 296
18th and 19th c. small furniture.

BURLINGTON HOUSE ANTIQUES
25 North Bridge Street
Hawick, Borders, Scotland
Tel: (0450) 2984
Georgian and Victorian furniture.

CIRCA 1800
8 Deanhaugh Street
Stickbridge
Edinburgh, Scotland
Tel: (031) 332 5171
18th and 19th c. pine, oak and upholstered furniture.

COACH HOUSE ANTIQUES LTD
8–12 North Port
Perth, Tayside, Scotland
Tel: (0738) 29835
Georgian mahogany furniture.

JOHN CORRIN ANTIQUES
92 Rosemount Place
Aberdeen, Grampian, Scotland
Tel: (0224) 630436
Victorian small furniture.

PAUL COUTS LTD
101–107 West Bow
Edinburgh, Scotland
Tel: (031) 225 3238
18th c. English and Continental furniture.

CRIEFF ANTIQUES
Comrie Road
Crieff, Tayside, Scotland
Tel: (0764) 3322
Victorian small furniture.

CRANFORD GALLERIES
10 Knut Street
Knutsford, Cheshire
Tel: (0565) 3646
Pine furniture and Victoriana.

CROWN ARCADE ANTIQUES
42 Miller Street
Glasgow, Strathclyde, Scotland
Tel: (041) 248 2626
Georgian and Victorian furniture.

ERIC DAVIDSON ANTIQUES LTD
4 Grassmarket
Edinburgh, Lothian, Scotland
Tel: (031) 225 5815
18th and 19th c. English and Continental furniture.

DUNEDIN ANTIQUES LTD
4 North West Circus Parade
Edinburgh, Lothian, Scotland
Tel: (031) 226 3074
18th and 19th c. furniture.

DUNKELD ANTIQUES
Atholl Street
Dunkeld, Tayside, Scotland
Tel: (035 02) 578
18th and 19th c. furniture.

DONALD ELLIS ANTIQUES
St Ninian Road
Nairn, Highland, Scotland
Tel: (0667) 53303
18th and early 19th c. furniture.

EUREKA ANTIQUES
18 Northenden Road
Sale, Cheshire M33 3BR
Tel: (061) 962 5629
18th and 19th c. furniture.

FELTON PARK ANTIQUES
Felton Park
Felton, Northld NE65 9HN
Tel: (067 087) 652 and 319 (Home)
18th and 19th c. small furniture.

FENTON ANTIQUES
The Cottage
Travebank
Barry, Tayside, Scotland
Tel: (0241) 2326
18th and early 19th c. furniture.

J. FOSTER AND SON
19–21 Bell Street
St Andrews, Fife, Scotland
Tel: (0334) 72080
19th c. furniture.

JOAN FRERE ANTIQUES
Drambuie House
Drumnadrochit, Highland, Scotland
Tel: (045 62) 210
Pre–1800 English oak furniture.

GALLERIES DE FRESNES
Cessnock Castle
Galston, nr Kilmarnock
Strathclyde, Scotland
Tel: (0563) 820314
17th c. oak furniture.

GLYNN INTERIORS
92 King Street
Knutsford, Cheshire
Tel: (0565) 4418
English furniture from 1780–1910.

WM GOODFELLOW ANTIQUES
The Green
Over Kellet
Carnforth, Lancs LA6 1PU
Tel: (0524) 733030
English furniture, pre 1850.

Right: Sheraton period inlaid mahogany dressing table, circa 1860, courtesy of Charles Hay Antiques.

GROSVENOR ANTIQUES
22 Watergate Street
Chester, Cheshire CH1 2LA
Tel: (0244) 315201
18th c. furniture.

HAREWOOD ANTIQUES
26–27 Harrogate Road
Harewood, Leeds, W Yorkshire LS17 9LH
Tel: (0532) 886327
Occasional furniture in oak, mahogany and rosewood.

CHARLES HAY ANTIQUES
44 High Street
Coldstream, Borders, Scotland
Tel: (0890) 2552
18th and early 19th c. furniture.

HOLDEN WALKER
15 Manchester Road
Chapel-en-le-Frith, Derbs
Tel: (029 881) 4744
Pine furniture.

ICHMARTINE HOUSE ANTIQUES
Inchture, Tayside, Scotland
Tel: Not Available
17th to 19th c. furniture.

IMRIE ANTIQUES
Back Street
Bridge of Earn, Tayside, Scotland
Tel: (073 881) 2784
Georgian and Victorian furniture.

KENNETH JACKSON
74 Thistle Street
Edinburgh, Lothian, Scotland
Tel: (031) 225 9634
17th and 18th c. English and Continental furniture.

KILMACOLM ANTIQUES
29 Stewart Place
Kilmacolm, Strathclyde, Scotland
Tel: (050 587) 3149
Georgian and Victorian furniture.

R. MCASLAN
188 Woodlands Road
Glasgow, Strathclyde G3 6LL, Scotland
Tel: (041) 332 4247
17th to 19th c. oak, walnut and mahogany furniture.

MUIRHEAD MOFFATT AND COMPANY
182 West Regent Street
Glasgow, Strathclyde, Scotland
Tel: (041) 226 4683/3406
18th and early 19th c. furniture.

MONALTRIE ANTIQUES
Bridge Square
Ballater, Grampian, Scotland
Tel: (033 82) 429
Victorian furniture.

MONKLAND ANTIQUES LTD
110 Deedes Street
Airdrie, Strathclyde, Scotland
Tel: (023 64) 60131/62216
Oak, mahogany and inlaid furniture.

NEWGATE ANTIQUES
59 Newgate Street
Morpeth, Northld
Tel: (0670) 56875
Regency, Victorian and Edwardian furniture.

NICHOLSON ANTIQUES
3 Cranston Street
and
297 Canongate
Edinburgh, Lothian, Scotland
Tel: (031) 556 1842
17th to 19th c. country furniture.

NORWOOD ANTIQUES
1 Norwood
Beverley, N Humberside
Tel: (0482) 868851
18th to early 20th c. furniture.

OLDMILL ANTIQUES
68 Claremont Street
Aberdeen, Grampian, Scotland
Tel: (0224) 573562
Victorian small furniture.

PARK GALLERIES ANTIQUES
167 Mayor Street
Bolton, Lancs
Tel: (0204) 29827
(By appointment 061 764 5853)
16th to 20th c. furniture.

R. PARRY ANTIQUES
7 Cowgatehead
Edinburgh, Lothian, Scotland
Tel: (031) 225 5918
19th c. furniture.

THE PENNY FARTHING
8 Beaufort Road
Edinburgh, Scotland
Tel: (031 447) 2410
18th and 19th c. furniture

ELAINE PHILLIPS ANTIQUES
2 Royal Parade
Harrogate, N Yorks
Tel: (0423) 69745
17th and 18th c. oak furniture.

BARBARA SCOTT-BEVERIDGE
Dunkeld Road
Bankfoot, Tayside, Scotland
Tel: (073 887) 333
18th and 19th c. furniture.

CAROLYN SCOTT ANTIQUES AND CURIOS
16 Victoria Street
Edinburgh, Lothian, Scotland
Tel: (031) 225 5714
Stripped pine furniture.

THE SHIP'S WHEEL
2 Traill Street
Thurso, Highland, Scotland
Tel: (0847) 2485
18th and 19th c. furniture.

TANTALUS ANTIQUES
41 St Stephen Street
Edinburgh, Lothian, Scotland
Tel: (031) 226 5984
Small furniture from 1800–1920.

TEMPLEMANS
1 George Street
Perth, Tayside, Scotland
Tel: (0783) 25550
Georgian mahogany furniture.

TREASURE HOUSE
16 Holburn Street
Aberdeen, Grampian, Scotland
Tel: (0224) 20219
Georgian and Victorian small furniture.

Left: Early 18th c. oak dresser crossbanded with walnut. On top, 18th c. Italian altar Candlesticks and 19th c. brass jardinière.

HIBERNIAN ANTIQUES
1 Molesworth Place
2 and 16 North Street
Dublin, Rep of Ireland
Tel: Dublin 763834
18th and 19th c. furniture.

HILLSIDE ANTIQUES
16 Main Street
Hillsborough, Co Down, N Ireland
Tel: (0846) 682498
Stripped pine furniture.

LOUGH CUTRA CASTLE ANTIQUES
Gort, Galway
Co Galway, Rep of Ireland
Tel: Not Available
17th to 19th c. furniture.

MOYALLON ANTIQUES
54 Moyallon Road
Portadown, Co Armagh, N Ireland
Tel: (0762) 615
19th c. furniture, specialising pine and country pieces.

OLD CROSS ANTIQUES
3–5 Main Street
Greyabbey, Co Down, N Ireland
Tel: (024 774) 346
Small furniture from 1800–1920.

ORMOND ANTIQUES
32 Lower Ormond Quay
Dublin, Rep of Ireland
Tel: (0001) 741569
18th and 19th c. furniture.

JANE WILLIAMS ANTIQUES LTD
23 Molesworth Street
Dublin, Rep of Ireland
Tel: (0001) 767857
18th and early 19th c. furniture.

Below: Minsterley dresser (from Shropshire) in oak, crossbanded in mahogany, circa 1770, courtesy of E.W. Webster.

VICTORIANA ANTIQUES
70 Rosemount Viaduct
Aberdeen, Grampian, Scotland
Tel: (0224) 20219
Victorian and Edwardian furniture, especially roll-top desks and chairs.

E.W. WEBSTER
Wash Farm
Bickerstaffe
Nr Ormskirk, Lancs
Tel: (0695) 24322
Pre-1840 furniture, especially dressers.

WHEELWRIGHTS ANTIQUES
Pinfold Lane
Fishlake, Doncaster, S Yorkshire DN7 5LA
Tel: (0302) 841411
Stripped pine furniture including country chairs and chests.

JOHN WHITELAW
156 High Street
Auchterarder, Tayside, PH3 1AD
Scotland
Tel: (076 46) 2482
17th to early 19th c. furniture.

WHYTOCK AND REID
Sunbury House
Belford Mews
Edinburgh, Scotland EH4 3DN
Tel: (031) 226 4911
18th and early 19th c. furniture.

COLIN R. WOOD
25 Rose Street
Aberdeen, Grampian, Scotland AB1 2DP
Tel: (0224) 23019
18th and 19th c. furniture.

MICHAEL YOUNG
Invercowie House
Stonehaven, Grampian, Scotland
Tel: (0569) 63264/62364
18th and 19th c. English furniture.

JOHN YATES AND SON
5½ Spittal Street
and
5 Bank Street
Stirling, Central, Scotland
Tel: (0786) 3875
18th and early 19th c. furniture.

NORTHERN IRELAND AND REPUBLIC OF IRELAND

THE ANTIQUE SHOP
Main Street
Templepatrick, Antrim, N Ireland
Tel: (084 94) 32645
18th c. furniture.

ANTIQUES OF COMBER
13 High Street
Comber, Co Down, N Ireland
Tel: (0247) 872690
18th and 19th c. pine furniture.

EDWARD BUTLER
14 Batchelor's Walk
Dublin, Rep of Ireland
Tel: (0001) 743485
17th to 19th c. furniture.

TOM CALDWELL GALLERIES
40 and 56 Bradbury Place
Belfast, N Ireland
Tel: (0232) 23311
18th and early 19th c. furniture.

DUNLUCE ANTIQUES
33 Ballytober Road
Bushmills, Co. Antrim BT57 8UU, N Ireland
Tel: (02657) 31140
Georgian furniture.

GEORGIAN SHOP
54 South William Street
Dublin, Rep of Ireland
Tel: (0001) 774434
18th c. furniture.

Right: Facet stem English wine glass, the bowl engraved with ships sailing between two ports, circa 1780, courtesy of Asprey and Company Ltd.

LONDON

NORMAN ADAMS LTD
8/10 Hans Road
London SW3
Tel: (01) 589 5266
18th c. glass.

ADAMS ROOM LTD
18–20 Ridgway
London SW19
Tel: (01) 946 7047
18th and 19th c. glass.

ANNO DOMINI ANTIQUES
66 Pimlico Road
London SW1
Tel: (01) 730 5496/373 1944
17th to 19th c. glass.

ANTIQUES AND FINE ARTS
152 Upper Richmond Road
London SW15
Tel: (01) 788 9123
19th c. glass.

ANTIQUUS
90–92 Pimlico Road
London SW1
Tel: (01) 730 8681
Classical, mediaeval and Renaissance glass.

ASPREY AND COMPANY LTD
165–169 New Bond Street
London W1Y OAR
Tel: (01) 493 6767
18th and 19th c. glass.

ASTORIA
222 Munster Road
London SW6
Tel: (01) 385 9888
Art Deco glass.

BARNES ANTIQUES
16 Lower Richmond Road
London SW15
Tel: (01) 789 3371
Art glass.

SUSAN BECKER
18 Lower Richmond Road
London SW15
Tel: (01) 788 9082
Opaline glass.

WILLIAM BEDFORD ANTIQUES LTD
327 Upper Street
Islington Green
London N1
Tel: (01) 226 9648
Glass from 1650–1830.

PHILIP BRADY
3 Blenheim Crescent
London W11
Tel: (01) 727 7536
18th and 19th c. glass.

WILLIAM BRAY
58 Fulham Road
London SW6
Tel: (01) 731 1170
Georgian glassware.

BEVERLEY BROOK ANTIQUES
22 High Street
London SW13
Tel: (01) 878 4899 and 878 5656 (Home)
Regency, Victorian and Edwardian glass.

F.G. BRUSCHWEILER ANTIQUES LTD
3 Lonsdale Road
London W11
Tel: (01) 229 3106
18th and 19th c. glass.

W.G.T. BURNE LTD
11 Elystan Street
London SW3 3NT
Tel: (01) 589 6074
18th and 19th c. English and Irish collector's glass plus tableware, decanters and lustre glass.

LEWIS CAPLAN ASSOCIATES LTD
50 Fulham Road
London SW3
Tel: (01) 589 3108 and 584 6328
Art Nouvean and Art Deco glass from 1890–1945.

CHAPMAN AND DAVIES ANTIQUES
10 Theberton Street
London N1 OQX
Tel: (01) 226 5565/348 4846/359 4330
Stained glass panels, especially those just before and after turn of the century.

GLASS

Above: Victorian turquoise cameo glass vase, courtesy of The Hay Loft.

JOHN CLYNE
3 and 10 Blenheim Crescent
London W11
Tel: (01) 727 7536
Victorian and Edwardian glass.

COBWEB
2 Englands Lane
London NW3
Tel: (01) 586 4605
Ancient and antique European and Far Eastern glass.

THE COLLECTOR ON LAVENDER HILL
43 Lavender Hill
London SW11
Tel: (01) 223 8683
Victorian to Art Deco glass.

COLLET'S CHINESE GALLERY
40 Great Russell Street
London WC1
Tel: (01) 580 7538
18th and 19th c. Chinese snuff bottles.

THE CORNER CUPBOARD
679 Finchley Road
London NW2
Tel: (01) 435 4870
18th and 19th c. glass.

CREST ANTIQUES
313–315 and 287 Putney Bridge Road
London SW15
Tel: (01) 789 3165
19th and 20th c. glass.

TONY DAVIS INC
235–9 Lavender Hill
London SW11
Tel: (01) 228 1370/1 and 223 9532 (Home)
Victorian and Edwardian glass.

DELOMOSNE AND SON LTD
4 Campden Hill Road
London W8 7DU
Tel: (01) 937 1804
English and Irish glass, specialising in 18th c. wineglasses.

DENTON ANTIQUES
87 Marylebone High Street
London W1
Tel: (01) 935 5831
Cut glass specialists, with emphasis on chandeliers.

H. AND W. DEUTSCH ANTIQUES
111 Kensington Church Street
London W8
Tel: (01) 727 5984
18th and 19th c. English and Continental glassware.

DODO
185 Westbourne Grove
London W11
Tel: (01) 229 3132
Wine, beer and scent bottles.

FOREST HILL ANTIQUES
7 Davids Road
London SE23
Tel: (01) 699 4061 and 693 5050 (Home)
18th to early 20th c. glass, including Art Nouveau and Art Deco.

PETER FRANCIS
26 Museum Street
London WC1
Tel: (01) 637 0165
Glass from 1760–1860.

GALERIE 1900
267 Camden High Street
London NW1
Tel: (01) 485 1001 and 969 1803 (Home)
Art Nouveau and Art Deco glass.

GALLERY 25
4 Halkin Arcade
London SW1
Tel: (01) 235 5178
Art glass from 1900–1930.

ELIA GRAHAME ANTIQUES
97c Kensington Church Street
London W8
Tel: (01) 727 4132
18th c. glass.

GREAT EXPECTATIONS
62 Old Church Street
London SW3
Tel: (01) 352 9850
19th c. glass.

GORDON GRIDLEY
41 Camden Passage
London N1
Tel: (01) 226 0643/9033
17th to 19th c. glass.

SHERRY HATCHER
15 Pierrepont Arcade
Camden Passage
London N1
Tel: (01) 226 5679/8496
Victorian glass, specialising in perfume bottles.

THE HAY LOFT
332 Upper Richmond Road
London SW14
Tel: (01) 876 5020
Glass from 1800–1930, specialising in Victorian pieces.

HELGATO
50 Highgate High Street
London N6 5HX
Tel: (01) 348 3864
British glass to 1880.

LESLEY HEPHERD ANTIQUES
47 Camden Passage
London N1
Tel: (01) 359 1755
English glass from 1740–1840.

J.T. ANTIQUES
11 Webb's Road
London SW11
Tel: (01) 228 7171
18th to early 20th c. glass.

MELVYN AND GARY JAY ANTIQUES
64a Kensington Church Street
London W8 4DB
Tel: (01) 937 6832
19th c. glass.

THOMAS KERR ANTIQUES LTD
11 Theberton Street
London N1 0QY
Tel: (01) 226 0626
18th c. glassware.

RICHARD KIHL WINE ANTIQUES
164 Regents Park Road
London NW1
Tel: (01) 586 3838
Wine-related antiques including glass decanters, claret jugs, funnels and old bottles, all from 1750–1910.

RICHARD LALLY LTD
152 Upper Richmond Road
London SW15
Tel: (01) 788 9123
18th and 19th c. glassware.

JILL LEWIS
Collector's Corner
138 Portobello Road
London W11
Tel: (040) 372 2357
Scent bottles.

ERIC LINEHAM ANTIQUES
62 Kensington Church Street
London W8
Tel: (01) 937 9650
English and Continental art glass, including cameo overlay and other unusual pieces.

LYONS GALLERY
47–49 Mill Lane
London NW6
Tel: (01) 794 3537
Art Nouveau and Art Deco glass, including Lalique.

MARTINS-FORREST ANTIQUES
8 Halkin Arcade, Motcomb Street
London SW1
Tel: (01) 235 8353 and 341 0673 (Home)
Art Nouveau and Art Deco glass.

MERCURY ANTIQUES
1 and 1b Ladbroke Road
London W11
Tel: (01) 727 5106
Glass from 1800–1850.

MOMTAZ GALLERY LTD
42 Pembridge Road
London W11
Tel: (01) 229 5579
Persian and Islamic glass.

NAYLORS
131 Munster Road
London SW6
Tel: (01) 731 3679
Glass, from 1850–1950.

H.W. NEWBY
130c Brompton Road
London SW3
Tel: (01) 589 2752
English and Continental glass, pre-1830.

PAT NYE
Collector's Corner
138 Portobello Road
London W11
Tel: (01) 948 4314
18th and early 19th c. drinking glasses.

P.J. ANTIQUES
12 Lower Richmond Road
London SW15
Tel: (01) 789 3198
18th and 19th c. glass.

HOWARD PHILLIPS
11a Henrietta Place
London W1
Tel: (01) 580 9844
Pre-1830 and pre-Roman glass.

PORTMEIRION ANTIQUES
5 Pont Street
London SW1
Tel: (01) 235 7601
Glass from 1700–1900.

THE PURPLE SHOP
15 Flood Street, London SW3
Tel: (01) 352 1127
Art Nouveau and Art Deco glass.

Right: Early 19th c. goblet decorated by the process patented by Davenport in 1806, courtesy of A. Henning.

ROCHFORT ANTIQUES GALLERY
32–34 The Green
Winchmore Hill
London N21
Tel: (01) 886 4779
18th and 19th c. glass.

RUTLAND STREET GALLERY
8 Rutland Street
London SW7
Tel: (01) 581 3761
Cameo glass.

GERALD SATTIN LTD
25 Burlington Arcade
London W1
Tel: (01) 493 6557
English glass to 1880.

SHEPPARD AND COOPER LTD
5–6 Cork Street
London W1
Tel: (01) 734 9179
Glass from 1400 B.C. on.

SOUTH AUDLEY ART GALLERIES LTD
36 South Audley Street
London W1
Tel: (01) 499 3178/3195
Specialists in Gallé glass.

SPINK AND SON LTD
5, 6 and 7 King Street
London SW1
Tel: (01) 930 7888
19th c. glass including paperweights.

STAIR AND COMPANY LTD
120 Mount Street
London W1Y 5HB
Tel: (01) 499 1784/5
English cut-glass chandeliers.

SUNDRIDGE ANTIQUES
564 Kings Road
London SW6
Tel: (01) 736 0828
Glass from 1750–1920.

Above: "Trade Mark" and "Jackal" Dutch gin bottles with typical case shape used to export the product around the world, circa 1890, courtesy of Keith Shotter.

MAUREEN THOMPSON
34 Kensington Church Street
London W8
Tel: (01) 937 9919
17th and 18th c. glass.

EARLE D. VANDEKAR
138 Brompton Road
London SW3 1HY
Tel: (01) 589 8481/3398
European and English glassware, pre-1830.

W.13 ANTIQUES
10 The Avenue
London W13
Tel: (01) 998 0390
18th and 19th c. glass.

RON WELDON
109 Regents Park Road
London NW1
Tel: (01) 485 6210/4433
18th and 19th c. glass.

P. AND L. WOOLMAN
351 Upper Street
London N1
Tel: (01) 359 7648
Specialists in Gallé glass.

SOUTH AND SOUTHEAST ENGLAND

ABBEY ANTIQUES AND ARTS
97 High Street
Hemel Hempstead, Herts
Tel: (0442) 64667
18th and 19th c. glass.

APOLLO GALLERIES
61, 65 and 67 South End
Croydon, Surrey
Tel: (01) 681 3727/680 1968
18th and 19th c. English and Continental glass.

ARTBRY'S ANTIQUES
44 High Street
Orpington, Kent
Tel: (01) 868 0834 and 954 1840 (Home)
18th and 19th c. glass.

C. CLEALL ANTIQUES
16 Brewers Lane
Richmond, Surrey
Tel: (01) 940 8069
Art Nouveau and Art Deco glass.

COLLECTOR'S CORNER
73 High Street
Teddington, Middx
Tel: (01) 977 1079 and 977 6450 (Home)
Georgian and Victorian glass.

DAVID FILEMAN
Squirrels Bayards, Horsham Road
Steyning, Sussex
Tel: (0903) 813229
18th and 19th c. glass chandeliers, cut table glass and 18th c. collector's glass, including French paperweights.

A. HENNING
48 Walton Street
Walton-on-the-Hill
Tadworth, Surrey
Tel: Tadworth 3337
English glassware from 1700 to 1840.

HILL RISE ANTIQUES
26 Hill Rise
Richmond, Surrey
Tel: (01) 948 1140 and 876 4114 (Home)
19th c. glass.

SHIRLEY KING
2 Johnston Road
Woodford Green, Essex
Tel: (01) 505 5774
19th c. glass.

LAYTON ANTIQUES
1 Paved Court, The Green
Richmond, Surrey
Tel: (01) 940 2617
Victorian glass.

ANTHONY J. LESTER
The Dower House
Hithercroft, nr Wallingford, Oxon
Tel: (0491) 36683 (By appointment only)
18th c. English wine glasses.

THE OLD HOUSE
15/17 High Street
Seaford, Sussex
Tel: (0323) 892091
18th to early 20th c. glass.

PAMELA AND BARRY ANTIQUES
126 Sandridge Road
St Albans, Herts
Tel: St Albans 51109
18th and 19th c. glass.

PENNY FARTHING ANTIQUES
71 High Street
Chobham, Surrey
Tel: (099 05) 7718
Unusual glass including Cranberry and Bristol pieces.

KEITH SHOTTER
81 Regent Street
Shanklin, Isle of Wight PO37 7AP
Tel: (098 386) 2334
Glass bottles from Roman period to 1930.

STANMORE HILL ANTIQUES
105 Stanmore Hill
Stanmore, Middx
Tel: (01) 954 0490
18th and 19th c. English and Continental glass.

SUNDRIDGE ANTIQUES
4 Sundridge Parade
Plaistow Lane
Bromley, Kent
Tel: (01) 460 8164
Glass from 1780–1920.

NORMAN WITHAM
2 High Street
Beckenham, Kent
Tel: (01) 650 4651
Victorian glass.

SOUTHWEST ENGLAND AND WALES

ALDERSON AND ALDERSON
23 Brook Street
Bath, Avon
Tel: (0225) 21652
18th and 19th c. glass.

BELL PASSAGE ANTIQUES
28 High Street
Wickwar
Wotton-under-Edge, Glos GL12 8NP
Tel: (045 424) 251
Early drinking glasses.

ANGELA CLEMENT ANTIQUES
First Floor
37 East Street
Blandford Forum, Dorset
Tel: (0258) 53472
Victorian and Regency glass

EIFIONA HUGHES
The Antique Shop
High Street
Criccieth, Gwynedd, Wales
Tel: (076 671) 2160
18th and early 19th c. glass.

OLD BARN ANTIQUES COMPANY
The Abbey Antique Shop
Half Moon Street
Sherborne, Dorset
Tel: (093 581) 2068
18th and 19th c. glass.

SHIP STREET GALLERIES
14 Ship Street
Brecon, Powys, Wales
Tel: (0874) 3926
18th and early 19th c. glass.

SOMERVALE ANTIQUES
6 Radstock Road
Midsomer Norton
Bath, Avon BA3 2AJ
Tel: (0761) 412686
18th and early 19th English glass including decanters, cut and coloured, plus Bristol and Nailsea glass.

MIDLANDS AND EAST ANGLIA

JOHN A. BROOKS
2 Knights Crescent
Rothley, Leics LE7 7PN
Tel: (0533) 302625 (By appointment only)
18th and early 19th c. glassware, particularly pressed glass and drinking glasses.

Below: Selection of 18th c. English drinking glasses with opaque and air twist stems; in foreground, 19th c. tumbler with engraving showing clipper ship going under the iron Sunderland Bridge, whose opening in 1796 the glass commemorates, courtesy of Somervale Antiques.

GAVINA EWART
37 Sheep Street
Stratford-upon-Avon, Warks
Tel: (0789) 293917
18th c. drinking glasses and stemware plus 19th c. paperweights.

NORTH OF ENGLAND AND SCOTLAND

ALADIN
114–116 Strathmartine Road
Dundee, Tayside, Scotland
Tel: (0382) 86649
17th to 19th c. glass.

ANDERSON AND SLATER ANTIQUES
8 King Street
Knutsford, Cheshire WA16 6DL
Tel: (0565) 2917
18th and 19th c. glass.

Left: Wine glass with bell bowl on a slender six-sided Silesian stem and folded foot, circa 1725, courtesy of John Brooks.

BIELDSIDE ANTIQUES
85 North Deeside Road
Bieldside, Aberdeen
Grampian Scotland
Tel: (033 82) 296
18th and 19th c. glass.

DRAGON ANTIQUES
10 Dragon Road
Harrogate, N Yorkshire
Tel: (0423) 62037
Victorian art glass including Art Nouveau.

WILLIAM GOODFELLOW
The Green, Over Kellet
Carnforth, Lancs LA6 1BU
Tel: (0524) 733030
English glass, pre-1850.

WILLIAM MACADAM
86 Pilrig Street
Edinburgh, Lothian, Scotland
Tel: (031) 553 1364
18th c. drinking glasses plus 18th and 19th c. coloured and pressed glass.

SUNFIELD COTTAGE ANTIQUES
Inchmarlo, Banchory
Grampian, Scotland
Tel: (033 02) 2703
18th and 19th c. glass.

NORTHERN IRELAND

COOKSTOWN ANTIQUES
11a Oldtown Street
Cookstown, Co Tyrone, N Ireland
Tel: (064 87) 65279
Victorian glass.

HAMILTON ANTIQUES
19 Shore Road
Holywood, Co Down, N Ireland
Tel: (023 17) 4404
18th c. Irish glass.

LONDON

MARIA ANDIPA ICON GALLERY
162 Walton Street
London SW3
Tel: (01) 589 2371
Ethnic jewellery from the 15th c. on.

ANNABO AND CROESUS
Stand 324
Grays Antique Market
Davies Street
London W1
Tel: (01) 493 0624
18th to early 20th c. jewellery.

PHILIP ANTROBUS LTD
11 New Bond Street
London W1
Tel: (01) 493 4557
*Antique jewellery including Georgian
diamonds, gold pieces and Victorian jewellery.*

ARMITAGE CLARKE
9 Blenheim Street
New Bond Street
London W1
Tel: (01) 493 8828/629 0308
18th and 19th c. jewellery.

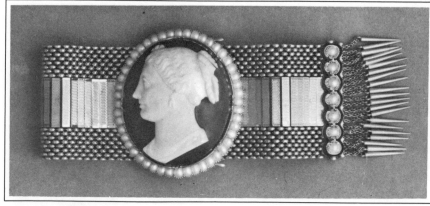

ARMOUR-WINSTON LTD
43 Burlington Arcade
London W1
Tel: (01) 493 8937
Specialists in Victorian jewellery.

ASPREY AND COMPANY LTD
153 Fenchurch Street
London EC3
Tel: (01) 626 2160
18th to early 20th c. jewellery.

*Above: Gold, pearl and hardstone cameo
bracelet, circa 1840, courtesy of Ronald
Benjamin Antiques.*

ASTORIA
222 Munster Road
London SW6
Tel: (01) 385 9888
*Art Deco jewellery, including cocktail and
smoking accessories.*

C. BARRETT AND COMPANY
51 Burlington Arcade
London W1
Tel: (01) 493 2570
*European and Oriental ivory, jade, coral plus
Russian silver and enamels.*

BELLAMY
15 Flood Street
London SW3
Tel: (01) 352 3334
*19th and 20th c. jewellery, including Art
Nouveau and Art Deco items.*

RONALD BENJAMIN ANTIQUES
25b Hatton Garden
(Entrance in Greville Street)
London EC1
Tel: (01) 242 6188/9105
*Jewellery from 1700, including signed pieces
such as Fabergé's.*

BROMET
55 Burlington Arcade
London W1
Tel: (01) 493 6582
Georgian jewellery.

BUTLER AND WILSON
189 Fulham Road
London SW3
Tel: (01) 352 3045
Art Deco jewellery, including Rolex watches.

THE BUTTON QUEEN
19 Marylebone Lane
London W1
Tel: (01) 935 1505
*19th c. and Edwardian jewellery, specialising
in buckles, buttons and unusual cuff links.*

CAMEO CORNER LTD
c/o Liberty's, Regent Street
London W1
Tel: (01) 734 1234
*Established in 1908, dealing in antique
jewellery including Art Nouveau and Art
Deco pieces, as well as cameos.*

*Left: Engraved chrome and black bakelite
choker and earring; engraved and pierced ring
in silver and black onyx; and aluminium and
black bakelite bracelet, all circa 1930, courtesy
of Astoria.*

*Right: Mid-Victorian Holbeinesque pendant
set with diamonds and emeralds (right) and an
early Victorian gold bow brooch (left),
courtesy of Ronald Benjamin Antiques.*

LEWIS M. CAPLAN ASSOCIATES LTD
50 Fulham Road
London SW3
Tel: (01) 589 3108/584 6328
Signed Art Nouveau and Art Deco jewellery.

ARMITAGE CLARKE
9 Blenheim Street
New Bond Street
London W1
Tel: (01) 493 8828/629 0308
18th and 19th c. jewellery.

COBRA AND BELLAMY
149 Sloane Street
London SW1
Tel: (01) 730 2823
Late 19th and early 20th c. jewellery.

THE CORNER CUPBOARD
679 Finchley Road
London NW2
Tel: (01) 435 4870
18th and 19th c. jewellery.

CREST ANTIQUES
313–315 and 287 Putney Bridge Road
London SW15
Tel: (01) 789 3165
19th and early 20th c. jewellery.

DEMAS
31 Burlington Arcade
London W1
Tel: (01) 493 9496
*Specialists in Georgian and Victorian
jewellery.*

DONOHOE
175 Portobello Road
London W11
Tel: (01) 727 4681 and 455 5507 (Home)
Georgian and Victorian jewellery.

M. EKSTEIN LTD
90 Jermyn Street
London SW1
Tel: (01) 930 2024
Continental jewellery.

J.F. EWING
11 High Street
London SW19
Tel: (01) 946 4700
Jewellery from 1800–1930.

THE GOLDEN PAST
6 Brook Street
London W1
Tel: (01) 493 6422
*Gold and silver brooches, necklaces, guards,
rings, earrings, bracelets, seals and charms,
and pinchbeck pieces.*

GREEN'S ANTIQUE GALLERIES
117 Kensington Church Street
London W8
Tel: (01) 229 9618/9
Jewellery, 18th to early 20th c.

M. HAKIM
4 The Royal Arcade
Old Bond Street
London W1
Tel: (01) 629 2643
18th c. jewellery.

HANCOCKS AND COMPANY LTD
1 Burlington Gardens
London W1
Tel: (01) 493 8904/5
Jewellery from 1830–1940, especially cameos.

JAMES HARDY AND COMPANY
235 Brompton Road
London SW3
Tel: (01) 589 5050
Jewellery, specialising in silver items.

HARRIS AND FRANK LTD
53 Holland Park
London W11 3RS
Tel: (01) 727 4769 (By appointment only)
16th to 19th c. jewellery.

THE HAY LOFT
332 Upper Richmond Road
London SW14
Tel: (01) 876 5020
Jewellery from 1800–1930.

HEIRLOOM AND HOWARD LTD
1 Hay Hill
Berkeley Square
London W1
Tel: (01) 493 5868
*Armorial jewellery, ie pieces with crests or
coats-of-arms on them, such as signet rings.*

R. HOLT AND COMPANY LTD
98 Hatton Garden
London EC1
Tel: (01) 405 5286
Chinese jewellery.

THE HOUSE OF ANDOR
17a The Burroughs
London NW4
Tel: Not Available
18th and 19th c. jewellery.

INHERITANCE
98 Islington High Street
London N1
Tel: (01) 226 8305
*19th c. rings, bracelets and diamond
pendants.*

*FOR MAP OF LONDON'S POSTAL
DISTRICTS, SEE PAGE 61.*

KLABER AND KLABER
2b Hans Road
London SW3
Tel: (01) 589 7728
Fine European enamels.

DAN KLEIN LTD
11 Halkin Arcade
Motcomb Street
London SW1
Tel: (01) 245 9868
*Jewellery from 1850–1960 including Art Deco
and Art Nouveau.*

H. KNOWLES-BROWN LTD
27 Hampstead High Street
London NW3
Tel: (01) 435 4775
Antique and Renaissance jewellery.

MARTINS-FORREST ANTIQUES
8 Halkin Arcade
Motcomb Street
London SW1
Tel: (01) 235 8353 and 341 0673 (Home)
Art Nouveau and Art Deco jewellery.

RENEE MATYAS GALLERY
746 Finchley Road
London NW11
Tel: (01) 455 9306/458 8911
*17th to 19th c. English and Continental
jewellery.*

M. MCALEER
1a St Christopher's Place
London W1
Tel: (01) 486 1171
Victorian jewellery.

NIGEL MILNE
91 Mount Street
London W1
Tel: (01) 493 9646
*Early Victorian to 1930's jewellery, including
Art Nouveau and Art Deco.*

THE MINERAL KINGDOM
3 Pierrepont Arcade, Camden Passage
London N1
Tel: Not Available
*Jewellery, especially pieces set with
semi-precious stones- jade, coral, agate, jet
and ivory.*

L. NEWLAND
17 Picton Place
London W1
Tel: (01) 935 2864
18th to early 20th c. jewellery.

NOVISSIMO ANTIQUES
99 Church Road
London SW13
Tel: (01) 748 8151
17th to 19th c. jewellery.

JACK OGDEN
42 Duke Street
London SW1
Tel: (01) 930 3353
Ancient Greek, Roman, Egyptian and Byzantine gold jewellery.

RICHARD OGDEN LTD
28 and 29 Burlington Arcade
London W1
Tel: (01) 493 9136/7
Jewellery, specialising in rings.

A.H. PAGE
66 Gloucester Road
London SW7 4QT
Tel: (01) 584 7349
Victorian and Edwardian jewellery.

S.J. PHILLIPS LTD
139 New Bond Street
London W1A 3DL
Tel: (01) 629 6261
Early 19th c. jewellery.

Below: Selection of ancient Greek and Roman jewellery, courtesy of Jack Ogden.

MADELINE POPPER
Stand L18–L21
Gray's Mews
1–7 Davies Mews
London W1
Tel: (01) 408 1089
18th to early 20th c. jewellery including Art Deco and Art Nouveau plus cameos, Berlin iron, mourning jewellery, cut steel, coloured gold and gemstones.

PRIORY ANTIQUES
45 Cloth Fair
West Smithfield
London EC1
Tel: (01) 606 9060
Victorian jewellery.

THE PURPLE SHOP
15 Flood Street
London SW3
Tel: (01) 352 1127
Jewellery, especially Art Nouveau and Art Deco.

ROCHFORT ANTIQUES GALLERY
32–34 The Green
Winchmore Hill
London N21
Tel: (01) 886 4779
18th and 19th c. jewellery.

SAC FRERES
45 Old Bond Street
London W1
Tel: (01) 493 2333
Jewellery, specialising in amber.

SIMEON
19 Burlington Arcade
London W1V 9AB
Tel: (01) 493 3353
Jewellery up to and including Art Deco.

SPINK AND SON LTD
5, 6 and 7 King Street
London SW1
Tel: (01) 930 7888
17th to 19th c. jewellery.

THE TRINKET BOX
1 Goldhurst Terrace
London NW6
Tel: (01) 624 4264
Georgian and Victorian jewellery.

A.R. AND J.S. ULLMANN LTD
10 Hatton Garden
London EC1N 8AH
Tel: (01) 405 1877
19th and early 20th c. gold, silver and diamond jewellery.

VALE STAMPS AND ANTIQUES
21 Tranquil Vale
London SE3
Tel: (01) 852 9817
Jewellery from 3000 B.C.–500 A.D.

WARTSKI
14 Grafton Street
London W1
Tel: (01) 493 1141/2/3
Russian goldsmiths' work, Fabergé in particular, plus other antique jewellery from 18th to 20th c. See "Specialist Dealers, Semi-Precious Materials" for illustration.

YOUNG STEPHEN ANTIQUES
Bond Street Antique Centre
124 New Bond Street
London W1
Tel: (01) 499 7927
19th and 20th c. jewellery especially Edwardian, Art Nouveau and Art Deco pieces. See overleaf for illustration.

SOUTH AND SOUTHEAST ENGLAND

C. CLEALL ANTIQUES
16 Brewers Lane
Richmond, Surrey
Tel: (01) 940 8069
Art Nouveau and Art Deco jewellery.

THE CLOCK SHOP
284 Wickham Road
Shirley, Surrey
Tel: (01) 656 2800
18th and 19th c. jewellery.

J.D. GOLD
20 Prince Albert Street
Brighton, Sussex
Tel: (0273) 28813
Georgian and Victorian jewellery including gold and silver enamel watches.

PETER AND DEBBIE GOODAY
20 Richmond Hill
Richmond, Surrey
Tel: (01) 940 8652
Art Nouveau and Art Deco jewellery.

GREAT GROOMS ANTIQUES LTD
Parbrook
Billingshurst, Sussex
Tel: (040 381) 2263
Jewellery from 1860.

HOUSE OF ANTIQUES
4 College Street
Petersfield, Hants
Tel: (0730) 2172
18th and 19th c. jewellery.

SHIRLEY KING
2 Johnston Road
Woodford Green, Essex
Tel: (01) 505 5774
19th c. jewellery.

THE MAGPIE
25 Sandrock Hill Road
Wrecclesham, Farnham, Surrey
Tel: (025 13) 3129
Jewellery including ivory and mother-of-pearl items.

THE OLD FORGE
Pilgrims Way
Hollingbourne, Kent ME17 1UW
Tel: (062 780) 360
17th and 18th c. jewellery.

PAYNE AND SON LTD
131 High Street
Oxford, Oxon OX1 4DH
Tel: (0865) 43787
18th to early 20th c. jewellery.

RICHARD AND CAROLINE PENMAN
Cockhaise Mill
Lindfield, Sussex
Tel: (04447) 2514
Georgian and Victorian jewellery including gold chains, parures, coral, fans, and Georgian paste.

TRINITY ANTIQUES CENTRE
7 Trinity Street
Colchester, Essex
Tel: (0206) 77775
Victorian jewellery.

TURPINS ANTIQUES
4 Stoney Lane
Thaxted, Essex
Tel: (0371) 830 495
Fine antique jewellery.

S. WARRENDER AND COMPANY
4 Cheam Road
Sutton, Surrey
Tel: (01) 643 4381
Jewellery from 1790 on.

JOHN WESTLEY
41–42 Windsor Street
Uxbridge, Middx
Tel: (0895) 34933
Victorian jewellery.

WITHAM ANTIQUES
27a Bridge Street
Witham, Essex
Tel: (0376) 512407
Victorian silver and gold jewellery.

SOUTHWEST ENGLAND AND WALES

ABBEY GALLERIES
9 Abbey Churchyard
Bath, Avon
Tel: (0225) 60565
18th and 19th c. jewellery.

Right: A selection of diamond and pearl jewellery, courtesy of Young Stephen Antiques.

ABOYNE ANTIQUES
13 York Street
Bath, Avon
Tel: (0225) 64850 and 319961 (Home)
18th and early 19th c. jewellery.

BATH GALLERIES
33 Broad Street
Bath, Avon
Tel: (0225) 62946
18th and 19th c. jewellery.

G.M.S. ANTIQUES
36 High Street
Wickwar
Wotton-under-Edge, Glos GL12 8NP
Tel: (0454 24) 251
Victorian jewellery.

EDWARD A. NOWELL
21/23 Market Place
Wells, Somerset BA5 2RF
Tel: (0749) 72415
18th and 19th c. jewellery, including Victorian pieces.

OAK CHEST JEWELLERS
1 Oak Street
Llangollen, Clwyd, Wales
Tel: (0978) 860095
Victorian jewellery.

SOMERVALE ANTIQUES
6 Radstock Road
Midsomer Norton
Bath, Avon BA3 2AJ
Tel: (0761) 412686
Bijouterie, i.e. jewellery noted for the delicacy of the work rather than value of the materials or stones.

TAMAR GALLERY
5 Church Street
Launceston, Cornwall
Tel: (0566) 4233
19th and 20th c. jewellery.

MIDLANDS AND EAST ANGLIA

MELVILLE KEMP LTD
89–91 Derby Road
Nottingham, Notts NG1 5BB
Tel: (0602) 417055
18th and 19th c. jewellery.

MERIDIAN HOUSE ANTIQUES
Meridian House
Market Street
Stourbridge, W Midland
Tel: (038 43) 5384
Victorian jewellery.

JAMES AND ANN TILLETT
Tombland House
12 and 13 Tombland
Norwich, Norfolk NR3 1HF
Tel: (0603) 24914
18th and 19th c. jewellery.

NORTH OF ENGLAND AND SCOTLAND

JOSEPH H BONNAR
60 Thistle Street
Edinburgh, Lothian, Scotland
Tel: (031) 556 9003
Jewellery, specialising in Art Nouveau and Art Deco.

HAMISH M. EDWARD
50 Wellington Street
Glasgow, Scotland
Tel: (041) 248 7723
18th and 19th c. jewellery.

FILLANS ANTIQUES
2 Market Walk
Huddersfield, W. Yorks
Tel: (0484) 20889
Jewellery from 1800 on.

GROSVENOR ANTIQUES
22 Watergate Street
Chester, Cheshire Ch1 2LA
Tel: (0244) 315201
Jewellery from all periods including Art Deco.

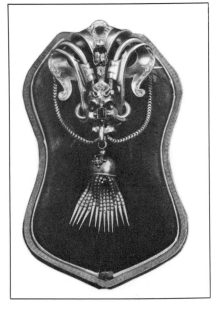

Above: Victorian bloomed gold brooch set with emeralds and diamonds in original fitted case, circa 1860, courtesy of Melville Kemp Ltd.

THORNTON TAYLOR ANTIQUES
2c Fernleigh Road
Glasgow, Scotland
Tel: (041) 637 7749
Georgian and Victorian jewellery.

CHRISTOPHER WARNER
15 Princes Street
Harrogate, N Yorkshire HG1 1NG
Tel: (0423) 503617
18th and 19th c. jewellery.

NORTHERN IRELAND

GREYABBEY TIMECRAFT LTD
18 Main Street
Greyabbey, Co Down, N Ireland
Tel: (024 774) 416
19th and early 20th c. jewellery.

J.A. JOHNSTON LTD
29 English Street
Armagh, Co Armagh, N Ireland
Tel: (0861) 522753
Georgian and Victorian jewellery.

KNOCK ANTIQUES
284 Upper Newtownards Road
Belfast, Antrim, N Ireland
Tel: (0232) 662998
Victorian jewellery.

SINCLAIRS ANTIQUE GALLERY
19 Arthur Street
Belfast, Antrim, N Ireland
Tel: (0232) 662998
Victorian jewellery.

KITCHENWARE

LONDON

T. AND S. LEMKOW
8–9 Pierrepoint Arcade, London N1
Tel: (01) 226 2997
Kitchen utensils, including copper and brass ware.

JILL LEWIS
Collector's Corner 138 Portobello Road
London W11
Tel: (040) 372 2357
Sewing accessories including thimbles.

STEPHEN LONG
348 Fulham Road, London SW10
Tel: (01) 352 8226
18th and 19th c. kitchen items.

ORCHARD ANTIQUES
52 Porchester Road
London W2
Tel: (01) 221 0154
Early kitchenware.

PEEL ANTIQUES
131d Kensington Church Street
London W8
Tel: (01) 727 8928
18th to early 20th c. household items.

PUTNAMS KITCHEN ANTIQUES
72 Mill Lane
London NW6
Tel: (01) 431 2935
Victorian and country kitchenware, and bathware.

TWENTY ONE ANTIQUES
21 Chalk Farm Road
London NW1
Tel: (01) 485 1239
Victorian kitchenware.

SOUTH AND SOUTHEAST ENGLAND

PAUL FEWINGS LTD
38 South Street
Titchfield, Nr Fareham, Hants
Tel: (0329) 43952
Kitchenware from 1750–1900.

GRAYS ANTIQUES
Volunteer
Queen Street
Twyford, Hants
Tel: (0962) 712 866
Kitchen antiques including early metalware.

Above: American pottery tobacco jar, circa 1800, courtesy of Market Place Antiques.

MARKET PLACE ANTIQUES
35 Market Place
Henley-on-Thames, Oxon RG9 2AA
Tel: (04902) 2387
Kitchen and household items.

SPENCER SWAFFER
30 High Street
Arundel, W Sussex
Tel: (0903) 882132
Victorian kitchenware.

LONDON

ANTIQUE RESTORATIONS
211 Westbourne Park Road
London W11
Tel: (01) 727 0469
English and Oriental lacquer.

THE ARK ANGEL
14 Camden Passage
London N1
Tel: (01) 226 1644
Small lacquer objects.

CARSON BOOTH ANTIQUES
80/82 Pimlico Road
London SW1
Tel: (01) 730 7004/235 1512
Oriental lacquer including furniture.

CIANCIMINO LTD
104 Mount Street
London W1
Tel: (01) 499 2672
Japanese lacquer screens.

THE CORNER CUPBOARD
28 Camden Passage
London N1
Tel: (01) 226 4539/(047 333) 206
Papier maché samplers.

SHIRLEY DAY LTD
59/60 Jermyn Street
London SW1
Tel: (01) 491 1916
Japanese lacquer.

PETER FRANCIS
26 Museum Street
London WC1
Tel: (01) 637 0165
Papier mâché and tôle from 1760–1860.

ROBIN GAGE
50 Pimlico Road
London SW1
Tel: (01) 730 2878
English and Chinese lacquer from 1700–1900.

GRACE ANTIQUES
28 Pembridge Villas
London W11 3EL
Tel: (01) 229 4415
18th and 19th c. papier mâché and tôle-painted trays.

IMOGEN GRAHAM
585 Kings Road
London SW6
Tel: (01) 736 2465
Painted furniture and bamboo and lacquer.

GWYNETH ANTIQUES
56 Ebury Street
London SW1
Tel: (01) 730 2513
Lacquer objects including furniture.

HALCYON DAYS
14 Brook Street
London W1Y 1AA
Tel: (01) 629 8111
Selection of small tôle items.

Above: 18th c. lac Burgouté tea box with original zinc liner, courtesy of Gwyneth Antiques.

LOOT
76/78 Pimlico Road
London SW1W 8PL
Tel: (01) 730 8097
Oriental lacquer.

MALLETT AND SON LTD
40 New Bond Street
London W1Y OBS
Tel: (01) 499 7411
18th c. lacquer furniture including clocks.

DAVID MARTIN-TAYLOR ANTIQUES LTD
592 Kings Road
London SW6
Tel: (01) 731 5054
Oriental lacquer, including furniture.

JEREMY J. MASON ORIENTAL ART
145 Ebury Street
London SW1
Tel: (01) 730 6971 and 874 4173 (Home)
Japanese lacquer.

NASH ANTIQUES
183 Westbourne Grove
London W11
Tel: (01) 727 3796
Lacquerware including furniture.

NIHON TOKEN
23 Museum Street
London WC1
Tel: (01) 580 6511/444 6726
Japanese lacquer including furniture.

PARK ANTIQUES
62 New Kings Road
London SW6 4LT
Tel: (01) 736 6222
Lacquer and papier mâché boxes of all kinds.

MICHAEL AND MARGARET PARKER
24 Cheval Place
London SW7
Tel: (01) 589 0133
Early English lacquer, papier mâché and tôle.

Left: English 18th c. domed coffer with carrying handles, decorated in scarlet lacquer with gold chinoiserie, on its original stand with cabriole legs, circa 1710, courtesy of Mallett and Son Ltd.

Above: Early 18th c. Mitsuda-E lacquer tray showing children with a snowball, courtesy of Nihon Token.

A.J. REFFOLD AND PARTNERS LTD
28 Pimlico Road
London SW1
Tel: (01) 730 6788
Lacquer and papier mâché boxes.

PETER REYNOLDS
67 New Kings Road
London SW6
Tel: (01) 736 7797
Painted and lacquered furniture.

BARRY SAINSBURY
145 Ebury Street
London SW1
Tel: (01) 730 3393
Specialist in 17th to 19th c. Chinese and Japanese lacquer, including hardwood and lacquer furniture.

GEORGE SHERLOCK
588 Kings Road
London SW6
Tel: (01) 736 3955
Lacquered pieces, including furniture, from 1650–1900.

Above: Early 19th c. Japanese trunk in black lacquer with Imperial mountings, courtesy of Barry Sainsbury.

KEITH SKEEL ANTIQUES
94 Islington High Street
London N1
Tel: (01) 359 9894
Bamboo and lacquer furniture.

TEMPUS ANTIQUES LTD
43 Kensington Church Street
London W8
Tel: (01) 937 4359
Japanese lacquer.

SOUTHWEST ENGLAND AND WALES

E.R. HYATT
Regency House
Old Fore Street
Sidmouth, Devon
Tel: (0395) 4284
19th c. papier mâché.

NORTH OF ENGLAND AND SCOTLAND

CHARLES HAY ANTIQUES
44 High Street
Coldstream, Borders, Scotland
Tel: (0890) 2552
18th and early 19th c. papier mâché.

LIGHTING

LONDON

ACTINO ANTIQUES
136 Lee High Road
London SE13
Tel: (01) 318 1273
19th and early 20th c. lighting.

AFTER DARK
20 Chalk Farm Road
London NWL
Tel: (01) 267 3300
Victorian to Art Deco lamps and lighting fixtures.

ANTIQUE PUSSY
965 Fulham Road
London SW6
Tel: (01) 731 2814
Copper and brass light fixtures to 1939.

W.G.T. BURNE
11 Elystan Street
London SW3
Tel: (01) 589 6074
Lighting fittings, especially for glass lamps and chandeliers.

FOR A MAP OF LONDON'S POSTAL DISTRICTS, SEE PAGE 61

MRS M.E. CRICK
166 Kensington Church Street
London W8
Tel: (01) 229 1338
English and Continental chandeliers from 18th c. on in crystal, cut glass and ormolu.

T. CROWTHER AND SON LTD
282 North End Road
London SW6 1NH
Tel: (01) 385 1375/7
18th c. lighting fixtures.

DELOMOSNE AND SON LTD
4 Campden Hill Road
London W8
Tel: (01) 937 1804
Glass chandeliers, all pre-1830.

DENTON ANTIQUES
87 Marylebone High Street
London W1
Tel: (01) 935 5831
Specialists in cut-glass chandeliers.

THE FACADE
196 Westbourne Grove
London W11
Tel: (01) 727 2159
Light fixtures from 1900–1930.

GALERIE 1900
267 Camden High Street
London NW1
Tel: (01) 485 1001 and 969 1803 (Home)
Art Nouveau and Art Deco lighting.

GODDARD AND FARMER
8 Thackeray Street
London W8
Tel: (01) 937 4917
Victorian lamps and lampshades.

GREAT EXPECTATIONS
62 Old Church Street
London SW3
Tel: (01) 352 9850
19th c. lamps.

J. GROTTY AND SON LTD
74 New Kings Road
London SW6
Tel: (01) 385 1789
18th and 19th c. light fittings.

HOLLINGSHEAD AND COMPANY
783 Fulham Road
London SW6
Tel: (01) 385 8519
Specialists in chandeliers.

LIGHTING

LYONS GALLERY
47–49 Mill Lane
London NW6
Tel: (01) 794 3537
Art Nouveau and Art Deco lighting.

M. AND W. ANTIQUES
2 Parsifal Road
London NW6
Tel: (01) 959 0753
French candelabra and lamps in ormolu, marble and bronze.

DAVID MALIK
112 Kensington Church Strret
London W8
Tel: (01) 229 2987
Specialists in chandeliers.

MARTINS-FORREST ANTIQUES
8 Halkin Arcade
Motcomb Street
London SW1
Tel: (01) 235 8353 and 341 0673 (Home)
Art Nouveau and Art Deco lighting.

PETER METCALFE
2 Parsifal Road
London NW6 1UH
Tel: (01) 435 5025
Antique lamps in French marble or porcelain with ormolu mounts or vases, supplied with silk lampshades.

TOBY MITCHELL
17 Chalk Farm Road
London NW1
Tel: (01) 485 0831
Lanterns and wall lights.

PERIOD BRASS LIGHTS
9a Thurloe Place
London SW7
Tel: (01) 589 8305
Brass and gilt light fittings.

Below: Oil lamp in cast brass with white china font, patented "Hinks" burner and crimpled-top, opal flint glass shade, courtesy of Christopher Wray's Lighting Emporium.

Above: Cameo table lamp etched in red over yellow, signed on base and shade by Emile Gallé, courtesy of Leinster Fine Art.

JONES
194 Westbourne Grove
London W11
Tel: (01) 229 6866
Lighting from 1850–1950, especially Art Nouveau and Art Deco.

JULIAN ANTIQUES
67 Park Road
London NW1
Tel: (01) 723 0653
French ormolu candelabra, chandeliers, lamps and wall brackets, from 16th to 19th c.

KEEBLE LTD
13 Walton Street
London SW3
Tel: (01) 581 3676
18th c. light fittings.

THE LAMP SHOP
24 Bedfordbury
London WC2
Tel: (01) 836 3852 and 402 4337 (Home)
Lamps and lighting from 1860–1940.

LEINSTER FINE ART
9 Hereford Road
London W2 4AB
Tel: (01) 229 9985
Art Nouveau lighting.

T. AND S. LEMKOW
8–9 Pierrepoint Arcade
London N1
Tel: (01) 226 2997
Specialists in oil lamps.

MELVYN LIPITCH
120–124 Fulham Road
London SW3 6HV
Tel: (01) 373 3328
18th c. English lanterns.

LIGHTING

ODDIQUITIES
61 Waldram Park Road
and
20 Sunderland Road
London SE23
Tel: (01) 699 9574
Oil, lamps, gas and electric light fittings, from 1800–1920.

PORTMEIRION ANTIQUES
5 Pont Street
London SW1
Tel: (01) 235 7601
Lamps from 1700–1900.

H.W. POULTER AND SON
279 Fulham Road
London SW10
Tel: (01) 352 7268
Brass chandeliers.

PRATT AND BURGESS LTD
7 Old Brompton Road
London SW7
Tel: (01) 589 8501
Brass chandeliers and lanterns.

W. SITCH AND COMPANY LTD
48 Berwick Street
London W1
Tel: (01) 437 3776
Late 19th and early 20th c. wall brackets, chandeliers, standard lamps and glass bowls.

SMIFFS ANTIQUES
121 High Road
London N2
Tel: (01) 883 6121
Brass lighting from Victorian to Art Deco.

SOUTH AUDLEY ART GALLERIES LTD
34 South Audley Street
London W1
Tel: (01) 499 3178/3195
English and Continental chandeliers.

PHILIP TURNER LTD
16 Crawford Street
London W1
Tel: (01) 935 6074
18th and 19th c. light fittings.

M. TURPIN LTD
21 Manson Mews
Queen's Gate
London SW7
Tel: (01) 373 8490/736 3417
18th c. chandeliers.

EARLE D. VANDEKAR
138 Brompton Road
London SW3 1HY
Tel: (01) 589 8481/3398
Chandeliers and candelabra.

WILKINSON GLASS
43–45 Wastdale Road
London SE23
Tel: (01) 699 4420
18th c. glass chandeliers.

WINDSOR HOUSE ANTIQUES
298 Westbourne Grove
London W11
Tel: (01) 221 4883
Brass lighting including oil lamps.

CHRISTOPHER WRAY'S LIGHTING EMPORIUM
600 Kings Road
London SW6
Tel: (01) 736 8434
Oil, gas and early electric lamps from 1850–1940.

SOUTH AND SOUTHEAST ENGLAND

ADRIAN ALAN LTD
4 Frederick Place
Brighton, Sussex BN1 4EA
Tel: (0273) 25277/25015
19th c. lighting.

ANTIQUES
314 Carshalton Road
Carshalton, Surrey
Tel: (01) 642 5865
Victorian and Edwardian oil lamps.

THE ENGLISH STREET FURNITURE COMPANY
Somers House, Linnfield Corner
Redhill, Surrey
Tel: Redhill 60986
Specialist in all kinds of street furniture including period street lights.

DAVID FILEMAN
Squirrels Bayards
Horsham Road
Steyning, W Sussex
Tel: (0903) 813229
18th and 19th c. glass chandeliers, table lights and wall lights.

JULIAN ANTIQUES
124 High Street
Hurstpierpoint, Sussex
Tel: (0273) 832145
French ormolu candelabra, chandeliers, lamps and wall brackets from 16th to 19th c. See "Stoves and Fireplaces" for illustration.

Above: Victorian, gas-fired, cast iron lamp post, courtesy of The English Street Furniture Company.

J. RANGER
148 Nine Mile Ride
Wokingham, Berks
Tel: (0734) 732754
Art Nouveau and Art Deco lamps.

H. SARGEANT
21 The Green
Westerham, Kent TN16 1AY
Tel: Westerham 62130
Glass chandeliers, candelabra, lustres, and wall lights.

SOUTHWEST ENGLAND AND WALES

ALICE LIGHTING AND ANTIQUES
3 Wellfield Road
Cardiff, S Glamorgan, Wales
Tel: (0222) 499156
Victorian lighting.

FINE FEATHERS ANTIQUES
7 King Street
Llandeilo, Dyfed, Wales
Tel: (0269) 850561
Victorian oil lamps.

IAN MCCARTHY
Arcadian Cottage
112 Station Road
Clutton, Avon
Tel: Not Available
Antique and decorative lamps from every period, as well as parts and lampshades.

NORTH OF ENGLAND AND SCOTLAND

HAREWOOD ANTIQUES
26/27 Harrogate Road
Harewood, Leeds, W Yorkshire LS17 9LH
Tel: (0532) 886327
Victorian oil lamps and converted gas lights.

KELLY'S OF KNARESBOROUGH
96 High Street
Knaresborough, N Yorkshire
Tel: (0423) 862041
Late 18th to early 20th c. lighting including chandeliers, wall lights and lustres.

METALWARE

LONDON

ALBANY ANTIQUES LTD
79 Albany Street
London NW1
Tel: (01) 387 3187
18th and 19th c. metalware.

THE ANTIQUE GALLERY
40 Peckham Rye
London SE15
Tel: (01) 732 7808
18th and 19th c. brass and copper.

AXIA
43 Pembridge Villas
London W11
Tel: (01) 727 9724
Islamic and Byzantine metalware.

BALCOMBE GALLERIES
7 Stanley Studios
Park Walk
London SW10
Tel: (01) 352 4353 and 352 9996 (Home)
Pewter including Art Nouveau items.

BARNES ANTIQUES
16 Lower Richmond Road
London SW15
Tel: (01) 789 3371
19th c. brass and copper.

WILLIAM BEDFORD ANTIQUES LTD
327 Upper Street
Islington Green
London N1
Tel: (01) 226 9648
Late 17th to early 19th c. brass.

JAMES BILLINGS
352 Kings Road
London SW3
Tel: (01) 352 1393 and 9635 (Home)
Metalware, pre-1880.

WILLIAM BRAY
58 Fulham Road
London SW6
Tel: (01) 731 1170
Georgian brassware.

BURGUNDY ANTIQUES
95 Pimlico Road
London SW1
Tel: (01) 730 0044
18th and 19th c. English and Continental metalware.

JACK CASIMIR LTD
The Brass Shop
23 Pembridge Road
London W11 3HG
Tel: (01) 727 8643
16th to 18th c. English and Continental brass, copper, bronze, pewter and steel.

CATSPA
116–118 Islington High Street
London N1
Tel: (01) 359 7616/883 3992
Art Nouveau and Art Deco pewter.

CHATTELS
53 Chalk Farm Road
London NW1
Tel: (01) 267 0877
18th and 19th c. rural metalware.

CHELSEA BRIC-A-BRAC SHOP LTD
16 Hartfield Road
London SW19
Tel: (01) 946 6894 and 542 5509/8112
Brass, copper and steel, Victorian onwards.

SIMON COLEMAN ANTIQUES
51 High Street
London SW13
Tel: (01) 878 5037
18th and 19th c. metalwork.

COUNTRY PINE LTD
13 Chalk Farm Road
London NW1
Tel: (01) 485 9697
Brass and copper from 1850–1950.

JOHN CREED ANTIQUES LTD
3 and 5a Camden Passage
London N1
Tel: (01) 226 8867
Metalware, especially brass and copper from 1600–1850.

THE CURIO SHOP
21 Shepherd Market
London W1Y 7HR
Tel: (01) 493 5616
Brass, pewter and copper from George III to Victorian period.

Below: Gothic oak stool and a brass "Three Kings" candlestick, courtesy of Arthur Davidson Ltd.

ARTHUR DAVIDSON LTD
78–79 Jermyn Street
London SW1
Tel: (01) 930 6687
16th to 18th c. metalware.

DEN OF ANTIQUITY
96 Coombe Lane
London SW20
Tel: (01) 947 0850
Victorian and Edwardian copper and brass.

R. DICKSON
819 Fulham Road
London SW6
Tel: (01) 731 5778
18th and early 19th c. English and Continental bronzes.

FAYME ANTIQUES
56 Elgin Crescent
London W11 2JJ
Tel: (01) 727 9526
Fine quality brass and copperware from 17th to 19th c.

FINE AND RARE
Top Floor
Macneill's Warehouse, Newhams Row

METALWARE

FINE AND RARE (CON'T)
175 Bermondsey Street
London SE1
*Brassware including escutcheons and drawer
pulls.*

GALERIE 1900
267 Camden High Street
London NW1
Tel: (01) 485 1001 and 969 1803 (Home)
*Art Nouveau and Art Deco metalware
including pewter.*

GEE BEE ANTIQUES
201 Brompton Road
London SW3
Tel: (01) 589 3317
Brass, copper and pewter.

GORDON GRIDLEY
41 Camden Passage
London N1
Tel: (01) 226 0643/9033
17th to 19th c. brass and pewter.

JOHN HAINE ANTIQUES LTD
133 Kensington Church Street
London W8
Tel: (01) 221 4420
17th and 18th c. metalwork.

THE HAY LOFT
332 Upper Richmond Road
London SW14
Tel: (01) 876 5020
Brass and copper from 1800–1930.

FELIX HILTON
45 St John's Wood High Street
London NW8
Tel: (01) 722 7634
*18th and 19th c. bronze, ormolu, pewter,
copper and brass.*

J.C. ANTIQUES
12 Warwick Terrace
London E17
Tel: (01) 539 4275 and 802 0582 (Home)
19th c. brassware.

JELLINEK AND SAMPSON
156 Brompton Road
London SW3
Tel: (01) 589 5272
17th and 18th c. metalwork.

WILLIAM JOB LTD
86–88 Pimlico Road
London SW1 8PL
Tel: (01) 730 7374
17th and 18th c. brass and wrought iron.

T. AND S. LEMKOW
8–9 Pierrepoint Arcade
London N1
Tel: (01) 226 2997
18th and 19th c. brass and copper.

NELLIE LENSON AND ROY SMITH
16 Pierrepont Row
London N1
Tel: (01) 226 2423
Early brass.

PETER MARTIN
44 Ledbury Road
London W11
Tel: (01) 727 1301
Early metalware including pewter.

MASSEY ANTIQUES
11 The Mall
Camden Passage
London N1
Tel: (01) 359 7966
19th c. brass and copper.

JOY MCDONALD
50 Station Road
London SW13
Tel: (01) 876 6184
18th and 19th c. brass and copper.

MOMTAZ GALLERY LTD
42 Pembridge Road
London W11
Tel: (01) 229 5579
Persian and Islamic metalwork.

RICHARD MUNDEY
19 Chiltern Street
London W1M 1HE
Tel: (01) 935 5613/3302
*17th c. to Victorian pewter, including flagons,
chargers, plates, candlesticks, porringers and
measures.*

NICODEMUS
27 Lacy Road
London SW15
Tel: Not Available
Copper and brassware from 1805–1910.

NIHON TOKEN
23 Museum Street
London WC1A 1JT
Tel: (01) 580 6511
Japanese metalwork.

KEVIN A. PAGE ANTIQUES
5 Camden Passage
and
6 Gateway Arcade
Camden Passage
London N1
Tel: (01) 226 8559
Continental pewter.

PHILIP AND RICHARD PARKER
98 Fulham Road
London SW3
Tel: (01) 589 7327 and 947 5569 (Home)
17th to late 19th c. metalware.

PETER PLACE
156 Walton Street
London SW3
Tel: (01) 584 2568
*17th and 18th c. English and Continental
brass.*

ROBERT PRESTON
121b Kensington Church Street
London W8
Tel: (01) 727 4872
Brass, pewter and copper items.

PUG ANTIQUES
191–193 Hartfield Road
London SW19
Tel: (01) 542 3409 and Ashtead 77342
(Home)
Copper, brass and pewter from 1800.

RENDLESHAM AND DARK
498 Kings Road
London SW10
Tel: (01) 351 1442
Pre-18th c. pewter.

ROD'S ANTIQUES
79 Portobello Road
London W11
Tel: (01) 229 2544
English and European copper and brass.

*Left: Collection of rare pewter, courtesy of
Richard Mundey. Bottom shelf: In centre,
Charles I flagon, flanked by William III and
George I flagon (2nd from left). Centre shelf:
James I, 1610 flagon flanked on each side by
"Bun-lid" Charles I flagon. Third from left: A
Scottish tappit hen, circa 1740. Top shelf: In
the centre, an Elizabethan engraved rose-water
dish, two early candlesticks, circa 1670, a
Stuart (Charles II) flat lid tankard and two
William and Mary lidded tankards. At the
back, broad rimmed plates and a narrow
rimmed dish, circa 1600–1650.*

ROCHFORT ANTIQUES GALLERY
32–34 The Green
Winchmore Hill
London N21
Tel: (01) 886 4779
18th and 19th c. copper.

ROGERS DE RIN ANTIQUES
76 Royal Hospital Road
London SW3
Tel: (01) 352 9007
17th to 19th c. brassware.

DAVID SLATER
170 Westbourne Grove
London W11
Tel: (01) 727 3336
Early metalwork including pewter.

TRAFALGAR ANTIQUES
117 Trafalgar Road
London SE10
Tel: (01) 858 3709
Metalware from 1750–1900.

TWENTY ONE ANTIQUES
21 Chalk Farm Road
London NW1
Tel: (01) 485 1239
Pennsylvania and "canal" painted metalware.

VILLAGE GREEN ANTIQUES
348 Upper Street
London N1
Tel: (01) 359 3942
18th and 19th c. brass and copper.

W.13 ANTIQUES
10 The Avenue
London W13
Tel: (01) 998 0390
18th and 19th c. brass and copper.

JOANNA WARRAND
99 Kensington Church Street
London W8
Tel: (01) 727 2333
18th and 19th c. brassware.

RON WELDON
109 Regents Park Road
London NW1
Tel: (01) 485 6210/4433
18th and 19th c. polished iron.

SOUTH AND SOUTHEAST ENGLAND

ABBEY ANTIQUES AND ARTS
97 High Street
Hemel Hempstead, Herts
Tel: (0442) 64667
18th and 19th c. metalware.

CEDAR ANTIQUES
High Street
Hartley Wintney, Hants
Tel: (025 126) 3252
17th and 18th c. metalware.

COURT HOUSE ANTIQUES
19 Market Place
Brentford, Middx
Tel: (01) 560 7074 and Walton-on-Thames 27186
18th and 19th c. copper and brass.

EDGWARE ANTIQUES
19 Whitchurch Lane
Edgware, Middx
Tel: (01) 952 1606
Victorian and Edwardian brassware.

Above: Early 18th c. engraved brass lock, courtesy of A. and E. Foster.

MOLLIE EVANS
84 Hill Rise
Richmond, Surrey
Tel: (01) 948 0182 and 940 3720 (Home)
Copper and brass, including Art Nouveau and Art Deco.

A. AND E. FOSTER
Little Heysham
Naphill, Bucks
Tel: (024 024) 2024 (By appointment only)
Early metalwork.

PETER GOODAY
20 Richmond Hill
Richmond, Surrey
Tel: (01) 940 8652
Art Nouveau and Art Deco metalwork, especially Liberty pewter.

GRAY ANTIQUES
Volunteer
Queen Street
Twyford, Hants
Tel: (0962) 712 866
Kitchen antiques including early metalware.

GREAT GROOMS ANTIQUES LTD
Parbrook
Billingshurst, Sussex
Tel: (040 381) 2263
18th to early 20th c. brass and copper.

GUMBRELLA
3 Church Road
Farnborough Village, Kent BR6 7DG
Tel: Farnborough 56642
19th and early 20th c. brass and copper.

ANN AND RICHARD HAGEN
Bakehouse Cottage
Northwood End
Haynes, Bedford, Beds
Tel: (023 066) 424
Metalwork from 1690–1840.

HOUSE OF ANTIQUES
4 College Street
Petersfield, Hants
Tel: (0730) 2172
18th and 19th c. metalware.

JOAN JARMAN ANTIQUES
81a High Street
Teddington, Middx TW11 8HG
Tel: (01) 977 4260
Brass and copper from 1800 onwards.

PAUL JONES ANTIQUES
10 Market Place
Chalfont St Peter, Bucks SL9 9LA
Tel: Gerrards Cross 83367
19th c. brass and copper.

KELVEDON ANTIQUES
90 High Street
Kelvedon, Colchester, Essex
Tel: (0376) 70557
18th c. brass and pewter.

JEAN KERSHAW
West Farm Antiques
High Street
Orwell, nr Royston, Herts
Tel: (022 020) 464
Eary metalwork.

SHIRLEY KING
2 Johnston Road
Woodford Green, Essex
Tel: (01) 505 5774
19th c. copper and brass.

MARGARET MCCLOY ANTIQUES
49 Surbiton Road
Kingston, Surrey
Tel: (01) 549 6423
Victorian and Edwardian copper and brass.

THE OLD FORGE
Pilgrims Way
Hollingbourne, Kent ME17 1UW
Tel: (062 780) 360
17th and 18th c. copper and brass.

W.A. PINN AND SONS
124 Swan Street
Sible Hedingham
Halstead, Essex
Tel: (0787) 61127
17th to early 19th c. metalwork.

RICHARD QUINNELL LTD
Rowhurst Forge
Oxshott Road
Leatherhead, Surrey KT22 OEN
Tel: (0372) 375148
*Restoration and reproduction of items in
brass, bronze, wrought and cast iron, steel and
aluminium.*

TAURUS ANTIQUES LTD
145 Masons Hill
Bromley, Kent BR2 9HY
Tel: (01) 464 8746
Brass and copper from 1800 on.

THE TOKEN HOUSE
7 Market Parade, High Street
Ewell
Epsom, Surrey
Tel: (01) 393 9654
19th c. copper and brass.

TURPINS ANTIQUES
4 Stoney Lane
Thaxted, Essex
Tel: (0371) 830495
17th to 19th c. metalware.

WARNER AND WOOD
The Workshop
Phillips Chase, off Bradford Street
Braintree, Essex
Tel: (0376) 25270
17th to early 20th c. pewter.

W.H. WELLER AND SON
12 Worth Street
Eastbourne, E Sussex
Tel: (0323) 23592
*Specialists in small unusual items of
metalware.*

SOUTHWEST ENGLAND AND WALES

ALDERSON AND ALDERSON
23 Brook Street, Bath, Avon
Tel: (0225) 21652
18th and 19th c. metalwork.

COUNTRY ANTIQUES
Castle Mill
The Bridge
Kidwelly, Dyfed, Wales
Tel: (0554) 890534
Pre-1900 copper and pewter.

FINE FEATHERS ANTIQUES
7 King Street
Llandeilo, Dyfed, Wales
Tel: (0269) 850561
19th c. brass and copper.

P.G. KYDD
Cannon Antiques
70 Colston Street
Bristol, Avon BS1 5AZ
Tel: (0272) 299265
*17th to 19th c. pewter, brass, copper and
wrought iron domestic metalware.*

MACELAND ANTIQUES
3 and 3a Carmarthen Street
Llandeilo, Dyfed, Wales
Tel: (055 03) 509
18th and 19th c. metalware.

DAVID PATTERSON
20 Queen Street
Lostwithiel, Cornwall
Tel: (0208) 872879
Victorian copper and brass.

MIDLANDS AND EAST ANGLIA

LIZ ALLPORT
Corner Antiques
Coltishall Antiques Centre
Coltishall, Norfolk
Tel: (0603) 737631
19th c. copper and brass.

MRS A.G. BANNISTER
Abode
The Shrieve's House
40 Sheep Street
Stratford-upon-Avon, Warks
Tel: (0789) 68755
Brassware.

E.M. CHESHIRE
The Manor House
Market Place
Bingham, Notts
Tel: (0949) 38861
17th to 19th c. metalware.

PAUL HOPWELL ANTIQUES
30 High Street
West Haddon, Northants
Tel: (078 887) 636
*17th and 18th c. brass, copper and ironwork
pieces. See entry under "Furniture" for
illustration.*

MERIDIAN HOUSE ANTIQUES
Meridian House
Market Street
Stourbridge, W Midlands
Tel: (038 43) 5384
18th and 19th c. brass and copper.

NEVILL ANTIQUES
9/10 Milk Street
and
30/31 Princess Street
Shrewsbury, Shropshire
Tel: (0743) 51013
18th and 19th c. metalware.

NORTH OF ENGLAND AND SCOTLAND

ATTICA ANTIQUES
62 Candlemaker Row
Edinburgh, Lothian, Scotland
Tel: (031) 225 9400
17th to 19th c. copper and brass.

COACH HOUSE ANTIQUES LTD
8–10 North Port
Perth, Tayside, Scotland
Tel: (0783) 29835
Georgian metalware.

HAREWOOD ANTIQUES
26–27 Harrogate Road
Harewood, Leeds, W Yorkshire LS17 9LH
Tel: (0532) 886327
Victorian brass and copper.

THE PENNY FARTHING
8 Beaufort Road
Edinburgh, Lothian, Scotland
Tel: (031) 447 2410
Pewter, copper and brass items.

ELAINE PHILLIPS ANTIQUES LTD
2 Royal Parade
Harrogate, N Yorkshire
Tel: (0423) 69745
*17th to 19th c. metalware. See "Specialist
Dealers, Furniture" for selection.*

E.W. WEBSTER
Wash Farm
Bickerstaffe
Nr Ormskirk, Lancs.
Tel: (0695) 24322
Pre-1830 metalware.

NORTHERN IRELAND

ANTIQUES OF COMBER
13 High Street
Comber, Co Down, N Ireland
Tel: (0247) 872690
Cast iron metalware and copper.

THE ANTIQUE SHOP
Main Street
Templepatrick, Antrim, N Ireland
Tel: (084 94) 32645
18th c. metalware.

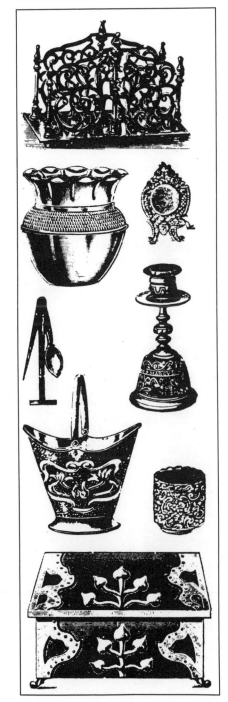

LONDON

NORMAN ADAMS LTD
8–10 Hans Road
London SW3
Tel: (01) 589 5266
18th c. mirrors.

ANNO DOMINI
66 Pimlico Road
London SW1
Tel: (01) 730 5496
18th and early 19th c. mirrors.

ANTIQUE RESTORATIONS
211 Westbourne Park Road
London W11
Tel: (01) 727 0467
Gilded mirrors.

WILLIAM BEDFORD ANTIQUES LTD
327 Upper Street
Islington Green
London N1
Tel: (01) 226 9648
Late 17th to early 19th c. mirrors.

R. DICKSON
819 Fulham Road
London SW6
Tel: (01) 731 5778
18th and early 19th c. mirrors.

FERNANDES AND MARCHE
23 Motcomb Street
London SW1
Tel: (01) 235 6773
18th and 19th c. gilt mirrors.

ANTHONY JAMES AND SON LTD
253 New Kings Road
London SW6
Tel: (01) 731 3474
Mirrors, pre-1830.

JULIAN ANTIQUES
67 Park Road
London NW1
Tel: (01) 723 0653
French gilt and Venetian glass mirrors.

THE LACQUER CHEST
75 Kensington Church Street
London W8
Tel: (01) 937 1306
Mirrors from 1800–1900, specialising in the unusual.

MELVYN LIPITCH
120–124 Fulham Road
London SW3 6HV
Tel: (01) 373 3328
18th c. English mirrors.

PAUL MITCHELL
99 New Bond Street
London W1Y 9LF
Tel: (01) 493 8732/0860
Carved and/or gilded picture frames.

ALEC OSSOWSKI
83 Pimlico Road
London SW1
Tel: (01) 730 3256
Carved and uncarved gilt mirrors.

Below: Chippendale mirror, circa 1765, (left), and oval Chippendale mirror, circa 1765, both courtesy of Fernandes and Marche.

GERALD SPYER AND SON LTD
18 Motcomb Street
London SW1
Tel: (01) 235 3348
18th c. and Regency gilt mirrors.

STRATTON ANTIQUES ETC
165 Thames Road
London W4
Tel: (01) 994 3140
18th and 19th c. mirrors.

THROUGH THE LOOKING GLASS LTD
563 Kings Road
London SW6
Tel: (01) 736 7799
18th and 19th c. mirrors.

FERENC TOTH
598a Kings Road
London SW6
Tel: (01) 731 2063 and 602 1771 (Home)
19th c. mirrors.

M. TURPIN LTD
21 Manson Mews
Queen's Gate
London SW7
Tel: (01) 373 8490/736 3417
18th c. mirrors.

J. WOLFF AND SON LTD
1 Chester Court
Albany Street
London NW1
Tel: (01) 935 3636
18th and 19th c. English and French mirrors.

Above: One of a pair of George II walnut and parcel gilt wall mirrors, circa 1750, courtesy of Gerald Spyer and Son Ltd

CLIFFORD WRIGHT
171 Dawes Road
London SW6
Tel: (01) 385 9175
Mirrors from 1685–1820.

SOUTH AND SOUTHEAST ENGLAND

JULIAN ANTIQUES
124 High Street
Hurstpierpoint, Sussex
Tel: (0273) 832 145
French gilt and Venetian glass mirrors.

MIDLANDS AND EAST ANGLIA

THOMAS COULBORN AND SONS
Vesey Manor
64 Birmingham Road
Sutton Coldfield, W Midlands B72 1QF
Tel: (021 354) 3974/3139
18th c. and Regency mirrors.

Right: Louis XVI-style marble mantelpiece with gilt overmantel mirror, courtesy of Julian Antiques.

MODELS
LONDON

LANGFORDS
46–47 Chancery Lane
London WC2
Tel: (01) 405 6402
Cased model ships and boats.

PAUL MASON GALLERY
149 Sloane Street
London SW1
Tel: (01) 730 3683
Ship models.

RELCY ANTIQUES
9 Nelson Road
London SE10
Tel: (01) 858 2812 and 858 7218 (Home)
18th and 19th c. ship models.

ROD'S ANTIQUES
79 Portobello Road
London W11
Tel: (01) 229 2544
Boat models.

SOUTH AND SOUTHEAST ENGLAND

ART AND MARINE
19 Lion Street
Rye, E Sussex
Tel: (07973) 4200
Nautical antiques including ship models.

NORTH OF ENGLAND AND SCOTLAND

QUADRANT ANTIQUES
5 North West Circus Parade
Stockbridge, Edinburgh
Lothian, Scotland
Tel: (031) 226 7282
18th and 19th c. ship builder's models.

LONDON

JOHN AND ARTHUR BEARE
7 Broadwick Street
London W1
Tel: (01) 437 1449
Specialists in violins, cellos, and bows.

TONY BINGHAM
11 Pond Street
London NW3 29N
Tel: (01) 794 1596
Musical instruments and music.

RICHARD BURNETT
3 Macaulay Road
London SW4
Tel: (01) 622 9393/4 (By appointment only)
Keyboard and other musical instruments, plus music stands and other items related to music.

LAMONT ANTIQUES
Newhams Row
175 Bermondsey Street
London SE1
Tel: (01) 403 0126
Victorian and Edwardian pianos.

M.A.D.D. ANTIQUES
193 Queens Road
London SE15
Tel: (01) 639 5834
Early 20th c. pianos.

N.P. MANDER LTD
St Peters Organ Works
London E2
Tel: Not Available
Antique pipe organs.

MORLEY GALLERIES
4 Belmont Hill
London SE13
Tel: (01) 852 6151
Harpsichords, clavichords, spinets, harps and pianos.

PRINCIPIA FINE ART
28 Victoria Grove
London W8
Tel: (01) 584 8080
Musical instruments of all kinds.

ST PETERS ORGAN WORKS
St Peters Close
Warner Place
London E2
Tel: (01) 739 4747
Antique pipe organs.

SUSAN SPITZ ANTIQUES
561 Kings Road
London SW6
Tel: (01) 736 0375
Georgian and Victorian music stands.

IGOR TOCIAPSKI
39–41 Ledbury Road
London W11
Tel: (01) 229 8317
Mechanical music machines from 1500–1900.

SOUTH AND SOUTHEAST ENGLAND

W.E. HILL & SON
Havenfields
Great Missenden, Bucks
Tel: (02406) 3655
Makers, dealers and restorers of instruments and accessories of the violin family.

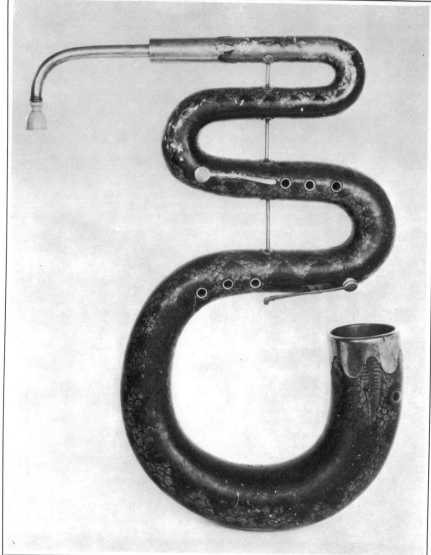

SOUTHWEST ENGLAND AND WALES

ARTHUR S. LEWIS
Link End House
Corse Lawn, Glos GL1 94LZ
Tel: (0452) 78258
Specialists in cylinder and disc music boxes.

SAN DOMENICO STRINGED INSTRUMENTS
177 Kings Road
Cardiff, S Glamorgan, Wales
Tel: (0222) 35881
Violins, cellos and bows, specialising in old violins.

Above: English serpent horn with painted decoration, circa 1820, and Pardessus de viole by Louis Guersan of Paris with carved head (close-up), dated 1761, both courtesy of Tony Bingham.

LONDON

THOMAS AGNEW AND SONS LTD
43 Old Bond Street
London W1X 4BA
Tel: (01) 629 6176
Persian manuscripts.

ALBANY ANTIQUES LTD
79 Albany Street
London NW1
Tel: (01) 387 3187
18th and 19th c. Chinese pottery and porcelain.

DAVID ALEXANDER
102 Waterford Road
London SW6
Tel: (01) 731 4644
Chinese ceramics, works of art and snuff bottles.

ANCHOR ANTIQUES LTD
26 Charing Cross Road
London WC2
Tel: (01) 836 5686 (By appointment only)
Oriental pottery and porcelain.

ARCADE GALLERY LTD
28 Old Bond Street
London W1
Tel: (01) 493 1879
Indian miniatures and African tribal sculpture.

ASTLEYS
109 Jermyn Street
London SW1
Tel: (01) 930 1687
Oriental pipes.

AXIA
43 Pembridge Villas
London W11
Tel: (01) 727 9724
Islamic and Byzantine icons, textiles, metalwork, woodwork, ceramics.

BARHAM FINE ART
83–85 Portobello Road
London W11
Tel: (01) 727 3845
Chinese porcelain.

BARLING OF MOUNT STREET LTD
112 Mount Street
London W1
Tel: (01) 499 2858
Oriental works of art, up to 12th c.

STANLEY BEAL
41 Fairfax Road
London NW6
Tel: (01) 328 7527
Oriental porcelain.

SUSAN BECKER
18 Lower Richmond Road
London SW15
Tel: (01) 788 9082
Oriental pottery and porcelain.

RAYMOND BENARDOUT LTD
4 and 5 William Street
London SW1X 9HL
Tel: (01) 235 9588
Oriental carpets, rugs, textiles and furniture.

RAYMOND LE BRUN
39 Ovington Street
London SW3 2JA
Tel: (01) 589 7945 (By appointment only)
17th to 19th c. Oriental furniture, statuary and works of art.

CALE ANTIQUES
24 Cale Street
Chelsea Green
London SW3
Tel: (01) 589 6146
Pre-1700 Chinese ceramics.

CARSON BOOTH ANTIQUES
80–82 Pimlico Road
London SW1
Tel: (01) 730 7004/235 1512
Oriental furniture including lacquer.

BEURDELEY, MATTHEWS AND COMPANY LTD
16 Savile Row
London W1
Tel: (01) 734 8557
Oriental ceramics, bronzes and sculpture

HELEN BUXTON ANTIQUES
Georgian House
84 Portobello Road
London W11
Tel: (01) 229 9458
Satsuma ware and Japanese works of art.

DAVID BROWER ANTIQUES
113 Kensington Church Street
London W8
Tel: (01) 221 4155
Oriental decorative porcelain, furniture and bronzes.

CATHAY ANTIQUES
12 Thackeray Street
London W8
Tel: (01) 937 6066
18th c. Chinese and Japanese porcelain, pottery, paintings, prints, bronzes, lacquer, sculpture and works of art.

ODILE CAVENDISH
14 Lowndes Street
London SW1
Tel: (01) 235 2491
Oriental furniture, Japanese screens, Chinese paintings and miscellaneous works of art.

CHANCERY ANTIQUES LTD
357 Upper Street
London N1 OPD
Tel: (01) 359 9035
Chinese and Japanese porcelain, bronzes, ivories, cloisonné and Satsuma ware.

Left: Bronze figure of a disciple of Buddha, from Siam, circa 1650, courtesy of Raymond Le Brun.

CIANCIMINO LTD
104 Mount Street
London W1
Tel: (01) 499 2672
Japanese lacquer screens plus Chinese, Japanese and Indian works of art.

COBWEB
2 Englands Lane
London NW3
Tel: (01) 586 4605
Ancient and antique Far Eastern sculpture including bronzes, woodstone carvings, ivories, jades, pottery and glass.

COHEN AND PEARCE
84 Portobello Road
London W11
Tel: (01) 229 9458
Chinese porcelain, bronzes and works of art; Japanese prints.

COLLET'S CHINESE GALLERY
40 Great Russell Street
London WC1
Tel: (01) 580 7538
17th to 19th c. Chinese paintings, porcelain, carvings, wood, semi-precious stones, jade, ivory and snuff bottles.

JOHN CRICHTON
34 Brook Street
London W1
Tel: (01) 629 7926 and 398 1933 (Home)
Chinese and Japanese porcelain and works of art, not later than 18th c.

SHIRLEY DAY LTD
59–60 Jermyn Street
London SW1
Tel: (01) 491 1916
Japanese paintings, screens, sculpture, ceramics and lacquer.

H. AND W. DEUTSCH ANTIQUES
111 Kensington Church Street
London W8
Tel: (01) 727 5984
Oriental porcelain.

DIPPERVALE LTD
25 Chepstow Corner
Chepstow Place
London W2 4TY
Tel: (01) 229 8456
Specialists in papier mâché and lacquer furniture and objects.

EAST ASIA BOOKS AND ART COMPANY
277 Eversholt Street
London NW1
Tel: (01) 387 3531
Oriental antiquarian books, plus Japanese and Chinese paintings, prints, jade and netsuke.

EVANS ANTIQUES LTD
81 Kensington Church Street
London W8
Tel: (01) 937 3754
Chinese porcelain and works of art.

EYRE AND HOBHOUSE LTD
39 Duke Street
London SW1
Tel: (01) 930 9308
19th c. paintings, drawings, aquatints and prints relating to subjects by European artists in India and the Far East.

S. FRANSES AND COMPANY LTD
71–73 Knightsbridge
London SW1
Tel: (01) 235 1888/3609
Oriental carpets, rugs, needlework and textiles.

KENNETH GILL
112 Crawford Street
London W1
Tel: (01) 486 1502
Oriental porcelain, furniture, and objects.

MARTIN GREGORY GALLERY
34 Bury Street
London SW1
Tel: (01) 839 3731
18th and 19th c. English and Dutch watercolours and oil paintings, specialising in pictures relating to China.

NICHOLAS GRINDLEY
37 Bury Street
London SW1
Tel: (01) 930 6670
Oriental paintings, furniture and works of art.

GWYNETH ANTIQUES
56 Ebury Street
London SW1
Tel: (01) 730 2513
Oriental furniture, textiles and small objects. For illustration see entry under "Lacquer".

HART AND ROSENBERG
2 and 3 Gateway Arcade
355 Upper Street
London N1
Tel: (01) 359 6839
Chinese and Japanese porcelain and works of art.

HEIRLOOM AND HOWARD LTD
1 Hay Hill
Berkeley Square
London W1
Tel: (01) 493 5868
17th to 19th c. Chinese porcelain. See entry under "Porcelain" for illustration.

MILNE HENDERSON
99 Mount Street
London W1
Tel: (01) 499 2507
Chinese and Japanese paintings, screens, prints and drawings.

HESKIA
19 Mount Street
London W1
Tel: (01) 629 1483
Oriental carpets, rugs and tapestries.

R. HOLT AND COMPANY LTD
98 Hatton Garden
London EC1
Tel: (01) 405 5286
Chinese jewellery and swords.

ERIC HUDES
142 Portobello Road
London W11
Tel: (0376) 83767 (Home)
Open Saturday only
Oriental ceramics from A.D. 900–1830.

JAPANESE GALLERY
66d Kensington Church Street
London W8
Tel: (01) 229 2934 and 226 3347 (Home)
Japanese wood-cut prints, books, porcelain and other antiquities.

Above: Chinese calligraphy table of Huang Hua-li with an inset burr panel, skimmed in thin red lacquer; the oval slightly splayed legs are tenoned into the top to contain the shaped frieze and capped with European brass sabots; from the end of the 16th c., courtesy of Nicholas Grindley.

R. AND J. JONES
44a Kensington Church Street
London W8
Tel: (01) 937 9216
Russian works of art, including sculpture, pottery, porcelain.

PETER KEMP
174a Kensington Church Street
London W8
Tel: (01) 229 2988
10th to 19th c. Chinese porcelain and 17th to 19th c. Japanese porcelain.

ROBIN KENNEDY
Grays Mews
1–7 Davies Mews
London W1
Tel: (01) 408 1238
Fine Japanese prints and Indian miniature paintings.

KHALILI GALLERY
15c Clifford Street
London W1
Tel: (01) 734 4202
Persian, Islamic and other ancient works of art.

ERIC KING ANTIQUES
203 New Kings Road
London SW6
Tel: (01) 736 3162 and 731 2554 (Home)
Oriental furniture.

COLIN LACY GALLERY
38 Ledbury Road
London W11
Tel: (01) 229 9105
Indian miniatures.

LENNOX MONEY LTD
68 and 99 Pimlico Road
London SW1
Tel: (01) 730 2151/3070
Indian ebony and ivory furniture.

LOOT
76–78 Pimlico Road
and
26 Holbein Place
London SW1
Tel: (01) 730 8097 and 352 0135 (Home)
Oriental objects from 1650–1900.

L.P.J. ANTIQUES LTD
c/o Laurence Mitchell Antiques
27 Camden Passage
London N1
Tel: (01) 359 7579
Chinese and Japanese porcelain including vases plus Chinese furniture, ivories and bronzes.

LUNN ANTIQUES
86 New Kings Road
London SW6
Tel: (01) 736 4638
Oriental embroidery.

MANSOUR GALLERY
46 Davies Street
London W1
Tel: (01) 491 7444
Islamic works of art, miniatures, carpets, ancient glass and glazed wares.

S. MARCHANT AND SON
120 Kensington Church Street
London W8
Tel: (01) 229 5319
Chinese and Japanese pottery, porcelain, netsuke, ivories, jades and cloisonné.

G. AND M. MARDELLIS
109 Kensington Church Street
London W8
Tel: (01) 727 7413
Oriental pottery and porcelain.

THE MARK GALLERY
9 Porchester Place
London W2
Tel: (01) 262 4906
16th to 19th c. Russian icons.

DAVID MARTIN-TAYLOR ANTIQUES LTD
592 Kings Road
London SW6
Tel: (01) 731 5054
Oriental furniture, lacquer and bronzes.

JEREMY J. MASON ORIENTAL ART
145 Ebury Street
London SW1
Tel: (01) 730 6971 and 874 4173 (Home)
Oriental art including Chinese ceramics and jades and Japanese lacquer.

MOMTAZ GALLERY LTD
42 Pembridge Road
London W11
Tel: (01) 229 5579
Luristan bronzes, Islamic pottery from 9th to 14th c, Nishapur, Gurpan, Ravy, and Kashan 9th thru 11th c; plus glass and metalwork.

D.C. MONK AND SON
132–134 Kensington Church Street
London W8
Tel: (01) 229 3727
Oriental porcelain.

HUGH MOSS LTD
23 Bruton Lane.
London W1
Tel: (01) 492 1835
Oriental porcelain, paintings, furniture and Chinese snuff boxes.

SYDNEY L. MOSS LTD
51 Brook Street
London W1
Tel: (01) 629 4670/493 7374
Chinese and Japanese ceramics from 1500 B.C. to 20th c. A.D. plus Japanese netsuke 18th to 20th c.

SYLVIA NAPIER LTD
32 Ledbury Road
London W11
Tel: (01) 229 9986/7
Decorative Oriental furniture including screens and boxes.

NASH ANTIQUES
183 Westbourne Grove
London W11
Tel: (01) 727 3796
Oriental and Japanese furniture, porcelain, bronzes, jade, ivory, netsuke and lacquer.

NIHON TOKEN
23 Museum Street
London WC1
Tel: (01) 580 6511 and 444 6726 (Home)
Japanese swords, lacquer, armour, metalwork, fabrics, bronzes, furniture, prints, pottery, porcelain, netsuke, paintings, sculpture, books, mirrors and inro. For additional illustrations, see "Specialist Dealers, Arms and Armour", "Pottery and Porcelain" and "Lacquer".

ORMONDE ORIENTAL ANTIQUES
181 Westbourne Grove
London W11
and
Portwine Arcade
173 Portobello Road
London W11
Tel: (01) 221 4219
Indian, Tibetan, Chinese, Japanese, Burmese and Thai ivories, paintings, porcelain, bronzes, cloisonné and enamels.

KEVIN A. PAGE ANTIQUES
5 Camden Passage
and
6 Gateway Arcade
Camden Passage
London N1
Tel: (01) 226 8559
19th c. Oriental porcelain, cloisonné, bronzes, ivories.

PEEL ANTIQUES
131d Kensington Church Street
London W8
Tel: (01) 727 8928
18th and early 19th c. Chinese pottery and porcelain.

RAPHAEL FINE ARTS LTD
DRC House
2 Cornwall Terrace
London NW14 4QP
Tel: (01) 486 9931 (By appointment only)
Oriental ceramics and ivories.

Above: Late 17th c. lacquer inro signed Kajikawa Bunryusai, showing a fox-priest, courtesy of Nihon Token.

J.S. RASMUSSEN FINE ARTS
5 Logan Mews, Logan Place
London W8
Tel: (01) 373 6527
Japanese art.

GRAHAM ROSENTHAL
The London Oriental and Fine Art Galleries
Georgian House
84 Portobello Road
London W11
Tel: (01) 229 9458
Oriental porcelain.

MARCUS ROSS ANTIQUES
14 Pierrepoint Row
Camden Passage
London N1
Tel: (01) 359 8494
Oriental porcelain.

HANS RYDEN
2 Mallord Street
London SW3
Tel: (01) 352 3692
Chinese ceramics.

BARRY SAINSBURY
145 Ebury Street
London SW1
Tel: (01) 730 3393
17th and 18th c. Chinese and Japanese lacquer, including furniture. See "Lacquer" for illustration.

SCHWARTZ
93 Blackheath Road
London SE10
Tel: (01) 692 1652
Oriental pottery, porcelain and bronzes, Japanese prints, Indian miniatures and statues.

Left: Interior view showing a selection of Oriental antiques, courtesy of Sylvia Napier Ltd.

SIMEON
19 Burlington Arcade
London W1V 9AB
Tel: (01) 493 3353
*Oriental works of art including Japanese
netsuke and inro plus Chinese snuff bottles.*

JOHN SPARKS LTD
128 Mount Street
London W1
Tel: (01) 499 1932/2265
*Chinese pottery, porcelain, jade and
hardstones, B.C. to late 18th c.*

AUBREY SPIERS ANTIQUES
Shop C3, Chenil Galleries
183 Kings Road
London SW3
Tel: (01) 352 2123 and 954 0850 (Home)
17th and 18th c. Oriental porcelain.

SPINK AND SON LTD
5, 6 and 7 King Street
London SW1
Tel: (01) 930 7888
*Chinese, Japanese, Indian, South-East Asian
and Islamic art.*

STAIR AND COMPANY LTD
120 Mount Street
London W1Y 5HB
Tel: (01) 499 1784/5
18th c. Chinese porcelain.

M. AND C. TELFER-SMOLLETT
88 Portobello Road
London W11
Tel: (01) 727 0117 and 229 8028 (Home)
*Oriental furniture and fabrics plus Middle
Eastern screens and tables.*

TEMPUS ANTIQUES LTD
43 Kensington Church Street
London W8
Tel: (01) 937 4359
*Japanese ivories, bronzes, cloisonné, pottery,
porcelain and lacquer.*

TOYNBEE AND CLARKE LTD
95 Mount Street
London W1
Tel: (01) 499 4472
*17th to 19th c. Chinese and Japanese paintings
and screens.*

EARLE D. VANDEKAR
138 Brompton Road
London SW3 1HY
Tel: (01) 589 8481/3398
Oriental ceramics.

WAN LI
7 Gateway Arcade
355 Upper Street
London N1
Tel: (01) 226 0997
*Chinese works of art including porcelain and
fans.*

JOANNA WARRAND
99 Kensington Church Street
London W8
Tel: (01) 727 2333
18th and 19th c. Oriental porcelain.

WARTSKI
14 Grafton Street
London W1
Tel: (01) 493 1141/2/3
Russian works of art including jewellery

WELBANK
Shop 10
Angel Arcade
London N1
Tel: (01) 359 9558
Oriental porcelain.

MARY WISE
27 Holland Street
London W8
Tel: (01) 937 8649
Chinese antiquities, pre-1800.

DOUGLAS WRIGHT LTD
34 Curzon Street
London W1
Tel: (01) 629 9993
*Japanese and Chinese works of art including
netsuke, bronzes, ivories and hardstones.*

SOUTH AND SOUTHEAST ENGLAND

THE GALLERY
18 Endwell Road
Bexhill-on-Sea, E Sussex
Tel: (0424) 212127
*Furniture and china from 17th to late 19th c.
See "Furniture" for illustration.*

*Right: Pottery model of a seated female
figure holding a spray of lingxi fungus on one
hand. Glazed in cream, green and amber
splashes, with traces of pigment remaining on
the face, Tang dynasty (618–906 AD),
courtesy of Spink and Son Ltd.*

ERIC HUDES
Paigles, Perry Green
Bradwell, Braintree, Essex CM7 8ES
Tel: (0376) 83767
Oriental ceramics from 900–1830.

SOUTHWEST ENGLAND AND WALES

ARTS OF LIVING
18 Green Street
Bath, Avon
Tel: (0225) 64270
Persian, Afghan, Caucasian, Turkoman, and old tribal rugs, grain bags plus embroidered Chinese panels.

Above: A selection of Japanese sword fittings, courtesy of Andrew Spencer.

R. AND D. COOMBES
Aldbourne
Marlborough, Wilts
Tel: (0672) 40241
Oriental art including ceramics, paintings, embroideries, costume, jades, netsuke, sword fittings and Japanese prints, all pre-1700.

ANDREW DANDO
4 Wood Street
Queen Square
Bath, Avon
Tel: (0225) 22702
Oriental pottery and porcelain, 17th to mid-19th c.

ORIENTAL ANTIQUES
4 Belvedere
Lansdown Road
Bath, Avon BA1 5ED
Tel: (0225) 315987
Oriental ivories, costume, embroidery and furniture.

MIDLANDS AND EAST ANGLIA

WESTLEY RICHARDS AND COMPANY LTD
Grange Road
Birmingham, W Midlands B29 6AR
Tel: (021) 472 2953
Oriental, specialising in Indian works of art.

NORTH OF ENGLAND AND SCOTLAND

PAUL M. PETERS ANTIQUES
15 Bower Road
Harrogate, N Yorkshire
Tel: (0423) 60118
17th to 19th c. Japanese and Chinese ceramics, bronzes, ivories and lacquer.

SCOTT-ALLAN ORIENTAL ANTIQUES
35 Buccleuch Street
Edinburgh, Lothian, Scotland
Tel: (031) 667 3350
Chinese porcelain.

ANDREW SPENCER
32 Rotcher Hill
Holmfirth, Yorkshire
Tel: (048 489) 5234
Japanese sword fittings.

SEE ALSO ENTRIES UNDER "SPECIALIST DEALERS, CARPETS AND RUGS."

PHOTOGRAPHICA

LONDON

H. BARON
136 Chatsworth Road   London NW2 5QU
Tel: (01) 459 2035 (By appointment only)
Signed and unsigned photographs of musicians.

ROBERT HERSHKOWITZ LTD
5 Kynance Mews   London SW7
Tel: (01) 589 9937 and (079 156) 442
(Home) (By appointment only)
19th c. photographs.

Left: "The King's Own" tropical deluxe camera by the London Stereoscopic Company, circa 1912, here in teak, bound with inset brass, courtesy of Vintage Cameras.

CINEMA BOOKSHOP
13–14 Great Russell Street
London WC1
Tel: (01) 637 0206
Stills from the cinema.

HUMBLEYARD FINE ART
Waterfall Cottage
Mill Street
Swanton Morley, Norfolk
Tel: (036 283) 793
Photographic instruments.

N.W. LOTT AND H.J. GERRISH LTD
14 Masons Yard, Duke Street
London SW1
Tel: (01) 930 1353
Victorian photographs.

HOWARD RICKETTS LTD
180 New Bond Street
London W1
Tel: (01) 499 7357/409 1071
Early photographic material.

VINTAGE CAMERAS LTD
254 and 256 Kirkdale
London SE26
Tel: (01) 778 5416/5841/9052
Vintage cameras from 1840–1950.

CHRISTOPHER WOOD GALLERY
15 Motcomb Street
London SW1
Tel: (01) 235 9141/2
Victorian photography.

NORTH OF ENGLAND AND SCOTLAND

MARTIN ANTIQUES
36 St Stephen Street
Edinburgh, Lothian, Scotland
Tel: (031) 556 3527
Photographic instruments.

PHOTOGRAPHER.

Above: "A Farm Cart Fording A Stream",
gouache painting by George Barret R.A., circa
1770, courtesy of Abbott and Holder.

LONDON

ABBOTT AND HOLDER
73 Castlenau
London SW13
Tel: (01) 748 2416 (By appointment only)
18th to early 20th c. watercolours and oil
paintings.

ARTHUR ACKERMANN AND SON
3 Old Bond Street
London W1
Tel: (01) 493 3288/629 0592
English sporting paintings.

NORMAN ADAMS LTD
8–10 Hans Road
London SW3
Tel: (01) 589 5266.
18th c. paintings.

ADAMS ROOM LTD
18–20 Ridgway
London SW19
Tel: (01) 946 7047
18th and 19th c. oil paintings, specialising in
English landscapes.

THOMAS AGNEW AND SONS LTD
43 Old Bond Street
London W1X 4BA
Tel: (01) 629 6176
Paintings by Old Master from all schools as
well as English watercolours.

ALEXANDER GALLERY
13 Duke Street
London SW1
Tel: (01) 930 3062/3
Old Master paintings.

ANFORA ANTIQUES LTD
20 Motcomb Street
London SW1
Tel: (01) 235 6317 and 229 2342 (Home)
15th to 19th c. Continental paintings,
specialising in works by Italian artists.

ANTIQUES AND FINE ARTS
152 Upper Richmond Road
London SW15
Tel: (01) 788 9123
19th c. oil paintings.

ANTIQUES LTD
18 Parson Street
London NW4 1QB
Tel: (01) 203 1194
18th and 19th c. oil paintings and
watercolours.

ANTIQUE PUSSY
965 Fulham Road
London SW6
Tel: (01) 731 2814
Oil paintings and watercolours from
1650–1939.

APOLLO GALLERIES
61/65 and 67 South End
Croydon, Surrey
Tel: (01) 681 3727/680 1968
19th c. oil paintings and watercolours.

APPLEBY BROTHERS LTD
8–10 Ryder Street
London SW1
Tel: (01) 930 2209/6507
19th c. English watercolours.

ASTORIA
222 Munster Road
London SW6
Tel: (01) 385 9888
Art Deco watercolours and oil paintings.

BALCOMBE GALLERIES
Stanley Studios
Park Walk
London SW10
Tel: (01) 352 4353
Paintings from 1830–1920.

BALFOUR AND NORMAN LTD
26 Curzon Street
London W1
Tel: (01) 409 0050
Large stock of 16th to early 20th c. oil
paintings.

BARHAM ANTIQUES
83 Portobello Road
London W11
Tel: (01) 727 3845
Old Master and Victorian oil paintings.

BAUMKOTTER GALLERY
63a Kensington Church Street
London W8
Tel: (01) 937 5171
17th to 19th c. oil paintings.

WILLIAM BEDFORD ANTIQUES LTD
327 Upper Street
Islington Green
London N1
Tel: (01) 226 9648
Oil paintings and watercolours from
1650–1830, plus reverse painted glass
pictures.

CHRIS BEETLES LTD
104 Randolph Avenue
London W9
Tel: (01) 286 1404
English watercolours, 1750–1930.

ANTHONY BELTON
Collector's Corner
138 Portobello Road
London W11
Tel: (01) 937 1012
Topographical and marine picture, pre-1830.

BELGRAVE GALLERY
33 Sackville Street
London W1
Tel: (01) 734 4119
British paintings from 1890–1940.

SOPHIA BAYNE POWELL
19 St Andrews Chambers
Well Street
London W1
Tel: (01) 637 5761
Specialists in 19th c. primitive pictures.

M. BERNARD
21 Ryder Street
London SW1
Tel: (01) 930 6894
18th and 19th c. English paintings,
specialising in Venetian views and flower
subjects.

JAMES BILLINGS
352 Kings Road
London SW3
Tel: (01) 352 1393 and 9635 (Home)
18th and 19th c. paintings.

ANDREW BLAIN
12 Somerset Road
London W4
Tel: (01) 994 3744 (By appointment only)
19th c. oil paintings and watercolours.

H. BLAIRMAN AND SONS LTD
119 Mount Street
London W1
Tel: (01) 493 0444
Chinese mirror paintings.

WILLIAM BRAY
58 Fulham Road
London SW6
Tel: (01) 731 1170
Oil paintings from the Georgian period.

BROD GALLERY
24 St James's Street
London SW1
Tel: (01) 839 3871/2
17th c. Dutch paintings plus Flemish
paintings, drawings and watercolours of all
periods.

BEVERLEY BROOK ANTIQUES
22 High Street
London SW13
Tel: (01) 878 4899 and 878 5656 (Home)
Regency, Victoriana and Edwardian
watercolours.

Right: "The Piazzetta" by Canaletto, courtesy of Thomas Agnew and Sons Ltd.

THE BROTHERTON GALLERY LTD
77 Walton Street
London SW3
Tel: (01) 589 6848
19th c. landscape and natural history oil paintings and watercolours.

CAELT GALLERY
182 Westbourne Grove
London W11
Tel: (01) 229 9309 and 229 0303 (Home)
Irish, Middle Eastern, Canadian, South African, and Australian paintings.

CATHAY ANTIQUES
12 Thackeray Street
London W8
Tel: (01) 937 6066
18th c. Chinese and Japanese paintings.

ODILE CAVENDISH
14 Lowndes Street
London SW1
Tel: (01) 235 2491
Oriental paintings.

THE CAVENDISH GALLERY
1 Marylebone Street
London W1M 7PN
Tel: (01) 935 5143
British oil paintings and watercolours

CENTAUR GALLERY
82 Highgate High Street
London N6
Tel: (01) 340 0087
18th and early 19th c. oil paintings and watercolours.

CHAPMAN AND DAVIES ANTIQUES
10 Theberton Street
London N1
Tel: (01) 226 5565/348 4846/359 4330
17th to early 20th c. oil paintings.

CHAUCER AND VAN DAM GALLERIES
45 Pimlico Road
London SW1
Tel: (01) 235 8235
Old Master paintings.

CHENIL GALLERY
181 Kings Road
London SW3
Tel: (01) 352 2163/5574
Military, marine, and sporting prints and watercolours.

CLARGES GALLERY
158 Walton Street
London SW3
Tel: (01) 584 3022
19th and 20th c. British oil paintings and watercolours.

GERALD CLARK
1 High Street
London NW7
Tel: (01) 906 0342
18th and 19th c. English watercolours.

COBRA AND BELLAMY
149 Sloane Street
London SW1
Tel: (01) 730 2823
Late 19th and early 20th c. paintings.

COBWEB
2 Englands Lane
London NW3
Tel: (01) 586 4605
19th and 20th c. oil paintings and watercolours.

EDWARD COHEN
40 Duke Street
London SW1
Tel: (01) 839 5180
Old Master and 19th c. oil paintings.

COLLET'S CHINESE GALLERY
40 Great Russell Street
London WC1
Tel: (01) 580 7538
17th to early 20th c. Chinese paintings.

COLNAGHI AND CO
14 Old Bond Street
London W1
Tel: (01) 491 7408
Old Master paintings.

THE COTTAGE GALLERY
9 Hereford Road
London W2
Tel: (01) 221 4578
18th to early 20th c. German paintings.

COVENT GARDEN GALLERY LTD
Flat 8, St James's Chambers
2–10 Ryder Street
London SW1
Tel: (01) 930 9696
17th to 19th c. British and Continental oil paintings and watercolours.

CRANE ARTS LTD
321 Kings Road
London SW3
Tel: (01) 352 5857
18th to early 20th c. naive paintings.

ANTHONY DALLAS AND SONS LTD
9 Old Bond Street
London W1
Tel: (01) 491 8662
Old Masters.

SHIRLEY DAY LTD
59–60 Jermyn Street
London SW1
Tel: (01) 491 1916
Japanese paintings, including screens.

DENBIGH GALLERIES
3 Denbigh Road
London W11
Tel: (01) 229 6765
18th and 19th c. oil paintings and frames.

JOHN DENHAM
The Gallery
50 Mill Lane
London NW6
Tel: (01) 794 2635
17th to early 20th c. oil paintings and watercolours. See overleaf for illustration.

COLIN DENNY LTD
18 Cale Street
London SW3
Tel: (01) 584 0240
19th c. marine paintings.

DE VILLIERS ANTIQUES
311 Fulham Palace Road
London SW6
Tel: (01) 731 3859
18th and 19th c. paintings.

DOUWES FINE ART
38 Duke Street
London SW1
Tel: (01) 839 5795
Old Master oil paintings and watercolours.

WILLIAM DROWN
41 St James's Place
London Sw1
Tel: (01) 493 4711
Old Master paintings.

EALING ANTIQUES
34 St Mary's Road
London W5
Tel: (01) 567 6192
18th and 19th c. oil paintings.

FINCHLEY FINE ART GALLERIES
983 High Road
London N12
Tel: (01) 446 4848
English watercolours and oil paintings.

FINE PICTURE INVESTMENTS LTD
75 Randolph Avenue
London W9
Tel: (01) 286 5018
17th and 18th c. paintings.

FIVE FIVE SIX ANTIQUES
c/o Patricia Harvey
556 Kings Road
London SW6
Tel: (01) 731 2016 and 624 5173 (Home)
*18th and early 19th c. primitive paintings
with children, animals and landscape subjects.*

FLEUR DE LYS GALLERY
82–83 Cornwall Gardens
London SW7 4AZ
Tel: (01) 937 6804
*19th c. English, Dutch and Continental
paintings.*

EAST ASIA COMPANY
103 Camden High Street
London NW1
Tel: (01) 388 5793
Japanese and Chinese paintings.

**THE ENGLISH WATERCOLOUR
GALLERY**
Barry Kendall
2 Warwick Place
London W9
Tel: (01) 286 9902
18th and 19th c. English watercolours.

EYRE AND HOBHOUSE LTD
39 Duke Street
London SW1
Tel: (01) 930 9308
*19th c. oil paintings and watercolours,
relating to European artists in India and the
Far East.*

*Above: "Fisherfolk on the Shore", a
watercolour by William Collins, circa 1840,
courtesy of John Denham.*

FAUSTUS GALLERIES LTD
67–68 Jermyn Street
London SW1
Tel: (01) 930 1864
Old Master paintings.

FIDDES WATT GALLERY
Studio 7
249 Kensal Road
London W10
Tel: (01) 864 0766
*Oil paintings and watercolours, specialising
in those by Scottish artists.*

JOCELYN FIELDING FINE ART LTD
17 Ryder Street
London SW1
Tel: (01) 839 5040
*Old Master oil paintings, plus English oil
paintings and watercolours.*

FORES GALLERY LTD
15 Sicilian Avenue
London Wc1
Tel: (01) 404 3063
*17th to early 20th c. British sporting oil
paintings and watercolours.*

FORTESCUE SWAN GALLERIES
238 Brompton Road
London SW3
Tel: (01) 584 4736
19th and early 20th c. watercolours.

A. AND J. FOWLE
542 Streatham High Road
London SW16
Tel: (01) 764 2896
Victorian and Edwardian paintings.

*Below: "View on the Thames", a
watercolour by Peter de Wint (1784–1840),
courtesy of the Fry Gallery.*

FRY GALLERY
58 Jermyn Street
London SW1Y 6LX
Tel: (01) 493 4496
17th to 19th c. English watercolours.

GAFIT LTD
Lower Ground Floor Stockrooms
496 Kings Road
London SW10
Tel: (01) 352 4751
19th c. oil paintings.

GALLERY KALEIDOSCOPE
66 Willesden Lane
London NW6
Tel: (01) 328 5833
*18th to early 20th c. oil paintings and
watercolours.*

ROBIN GARTON
9 Lancashire Court
New Bond Street
London W1
Tel: (01) 493 2820
English watercolours from 1850–1940.

CHRISTOPHER GIBBS LTD
118 New Bond Street
London W1
Tel: (01) 629 2008/9
18th and 19th c. oil paintings.

THOMAS GIBSON FINE ARTS LTD
9a New Bond Street
London W1
Tel: (01) 499 8572
*19th and early 20th c. Impressionist sculpture
and paintings.*

DAVID GILL
25 Palace Gate
London W8
Tel: (01) 584 9184 (By appointment only)
Paintings from 1900–1930.

GOLFIANA MISCELLANEA LTD
84 Kingsway
London WC2
Tel: (01) 405 7711
Paintings with golf as subject matter.

GORE AND PLAYER
49 Church Road
London SW13
Tel: (01) 748 8850 and 748 7644 (Home)
*18th and 19th c. oil paintings and
watercolours.*

GAVIN GRAHAM GALLERY
47 Ledbury Road
London W11 2AA
Tel: (01) 229 4848
19th c. English and Continental oil paintings.

MARTIN GREGORY GALLERY
34 Bury Street
London SW1
Tel: (01) 839 3731
*18th and 19th c. English and Dutch oil
paintings and watercolours, specialising in
pictures relating to China.*

GREEN AND HEWETT
188 Dartmouth Road
London SE26
Tel: (01) 699 5461
Early English watercolours.

NICHOLAS GRINDLEY
37 Bury Street
London SW1
Tel: (01) 930 6670
Oriental paintings.

GUNTER FINE ART
4 Randall Avenue
London NW2
Tel: (01) 452 3997 (By appointment only)
*18th and 19th c. watercolours and 19th c. oil
paintings.*

HAHN AND SONS FINE ART
47 Albemarle Street
London W1
Tel: (01) 493 9196
*17th to 19th c. English and Continental oil
paintings.*

JOHN HALL ANTIQUES AND PRINTS
17 Harrington Road
London SW7
Tel: (01) 584 1307
Theatrical paintings from 1700–1900.

HAMLET GALLERY
5 Pond Street
London NW3
Tel: (01) 442 0056/794 3511
Early 19th c. to early 20th c. paintings.

A. AND K. HART-DAVIS
10 Hampstead Way
London N11
Tel: (01) 455 6581/458 4000
18th and 19th c. watercolours.

*Left: "Sunday Lunch" signed by Frederick
Daniel Hardy, crica 1865, courtesy of the
Gavin Graham Gallery.*

*Above: "The Hongs of Canton", a gouache
painting, circa 1840, courtesy of the Martin
Gregory Gallery.*

JULIAN HARTNOLL
Second Floor
14 Mason's Yard, Duke Street
London SW1
Tel: (01) 839 3842
*19th c. British paintings, especially
Pre-Raphaelite.*

W.R. HARVEY AND COMPANY LTD
67–70 Chalk Farm Road
London NW1 8AN
Tel: (01) 485 1504/267 2767
Oil paintings from 1650–1830.

HAZLITT, GOODEN AND FOX LTD
38 Bury Street
London SW1
Tel: (01) 930 6422/3
Old Master paintings.

HEIM GALLERY
59 Jermyn Street
London SW1
Tel: (01) 493 0688
Old Master paintings.

HEIRLOOM AND HOWARD LTD
1 Hay Hill
Berkeley Square
London W1
Tel: (01) 493 5868
*Armorial paintings, ie those works with crests
or coats-of-arms as subject matter.*

HELGATO
50 Highgate High Street
London N6 5HX
Tel: (01) 348 3864
*English oil paintings and watercolours to
1900.*

MILNE HENDERSON
99 Mount Street
London W1
Tel: (01) 499 2507
Chinese and Japanese paintings.

MARTIN HENMAN ANTIQUES
218 High Road
London N2
Tel: (01) 444 5274
Paintings from 1650–1900.

HERITAGE ANTIQUES
97 Pimlico Road
London SW1
Tel: (01) 730 1973 and 435 5993 (Home)
17th to 19th c. oil paintings and watercolours.

HOLBEIN GALLERIES
70 Pimlico Road
London SW1
Tel: (01) 730 8673
Old Master paintings.

THE HON. MAURICE HOWARD
3 Walpole Street
London SW3
Tel: (01) 730 3752 (By appointment only)
Old English watercolours.

DAVID HUGHES
45 Moore Park Road
London SW6
Tel: (01) 736 0412
Late 19th to early 20th c. paintings including Symbolist and Belle Epoque works.

MALCOLM INNES AND PARTNERS
172 Walton Street
London SW3
Tel: (01) 584 0575/5559
Scottish and sporting paintings. See entry under "Specialist Dealers, Paintings, North of England and Scotland" for illustration.

IONA ANTIQUES
Stand 11
Antique Hypermarket
26 Kensington High Street
London W8 4PF
Tel: (01) 937 7435
19th c. English animal paintings.

IVOR FINE ART
13 Dover Street (First Floor)
London W1
Tel: (01) 491 4866
18th to early 20th c. English watercolours.

ALAN JACOBS GALLERY
8 Duke Street
London SW1Y 6EN
Tel: (01) 930 3709
17th c. Dutch and Flemish Old Master paintings.

JELLINEK AND SAMPSON
156 Brompton Road
London SW3
Tel: (01) 589 5272
Primitive paintings.

Below: Portrait of Sigrid Kursal, wife of Henry Fleming, a Swedish noblemen, by an unknown artist dated 1639, courtesy of Lane Fine Art Ltd.

OSCAR AND PETER JOHNSON LTD
Lowndes Lodge Gallery
27 Lowndes Street
London SW1
Tel: (01) 235 6464
18th and 19th c. English paintings.

THOMAS KERR ANTIQUES LTD
11 Theberton Street
London N1 0QY
Tel: (01) 226 0626
16th to early 20th c. English and Continental furniture.

RICHARD KNIGHT
3rd and 4th Floor
9 Old Bond Street
London W1
Tel: (01) 629 2985
Old Master paintings.

COLIN LACY GALLERY
38 Ledbury Road
London W11
Tel: 229 9105
18th and 19th c. oil paintings and watercolours.

RICHARD LALLY LTD
152 Upper Richmond Road
London SW15
Tel: (01) 788 9123
18th and 19th c. paintings.

LANE FINE ART LTD
86–88 Pimlico Road
London SW1
Tel: (01) 730 7374
16th and 17th c. portraits, English sporting pictures and Old Master paintings.

LASSON GALLERY
82–84 Jermyn Street
London SW1
Tel: (01) 629 6981
19th and early 20th c. Old Master and French paintings.

RAYMOND LE BRUN
39 Ovington Street
London SW3 2JA
Tel: (01) 589 7945
17th to 19th c. Continental and Oriental paintings.

LEE AND STACY
5 Pond Street
London NW3
Tel: (01) 794 7904/452 0056
18th to early 20th c. oil paintings and watercolours.

LEFEVRE GALLERY
30 Bruton Street
London W1
Tel: (01) 629 2250/493 1572
19th and early 20th c. Impressionist paintings.

LEGGATT BROTHERS
17 Duke Street
London SW1
Tel: (01) 930 3772
17th to early 19th c. oil paintings.

LILLIE ANTIQUES
244–246 Lillie Road
London SW6
Tel: (01) 385 9852 and 385 2100 (Home)
18th and 19th c. paintings.

LIMNER ANTIQUES
Bond Street Antique Centre
124 New Bond Street
London W1
Tel: (01) 629 5314 and 493 6115 (Home)
16th to early 19th c. portrait miniatures.

LITTLE WINCHESTER GALLERY
36a Kensington Church Street
London W8
Tel: (01) 937 8444
19th c. Continental oil paintings.

N.W. LOTT AND H.J. GARRISH LTD
14 Mason's Yard
Duke Street
London SW1
Tel: (01) 930 1353
19th and early 20th c. watercolours.

PETER LOVEDAY PRINTS
46 Norland Square
London W11
Tel: (01) 221 4479 (By appointment only)
Oil paintings and watercolours, especially of British sporting life from 1700–1940.

LYONS GALLERY
47–49 Mill Lane
London NW6
Tel: (01) 794 3537
Art Nouveau and Art Deco paintings including gouaches and oils.

MAAS GALLERY
15a Clifford Street
London W1
Tel: (01) 734 2302
Victorian oil paintings and watercolours.

MACCONNAL MASON GALLERY
14 Duke Street
London SW1
Tel: (01) 839 7693/499 6991
19th and 20th c. oil paintings.

MACKAY GALLERY
821 Fulham Road
London SW6
Tel: (01) 731 5888
19th and 20th c. English oil paintings and 19th c. English watercolours.

Below: "Portrait of Penelope, Mrs Bayfield" by Thomas Hudson, courtesy of Leggatt Brothers.

Above: "The Old Flirt", oil on canvas by Eugene Delfosse, signed and dated 1859, courtesy of the Little Winchester Gallery.

MADDEN GLALLERIES
77 Duke Street
London W1
Tel: (01) 493 5854
French Impressionist and Post-Impressionist paintings and sculpture.

MANGATE GALLERY
3 Chiswick Lane
London W4 2LR
Tel: (01) 995 9867 (By appointment only)
England watercolours from 1750–1950.

PAUL MASON GALLERY
149 Sloane Street
London SW1X 9BZ
Tel: (01) 730 3683
18th and 19th c. marine and sporting paintings.

MASSEY ANTIQUES
11 The Mall
Camden Passage
London N1
Tel: (01) 359 7966
19th c. oil paintings.

MATHAF GALLERY LTD
24 Motcomb Street
London SW1X 8JU
Tel: (01) 235 0010
19th c. paintings with Arabian subjects.

MATTHIESEN FINE ART LTD
7/8 Mason's Yard
Duke Street
London SW1
Tel: (01) 930 2437
Old Master paintings and selected 20th c. masterpieces.

RENEE MATYAS GALLERY
746 Finchley Road
London NW11
Tel: (01) 455 9306/458 8911
17th and 19th c. English and Continental oil paintings.

J. AND J. MAY
40 Kensington Church Street
London W8
Tel: (01) 937 3575
Reverse-painted glass pictures.

ROY MILES FINE PAINTINGS
6 Duke Street
London SW1
Tel: (01) 930 8665
19th c. oil paintings.

JOHN MITCHELL AND SON
8 New Bond Street
First Floor
London W1
Tel: (01) 493 7567
17th c. Dutch, 18th c. English and 19th c. French oil paintings and watercolours.

THE MOORLAND GALLERY
23 Cork Street
London W1
Tel: (01) 734 6961
Sporting and wildlife paintings.

MORTON MORRIS AND CO
32 Bury Street
London SW1
Tel: (01) 930 3825
17th to 19th c. Old Master paintings including English paintings.

HUGH MOSS LTD
23 Bruton Lane
London W1
Tel: (01) 492 1835
Oriental paintings.

M. NEWMAN LTD
43a Duke Street
London SW1
Tel: (01) 930 6068
Oil paintings and watercolours from 1800–1930.

NIHON TOKEN
23 Museum Street
London WC1A 1JT
Tel: (01) 580 6511
Ancient and antique Japanese paintings.

ROBERT NOORTMAN GALLERY
8 Bury Street
London SW1
Tel: (01) 839 2606
17th to 19th c. oil paintings, including Old Masters.

Above: "After Prayer" signed by Rudolph Ernst (1854–1935), courtesy of the Mathaf Gallery Ltd.

OLD TIMES FURNISHING COMPANY
135 Lower Richmond Road
London SW15
Tel: (01) 788 3551
18th and 19th c. paintings.

N.R. OMELL
6 Duke Street
London SW1
Tel: (01) 839 6223/4
19th c. English landscape and marine oil paintings.

Below: "In The Meadows, Early Morning, Bristol", signed by Thomas Pyne RA, circa 1930, courtesy of the Mangate Gallery.

Above: "Shipping in the Pool of London" signed by C.J. De Lacy, dated 1893, courtesy of Omell Galleries.

OMELL GALLERIES
22 Bury Street
London SW1Y 6AL
Tel: (01) 839 4274
English and Continental oil paintings from 1860–1910.

HAL O'NIANS
6 Ryder Street
London SW1
Tel: (01) 930 9392
15th to 18th c. Old Master paintings.

ORMONDE ORIENTAL ANTIQUES
181 Westbourne Grove
and
Portwine Arcade
173 Portobello Road
London W11
Tel: (01) 221 4219
Indian, Tibetan, Chinese, Japanese, Burmese and Thai paintings.

GERALD OSOSKI
7 Heath Hurst Road
London NW3
Tel: (01) 435 2959
16th to early 20th c. oil paintings and watercolours.

PAISNEL GALLERY
768 Fulham Road
London SW6
Tel: (01) 736 7898
19th and early 20th c. oil paintings and watercolours.

PARK GALLERIES
21 Hendon Lane
London N3
Tel: (01) 346 2176
18th to early 20th c. English watercolours and oil paintings.

MICHAEL PARKIN FINE ART LTD
11 Motcomb Street
London SW1
Tel: (01) 235 8144
British oil paintings and watercolours from 1840 to 1940.

PARTRIDGE FINE ARTS LTD
144–146 New Bond Street
London W1
Tel: (01) 629 0834
Paintings of the English and Italian school.

W.H. PATTERSON FINE ARTS LTD
19 Albemarle Street
London W1
Tel: (01) 629 1910/4119
18th and 19th c. Old Master oil paintings.

PAWSEY AND PAYNE LTD
4 Ryder Street
London SW1
Tel: (01) 930 4221
18th to early 20th c. English and European oil paintings and watercolours, specialising in landscape, sporting, and portraiture.

DAVID PETTIFER LTD
269 Kings Road
London SW3
Tel: (01) 352 3088
18th and 19th c. oil paintings and watercolours.

PHOENIX ANTIQUES LTD
235 Westbourne Grove
London W11
Tel: (01) 221 7218
18th c. oil paintings.

THE PINK SHOP
82 Portobello Road
London W11
Tel: (01) 727 8851
18th and 19th c. oil paintings and watercolours.

PHILIP
59 Ledbury Road
London W11
Tel: (01) 727 7915
16th and 17th c. oil paintings and primitive paintings.

POLAK GALLERY
21 King Street
London SW1
Tel: (01) 930 9245
19th and 20th c. British and European oil paintings and watercolours.

ANNABEL POPOVIC
11 Shafto Mews
Cadogan Square
London SW1
Tel: (01) 727 9705/1207 (By appointment only)
Old Master watercolours.

POTTLES
6 Camden Walk
Camden Passage
London N1
Tel: (01) 226 9348
Primitive paintings.

BLAISE PRESTON LTD
44 Duke Street
London SW1
Tel: (01) 839 6222
17th to 19th c. Dutch and English paintings.

RUPERT PRESTON LTD
44 Duke Street
London SW1
Tel: (01) 727 9878 (By appointment only)
17th c. marine paintings of the Netherlands.

Left: "Landscape with Figures by Cottage" by John Knox (1778–1845), courtesy of Pawsey and Payne Ltd.

PAINTINGS

Above: "Washing Day" by Edward Frere, signed and dated 1870, courtesy of the Polak Gallery.

NORMAN PRIMROSE GALLERY
10 Princes Arcade
London SW1
Tel: (01) 439 4471
18th and 19th c. English watercolours and 19th c. English oil paintings.

PYMS GALLERY
13 Motcomb Street
London SW1
Tel: (01) 235 3050
19th to mid 20th c. oil paintings and watercolours, specialising in genre, landscape and marine subjects.

ANTHONY REED
3 Cork Street
London W1
Tel: (01) 437 0157
18th and 19th c. English paintings plus early English watercolours.

Below: "The Old Holland", signed and dated by the artist, Thomas Bush Hardy (1842–1897), courtesy of the Rosendale Gallery.

PAUL REEVES
102 Bennerley Road
London SW11
Tel: (01) 223 3399
English paintings, especially Arts and Crafts, from 1850–1950.

RELCY ANTIQUES
9 Nelson Road
London SE10
Tel: (01) 858 2812 and 858 7218 (Home)
18th and 19th c. English and Continental paintings, especially those with marine or sporting subject.

RICHMOND GALLERY
8 Cork Street
London W1
Tel: (01) 437 0264
19th and early 20th c. French paintings.

THE ROSENDALE GALLERY
114 Rosendale Road
London SE21
Tel: (01) 670 8747
English watercolours from 1780–1914

ROSS GALLERIES
18 Dover Street
London W1
Tel: (01) 629 0975/6
19th c. English and Continental paintings.

ROYAL EXCHANGE ART GALLERY
14 Royal Exchange
London EC3
Tel: (01) 283 4400
19th and early 20th c. oil paintings and watercolours specialising in marine and landscape subjects.

RUTLAND GALLERY
32a St George Street
London W1
Tel: (01) 499 5636
British and American primitive paintings.

SABIN GALLERIES LTD
4 Cork Street
London W1
Tel: (01) 734 6186
Georgian paintings.

Caption: "Nijinski in the Ballet L'après-midi d'un Faune" by George Barbier in 1913, courtesy of the Charles Spencer Gallery.

SCHWARTZ
93 Blackheath Road
London SE10
Tel: (01) 692 1652
Indian miniatures.

SIMEON
19 Burlington Arcade
London W1V 9AB
Tel: (01) 493 3353
English and European miniatures.

JULIAN SIMON FINE ART
135 Kings Road
London SW3
Tel: (01) 351 1096
18th to early 20th c. British and Continental watercolours and oil paintings.

CAROLINE SMITH
100 Warwick Gardens
London W14
Tel: (01) 602 2281 (By appointment only)
British watercolours.

ANDREW SMITHSON MASTER DRAWINGS
50 South Molton Street
London W1
Tel: (01) 629 4434
16th to 18th c. Dutch and Italian Old Master paintings.

SOOLE AND MERKEL
69 Kensington Church Street
London W8
Tel: (01) 937 2410
17th to 19th c. paintings.

EDWARD SPEELMAN
175 Piccadilly
London W1
Tel: (01) 493 0657
Old Master paintings.

CHARLES SPENCER THEATRE GALLERY
82 York Street
London W1H 1DP
Tel: (01) 723 5772
Paintings and portraits for the theatre over four centuries, including designs for Irving, Bernhardt, the Ballets Russes, the Folies Bergère, and the Royal Ballet and Opera Company.

H.J. SPILLERS LTD
37 Beak Street
London W1
Tel: (01) 437 4661
Old Master oil paintings,

PAINTINGS

MARSHALL SPINK
18 Albemarle Street
London W1
Tel: (01) 493 2575/5280
Old Master paintings from Italian primitives to Constable.

SPINK AND SON LTD
5, 6, and 7 King Street
London SW1
Tel: (01) 930 7888
17th to 19th c. English oil paintings and watercolours.

SPREAD EAGLE ANTIQUES
8 Nevada Street
London SE10
Tel: (01) 692 1618/858 9713
English watercolours and oil paintings.

STERN GALLERY
40 Ledbury Road
London W11
Tel: (01) 229 6187
18th and 19th c. oil paintings.

LAURI STEWART ANTIQUES
36 Church Lane
London N2
Tel: (01) 883 7719
Victorian watercolours and oil paintings.

SUNDRIDGE ANTIQUES
564 Kings Road
London SW6
Tel: (01) 736 0828
Oil paintings and watercolours from 1780–1920.

F. TELTSCHER LTD
17 Crawford Street
London W1H 1PE
Tel: (01) 935 0525
17th to 19th c. oil paintings.

TOPOGRAPHICAL ARTS
2 Cecil Court
Charing Cross Road
London WC2
Tel: (01) 836 2922
18th and 19th c. topographical watercolours.

FERENC TOTH
598a Kings Road
London SW6
Tel: (01) 731 2063 and 602 1771 (Home)
19th c. paintings.

TOYNBEE AND CLARKE LTD
95 Mount Street
London W1
Tel: (01) 499 4472
17th to 19th c. Chinese and Japanese paintings.

TRAFALGAR GALLERIES
35 Bury Street
London SW1
Tel: (01) 839 6466
19th c. and Old Master paintings.

TRENGROVE
46 South End
Croydon, Surrey
Tel: (01) 688 2155
18th and 19th c. oil paintings and watercolours.

TROVE
71 Pimlico Road
London SW1
Tel: (01) 730 6514
Sporting paintings from 1750 on.

TRYON AND MOORLAND GALLERY
23–24 Cork Street
London W1
Tel: (01) 734 6961
Sporting and natural history pictures.

LEIGH UNDERHILL GALLERY
100 Islington High Street
London N1
Tel: (01) 226 5673
British paintings from 1900–1940.

RAFAEL VALLS
34 Bury Street
London SW1
Tel: (01) 839 2713/1092
Old Master and 19th c. paintings.

SABIN VANDERKAR LTD
43 Duke Street
London SW1
Tel: (01) 839 1091
Dutch and Flemish paintings from all periods.

JOHNNY VAN HAEFTEN LTD
180 New Bond Street
London W1
Tel: (01) 499 1885 and 373 0953 (Home)
16th and 17th c. Dutch and Flemish Old Master paintings.

VERMOUTIER AND BANKS
25a Holland Street
London W8
Tel: (01) 937 3262
18th and 19th c. primitive paintings.

WALKER-BAGSHAWE
46a Ockendon Road
London N1
Tel: (01) 226 9904 (By appointment only)
19th c. oil paintings and watercolours.

THE WELBECK GALLERY
18 Thayer Street
London W1
Tel: (01) 493 1141/2/3
17th to early 20th c. topographical, natural history, military and bird prints, etchings and engravings.

Right: "Travelling Harvesters" by Henry Herbert la Thangue painted in 1897, courtesy of the Louise Whitford Gallery.

Above: "The Rialto, Venice" by William Callow, R.W.S. (1812–1908), in pencil and watercolour, signed and dated August 1846, courtesy of Spink and Son Ltd.

LOUISE WHITFORD GALLERY
25a Lowndes Street
London SW1
Tel: (01) 235 3155
Oil paintings from 1880–1920 including Vienna Secession, Belle Epoque, Symbolist, Post-Impressionist, and Australian.

WILDENSTEIN AND COMPANY LTD
147 New Bond Street
London W1
Tel: (01) 629 0602
Old Master and Impressionist paintings.

WILLIAMS AND SON
2 Grafton Street
London W1
Tel: (01) 493 4985/5751
19th c. British and European paintings.

CHRISTOPHER WOOD GALLERY
15 Motcomb Street
London SW1
Tel: (01) 235 9141/2
Victorian oil paintings and watercolours.

Above: "A Little Girl with a Cat" by Sophie Anderson, circa 1870, courtesy of Christopher Wood Gallery.

ANDREW WYLD
3 Cork Street
London W1
Tel: (01) 437 2741
18th and 19th c. English watercolours and oil paintings.

CHARLES YOUNG FINE PAINTINGS
Second Floor, Old Bond Street House
6–8 Old Bond St
London W1
Tel: (01) 499 1117
English oil paintings from 1600–1900 and 19th c. watercolours.

SOUTH AND SOUTHEAST ENGLAND

ABBEY ANTIQUES AND ARTS
97 High Street
Hemel Hempstead, Herts
Tel: (0442) 64667
Early English watercolours.

ARTBRY'S ANTIQUES
44 High Street
Orpington, Kent
Tel: (01) 868 0834 and 954 1840 (Home)
17th to 19th c. oil paintings.

BALCOMBE GALLERIES
Balcombe, Sussex
Tel: (044 483) 439
Paintings from 1880–1920.

BOURNE GALLERY
31–33 Lesbourne Road
Reigate, Surrey
Tel: Reigate 41614
19th c. oil paintings and watercolours.

CAMBRIDGE FINE ART LTD
68 Trumpington Street
Cambridge, Cambs CB2 1RJ
Tel: (0223) 68488
Victorian oil paintings. See overleaf for illustration.

EASTBOURNE FINE ART
47 South Street
Eastbourne, Sussex
Tel: (0323) 25634/23769
19th c. English and Continental oil paintings and watercolours.

EDGWARE ANTIQUES
19 Whitchurch Lane
Edgware, Middx
Tel: (01) 952 1606
Victorian and Edwardian watercolours.

GALLERY 10
10 Richmond Hill
Richmond, Surrey
Tel: (01) 948 3314
19th and early 20th c. British and European oil paintings, including Art Nouveau and Art Deco.

GREAT GROOMS ANTIQUES LTD
Parbrook
Billingshurst, Sussex
Tel: (040 381) 2263
Early 20th c. oil paintings.

GREEN LANE ANTIQUES
1 Maxwell Road
Northwood, Middx
Tel: Northwood 22177
19th c. watercolours.

THE HAMPTON HILL GALLERY LTD
203–205 High Street
Hampton Hill, Middx TW12 1NP
Tel: (01) 977 5273
18th to early 20th c. watercolours.

HUGHENDEN HOUSE GALLERY
35 Park Road
Teddington, Middx
Tel: (01) 977 4460
17th to 19th c. oil paintings.

ANTHONY J. LESTER
The Dower House
Hithercroft, nr Wallingford, Oxon
Tel: (0491) 36683 (By appointment only)
18th to early 20th c. watercolours. See overleaf for illustration.

THE MAGPIE
25 Sandrock Hill Road
Wrecclesham, Farnham, Surrey
Tel: (025 13) 3129
Victorian watercolours.

MARBLE HILL GALLERY
72 Richmond Road
Twickenham, Middx
Tel: (01) 892 1488
Victorian watercolours.

NORTON ANTIQUES
56 London Road
Beaconsfield, Bucks HP9 2JH
Tel: (049 46) 3674
18th and 19th c. oil paintings.

Below: "Going to Market with Geese and Goslings", monogrammed by the artist, Myles Birket Foster R.W.S. (1825–1899), courtesy of Abbey Antiques and Arts.

Above: "Building Haystacks" by Tomson Laing, courtesy of Cambridge Fine Art Ltd

OLD HALL GALLERY
Crown Lodge
Crown Road
Morden, Surrey
Tel: (01) 540 9918 (By appointment only)
17th to 19th c. oil paintings.

PICTURE CARE LTD
30–32 Hill Rise
Richmond, Surrey
Tel: (01) 948 4638/9/940 5790
18th to early 20th c. oil paintings and watercolours.

PRIESTS ANTIQUES AND FINE ARTS
56 North Street
Thame, Oxon
Tel: (084 421) 4461
17th to 19th c. oil paintings.

CYRIL STONE
30 Palmeira Square
Hove, Sussex BN2 2JB
Tel: (0273) 739523
18th and 19th c. oil paintings and watercolours.

Below: "Over the Stepping Stones", a watercolour by Henry John Sylvester Stannard, R.B.A. (1870–1951), courtesy of Anthony J. Lester.

STOTFOLD ANTIQUES
21 High Street
Westerham, Kent
Tel: (0959) 63055
19th c. oil paintings and watercolours.

SUNDRIDGE ANTIQUES
4 Sundridge Parade
Plaistow Lane
Bromley, Kent
Tel: (01) 460 8614
Oil paintings and watercolours from 1780–1920.

IVOR AND JOAN WEISS
57a Priory Street
Colchester, Essex C01 2QE
Tel: (0206) 868224
Oil paintings and watercolours from 17th to 19th c.

H.S. WELLBY LTD
The Malt House
Church End
Haddenham, Bucks
Tel: (0844) 290 036
18th and 19th c. oil paintings.

THE WHITGIFT GALLERIES
77 South End
Croydon, Surrey
Tel: (01) 688 0990
19th and early 20th c. oil paintings.

Above: A German prince by an unknown artist, oil on canvas, circa 1750, courtesy of H.S. Wellby.

YELLOW LANTERN ANTIQUES LTD
34/65B Holland Road
Hove, Sussex BU3 771572
Tel: (0273) 771572
19th c. oil paintings.

SOUTHWEST ENGLAND AND WALES

ABOYNE ANTIQUES
13 York Street
Bath, Avon
Tel: (0225) 64850 and 319961 (Home)
18th and 19th c. watercolours and oil paintings.

ANGHARAD'S ANTIQUES
106 Chester Road
Shotton, Clywd, Wales
Tel: (0244) 812240
19th c. portrait miniatures.

Below: Painting by Henry Frederick Lucas, signed and dated 1888, oil on canvas in hand-made gilt frame, courtesy of J. Collins and Son.

Above: "Figures in a Landscape" by William Shayer Snr, signed and dated 1832, courtesy of the Hampshire Gallery.

JOHN. H. COLLINGS LTD
Prospect House, Knightcott
Banwell, Avon
Tel: (0934) 823181
Paintings from 1800–1900.

J. COLLINS AND SON
63 and 28 High Street
Bideford, Devon
Tel: (023 72) 3103
Victorian watercolours and oil paintings.

COTSWOLD GALLERIES
High Street
Moreton-in-Marsh, Glos
Tel: (0608) 50601
Victorian oil paintings.

MICHAEL DANNY
6 Old King Street
Bath, Avon
Tel: (0225) 331694 and 832027 (Home)
British watercolours from 1750.

GASTRELL HOUSE
33 Long Street
Tetbury, Glos GL8 8AA
Tel: (0666) 52228
17th to early 19th c. oil paintings.

GWYNEDD GALLERIES
Paris House, Snowdon Street
Penygroes, Nr Caernarvon
Gwynedd, Wales
Tel: (028 681) 329
18th and 19th c. oil paintings and watercolours.

HAMPSHIRE GALLERY
18 Landsdowne Road
Bournemouth, Dorset BH1 1SD
Tel: (0202) 21211
17th to 19th c. English and Continental oil paintings and watercolours.

GEOFFREY LAMBERT FINE ART
Jardin Clouet
St Andrew, Guernsey, Channel Islands
Tel: (04 81) 36151
19th and early 20th c. British and Continental oil paintings and watercolours including landscape, marine, still life and sporting subjects.

Above: "Caernarvon Castle", a watercolour by Samuel Jackson (1794–1865), courtesy of the Heather Newman Gallery.

HEATHER NEWMAN GALLERY
Milidouwa, Cranham
Painswick, Glos GL6 6TX
Tel: (0452) 812230
British watercolours from 1750 on.

C.J. ORSON
London House
Ruardean, Glos GL17 9UT
Tel: (0594) 542309
18th to early 20th c. English paintings, specialising in works by Gerald Ososki R.B.A.

SKEAPING GALLERY
Townend House
Lydford
Okehampton, Devon
Tel: (0822) 82 383
18th, 19th and early 20th c. oil paintings and watercolours.

TAMAR GALLERY
5 Church Street
Launceston, Cornwall
Tel: (0566) 4233
18th to early 20th c. watercolours.

MORRIS TUCKER
Lower Town House
Chudleigh Knighton, Devon TQ13 OME
Tel: (0626) 852123
Specialist in maritime history with ship portraits, wool pictures, primitives, samplers, and sea shell valentines.

MIDLANDS AND EAST ANGLIA

BROBURY HOUSE GALLERY
Brobury, nr, Hay-on Wye
Heref & Worcs
Tel: (0497) 229
Late 19th and early 20th c. watercolours.

SIMON CARTER GALLERY
23 Market Hill
Woodbridge, Suffolk
Tel: (03943) 2242
Early British paintings including 17th to 19th c. portraits, and watercolours from 1750 to 1900. See overleaf for illustration.

THE ENCHANTED AVIARY
Long Melford
Sudbury, Suffolk
Tel: (0787) 78814
Victorian paintings with natural history subjects.

GAVINA EWART
37 Sheep Street
Stratford-upon-Avon, Warks
Tel: (0789) 293917
19th c. oil and watercolour paintings.

FAIRHURST ART GALLERY
13 Bedford Street
Norwich, Norfolk
Tel: (0603) 614214
18th and 19th c. oil paintings, as well as selection of Dutch paintings and 19th c. English primitives.

HUMBLEYARD FINE ART
Waterfall Cottage, Mill Street
Swanton Morley, Norfolk
Tel: (036 283) 793
18th and 19th c. oil paintings and watercolours, especially marine.

KESTREL HOUSE
72 Gravelly Hill
North Erdington
Birmingham, W Midlands B23 6BB
Tel: (021) 373 2375
Victorian watercolours and oil paintings.

LOWER NUP-END GALLERY LTD
Cradley
Nr Malvern, Heref & Worcs
Tel: (088 684) 334 (By appointment only)
18th and 19th c. English watercolours and oil paintings. See overleaf for illustration.

SALLY MITCHELL FINE ARTS
Thornlea, Askham
Newark, Notts NG22 0RN
Tel: (077783) 234
18th to early 20th c. country and sporting paintings.

JOHN NOOTT FINE PAINTINGS
Picton House Gallery
Broadway, Heref & Worcs
Tel: (0386) 852787
Oil paintings from 1840–1940. See overleaf for illustration.

OWNART GALLERY
22 Bore Street
Lichfield, Staffs
Tel: (05432) 53626
*19th and early 20th c. oil paintings and
watercolours.*

NORTH OF ENGLAND AND SCOTLAND

ADAMS ANTIQUES
65 Waterloo Row
Chester, Cheshire CH1 2LE
Tel: (0244) 319421
18th and 19th oil paintings and watercolours.

ANDERSON AND SLATER ANTIQUES
8 King Street
Knutsford, Cheshire WA16 6DL
Tel: (0565) 2917
18th and 19th c. paintings.

ATHOLL ANTIQUES
322 Great Western Road
Aberdeen, Grampian, Scotland
Tel: (0224) 53547
Scottish Victorian oil paintings.

CAMPBELL-GIBSON FINE ARTS
Star Brae
Oban, Strathclyde, Scotland
Tel: (0631) 2303
Victorian watercolours.

DEAN GALLERY
42 Dean Street
Newcastle-upon-Tyne, Tyne & Wear NE1
1PG
Tel: (0632) 325923
*19th and early 20th c. paintings, with
emphasis on local subjects by local artists.*

DUNKELD ANTIQUES
Atholl Street
Dunkeld, Tayside, Scotland
Tel: (035 02) 578
18th and 19th c. Scottish oil paintings.

THE FINE ART SOCIETY LTD
12 Great King Street
Edinburgh, Lothian, Scotland
Tel: (031) 557 1903
*British, especially Scottish, oil paintings and
watercolours from 1800 on.*

GALLERIES DE FRESNES
Cessnock Castle
Galston, nr Kilmarnock, Strathclyde
Scotland
Tel: (0563) 820314
19th and early 20th c. oil paintings.

WILLIAM GOODFELLOW
The Green
Over Kellet
Carnforth, Lancs LA6 1BU
Tel: (0524) 733030
English paintings, pre-1900.

*Above right: Oil painting of Peg Woffington
in "As You Like It" painted by Edward Perry
in 1757, courtesy of the Simon Carter Gallery.*

*Centre right: "An Evening on the Llugwy,
North Wales" by B.W. Leader, R.A., oil on
canvas and signed by artist, courtesy of Lower
Nup-End Gallery Ltd.*

*Bottom right: "Charles II Before His Peers" by
Edgar Bundy, circa 1900, courtesy of John
Noott Fine Paintings.*

*Above: Victorian watercolour by T.B. Hardy,
courtesy of the Dean Gallery.*

CHARLES HAY ANTIQUES
44 High Street
Coldstream, Borders, Scotland
Tel: (0890) 2552
*18th and early 19th c. reverse-painted glass
pictures.*

MALCOLM INNES GALLERY
67 George Street
Edinburgh, Lothian, Scotland
Tel: (031) 226 4151
*18th and 19th c. Scottish landscape sporting
and natural history paintings.*

JAYS FINE ART DEALERS
Cambridge Gallery
4 Cambridge Arcade
Southport, Merseyside PR8 1AS
Tel: (0704) 34488
*18th and 19th c. watercolours and 17th to
19th c. oil paintings.*

THE KELVIN GALLERY
117 Bath Street
Glasgow, Scotland
Tel: (041) 221 1367
19th c. oil paintings and watercolours.

THE MCEWAN GALLERY
Glengarden.
Ballater, Aberdeen, Grampian, Scotland
Tel: (033 82) 429
and
Castleton Lane
Braemar, Aberdeen, Grampian, Scotland
Tel: (033 83) 429
*18th and 19th c. oil paintings and
watercolours.*

ANDREW PATTERSON GALLERY
The Studio
19 Academy Street
Inverness, Highland, Scotland
Tel: (0463) 34576
*17th and 18th c. Continental and Scottish
paintings, including marine oil paintings and
watercolours.*

QUADRANT ANTIQUES
5 North West Circus Parade
Stockbridge, Edinburgh
Lothian, Scotland
Tel: (031) 226 7282
18th and 19th c. marine paintings.

THE RENDEZVOUS GALLERY
100 Forest Avenue
Aberdeen, Grampian, Scotland
Tel: (0224) 323247
*Art Nouveau paintings, especially of the
Scottish school.*

JOHN SCOTT-ADIE
16 St John Street
Perth, Tayside, Scotland
Tel: (0783) 25550
*19th c. oil paintings and watercolours
specialising in Scottish works and landscapes.*

*Above: "Fishing a Highland River" by
Edmund Nemann and Joseph Adam, dated
1865 and signed by both artists, courtesy of
the Malcolm Innes Gallery.*

STEIGAL FINE ARTS
6 North West Circus Place
Edinburgh, Lothian, Scotland
Tel: (031) 226 4563
*British paintings from 1800–1930,
specialising in the Decorative Arts period.*

WALKER GALLERIES LTD
90–92 Station Parade
Harrogate, N Yorkshire HG1 1ST
Tel: (0423) 67933
*19th and early 20th c. English and
Continental oil paintings and watercolours.*

WELLINGTON FINE ART
14 Park Circus
Glasgow, Scotland
Tel: (041) 331 2896
19th and early 20th c. oil paintings.

NORTHERN IRELAND

THE BELL GALLERY
Abbotsford
2 Malone Road
Belfast, Antrim, N Ireland
Tel: (0232) 662998
*19th c. British and Irish oil paintings and
watercolours.*

DUNLUCE ANTIQUES
33 Ballytober Road
Bushmills, Co Antrim BT57 8UU
N Ireland
Tel: (02657) 31140
18th and 19th c. Irish paintings.

*Left: "Farm Cottage in a Wooded Landscape"
by John Laporte, signed and dated 1815,
courtesy of Jays Fine Art Dealers.*

LONDON

ADAMS ROOM LTD
18–20 Ridgway
London SW19
Tel: (01) 946 7047
18th and 19th c. porcelain.

ALBERT AMOR LTD
37 Bury Street
London SW1
Tel: (01) 930 2444
English ceramics, especially first period Worcester and blue and white porcelain.

ANTIQUE PORCELAIN COMPANY LTD
149 New Bond Street
London W1
Tel: (01) 629 1254
18th c. porcelain and faience, especially French.

THE ANTIQUE SHOP
9 Fortis Green
London N2 ·
Tel: (01) 883 7651
19th c. Canton, Imari and Satsuma ware.

ARTINERIAS LTD
3 New Cavendish Street
London W1
Tel: (01) 935 6912 or 459 0782 (Home)
Louis Philippe porcelain.

BARHAM ANTIQUES
83 Portobello Road
London W11
Tel: (01) 727 3845
Victorian, European and Oriental porcelain.

BARNET ANTIQUES AND FINE ART
1180 High Road
London N20
Tel: (01) 445 9695
18th c. porcelain.

STANLEY BEAL
41 Fairfax Road
London NW6
Tel: (01) 328 7525
Oriental porcelain.

SUSAN BECKER
18 Lower Richmond Road
London SW15
Tel: (01) 788 9082
Porcelain 18th and 19th c., especially Worcester, Moore Brothers, Doulton, Derby, Coalport, Meissen and Oriental pieces.

R. BONNETT
582 Kings Road
London SW6
Tel: (01) 736 4593 and 788 2763 (Home)
Staffordshire figures.

PHILIP BRADY
3 Blenheim Crescent
London W11
Tel: (01) 727 7536
18th and 19th c. porcelain.

WILLIAM BRAY
58 Fulham Road
London SW6
Tel: (01) 731 1170
Porcelain from the Georgian period.

DAVID BROWER ANTIQUES
113 Kensington Church Street
London W8
Tel: (01) 221 4155
Oriental and Continental decorative porcelain.

Above: "The Apple Pickers" porcelain grouping by Meissen, circa 1880, courtesy of Susan Becker.

F.G. BRUSCHWEILER ANTIQUES LTD
3 Lonsdale Road
London W11
Tel: (01) 229 3106 and (062 185) 1252 (Home)
19th c. porcelain.

CATHAY ANTIQUES
12 Thackeray Street
London W8
Tel: (01) 937 6066
Chinese and Japanese porcelain.

CHANCERY ANTIQUES
22 Park Walk
London SW10
Tel: (01) 352 6016 (By appointment only)
Georgian and early Victorian porcelain.

CHANCERY ANTIQUES LTD
357 Upper Street
London N1 0PD
Tel: (01) 359 9035
Chinese and Japanese porcelain, including Satsuma ware.

CHINA CHOICE
New Cavendish Street
London W1
Tel: (01) 935 0184
18th c. English porcelain.

JOHN CLYNE
3 and 10 Blenheim Crescent
London W11
Tel: (01) 727 7536
Victorian and Edwardian porcelain.

COHEN AND PEARCE
84 Portobello Road
London W11
Tel: (01) 229 9458
Chinese porcelain.

COLLET'S CHINESE GALLERY
40 Great Russell Street
London WC1
Tel: (01) 580 7538
17th to 19th c. Chinese porcelain.

CRAVEN ANTIQUES
17 Garson House
Gloucester Terrace
London W1
Tel: (01) 262 4176 (By appointment only)
English porcelain from 1780–1830.

CREST ANTIQUES
313–315 and 287 Putney Bridge Road
London SW15
Tel: (01) 789 3165
19th and early 20th c. porcelain.

JOHN CRICHTON
34 Brook Street
London W1
Tel: (01) 629 7926 and 398 1933 (Home)
Chinese and Japanese porcelain.

DELOMOSNE AND SON LTD
4 Campden Hill Road
London W8 7DU
Tel: (01) 937 1804
18th and early 19th c. porcelain.

DEN OF ANTIQUITY
96 Coombe Lane
London SW20
Tel: (01) 947 0850
Victorian and Edwardian porcelain.

EALING ANTIQUES
34 St Mary's Road
London W5
Tel: (01) 567 6192
18th and 19th c. porcelain.

M. EKSTEIN LTD
90 Jermyn Street
London SW1
Tel: (01) 930 2024
Continental porcelain.

PETER FRANCIS
26 Museum Street
London WC1
Tel: (01) 637 0165
Porcelain from 1760–1860.

ELAINE FREEDMAN ANTIQUES
Camden Passage
London N1
Tel: Not Available
Continental and English porcelain.

VINCENT FREEMAN
8–10 Gateway Arcade
Camden Passage
London N1
Tel: (01) 226 6178
Porcelain from 1800–1900.

GAY ANTIQUES
1 Beauchamp Place
London SW3
Tel: (01) 584 9615
Continental porcelain including Sèvres, Vienna, Meissen, plus 19th c. Minton and Crown Derby and Royal Worcester fruit and cattle.

GLAISHER AND NASH LTD
Lowndes Lodge
Cadogan Place
London SW1
Tel: (01) 235 2285/6
Porcelain from 1700–1820.

JOHN HALL ANTIQUES AND PRINTS
17 Harrington Road
London SW7
Tel: (01) 584 1307
Staffordshire figures from 1760–1860.

HARCOURT ANTIQUES
5 Harcourt Street
London W1
Tel: (01) 723 5919
English, Continental and Oriental porcelain, pre-1830.

HART AND ROSENBERG
2–3 Gateway Arcade
355 Upper Street
London N1
Tel: (01) 359 6839
Chinese, Japanese and European porcelain.

HEIRLOOM AND HOWARD LTD
1 Hay Hill
Berkeley Square, London W1
Tel: (01) 493 5868
17th to 19th c. English and Chinese armorial porcelain.

HELGATO
50 Highgate High Street
London N6 5HX
Tel: (01) 348 3864
British porcelain to 1880.

MARTIN HENMAN ANTIQUES
218 High Road
London N2
Tel: (01) 444 5274
Porcelain from 1750–1910.

FELIX HILTON
45 St John's Wood High Street
London NW8
Tel: (01) 722 7634
18th and 19th c. porcelain.

HOFF ANTIQUES
66a Kensington Church Street
London W8 4BY
Tel: (01) 229 5516
Fine 18th c. European porcelain including German Meissen, French softpastes, and pieces from most important Italian and English factories.

Above: A Chinese armorial mug with the arms of Admiral Sir Edward Hughes K.B., circa 1780, courtesy of Heirloom and Howard Ltd.

MICHAEL HOGG ANTIQUES
172 Brompton Road
London SW3
Tel: (01) 589 8629
Chinese porcelain.

HARCOURT ANTIQUES
5 Harcourt Street
London W1
Tel: (01) 723 5919
Oriental porcelain, pre-1830.

J.T. ANTIQUES
11 Webb's Road
London SW11
Tel: (01) 228 7171
18th to early 20th c. porcelain.

Below: Early Worcester first period tea bowl and saucer, painted in pink and green with landscapes and flowers, circa 1755, courtesy of Klaber and Klaber.

JAPANESE GALLERY
66d Kensington Church Street
London W8
Tel: (01) 229 2934 and 226 3347 (Home)
Japanese porcelain.

MELVYN AND GARY JAY ANTIQUES
64a Kensington Church Street
London W8 4DB
Tel: (01) 937 6832
19th c. porcelain.

KENWAY ANTIQUES
70 Kenway Road
London SW5
Tel: (01) 373 1631
Oriental porcelain.

KLABER AND KLABER
2a Bedford Gardens
Kensington Church Street
London W8 7EH
Tel: (01) 727 4573
18th c. European porcelain and English enamels.

L.P.J. ANTIQUES LTD
c/o Laurence Mitchell Antiques
27 Camden Passage
London N1
Tel: (01) 359 7579
18th and 19th c. English porcelain and ironstone including Meissen, Nankin and blue and white ware.

RAYMOND LE BRUN
39 Ovington Street
London SW3 2JA
Tel: (01) 589 7945
17th to 19th c. Continental and Oriental porcelain.

LILLIE ANTIQUES
244–246 Lillie Road
London SW6
Tel: (01) 385 9852 and 385 2100 (Home)
18th and 19th c. Continental porcelain.

ERIC LINEHAM AND SONS
62 Kensington Church Street
London W8
Tel: (01) 937 9650
19th c. English, Continental and Oriental porcelain.

J. LIPITCH LTD
177 Westbourne Grove
London W11
Tel: (01) 229 0783
18th c. porcelain.

THE LITTLE ANTIQUE SHOP
9 Hereford Road
London W2
Tel: (01) 221 4578
18th to early 20th c. fine German porcelain.

THE LITTLE CURIOSITY SHOP
24 The Green
Winchmore Hill
London N21
Tel: (01) 886 0925
Victorian porcelain.

MASSEY ANTIQUES
11 The Mall
Camden Passage
London N1
Tel: (01) 359 7966
19th c. English and Continental porcelain.

PORCELAIN

D.C. MONK AND SON
132–134 Kensington Church Street
London W8
Tel: (01) 229 3727
Oriental porcelain.

HUGH MOSS LTD
23 Bruton Lane
London W1
Tel: (01) 492 1835
Oriental porcelain.

MRS MUNRO ANTIQUES LTD
11 Montpelier Street
London SW7
Tel: (01) 589 0686/5052
18th and 19th c. porcelain.

NASH ANTIQUES
183 Westbourne Grove
London W11
Tel: (01) 727 3796
Oriental and Japanese porcelain.

NING LTD
8 Symons Street
London SW3
Tel: (01) 730 9111
Spode, Wedgwood, Davenport and blue and white porcelain.

CHARLES L. NYMAN AND COMPANY LTD
230 and 242 Camden High Street
London NW1
Tel: (01) 485 1907 (Trade only)
19th c. English and Continental porcelain.

ORMONDE ORIENTAL ANTIQUES
181 Westbourne Grove
and
Portwine Arcade
173 Portobello Road
London W11
Tel: (01) 221 4219
Indian, Tibetan, Chinese, Japanese, Burmese and Thai porcelain.

RAYMOND O'SHEA GALLERY
6 Ellis Street
(Off Sloane Street)
London SW1
Tel: (01) 730 0082
Porcelain with cartographic motifs.

KEVIN PAGE ANTIQUES
5 Camden Passage
London N1
Tel: (01) 226 8558
19th c. Oriental porcelain.

PORTOBELLO ANTIQUE COMPANY
133 Portobello Road
London W11
Tel: (01) 221 0344
Porcelain from 1800.

RELCY ANTIQUES
9 Nelson Road
London SE10
Tel: (01) 858 2812
18th c. porcelain.

ROCHEFORT ANTIQUES GALLERY
32–34 The Green
Winchmore Hill
London N21
Tel: (01) 886 4779/363 0910
18th and 19th c. English and Continental porcelain.

GRAHAM ROSENTHAL
The London Oriental and Fine Art
Galleries
Georgian House
84 Portobello Road
London W11
Tel: (01) 229 9458
Oriental porcelain.

MARCUS ROSS ANTIQUES
14 Pierrepoint Row
Camden Passage
London N1
Tel: (01) 359 8494
Oriental porcelain.

EDWARD SALTI
43 Davies Street
London W1
Tel: (01) 629 2141
French porcelain specialising in Meissen and Sèvres and English enamel.

GERALD SATTIN LTD
25 Burlington Arcade
London W1
Tel: (01) 493 6557
English and Continental porcelain to 1880.

SENSATION LTD
66 Fulham High Street
London SW6 3LQ
Tel: (01) 736 4135
18th and 19th c. porcelain.

JEAN SEWELL LTD
3 Camden Street
London W8 7EP
Tel: (01) 727 3122
18th and 19th c. pottery and porcelain, specialising in tableware.

SOUTH AUDLEY ART GALLERIES LTD
36 South Audley Street
London W1
Tel: (01) 499 3178/3195
19th c. English and Continental porcelain.

AUBREY SPIERS ANTIQUES
Shop C3
Chenil Galleries
183 Kings Road
London SW3

AUBREY SPIERS (CON'T)
Tel: (01) 352 2123 and 954 0850 (Home)
17th and 18th c. Oriental porcelain plus 18th and 19th c. English and Continental porcelain.

STAIR AND COMPANY LTD
120 Mount Street
London W1Y 5HB
Tel: (01) 499 1784/5
18th c. Chinese porcelain.

TRAFALGAR ANTIQUES
117 Trafalgar Road
London SE10
Tel: (01) 858 3709
Porcelain from 1750–1900.

THE TRINKET BOX
1 Goldhurst Terrace
London NW6
Tel: (01) 624 4264
Victorian and Edwardian porcelain.

JOANNA WARRAND
99 Kensington Church Street
London W8
Tel: (01) 727 2333
18th and 19th c. English, Continental, and Oriental porcelain.

WELBANK
Shop 10, Angel Arcade
London N1
Tel: (01) 359 9558
Oriental porcelain.

WELLINGTON ANTIQUES
4 Wellington Terrace
London W2
Tel: (01) 221 6083
19th c. European porcelain.

WILBERRY ANTIQUES
32 Crawford Street
London W1
Tel: (01) 724 0606
Specialists in Staffordshire figures.

WINIFRED WILLIAMS
3 Bury Street
London SW1
Tel: (01) 930 4732
18th c. European porcelain of museum standard.

SOUTH AND SOUTHEAST ENGLAND

ADRIAN ALAN LTD
4 Frederick Place
Brighton, Sussex BN1 4EA
Tel: (0273) 25277/25015
18th and 19th c. porcelain.

APOLLO GALLERIES
61, 65 and 67 South End
Croydon, Surrey
Tel: (01) 681 3727/680 1968
18th and 19th c. English and Continental porcelain.

COLLECTOR'S CORNER
73 High Street
Teddington, Middx
Tel: (01) 977 1079 and 977 6450 (Home)
Late 18th to 19th c. porcelain.

COURT HOUSE ANTIQUES
19 Market Place
Brentford, Middx
Tel: (01) 560 7074 and Walton-on-Thames 27186
18th and 19th c. porcelain.

GREEN LANE ANTIQUES
1 Maxwell Road
Northwood, Middx
Tel: Northwood 22177
English porcelain, especially Worcester and Derby.

HOUSE OF ANTIQUES
4 College Street
Petersfield, Hants
Tel: (0730) 2172
18th and 19th c. porcelain.

SHIRLEY KING
2 Johnston Road
Woodford Green, Essex
Tel: (01) 505 5774
19th c. porcelain.

MALDWYN ANTIQUES
12–12a Beynon Parade
Carshalton, Surrey
Tel: (01) 669 0793 and 393 4530 (Home)
Porcelain from 1780 on.

MANOR HOUSE ANTIQUES
The Green
Datchet, Berks
Tel: (0753) 42164/41460
Oriental porcelain.

W.A. PINN AND SONS
124 Swan Street
Sible Hedingham
Halstead, Essex
Tel: (0787) 61127
17th to early 19th c. porcelain.

STANMORE HILL ANTIQUES
105 Stanmore Hill
Stanmore, Middx
Tel: (01) 954 0490
18th and 19th c. porcelain.

STEPPES HILL FARM ANTIQUES
Steppes Hill Farm
Stockbury
Sittingbourne, Kent
Tel: (0795) 842205
18th to 20th c. English porcelain.

THE TOKEN HOUSE
7 Market Parade, High Street
Ewell, Epsom, Surrey
Tel: (01) 393 9654
19th c. porcelain.

TRINITY ANTIQUES
7 Trinity Street
Colchester, Essex
Tel: (0206) 77775
Porcelain from 1720–1850.

VALION ANTIQUES
42 Chancery Lane
Beckenham, Kent
Tel: (01) 658 6644
18th and 19th c. porcelain.

WALTON ANTIQUES
7 Duke Street
Richmond, Surrey
Tel: (01) 948 2258 and 940 6519 (Home)
17th to 19th c. Chinese porcelain.

WINSTON GALLERIES
68 High Street
Harrow, Middx
Tel: (01) 422 4470
18th and 19th c. porcelain.

NORMAN WITHAM
2 High Street
Beckenham, Kent
Tel: (01) 650 4651
Victorian porcelain.

SOUTHWEST ENGLAND AND WALES

ABOYNE ANTIQUES
13 York Street
Bath, Avon
Tel: (0225) 64850 and 319961 (Home)
18th and 19th c. porcelain.

ALDBURY ANTIQUES
High Street, Blockley
Nr Moreton-in-Marsh, Glos
Tel: (0386) 700280
18th c. English porcelain.

BELL PASSAGE ANTIQUES
38 High Street, Wickwar
Wotton-under-Edge, Glos GL12 8NP
Tel: (045 424) 251
18th and 19th c. porcelain.

THE CELLAR ANTIQUES
17 High Street
Lampeter, Dyfed, Wales
Tel: (0570) 422531
Nantgarw, Swansea, English and Continental porcelain plus Delftware.

JOHN CROFT ANTIQUES
3 George Street
Bath, Avon
Tel: (0225) 66211
17th to early 19th c. porcelain.

DOLWEN ANTIQUES
430 Abergele Road
Old Colwyn, Colwyn Bay
Clwyd, Wales
Tel: (0492) 57823
Victorian and Edwardian porcelain vases and figures.

D.S. HUTCHINGS
The Annexe
210 Chepstow Road
Newport, Gwent, Wales
Tel: (0633) 65511
English and Welsh porcelain, especially Swansea and Nantgarw.

NIKKI ANTIQUES
123a Commercial Road
Lower Parkstone
Poole, Dorset BH14 0JD
Tel: (0202) 740939
English and Continental porcelain.

OLD BARN ANTIQUES COMPANY
The Abbey Antique Shop
Half Moon Street
Sherborne, Dorset
Tel: (093 581) 2068
18th and 19th c. porcelain.

OLD MARKET ANTIQUES
37 Old Market Street
Usk, Gwent, Wales
Tel: (029 13) 2813
Swansea, Nantgarw and Derby porcelain.

Left: A first period Worcester lozenge-shaped dish on scale blue ground, painted in the vase and mirror shaped reserves with exotic birds and flowers, from the Lady Mary Wortley Montagu service, courtesy of Steppes Hill Farm Antiques.

PENYGROES ANTIQUES
19a Water Street
Penygroes, Gwynedd, Wales
Tel: (028 689) 332
19th c. Oriental and British porcelain.

SHIRLEY VARLEY ANTIQUES
3 Lewis Buildings
Newton, nr Porthcawl
Mid Glamorgan, Wales
Tel: (065 671) 6460
18th and 19th c. English pottery and porcelain.

WEST WALES ANTIQUES
18 Manselfield Road
Bishopston, nr Swansea
W Glamorgan
Tel: (044 128) 4318
and
6a Crovus Terrace
St Clears, Dyfed, Wales
Tel: (0994) 230 576
18th c. porcelain, including Welsh porcelain from 1814–1820.

MIDLANDS AND EAST ANGLIA

ROBERT AND ELIZABETH ALLPORT
Corner Antique
Coltishall, Norfolk
Tel: (0603) 737631
18th and 19th c. porcelain.

COLIN DAVIES ANTIQUES
15 Wolverhampton Road
Stafford, Staffs
Tel: (0785) 40545
French porcelain.

GAVINA EWART
37 Sheep Street
Stratford-upon-Avon, Warks
Tel: (0789) 293917
18th and 19th c. English and Continental porcelain, specialising in pot lids and Prattware.

FEARNS ANTIQUES
9 Coleshill Street
Fazeley, nr Tamworth, Staffs
Tel: (0827) 54233
18th to early 20th c. porcelain.

ALAN GRANT ANTIQUES
Clifton
Rugby, Warks
Tel: (0788) 71165
Oriental porcelain.

NEVILL ANTIQUES
9–10 Milk Street
and
30–31 Princess Street
Shrewsbury, Shropshire
Tel: (0743) 51013
18th and 19th c. porcelain.

PATRICK TAYLOR ANTIQUES
First Floor Under Arch
13 St Peter's Street
Ipswich, Suffolk 1PI 1XF
Tel: (0473) 50774 (By appointment only)
18th and 19th c. English and Continental porcelain.

NORTH OF ENGLAND AND SCOTLAND

ADAMS ANTIQUES
65 Waterloo Row
Chester, Cheshire CH1 2LE
Tel: (0244) 319421
18th and 19th c. porcelain.

ALEXANDER ADAMSON
Hawthornden Castle
Lasswade, Lothian, Scotland
Tel: (031) 440 2180
and
48 St Stephen Street
Edinburgh, Lothian, Scotland
Tel: (031) 225 7310
18th and early 19th c. porcelain.

SCOTT ALLAN ORIENTAL ANTIQUES
35 Buccleuch Street
Edinburgh, Lothian, Scotland
Tel: (031) 667 3350
Chinese porcelain.

BIELDSIDE ANTIQUES
85 North Deeside Road
Bieldside, Aberdeen, Grampian, Scotland
Tel: (033 82) 296
18th and 19th c. porcelain.

CRIEFF ANTIQUES
Comrie Road
Crieff, Tayside, Scotland
Tel: (0764) 3322
Victorian porcelain.

THE EDWARDS GALLERY
20 Dundas Street
Edinburgh, Lothian, Scotland
Tel: (031) 557 1903
English and Continental porcelain, especially Royal Worcester.

J. FOSTER AND SON
19–21 Bell Street
St Andrews, Fife, Scotland
Tel: (0334) 72080
19th c. porcelain.

GROSVENOR ANTIQUES
22 Watergate Street
Chester, Cheshire CH1 2LA
Tel: (0244) 315201
Porcelain from all periods, including Art Deco.

HAREWOOD ANTIQUES
26–27 Harrogate Road
Harewood, Leeds, W Yorkshire LS17 9LH
Tel: (0532) 886327
Victorian porcelain.

THORNTON TAYLOR ANTIQUES
2c Fernleigh Road
Glasgow, Strathclyde, Scotland
Tel: (041) 637 7749
Porcelain from 1750–1850.

NORTHERN IRELAND

DUNLUCE ANTIQUES
33 Ballytober Road
Bushmills, Co Antrim BT57 8UU
N Ireland
Tel: (02657) 31140
18th and 19th c. porcelain, specialising in English manufacturers.

HAMILTON ANTIQUES
19 Shore Road
Holywood, Co Down, N Ireland
Tel: (023 17) 4404
19th c. porcelain.

POTTERY

LONDON

ANCHOR ANTIQUES LTD
26 Charing Cross Road
London WC2
Tel: (01) 836 5686 (By appointment only)
Continental and Oriental pottery.

THE ANTIQUE SHOP
6 Bellevue Road
London SW17
Tel: Not Available
Staffordshire pottery.

IAN AULD
1 Gateway Arcade
Camden Passage
London N1
Tel: (01) 359 1440
Pottery, including 18th c. English slipware.

ANTHONY BELTON
14 Holland Street
London W8
Tel: (01) 937 1012
and

ANTHONY BELTON (CON'T)
Collector's Corner
138 Portobello Road
London W11
Tel: (01) 748 2476
Pre-1830 English and European pottery including Wedgwood.

BRISIGOTTI ANTIQUES
186 Westbourne Grove
London W11
Tel: (01) 727 3493
Italian majolica.

CLUNES AND FOSTER ANTIQUES
9 West Place
Wimbledon Common
London W19
Tel: (01) 946 1643
Staffordshire figures.

COBWEB
2 Englands Lane
London NW3
Tel: (01) 586 4605
European and Far Eastern pottery.

JOHN CREED ANTIQUES LTD
3–5a Camden Passage
London N1
Tel: (01) 226 8867
Pottery, especially blue-printed earthenware 1780–1840.

RICHARD DENNIS
144 Kensington Church Street
London W8
Tel: (01) 727 2061
English studio pottery, especially Doulton, from 1870–1930.

JUDY FOX
81 Portobello Road
London W11
Tel: (01) 229 8130
Late 19th to early 20th c. pottery including Art Deco.

GALERIE 1900
267 Camden High Street
London NW1
Tel: (01) 485 1001 and 969 1803 (Home)
Art Nouveau and Art Deco pottery.

LESLEY HEPHERD ANTIQUES
47 Camden Passage
London N1
Tel: (01) 359 1755
Early 19th c. blue-and-white transferware and Masons ironstone.

JONATHAN HORNE
66c Kensington Church Street
London W8
Tel: (01) 221 5658
Early English and Continental pottery including Delftware, slipware, creamware, Staffordshire pottery and saltglazed stoneware, as well as 17th and 18th c. English and Dutch tiles.

ERIC HUDES
142 Portobello Road
London W11
Tel: (0376) 83767 (Home)
Early English pottery.

JELLINEK AND SAMPSON ANTIQUES
156 Brompton Road
London SW3
Tel: (01) 589 5272
17th and 18th c. English pottery.

LIBRA ANTIQUES
131e Kensington Church Street
London W8
Tel: (01) 727 2990
Blue-and-white pottery and lustreware.

TOBIAS JELLINEK LTD
18 Chepstow Corner
Chepstow Villas
London W2
Tel: (01) 727 5980
17th and 18th c. Continental pottery.

STEPHEN LONG
348 Fulham Road
London SW10
Tel: (01) 352 8226
18th and 19th c. English pottery.

LYONS GALLERY
47–49 Mill Lane
London NW6
Tel: (01) 794 3537
Art Nouveau and Art Deco pieces, including studio ceramics.

NOVISSIMO ANTIQUES
99 Church Road
London SW13
Tel: (01) 748 8151
Specialists in Mason's ironstone china.

E.R. O'CONNOR AND D. WALTER-ELLIS
19 Crawford Street
London W1
Tel: (01) 935 1245
Specialists in Majolica and Delft.

OLIVER-SUTTON ANTIQUES
34c Kensington Church Street
London W8 4HA
Tel: (01) 937 0633
Specialists in 19th c. Staffordshire pottery figures, claiming the largest and most comprehensive collection in the world. Additionally, other animals, cottages, pot lids and Parian ware.

THE PURPLE SHOP
15 Flood Street
London SW3
Tel: (01) 352 1127
Art Nouveau and Art Deco studio pottery.

RABIRAFFI ANCIENT ART
36 Davies Street
London W1
Tel: (01) 499 9363/9384
9th to 13th c. Islamic pottery.

RAPHAEL FINE ARTS LTD
DRC House, 2 Cornwall Terrace
London NW1 4QP
Tel: (01) 486 9931 (By appointment only)
Dutch Delft and tiles.

ROGERS DE RIN ANTIQUES
76 Royal Hospital Road
London SW3
Tel: (01) 352 9007
18th and 19th c. Scottish Wemyss ware and Staffordshire pottery.

SCHWARTZ
93 Blackheath Road
London SE10
Tel: (01) 692 1652
Early English and Oriental pottery.

CONSTANCE STOBO
31 Holland Street
London W8
Tel: (01) 937 6286
18th and 19th c. English lustreware and pottery.

VALE STAMPS AND ANTIQUES
21 Tranquil Vale
London SE3
Tel: (01) 852 9817
Pottery from 3000 BC–500 AD.

VERMOUTIER AND BANKS
25a Holland Street
London W8
Tel: (01) 937 3262
17th and 18th c. English pottery.

RON WELDON
109 Regents Park Road
London NW1
Tel: (01) 485 6210/4433
18th and 19th c. Staffordshire pottery.

CHRISTOPHER WOOD GALLERY
15 Motcomb Street
London SW1
Tel: (01) 235 9141/2
Victorian pottery including studio ceramics.

ROBERT YOUNG ANTIQUES
68 Battersea Bridge Road
London SW11
Tel: (01) 228 7847
Provinicial English pottery.

SOUTH AND SOUTHEAST ENGLAND

BIZZY LIZZY
6–8 Paved Court
Richmond, Surrey
Tel: (01) 940 1813
Victorian pottery.

MOLLIE EVANS
84 Hill Rise
Richmond, Surrey
Tel: (01) 948 0182 and 940 3720 (Home)
Studio pottery.

Left: "The Murder in the Red Barn" by Obadiah Sherratt, circa 1828, and "Travelling Menagerie Leopards", circa 1845 (below), both courtesy of Oliver-Sutton Antiques.

HOUSE OF MALLETT
67–69 Brighton Road
Surbiton, Surrey
Tel: (01) 390 3796
Art pottery.

ERIC HUDES
Paigles, Perry Green
Bradwell, Braintree, Essex CM7 8ES
Tel: (0376) 83767
Early English pottery.

MARKET PLACE ANTIQUES
35 Market Place
Henley-on-Thames, Oxon RG9 2AA
Tel: (04912) 2387
18th and 19th c. pottery. For illustrations, see entries under "Specialist Dealers, Kitchenware" and "Primitives".

THE OLD FORGE
Pilgrims Way
Hollingbourne, Kent ME17 1UW
Tel: (062 780) 360
Staffordshire pot lid and figures.

J. RANGER
148 Nine Mile Ride
Wokingham, Berks
Tel: (0734) 732754
Pottery including Staffordshire and Bisque figures, Clarice Cliff pottery plus early and Victorian Staffordshire portrait figures, animals, cottages and castles.

SPENCER SWAFFER
50 High Street
Arundel, W Sussex
Tel: (0903) 882132
Blue and white pottery.

TAURUS ANTIQUES LTD
145 Masons Hill
Bromley, Kent BR2 9HY
Tel: (01) 464 8746
Pottery and porcelain from 1800 on, including blue and white transfer ware.

SOUTHWEST ENGLAND AND WALES

FRAMFAM LTD
High Street
Moreton-in-Marsh, Glos
Tel: (0608) 50648
18th and 19th c. Staffordshire pottery.

LLANDOGO ANTIQUES
The Old Post Office
Llandogo, Gwent, Wales
Tel: (059 453) 213
Pottery from 1760–1880.

LONDON

DAVID ALEXANDER ANTIQUES
102 Waterford Road
London SW6
Tel: (01) 731 4644
Chinese pottery and porcelain.

ALBANY ANTIQUES LTD
79 Albany Street
London NW1
Tel: (01) 387 3187
18th and 19th c. English and Chinese pottery and porcelain.

ANCHOR ANTIQUES LTD
26 Charing Cross Road
London WC2
Tel: (01) 836 5686 (By appointment only)
Oriental pottery and porcelain.

Above: Pair of rare Staffordshire pointers, circa 1855, and a Staffordshire pastille burner, circa 1845, courtesy of J. Ranger.

MINETY ANTIQUES
Malmesbury, Wilts
Tel: (066 640) 255 (By appointment only)
Early pottery and creamware.

NORTH DEVON ANTIQUES
113 East Street
South Molton, N Devon
Tel: (076 95) 3184
18th c. pottery specialising in Mason's ironstone.

PETER PHILP
77 Kimberley Road
Cardiff, Glamorgan CF2 5DP, Wales
Tel: (0222) 493826
17th to 19th c. English and Welsh pottery.

MIDLANDS AND EAST ANGLIA

BITS AND PIECES
34 High Street
Higham Ferrers, Northants
and
3a Church Street
Finedon, Northants
Tel: (0933) 680430
Country-style pottery including blue transferware.

ANTIQUES LTD
18 Parson Street
London NW4
Tel: (01) 203 1194
18th and 19th c. pottery and porcelain.

ANTIQUE PUSSY
965 Fulham Road
London SW6
Tel: (01) 731 2814
Pottery and porcelain from 1650–1939.

ASTLEYS
109 Jermyn Street
London SW1
Tel: (01) 930 1687
Pottery and porcelain pipes.

NORTH OF ENGLAND AND SCOTLAND

DRAGON ANTIQUES
10 Dragon Road
Harrogate, N Yorkshire
Tel: (0423) 62037
Art Pottery including Art Nouveau and Art Deco pieces.

IMPERIAL FINE ARTS
304 Preston Road
Clayton-Le-Woods
Chorley, Lancs
Tel: (025 72) 63214
Specialists in early Mason's ironstone china.

OLDMILL ANTIQUES
68 Claremont Street
Aberdeen, Grampian, Scotland
Tel: (0224) 573562
Victorian pottery.

JANE POLLOCK ANTIQUES
4 Castlegate
Penrith, Cumbria
Tel: (0768) 67211 (By appointment only)
19th c. pottery specialising in blue-and-white and lustreware.

SUNFIELD ANTIQUES COTTAGE
Inchmarlo, Banchory,
Grampian, Scotland
Tel: (033 02) 2703
18th and 19th c. pottery.

ASTORIA
222 Munster Road
London SW6
Tel: (01) 385 9888
Art Deco pottery and porcelain.

AXIA
43 Pembridge Villas
London W11
Tel: (01) 727 9724
Islamic and Byzantine pottery and porcelain.

BARNES ANTIQUES
16 Lower Richmond Road
London SW15
Tel: (01) 789 3371
19th c. pottery and porcelain including Wedgwood and ironstone.

POTTERY AND PORCELAIN

G.P. BASTILLO AND SONS ANTIQUES
27 Battersea Rise
London SW11
Tel: (01) 223 5341 and 673 1792 (Home)
Georgian, Victorian and Edwardian pottery and porcelain.

SUSAN BECKER
18 Lower Richmond Road
London SW15
Tel: (01) 788 9082
English and Oriental pottery and porcelain.

BEVERLEY BROOK ANTIQUES
22 High Street
London SW13
Tel: (01) 878 4899 and 878 5656 (Home)
Regency, Victorian and Edwardian pottery and porcelain.

CALE ANTIQUES
24 Cale Street
Chelsea Green
London SW3
Tel: (01) 589 6146
Pre-1700 European and Chinese ceramics including Delft, majolica and faience.

CATHAY ANTIQUES
12 Thackeray Street
London W8
Tel: (01) 937 6066
18th c. Chinese and Japanese pottery and porcelain.

GERALD CLARK
1 High Street
London NW7
Tel: (01) 906 0342
18th and 19th c. English pottery and porcelain, specialising in animals, figures, burners and plaques.

DAVID CLARKE
Unit 1
105 Portobello Road
London W11
Tel: (085 886) 246 (after 6 pm)
English pottery and porcelain prior to 1760, specialising in useful pieces and those with rare shapes.

THE COLLECTOR ON LAVENDER HILL
43 Lavender Hill
London SW11
Tel: (01) 223 8683
Victorian and Art Deco pottery and porcelain.

JEREMY COOPER LTD
9 Galen Place
Bury Place
London WC1A 2JR
Tel: (01) 242 5138/404 0336
Pottery and porcelain from 1830–1940, including studio ceramics.

THE CORNER CUPBOARD
679 Finchley Road
London NW2
Tel: (01) 435 4870
18th and 19th c. pottery and porcelain.

TONY DAVIS INC
235–9 Lavender Hill
London SW11
Tel: (01) 228 1370/1 and 223 9532 (Home)
Victorian and Edwardian pottery and porcelain.

SHIRLEY DAY LTD
59–60 Jermyn Street
London SW1
Tel: (01) 491 1916
Japanese ceramics.

H. AND W. DEUTSCH ANTIQUES
111 Kensington Church Street
London W8
Tel: (01) 727 5984
18th and 19th c. English and Continental pottery and porcelain.

FINCHLEY FINE ART GALLERIES
983 High Road
London N12
Tel: (01) 446 4848
18th to early 20th c. pottery and porcelain.

FOREST HILL ANTIQUES
7 Davids Road
London SE23
Tel: (01) 699 4061 and 693 5050 (Home)
18th to early 20th c. pottery and porcelain, including Art Nouveau and Art Deco.

GODDARD AND FARMER
8 Thackeray Street
London W8
Tel: (01) 937 4917
Victorian pottery and porcelain.

GORE AND PLAYER
49 Church Road
London SW13
Tel: (01) 748 8850 and 748 7644 (Home)
18th and 19th c. pottery and porcelain.

GOSSLAND COLLECTABLES
286 Westbourne Grove
London W11
Tel: Not Available
Commemoratives, Prattware, Parian ware, pot lids, Goss and crested china, Old Bill pottery, Wemyss, Moorcroft and Doulton ware, fairings and Victorian pieces.

GRACE ANTIQUES
28 Pembridge Villas
London W11 3EL
Tel: (01) 229 4415
18th and 19th c. pottery and porcelain.

GRAHAM AND OXLEY LTD
101 Kensington Church Street
London W8 7LN
Tel: (01) 229 1850
18th and early 19th c. English pottery and porcelain.

ELIA GRAHAME
97a Kensington Church Street
London W8
Tel: (01) 727 4132
18th c. pottery and porcelain.

GREAT EXPECTATIONS
62 Old Church Street
London SW3
Tel: (01) 352 9850
19th c. pottery and porcelain.

GORDON GRIDLEY
41 Camden Passage
London N1
Tel: (01) 226 0643/9033
17th to early 19th c. English, Continental and Oriental pottery and porcelain.

JOHN HALL ANTIQUES AND PRINTS
17 Harrington Road
London SW7 3ES
Tel: (01) 584 1307
18th and 19th c. pottery and porcelain figures including named Victorian Staffordshire portrait figures. See overleaf for illustration.

THE HAY LOFT
332 Upper Richmond Road
London SW14
Tel: (01) 876 5020
Pottery and porcelain from 1800–1930. See overleaf for illustration.

HOLBEIN ANTIQUES LTD
8 Holbein Place
London SW1
Tel: (01) 730 1957
Specialists in jardinières.

Left: Longton Hall Middle Period spoon tray by the castle painter, John Hayfield, circa 1753, courtesy of David Clarke.

THE HOUSE OF ANDOR
17a The Burroughs
London NW4
Tel: Not Available
18th and 19th c. porcelain and pot lids.

J.C. ANTIQUES
12 Warwick Terrace
London E17
Tel: (01) 539 4275 and 802 0582 (Home)
19th c. pottery and porcelain.

JAPANESE GALLERY
66d Kensington Church Street
London W8
Tel: (01) 229 2934 and 226 3347 (Home)
Japanese ceramics.

JONES
194 Westbourne Grove
London W11
Tel: (01) 229 6866
*Decorative ceramics, from 1880–1940,
especially Moorcroft.*

JUST A SECOND ANTIQUES
40 Fulham High Street
London SW6
Tel: (01) 731 1919 and 673 1793 (Home)
*Pottery and porcelain, Georgian to
Edwardian.*

JUSTUS ANTIQUES
82 Buckingham Gate
London SW1
Tel: (01) 222 5251
Specialists in commemorative ware.

THE LACQUER CHEST
75 Kensington Church Street
London W8
Tel: (01) 937 1306
*Pottery and porcelain from 1800, specialising
in the unusual.*

*Below: Selection of Victorian pottery and
porcelain including two Staffordshire figures,
courtesy of The Hay Loft.*

LEDGER ANTIQUES LTD
101a Fulham Road
London SW3
Tel: (01) 581 0922 and 584 6436 (Home)
*Mason's patent ironstone china from
1800–1840; Staffordshire houses and castles
from 1780–1860; naval and military figures
from 1800–1860.*

*Above: Interior view showing a selection of
figures available at John Hall Antiques and
Prints.*

PETER MANHEIM LTD
69 Upper Berkeley Street
London W1
Tel: (01) 723 6596
English pottery, and porcelain.

POTTERY AND PORCELAIN

S. MARCHANT AND SON
120 Kensington Church Street
London W8
Tel: (01) 229 5319
Chinese and Japanese pottery and porcelain.

G. AND M. MARDELLIS
109 Kensington Church Street
London W8
Tel: (01) 727 7413
Oriental pottery and porcelain.

MARTINS-FORREST ANTIQUES
8 Halkin Arcade
Motcomb Street
London SW1
Tel: (01) 235 8353 and 341 0673 (Home)
Art Nouveau and Art Deco pottery and porcelain.

JEREMY J. MASON ORIENTAL ART
145 Ebury Street
London SW1
Tel: (01) 730 6971 and 874 4173 (Home)
Chinese pottery and porcelain.

J. AND J. MAY
40 Kensington Church Street
London W8
Tel: (01) 937 3575
Commemorative pottery and porcelain from 1750–1850.

MERCURY ANTIQUES
1–1b Ladbroke Road
London W11
Tel: (01) 727 5106
English porcelain from 1750–1850, English pottery and Delft from 1720–1850.

SYDNEY L. MOSS LTD
51 Brook Street
London W1
Tel: (01) 629 4670/493 7374
Chinese and Japanese ceramics from 1500 B.C. to 1900 A.D.

NAYLORS
131 Munster Road
London SW6
Tel: (01) 731 3679
Pottery and porcelain from 1850–1950.

Below: A selection of Victorian jardinières, courtesy of Barrie Quinn Antique.

Above: 18th c. porcelain sake ewer from Arita, Japan, courtesy of Nihon Token.

H.W. NEWBY
130c Brompton Road
London SW3
Tel: (01) 589 2752
Porcelain, faience, and pottery, all pre-1830.

NIHON TOKEN
23 Museum Street
London WC1
Tel: (01) 580 6511 and 444 6726 (Home)
Japanese pottery and porcelain.

PEEL ANTIQUES
131d Kensington Church Street
London W8
Tel: (01) 727 8928
18th and early 19th c. English and Chinese porcelain and pottery.

PORTMEIRION ANTIQUES
5 Pont Street
London SW1
Tel: (01) 235 7601
Pottery and porcelain from 1700–1900.

BARRIE QUINN ANTIQUES
1, 3 and 4 Broxholme House
New Kings Road
London SW6
Tel: (01) 736 4747
Specialist in Victorian jardinières.

RAVEN ANTIQUES
256 Lee High Road
London SE13
Tel: (01) 852 5066
Staffordshire figures from 1790–1900 plus English and Continental porcelain from 1780–1900.

SCHWARTZ
93 Blackheath Road
London SE10
Tel: (01) 692 1652
Early English pottery and Oriental pottery and porcelain.

SENSATION LTD
62 and 66 Fulham High Street
London SW6
Tel: (01) 736 4135
17th to 19th c. pottery and porcelain.

JEAN SEWELL ANTIQUES LTD
3 Campden Street
London W8
Tel: (01) 727 3122
18th and 19th c. porcelain and 19th c. pottery.

SPREAD EAGLE ANTIQUES
22 and 23 Nelson Road
London SE10
Tel: (01) 692 1618
19th c. pottery and porcelain.

LAURI STEWART ANTIQUES
36 Church Lane
London N2
Tel: (01) 883 7719
Victorian, European pottery and porcelain.

JACOB STODEL ANTIQUES
116 Kensington Church Street
London W8 4BH
Tel: (01) 221 2652
17th to 19th c. European pottery and porcelain.

SUNDRIDGE ANTIQUES
564 Kings Road
Londons SW6
Tel: (01) 736 0828
Pottery and porcelain from 1750–1920.

OLIVER SUTTON ANTIQUES
34c Kensington Church Street
London W8
Tel: (01) 937 0633
Staffordshire portrait figures, pot lids, and marked Parian ware.

TEMPUS ANTIQUES
43 Kensington Church Street
London W8
Tel: (01) 937 4359
Japanese pottery and porcelain.

J. VAN BEERS
1–7 Davies Mews
London W1
Tel: (01) 408 0434
Oriental and European ceramics.

EARLE D. VANDEKAR
138 Brompton Road
London SW3 1HY
Tel: (01) 589 8481/3398
Oriental porcelain, European (including English) faience and pottery.

Right: One of a pair of 19th c. rosewood Oriental-style tables with marble tops, a blue-and-white tureen, circa 1820, and a late 19th c. Tibetan rug, courtesy of The Gallery.

VENNERS ANTIQUES
7 New Cavendish Street
London W1
Tel: (01) 935 0184
18th and 19th c. English pottery and porcelain.

W. 13 ANTIQUES
10 The Avenue
London W13
Tel: (01) 998 0390
18th and 19th c. pottery and porcelain.

WALBROOK
c/o Betty and Vera Vandekar
101b Kensington Church Street
London W8
Tel: (01) 727 2471
18th and 19th c. Oriental and Continental pottery and porcelain.

WATERBYRN LTD
11 St John's Wood High Street
London NW8
Tel: (01) 722 7058
19th c. pottery and porcelain.

MARY WISE
27 Holland Street
London W8
Tel: (01) 937 8649
18th and 19th c. English, Continental and Chinese pottery and porcelain.

P. AND L. WOOLMAN
351 Upper Street
London N1
Tel: (01) 359 7648 and 340 2468 (Home)
Pottery and porcelain from 1800–1930.

SOUTH AND SOUTHEAST ENGLAND

C. CLEALL ANTIQUES
16 Brewers Lane
Richmond, Surrey
Tel: (01) 940 8069
Art Nouveau and Art Deco pottery and porcelain.

BELINDA COOTE ANTIQUES
63 High Street
Hartley Wintney, Hants
Tel: (025 126) 2213
18th and 19th c. pottery and porcelain, specialising in ironstone.

THE GALLERY
18 Endwell Road
Bexhill-on-Sea, E Sussex
Tel: (0424) 212127
Pottery and porcelain from 17th to late 19th c.

HILL RISE ANTIQUES
26 Hill Rise
Richmond, Surrey
Tel: (01) 948 1140 and 876 4114 (Home)
19th c. pottery and porcelain.

JOHN LESLIE ANTIQUES
14 Foxfield Close
Northwood, Middx
Tel: Northwood 21184 (By appointment only)
18th and 19th c. English porcelain and pottery, especially blue and white.

MARGARET MCCLOY ANTIQUES
49 Surbiton Road
Kingston, Surrey
Tel: (01) 549 6423
Victorian and Edwardian pottery and porcelain.

B.M. NEWLOVE
139–141 Ewell Road
Surbiton, Surrey
Tel: (01) 399 8857
18th and 19th c. pottery and porcelain.

THE OLD HOUSE
15–17 High Street
Seaford, Sussex
Tel: (0323) 892091
18th to early 20th c. pottery and porcelain.

PAMELA AND BARRY ANTIQUES
126 Sandridge Road
St Albans, Herts
Tel: St Albans 51109
18th and 19th c. pottery and porcelain.

PENNY FARTHING ANTIQUES
71 High Street
Chobham, Surrey
Tel: (099 05) 7718
18th and 19th c. English and Continental porcelain and pottery.

SUNDRIDGE ANTIQUES
4 Sundridge Parade
Plaistow Lane
Bromley, Kent
Tel: (01) 460 8164
Pottery and porcelain from 1750–1920.

SOUTHWEST ENGLAND AND WALES

AUSTIN ANTIQUES
Stoke St Gregory
Taunton, Somerset
Tel: (082 349) 481
Mason's ironstone, Miles Mason porcelain, Staffordshire figures and pottery.

CASTLE ANTIQUES
41 Old Market Street
Usk, Gwent, Wales
Tel: (029 13) 2424
English and Welsh pottery and porcelain including blue and white transfer ware.

ANGELA CLEMENT ANTIQUES
First Floor
37 East Street
Blandford Forum, Dorset
Tel: (0258) 53472
Victorian and Regency pottery and porcelain.

R. AND D. COOMBES
The Old Priest House
Aldbourne
Marlborough, Wilts
Tel: (0672) 40241
Oriental ceramics, 18th c. and earlier.

CORNER HOUSE ANTIQUES
31a Rivers Street
Bath, Avon
Tel: Not Available
18th to early 20th c. pottery and porcelain and Victorian tiles.

ANDREW DANDO
4 Wood Street
Queen Square
Bath, Avon
Tel: (0225) 22702
English, Continental and Oriental 17th to mid-19th c. pottery and porcelain.

GERALD DEACON
2 Wood Street
Queen Square
Bath, Avon
Tel: (0225) 25907
18th and early 19th c. English pottery and porcelain.

RAGLAN ANTIQUES
High Street
Raglan, Gwent, Wales
Tel: (0291) 690327
*17th and 18th c. pottery and porcelain
including Delft.*

TAMAR GALLERY
5 Church Street
Launceston, Cornwall
Tel: (0566) 4233
*18th and early 19th c. English blue and white
pottery and porcelain.*

MORRIS TUCKER
Lower Town House
Chudleigh Knighton, Devon TQ13 0ME
Tel: (0626) 852123
*Specialist in maritime and country pottery and
porcelain.*

MIDLANDS AND EAST ANGLIA

LIZ ALLPORT
Corner Antiques
Coltishall Antiques Centre
Coltishall, Norfolk
Tel: (0603) 737631
*19th c. pottery and porcelain including pot
lids and Prattware.*

MELVILLE KEMP LTD
89–91 Derby Road
Nottingham NG1 5BB
Tel: (0602) 417055
18th and 19th c. pottery and porcelain.

LINDUM ANTIQUES
Donington-on-Bain
Louth, Lincs
Tel: (0507) 84639
Early pottery and porcelain.

NORTH OF ENGLAND AND SCOTLAND

ANDERSON AND SLATER ANTIQUES
8 King Street
Knutsford, Cheshire WA16 6DL
Tel: (0565) 2917
18th and 19th c. pottery and porcelain.

*Below: Porcelain jug decorated in polychrome
commemorating a perjury trial in Cornwall in
1830, courtesy of Morris Tucker.*

**BURNLEY ANTIQUES AND FINE
ARTS LTD**
336a Colne Road
Burnley, Lancs
Tel: (0282) 20143
Pottery and porcelain.

ELM HOUSE ANTIQUES
The Sands, Church Street
Haddington, Lothian, Scotland
Tel: (062 082) 3413
*18th and 19th c. English porcelain,
specialising in blue and white earthenware
and Scottish pottery.*

FAIR MAID'S HOUSE
North Port
Perth, Tayside, Scotland
Tel: (0783) 25976
*Scottish and English porcelain; Doulton and
Art Pottery.*

FELTON PARK ANTIQUES
Felton Park
Felton, Northld NE65 9HN
Tel: (067 087) 652 and 319 (Home)
*Pottery and porcelain including Newhall,
Sunderland lustreware and blue and white
transferware.*

WILLIAM GOODFELLOW
The Green
Over Kellet
Carnforth, Lancs LA6 1BU
Tel: (0524) 733030
*English pottery and porcelain pre-1850 and
Oriental porcelain 1700 to 1870.*

NEWGATE ANTIQUES
59 Newgate Street
Morpeth, Northld
Tel: (0670) 56875
*19th c. Newcastle and Sunderland pottery;
18th and 19th c. porcelain, including first
period Worcester and Royal Worcester.*

PAUL M. PETERS ANTIQUES
15 Bower Road
Harrogate, N Yorkshire
Tel: (0423) 60118
*17th to 19th c. European, Chinese and
Japanese ceramics.*

*Right: Selection of English pottery,
porcelain and glass, courtesy of William
Goodfellow Antiques.*

JAN STRUTHER
13 Randolph Place
Edinburgh, Lothian, Scotland
Tel: (031) 226 4563
*English pottery and porcelain, especially
English Delftware.*

TREASURE HOUSE
16 Holburn Street
Aberdeen, Grampian, Scotland
Tel: (0224) 20219
Georgian and Victorian pottery and porcelain.

NORTHERN IRELAND

COOKSTOWN ANTIQUES
11a Oldtown Street
Cookstown, Co Tyrone, N Ireland
Tel: (064 87) 65279
Victorian pottery and porcelain.

OLD CROSS ANTIQUES
3–5 Main Street
Greyabbey, Co Down, N Ireland
Tel: (024 774) 346
*Porcelain and Staffordshire pottery from
1800–1900.*

LONDON

THE ARK ANGEL
14 Camden Passage
London N1
Tel: (01) 226 1644
Primitive paintings.

ASTLEYS
109 Jermyn Street
London SW1
Tel: (01) 930 1687
16th to 18th c. "primitive" pipes.

CENTAUR GALLERY
82 Highgate High Street
London N6
Tel: (01) 340 0087
18th and early 19th c. folk art and primitives.

CRANE ARTS LTD
321 Kings Road
London SW3
Tel: (01) 352 5857
18th to early 20th c. naive paintings.

FIVE FIVE SIX ANTIQUES
556 Kings Road
London SW6
Tel: (01) 731 2016 and 624 5173 (Home)
18th and early 19th c. primitive paintings with children, animal and landscape subjects.

JELLINEK AND SAMPSON
156 Brompton Road
London SW3
Tel: (01) 589 5272
Primitive pictures.

PHILIP
59 Ledbury Road
London W11
Tel: (01) 727 7915
16th and 17th c. primitive paintings.

POTTLES
6 Camden Walk
Camden Passage
London N1
Tel: (01) 226 9438
Primitive paintings.

RUTLAND GALLERY
32a St George Street
London W1
Tel: (01) 499 5636
British and American primitive paintings.

VERMOUTIER AND BANKS
25a Holland Street
London W8
Tel: (01) 937 3262
18th and 19th c. primitive paintings.

SOUTH AND SOUTHEAST ENGLAND

ANGELA PAGE ANTIQUES
Sion House
15 Mount Sion
Tunbridge Wells, Kent
Tel: (0892) 22217
English and N European folk art.

MARKET PLACE ANTIQUES
35 Market Place
Henley-on-Thames, Oxon RG9 2AA
Tel: (04912) 2387
Primitives including treen.

Above: From left to right, a Scandinavian horn ladle, 19th c. saltglaze tobacco jar, oil painting of dog with two monkeys in maple frame, circa 1825, and an inland wooden "Fox and Geese" board with turned pegs, courtesy of Market Place Antiques.

SOUTHWEST ENGLAND AND WALES

MORRIS TUCKER
Lower Town House
Chudleigh Knighton, Devon TQ13 OME
Tel: (0626) 852123
Specialist in maritime and country items including primitive portraits and American Indian artifacts.

LONDON

ABBOTT AND HOLDER
73 Castlenau
London SW13
Tel: (01) 748 2416
18th to early 20th c. prints under £500.

ARTHUR ACKERMANN AND SON
3 Old Bond Street
London W1
Tel: (01) 493 3288/629 0592
English sporting prints.

THOMAS AGNEW AND SONS LTD
43 Old Bond Street
London W1X 4BA
Tel: (01) 629 6176
English prints and engravings of all schools.

J. ASH RARE BOOKS
25 Royal Exchange
London EC3
Tel: (01) 626 2665
Maps and prints from 1550–1900.

ASTORIA
222 Munster Road
London SW6
Tel: (01) 385 9888
Art Deco etchings, engravings, lithographs and woodcuts.

M. AYRES
31 Museum Street
London WC2
Tel: (01) 636 2844
Antiquarian etchings.

H. BARON
136 Chatsworth Road
London NW2 5QU
Tel: (01) 459 2035 (By appointment only)
Engraved or lithographed musicians' portraits.

BASKETT AND DAY
173 New Bond Street
London W1
Tel: (01) 629 2991
16th to 19th c. Old Master prints.

BAYNTON-WILLIAMS
18 Lowndes Street
London SW1
Tel: (01) 235 6595/6
Sporting, marine and decorative prints and maps up to 1850.

TONY BINGHAM
11 Pond Street
London NW3 2PN
Tel: (01) 794 1596
Engravings of musicians or of musical subjects.

THE BRAMPTONS
70 Marchmont Street
London WC1
Tel: (01) 837 5584
Maps and prints, especially of London and including Dickens.

FOR MAP OF LONDON'S POSTAL DISTRICTS, SEE PAGE 61

Left: Etching and aquatint printed in sepia, by and after D. Sandlay, 1777, courtesy of the Burlington Gallery Ltd.

STANLEY CROWE LTD
5 Bloomsbury Street
London WC1
Tel: (01) 580 3976
Views and maps of Great Britain including Ireland.

DAVIES ANTIQUES
10 Gloucester Road
London SW7
Tel: (01) 584 8271
18th and 19th c. maps and prints.

DAWSON RARE BOOKS
16–17 Pall Mall
London SW1
Tel: (01) 930 2515
Maps from 1500 to 1900.

JOHN DENHAM
The Gallery
50 Mill Lane
London NW6
Tel: (01) 794 2635
17th to early 20th c. prints.

SEBASTIAN D'ORSAI LTD
39 Theobalds Road
London WC2
Tel: (01) 405 6663
Framed prints.

DOUWES FINE ART
38 Duke Street
London SW1
Tel: (01) 839 5795
Old Master prints.

ROBERT DOUWMA LTD
93 Great Russell Street
London WC1
Tel: (01) 636 4895
Maps and engravings to late 19th c. See overleaf for illustration.

Below: Etching and aquatint of Coraig Castle, Carmarthenshire, after Paul Sandby, RA, circa 1810, courtesy of John Denham.

THE BROTHERTON GALLERY LTD
77 Walton Street
London SW3
Tel: (01) 589 6848
19th c. landscape, natural history and sporting prints.

CLIVE BURDEN LTD
13 Cecil Court
Charing Cross Road
London WC2
Tel: (01) 836 2177 (By appointment only)
Maps from 1500–1860 and prints from 1720–1870.

BURLINGTON GALLERY LTD
10 Burlington Gardens
London W1X 1LG
Tel: (01) 734 9228
18th and 19th c. topographical, sporting and decorative prints.

JOHN CAMPBELL
164 Walton Street
London SW3
Tel: (01) 584 9268
19th and 20th c. posters and lithographs.

CATHAY ANTIQUES
12 Thackeray Street
London W8
Tel: (01) 937 6066
18th c. Japanese and Chinese prints.

CENTAUR GALLERY
82 Highgate High Street
London N6
Tel: (01) 340 0087
18th and early 19th c. prints.

CHAPMAN AND DAVIES ANTIQUES
10 Theberton Street
London N1
Tel: (01) 226 5565/348 4846/359 4330
17th to early 20th c. prints.

CHELSEA RARE BOOKS
313 Kings Road
London SW3
Tel: (01) 351 0950
Antiquarian maps and prints.

CINEMA BOOKSHOP
13–14 Great Russell Street
London WC1
Tel: (01) 637 0206
Cinema posters.

ARMITAGE CLARKE
9 Blenheim Street
New Bond Street
London W1
Tel: (01) 493 8828/629 0308
Sporting and marine prints.

J. CLARKE-HALL LTD
7 Bride Court
Off Fleet Street
London EC4
Tel: (01) 353 4116
19th c. prints.

COHEN AND PEARCE
84 Portobello Road
London W11
Tel: (01) 229 9458
Japanese prints.

CRADDOCK AND BARNARD
32 Museum Street
London WC1
Tel: (01) 636 3937
Engravings, etchings and woodcuts from the 15th c. on.

CHRISTOPHER DRAKE
10 Maddox Street
London W1
Tel: (01) 629 5571
Old Master prints.

DUNDON FINE ART LTD
55 Teddington Park
Teddington, Middx TW11 8DE
Tel: (01) 977 8416
*British and European prints from 1800
onwards.*

DODO
185 Westbourne Grove
London W11
Tel: (01) 229 3132
*Printed ephemera including advertisement
posters, signs, plus tin and crate labels.*

MADAME J. DUPONTS ET FILS
68 Lincoln Road
London N2
Tel: (01) 883 7852 (By appointment only)
18th and 19th c. maps and prints.

EAST ASIA COMPANY
103 Camden High Street
London NW1
Tel: (01) 388 5783
Japanese and Chinese prints.

EYRE AND HOBHOUSE LTD
39 Duke Street
London SW1
Tel: (01) 930 9308
*19th c. aquatints and prints relating to
subjects by European artists in India and the
Far East.*

FAUSTUS
94 Jermyn Street
London SW1
Tel: (01) 930 1864
Old Master etchings.

FIDDES WATT GALLERY
Studio 7, 249 Kensal Road
London W10
Tel: (01) 864 0766
*Prints, specialising in those by Scottish
artists.*

FORTESCUE SWAN GALLERIES
238 Brompton Road
London SW3
Tel: (01) 584 4736
Sporting prints.

J.A.L. FRANKS LTD
180 Fleet Street
London EC4
Tel: (01) 405 0274
Antiquarian maps.

GALLERY KALEIDOSCOPE
66 Willesden Lane
London NW6
Tel: (01) 328 5833
18th to early 20th c. prints.

ROBIN GARTON
9 Lancshire Court, New Bond Street
London W1
Tel: (01) 493 2820
*Old Master and British prints from
1850–1940.*

STANLEY GIBBONS
391, 395 and 399 Strand
London WC2
Tel: (01) 836 8444
Antique maps and topographic prints.

GORE AND PLAYER
49 Church Road
London SW13
Tel: (01) 748 8850 and 748 7644 (Home)
18th and 19th c. engravings.

ELIA GRAHAME
97a Kensington Church Street
London W8
Tel: (01) 727 4132
Early prints.

GODDARD AND FARMER
8 Thackeray Street
London W8
Tel: (01) 937 4917
Victorian prints.

RICHARD GREEN
36 and 44 Dover Street
London W1
Tel: (01) 493 7997/491 3277
*Old Masters, sporting and 19th c. English
prints.*

JOHN HALL ANTIQUES AND PRINTS
17 Harrington Road
London SW7
Tel: (01) 584 1307
*Theatrical prints and playbills from
1760–1900; engraved and lithographed music
fronts; greetings cards and postcards from
1800–1900.*

HALCYON DAYS
14 Brook Street
London W1Y 1AA
Tel: (01) 629 8111
18th and 19th c. prints.

JULIAN HARTNOLL
Second Floor
14 Mason's Yard
Duke Street
London SW1
Tel: (01) 839 3842 (By appointment only)
Victorian engravings.

*Right: "Woman After Her Bath", a
woodcut by Hashiguchi Goyo, first published
in 1920, courtesy of the Japanese Gallery.*

*Above: De Wit's panorama of London, circa
1680, courtesy of Robert Douwma Ltd.*

HELGATO
50 Highgate High Street
London N6 5HX
Tel: (01) 348 3864
English maps and prints to 1900.

B. HIRSCHLER
62 Portland Avenue
and
71 Dunsmore Road
London N16
Tel: (01) 800 6395
Maps of Palestine.

THE HOLLAND PRESS LTD
37 Connaught Street
London W2 2A2
Tel: (01) 262 6184
Antique maps.

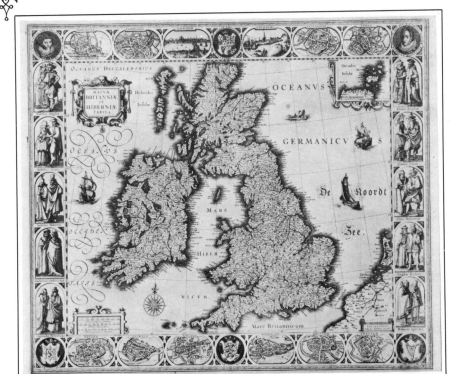

J.C. ANTIQUES
12 Warwick Terrace
London E17
Tel: (01) 539 4275 and 802 0582 (Home)
17th to early 19th c. prints.

JAPANESE GALLERY
66d Kensington Church Street
London W8
Tel: (01) 229 2934 and 226 3347 (Home)
Japanese wood-cut prints.

JUSTUS ANTIQUES
82 Buckingham Gate
London SW1
Tel: (01) 222 5251
Specialists in ''Spy'' cartoons.

Above: Copper plate engraving map of the British Isles, published in Amsterdam by Jodocus Hondius, circa 1625, courtesy of The Map House.

RICHARD KRUML
47 Albemarle Street
London W1
Tel: (01) 629 3017 (By appointment only)
Japanese prints.

COLIN LACY GALLERY
38 Ledbury Road
London W11
Tel: (01) 229 9105
Decorative, sporting and marine prints.

LEINSTER FINE ART
9 Hereford Road
London W2 4AB
Tel: (01) 229 9985
Belle Epoque prints and posters.

LONDON POSTCARD CENTRE
21 Kensington Park Road
London W11
Tel: (01) 229 1888 and 727 0505
Posters, photographs and advertising ephemera.

LORDS GALLERY
26 Wellington Road
London NW8
Tel: (01) 722 4444
19th and early 20th c. original posters, including Kurt Schwitters and Friedrich Meckseper.

N.W. LOTT AND H.J. GERRISH LTD
14 Mason's Yard, Duke Street
London SW1
Tel: (01) 930 1353
19th and 20th c. etchings.

PETER LOVEDAY PRINTS
46 Norland Square
London W11 4PZ
Tel: (01) 221 4479
Prints, especially of British sporting life.

LUMLEY CAZALET LTD
24 Davies Street
London W1
Tel: (01) 499 5058
Late 19th and early 20th c. prints.

FINBAR MACDONNELL
17 Camden Passage
London N1
Tel: (01) 226 0537
Prints and maps, pre-1850.

THE MAP HOUSE
54 Beauchamp Place
London SW3
Tel: (01) 589 4325/9821
Antique and rare maps.

Below: Map of the world in two hemispheres, published by Gerald Mercator in 1595, courtesy of Mapsellers Ltd.

Below: ''The Wheelwright'', a line engraving by Stanley Anderson, dated 1939, from an edition of 50, courtesy of N.W. Lott and H.J. Gerrish Ltd.

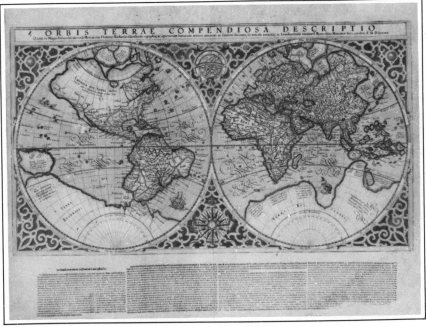

MAPSELLERS LTD
37 Southampton Street
London WC2E 7HE
Tel: (01) 836 8444
16th to late 19th c. European and world maps.
See previous page for illustration.

PAUL MASON GALLERY
149 Sloane Street
London SW1X 9BZ
Tel: (01) 730 3683
18th and 19th c. marine and sporting prints.

MATTHIESEN FINE ART LTD
6 Mason's Yard, Duke Street
London SW1
Tel: (01) 930 2437
19th and early 20th c. British and Continental prints.

CHRISTOPHER MENDEZ
51 Lexington Street
London W1
Tel: (01) 734 2385
Old Master engravings, etchings and woodcuts, up to 1800; 18th c. English prints.

MILNE HENDERSON
99 Mount Street
London W1
Tel: (01) 499 2507
Chinese and Japanese prints.

THE MOORLAND GALLERY
23 Cork Street
London W1
Tel: (01) 734 6961
Sporting and wildlife prints.

MRS MUNRO ANTIQUES LTD
11 Montpelier Street
London SW7
Tel: (01) 589 0686/5052
18th and 19th c. prints.

NICODEMUS
27 Lacy Road
London SW15
Tel: (01) 789 2838
Pre-Edwardian prints.

NIHON TOKEN
23 Museum Street
London WC1
Tel: (01) 580 6511 and 444 6726 (Home)
Japanese prints.

OLD LONDON GALLERY
15 Royal Opera Arcade
Pall Mall
London SW1
Tel: (01) 930 7679
18th and 19th c. prints, some hand-coloured and some London subjects.

RAYMOND O'SHEA GALLERY
6 Ellis Street
London SW1
Tel: (01) 730 0082
Maps and prints from 1486–1850, including celestial charts.

GERALD OSOSKI
7 Heath Hurst Road
London NW3
Tel: (01) 435 2959
16th to early 20th c. Old Master prints.

Right: Original softground etching, "La Danse à la Campagne" by Pierre Auguste Renoir, dated 1897, courtesy of the William Weston Gallery Ltd.

PARK GALLERIES
20 Hendon Lane
London N3
Tel: (01) 346 2176
18th to earth 20th c. prints.

MICHAEL PARKIN FINE ART LTD
11 Motcomb Street
London SW1
Tel: (01) 235 8144
British prints from 1840–1940.

PLEASURES OF PAST TIMES
11 Cecil Court
London WC2
Tel: (01) 836 1142
19th c. Posters and playbills.

JONATHAN POTTER LTD
1 Grafton Street
London W1
Tel: (01) 491 3520
16th to 19th c. maps and 18th and 19th c. prints.

ROYAL EXCHANGE ART GALLERY
14 Royal Exchange
London EC3
Tel: (01) 283 4400
19th and early 20th c. etchings specialising in marine and landscape subjects.

SARUM
10 Chapel Street
Belgrave Square
London SW1
Tel: (01) 235 6744
16th to 18th c. maps.

SCHWARTZ
93 Blackheath Road
London SE10
Tel: (01) 692 1652
Japanese prints.

JULIAN SIMON FINE ART
135 Kings Road
London SW3
Tel: (01) 351 1096
18th and 19th c. British and European watercolours.

HENRY SOTHERAN LTD
2–5 Sackville Street
London W1X 2DP
Tel: (01) 734 1150
18th and early 20th c. maps and prints.

CHARLES SPENCER THEATRE GALLERY
82 York Street
London W1H 1DP
Tel: (01) 723 5772
Prints and portraits for the theatre over four centuries, including designs for Irving, Bernhardt, the Ballets Russes, the Folies Bergère and the Royal Ballet and Opera companies. For illustration, see entry under "Specialist Dealers Paintings".

SPREAD EAGLE ANTIQUES
8 Nevada Street
London SE10
Tel: (01) 692 1618
19th c. prints.

HAROLD T. STOREY
3 Cecil Court
Charing Cross Road
London WC2
Tel: (01) 836 3777
19th c. engravings.

TAURUS GALLERY
637 Fulham Road
London SW6
Tel: (01) 736 1031
17th to 19th c. engravings and prints.

TRAVIS AND EMERY
17 Cecil Court
London WC2
Tel: (01) 240 2129
Prints with musical themes.

TRYON GALLERY
23–24 Cork Street
London W1
Tel: (01) 734 6961
Sporting and natural history prints.

UNDER TWO FLAGS
4 St Christopher's Place
London W1
Tel: (01) 935 6934
Old military prints.

LEIGH UNDERHILL GALLERY
100 Islington High Street
London N1
Tel: (01) 226 5673
British prints from 1900–1940.

WALKER-BAGSHAWE
46a Ockendon Road
London N1
Tel: (01) 226 9904 (By appointment only)
19th c. prints.

WARWICK LEADLAY GALLERY
5 Nelson Road
London SE10 9JB
Tel: (01) 858 0317/852 7484
Antiquarian maps and prints, specialising in SE London and Kent. Also worldwide selection of topographical prints, shipping, fashion, flowers and animals.

WELBECK GALLERY
18 Thayer Street
London W1M 5LD
Tel: (01) 935 4825
Antiquarian prints, specialising in natural history, especially birds and flowers. Also antique maps of London's topography.

WILLIAM WESTON GALLERY LTD
7 Royal Arcade
Albemarle Street
London W1
Tel: (01) 493 0722
*19th and early 20th c. etchings and
lithographs by European and British artists.*

EDNA WHITESON LTD
343 Bowes Road
London N11
Tel: (01) 361 1105 and 449 8860 (Home)
Early 17th c. maps and prints.

CHRISTOPHER WOOD GALLERY
15 Motcomb Street
London SW1
Tel: (01) 235 9141/2
Pre-Raphaelite prints.

SOUTH AND SOUTHEAST ENGLAND

ASPIDISTRA
46 St James Parade
Bath, Avon
Tel: (0225) 61948
19th and early 20th c. prints.

COLLECTORS TREASURES LTD
Hogarth House
High Street
Wendover, Bucks HP22 6DU
Tel: (0296) 624402
and
91 High Street
Amersham Bucks
Tel: (024 03) 7213
18th and 19th c. maps and prints.

ANN AND RICHARD HAGEN
Bakehouse Cottage
Northwood End
Haynes, Beds
Tel: (023 066) 424
Maps and prints from 1690–1840.

HAMPTON HILL GALLERY
203 and 205 High Street
Hampton Hill, Middx
Tel: (01) 977 1379/5273
18th to early 20th c. prints.

ANDREW LEVERTON
12 Walton Court
Lyonsdown Road
New Barnet, Herts
Tel: (01) 440 2279/886 6038
Decorative prints and maps.

THE LITCHFIELD GALLERY
1062 Christchurch Road
Bournemouth, Dorset
Tel: (0202) 425454
18th to early 20th c. maps, charts and prints.

NORTHWOOD MAPS LTD
71 Hallowell Road
Northwood, Middx.
Tel: Northwood 21525 (By appointment only)
16th to early 20th c. maps.

PERIWINKLE PRESS
Chequers Hill Doddington
Sittingbourne, Kent ME9 OBN
Tel: (079 586) 246
17th to 19th c. prints.

WARNER'S MILITARY SPECIALISTS
2 The Apple Market
Eden Street
Kingston-upon-Thames, Surrey
Tel: Not Available (Mail Order Only)
Military prints.

SOUTHWEST ENGLAND AND WALES

R. AND D. COOMBES
The Old Priest House
Aldbourne
Marlborough, Wilts
Tel: (0672) 40241
Japanese woodblock prints and early English prints of China, all pre-18th c.

MAPS PRINTS AND BOOKS
7 The Struet
Brecon, Powys, Wales
Tel: (0874) 2714
17th c. maps and prints.

REGENT GALLERY
10 Montpelier Arcade
Cheltenham, Glos GL50 1SU
Tel: (0242) 512826
One of the largest dealers in antiquarian maps and topographical prints. Catalogue also available.

MIDLANDS AND EAST ANGLIA

BROBURY HOUSE GALLERY
Brobury, nr Hay-on-Wye
Heref & Worcs
Tel: (0497) 229
17th to early 20th c. Old Master and decorative prints.

HUMBLEYARD FINE ART
Waterfall Cottage
Mill Street
Swanton Morley, Norfolk
Tel: (036 283) 793
18th and 19th c. prints, especially with marine subjects.

Below: Map of Derbyshire by Owen Baven, circa 1720, courtesy of Collectors Treasures Ltd.

SALLY MITCHELL FINE ARTS
Thornlea, Askham
Newark, Notts NG22 0RN
Tel: (077783) 234
18th to early 20th c. country and sporting prints.

OWNART GALLERY
22 Bore Street
Lichfield, Staffs
Tel: (05432) 53626
19th and early 20th c. etchings.

NORTH OF ENGLAND AND SCOTLAND

ABOYNE ANTIQUES OF ROYAL DEESIDE
Station Square
Aboyne, Aberdeen, Grampian, Scotland
Tel: (0339) 2231
19th c. prints.

AITKEN DOTT AND SON
26 Castle Street
Edinburgh, Lothian, Scotland
Tel: (031) 225 7310
Scottish engravings, lithographs and maps.

CAMPBELL-GIBSON FINE ARTS
Star Brae
Oban, Grampian, Scotland
Tel: (0631) 2303
Victorian engravings and prints.

JOHN GRANT
13c and 15a Dundas Street
Edinburgh, Lothian, Scotland
Tel: (031) 556 9698
Scottish topographical prints and maps from 1790–1870.

THE MCEWAN GALLERY
Glengarden
Ballater, Aberdeen, Grampian, Scotland
Tel: (033 82) 429
17th to 19th c. etchings.

NEWGATE ANTIQUES
59 Newgate Street
Morpeth, Northumberland
Tel: (0670) 56875
17th to 19th c. maps and engravings

NICHOLSON ANTIQUES
3 Cranston Street
and
297 Cannongate
Edinburgh, Lothian, Scotland
Tel: (031) 225 5918
Maps and prints from 1600–1800.

ALAN RANKIN
72 Dundas Street
Edinburgh, Lothian, Scotland
Tel: (031) 556 3705
Maps and prints to 1860.

THE SHIP'S WHEEL
2 Traill Street
Thurso, Highland, Scotland
Tel: (0847) 2485
17th to 19th c. maps and prints.

NORTHERN IRELAND

PHYLLIS ARNOLD STUDIO GALLERY
First Floor
113 High Street
Bangor, Co Down, N Ireland
Tel: (0247) 853322
19th c. maps and prints of Ireland and Scotland.

SCIENTIFIC INSTRUMENTS AND TOOLS

LONDON

ARTIFACTS
9 Camden Passage
London N1
Tel: (01)
18th and 19th c. scientific instruments.

ASPREY AND COMPANY LTD
165–169 New Bond Street
London W1Y 0AR
Tel: (01) 493 6767
Ships' chronometers.

JOHN BALL ANTIQUES
178a Westbourne Grove
London W11
Tel: (01) 727 3607 and 452 9049 (Home)
Marine instruments.

WILLIAM BEDFORD ANTIQUES LTD
327 Upper Street
Islington Green
London N1
Tel: (01) 226 9648
Barometers from 1650–1830.

CHELSEA CLOCKS
479 Fulham Road
London SW6
Tel: (01) 731 5704
19th and early 20th c. barometers and scales.

ARTHUR DAVIDSON LTD
78/79 Jermyn Street
London SW1
Tel: (01) 930 6687
17th to 19th c. scientific instruments.

DELEHAR
146 Portobello Road
London W11
Tel: (01) 727 9860 or 262 7824
Scientific instruments.

JACK DONOVAN
93 Portobello Road
London W11
Tel: (01) 727 1485
Early gramophones and phonographs.

FAGIN'S PHONOGRAPH EMPORIUM
189 Blackstock Road
London N5
Tel: (01) 359 4793
Phonograph equipment including gramophones and spares, early wireless equipment and early records.

GARNER AND MARNEY LTD
41–43 Southgate Road
London N1
Tel: (01) 226 1535
18th and 19th c. mercurial barometers.

W.R. HARVEY AND COMPANY LTD
67–70 Chalk Farm Road
London NW1 8AN
Tel: (01) 485 1504/267 2767
Barometers from 1650–1830.

E. HOLLANDER
80 Fulham Road
London SW3
Tel: (01) 589 7239
18th and 19th c. English barometers.

JUBILEE
10 Pierrepoint Row
Camden Passage
London N1
Tel: (01) 607 5462 (Home)
Photographic apparatus and images including magic lanterns and stereoscopic slides.

Above: Mahogany 20" Hadley quadrant owned by Thomas Hammond, dated 1758, courtesy of Harriet Wynter Ltd.

SIMON KAYE LTD
1½ Albemarle Street
London W1
Tel: (01) 493 7658
Medical instruments.

LANGFORDS
46–47 Chancery Lane
London WC2
Tel: (01) 405 6402
Scientific and marine instruments.

LOTS ARTIFACTS
9 Camden Passage
London N1
Tel: Not Available
Scientific instruments, mechanical antiques and tools.

MARINER ANTIQUES LTD
55 Curzon Street
London W1
Tel: (01) 499 0171/2
Scientific instruments and marine items.

PETER MARTIN
44 Ledbury Road
London W11
Tel: (01) 727 1301
Scientific instruments.

MASSEY ANTIQUES
11 The Mall
Camden Passage
Tel: (01) 359 7966
19th c. marine instruments including telescopes.

RICHARD MAUDE TOOLS
6 Malbrook Road
London SW15
Tel: (01) 788 2991 (By appointment only)
18th and 19th c. woodworking tools including 19th c. ornamental turning lathes.

ARTHUR MIDDLETON LTD
12 New Row
London WC2
Tel: (01) 836 7042/7062
18th and 19th c. scientific instruments including those for navigation, astronomy, surveying and medicine.

PORTOBELLO ANTIQUE COMPANY
133 Portobello Road
London W11
Tel: (01) 221 0344
Victorian barometers, from 1860.

PRINCIPIA FINE ART
28 Victoria Grove
London W8
Tel: (01) 584 8080
Scientific instruments.

RELCY ANTIQUES
9 Nelson Road
London SE10
Tel: (01) 858 2812 and 858 7218 (Home)
Scientific instruments, especially marine items such as 18th and 19th c. sextants and telescopes.

A. ROCH AND SONS LTD
99 Crawford Street
London W1
Tel: (01) 724 0563
18th and 19th c. barometers.

ROD'S ANTIQUES
79 Portobello Road
London W11
Tel: (01) 229 2544
Scientific instruments including barometers.

STAIR AND COMPANY LTD
120 Mount Street
London W1Y 5HB
Tel: (01) 499 1784/5
18th c. English barometers.

MALCOLM D. STEVENS
350 Upper Street
London N1
Tel: (01) 359 1020/787 4607
Fine barometers and marine chronometers.

STRIKE ONE LTD
51 Camden Passage
London N1
Tel: (01) 226 9709/359 7022/878 2769
18th and 19th c. barometers.

TALKING MACHINE
30 Watford Way
London NW4
Tel: (01) 202 3474
Dealers in old radios, gramophones, typewriters and sewing machines. They have a selection of spare parts.

IGOR TOCIAPSKI
39–41 Ledbury Road
London W11
Tel: (01) 229 8317
16th to 19th c. scientific instruments.

HARRIET WYNTER LTD
50 Redcliffe Road
London SW10
Tel: (01) 352 6494 (By appointment only)
16th to 19th c. scientific instruments.

VINTAGE CAMERAS LTD
254–256 Kirkdale
London SE26
Tel: (01) 778 5416/5841/9052
Scientific instruments from 18th c. on.

V.C. YOULTEN AND B.J. RAPER
Antiquarius
15 Flood Street
London SW3
Tel: (01) 821 9734
Antique pharmaceutical items.

SCULPTURE

Above: One of a pair of figures entitled "Gratitude" (the other is "Innocence Defended by Fidelity") by Giovanni M Benzoni (1809–1873). Both were awarded a medal at the Great Exhibition of 1851, courtesy of Crowther of Syon Lodge Ltd.

NIHON TOKEN
23 Museum Street
London WC1
Tel: (01) 580 6511 and 444 6726 (Home)
Japanese sculpture including netsuke.

JACK OGDEN
42 Duke Street
London SW1
Tel: (01) 930 3353
Greek, Roman, Egyptain and Byzantine bronze and marble sculpture.

ALEC OSSOWSKI
83 Pimlico Road
London SW1
Tel: (01) 730 3256
Specialist in gilded items with a selection of wood carvings.

PHILIP
59 Ledbury Road
London W11
Tel: (01) 727 7915
16th and 17th c. sculpture.

SCHWARTZ
93 Blackheath Road
London SE10
Tel: (01) 692 1652
Indian statuary, including Buddhas.

MARSHALL SPINK
18 Albemarle Street
London W1
Tel: (01) 493 2575/5280
13th to 16th c. sculpture.

SPINK AND SON LTD
5, 6 and 7 King Street
London SW1
Tel: (01) 930 7888
Ancient and antique European and Oriental sculpture.

ROBIN SYMES LTD
3 Ormond Yard
Duke of York Street
London SW1
Tel: (01) 930 9856/7
Roman, Greek and Egyptian bronzes and marbles.

F. TELTSCHER LTD
17 Crawford Street
London W1H 1PE
Tel: (01) 935 0525
15th to 19th c. wood carvings.

GEOFFREY VAN LTD
107 Portobello Road
London W11
Tel: (01) 229 5577
European wood carvings.

CHRISTOPHER WOOD GALLERY
15 Motcomb Street
London SW1
Tel: (01) 235 9141/2
Victorian sculpture.

Above: "The Age of Innocence" by Alfred Drury R.A., inscribed by the artist in 1897, courtesy of the Christopher Wood Gallery.

SOUTH AND SOUTHEAST ENGLAND

ART AND MARINE
19 Lion Street
Rye, Sussex
Tel: (07973) 4200
Scrimshaw carvings.

CROWTHER OF SYON LODGE LTD
Busch Corner, London Road
Isleworth, Middx
Tel: (01) 560 7978
Architectural statuary.

FARNBOROUGH ANTIQUES
10 Church Road
Farnborough, Orpington, Kent
Tel: (0689) 51834
Early woodcarvings.

WALTON ANTIQUES
7 Duke Street
Richmond, Surrey
Tel: (01) 948 2258 and 940 6519 (Home)
17th to 19th c. carved giltwood figures.

SOUTHWEST ENGLAND AND WALES

R. AND D. COOMBES
The Old Priest House
Aldbourne, Marlborough, Wilts
Tel: (0672) 40241
Pre-18th c. Oriental sculpture, including bronzes.

PETER PHILP
77 Kimberley Road
Cardiff, Glamorgan CF2 5DP, Wales
Tel: (0222) 493826
17th to early 19th c. woodcarvings.

NORTH OF ENGLAND AND SCOTLAND

THE FINE ART SOCIETY LTD
12 Great King Street
Edinburgh, Lothian, Scotland
Tel: (031) 557 1903
British, especially Scottish, sculpture from 1800 on.

Left: 16th c. oak carving of a Turk, artist unknown, courtesy of Farnborough Antiques.

SEMI-PRECIOUS MATERIALS

LONDON

ROBERT BARLEY ANTIQUES
48 Fulham Road
London SW6
Tel: (01) 736 4429
16th to 19th c. ivories.

C. BARRETT AND COMPANY
51 Burlington Arcade
London W1
Tel: (01) 493 2570
European and Oriental ivories.

THE BUTTON QUEEN
19 Marylebone Lane
London W1
Tel: (01) 935 1505
*Old and antique buttons and buckles,
including those made from ivory, bone, horn,
etc.*

CHANCERY ANTIQUES LTD
357 Upper Street
London N1 0PD
Tel: (01) 359 9035
*Chinese and Japanese ivories and cloisonné.
See entry under "Specialist Dealers, Toys and
Games" for illustration.*

CHANTICLEER ANTIQUES
105 Portobello Road
London W11
Tel: (01) 385 0919 (By appointment only)
*Chinese and European ivory chess sets,
tortoiseshell items, and Sorrento work.*

COBWEB
2 Englands Lane
London NW3
Tel: (01) 586 4605
*Ancient and antique European and Far
Eastern ivories and jades.*

COLLET'S CHINESE GALLERY
40 Great Russell Street
London WC1
Tel: (01) 580 7538
*18th and 19th c. semi-precious stones, jade
and ivory.*

H. AND W. DEUTSCH ANTIQUES
111 Kensington Church Street
London W8
Tel: (01) 727 5984
*18th and 19th c. English and Continental
cloisonné.*

DONOHOE
175 Portobello Road
London W11
Tel: (01) 727 4681 and 455 5507 (Home)
European ivories.

EAST ASIA COMPANY
103 Camden High Street
London NW1
Tel: (01) 388 5783
Japanese and Chinese netsuke.

GAY ANTIQUES
1 Beauchamp Place
London SW3
Tel: (01) 584 9615
French ivories.

GRACE ANTIQUES
28 Pembridge Villas
London W11
Tel: (01) 229 4415
Early 19th c. enamels.

GREGORY, BOTTLEY AND LLOYD
8–12 Rickett Street
London SW6
Tel: (01) 381 5522
Collection of minerals and fossils.

M. HAKIM
4 The Royal Arcade
Old Bond Street
London W1
Tel: (01) 629 2643
English enamels.

HALCYON DAYS
14 Brook Street
London W1Y 1AA
Tel: (01) 629 8111
*Small itmes in enamels, tortoiseshell and
papier mâché.*

LESLEY HEPHERD ANTIQUES
47 Camden Passage
London N1
Tel: (01) 359 1755
Tortoiseshell.

ANTHONY JAMES AND SON LTD
253 New Kings Road
London SW6
Tel: (01) 731 3474
Ormolu, pre-1830.

JAPANESE GALLERY
66d Kensington Church Street
London W8
Tel: (01) 229 2934 and 226 3347 (Home)
Japanese netsuke.

L.P.J. ANTIQUES LTD
c/o Laurence Mitchell Antiques
27 Camden Passage
London N1
Tel: (01) 359 7579
Chinese ivories.

ERIC LINEHAM AND SONS
62 Kensington Church Street
London W8
Tel: (01) 937 9650
*19th c. English, Continental and Oriental
enamels.*

*Right: Spar tower made by a West
Cumberland miner from minerals found in the
Egremont area, circa 1880, courtesy of
Gregory, Bottley and Lloyd.*

*Above: Two enamel scent bottles and an etui,
circa 1770, courtesy of Halcyon Days.*

BRIAN LLOYD MINERALS
15a Pall Mall
London SW1
Tel: (01) 930 6921 and 352 5375 (Home)
*Mineral specimens, fossils, and objects made
from minerals.*

S. MARCHANT AND SON
120 Kensington Church Street
London W8
Tel: (01) 229 5319
*Chinese and Japanese cloisonné ivories and
jades.*

PETER MANHEIM LTD
69 Upper Berkeley Street
Portman Square
London W1
Tel: (01) 723 6595
English enamels.

JEREMY J. MASON ORIENTAL ART
145 Ebury Street
London SW1
Tel: (01) 730 6971 and 874 4173 (Home)
Chinese jades.

NASH ANTIQUES
183 Westbourne Grove
London W11

SOUTH AUDLEY ART GALLERIES LTD
36 South Audley Street
London W1
Tel: (01) 499 3178/3195
English and Continental ivories and enamels.

SPINK AND SON LTD
5, 6 and 7 King Street
London SW1
Tel: (01) 930 7888
Chinese and Japanese jades.

GERALD SPYER AND SON LTD
18 Motcomb Street
London SW1
, Tel: (01) 235 3348
18th c. ormolu items.

TEMPUS ANTIQUES LTD
43 Kensington Church Street
London W8
Tel: (01) 937 4359
Japanese ivories and cloisonné.

WARTSKI
14 Grafton Street
London W1
Tel: (01) 493 1141/2/3
Semi-precious objects, including some by Fabergé.

WINIFRED WILLIAMS
3 Bury Street
London SW1
Tel: (01) 930 4732
18th c. European enamels of museum standard.

MARY WISE
27 Holland Street
London W8
Tel: (01) 937 8649
18th and 19th c. jade.

DOUGLAS WRIGHT LTD
34 Curzon Street
London W1
Tel: (01) 629 9993
Japanese and Chinese ivories.

NASH ANTIQUES (CON'T)
Tel: (01) 727 3796
Oriental and Japanese jade and ivory, including netsuke.

NIHON TOKEN
23 Museum Street
London WC1A 1JT
Tel: (01) 580 6511
Japanese lacquer, netsuke, and inro.

ORMONDE ORIENTAL ANTIQUES
181 Westbourne Grove
London W11
and
Portwine Arcade
173 Portobello Road
London W11
Tel: (01) 221 4219
Indian, Tibetan, Chinese, Japanese, Burmese and Thai cloisonné and enamels.

KEVIN A. PAGE ANTIQUES
5 Camden Passage
and
6 Gateway Arcade
Camden Passage
London N1
Tel: (01) 226 8558
19th c. Oriental enamels, cloisonné and ivories.

Above: Jade group of two perched cranes, a mother and young holding peach sprays, in a pale whitish celadon tone, courtesy of Spink and Son Ltd.

PARK ANTIQUES
62 New Kings Road
London SW6 4LT
Tel: (01) 736 6222
Horn, tortoiseshell and mother-of-pearl snuff boxes and card cases.

RAPHAEL FINE ARTS LTD
DRC House
2 Cornwall Terrace
London NW1 4QP
Tel: (01) 486 9931 (By appointment only)
Fine Oriental and European ivories.

J.S. RASMUSSEN FINE ARTS
5 Logan Mews, Logan Place
London W8
Tel: (01) 373 6527
Early 18th to early 20th c. Japanese netsuke and inro.

COLIN SMITH AND GERALD ROBINSON ANTIQUES
Geoffrey Van Arcade
107 Portobello Road
London W11
Tel: (01) 998 8160 and 579 5620
Ivory and tortoiseshell items, with visiting card cases a speciality.

SOUTH AND SOUTHEAST ENGLAND

ART AND MARINE
19 Lion Street
Rye, East Sussex
Tel: (07973) 4200
Scrimshaw carvings.

ELIOT ANTIQUES
Stanford Dingley
Reading, Berks
Tel: (0734) 744649
18th c. English enamels. See overleaf for illustration.

HORN ANTIQUES
c/o Paula Hardwick
Glenn Cottage
Hindhead, Surrey GU26 6EL
Tel: (042 873) 4868 (By appointment only)
Specialist in objects made from horn. See overleaf for illustration.

Left: Carved agate rabbit by Carl Fabergé and gold-mounted, double-opening agate snuff box, circa 1740, courtesy of Wartski.

SEMI-PRECIOUS MATERIALS / SILVER AND SILVER PLATE

Left: Mid-19th c. oxhorn goblet with turned stem and base, courtesy of Paula Hardwick of Horn Antiques.

SOUTHWEST ENGLAND AND WALES

R. AND D. COOMBES
The Old Priest House
Aldbourne
Marlborough, Wilts
Tel: (0672) 40241
Pre-18th c. jades, ivories and netsuke.

ORIENTAL ANTIQUES
4 Belvedere
Lansdown Road
Bath, Avon, BA1 5ED
Tel: (0225) 315987
Oriental ivories.

MIDLANDS AND EAST ANGLIA

COLIN DAVIES ANTIQUES
15 Wolverhampton Road
Stafford, Staffs
Tel: (0785) 40545
French enamels.

Above: Selection of 18th c. enamels, courtesy of Eliot Antiques.

NORTH OF ENGLAND AND SCOTLAND

JANET G. LUMSDEN
51a George Street
Edinburgh, Lothian, Scotland
Tel: (031) 225 2911
18th and 19th c. jade carvings and netsuke.

PAUL M. PETERS
15 Bower Road
Harrogate, N Yorkshire
Tel: (0423) 60118
17th to 19th c. Chinese and Japanese ivories.

SILVER AND SILVER PLATE

LONDON

ADAMS ROOM LTD
18–20 Ridgway
London SW19
Tel: (01) 946 7047
18th and 19th c. silver and silver plate.

ANTIQUES LTD
18 Parsons Street
London NW4 1QB
Tel: (01) 203 1194
Silver from 1860–1900.

ASPREY AND COMPANY LTD
153 Fenchurch Street, London EC3
Tel: (01) 626 2160
and
165–169 New Bond Street, London W1
Tel: (01) 493 6767
18th to 20th c. silver.

G.P. BASTILLO AND SONS
27 Battersea Rise
London SW11
Tel: (01) 223 5341 and 673 1792 (Home)
Georgian, Victorian and Edwardian silver.

STANLEY BEAL
41 Fairfax Road
London NW6
Tel: (01) 328 7525
Silver from 1700, Sheffield plate from 1750–1820, and Victorian plate from 1840–1900.

PAUL BENNETT
75 George Street
London W1
Tel: (01) 935 1555
Silver from 1740–1963 and Sheffield plate.

J.H. BOURDON-SMITH LTD
24 Mason's Yard
Duke Street
London SW1
Tel: (01) 839 4714/5
17th to early 20th c. silver.

BRAND INGLIS
9 Halkin Arcade
Motcomb Street
London SW1
Tel: (01) 235 6604
English and European silver, all periods.

BRUFORD AND HEMMING LTD
28 Conduit Street
London W1
Tel: (01) 499 7644/629 4289
Domestic silverware, especially flatware.

BUTLER AND WILSON
189 Fulham Road
London SW3
Tel: (01) 352 3045
Silver card cases, flasks and cigarette holders.

Below: Silver tea and coffee service decorated with the arms of the Countess of Cadogan, by R. and S. Garrard, London, circa 1840, courtesy of Asprey and Company Ltd.

CHANCERY ANTIQUES
22 Park Walk
London SW10
Tel: (01) 352 6016 (By appointment only)
Georgian and early Victorian silver and silver plate.

J. CHRISTIE
26 Burlington Arcade
London W1V 9AD
Tel: (01) 629 3070
English and Continental silver and Sheffield plate.

JOHN CLAY
263 New Kings Road
London SW6
Tel: (01) 731 5677
18th and 19th c. silver.

COBRA AND BELLAMY
149 Sloane Street
London SW1
Tel: (01) 730 2823
Late 19th and early 20th c. silver.

MARY COOKE ANTIQUES LTD
1 Barnes High Street
London SW13 9LB
Tel: (01) 878 2057
18th and 19th c. silver.

THE CORNER CUPBOARD
679 Finchley Road
London NW2
Tel: (01) 435 4870
18th and 19th c. silver.

CREST ANTIQUES
313–315 and 287 Putney Bridge Road
London SW15
Tel: (01) 789 3165
19th and early 20th c. silver.

THE CURIO SHOP
21 Shepherd Market
London W1Y 7HR
Tel: (01) 493 5616
Silver and silver plate from George III to the Victorian period.

DE HAVILLAND ANTIQUES LTD
48 Sloane Street
London SW1
Tel: (01) 235 3534
Fine 17th and 18th c. silver.

DELIEB ANTIQUES LTD
31 Woodville Road
London NW11
Tel: (01) 458 2083 (By appointment only)
Silver, specialising in rare pieces.

DE VILLIERS ANTIQUES
311 Fulham Palace Road
London SW6
Tel: (01) 731 3859
18th and 19th c. silver.

DONOHOE
175 Portobello Road
London W11
Tel: (01) 727 4681 and 455 5507 (Home)
17th to early 19th c. collector's silver.

EDWARD AND JOANNA DONOHOE
1–7 Davies Mews
London W1
Tel: (01) 629 5633 and 455 5507 (Home)
Antique silver

E. AND A. ANTIQUES
36 Ledbury Road
London W11
Tel: (01) 229 1823
Silver and silver plate.

EALING ANTIQUES
34 St Mary's Road
London W5
Tel: (01) 567 6192
18th and 19th c. silver.

M. EKSTEIN LTD
90 Jermyn Street
London SW1
Tel: (01) 930 2024
Continental silver.

PETER FRANCIS
26 Museum Street
London WC1
Tel: (01) 637 0165
Sheffield plate from 1760–1860.

Above: A coach-fitting with the arms of King George IV, circa 1820, courtesy of Heirloom and Howard Ltd.

I. FREEMAN AND SON LTD
18 Leather Lane
London EC1
Tel: (01) 405 4633
Silver and old Sheffield plate.

J. FREEMAN
85a Portobello Road
London W11
Tel:(01) 221 5076
Victorian silver plate from 1830–1870; Sheffield plate from 1790–1830; Victorian and later silver.

JAMES HARDY AND COMPANY
235 Brompton Road
London SW3
Tel: (01) 589 5050
Silver, including silver tableware.

SHERRY HATCHER
15 Pierrepoint Arcade
Camden Passage
London N1
Tel: (01) 226 5679/8496
Georgian to Edwardian silver.

HEATHER ANTIQUES
144 Islington High Street
London N1
Tel: (01) 226 2412
Silver and silver plate.

HEIRLOOM AND HOWARD LTD
1 Hay Hill
Berkeley Square
London W1
Tel: (01) 493 5868
Specialists in armorial antiques, ie those with crests or costs-of-arms on them, in silver and Sheffield plate.

HOW OF EDINBURGH
2–3 Pickering Place
St James's Street
London SW1
Tel: (01) 930 7140
English silver prior to 1750, including English provincial silver and Scottish silver.

HUNDRED AND ONE
101 Notting Hill Gate
London W11
Tel: (01) 727 2326
18th and 19th c. silver and 19th c. silver plate.

HYDE PARK ANTIQUES
191 Westbourne Grove
London W11
Tel: (01) 727 1585
Silver and silver plate from 1700–1900.

GOWLAND BROTHERS LTD
48 Cornhill
London EC3
Tel: (01) 626 9155/4670
17th to 19th c. silver.

GREAT EXPECTATIONS
62 Old Church Street
London SW3
Tel: (01) 352 9850
19th c. silver plate.

SIMON GRIFFIN ANTIQUES
3 Royal Arcade
28 Old Bond Street
London W1
Tel: (01) 491 7367 and (0525 220) 256
(Home)
Small silver pieces, old Sheffield plate and Victorian electro-plate

HANCOCKS AND CO LTD
1 Burlington Gardens
London W1
Tel: (01) 493 8904/5
17th to early 20th c. small silver.

HARRIS AND FRANK LTD
53 Holland Park
London W11 3RS
Tel: (01) 727 4769 (By appointment only)
16th to 19th c. silver and Sheffield plate.

ROSEMARY HART
4 Gateway Arcade
and
355 Upper Street
London N1
Tel: (01) 359 6839
18th and early 19th silver and silver plate.

THE HAY LOFT
332 Upper Richmond Road
London SW14
Tel: (01) 876 5020
Silver plate from 1800–1930.

E. HOLLANDER
80 Fulham Road
London SW3
Tel: (01) 589 7239
18th and 19th c. silver and Sheffield plate.

THE HOUSE OF ANDOR
17a The Burroughs
London NW4
Tel: Not Available
18th and 19th c. silver.

HUNDRED AND ONE
49 Beauchamp Place
London SW3
Tel: (01) 589 0396
18th and 19th c. silver and 19th c. silver plate.

MELVYN AND GARY JAY ANTIQUES
64a Kensington Church Street
London W8 4DB
Tel: (01) 937 6832
19th c. silver and silver plate.

H.R. JESSOP LTD
3 Motcomb Street
Belgrave Square
London SW1
Tel: (01) 235 2978
17th to 19th c. English silver.

JUST A SECOND ANTIQUES
40 Fulham High Street
London SW6
Tel: (01) 731 1919 and 673 1793 (Home)
Georgian to Edwardian silver.

SIMON KAYE LTD
1½ Albemarle Street
London W1
Tel: (01) 493 7658
*Georgian silver, 18th c. Sheffield plate and
more recent silver.*

RICHARD KIHL WINE ANTIQUES
164 Regents Park Road
London NW1
Tel: (01) 586 3838
*Wine-related antiques, including silver jugs,
coasters, corkscrews from 1750–1910.*

H. KNOWLES-BROWN LTD
27 Hampstead High Street
London NW3
Tel: (01) 435 4775
Silver from the Renaissance on.

LANGFORDS
46–47 Chancery Lane
London WC2
Tel: (01) 405 6402
18th and 19th c. silver plate.

JOHN LAURIE
352 Upper Street
London N1
Tel: (01) 226 0913
18th and 19th c. silver and Sheffield plate.

STANLEY LESLIE
15 Beauchamp Place
London SW3
Tel: (01) 589 2333
Silver and Sheffield plate from all periods.

M.P. LEVENE LTD
5 Thurloe Place
London SW7
Tel: (01) 589 3755
18th and 19th c. silver and Sheffield plate.

SANDA LIPTON
22 Farringdon Lane
London EC1
Tel: (01) 253 5299
17th to 19th c. silver.

THE LITTLE CURIOSITY SHOP
24 The Green
Winchmore Hill
London N21
Tel: (01) 886 0925
Victorian silver.

**LONDON INTERNATIONAL SILVER
COMPANY LTD**
82 Portobello Road
London W11
Tel: (01) 221 5067
17th to early 20th c. silver and silver plate.

THE LONDON SILVER VAULTS
Chancery House
Chancery Lane
London WC2
Tel: (01) 242 3844
*18th and 19th c. silver plus Sheffield and
Victorian plate.*

THOMAS LUMLEY LTD
Standbrook House
2–5 Old Bond Street
London W1
Tel: (01) 629 2493
17th to 19th c. silver.

LYONS GALLERY
47–49 Mill Lane
London NW6
Tel: (01) 794 3537
Art Nouveau and Art Deco silver.

M. AND L. SILVER COMPANY LTD
131 Whitechapel Road
London E1
Tel: (01) 247 8906/8107
Silver and silver plate from 1750–1900.

MARKS ANTIQUES LTD
49 Curzon Street
London W1
Tel: (01) 499 1788
18th and 19th c. silver and Sheffield plate.

MARSHALL'S ANTIQUES
67 Chancery Lane
London WC2
Tel: (01) 405 4158
19th and early 20th c. silver.

MARTINS-FORREST ANTIQUES
8 Halkin Arcade
Motcomb Street
London SW1
Tel: (01) 235 8353 and 341 0673 (Home)
Art Nouveau and Art Deco silver.

M. MCALEER
1a St Christopher's Place
London W1
Tel: (01) 486 1171
*Small silver, including Irish and Scottish
silver pieces.*

JONATHAN MCCREERY
315 Kings Road
London SW3
Tel: (01) 352 5733 and (063 583) 680
(Home)
18th and 19th c. silver.

RAYMOND O'SHEA GALLERY
6 Ellis Street
London SW1
Tel: (01) 730 0082
Silver with cartographic motifs.

*Above: Pair of George I silver candlesticks by
Anthony Nelme, London 1722, courtesy of
S.J. Phillips Ltd.*

A.H. PAGE
66 Gloucester Road
London SW7 4QT
Tel: (01) 584 7349
Georgian silver.

PHILIP AND RICHARD PARKER
98 Fulham Road
London SW3
Tel: (01) 589 7327 and 947 5569 (Home)
17th to late 19th c. silver.

PAULINE PERETZ
16 Jacobs Well Mews, George Street
London W1H 6BD
Silver including hollow-ware and flatware.

*Below: From bottom left, George III silver
card case, circa 1812; George II nutmeg grater
in the form of an acorn embossed with floral
and scroll motif, circa 1740: George III crested
inkwell with a royal ducal crest, dated London
1763; Charles II silver-mounted shagreen
lancet case, circa 1685: George I oval silver
and tortoiseshell tobacco box, circa 1720;
George III silver travelling corkscrews, circa
1810, and Charles II silver drum shape comfit
box, circa 1670, all courtesy of Gerald Sattin
Ltd.*

SILVER AND SILVER PLATE

Above: George II coffee pot, made in London in 1750 by Thomas Whipham and engraved with a contemporary coat-of-arms, courtesy of S.J. Shrubsole Ltd.

S.J. PHILLIPS LTD
139 New Bond Street
London W1A 3DL
Tel: (01) 629 6261
Early 19th c. English and Continental silver.

PORTOBELLO SILVER GALLERIES LTD
82 Portobello Road
London W11
Tel: (01) 221 5067
Silver and silver plate from 1700, including cruet sets and cutlery.

THE PURPLE SHOP
15 Flood Street
London SW3
Tel: (01) 352 1127
Art Nouveau and Art Deco silver.

DAVID RICHARDS AND SONS
12 New Cavendish Street
London W1
Tel: (01) 935 3206
Georgian and Victorian silver, plus Sheffield and Victorian plate.

ROCHFORT ANTIQUES GALLERY
32–34 The Green
Winchmore Hill
London N21
Tel: (01) 886 4779
18th and 19th c. silver.

GERALD SATTIN LTD
25 Burlington Arcade
London W1
Tel: (01) 493 6557
English silver from 1700–1910, especially unusual pieces.

SCHREDDS OF PORTOBELLO
Shop 37
282 Portobello Road
London W11
Tel: (01) 348 3314
Pre-1870 silver, including Colonial and foreign pieces.

SENSATION LTD
62–66 Fulham High Street
London SW6
Tel: (01) 736 4135
17th to 19th c. silver.

S.J. SHRUBSOLE LTD
43 Museum Street
London WC1
Tel: (01) 405 2712
Late 17th to mid-19th c. silver and mid-18th to mid-19th c. Sheffield plate.

COLIN SMITH AND GERALD ROBINSON ANTIQUES
Geoffrey Van Arcade
107 Portobello Road
London W11
Tel: (01) 998 8160/579 5620
Silver, with visiting card cases a speciality.

SPINK AND SON LTD
5, 6 and 7 King Street
London SW1
Tel: (01) 930 7888
17th to 19th c. silver.

THE TRINKET BOX
1 Goldhurst Terrace
London NW6
Tel: (01) 624 4264
Victorian and Edwardian silver.

TWENTY ONE ANTIQUES
21 Chalk Farm Road
London NW1
Tel: (01) 485 1239
Silver and silver plate from 19th c. on.

A.R. AND J.S. ULLMANN LTD
10 Hatton Garden
London EC1N 8AH
Tel: (01) 405 1877
19th and early 20th c. English and Continental silver.

W. 13 ANTIQUES
10 The Avenue
London W13
Tel: (01) 998 0390
18th and 19th c. silver plate.

JOANNA WARRAND
99 Kensington Church Street
London W8
Tel: (01) 727 2333
18th and 19th c. English and Continental silver.

W.H. WILLSON LTD
15 King Street
London SW1
Tel: (01) 930 6463
English silver from 1600–1837.

P. AND L. WOOLMAN
351 Upper Street
London N1
Tel: (01) 359 7648 and 340 2468 (Home)
Silver and silver plate from 1750–1930.

SOUTH AND SOUTHEAST ENGLAND

APOLLO GALLERIES
61, 65 and 67 South End
Croydon, Surrey
Tel: (01) 681 3727/680 1968
18th and 19th c. English and Continental silver.

C. CLEALL ANTIQUES
16 Brewers Lane
Richmond, Surrey
Tel: (01) 940 8069
Art Nouveau and Art Deco Silver.

ELIOT ANTIQUES
Stanford Dingley
Reading, Berks
Tel: (0734) 744649
Specialist in silver snuff boxes and vinaigrettes. See overleaf for illustration.

GOLD CONNECTION ANTIQUES
40/44 St George's Walk
Croydon, Surrey
Tel: (01) 642 3772
Specialists in silver flatware.

GREAT GROOMS ANTIQUES LTD
Parbrook
Billingshurst, Sussex
Tel: (040 381) 2263
19th and 20th c. silver.

Left: Silver chamber pot by David Willaume, London 1743, once the property of George Booth, 2nd Earl of Warrington, whose coronet and cipher it bears, courtesy of Spink and Son Ltd.

HILL RISE ANTIQUES
26 Hill Rise
Richmond, Surrey
Tel: (01) 948 1140 and 876 4114 (Home)
19th c. silver plate.

HOUSE OF ANTIQUES
4 College Street
Petersfield, Hants
Tel: (0730) 2172
18th and 19th c. silver.

LAYTON ANTIQUES
1 Paved Court
The Green
Richmond, Surrey
Tel: (01) 940 2617
Victorian silver.

MALDWYN ANTIQUES
12 and 12a Beynon Parade
Carshalton, Surrey
Tel: (01) 669 0793 and 393 4530 (Home)
Silver from 1724.

NEALE ANTIQUES
21–21a Old Cross
Hertford, Herts SG14 1RE
Tel: Hertford 52561
Georgian to Edwardian silver.

THE OLD HOUSE
15–17 High Street
Seaford, Sussex
Tel: (0323) 892091
18th to early 20th c. silver and silver plate.

PAYNE AND SON LTD
131 High Street
Oxford, Oxon OX1 4DH
Tel: (0865) 43787
Antique and second-hand silver.

RICHARD AND CAROLINE PENMAN
Cockhaise Mill
Lindfield, Sussex
Tel: (04447) 2514
Georgian and Victorian silver including wine labels, vinaigrettes, card cases and watches, plus Sheffield plate.

PENNY FARTHING ANTIQUES
71 High Street
Chobham, Surrey
Tel: (099 05) 7718
19th c. silver and silverplate.

SURREY GALLERIES
295 High Street
Croydon, Surrey
Tel: (01) 681 0975 and 660 9294 (Home)
18th and 19th c. silver.

THE TOKEN HOUSE
7 Market Parade, High Street
Ewell, Epsom, Surrey
Tel: (01) 393 9654
19th c. silver and silver plate.

Right: (Top row, left to right) a Continental silver gilt vinaigrette, the lid with raised oval mosaic, circa 1850; a large oval silver gilt vinaigrette by Phipps and Robinson, London 1829, the lid set with moss agate; and a gold-mounted vinaigrette with cornelian cover and grey agate base, circa 1820; (bottom row, left to right) a small oval 18ct gold-mounted vinaigrette, the lid set with bloodstone, circa 1820; a silver "pebble" vinaigrette, the lid set with various coloured agates, Birmingham 1857; and a small silver gilt vinaigrette, the lid set with agate, London 1801; all courtesy of Eliot Antiques.

TRINITY ANTIQUES CENTRE
7 Trinity Street
Colchester, Essex
Tel: (0206) 77775
Georgian and Victorian silver.

VALION ANTIQUES
42 Chancery Lane
Beckenham, Kent
Tel: (01) 658 6644
18th and 19th c. silver.

S. WARRENDER AND COMPANY
4 Cheam Road
Sutton, Surrey
Tel: (01) 643 4381
Silver from 1762.

SOUTHWEST ENGLAND AND WALES

ABBEY GALLERIES
9 Abbey Churchyard
Bath, Avon

Above: Pair of George II rococo silver candlesticks, courtesy of Payne and Sons Ltd.

ABBEY GALLERIES (CON'T)
Tel: (0225) 60565
18th c. silver.

ALDERSON AND ALDERSON
23 Brook Street
Bath, Avon
Tel: (0225) 21652
18th and 19th c. silver.

BATH GALLERIES
33 Broad Street
Bath, Avon
Tel: (0225) 62946
18th c. silver.

ANGELA CLEMENT ANTIQUES
First Floor
37 East Street
Blandford Forum, Dorset
Tel: (0258) 53472
Victorian and Regency silver.

G.M.S. ANTIQUES
36 High Street
Wickwar
Wotton-under-Edge, Glos GL12 8NP
Tel: (0454 24) 251
Victorian silver and silver plate.

EDWARD A. NOWELL
21–23 Market Place
Wells, Somerset BA5 2RF
Tel: (0749) 72415
18th and early 19th c. English silver.

OAK CHEST JEWELLERS
1 Oak Street
Llangollen, Clwyd, Wales
Tel: (0978) 860095
Victorian silver.

OLD BARN ANTIQUES COMPANY
The Abbey Antique Shop
Half Moon Street
Sherborne, Dorset
Tel: (093 581) 2068
18th and 19th c. silver.

MIDLANDS AND EAST ANGLIA

ALAN GRANT ANTIQUES
Clifton, Rugby, Warks
Tel: (0788) 71165
19th c. silver and silver plate, specialising in the unusual.

MELVILLE KEMP LTD
89–91 Derby Road
Nottingham, Notts NG1 5BB
Tel: (0602) 417055
18th and 19th c. silver and Sheffield plate.

NEVILL ANTIQUES
9–10 Milk Street
and
30–31 Princess Street
Shrewsbury, Shropshire
Tel: (0743) 51013
18th and 19th c. silver and silver plate.

JAMES AND ANN TILLETT
Tombland House
12–13 Tombland
Norwich, Norfolk NR3 1HF
Tel: (0603) 24914
18th and 19th c. silver and Sheffield plate.

NORTH OF ENGLAND AND SCOTLAND

BIELDSIDE ANTIQUES
85 North Deeside Road
Bieldside, Aberdeen, Grampian, Scotland
Tel: (033 82) 296
18th and 19th c. Scottish provincial flatware.

COACH HOUSE ANTIQUES
8–10 North Port
Perth, Tayside, Scotland
Tel: (0783) 29835
Scottish provincial silver.

CRIEFF ANTIQUES
Comrie Road
Crieff, Tayside, Scotland
Tel: (0764) 3322
19th c. silver.

DUNNING ANTIQUES
Tron Square
Dunning, Tayside, Scotland
Tel: (076 484) 224
18th and 19th c. silver, 19th c. silver plate and Scottish provincial silver.

HAMISH M. EDWARD
50 Wellington Street
Glasgow, Strathclyde, Scotland
Tel: (041) 248 7723
18th and 19th c. silver.

FILLIANS ANTIQUES
2 Market Walk
Huddersfield, W Yorks
Tel: (0484) 20889
Silver and silver plate from 1700 on.

J. FOSTER AND SON
19–21 Bell Street
St Andrews, Fife, Scotland
Tel: (0334) 72080
19th c. silver.

WM GOODFELLOW
The Green, Over Kellet
Carnforth, Lancs LA6 1BU
Tel: (0524) 733030
English silver, pre-1850.

GROSVENOR ANTIQUES
22 Watergate Street
Chester, Cheshire CH1 2LA
Tel: (0244) 315201
Silver from all periods, including Art Deco.

LARGO ANTIQUES
Main Street
Upper Largo, Fife, Scotland
Tel: (033 36) 320219
18th and 19th c. silver, including Scottish provincial.

UNA MCVEIGH
98 West Bow
Edinburgh, Lothian, Scotland
Tel: (031) 226 7460
Small silver and silver plate.

MONALTRIE ANTIQUES
Bridge Square
Ballater, Aberdeen, Grampian, Scotland
Tel: (033 82) 429
18th and 19th c. silver and silver plate.

JAMES NISBET
49 West High Street
Forfar, Tayside, Scotland
Tel: (0307) 3434
Scottish silver from 1750 on.

JANE POLLOCK ANTIQUES
4 Castlegate
Penrith, Cumbria
Tel: (0768) 67211 (By appointment only)
Georgian and Victorian silver.

TREASURE HOUSE
16 Holburn Street
Aberdeen, Grampian, Scotland
Tel: (0224) 20219
Georgian and Victorian silver.

CHRISTOPHER WARNER
15 Princes Street
Harrogate, N Yorkshire HG1 1NG
Tel: (0423) 503617
18th and 19th c. silver.

NORTHERN IRELAND

BRIAN R. BOLT
Collectors Antiques
Portballintrae, Nr Bushmills
Antrim, N Ireland
Tel: (026 57) 31129
Small silver, specialising in spoons.

J.A. JOHNSTON LTD
29 English Street
Armagh, Co Armagh, N Ireland
Tel: (0861) 522753
Georgian and Victorian silver.

KNOCK ANTIQUES
284 Upper Newtownards Road
Belfast, Antrim, N Ireland
Tel: (0232) 662998
19th c. silver.

OLD CROSS ANTIQUES
3–5 Main Street
Greyabbey, Co Down, N Ireland
Tel: (024 774) 346
Silver from 1750–1920.

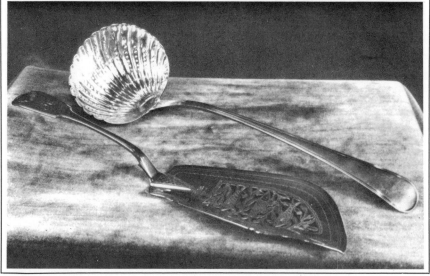

Left: Shell bowl soup ladle, made in London in 1792 by Richard Crossley, and fiddle shell fish slice engraved with fish and acorns, made in London in 1832, courtesy of Jane Pollock Antiques

LONDON

J.A.L. FRANKS LTD
7 Allington Street
London SW1
Tel: (01) 834 8697
and
180 Fleet Street
London EC4
Tel: (01) 405 0274
Stamps from all periods.

STANLEY GIBBONS
391, 395 and 399 Strand
London WC2
Tel: (01) 836 8444
Rare stamps and postal history.

VALE STAMPS AND ANTIQUES
21 Tranquil Vale
London SE3 0BU
Tel: (01) 852 9817
Postage stamps from 1840.

DAVID YOUNG
104 Chepstow Road
London W2
Tel: (01) 229 0660
British and Colonial stamps.

SOUTH AND SOUTHEAST ENGLAND

MALDWYN ANTIQUES
12 and 12a Beynon Parade
Carshalton, Surrey
Tel: (01) 669 0793 and 393 4530 (Home)
Stamps from 1600–1870.

SOUTHWEST ENGLAND AND WALES

CORRIDOR STAMP SHOP
7a The Corridor
Bath, Avon
Tel: (0225) 63368 and 316445 (Home)
Stamps and albums from 1700 to date.

TEXTILES AND NEEDLEWORK

LONDON

DAVID ADAM ORIENTAL CARPETS
118 Brompton Road
London SW3
Tel: (01) 584 6499
Oriental tapestries.

MARIA ANDIPA ICON GALLERY
162 Walton Street
London SW3
Tel: (01) 589 2371
Ethnic embroideries from the 15th c. on.

AND SO TO BED LTD
96b Camden High Street
London NW1
Tel: (01) 388 0364/5
and
638–640 Kings Road
London SW6
Tel: (01) 731 3593/4/5
and
7 New Kings Road
London SW6
Tel: (01) 731 3593
Victorian linen, patchwork quilts and mattress sets.

ANTIQUES
90–92 Pimlico Road
London SW1
Tel: (01) 730 8681
Classical, mediaeval and Renaissance textiles.

THE ARK ANGEL
14 Camden Passage
London N1
Tel: (01) 226 1644
Samplers and quilts.

AXIA
43 Pembridge Villas
London W11
Tel: (01) 727 9724
Islamic and Byzantine textiles.

BRIAN BALL
227 Ebury Street
London SW1
Tel: (01) 730 5000
Patchwork quilts.

RAYMOND BENARDOUT
5 William Street
London SW1X 9HL
Tel: (01) 235 3360
15th to 20th c. Oriental and tribal tapestries and textiles.

DAVID BLACK ORIENTAL CARPETS
96 Portland Road
London W11 4LN
Tel: (01) 727 2566
Carpet specialists who also have antique Near Eastern embroideries.

BOHUN AND BUSBRIDGE
c/o Celia Barker-Mill
24 Iverna Gardens
London W8
Tel: (01) 937 9145
Oriental woven artifacts including Kashmir, Paisley and Norwich shawls, lace, Oriental embroideries, folk costume, patchworks, chintz, Greek island embroideries, ikats and Rajastan silks, all from 16th to 19th c.

JOANNA BOOTH
247 Kings Road
London SW3
Tel: (01) 352 8998
17th to 19th c. tapestries and fabrics, including cushions.

L. AND G. BURNETT
290 Portobello Road
London W9
Tel: (01) 969 8899
Lace and linens.

ANARELLA CLARK
4 Holland Street
London W8
Tel: (01) 937 0614
Quilts, samplers and needlework.

EDWARD AND JOANNA DONOHOE
1–7 Davies Mews
London W1
Tel: (01) 629 5633 and 455 5507 (Home)
European textiles.

J. FAIRMAN LTD
218 Westbourne Grove
London W11
Tel: (01) 229 2262/3
Persian tapestries.

FIVE FIVE SIX ANTIQUES
556 Kings Road
London SW6
Tel: (01) 731 2016 and 624 5173 (Home)
18th and early 19th c. samplers, plus wool and silk works.

ROBERT FRANSES AND SON
5 Nugent Terrace
London NW8
Tel: (01) 286 6913
European and Oriental tapestries and needlework.

S. FRANSES AND COMPANY LTD
71–73 Knightsbridge
London SW1
Tel: (01) 235 1888/3609
15th to 18th c. European tapestries, plus Oriental needlework and textiles.

VICTOR FRANSES GALLERY
57 Jermyn Street
London SW1
Tel: (01) 493 6284/629 1144
Oriental and European tapestries and needlework.

GRACE ANTIQUES
28 Pembridge Villas
London W11 3EL
Tel: (01) 229 4415
18th and 19th c. samplers and textiles.

GWYNETH ANTIQUES
56 Ebury Street
London SW1
Tel: (01) 730 2513
Oriental textiles.

ROBERT HALES ANTIQUES LTD
131 Kensington Church Street
London W8
Tel: (01) 229 3887
17th to 19th c. European textiles and hangings.

HEIRLOOM AND HOWARD LTD
1 Hay Hill
Berkeley Square
London W1
Tel: (01) 493 5868
Armorial embroideries, ie those with crests or coats-of-arms on them.

HERAZ
32 Sloane Street
London SW1
Tel: (01) 730 6709
17th to 19th c. tapestries and textiles, plus 18th and 19th c. cushions.

JELLINEK AND SAMPSON
156 Brompton Road
London SW3
Tel: (01) 589 5272
17th and 18th c. needlework.

TEXTILES AND NEEDLEWORK

WILLIAM JOB LTD
86–88 Pimlico Road
London SW1 8PL
Tel: (01) 730 7374
17th and 18th c. needlework.

THE LACQUER CHEST
75 Kensington Church Street
London W8
Tel: (01) 937 1306
Fabrics from 1800–1900, specialising in the unusual.

JOSEPH LAVIAN
53–79 Highgate Road
London NW5
Tel: (01) 485 7955 and 346 3140 (Home)
18th and 19th c. kelims, tapestries and textiles.

JILL LEWIS
Collector's Corner
138 Portobello Road
London W11
Tel: (040) 372 2357
Sewing accessories, including thimbles.

STEPHEN LONG
348 Fulham Road
London SW10
Tel: (01) 352 8226
18th and 19th c. chintz, fabrics and patchwork quilts.

LOOT
76–78 Pimlico Road
London SW1
Tel: (01) 730 8097
18th and 19th c. textiles, including Oriental pieces.

LUCKY PARROT
2 Bellevue Parade
Bellevue Road
London SW17
Tel: (01) 672 7168
19th c. patchwork.

LUNN ANTIQUES
86 New Kings Road
London SW6
Tel: (01) 736 4638
Oriental embroidery, early lace, Victorian and Edwardian hand-worked linen, sheets, bedspreads, and tablecloths.

MALLETT AND SON LTD
40 New Bond Street
London W1Y 0BS
Tel: (01) 499 7411
18th c. needlework.

ALAN MARCUSON LTD
3 Warwick Place
London W9
Tel: (01) 286 7307/8
Central Asian textiles.

MAYORCAS LTD
38 Jermyn Street
London SW1
Tel: (01) 629 4195
Tapestries, textiles, embroideries, needlework, and church vestments.

NIHON TOKEN
23 Museum Street
London WC1A 1JT
Tel: (01) 580 6511
Ancient and antique Japanese textiles.

PAT NYE
Collector's Corner
138 Portobello Road

Above: Early 18th c. English crewelwork panel of a flowering tree with an exotic bird in its branches, all embroidered in bright colours, circa 1700, courtesy of Mallett and Son Ltd.

PAT NYE (CON'T)
London W11
Tel: (01) 948 4314 (Home)
18th and 19th c. needlework samplers.

THE PATCHWORK DOG AND THE CALICO CAT LTD
21 Chalk Farm Road
London NW1
Tel: (01) 485 1239
Patchwork quilts from 1800.

PINE AND DESIGN
28 Shelton Street
London WC2
Tel: (01) 836 1977/8
Victorian lace-edged tablecloths.

PORTMEIRION ANTIQUES
5 Pont Street
London SW1
Tel: (01) 235 7601
Quilts from 1700–1900.

PUTNAMS KITCHEN ANTIQUES
72 Mill Lane
London NW6
Tel: (01) 431 2935
Victorian quilts and tablecloths.

PETA SMITH ANTIQUE TEXTILES (AT ROBERT HALES)
133 Kensington Church Street
London W8
Tel: (01) 229 3887
17th to 19th c. European textiles including silks, velvets and embroideries.

LOUIS STANTON
299 Westbourne Grove
London W11
Tel: (01) 727 9336
Early English and Continental tapestries.

TRAFALGAR ANTIQUES
117 Trafalgar Road
London SE10
Tel: (01) 858 3709
Fabrics from 1750–1900.

TWENTY ONE ANTIQUES
21 Chalk Farm Road
London NW1
Tel: (01) 485 1239
English and American patchwork quilts from 1850–1930, and Victorian lace.

VERMOUTIER AND BANKS
25a Holland Street
London W8 4NA
Tel: (01) 937 3262
18th and 19th c. English needlework.

VIGO CARPET GALLERY
6a Vigo Street
London W1
Tel: (01) 439 6971
Textiles and tapestries.

VIGO-STERNBERG GALLERIES
37 South Audley Street
London W1
Tel: (01) 629 8307
European tapestries, from the 15th c. on.

TRUDE WEAVER
71 Portobello Road
London W11
Tel: (01) 229 8738
European and Continental tapestries.

SOUTH AND SOUTHEAST ENGLAND

CEDAR ANTIQUES
High Street
Hartley Wintney, Hants
Tel: (025 126) 3252
17th and 18th c. tapestries.

ANARELLA CLARK
19 High Street
Ditchling, Sussex
Tel: (07918) 4033
Quilts, samplers and needlework.

THE LEOPARD
41 Gloucester Road
Brighton, Sussex
Tel: (0273) 507619
18th to early 20th c. textiles, lace and lace-trimmed items such as tablecloths. See overleaf for illustration.

MARKET PLACE ANTIQUES
35 Market Place
Henley-on-Thames, Oxon RG9 2AA
Tel: (04912) 2387
Patchwork quilts from 1830.

PENNY FARTHING ANTIQUES
71 High Street
Chobham, Surrey
Tel: (099 05) 7718
19th c. lace and textiles.

THE TOKEN HOUSE
7 Market Parade, High Street
Ewell, Epson, Surrey
Tel: (01) 393 9654
19th c. samplers and embroideries.

TRINITY ANTIQUES
7 Trinity Street
Colchester, Essex
Tel: (0206) 77775
Victorian linens.

SOUTHWEST ENGLAND AND WALES

KATHERINE CHRISTOPHERS
St Catherines Court
St Catherines
Bath, Avon
Tel: (0225) 858159
14th to 17th c. tapestries, needlework and samplers.

R. AND D. COOMBES
The Old Priest House
Aldbourne
Marlborough, Wilts
Tel: (0672) 40241
Pre-18th c. Oriental embroideries and textiles.

RED BARN
Pontcanna Street
Cardiff, S Glamorgan
Tel: (0222) 513437
Welsh and patchwork quilts, lace and textiles.

MORRIS TUCKER
Lower Town House
Chudleigh Knighton, Devon TQ13 0ME
Tel: (0626) 852123
Specialist in maritime and country items with wool pictures, samplers and sea shell valentines.

MIDLANDS AND EAST ANGLIA

BITS AND PIECES
34 High Street
Higham Ferrers, Northants
and
3a Church Street
Finedon, Northants
Tel: (0933) 680430
Samplers and other embroideries.

MERIDIAN HOUSE ANTIQUES
Meridian House
Market Street
Stourbridge, W Midlands
Tel: (038 43) 5384
18th and 19th c. needlework samplers.

MRS A.M. PONSONBY
Upham House
Ashfield, nr Stowmarket, Suffolk
Tel: (072 882) 200
18th and 19th c. needlework pictures.

NORTH OF ENGLAND AND SCOTLAND

AND SO TO BED LTD
133 Deansgate
Bolton, Lancs
Tel: (0204) 392386
and
60 West Street
Sowerby Bridge
Halifax, W Yorkshire
Tel: (0422) 39759
and
65 Whitley Road
Whitley Bay
Tyne & Wear
Tel: (0632) 524611
Victorian linen, patchwork quilts and mattress sets.

Right: Finely-worked sampler by Ellen Preston, aged 11 years, Lancaster 1845, courtesy of Wm Goodfellow Antiques.

Above: Point-de-gaze needlepoint lace collar, courtesy of The Leopard.

WM GOODFELLOW
The Green
Over Kellet
Carnforth, Lancs LA6 1BU
Tel: (0524) 733030
English embroideries pre-1900.

HAND IN HAND
3 North West Circus Place
Edinburgh, Lothian, Scotland
Tel: (031) 556 8897
Victorian linen, embroidery, lace and tapestries.

CHARLES HAY ANTIQUES
44 High Street
Coldstream, Borders, Scotland
Tel: (0890) 2552
18th and early 19th c. needlework.

NORWOOD ANTIQUES
1 Norwood
Beverley, N Humberside
Tel: (0482) 868851
18th to early 20th c. lace, linen, crochet work, samplers, and tapestries.

THE OLD CURIO SHOP
Midsteeple
High Street
Dumfries, Dumfries and Galloway, Scotland
Tel: (0387) 4698
Victorian linen and lace.

OLDMILL ANTIQUES
68 Claremont Street
Aberdeen, Grampian, Scotland
Tel: (0224) 573562
Victorian linen and lace.

E.W. WEBSTER
Wash Farm
Bickerstaffe
Nr Ormskirk, Lancs
Tel: (0695) 24322
Pre-1850 samplers.

Left: Anglo-Indian ivory certofina and sandalwood chess and backgammon box/board, counters and shakers, in their original wood carrying-case, also containing a French ivory chess set, courtesy of Chanticleer Antiques.

UNDER TWO FLAGS
4 St Christopher's Place
London W1
Tel: (01) 935 6934
Model soldiers.

SOUTH AND SOUTHEAST ENGLAND

MALDWYN ANTIQUES
12 and 12a Beynon Parade
Carshalton, Surrey
Tel: (01) 669 0793 and 393 4530 (Home)
Models, Dinkies, Matchbox cars and railway accessories.

MARKET PLACE ANTIQUES
35 Market Place
Henley-on-Thames, Oxon RG9 2AA
Tel: (04912) 2387
Early wooden games. For illustration, see entry under "Primitives".

WARNER'S MILITARY SPECIALISTS
2 The Apple Market
Eden Street
Kingston-upon-Thames, Surrey
Tel: (Mail Order Only)
Model soldiers from 1900–1960.

MIDLANDS AND EAST ANGLIA

HUMBLEYARD FINE ART
Waterfall Cottage
Mill Street
Swanton Morley, Norfolk
Tel: (036 283) 793
18th and 19th c. games and accessories.

NORTH OF ENGLAND AND SCOTLAND

ANTIQUE MODELS AND MILITARIA
38 Union Place
Dundee, Tayside, Scotland
Tel: (0382) 86649
Dinky toys, die-cast and tinplate models from 1900 on.

LONDON

ANTIQUE TOY COENTRE
51 Camden Passage
London N1
Tel: (01) 226 4255/607 0846
Late 19th to early 20th c. tinplate toys, locomotives, dolls, and mechanical money boxes.

BARHAM ANTIQUES
83 Portobello Road
London W11
Tel: (01) 727 3845
Victorian wooden chess sets.

WILLIAM BEDFORD ANTIQUES LTD
327 Upper Street
London N1
Tel: (01) 226 9648
Late 17th to early 19th c. game boards, tables and boxes.

CHANTICLEER ANTIQUES
105 Portobello Road
London W11
Tel: (01) 385 0919 (By appointment only)
Chinese and European ivory chess sets.

JEREMY COOPER LTD
9 Galen Place
London WC1
Tel: (01) 242 5138/404 0336
Toys and games from 1830–1930.

GAME ADVICE
1 Holmes Road
London NW5
Tel: (01) 485 2188/4226
18th and 19th c. games, puzzles, chess sets and toys.

STANLEY GIBBONS
391, 395 and 399 Strand
London WC2
Tel: (01) 836 8444
Playing cards.

ANTHEA KNOWLES
42 Barnsbury Street
London N1
Tel: (01) 607 0846 (By appointment only)
Early tin toys.

STEPHEN LONG
348 Fulham Road, London SW10
Tel: (01) 352 8226
18th and 19th c. toys and games.

RAYMOND O'SHEA GALLERY
6 Ellis Street
(Off Sloane Street)
London SW1
Tel: (01) 730 0082
Cartographic specialist with topographical jigsaws

PETER STOCKHAM AT IMAGES
16 Cecil Court
London WC2
Tel: (01) 836 8661
Toys, especially wooden ones, and games.

TRADITION MILITARY ANTIQUES
5a–5b Shepherd Street
London W1
Tel: (01) 493 7452
Model soldiers.

Below: French hand-enamelled toy "Land Train", circa 1890, courtesy of Anthea Knowles.

LONDON

ANARELLA CLARK
4 Holland Street
London W8
Tel: (01) 937 0614
Treen from 17th c. on.

DONOHOE
175 Portobello Road
London W11
Tel: (01) 727 4681 and 455 5507 (Home)
European treen.

FAYME ANTIQUES
56 Elgin Crescent
London W11 2JJ
Tel: (01) 727 9526
17th to 19th c. decorative treen.

HALCYON DAYS
14 Brook Street
London W1Y 1AA
Tel: (01) 629 8111
Treen, specialising in small items.

HELGATO
50 Highgate High Street
London N6 5HX
Tel: (01) 348 3864
Treen to 1900.

LESLEY HEPHERD ANTIQUES
47 Camden Passage
London N1
Tel: (01) 359 1755
Treen from 17th c. on.

HOLLYWOOD ROAD ANTIQUES
1a Hollywood Road
London SW10
Tel: (01) 352 5248
Treen from 17th c. on.

WILLIAM JOB LTD
86–88 Pimlico Road
London SW1 8PL
Tel: (01) 730 7374
17th and 18th c. treen including snuff boxes.

PRINCIPIA FINE ART
28 Victoria Grove
London W8
Tel: (01) 584 8080
Treen from 17th c. on.

ROBERT YOUNG ANTIQUES
68 Battersea Bridge Road
London SW11
Tel: (01) 228 7847
17th and 18th c. English and European treen.

Above: James I cup and cover in pearwood with incised decoration, reputed to be one of 26 still in existence, courtesy of A. and E. Foster.

SOUTH AND SOUTHEAST ENGLAND

ANNARELLA CLARK ANTIQUES
19 High Street
Ditchling, Sussex
Tel: (07918) 4033
Primitive and country-style treen.

PAUL FEWINGS LTD
38 South Street
Titchfield, nr Fareham, Hants.
Tel: (0329) 43952
Treen from 1750–1900.

A. AND E. FOSTER
Little Heysham
Naphill, Bucks
Tel: (024 024) 2024 (By appointment only)
Early treen.

ANN AND RICHARD HAGEN
Bakehouse Cottage
Northwood End
Haynes, Beds
Tel:(023 066) 424
Treen from 1690–1840.

HOUSE OF ANTIQUES
4 College Street
Petersfield, Hants
Tel: (0730) 2172
18th and 19th c. treen.

THE MAGPIE
25 Sandrock Hill Road
Recclesham, Farnham, Surrey
Tel: (025 13) 3129
Treen from 17th c. on.

ANGELA PAGE ANTIQUES
Sion House, 14 Mount Sion
Tunbridge Wells, Kent
Tel: (0892) 22217
Treen from 17th c. on.

SOUTHWEST ENGLAND AND WALES

MACLEAN ANTIQUES
3–3a Carmarthen Street
Llandeilo, Dyfed, Wales
Tel: (055 03) 509
18th and 19th c. treen

PETER PHILP
77 Kimberley Road
Cardiff, Glamorgan CF2 5DP, Wales
Tel: (0222) 493826
17th to early 19th c. treen.

CHARLOTTE AND BETTE MORSE
Larks-in-the-Wood
Pentlow, Sudbury, Suffolk
Tel: (0787) 280377
17th and 18th c. oak furniture.

NORTH OF ENGLAND AND SCOTLAND

CHARLES HAY ANTIQUES
44 High Street
Coldstream, Borders, Scotland
Tel: (0890)
18th and early 19th c. treen.

E.W. WEBSTER
Wash Farm
Bickerstaffe, Nr Ormskirk, Lancs
Tel: (0695) 24322
Pre-1860 treen.

MISCELLANEOUS

LONDON

ASTLEYS
109 Jermyn Street
London SW1
Tel: (01) 930 1687
19th c. meerschaum pipes, smoking accessories, cigar boxes, smoking cabinets, tobacco jars, plus pottery, porcelain, primitive and Oriental pipes.

THE BUTTON QUEEN
19 Marylebone Lane
London W1
Tel: (01) 935 1505
Antique horn, silver, mother-of-pearl buttons. Will also cover buttons to match fabric.

GREGORY, BOTTLEY AND LLOYD
8–12 Rickett Street
London SW6
Tel: (01) 381 5522
Collections of minerals and fossils, collectors' cabinets and mining items including tools.

HEIRLOOM AND HOWARD LTD
1 Hay Hill
Berkeley Square
London W1
Tel: (01) 493 5868
Specialists in armorial antiques, ie those with crests or coats of arms on them. Selection includes pottery, porcelain, paintings, signet rings, etc. See entry under "Porcelain" for illustration.

Left: Pair of grey squirrels by Rowland Ward, circa 1900, courtesy of The Enchanted Aviary.

Left: Brown trout in bow-fronted glazed case, caught in 1928, weighing 7lbs 2oz, courtesy of Get Stuffed.

SOUTH AND SOUTHEAST ENGLAND

ART AND MARINE
19 Lion Street
Rye, E Sussex
Tel: (07973) 4200
Nautical antiques including scrimshaw carvings.

SPENCER SWAFFER
30 High Street
Arundel, W Sussex
Tel: (0903) 882132
19th and early 20th c. decoys.

SOUTHWEST ENGLAND AND WALES

ALDERSON AND ALDERSON
23 Brook Street
Bath, Avon
Tel: (0225) 21652
Silhouettes.

MIDLANDS AND EAST ANGLIA

THE ENCHANTED AVIARY
Long Melford
Sudbury, Suffolk
Tel: (0787) 78814
Victorian mounted birds, fish and animals.

NORTH OF ENGLAND AND SCOTLAND

MARTIN ANTIQUES
36 St Stephen Street
Edinburgh, Lothian EH3 5AL, Scotland
Tel: (031 556) 3527
Old woodworking tools.

GET STUFFED
105 Essex Road
London N1
Tel: (01) 226 1364
Stuffed birds, mammals, fish, butterflies, insects, plus horns, heads and mounted trophies.

BRIAN LLOYD MINERALS
15a Pall Mall
London SW1
Tel: (01) 930 6921 and 352 5375 (Home)
Mineral specimens and objects made from minerals.

THE MAP HOUSE
54 Beauchamp Place
London SW3
Tel: (01) 589 4325/9821
Cartographic specialists with a selection of antique globes.

M. ST CLARE
37 Mildmay Park
London N1
Tel: (01) 226 4587 (By appointment only)
Mounted birds, animals, fish and Victorian taxidermy items.

TALKING MACHINE
30 Watford Way
London NW4
Tel: (01) 202 3473
Mechanical music, old gramophones, phonographs, vintage records, early radios, typewriters, sewing machines and spare parts.

TAVERN TREASURES
7b Nelson Road
London SE10
Tel: (01) 853 5777 (By appointment only)
Wine and beer trade relics including corkscrews, barrel brushes, ashtrays, match strikers, and posters.

M. AND C. TELFER-SMOLLETT
88 Portobello Road
London W11
Tel: (01) 727 0117 and 229 8028 (Home)
Natural history specimens.

BRIAN R. VERRALL AND COMPANY
20 Tooting Bec Road
London SW17
Tel: (01) 672 1144
Vintage and veteran motor cycles and motor cars.

MARKETS AND WAREHOUSES

The antique markets in this section will carry a selection of objects from all periods. If you are looking for something in particular, phone the given number and ask if you can be put directly in touch with the relevant dealer(s). If you are more leisured, markets make terrific places for browsing. Days: Monday–Saturday unless otherwise indicated.

LONDON

ANGEL ARCADE
116–118 Islington High Street
London N1
Tel: (01) 226 2159
*Open: Saturday 8am–5pm, Wednesday 6.30am–3pm, otherwise individual shops by arrangement.
Number of Units: over 30
Stock: General antiques including old shop-fittings, advertising signs, cane and bamboo furniture.*

ALFIE'S ANTIQUE MARKET
13–25 Church Street
London NW8
Tel: (01) 723 6066
*Open: 10am–6pm, closed Monday
Number of Units: over 100
Stock: General antiques plus craft workshops and showrooms.*

ANTIQUARIUS
135 Kings Road
London SW3
Tel: (01) 351 5353
*Open: 10am–6pm
Number of Units: 150
Stock: General antiques including Art Nouveau, Art Deco and 1920's and 1930's fashions.*

ANTIQUE HYPERMARKET
26–40 Kensington High Street
London W8
Tel: (01) 937 1572
*Open: 10am–5.45pm
Number of Units: 85
Stock: General antiques including 19th c. furniture, silver, porcelain and icons.*

BERMONDSEY ANTIQUE MARKET
251–255 Long Lane, London SE1
Tel: (01) 937 1572
*Open: Friday 5am–2pm
Number of Units: 150
Stock: Silver, furniture, arms, carpets, toys, bric-à-brac, pictures, brass, copper and pewter.*

BERMONDSEY ANTIQUE WAREHOUSE
173 Bermondsey Street, London SE1 3UW
Tel: (01) 407 2040
*Open: Monday–Friday 9.30–5.30pm, otherwise by appointment
Number of Units: 6
Stock: General antiques including furniture and chandeliers.*

BOND STREET ANTIQUE CENTRE
124 New Bond Street
London W1
Tel: (01) 351 5353
*Open: Monday–Friday 10am–6pm, Saturday 10am–12pm
Number of Units: 44
Stock: Jewellery, silver, oriental items, arms, armour, small furniture, paintings, portrait miniatures and prints.*

BOND STREET SILVER GALLERIES
111–112 New Bond Street
London W1
Tel: (01) 493 6180
Open: 9am–5.30pm, closed Saturday
Number of Units: 15
Stock: Silver, plate, jewellery and Russian
    enamel.

**CAMDEN PASSAGE ANTIQUES
CENTRE (AND CAMDEN PASSAGE
SITES)**
357 Upper Street
Islington, London N1
Tel: (01) 359 0190
Open (shops and boutiques):
10.30am–5.30pm
Number of Units: 160
Stock: General antiques.

Open (stalls): Tuesday (general antiques)
    9am–4pm
    Wednesday (general antiques)
    8am–3pm
    Thursday and Friday (books)
    9am–4pm
    Saturday (general antiques)
    9am–5pm
Number of Units: 100

CHELSEA ANTIQUE MARKET
245a and 253 Kings Road,
London SW3
Tel: (01) 352 1425
Open: 10am–6pm
Number of Units: 100
Stock: General antiques.

CHENIL GALLERIES
181 Kings Road
London SW3
Tel: (01) 351 5153
Open: 10am–6pm
Number of Units: 140
Stock: Paintings, furniture, silver, jewellery,
    Art Nouveau and Art Deco.

**CORNER PORTOBELLO ANTIQUES
SUPERMARKET**
282, 284, 288, 290 Westbourne Grove
London W11
Tel: (01) 727 2027
Open: Friday 11am–4pm, Saturday
7am–6pm
Number of Units: 150
Stock: General antiques including silver,
    jewellery, and miniature antiques.

GEORGIAN VILLAGE
(facing Islington Green)
Camden Passage
London N1
Tel: (01) 226 7835
Open: Wednesday 6.30am–3pm, Saturday
    8am–5pm
Number of Units: 150
Stock: General antiques.

GRAYS ANTIQUE MARKET
58 Davies Street
London W1
Tel: (01) 629 7034
Open: Monday–Friday 10am–6pm, closed
    Saturday
Number of Units: 76
Stock: General antiques.

GRAYS MEWS
1–7 Davies Mews
London W1
Tel: (01) 493 7861

Open: Monday–Friday 10am–6pm, closed
    Saturday
Number of Units: over 70
Stock: General Antiques.

HAMPSTEAD ANTIQUE EMPORIUM
12 Heath Street
London NW3
Tel: (01) 794 3297
Open: 10am–6pm, closed Monday
Number of Units: 20
Stock: Jewellery, clocks, furniture, silver,
    paintings, prints, metalware, glass,
    Art Nouveau, Art Deco, linens and lace.

KNIGHTSBRIDGE PAVILION
112 Brompton Road
London SW3
Tel: (01) 589 5260
Open: Monday–Friday 10am–5.30pm,
    Saturday 11am–3pm
Number of Units: 17
Stock: General antiques.

LEWISHAM MONDAY MARKET
Riverdale Hall, Lewisham Centre
Rennell Street, London SE13
Tel: (01) 937 1246/693 7112
Open: Monday 8.30am–4.30pm
Number of Units: over 50
Stock: General antiques.

LONDON SILVER VAULTS
Chancery Lane
London WC2
Tel: (01) 242 3844/5
Open: Monday–Friday 9am–5.30pm,
    Saturday 9am–12pm
Number of Units: over 30
Stock: Silver, plate, jewellery, clocks, watches
    and collectors' items.

**MACNEILL'S ART AND ANTIQUES
WAREHOUSE**
Newnhams Row
175 Bermondsey Street
London SE1
Tel: (01) 403 0022
Open: 9.30am–6pm, Thursday
    9.30am–7.30pm, closed Saturday
Stock: Victorian furniture.

THE MALL ANTIQUES ARCADE
Camden Passage
London N1
Tel: (01) 359 0825
Open: 10am–5pm, Wednesday 7.30am–5pm,
    closed Monday
Number of Dealers: 38
Stock: General antiques including porcelain,
    furniture, jewellery, silver, pictures,
    clocks and bronzes.

NEW CRAWFORD MARKET
43 Crawford Street
London W1
Tel: (01) 723 2727
Open: 10am–6pm
Number of Units: 14
Stock: Furniture, china, glass, silver,
    pictures.

**PORTOBELLO ROAD AND
ENVIRONS**
Portobello Road
London W11
Open: 6am–6pm
Number of Units: 300
Stock: Wide range of general antiques.

SOUTH AND SOUTHEAST ENGLAND

THE ANTIQUES CENTRE
120 London Road
Sevenoaks, Kent
Tel: (0732) 52104
Open: 9am–1pm, 2pm–5.30pm
Number of units: 10
Stock: Mahogany, oak, Oriental and pine
    furniture, paintings, porcelain, dolls,
    silver, copper, brass, etc.
    all 17th–19th c.

BATTLESBRIDGE ANTIQUE CENTRE
Battlesbridge, Essex
Tel: Not Available
Open: Wednesday–Saturday
10.30am–5.30pm
Number of Units: 25
Stock: Large furniture and jewellery.

BRIGHTON ANTIQUES GALLERY
41 Meeting House Lane
Brighton, E Sussex
Tel: (0273) 26693/21059
Open: 10am–5.45pm
Number of Units: 22
Stock: Dolls, silver, jewellery, copper and
    brass, small furniture, arms and
    armour.

BROMLEY ANTIQUE MARKET
United Reformed Church Hall
Widmore Road
Bromley, Kent
Tel: (01) 334 8178
Open: Thursday 8.30am–3pm
Number of Units: 70
Stock: General antiques including jewellery,
    books, bric-à-brac, copper, brass, clocks,
    coins, furs, stamps and postcards.

DEDDINGTON ANTIQUE CENTRE
Laurel House
The Bull Ring
Deddington, Oxon
Tel: (0869) 38968
Open: Wednesday–Saturday 10am–5pm
Number of Units: 7 (in 9 rooms)
Stock: Furniture, copper and brass.

EPPING ANTIQUE GALLERIES
64–66 High Street
Epping, Essex
Tel: Epping 72102
Open: 10am–5pm, except Wednesday
Flea Market: Saturday 9am–5pm
Number of Units: 20
Stock: Furniture, paintings, porcelain and
    books, all 19th c.

ETON ANTIQUE MARKET
79 High Street, Eton, Berks
Tel: Not Available
Open: 10am–5.30pm, except Monday
Number of Units: 25
Stock: Jewellery, silver, china, glassware,
    ivory, Oriental works of art, furniture,
    paintings, brass, clocks, and coins.

HOUSE OF ANTIQUES
4 College Street
Petersfield, Hants
Tel: (0730) 2172
Open: 9.30am–1pm, 2pm–5.30pm, closed
Thursday
Number of Units: over 20
Stock: Furniture, boxes, porcelain, guns,
    swords, early glass, Staffordshire,
    metalware, clocks and paintings.

MIDHURST ANTIQUES MARKET
Curfew Garden Court
Knockhundred Row
Midhurst, W Sussex
Tel: (073 081) 4231
Open: 9.30am–5.30pm
Number of Units: 16
*Stock: Furniture, china, pictures, clocks,
    brass, copper, firearms and glass.*

SANDGATE ANTIQUES CENTRE
High Street
Sandgate, Kent
Tel: Not Available
Open: 10am–6pm, Sunday 11am–6pm
Number of Units: 8
Stock: General antiques.

TRINITY ANTIQUES CENTRE
7 Trinity Street
Colchester, Essex
Tel: (0206) 77775
Open: 9.30am–5pm, closed Thursday
Number of Units: 8
*Stock: Small furniture, copper, clocks, brass,
    porcelain, jewellery, silver, Victoriana,
    cameras, weapons, maps and prints.*

WALLINGTON ANTIQUE MARKET
St Elebheges Church Hall
Stafford Road
Wallington, Surrey
Tel: Not Available
Open: 8.30am–3.30pm
Number of Units: 20
Stock: General Antiques.

WOOD'S WHARF ANTIQUES BAZAAR
56 High Street
Haslemere, Surrey
Tel: (0428) 2125
Open: 9.30am–5pm
Number of Units: 14
Stock: General antiques.

SOUTHWEST ENGLAND

BATH ANTIQUE MARKET
Guinea Lane
The Paragon
Bath, Avon
Tel: (0225) 858467
Open: Wednesday 8am–3pm
Number of Units: 90
*Stock: Furniture, porcelain, pottery, glass,
    pictures, jewellery and metalware.*

BATH SATURDAY ANTIQUE MART
Walcot Street
Bath, Avon
Tel: (0225) 317837
Open: Saturday 8am–5pm
Number of Units: 50
Stock: General antiques.

BOURNEMOUTH ANTIQUES CENTRE
No.1 The Square
Bournemouth, Dorset
Tel: Not Available
Open: 10am–5pm
Number of Units: 21
Stock: General antiques.

CHELTENHAM ANTIQUE MARKET
54 Suffolk Road
Cheltenham, Glos
Tel: (0242) 29812
Open: 9am–5.30pm
Number of Units: 11
Stock: General antiques.

CIRENCESTER WAREHOUSE
Market Place
Cirencester, Glos
Tel: (01) 240 0428
Open: Friday 9am–4pm
Number of Units: about 60
Stock: General antiques.

CLIFTON ANTIQUES MARKET
26–28 The Mall
Clifton
Bristol, Avon
Tel: (0272) 741627
Open: Tuesday–Saturday 10am–6pm
Number of Units: 42
Stock: General antiques.

CORNISH ANTIQUE MARKET
Little Castle Street
Truro, Cornwall
Tel: (0872) 3970
Open: 9am–5pm, closed Thursday
Number of Units: about 20
*Stock: Jewellery, clothing, furs, silver, dolls,
    china, stamps, small furniture,
    postcards and books.*

GREAT WESTERN ANTIQUE CENTRE LTD
Bartlett Street
Bath, Avon
Tel: (0225) 24243/20686
Open: 9.30am–5pm
Number of Units: over 60
Stock: General antiques.

MARLBOROUGH ANTIQUES CENTRE
Cavendish House
High Street
Marlborough, Wilts
Tel: (0672) 2912/3570
Open: 10am–1pm, 2pm–5pm
Number of Units: 12
*Stock: Furniture, Victoriana, dolls and dolls'
    furnishings, weapons, silver, jewellery,
    coins and pictures.*

TAUNTON ANTIQUES CENTRE
27–29 Silver Street
Taunton, Somerset
Tel: (0823) 89327
Open: Monday 9am–4pm
Number of Units: 100
*Stock: General antiques including furniture,
    silver and porcelain.*

TORQUAY ANTIQUES CENTRE
250–252 Union Street
Torquay, Devon
Tel: (0803) 26621
*Open: Monday–Friday 9am–1pm,
    2pm–5.30pm*
Number of Units: 20
Stock: General antiques.

MIDLANDS AND EAST ANGLIA

BIRMINGHAM THURSDAY ANTIQUE FAIR (at a BTA Market)
141 Bromsgrove Street
Birmingham, W Midlands
Tel: (021) 622 2145
*Open: Thursday 9.30am–5pm, other times by
    appointment*
Number of Units: 30
Stock: General antiques.

NEWARK ART AND ANTIQUES CENTRE
Market Place and Chain Lane
Newark-on-Trent, Notts
Tel: (0636) 703959
Open: 9.30am–5.30pm, closed Thursday pm
Number of Units: 20
*Stock: Georgian and Victorian furniture,
    pottery, porcelain, glass, swords,
    militaria, coins, clocks, pictures, books,
    Victoriana, silver and jewellery.*

NORTH OF ENGLAND AND SCOTLAND

BOLTON THURSDAY ANTIQUE MARKET
St Paul's Parochial Hall
Newnham Street, Astley Bridge
Bolton, Gt Manchester
Tel: (0204) 51257
Open: Thursday 10am–4pm
Number of Units: about 20
*Stock: Silver, porcelain, jewellery, Goss china,
    postcards, Victoriana and small
    furniture.*

BUTTER LANE ANTIQUES CENTRE
40a King Street West
Manchester, Gt Manchester
Tel: (061) 834 1809
Open: 10.30am–5.30pm
Number of Units: 30
*Stock: Victoriana, bric-à-brac, costumes and
    silver.*

CHESTER ANTIQUE HYPERMARKET
41 Lower Bridge Street
Chester, Cheshire
Tel: (01) 240 0428
Open: 10am–5pm
Number of Units: 36
Stock: General antiques.

EDINBURGH ANTIQUE MARKET
64–78 St Stephen Street
Stockbridge
Edinburgh 3, Lothian, Scotland
Tel: Not Available
Open: 10am–5.30pm
Number of Units: 20
*Stock: General antiques including one
    gramophone specialist.*

NORTH WESTERN ANTIQUES CENTRE
New Preston Mill
New Hall Lane
Preston, Lancs
Tel: (0772) 798159
Open: Monday–Friday 8.30–5.30pm
Number of Units: 16
Stock: General antiques, mainly furniture.

THE VICTORIAN VILLAGE
53 West Regent Street
Glasgow, Strathclyde, Scotland
Tel: (041) 332 0703/5402
Open: 9am–5pm
Number of Units: 25
Stock: General antiques.

The following is a listing of some of the best-known antiques fairs in the U.K., arranged under the months in which they are held. Exact dates are unavailable, as they change from year to year, but can be obtained from the organizer, whose name and address are also given. In addition to these well-established events, many smaller fairs take place all over the country on an irregular basis, so it's worth watching for advertisements in local newspapers.

JANUARY

New Year Fair
St John's Hotel
Solihull, W Midlands
c/o S. and J. Petford
148 Highfield Road
Hall Green
Birmingham, W Midlands

Bristol Antique and Collectors' Fair
Bristol Exhibition Centre
Bristol, Avon
c/o G. Mosdell
Hillside, St. Issey
Nr. Wadebridge, Cornwall

Annual Norwich Antiques Fair
Blackfriars Hall
St. Andrew's Plain
Norwich, Norfolk
c/o Anthony Keniston
Old Rectory, Hopton Castle
Craven Arms, Shropshire
(Pre-1870)

West London Antiques Fair
Kensington New Town Hall
Hornton Street
London W8
c/o Caroline Penman
Cockhaise Mill, Lindfield
Haywards Heath, Sussex
(Pre-1870)

Devizes Antiques Fair
The Bear Hotel
c/o G. Mosdell
Hillside, St. Issey
Nr. Wadebridge, Cornwall

Annual Salisbury Fair
Red Lion Hotel
Salisbury, Wilts
c/o Anthony Keniston
Old Rectory, Hopton Castle
Craven Arms, Shropshire
(Pre-1870)

London Antique Dealers' Fair
Piccadilly Hotel
Piccadilly, London W1
c/o Mrs. J. Sumner
9 Market Square
Saffron Walden, Essex
(Furniture pre-1830)

FEBRUARY

Petersfield Antiques Fair
The Town Hall
Petersfield, Hants
c/o Eric Gamlin
20 Stroud Road
Gloucester, Glos
(Jewellery, silver, pictures, prints rugs and books pre-1920; all other items pre-1881)

Newcastle-Upon-Tyne Fair
Gosforth Park Hotel, High Gosforth Park
Newcastle-upon-Tyne, Tyne & Wear
c/o Mrs S. Brownson
Brownslow House, Gt. Budworth
Northwich, Cheshire
(Furniture pre-1860; jewellery, bronze, rugs and fine arts pre-1900; all other items pre-1880)

Annual Shropshire Antiques Fair
Lion Hotel
Shrewsbury, Shropshire
c/o Anthony Keniston
Old Rectory, Hopton Castle
Craven Arms, Shropshire
(All pre-1870)

St. James's Antiques Fair
Piccadilly Hotel
Piccadilly, London W1
c/o Mary Packham
7 Royal Well Place
Cheltenham, Glos
(Furniture and clocks pre-1840; pottery and porcelain pre-1870; jewellery pre-1900; all other items pre-1880)

Luton Fair
Chiltern Hotel
Dunstable Road, Walter Avenue
Luton, Beds
c/o R.J. Perry
61 Chesford Road
Luton, Beds
(All pre-1910 except jewellery, silver and dolls pre-1930)

Yeovil Antiques and Collectors' Fair
Johnson Hall
Yeovil, Somerset
c/o G. Mosdell
Hillside, St Issey
Nr Wadebridge, Cornwall

Annual Leicester Antiques Fair
Wigston Stage Motel
Welford Road
Leicester, Leics
c/o Anthony Keniston
Old Rectory, Hopton Castle
Craven Arms, Shropshire
(All pre-1870)

High Wycombe Spring Antiques Fair
Town Hall
High Wycombe, Bucks
c/o Tony and Norma Hepburn
Norton Antiques
56 London End
Beaconsfield, Bucks
(Furniture pre-1860; all other items pre-1900 except paintings, jewellery, carpets and rugs pre-1920)

South East Counties Antiques Dealers Fair
Goodwood House
Nr. Chichester, W Sussex
c/o S. Soper
Castle Gate
York, N Yorkshire
(All pre-1880)

MARCH

Chelsea Antiques Fair
Chelsea Old Town Hall
Kings Road
London SW3

Scottish Antiquarian Book Fair
The Roxburgh Hotel
Edinburgh, Lothian, Scotland
c/o Mrs E. Dean
The Burlington House Fair
4 Bloomsbury Square
London WC1
(Antiquity to 1930)

The Western Counties Fair
Weston Park
Shropshire
c/o S. Soper
Castle Gate
York, N Yorkshire
(All pre-1880)

The Burlington House Fair
Royal Academy of Arts
Burlington House
Piccadilly, London W1
c/o Mrs E. Dean,
4 Bloomsbury Square
London WC1
(Antiquity to 1930)

Antique Dealer To Dealer Show
Bristol Exhibition Centre
Bristol, Avon
c/o The Tony Gill Organisation
Chenil House
181–183 Kings Road
London SW3

Tatton Park Fair
Tatton Park
Knutsford, Cheshire
c/o Mrs S. Brownson
Brownslow House, Gt. Budworth
Northwich, Cheshire
(Furniture pre-1860; jewellery, bronze, rugs and fine art pre-1900; all other items pre-1880)

The Country Antique Dealers' Fair
Carlton Towers
Nr. Goole, Humberside
c/o S. Soper
Castle Gate
York, N Yorkshire
(All pre-1880)

Bristol Spring Antiques And Collectors Fair
Bristol Exhibition Centre
Bristol, Avon
c/o G. Mosdell
Hillside, St. Issey
Nr. Wadebridge, Cornwall

Kenilworth Antique Dealers' Fair
Chesford Grange,
Kenilworth, Warks
c/o Mrs J. Sumner
9 Market Square
Saffron Walden, Essex
(Furniture pre-1830)

Bristol Spring Fair
Victoria Rooms
Bristol, Avon
c/o Colin Gosling Exhibitions Ltd
Green Lane
Harwicke, Glos

Spring Guernsey Antiques Fair
Old Government House Hotel
St. Peter Port
Guernsey, C.I.
c/o J. Stevens Cox
The Lindens, Bas Courtils
St. Sampson, Guernsey, C.I.

Bath Spring Antiques Fair
Assembly Rooms
Bath, Avon
c/o Mary Packham Antiques Fairs
7 Royal Well Place
Cheltenham, Glos
(Furniture and clocks pre-1840; pottery and
porcelain pre-1870; jewellery pre-1900; all
other items pre-1880)

Antique Fair
Chelsea Old Town Hall
Kings Road
London SW3
c/o J. Raven and C. Stoddart-Scott
47 Drayton Place
London SW3
(Pre-1890)

Solihull Antiques Fair
The Civic Hall
Solihull, W Midlands
c/o Eric Gamlin
20 Stroud Road
Gloucester, Glos
(Jewellery, silver, pictures, prints, rugs and
books pre-1900; all other items pre-1860)

APRIL

Annual Cambridge Antiques Fair
Royal Cambridge Hotel
Cambridge, Cambs
c/o Anthony Keniston
Old Rectory, Hopton Castle
Craven Arms, Shropshire
(All pre-1870)

Portmeirion Antiques Fair
The Hercules Hall
Portmeirion, Penrhyndeudraeth
Gwynedd, Wales
c/o Mrs S. Jones
Angel Antiques
Portmeirion, Penrhyndeudraeth
Gwynedd, Wales

Camden Antiques Fair
Camden Arts Centre
Arkwright Road
London NW3
c/o Jeanette Jackson
Hampstead Artists' Council Ltd
(As above)

Farnham Antiques Fair
The Church House
Farnham, Surrey
c/o Eric Gamlin
20 Stroud Road
Gloucester, Glos
(Jewellery, silver, pictures, prints, rugs, and
books pre-1920; all other items pre-1881)

London Arms Fair
Royal Lancaster Hotel
Lancaster Terrace
Bayswater Road
London W2
c/o F. Wilkinson
40 Great James Street
London WC1

British International Antique Dealers' Fair
National Exhibition Centre
Birmingham, W Midlands
c/o National Exhibition Centre,
Birmingham
(English & European Furniture pre-1840; all
other items 1880 except carpets 1900)

Spring Antique Dealers Fair of Scotland
Hopetoun House
South Queensferry, Lothian, Scotland
c/o S. Soper
Castle Gate
York, N Yorkshire
(All pre-1880)

Norfolk Easter Antiques Fair
St. Andrew's and Blackfriars Halls
Norwich, Norfolk
c/o Donald Newby
Town Rooms
Halesworth, Suffolk
(Furniture pre-1851; all other items
1860–1899)

Thame Antiques Fair
Spread Eagle Hotel
Thame, Oxon
c/o Caroline Penman
Cockhaise Mill, Lindfield
Haywards Heath, W Sussex
(Pre-1880)

Solihull Easter Antiques Fair
St. John's Hotel
Solihull, W Midlands
c/o S. and J. Petford
148 Highfield Road, Hall Green
Birmingham, W Midlands
(Pre-1920)

Annual Brecon Antiques Fair
Castle of Brecon Hotel
Brecon, Powys, Wales
c/o Anthony Keniston
Old Rectory, Hopton Castle
Craven Arms, Shropshire
(All pre-1870)

Cheltenham Spring Antiques Fair
The Pump Room
Cheltenham, Glos
c/o Mary Packham
7 Royal Well Place
Cheltenham, Glos

Exeter Spring Antiques Fair
Rougemont Hotel
Exeter, Devon
c/o G. Mosdell
Hillside, St. Issey
Nr. Wadebridge, Cornwall

Buckinghamshire Antique Dealers' Fair
Stowe, Bucks
c/o S. Soper
Castle Gate
York, N Yorkshire
(All pre-1880)

MAY

Truro Spring Antiques And Collectors
Fair
City Hall
Truro, Cornwall
c/o G. Mosdell
Hillside, St. Issey
Nr. Wadebridge, Cornwall

Buxton Antiques Fair
Pavilion Gardens
Buxton, Derbs
c/o R. Heath-Bullock
8 Meadrow
Godalming, Surrey
(Furniture pre-1851; all other items pre-1860;
except fine arts pre-1903)

Annual Ludlow Antiques Fair
Overton Grange Hotel
Ludlow, Shropshire
c/o Anthony Keniston
Old Rectory, Hopton Castle
Craven Arms, Shropshire
(All pre-1870)

West of England Antiques Fair
Assembly Rooms
Bath, Avon
c/o A. Campbell Macinnes
9 George Street
Bath, Avon
(Clocks, barometers, metalwork pre-1830;
furniture pre-1840; porcelain pre-1850;
pictures, maps, books, silver, textiles,
scientific instruments pre-1860; glass,
netsuke, jewellery, bronzes, prints, orientalia
pre-1870)

East Midlands Antique Dealers Fair
Stapelford Park
Melton Mowbray, Leics
c/o S. Soper
Castle Gate
York, N Yorkshire
(All pre-1880)

Snape Antiques Fair
The Maltings
Snape, Suffolk
c/o Donald Newby
Town Rooms
Halesworth, Suffolk
(Furniture pre-1830; all other items
1860–1899)

Annual Aberdeen Antiques Fair
Amatola Hotel
Aberdeen, Grampian, Scotland
c/o Anthony Keniston
Old Rectory, Hopton Castle
Craven Arms, Shropshire
(All pre-1870)

North Devon Antique Dealers Fair
Queens Hall
Barnstaple, Devon
c/o G. Mosdell
Hillside, St. Issey
Nr. Wadebridge, Cornwall

JUNE

City of London Antique Dealers Fair
Syon Park, Isleworth
London W14
c/o S. Soper
Castle Gate
York, N Yorkshire
(All pre-1880)

Stratford Antiques Fair
Parish Hall
Sratford-upon-Avon, Warks
c/o Eric Gamlin
20 Stroud Road
Gloucester, Glos
(Jewellery, silver, pictures, prints, rugs and
books pre-1920; all other items pre-1881)

Antiquarian Book Fair
Europa Hotel, Grosvenor Square
London W1
c/o Mrs C. Perkins
Rectory Farm House, Church Enstone
Oxford, Oxon
(Incunabula to modern first editions)

The Fine Art and Antiques Fair
National Hall, Olympia
London W14
c/o M. Diviney
Earls Court Exhibition Centre
Warwick Road
London SW5
(Silver section pre-1930; gold section; furniture, clocks, scientific instruments, metalware pre-1830; jewellery pre-1900; paintings, carpets and textiles pre-1920; all other items pre-1860)

International Map Collectors' Society
Map Fair
Park Lane Hotel
Piccadilly, London W1
c/o Y. Beresiner
P.O. Box 70
London N3

The Border Antique Dealers' Fair
Alnwick Castle, Northumberland
c/o S.Soper
Castle Gate
York, N Yorkshire
(All pre-1880)

Petersfield Antiques Fair
The Town Hall
Petersfield, Hants
c/o Eric Gamlin
20 Stroud Road
Gloucester, Glos
(Jewellery, silver, pictures, prints, rugs and books pre-1920; all other items pre-1881)

Newton Abbot Giant Antiques' and
Collectors' Fair
Newton Abbot Racecourse, Devon
c/o G. Mosdell
Hillside, St. Issey
Nr. Wadebridge, Cornwall

South East Counties Antique Dealers'
Fair
Goodwood House
Nr. Chichester, W Sussex
c/o S. Soper
Castle Gate
York, N Yorkshire
(All pre-1880)

JULY

Brighton Antiques Fair
Corn Exchange
Brighton, E Sussex
c/o Caroline Penman
Cockhaise Mill, Lindfield
Haywards Heath, W Sussex
(Most items pre-1870)

Annual Welsh Antiques Fair
Hotel Metropole, Llandrindod Wells
Powys, Wales
c/o Anthony Keniston
Old Rectory, Hopton Castle
Craven Arms, Shropshire
(All pre-1870)

Lakeland Antiques Fair
Belsfield Hotel
Bowness-on-Windermere, Cumbria
c/o R. Ian Rawson-Lax
Woodclose House
Ripton Road
Pateley Bridge, N Yorkshire
(Furniture pre-1850; all other items pre-1870)

Annual Lincoln Antiques Fair
County Assembly Rooms
Linceln, Lincs
c/o Anthony Keniston
Old Rectory, Hopton Castle
Craven Arms, Shropshire
(All pre-1870)

Rudding Park Antique Dealers Fair
Rudding Park
Nr. Wetherby, W Yorkshire
c/o S. Soper
Castle Gate
York, N Yorkshire
(All pre-1880)

Plymouth Antiques Fair
The Guildhall
Plymouth, Devon
c/o G. Mosdell
Hillside, St. Issey
Nr. Wadebridge, Cornwall

AUGUST

Annual Highlands Antiques Fair
Caledonian Hotel
Inverness, Highland, Scotland
c/o Anthony Keniston
Old Rectory, Hopton Castle
Craven Arms, Shropshire
(All pre-1870)

Antique and Collectors' Giant Fair
Stafford County Showground, Staffs
c/o Mrs J. Sumner
9 Market Square
Saffron Walden, Essex
(Furniture pre-1830)

Annual Edinburgh Antiques Fair
The Roxburgh Hotel
Edinburgh, Lothian, Scotland
c/o Anthony Keniston
Old Rectory, Hopton Castle
Craven Arms, Shropshire
(All pre-1870)

Stratford Antiques Fair
Parish Hall
Stratford-upon-Avon, Warks
c/o Eric Gamlin
20 Stroud Road
Gloucester, Glos
(Jewellery, silver, pictures, prints, rugs and books pre-1920; all other items pre-1881)

Lindfield Antiques Fair
King Edward Hall, Lindfield
Nr. Haywards Heath, W Sussex
c/o Caroline Penman
Cockhaise Mill, Lindfield
Haywards Heath, W Sussex
(Most items pre-1890)

SEPTEMBER

Cheltenham Autumn Antiques Fair
The Pump Room
Cheltenham, Glos
c/o Mary Packham
7 Royal Well Place
Cheltenham, Glos
(Furniture and clocks pre-1840; pottery and porcelain pre-1870; jewellery pre-1900; all other items pre-1870)

Annual East Anglian Antiques Fair
Athenaeum
Bury St. Edmunds, Suffolk
c/o Anthony Keniston
Old Rectory, Hopton Castle
Craven Arms, Shropshire
(All pre-1870)

Tunbridge Wells Antiques Fair
The Spa Hotel
Mt. Ephraim, Kent
c/o Caroline Penman
Cockhaise Mill, Lindfield
Haywards Heath, W Sussex
(Most items pre-1880)

Petersfield Antiques Fair
Town Hall
Petersfield, Hants
c/o Eric Gamlin
20 Stroud Road
Gloucester, Glos
(Jewellery, silver, pictures, prints, rugs and books pre-1920; all other items pre-1881)

Torbay Antiques Fair
The Town Hall
Torquay, Devon
c/o G. Mosdell
Hillside, St. Issey
Nr. Wadebridge, Cornwall

Northumberland Antiques Fair
Lindon Hall Hotel
Morpeth, Northumberland
c/o Mrs. S. Brownson
Brownslow House, Gt. Budworth
Northwich, Cheshire
(Furniture pre-1860; jewellery, bronze, rugs and fine arts pre-1900)

Chelsea Antiques Fair
Chelsea Old Town Hall
Kings Road, London SW3
c/o Josephine Grahame-Ballin
21 George Street
St. Albans, Herts
(Carpets, rugs and bijouterie pre-1875; all other items pre-1830)

Exmouth Antiques and Collectors Fair
The Pavilion
Exmouth, Devon
c/o G. Mosdell
Hillside, St. Issey
Nr. Wadebridge, Cornwall

London Arms Fair
The Royal Lancaster Hotel
Lancaster Terrace
Bayswater Road
London W2
c/o F. Wilkinson
40 Great James Street
London WC1

Northern Antique Dealers' Fair
Royal Baths Assembly Rooms
Harrogate, N Yorkshire
c/o Northern Antique Dealer Fair
4 Corn Mill, Menston
Ilkley, W Yorkshire
(Furniture pre-1840; all other items pre-1860)

Solihull Antiques' and Collectors' Fair
Civic Hall
Solihull, W Midlands
c/o S. and J. Petford
148 Highfield Road
Hall Green, Birmingham, W Midlands
(Pre-1880)

Lilford Antiques Fair
Lilford Hall
Nr. Oundle, Northants
c/o F. and T. King
High Street
Attleborough, Norfolk

The Antique Dealers' Fair of Scotland
Hopetoun House
South Queensferry, Lothian, Scotland
c/o S. Soper
Castle Gate
York, N Yorkshire
(All pre-1880)

Annual Perthshire Antiques Fair
Station Hotel
Perth, Tayside, Scotland
c/o Anthony Keniston
Old Rectory, Hopton Castle
Craven Arms, Shropshire
(All pre-1870)

OCTOBER

Surrey Antiques Fair
Civic Hall
Guildford, Surrey
c/o R. Heath-Bullock
8 Meadrow
Godalming, Surrey
(Furniture pre-1830; all other items pre-1860; except fine arts pre-1900)

Park Lane Hotel Antiques Fair
Park Lane Hotel
Piccadilly, London W1
c/o P. Ruck
57 Mill Lane
London NW6
(Furniture, silver, porcelain pre-1830; textiles, paintings jewellery pre-1880; decorative arts section post-1880)

Luton Fair
Chiltern Hotel
Dunstable Road, Waller Avenue
Luton, Beds
c/o R.J. Perry
61 Chesford Road
Luton, Beds
(All pre-1910 except jewellery, silver and dolls pre-1930)

Annual York Antiques Fair
Assembly Rooms
York, N Yorkshire
c/o Anthony Keniston
Old Rectory, Hopton Castle
Craven Arms, Shropshire
(All pre-1870)

Annual Grasmere Fair
Grasmere Hall
Grasmere, Cumbria
c/o J.A. Saalmans
The Stables, College Street
Grasmere, Cumbria
(All items pre-1911)

Bath Autumn Antiques Fair
Assembly Rooms
Bath, Avon
c/o Mary Packham
7 Royal Well Place
Cheltenham, Glos
(Furniture, clocks pre-1840; pottery and porcelain pre-1870; jewellery pre-1900; all other items pre-1880)

Truro Autumn Antiques and Collectors'
Fair
City Hall
Truro, Cornwall
c/o G. Mosdell
Hillside, St. Issey
Nr. Wadebridge, Cornwall

Bristol Antiques Fair
Ashton Court Mansion
Bristol, Avon
c/o Eric Gamlin
20 Stroud Road
Gloucester, Glos
(Jewellery, silver, pictures, prints, rugs and books pre-1920; all other items pre-1881)

Antiques Fair
Chelsea Town Hall, Kings Road
London SW3
c/o J. Raven and C. Stoddart-Scott
47 Drayton Place
London, SW3
(Pre-1890)

Annual Hereford Antiques Fair
Green Dragon Hotel
Hereford, Heref & Worcs
c/o Anthony Keniston
Old Rectory, Hopton Castle
Craven Arms, Shropshire
(All pre-1870)

Bristol Autumn Antiques and Collectors'
Fair
Ashton Court Manor
Bristol, Avon
c/o G. Mosdell
Hillside, St. Issey
Nr. Wadebridge, Cornwall

The Dales Fair
Swinton Castle
Masham, N Yorkshire
c/o S. Soper
Castle Gate
York, N Yorkshire
(All pre-1880)

Kenilworth Antique Dealers' Fair
Chesford Grange
Kenilworth, Warks
c/o Mrs J. Sumner
9 Market Square
Saffron Walden, Essex
(Furniture pre-1830)

Lancashire Antique Dealers Fair
Stonyhurst College
Nr. Whalley, Lancs
c/o S. Soper
Castle Gate
York, N Yorkshire
(All pre-1880)

NOVEMBER

Autumn Guernsey Antiques Fair
Old Government House Hotel
St. Peter Port, Guernsey, C.I.
c/o J. Stevens Cox
The Lindens, Bas Courtils
St. Sampson, Guernsey, C.I.

Bristol Autumn Fair
Victoria Rooms
Bristol, Avon
c/o Colin Gosling Exhibitions Ltd
Green Lane
Harwicke, Glos

Bury St. Edmunds Antiques Fair
The Athenaeum
Bury St. Edmunds, Suffolk
c/o Donald Newby
Town Rooms
Halesworth, Suffolk
(Furniture pre-1851; all other items 1860–1899)

Kensington Antiques Fair
Kensington New Town Hall
Hornton Street
London W8
c/o R. Heath-Bullock
8 Meadrow
Godalming, Surrey
(Furniture pre-1830; all other items pre-1860 except fine arts pre-1900)

High Wycombe Autumn
Antiques Fair
Town Hall
High Wycombe, Bucks
c/o Tony and Norma Hepburn
56 London End
Beaconsfield, Bucks
(Furniture pre-1860; all other items pre-1900 except paintings, jewellery, carpets and rugs pre-1920)

The Ridings Antique Dealers Fair
Nostell Priory
Nr. Wakefield, W Yorkshire
c/o S. Soper
Castle Gate
York, N Yorkshire
(All pre-1880)

Exeter Autumn Antiques and Collectors
Fair
Rougemont Hotel
Exeter, Devon
c/o G. Mosdell
Hillside, St. Issey
Nr. Wadebridge, Cornwall

Shepton Mallet Antiques Fair
Bath & West Showground
Somerset
c/o Caroline Penman
Cockhaise Mill, Lindfield
Haywards Heath, W Sussex
(Pre-1930)

Chester Fair
Grosvenor Hotel
Chester, Chesire
c/o Mrs S. Brownson
Brownslow House, Gt. Budworth
Northwich, Cheshire
(Furniture pre-1881; jewellery, bronze and fine arts pre-1900; all other items pre-1850)

Farnham Antiques Fair
The Church House
Farnham, Surrey
c/o Eric Gamlin
20 Stroud Road
Gloucester, Glos
(Jewellery, silver, pictures, prints, rugs and books, pre-1920; all other items pre-1881)

Annual Bournemouth Antiques Fair
Anglo Swiss Hotel
Bournemouth, Dorset
c/o Anthony Keniston
Old Rectory, Hopton Castle
Craven Arms, Shrophire
(All pre-1870)

DECEMBER

The Christmas County Antiques Fair
Castle Howard
Nr. York, N Yorkshire
c/o S. Soper
Castle Gate
York, N Yorkshire
(All pre-1880)

Barnstaple Christmas Antiques' and
Collectors' Fair
Queens Hall
Barnstaple, Devon
c/o G. Mosdell
Hillside, St. Issey
Nr. Wadebridge, Cornwall

Annual Edinburgh Winter Fair
Roxburgh Hotel
Edinburgh, Lothian, Scotland
c/o Anthony Keniston
Old Rectory, Hopton Castle
Craven Arms, Shropshire
(All pre-1870)

AUCTION HOUSES AND SALEROOMS IN THE UNITED KINGDOM

Auctions may be divided into three types: the established London houses, their branches and representatives throughout the UK, provincial auction rooms, and informal country auctions often held in the front garden of a country cottage. The goods will be as variable as the venue but can be roughly divided into two categories: the specialist sale held when the auction house gets enough of a particular category, and the "mixed-lot sale" which usually comprises furniture and household effects.

The specialist sale, usually of valuable items, can take months or even years to prepare. It will be assigned a definite date(s) and a catalogue or list of the items in the sale is carefully prepared. (It is interesting to note that the catalogues from these sales have become collector's items in their own right.) A few days before the sale is held, it will be possible to view the items in the sale, and also to obtain a list of the anticipated prices or the "reserve" prices, below which the item will not be sold. If anything from these sales is found to be faulty, a forgery, or a fake, i.e. not as described in the catalogue, the auction house may allow for some kind of return policy within a stated, but limited time. It is important to note that if the catalogue says that an item is "in the style of" it means simply that, and the auction house cannot be taken to task. In any event, always read the conditions of sale before bidding.

The second type, the "mixed-lot sale", is often held weekly or bi-weekly with very little catalogue information available. Therefore, it is absolutely imperative to inspect the goods before these sales. Often the phrase "as seen" is used to describe a certain lot, which may be held to absolve the auctioneer from responsibility. However, if you are bargain-hunting or house-furnishing, these sales are a terrific source for unexpected and inexpensive finds.

BIDDING

If you have viewed the goods and would like to enter the bidding, but cannot attend the sale, it is usually possible to place an absentee bid. You can either ask the auctioneer to enter your bids, or, should you have to leave a sale before your lot comes up, you may be able to advise a porter of your maximum price. In the latter circumstance, should the porter be successful on your behalf, he/she should be tipped approximately 5% of the selling price.

When bidding in person, it is essential to catch the attention of the auctioneer. Raise your hand and state your bid, but should the bidding narrow to you and another, usually a glance to the auctioneer will do, followed by the improved bid. However, before you start to bid, it is sensible to establish a maximum price in your mind, thus preventing "auction fever".

CHARGES

Auction houses usually charge a commission of 10% to the seller – a result of the controversial buyer's premium introduced in 1975, and charged on everything except coins, stamps and wines. It is also normal for the buyer, unless he is well-known to the auctioneer, to pay at least 50% of the hammer price immediately after the sale, or once the auction is over.

As a seller, you should not have to pay a storage or warehousing fee, although if your lot fails to reach its reserve, a minimum charge may be levied. This may, however, be negotiable if you are selling a large number of goods or something particularly precious. Additional fees arise should you want to export an item. An export licence is needed for any of the following:

a work of art more than 50 years old and worth more than £8000;

any archaeological item, document, manuscript or archive over 80 years old;

any photograph more than 60 years old and having a value of over £200.

At the time of going to press, VAT is also charged to both sellers and to buyers, although foreign consignors who reside outside the UK and not in the EEC, do not pay the standard 15%. VAT is added to the fee charged by the auctioneer and to any additional services such as catalogue illustration, insurance and shipping. However, buyers do not pay VAT unless the item has been entered in the sale by a vendor who is registered for VAT for business purposes, in other words, a dealer.

There are a few categories on which VAT is not charged: paintings, drawings, engravings, prints, lithographs, sculptures, statuary and antiques over 100 years old, except loose pearls and loose gemstones. Collector's pieces of zoological, botanical, mineralogical, ethnographical and archaeological interest are also VAT exempt. In the Republic of Ireland, there is a 10% VAT on the buyer's premium and on the commission charged by the consignor, and also a 10% charge on goods imported into Ireland for sale at auction.

LONDON

BONHAMS MONTPELIER GALLERIES
Montpelier Street
London SW7 1HH
Tel: (01) 584 9161 (10 lines)/589 4577
and
Bonhams Chelsea
65–69 Lots Road, Kings Road
London SW10 0RN
Tel: (01) 352 0466 (furniture)/(01) 351 1380 (pictures)

Family-owned and -managed firm with as many as 12 auctions per week. Secondary saleroom in Chelsea opened at the end of the 1970's. Evening viewing to 7pm at Montpelier Street on Tuesdays and at Bonhams Chelsea on Mondays. Bonhams also carries out valuations, mostly for insurance purposes. Areas in which general auctions and specialist sales are held:

Arms and Armour	*Furniture*
Art Deco	*Jewellery*
Art Nouveau	*Manuscripts*
Books	*Paintings*
Ceramics	*Porcelain*
Chinese Works of Art	*Prints*
Clocks and Watches	*Rugs*
Coins	*Scientific Instruments*
Dolls	*Silver*
Drawings	*Stamps*
Engravings	*Wine*
Etchings	

CHRISTIE'S
8 King Street
London SW1Y 6QT
Tel: (01) 839 9060
and
Christie's South Kensington
85 Old Brompton Road
London SW7 3SS
Tel: (01) 581 223

Christie, Manson and Woods Ltd, the firm's full corporate name, has enjoyed a well-established reputation since its birth in 1766. James Christie first offered household goods and effects but, by the 19th c., its auctions included fine arts and property. Christie's became a public company in early 1970's but the family tradition still plays a strong role. Major emphasis is still on the fine arts, with experts in every field. There is a valuation and advisory tax service, for which there is a fee, but the traditional front counter service is free – at the main office in King Street a valuation and oral expert opinion will be given on any item brought to the front desk. Christie's South Kensington is devoted to lower priced properties. Areas in which general auctions and specialist sales are held:

Arms and Armour	Japanese Works of Art	Arms and Armour	Jewellery
Art Deco	Jewellery	Art Deco	Musical Instruments
Art Nouveau	Manuscripts	Art Nouveau	Paintings
Autographs	Maps	Automobilia	Pewter
Books	Medals	Baxter Prints	Photographica
Chinese Works of Art	Mediaeval Works of Art	Books	Photographic Instruments
Clocks and Watches	Musical Instruments	Chinese Works of Art	Porcelain
Coins	Paintings	Clocks and Watches	Postcards
Drawings	Pewter	Costume	Posters
Engravings	Porcelain	Cricketana	Pot Lids
Etchings	Prints	Dolls	Pre-Columbian Art
Ethnographica	Rugs	Drawings	Prints
Furniture	Russian Works of Art	Embroidery	Railwayana
Glass	Silver	Engravings	Rugs
Icons	Steam Models	Etchings	Scientific Instruments
Islamic Art	Wine	Firemarks	Silver
		Furniture	Sporting Items
		Glass	Stamps
		Icons	Toy Soldiers
		Islamic Art	Toys
		Japanese Works of Art	

PHILLIPS BLENSTOCK HOUSE
7 Blenheim Street
New Bond Street
London W1Y 0AS
Tel: (01) 629 6602
and
Phillips West Two
10 Salem Road
London W2 4BU
Tel: (01) 221 5303
and
Phillips Marylebone
Hayes Place
Lisson Grove
London NW1 6UA
Tel: (01) 723 2647

In 1796 James Christie's chief clerk decided to go into business for himself. Harry Phillips soon proved successful – so much so that when Queen Victoria decided to redecorate part of Buckingham Palace in the 1830's, it was Phillips who handled the sale of the unwanted furnishings. A privately held company, Phillips has become a multi-national concern in less than a decade. A few years ago, they also cleverly inaugurated a travelling appraisal service which publicizes its arrival beforehand, offering a free inspection and valuation service without any obligation to sell. The main branch has 10–12 sales per week in approximately 40 specialist areas. A quick glance at this list will tell you that Phillips is also interested in the more prosaic of collectibles. Areas in which general auctions and specialist sales are held:

SOTHEBY'S
34–35 New Bond Street
London W1A 2AA
Tel: (01) 493 8080
and
Sotheby's Aeolian Hall
Grosvenor Hill
Bond Street
London W1A 2AA
and
Sotheby's Conduit Street Gallery
26 Conduit Street
London W1A 2AA
and
Sotheby's Belgravia
19 Motcomb Street
London SW1X 8LB
Tel: (01) 235 4311
and
Sotheby's Hodgsons Rooms
115 Chancery Lane
London WC2A 1PX
Tel: (01) 405 7238

Founded by Samuel Baker, a bookseller and publisher in the 1730's, with the first recorded auction in 1744 when Baker sold his own as well as other people's books. Baker's nephew John Sotheby was taken into partnership in 1788, after Baker's death. During the 19th c., sales

were held not just in books, but also in pictures, jewellery, coins and wine. During the 1980's, another important development was made with the purchase of Parke-Bernet, the New York auction house. Aeolian Hall, acquired in 1979, sells jewellery and coins, while the Conduit Street gallery offers lots that do not exceed £1000 in value. Sotheby's Belgravia specialises in Victoriana. All branches will help with valuation, restoration before sale, and shipping. Areas in which general auction and specialist sales are held at Sotheby's New Bond Street:

Arms and Armour	Medals
Autographs	Mediaeval Works of Art
Books	Musical Instruments
Chinese Works of Art	Netsuke
Clocks and Watches	Paintings
Coins	Pewter
Drawings	Porcelain
Engravings	Pre-Columbian Art
Furniture	Prints
Glass	Rugs
Icons	Russian Works of Art
Islamic Art	Scientific Instruments
Japanese Works of Art	Silver
Judaica	Stamps
Manuscript	Wine
Maps	

Areas in which general auctions and specialist sales are held at Sotheby's Belgravia:

Art Deco	Photographica
Art Nouveau	Porcelain
Chinese Works of Art	Postcards
Clocks and Watches	Posters
Drawings	Railwayana
Furniture	Rugs
Glass	Scientific Instruments
Japanese Works of Art	Silver
Mechanical Musical	Steam Models
Instruments	Toys
Paintings	

Note: In 1980, the Veteran, Vintage and Special Interest Vehicle Dept moved to Glaspant Manor, Capel Iwan, Newcastle Emlyn, Dyfed, S Wales, c/o Michael Worthington-Williams. Tel: (0559) 370024.

AUCTION ROOMS THROUGHOUT THE BRITISH ISLES (LISTED ALPHABETICALLY BY TOWN)

AVON

Stanley Alder and Price
4 Princes Building
Bath, Avon
Tel: (0225) 62643

Aldridges
130–2 Walcot Street
Bath, Avon
Tel: (0225) 62830

Phillips (Bath)
The Auction Rooms
Old King Street
Bath BA1 1DD, Avon
Tel: (0225) 310709

Lalonde Bros and Parham
71 Oakfield Road
Bristol 8, Avon
Tel: (0272) 34052
and
Station Road
Weston-Super-Mare, Avon
Tel: (0934) 33174

Osmond Tricks and Son
Regent Street Saleroom
Regent Street, Clifton
Bristol BS8 4HG, Avon
Tel: (0272) 37201

Taviners
Prewett Street, Redcliffe
Bristol BS1 6PB, Avon
Tel: (0272) 25996

Alonzo Dawes and Hoddell
Sixways
Clevedon, Avon
Tel: (0272) 876011

Mart Auction Rooms
34–36 Baker Street
Weston-Super-Mare, Avon
Tel: (934) 28419

BEDFORDSHIRE

Robinson and Hall
14–15a St Paul's Square
Bedford, Beds
Tel: (0234) 52201

W.S. Johnson and Company
40 High Street
Leighton Buzzard, Beds
Tel: (05253) 2414

BERKSHIRE

Chancellors
31 High Street
Ascot, Berks
Tel: (0990) 20101

Tufnell and Partners
Chobham Road
Sunningdale
Ascot, Berks
Tel: (0990) 23411

Braxton and Son
108 Queen Street
Maidenhead, Berks
Tel: (0628) 25226

Dreweatt Watson and Barton
Donnington Priory
Newbury, Berks
Tel: (0635) 31234

Nicholas
13 Bridge Street, Caversham
Reading, Berks
Tel: (0734) 479665

Buckland and Son
7 Blagrave Street
Reading, Berks
Tel: (0734) 51370

V and V Auctions
6 Station Road
Reading, Berks
Tel: (0734) 53211

Martin and Pole
5a & 7 Broad Street
Wokingham, Berks
Tel: (0734) 780777

BUCKINGHAMSHIRE

Woods of Wycombe
20 London Road
Amersham, Bucks
Tel: (02403) 22186

Abbey Auctions
Midmede
Chapel Hill
Speen
Nr Aylesbury, Bucks
Tel: (0296) 583

W.S. Johnson and Company
10 Market Street
Buckingham, Bucks
Tel: (02802) 2120

Buckland and Son
Bringwood, East Common
Road
Gerrards Cross, Bucks
Tel: Gerrards Cross 85451

Barnard and Learmount
18 Bathurst Walk
Iver, Bucks
Tel: (0753) 652024

Foll and Parker
9 High Street ·
Woburn Sands
Milton Keynes MK17 8RG,
Bucks
Tel: (0908) 583231

CAMBRIDGESHIRE

Robert Arnold and Partners
55 Regent Street
Cambridge, Cambs CB2 1NS
Tel: (0223) 358285

Hammond & Company
The Auction Rooms
Cambridge Place
Cambridge, Cambs CB2 1NS
Tel: (0223) 356067

George Comins and Son
3 Chequer Lane
Ely, Cambs
Tel: (0353) 2265

Ekins Dilley and Handley
The Salerooms
St. Ives
Huntingdon, Cambs
Tel: (0480) 68144

Goldsmith and Bass
15 Market Place,
Oundle
Peterborough, Cambs
Tel: (08322) 2349

Raymond Munns
25 High Street
Willingham, Cambs
Tel: (0954) 60447

Grounds and Company
2 Nene Quay
Wisbech, Cambs
Tel: (0945) 5041

CHESHIRE

J.R. Bridgford and Sons
Heyes Lane
Alderley Edge, Cheshire
Tel: (0625) 585347

Richard Baker and Thomson
9 Hamilton Street
Birkenhead, Cheshire
Tel: (051) 647 9104

Robert I. Heyes and Associates
Hatton Buildings
Lightfoot Street, Hoole
Chester, Cheshire
Tel: (0244) 28941

Sotheby Beresford Adams
Duke Street
Chester, Cheshire
Tel: (0244) 315531

Swetenhams
Bold Place
Chester, Cheshire
Tel: (0244) 315333

Frank R. Marshall and Co
Church Street
Knutsford, Cheshire
Tel: (0565) 54361

Brocklehursts
King Edward Street
Macclesfield, Cheshire
Tel: (0625) 27555

Star Auction Gallery
Wheelock Street
Middlewich, Cheshire
Tel: (060684) 2590

Peter Wilson and Company
Victoria Gallery
Market Street
Nantwich, Cheshire
Tel: (0270) 63878

Andrew Hilditch and Son
19 The Square
Sandbach, Cheshire
Tel: (09367) 2048

Philip Davies and Sons
79 Wellington Road South
Stockport, Cheshire SE1 3SF
Tel: (061) 480 1137

Samuel Rains and Son
17 Warren Street
Stockport, Cheshire SK1 1UF
Tel: (061) 480 2252

CLEVELAND

Norman Hope and Partners
2 South Street
Hartlepool, Cleveland TS24
7SG
Tel: (0429) 67828

Lithgow Sons and Partners
The Auction Houses
Station Road
Stokesley
Middlesborough, Cleveland
Tel: (0642) 710158

CLWYD, WALES

K. Hugh Dodd and Partners
9 Chester Street
Mold, Clwyd, Wales
Tel: (0352) 2554

C. Wesley Haslam and Son
High Street
Rhyl, Clwyd, Wales
Tel: (0745) 4467

Seth Hughes and Son
St George's Crescent
Wrexham, Clwyd, Wales
Tel: (0978) 265123

Wingett and Sons
24–25 Chester Street
Wrexham, Clwyd, Wales
Tel: (0978) 53553

CORNWALL

Ruth Jones
8 Arwenack Street
Falmouth, Cornwall
Tel: (0326) 313444

Jose Collins and Harris
28 Coinagehall Street
Helston, Cornwall
Tel: (03265) 3355

May Whetter and Grose
Cornubia Hall
Par, Cornwall
Tel: (072681) 2271

Taylor Lane and Creber
Central Auction Rooms
Morrab Road
Penzance, Cornwall
Tel: (0736) 22867

Button Menhenitt and Mutton
Belmont Auction Rooms
Wadebridge, Cornwall
Tel: (020881) 2059

CUMBRIA

J. David King
14 Lowther Street
Carlisle, Cumbria
Tel: (0228) 25259

Thomson Roddick and Paurie
24 Lowther Street
Carlisle, Cumbria
Tel: (0228) 28939

James Thompson
64 Main Street
Kirby Lonsdale, Cumbria
Tel: (0468) 71555

Thornborrow and Co
St Andrew's Place
Penrith, Cumbria CA11 7XZ
Tel: (0768) 2095

Thomson Roddick and Laurie
25 King Street
Wigton, Cumbria
Tel: (09654) 3348

DERBYSHIRE

J.K. Hill, Hampson and
Company
8 The Quadrant
Buxton, Derbs
Tel: (0298) 3038

Eaton and Hollis
Exchange Buildings
Exchange Street
Derby, Derbs DE1 2DU
Tel: (0332) 49307

DEVON

Gribble Booth and Taylor
West Street
Axminster, Devon EX13 5NU
Tel: (0297) 32323

John C. Webber
Bristol & West House
Barnstaple, Devon
Tel: (0271) 73404

Phillips (Exeter)
Alphin Brook Road
Alphington, Exeter, Devon EX2
8TH
Tel: (0392) 39025

Tower Galleries (Exmouth)
Tower Street
Exmouth, Devon
Tel: (03952) 5853

Whitton and Laing
20 Queen Street
Exeter, Devon
Tel: (0392) 526621

T.D. Hussey and Son
99 High Street
Honiton, Devon
Tel: (0404) 2553

L. and M. Taylor
63 High Street
Honiton, Devon
Tel: (0404) 2404

Rendell's
13 Market Street
Newton Abbott, Devon
Tel: (0626) 3381

Taylor Lane and Creber
Central Auction Rooms
Trelawney Lane, Peverell
Plymouth, Devon
Tel: (0752) 20667

John Wood at Seaton
Salerooms
Harbour Road
Seaton, Devon
Tel: (0297) 20290

P.J. Eley
100 High Street
Sidmouth, Devon EX10 8EF
Tel: (03955) 2552

Ward and Chowen
1 Church Lane
Tavistock, Devon PL19 8AB
Tel: (0822) 2458

Sotheby Bearne
Rainbow
Avenue Road
Torquay, Devon
Tel: (0803) 26277

DORSET

House and Son
Lansdowne House
Christchurch Road
Bournemouth, Dorset
Tel: (0202) 26232

Riddett's
The Auction Rooms
Richmond Hill
Bournemouth, Dorset
Tel: (0202) 25686

H.Y. Duke and Son
40 South Street
Dorchester, Dorset
Tel: (0305) 4426

Rumsey and Rumsey
The Furniture Saleroom
Danecourt Road
Parkstone, Dorset
Tel: (0202) 748567

R.B. Taylor and Sons
Cheap Street
Sherborne, Dorset
Tel: (093581) 2099

Senior and Goodwin
Market Place
Sturminster Newton, Dorset
Tel: (0258) 72244

S.W. Cottee and Son
The Market
East Street
Wareham, Dorset
Tel: (09295) 2826

CO DURHAM

Tarn Bainbridge and Co
39 Grange Road
Darlington, Co Durham
Tel: (0325) 62553

Thomas Watson and Son
Northumberland Street
Darlington, Co Durham
Tel: (0325) 62559

DYFED, WALES

John Francis, Thomas Jones
and Sons
King Street
Carmarthen, Dyfed, Wales
Tel: (0267) 33111

R.G. Daniel and Partners
36 High Street
Lampeter, Dyfed, Wales
Tel: (0570) 422550

ESSEX

Cooper Hirst
Goldlay House
Parkway
Chelmsford Essex
Tel: (0245) 58141

J.P. Smith
1 Church Street
Coggeshall, Essex
Tel: (0376) 62051

Colchester Market Auctions
46 High Street
Colchester, Essex
Tel: (0206) 46161

Vost's
Layer Marney Tower
Colchester, Essex
Tel: (0206) 330250

Watsons
North Station Road
Colchester, Essex
Tel: (0206) 73733

J.M. Welch and Sons
The Old Town Hall
Dunmow, Essex
Tel: (0371) 2117

Epping Antique Auctions
64–66 High Street
Epping, Essex
Tel: Epping 73023

Ambrose and Son
149 High Road
Loughton IG10 4LZ, Essex
Tel: (01) 508 2121

C. White
132a Mill Road
Malden, Essex
Tel: (01) 892 5522

Gordon Long
1 King Street
Saffron Walden, Essex
Tel: (0799) 23553

Watsons
1 Market Street
Saffron Walden, Essex
Tel: (0799) 22058

Chapel and Chapel
543 London Road
Westcliff-on-Sea, Essex
Tel: (0702) 43734

GLOUCESTERSHIRE

G.H. Bayley and Sons
Vittoria House
Vittoria Walk
Cheltenham Glos GL50 1TW
Tel: (0242) 21102

Mallams
Grosvenor Galleries
26 Grosvenor Street
Cheltenham, Glos
Tel: (0242) 35712

D.N. Perry and Company
15 Royal Crescent
Cheltenham, Glos
Tel: (0242) 53722

Hobbs & Chambers
At the Sign of the Bell
Cirencester, Glos
Tel: (0285) 4736

Jackson Stops and Staff
Dollar Street
Cirencester, Glos
Tel: (0285) 3334

Moore Allen and Innocent
33 Castle Street
Cirencester, Glos
Tel: (0285) 2862

Bruton Knowles
Albion Chambers
53 Barton Street
Gloucester, Glos
Tel: (0452) 21267

Graham and Son
City Chambers
6 Clarence Street
Gloucester, Glos
Tel: (0452) 21177

Tayler and Fletcher
Stow-on-the-World
Glos GL54 1BL
Tel: (0451) 30383

Davis Champion and Payne
10–12 Kendrick Street
Stroud, Glos
Tel: (04536) 2275

Sandoe Luce Panes and
Company
Estate Offices
Wotton-under-Edge, Glos
Tel: (045385) 3193

GLAMORGAN, WALES

W.H. Cooke and Arkwright
92 Park Street
Bridgend
Glamorgan CF31 4BD, Wales
Tel: (0656) 55051

Davey, Hampton Jeffery and
Partners
273 Cowbridge Road East
Cardiff, Glamorgan CF5 1JB,
Wales
Tel: (0222) 30188

GWENT, WALES

J. Straker Chadwick
Market Street Chambers
Abergavenny, Gwent NP7
5SD, Wales
Tel: (0873) 2624

Davis and Sons
Bank Square
Chepstow, Gwent, Wales
Tel: (02912) 4908

GWYNEDD, WALES

Owens Gwynedd and
Company
56 High Street
Llangefni
Anglesey, Gwynedd, Wales
Tel: (0248) 722950

Bryan Davies and Associates
4 Mostyn Street
Llandudno
Gwynedd, Wales
Tel: (0492) 75125

HAMPSHIRE

Allen and May
18 Bridge Street
Andover Hants
Tel: (0264) 3417

Pearsons
99 Fleet Road
Fleet
Fordingbridge, Hants
Tel: (0425) 3166

Elliott and Green
40 High Street
Lymington, Hants
Tel: (0590) 77222

Jackman and Masters
53 High Street
Lymington, Hants
Tel: (0590) 77233

Jacobs and Hunt
Auction Rooms
Lavant Street
Petersfield, Hants
Tel: (0730) 2744

Whiteheads
34 High Street
Petersfield, Hants
Tel: (0730) 2691

Ormiston Knight and Paine
54 Southampton Road
Ringwood, Hants
Tel: (04254) 3333

Fox and Sons
30–43 London Road
Southampton, Hants
Tel: (0703) 25155

D.M. Nesbit and Company
7 Clarendon Road
Southsea
Hants PO5 2ED
Tel: (0705) 20785

Pearsons
Walcote Chambers
High Street
Winchester, Hants
Tel: (0962) 64444

HEREFORDSHIRE

C.T. and G.H. Smith
Lanark House
New Street
Ledbury, Heref & Worcs HR8
2DY
Tel: (0531) 2388

Russell Baldwin and Bright
Ryeland Road
Leominster, Heref & Worcs
Tel: (0568) 3897

Stooke Hill and Company
3 Broad Street
Leominster, Heref & Worcs
Tel: (0568) 3407

Coles Knapp and Kennedy
Palace Pound
Ross-on-Wye, Heref & Worcs
Tel: (0989) 2225

HERTFORDSHIRE

Sworder Salerooms
19 North Street
Bishop's Stortford, Herts
Tel: (0279) 52441

Watsons
1–2 Water Lane
Bishop's Stortford, Herts
Tel: (0279) 52361

Norris and Duvall
106 Fore Street
Hertford, Herts
Tel: Hertford 52249

HUMBERSIDE

Dickinson, Davy and Markham
10 Brawby Street
Brigg, S Humberside
Tel: (00652) 53666

Dee and Atkinson
The Exchange
Driffield
N Humberside
Tel: (0377) 43151

H. Evans and Sons
1 Parliament Street
Hull, N Humberside HU1 2AR
Tel: (0482) 23033

ISLE OF MAN

Chrystals
Bowring Road
Ramsey, Isle of Man
Tel: (0624) 812236

ISLE OF WIGHT

Way Riddett and Co
Town Hall Chambers
Lind Street
Ryde, Isle of Wight
Tel: (0983) 62255

Watson Bull and Porter
79–81 Regent Street
Shanklin, Isle of Wight
Tel: (098386) 3441

KENT

Burrows and Day
39–41 Bank Street
Ashford, Kent
Tel: (0233) 24321

Hobbs Parker
9 Tufton Street
Ashford, Kent
Tel: (0233) 22222

Stephen R. Thomas
76 Church Road
Ashford TW15 2TW, Kent
Tel: (0233) 57038

Kent Sales
13 Montpelier Avenue
Bexley, Kent
Tel: (01) 304 4556

Ashendens
10 Sun Street
Canterbury, Kent
Tel: (0227) 64711

G.W. Finn and Sons
Brooklands
Fordwich
Canterbury, Kent
Tel: (0227) 710200

Scarlett and Berthoud
29 Watling Street
Canterbury, Kent
Tel: (0227) 61489

Worsfolds
40 Station Road West
Canterbury, Kent
Tel: (0227) 68984

Baldwin and Partners
26 Railway Street
Chatham, Kent
Tel: (0634) 400121

James B. Terson and Sons
27–29 Castle Street
Dover, Kent
Tel: (0304) 202173

Smith-Woolley and Perry
24–26 Dover Road
Folkestone, Kent
Tel: (0303) 41967

Geering and Colyer
Highgate
Hawkhurst, Kent
Tel: (05805) 3181

Bulter and Hatch Waterman
86 High Street
Hythe, Kent
Tel: (0303) 66022

Stewart Gore
The Auction Rooms
Clifton Place
Margate, Kent
Tel: (0843) 21528

Lambert and Symes
77 Commerical Road
Paddock Wood, Kent
Tel: (089283) 2325

John Hogbin and Son
15 Cattle Market
Sandwich, Kent
Tel: (0304) 611044

Ibbett Moseley Card and
Company
125 High Street
Sevenoaks, Kent
Tel: (0732) 52246

Parsons Welch and Cowell
129 High Street
Sevenoaks, Kent
Tel: (0732) 51211

Butler and Hatch Waterman
102 High Street
Tenterden, Kent
Tel: (05806) 3233

John Hogbin and Son
53 High Street
Tenterden, Kent
Tel: (05806) 3200

Bracketts
22–29 High Street
Tunbridge Wells, Kent TN1
1UU
Tel: (0892) 33733

LANCASHIRE

J.R. Parkinson Son and Hamer
14 Bolton Street
Bury, Lancs
Tel: (061) 764 3341

Smith and Hodgkinson
53–55 St. Thomas's Road
Chorley, Lancs
Tel: (02572) 3633

Hothersall Forrest Mckenna
and Son
Bank Salerooms, Harris Court
Clitheroe, Lancs
Tel: (0200) 25446

Brand-Cotti and Partners
286 Poulton Road
Fleetwood, Lancs
Tel: (03917) 71157

Proctors
32 Market Square
Lancaster, Lancs
Tel: (0524) 2288

Warren and Wignall
55 Towngate
Leyland
Preston PR5 6EQ, Lancs
Tel: (0772) 23909

LEICESTERSHIRE

Ashby-De-La-Zouch Auction
Sales
Kilwardby Salerooms
Ashby-de-la-Zouch, Leics
Tel: (05304) 2766

Gilding Fine Arts
2 New Walk
Leicester, Leics
Tel: (0533) 551579

Heathcote Ball and Company
47 New Walk
Leicester, Leics
Tel: (0533) 544001

Geoffrey Snushall Auctions
171–3 Charles Street
Leicester, Leics
Tel: (0533) 59204

Tarrat-Ross Auctions
Midland Auction Mart
Market Street
Leicester, Leics
Tel: (0533) 22757

Warner Sheppard and Wade
16–18 Halford Street
Leicester, Leics LE1 1JB
Tel: (0533) 21613

Berry Bros
12 The Square
Market Harborough, Leics
Tel: (0858) 64091

Shoulder and Son
43 Nottingham Street
Melton Mowbray, Leics LE13
1NR
Tel: (0664) 3081

Walker, Walton and Hanson
4 Market Place
Oakham
Rutland, Leics
Tel: (0572) 2681

LINCOLNSHIRE

James Eley and Son
1 Main Ridge
Boston, Lincs
Tel: (0205) 61687

Lyall and Company
Market Place
Bourne, Lincs
Tel: (07782) 2431

John Wilson and Sons
41 High Street
Burgh-le-March, Lincs
Tel: (075483) 810477

Drewery and Wheeldon
10 Market Street
Gainsborough, Lincs
Tel: (0427) 4441

William H. Brown
31 St. Peters Hill
Grantham, Lincs
Tel: (0476) 66363

Escritt and Barrell
Elmer House
Grantham, Lincs
Tel: (0476) 5371

Golding
45 High Street
Grantham, Lincs NG31 6NE
Tel: (0476) 5456

Brogden and Company
38–39 Silver Street
Lincoln, Lincs
Tel: (0522) 31321

Thos. Mawer and Son
63 Monks Road
Lincoln, Lincs
Tel: (0522) 22215

Mawer Mason and Bell
Cornmarket
Louth, Lincs LN11 9QD
Tel: (0507) 602356

Martin Maslin
24 Market Place
Market Rasen, Lincs
Tel: (06732) 3783

A.E. Dowse and Son
7 Shelford Street
Scunthorpe, Lincs DN15 6NX

Earl and Lawrence
55 Northgate
Sleaford, Lincs
Tel: (0529) 302946

Geoffrey Collings and Co
High Street
Long Sutton
Spalding, Lincs P12 9DB
Tel: (0775) 362098

OTHER LONDON
AUCTION HOUSES

Bermondsey Auctions
175 Bermondsey Street
Newhams Row
London SE1
Tel: (01) 403 2065

Borough Auctions
9 Park Street
Off Stoney Street
London Bridge
London SE1
Tel: (01) 407 9577

Brillscote Architectural
Auctions
248 Camden High Street
London NW1
Tel: (01) 485 8072

Camden Auctions
The Salerooms
Hoppers Road
The Green
Winchmore Hill
London N21
Tel: (01) 886 1550

Dowell Lloyd and Company
4 Putney High Street
London SW15
Tel: (01) 788 7777

Harrods Auction Galleries
Arundel Terrace
Barnes
London SW13
Tel: (01) 748 2739

Highgate Auctions
Warehouse No. 8
Camden Goods Depot
Chalk Farm Road
London NW1
Tel: (01) 267 2124

Hollingsworth
56–58 Whitcomb Street
London WC2H 7DR
Tel: (01) 839 1875

Moore's Auction Rooms
143 Lewisham Way
London SE14
Tel: (01) 692 1970

Rippon, Boswell and Company
The Arcade
South Kensington Station,
London SW7
Tel: (01) 589 4242

Spink and Son
5–7 King Street
St. James's
London SW1
Tel: (01) 930 7888

Strutt and Parker
13 Hill Street
Berkeley Square
London W1X 8DL
Tel: (01) 629 7282

West London Auctions
Sandringham Mews
High Street
London W5
Tel: (01) 567 7096

GT MANCHESTER

F.S. Airey Entwhistle and
Company
Alliance House, 28–34 Cross
Street
Manchester M2 7AQ
Tel: (061) 834 9177

Capes Dunn and Company
38 Charles Street
Manchester M1 7DB
Tel: (061) 273 6060

Manchester Auction Mart
2–4 Atkinson Street
Off Deansgate
Manchester M3 3HH
Tel: (061) 834 3066

Edward Symmons and Partners
515–516 Royal Exchange
Manchester M2 7EN
Tel: (061) 832 8494

MERSEYSIDE

Outhwaite and Litherland
Kingsway Galleries
Fontenoy Street
Liverpool 3, Merseyside
Tel: (051) 236 6561

Eldon E. Worrall and Company
15 Seel Street
Liverpool, Merseyside L1 4AU
Tel: (051) 709 2950

Ball and Percival
132 Lord Street
Southport,
Merseyside
Tel: (0704) 36900

MIDDLESEX

Spa
24 Watford Road
Wembley
Middx HA0 3EP
Tel: (01) 908 2636

NORFOLK

G.A. Key
Market Place
Aylsham
Norfolk NR11 6EH
Tel: (026 373) 3195

Case and Dewing
Church Street
Dereham, Norfolk
Tel: (0362) 2004

Apthorpes
St. Nicholas Street
Diss, Norfolk
Tel: (0379) 2233

T.W. Gaze
Roydon Road
Diss, Norfolk
Tel: (0379) 2291

Charles Hawkins and Sons
Downham Market
Norfolk
Tel: (03663) 2112

Cruso and Wilkin
2 Northgate
Hunstanton, Norfolk
Tel: (04853) 33131

Ewings
Market Place
North Reepham
Norfolk NR10 4JJ,
Tel: (060526) 473

Ireland's
2 Upper King Street
Norwich, Norfolk
Tel: (0603) 610271

James (Norwich Auctions)
33 Timberhill
Norwich, Norfolk NR1 3LA
Tel: (0603) 24817

Norwich City Auctions
4 Bridewell Alley
Norwich, Norfolk
Tel: (0603) 29009

Noel D. Abel
32 Norwich Road
Watton, Norfolk
Tel: (0953) 881204

W.S. Hall and Palmer
Market Place
Wymondham, Norfolk
Tel: (0953) 603031

NORTHAMPTONSHIRE

Southam and Sons
Corn Exchange
Thrapston
Kettering, Northants
Tel: (0536) 2409

Northampton Auction Galleries
33–39 Sheep Street
Northampton, Northants
Tel: (0604) 37263

T.W. Arnold Corby and
Company
30 Brook Street
Raunds
Wellingborough, Northants
Tel: (0933) 623722

NORTHUMBERLAND

Ian A. Robertson
Narrowgate
Alnwick, Northld
Tel: (0665) 602725

NOTTINGHAMSHIRE

Edward Bailey and Son
17 Northgate
Newark, Notts
Tel: (0636) 3141

Neales of Nottingham
192 Mansfield Road
Nottingham, Notts
Tel: (0602) 624141

Turner Fletcher and Essex
7 Thurland Street
Nottingham, Notts
Tel: (0602) 45967

Walker Walton and Hanson
Byard Lane
Bridlesmith Gate
Nottingham, Notts
Tel: (0602) 54272

Henry Spencer and Sons
20 The Square
Retford, Notts
Tel: (0777) 706767

C.B. Sheppard and Son
The Auction Galleries
Chatsworth Street
Sutton-in-Ashfield, Notts
Tel: (0773) 87219

OXFORDSHIRE

Buckell and Ballard
49 Parsons Street
Banbury, Oxon
Tel: (0295) 53197

E.P. Messenger and Son
Pevensey House Salerooms
Manorsfield Road
Bicester, Oxon
Tel: (08692) 45985

Simmons and Lawrence
32 Bell Street
Henley-on-Thames, Oxon
Tel: (04912) 2525

Mallams
24 Michaels Street
Oxford, Oxon
Tel: (0865) 41358

Phillips (Oxford)
39 Park End Street
Oxford, Oxon
Tel: (0856) 723524

Green and Company
33 Market Place
Wantage, Oxon
Tel: (02357) 3561

Griffith and Partners
42 High Street
Watlington, Oxon
Tel: (049161) 2831

POWYS, WALES

Morris Marshall and Poole
2 Shortbridge Street
Newtown, Powys, Wales
Tel: (0686) 26160

Harry Ray and Company
Lloyds Bank Chambers
Broad Street
Welshpool, Powys
Tel: (0938) 2555

SHROPSHIRE

Richard J. Gannon's Auctions
13 The Square
Bishop's Castle, Shropshire
Tel: (05883) 240

Perry and Phillips
Newmarket Buildings
Listley Street
Bridgnorth, Shropshire
Tel: (07462) 2248

R.J. Garwood
55 Mill Street
Ludlow, Shropshire
Tel: (0584) 3242

McCartney Morris Barker
Corve Street
Ludlow, Shropshire
Tel: (0584) 2251

Nock Deighton
10 Broad Street
Ludlow, Shropshire
Tel: (0584) 2364

Hall Wateridge and Owen
Welsh Bridge Salerooms
Shrewsbury, Shropshire
Tel: (0743) 57074

Barber and Son
1 Church Street
Wellington,
Telford, Shropshire
Tel: (0952) 42155

SOMERSET

King Miles and Company
The Square
Axbridge, Somerset
Tel: (0934) 732268

Tamlyn and Son
56 High Street
Bridgwater, Somerset
Tel: (0278) 58241

Lawrences Fine Art of
Crewkerne
Falkland Square
Crewkerne, Somerset
Tel: (0460) 73041

John D. Fleming and Co
Melton House
High Street, Dulverton
Somerset
Tel: (0398) 23597

F.L. Hunt and Sons
Market Place
Somerton, Somerset
Tel: (0458) 72998

W.R.J. Greenslade
Priory Salerooms
Taunton, Somerset
Tel: (0823) 77121

STAFFORDSHIRE

Fletcher and Associates
7 High Street
Church Eaton, Staffs
Tel: (0785) 823014

Louis Taylor and Sons
Percy Street
Hanley
Stoke-on-Trent, Staffs
Tel: (0782) 22373

SUFFOLK

Tuohy and Son
18 High Street
Aldeburgh, Suffolk
Tel: (072885) 2066

Lacy Scott and Sons
3 Hatter Street
Bury St. Edmunds, Suffolk
Tel: (0284) 63531

Robert Dove and Partners
Dover House
Wolsey Street
Ipswich, Suffolk
Tel: (0473) 55137

Garrod Turner
50 St. Nicholas Street
Ipswich, Suffolk
Tel: (0473) 54664

Notleys
Royal Thoroughfare
Lowestoft, Suffolk
Tel: (0502) 2024

Newmarket Auctions
156 High Street
Newmarket, Suffolk
Tel: (0638) 61183

G.J. Warner Auctions
The Rectory
Redgrave
Nr Diss, Suffolk
Tel: (037 989) 545

Flick and Son
Old Bank House
Saxmundham, Suffolk
Tel: (0728) 3232

R.C. Knight and Sons
Market Place
Stowmarket, Suffolk
Tel: (04492) 2384

Oliviers
23–4 Market Hill
Sudbury, Suffolk
Tel: (0787) 72247

Spear and Son
The Hill
Wickham Market, Suffolk
Tel: (0728) 746321

Arnott and Calver
14 Church Street
Woodbridge, Suffolk
Tel: (03943) 2244

SURREY

F.G. Lawrence and Sons
Norfolk House
High Street
Bletchingley, Surrey
Tel: (0883) 843323

Parkins and Company
18 Malden Road
Cheam, Surrey
Tel: (01) 644 6127

Surrey Antique Auctions
10 Windsor Street
Chertsey, Surrey
Tel: (09328) 63313

Barbers (Chobham)
Town Mill
Vicarage Road
Chobham, Surrey
Tel: (09905) 7341

P.F. Windibank
The Dorking Halls
19–20 Reigate Road
Dorking, Surrey
Tel: (0306) 884556

Weller Eggar
74 Castle Street
Farnham, Surrey
Tel: (0252) 716221

Messenger May Baverstock
93 High Street
Godalming, Surrey
Tel: (04868) 23567

Clarke Gammon
Guildford Auction Rooms
Bedford Road
Guildford, Surrey
Tel: (0483) 72266

Cubitt and West
Millmead
Guildford, Surrey
Tel: (0483) 504030

Bonsor Penningtons
82 Eden Street
Kingston-on-Thames
Surrey
Tel: (01) 546 0022

Harold Williams Bennett and
Partners
2–3 South Parade
Merstham, Surrey
Tel: (073 74) 2234

Wentworth Auction Gallery
22 Station Approach
Virginia Water, Surrey
Tel: (099 04) 3711

EAST SUSSEX

Brighton Central Auction
Rooms
39 Upper Gardener Street
Brighton, E Sussex
Tel: (0273) 687968

Raymond P. Inman
35 Temple Street
Brighton, Sussex
Tel: (0273) 774777

Meads of Brighton
Film Studio Auction Rooms
St. Nicholas Road
Brighton, E Sussex
Tel: (0273) 202997

Heathfield Furniture Auctions
The Market
Heathfield, E Sussex
Tel: (04352) 3132

Wallis and Wallis
Regency House
1 Albion Street
Lewes, E Sussex
Tel: (07916) 3137

Vidler and Company
Auction Offices
Cinque Ports Street
Rye, E Sussex
Tel: (07973) 2124

Harold Bennett
115 Church Road
Hove, E Sussex
Tel: (0273) 736207

Burtenshaw Walker
66 High Street
Lewes, E Sussex
Tel: (07916) 4225

Gorringes
15 North Street
Lewes, E Sussex
Tel: (07916) 2503

WEST SUSSEX

Stride and Son
Southdown House
St. John's Street
Chichester, W Sussex
Tel: (0243) 782626

Wyatt and Sons
Baffins Hall
59 East Street
Chichester, W Sussex
Tel: (0243) 786581

Turner Rudge and Turner
29 High Street
East Grinstead, W Sussex
Tel: (0342) 24101

T. Bannister and Company
Market Place
Haywards Heath, W Sussex
Tel: (0444) 412402

Sotheby King and Chasemore
Station Road
Pulborough, W Sussex
Tel: (07982) 3831

Churchmans Auction Galleries
Church Street
Steyning, W Sussex
Tel: (0903) 813815

Fox and Sons, Jordan and Cook
Rivoli Salerooms
Chapel Road
Worthing, W Sussex
Tel: (0903) 30121

TYNE & WEAR

Anderson and Garland
Anderson House
Market Street
Newcastle-upon-Tyne
Tyne & Wear
Tel: (0632) 26278

Thomas N. Miller
18–22 Gallowgate
Newcastle-upon-Tune
Tyne & Wear
Tel: (0632) 25617

WARWICKSHIRE

Charles R. Phillips
The Estate Office
Evesham Road
Cookhill, Alcester, Warks
Tel: (078971) 763615

Bell Court Auction Rooms
67 High Street
Bidford-on-Avon, Warks
Tel: (078988) 2611

Chas. B. Odell and Company
7 Smalley Place
Kenilworth, Warks
Tel: (0926) 54869

Locke and England
1–2 Euston Place
Leamington Spa, Warks
Tel: (0926) 27988

Seamans of Rugby
20 Little Church Street
Rugby, Warks
Tel: (0788) 2367

Edwards Bigwood and Bewlay
The Old School
Tiddington
Stratford-on-Avon, Warks
Tel: (0789) 69415

WEST MIDLANDS

Biddle and Webb
Enfield Hall
Islington Row
Five Ways
Birmingham B15
Tel: (021) 643 4380

James and Lister Lea
11 Newhall Street
Birmingham B3
Tel: (021) 236 1751

Phillips Knowle
The Old House
Station Road
Knowle
Solihull West Midlands
Tel: (05645) 6151

Giles Haywood and Co
14 Foster Street
Stourbridge
West Midlands
Tel: (03843) 70891

Walker Barnett and Hill
3 Waterloo Road
Wolverhampton, West
Midlands
Tel: (0902) 771511

WILTSHIRE

Dennis Pocock and Son
High Street Saleroom
Marlborough, Wilts
Tel: (0672) 53471

Sandoe and Sandoe
10 High Street
Pewsey, Wilts
Tel: (06726) 3101

Woolley and Wallis
Castle Auction Mart
Salisbury, Wilts
Tel: (0722) 27405

WORCESTERSHIRE

Blinkhorn and Co
41–43 North Street
Broadway, Heref & Worcs
Tel: (038681) 852456

J.G. Lear and Son
215 Worcester Road
Malvern Link, Heref & Worcs
Tel: (06845) 5235

Arthur Griffiths and Son
57 Foregate Street
Worcester, Heref & Worcs
Tel: (0905) 26464

J.G. Lear and Son
46 Foregate Street
Worcester, Heref & Worcs
Tel: (0905) 25184

NORTH YORKSHIRE

M. Philip Scott
East View
Langthorne
Bedale, N Yorkshire
Tel: (06772) 3325

Morphets
4–6 Albert Street
Harrogate, N Yorkshire
Tel: (0423) 502282

Renton and Renton
16 Albert Street
Harrogate, N Yorkshire
Tel: (0423) 61531

Phillips (Leeds)
17a East Parade
Leeds LS1, N Yorkshire
Tel: (0532) 448011

Boulton and Cooper
St. Michael's House
Malton, N Yorkshire
Tel: (0653) 2151

J.E. and R.M. Tennant
The Old Chapel
Market Place
Richmond, N Yorkshire
Tel: (0748) 4241

SOUTH YORKSHIRE

Stanilands
28 Netherhall Road
Doncaster, S Yorkshire
Tel: (0302) 27121

A.E. Dowse and Son
Sheffield Auction Centre
82 West Street
Sheffield, S Yorkshire
Tel: (0742) 25858

WEST YORKSHIRE

Dacre Son and Hartley
5 The Grove
Ilkley, W Yorkshire
Tel: (0943) 600655

Andrew Sharpe and Partners
2 The Grove
Ilkley, W Yorkshire
Tel: (0943) 600456

W. Mackay Audsley
5 King Street
Leeds 1, West Yorkshire
Tel: (0532) 446991

Laidlaws
1 Crown Court
Wakefield, W Yorkshire
Tel: (0924) 75301

SCOTLAND

DUMFRIES & GALLOWAY

Thomson Roddick and Laurie
20 Murray Street
Annan
Dumfries, Scotland
Tel: (0387) 2575

GRAMPIAN

John Milne
The Bon-Accord Auction
Rooms
9–11 North Silver Street
Aberdeen, Grampian, Scotland
Tel: (0224) 50336

LOTHIAN

Phillips (Edinburgh)
63–65 George Street
Edinburgh, Lothian, Scotland
Tel: (031) 225 2575

STRATHCLYDE

Afflecks of Ayr
Nile Court
Ayr, Strathclyde, Scotland
Tel: (0292) 65187

Christie's and Edmiston's
164–166 Bath Street
Glasgow G2, Strathclyde,
Scotland
Tel: (041) 332 8134

Phillips (Glasgow)
98 Sauchiehall Street
Glasgow, Strathclyde, Scotland
Tel: (041) 332 3386

TAYSIDE

Taylor's Auction Rooms
Panmure Row
Montrose, Tayside, Scotland
Tel: (0674) 2275

Thomas Love and Sons
St. John's Place
Perth, Scotland
Tel: (0738) 24111

CHANNEL ISLANDS

Langlois of Guernsey
Sir William Place
St. Peter Port
Guernsey, C1
Tel: (0481) 23421

Martel, Maides and Lepelley
50 High Street
St. Peter Port
Guernsey, C1
Tel: (0481) 21203

F. Legallais and Sons
Bath Street
Jersey, C1
Tel: (0534) 30202

NORTHERN IRELAND

Osborne King and Megran
14 Montgomery Street
Belfast BT1, N Ireland
Tel: (0232) 20233

REPUBLIC OF IRELAND

Alain Chawner Ltd
Stable Galleries
Charlesrown, Ardee
Co Louth, Rep of Ireland
Tel: Drogheda 53259

Goerge Mealy and Sons
46–50 Kilkenny Street
Castlecomer
Co Kilkenny, Rep of Ireland
Tel: Castlecomer 41229

Marsh's Auction Rooms
70 South Mell,
Cork, Rep of Ireland
Tel: (0002) 20347

James Adam and Son
26 St. Stephen's Green N
Dublin 2, Rep of Ireland
Tel: (0001) 760261

Hamilton and Hamilton
15 Molesworth Street
Dublin 2, Rep of Ireland
Tel: (0001) 765501

Keane Mahony Smith
35 Molesworth Street
Dublin 2, Rep of Ireland
Tel: (0001) 682468

Denis S. Drum
New Street
Malahide
Co Dublin, Rep of Ireland
Tel: Malahide 452819

CARING FOR ANTIQUES

Antiques deserve the best care you can give them – whether it's a simple polishing from time to time, or extensive restoration. This section, devoted to caring for antiques, will help you in your search for an expert restorer, a specialist product or a course in restoration.

The first division lists 850 restorers arranged by the type of material they work on, such as glass, or by the type of goods they deal with, such as furniture. Occasionally, some restorers may appear in more than one section because their skill may be of use in differing circumstances. For example, a person who restores gilding may be listed under both "Picture Frames" and "Furniture", because both those items may be gilded as well as needing attention to other areas, such as plaster work or veneer. In this case, the restorer would also be listed under "Gilding".

When searching for the ideal craftsperson to undertake the item in question, bear in mind the important distinction between repairs, restoration and conservation. The majority of the people in this section are restorers, although a few specify that they only undertake repairs, or that conservation is their goal.

To clarify, restoration means attempting to make the article as good as new and may include the manufacture of new parts or fittings. For example, with an article of furniture, a missing splat would be crafted from matching wood, fitted, and then stained and polished to perfection. Repairs, on the other hand, generally involve merely fixing what is already there, such as glueing loose joints. Conservation is very different – it means salvaging what is left and preserving it for the future without trying to make the article look as it did originally. The term is often applied to textiles, when, as often as not, a total reweaving is impractical. Instead, a strengthening operation is undertaken. In this case, a stronger backing cloth may be sewn on, without sacrificing the appearance of the article, but, at the same time, not trying to reproduce the original effect of a perfectly-woven piece.

Having drawn the above distinction only gives rise to another serious question – should an item always be restored? Restorative processes should never be carried out to cover a serious fault or to affect a period or date which gives lie to the truth. However, dirt and deterioration are another matter, and there are very few things which are not improved by careful cleaning. Anything to arrest the ravages of time should be considered and any means employed to preserve the piece for future generations, provided that the treatment is sensitive.

A word of caution: although this section is compiled with the best intentions, it is obviously impossible to have personal experience of all the restorers listed herein. Therefore, the author can take no responsibility for an individual restorer's skills or fees. If there are several possible restorers in your area, it might be a good idea to make a few enquiries by telephone, before deciding to place the work. In this way, you can get a feeling for the person you will be dealing with by discussing the details of the item in question.

For his or her part, the restorer will want to know the approximate period of the piece, how extensive the damage is, which parts need his or her attention, and whether you have any of the missing bits. (The need to be explicit is most critical with furniture, because of the complex nature of its manufacture, and with antiquities, because of their age.)

Once an appointment is made, take the damaged piece with you if possible, plus any broken-off pieces. If the item is not portable, the restorer may be prepared to visit you. However, if possible visit the restorer's workshop – it will help you to judge the quality of their workmanship if you inspect the piece they are currently working on. Once you have spoken to the restorer, you will have an idea of the complexity of the job and the time it will take. You should also be given an estimate of the approximate cost; a small deposit may be requested. Do not be concerned if the restorer asks for what seems like a long time to do the work. Never hurry the restorer. Time is very important in obtaining the best possible results, and, if the restorer is a good one,

there may already be a waiting list. The cost of restoration is rarely prohibitive – damaged pieces only get more damaged as time goes on, so an investment in restoration is always a good one.

The second division of this section lists courses on restoration throughout the U.K. All manner and types of instruction are listed – whether it's a one-week summer seminar or a two-year degree course. Most people will opt for a smattering of knowledge, which is arguably better than knowing nothing. If you are a collector or merely interested in a certain area of antiques, it certainly does no harm to know more of their construction. It follows that once you understand the material, the better you can care for the piece.

However, never attempt restoration unless you have a deft hand and/or some experience. More antiques are devalued through inept restoration than by any other misfortune. Even simple cleaning and polishing should be preceded by consulting a reference book or two (or another restorer). There is a sad story of a friend who purchased a lovely beaded chemise of the 1920's. In her excitement to wear it that evening, she rushed home, dipped it into sudsy water, and watched in horror as every bead and sequin dissolved immediately (being cellulose-based, not plastic- or metal- as they sometimes were). Do not attempt anything which might spoil your beloved piece. Consult the experts.

If you decide to undertake restoration yourself, the final pages of this section will prove invaluable. Specialist products such as polishes, paints, cabinet fittings, veneers, tools, chemicals, adhesives and tools to facilitate your work are listed, as well as unusual items such as display stands, coloured glasses and imported yarns. Most of the manufacturers offer a mail order service, so there is no excuse for starting the job with the wrong materials.

When working with antiques, remember that they have already survived for many years and that are only in your care for a relatively short time – so give them the best possible home by taking care of them properly.

CHAIR-MAKER.

CARPENTER.

CABINET-MAKER.

SEE ALSO THE RESTORERS
UNDER VARIOUS RELATED
MATERIALS SUCH AS
METALWARE AND STONEWARE

LONDON

**THE ARCHITECTURAL ANTIQUE
MARKET**
4–8 Highgate High Street
London N6
Tel: (01) 341 3761/348 4846/340 8476/359
4330 and 830 5256
*Restoration of cast ironwork, woodwork and
stained glass.*

ASHBY AND HORNER
32 Earl Street
London EC2A 2JD
Tel: (01) 377 0266
*Restoration, repair and renewal of stonework
plus restoration, repair and replacement of
architectural joinery including panelling and
staircases.*

GUY F. BAGSHAW
96 Webber Street
London SE1 OQN
Tel: (01) 928 3624
*Architectural renovation and joinery
specialising in 18th c. staircases and porches.*

BOSTOCK AND GERRISH
London NW1
Tel: (01) 723 9912 (by appointment only)
Restoration of carved and painted woodwork.

IAN CLAYTON LTD
277 Grays Inn Road
London WC1X 8PF
Tel: (01) 278 0281
*Statuary and monument consolidation,
including cleaning and preservation to
international museum standards.*

EATON-GAZE LTD
86 Teesdale Street
London E2 6 PU
Tel: (01) 739 7272
*Restoration of fibrous plasterwork including
mantelpieces, internal and external mouldings
and composition ornamentation.*

V.A. MANNERS AND SON
47 Chilham Road
Mottingham
London SE19 4BE
Tel: (01) 857 2592
*Restoration and polishing in situ of panelling,
doors, staircases and furniture.*

PINECRAFT
132a Liverpool Road
London N1
Tel: (01) 609 2653
*Stripping of pine furniture and architectural
fittings. See overleaf for illustration.*

*Above right: Removing sulphations by
micro-silica blasting from 16th and 17th c.
Italian marble statuary at the Orangery,
Kensington Palace, London, courtesy of Ian
Clayton Ltd.*

*Right: Plain Ionic columns supporting a
balcony entablature in the Mail Hall at the
Bath Assembly Rooms, restored by Eaton-
Gaze Ltd.*

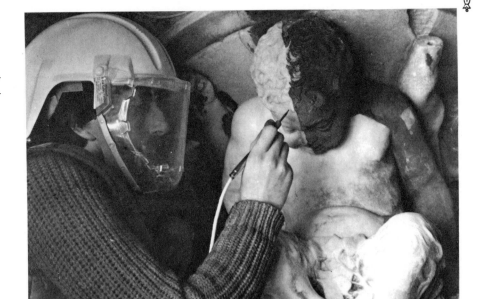

Above: "Before" and "After" of a painted door, stripped and finished by Pinecraft.

THOMAS AND WILSON
454 Fulham Road
London SW6 1BY
Tel: (01) 381 1161/7
Restoration and reproduction of decorative plasterwork plus the reinstatement of external stucco in cement and sand or fibreglass.

WATTS AND COMPANY LTD
7 Tufton Street
London SW1 3QE
Tel: (01) 222 2893/7169
Restoration of wallpaper. See entry under "Paintings and Prints Restorers" for illustration.

SOUTH AND SOUTH EAST ENGLAND

ENGLISH STREET FURNITURE COMPANY
Somers House
Linnfield Corner
Redhill, Surrey
Tel: Redhill 60986
Specialists in all kinds of street furniture from telephone kiosks to village water pumps to original gas-fired lamp posts. See "Lighting" for illustration.

DAVID GILLESPIE ASSOCIATES LTD
Dippenhall
Farnham, Surrey GU10 5DW
Tel: (0252) 723531
Restoration of mouldings, carvings or sculptures in plaster.

Right: Decorative classical plasterwork as installed in a palace in Riyadh, Saudi Arabia; courtesy of Thomas and Wilson.

HAGEN RESTORATIONS
Bakehouse Cottage
Northwood End
Haynes, Beds
Tel: (023 066) 424
Restoration and repair to woodwork.

IN SITU PAINT STRIPPING COMPANY
Rowan Garth
Upper Hartfield, E Sussex
Tel: (0892 77) 292
Stripping of paint or varnish from interior fitted woodwork such as staircases, architraves, skirtings, doors, shutters etc. Will also sand floors and reseal parquet and floorboards as well as bleach, stain, polish and varnish any wood surfaces.

J.S.R. JOINERY
Poole Street
Great Yeldham
Halstead, Essex
Tel: (0787) 237722
Architectural reproduction including wood turning. Staircase balusters, newel posts plus windows and doors copied from photo reference.

BERTRAM NOLLER
14a London Road
Reigate, Surrey RH1 5RY
Tel: (073 72) 42548
Restoration and supply of marble.

D.J. SMITH
34 Silchester Road
Pamber Heath, nr Basingstoke
Hants RG2 6EF
Tel: (0734) 700595
Restoration of carving, specialising in 18 c.

STUART J. SMITH
5 Hillmead Gardens
Bedhampton, Hants PO9 3NL
Tel: (0705) 477576
Restoration of plaster or stucco mouldings, using templates in situ, and the reproduction of small embellishments in cast plaster using the jelly mould method.

M.P. WALLIS
Norfolk Cottage, 1 The Row
Hawdridge Common, nr Chesham,
Bucks
Tel: (024 029) 8172
Polishing and restoration including large projects like panelling and staircases in situ.

D.W. WINDSOR LTD
Netherfield Lane
Stanstead Abbots
Ware, Herts
Tel: (0920) 870567
Specialists in restoration of antique lanterns for public, commercial and private use.

R.J. YOUNG
15 Station Road East
Ash Vale
Aldershot, Hants GU12 5LT

R.J. YOUNG (CON'T)
Tel: (0252) 542789
Restoration and reproduction of ornamental plasterwork and stucco fascias

SOUTHWEST ENGLAND AND WALES

L.G. AND K.L. DISNEY
The Forge
Kewstoke Road
Worle, Weston-super-Mare, Avon
Tel: (0934) 512423
Restoration of ornamental ironwork.

ROGER LESLIE HARDY
10 Heol Hyfrydle
Coedpoeth, nr Wrexham
Clwyd LL11 3NL, Wales
Tel: (0352) 771 611
Duplication of wooden mouldings, pillars, turnings or carvings, large or small.

WING AND STAPLES
The Forge
Motcombe
Shaftesbury, Dorset SP7 9PE
Tel: (0747) 3104
Manufacture and restoration of hand-wrought metalwork.

MIDLANDS AND EAST ANGLIA

DAVID ACKROYD.
Bleathwood Manor Farm
Bleathwood
Ludlow, Shropshire
Tel: (0584) 810726
Architectural restoration of wood.

W.G. CROTCH AND SON
119 Fore Street
Ipswich, Suffolk
Tel: (0473) 50349
Restoration of architectural plaster mouldings.

KINGFISHER RESTORATION
2 Westgate Terrace
Long Melford
Sudbury, Suffolk CO10 9HB
Tel: (0787) 310677
Paint-stripping on site, sand-blasting off site. Collection service.

Right: Fibrous plaster moulding of a sculpture from the Great Hall at University College, Frognal, reproduced and stained to look like wood, courtesy of David Gillespie Associates Ltd.

H.B. MOORE
The Forge
Bradeston, Woodbridge, Suffolk
Tel: (072 882) 354
Restoration of wrought metalwork.

ANDREW NAYLOR
Unit H3
Halesfield 19
Telford, Shropshire
Tel: (0952) 583116
Conservation and restoration of metalwork, specialising in lead garden sculpture and architectural ornament. See entry under 'Restorers, Metalware' for illustration.

NORTH OF ENGLAND AND SCOTLAND

JOHN HENDERSON LTD
Inglis Lane
Castleblair
Dunfermline, Fife, Scotland
Tel: (0383) 21123/23714
Restoration of wrought and cast iron metalwork. Architectural work carried out in situ.

STRIP SHOP
Unit 3
Country Road
Ormskirk, Lancs
Tel: (0695) 78766
Wood-stripping service, using "Patinex" system, a non-caustic solution which does not affect the colour of the wood.

Left: Exterior lantern created by Wing and Staples.

SOUTHWEST ENGLAND

THE FLINTLOCK
17a High Street
Glastonbury, Somerset
Tel: (0458) 31525
Restoration of arms and armour, specialising in the unusual.

NORTH OF ENGLAND AND SCOTLAND

ALTECH SERVICES
c/o Ron Field
Langley Park Industrial Estate
Witton, Gilbert, Co Durham
Tel: (0385) 730491
Mechanical repairs to weapons.

A. WALTER
THE COUNTRY GUN SHOP
Lilliesleaf, Melrose
Roxburghshire TD6 9JD, Scotland
Tel: (083 57) 315
Repairs to all types of sporting firearms. Stocks, fore-ends and barrels re-made if necessary.

LONDON

EUROBIND BOOKBINDERS LTD
St George's Works
72 Conington Road
London SE13
Tel: (01) 318 5757/5069
Hand bookbinding including gold blocking and hand finishing of single copies.

GREEN AND STONE OF CHELSEA
259 Kings Road
London SW3
Tel: (01) 352 6521
Agents for bookbinders and calligraphers.

W.T. MORRELL AND COMPANY LTD
4–7 Nottingham Court
Shorts Gardens
London WC2
Tel: (01) 836 6066
Restoration since 1860 of leather bookbindings.

Above and opposite: "Before" and "After" photographs of a volume on French history, restored by Zaehnsdorf Ltd.

ROGER TURNER BOOKS LTD
22 Nelson Road
London SE10
Tel: (01) 853 5271
Restoration of books including rebinding.

ZAEHNSDORF LTD
175r Bermondsey Street
London SE1 3UW
Tel: (01) 407 1244
Restoration, conservation and repair of antiquarian books.

Below: Two views of the interior of W.T. Morrell's premises. On the right the presses for the books, on the left the tooling and lettering area.

SOUTH AND SOUTHEAST ENGLAND

DAVID COLVER
19 Hall Place Drive
Weybridge, Surrey KT13 OA5
Tel: (0932) 45476
Restoration of books including bespoke binding in fine leathers and gold tooling. Also repairs, re-backs and conserves paper documents. Will also lecture and provide demonstrations of his craft.

JARVIS BOOKBINDERS LTD
28 Broad Street
Ramsgate, Kent CT11 8QY
Tel: (0843) 51797
Specialists in hand sewing and binding. Projects up to 500 volumes undertaken.

M.H. WILLMOT
42 Lower High Street
Thame, Oxon OX9 2AA

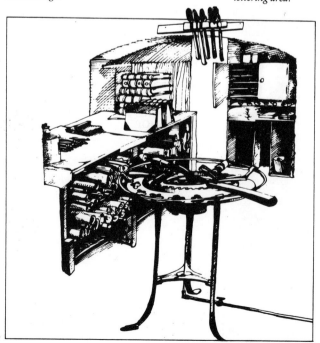

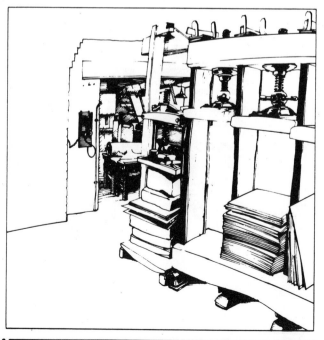

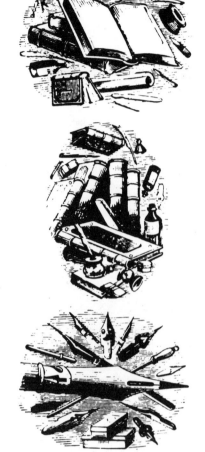

M.H. WILLMOT (CON'T)
Tel: (084 421) 3350
*New and antique bindings undertaken,
specialising in single copies and unusual
projects.*

SOUTHWEST ENGLAND AND WALES

JEREMY LAST
56A Goose Street
Beckington, Bath, Avon BA3 6SS
Tel: (0373) 830463
*Bookbinding and conservation by family
business. Will work in any style, any
material, and also repair in original materials.*

WINSTANLEY BOOKBINDERS
213 Devizes Road
Salisbury, Wilts SP2 9LT
Tel: (0722) 4998
*Rebacking and restoration of antiquarian books
and archival papers.*

MIDLANDS AND EAST ANGLIA

RICHARD LANE
Heath House, Smiths Lane
Fakenham, Norfolk
Tel: (0328) 2151
*Restoration of books. Almost any bookbinding
project undertaken from the finest antiquarian
restoration to new leather or cloth bindings.
Also have own marbled papers and aim to
complete all work within six weeks.*

*Below: Bible rebound in pigskin with sewn
raised cords, silk sewn headbands, gilt edges
all round, and individually created endpapers
courtesy of Winstanley Bookbinders.*

*Far left: David Colver "finishing" the spine of
a book.*

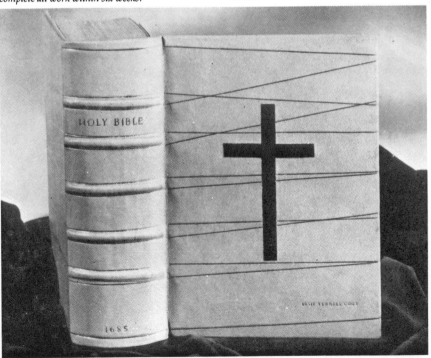

Above: Pair of ladderback chairs with new rush seats, courtesy of the Basketmakers Association.

Above right: Ricky Holdstock re-rushing a country ladderback chair.

LONDON

JOHN HAYES AND SONS
The Old Fire House
St Mary's Square
St Mary's Road, London W5 4QX
Tel: (01) 840 4022
Restoration of cane and rush seating.

M. AND F. CANERS
14 Second Avenue
London, E17
Tel: (01) 521 3409
Fortnightly collection and delivery service in London area. All patterns and periods undertaken but speciality Bergère suites.

Below: "Before" and "After" photos showing a Bergère-style armchair, as restored by the Centre of Restoration and Arts.

SOUTH AND SOUTHEAST ENGLAND

BASKETMAKERS ASSOCIATION
Mrs Olivia Elton Barratt,
Millfield Cottage
Little Hadham, Ware, Herts
Tel: (0279) 51497
Restoration of cane, close cane, willow skeining and rush work on furniture, baskets, or antique carriage panels.

MOREN BROWN
The Green South
Warborough, Oxford
Oxon OX9 8DR
Tel: (086 732) 8354
Restoration of cane and rush seating.

BRIAN EDWIN CAUDELL
55 Stowe Road
Orpington, Kent
Tel: Orpington 73631
Re-caning service.

CENTRE OF RESTORATION AND ARTS
20 Folly Lane
St Albans, Herts
Tel: (0727) 51555
Re-caning in any pattern as well as re-seating in rush and seagrass. Supplies shop on premises.

TONY AND KATE HANDLEY
Home Farm
School Road
Ardington, Wantage, Oxon
Tel: (023 588) 614 and 362
Restoration of cane and rush seating.

RICKY HOLDSTOCK
Hillside Cottage,
The Forstal, Hernhill
Faversham, Kent ME13 9JQ
Tel: (022) 775 204
Restoration of all styles of rush and cane seating. Collection and delivery in South East; large pieces can be repaired in situ.

J.M. SELLORS ANTIQUES
28 St James Road
Croydon, Surrey
Tel: (01) 689 1004/647 1768
Restoration of rush seating.

SOUTHWEST ENGLAND AND WALES

COTSWOLD CANERS
Mrs Janet Gibbs
Workshop No 5
Cricklade Street
Cirencester, Glos
Tel: (0285) 61790
Re-caning firm capable of restoring difficult patterns such as spiderwork, fanbacks, and double-caned Bergères.

MIDLANDS AND EAST ANGLIA

ALMA ANTIQUE RESTORERS
The Old Gospel Hall
Dereham Road
Norwich, Norfolk
Tel: (0603) 613184
Re-caning service.

Above left: Restoration of spiderback cane work by Wood Graphics.

Above: Re-rushing a spindleback chair, courtesy of I. and J. Brown.

I. AND J. BROWN
58 Commercial Road
Hereford, Heref & Worcs HR1 2BP
Tel: (0432) 58895
Restoration of rush seating.

CANE CRAFT
Lowestoft Road
Hopton
Great Yarmouth, Norfolk NR31 9AH
Tel: (0502) 731571
Restoration of cane-covered handles on ceramic or metal teapots.

K.J. TRAYLER
Fir Close
Frostenden
Wangford, Suffolk
Tel: (050 278) 261
Chair caning and seagrass or rush seating repairs for antique or modern furniture.

Left: Mrs Janet Gibbs replacing fanback caning on Regency chair.

WOOD GRAPHICS
39 Greenwood Crescent
Boughton, Notts NG22 9HX
Tel: (0623) 860298
Restoration of rush and cane seating.

NORTH OF ENGLAND AND SCOTLAND

JOCELYN ANTIQUES
161 West George Street
Glasgow G2 2JJ, Scotland
Tel: (041) 248 3024
Restoration of cane seating.

DAVID OFFLEY
7 Shipley Common Lane
Ilkeston, Derbs DE7 8TR
Tel: (0602) 321653
Chair seating in cane and seagrass.

PETER SNART
Willowbog Farm
Wark, Hexham, Northld
Tel: (043 481) 217
Rush seating and rattan cane work.

LONDON

BENARDOUT
31a Buckingham Palace Road
London SW1
Tel: (01) 834 8241
*Restoration of hand-made antique and modern
Oriental rugs and carpets.*

RAYMOND BENARDOUT
5 William Street
London SW1X 9HL
Tel: (01) 235 3360
*Cleaning and restoration of antique rugs and
carpets.*

DAVID BLACK ORIENTAL CARPETS
96 Portland Road
London W11
Tel: (01) 727 2566
*Cleaning, repair and restoration of village and
nomad tribal rugs.*

BOHUN AND BUSBRIDGE
8 Clarendon Road
London W11
Tel: (01) 229 7825
*Cleaning and repair of all types of carpets and
textiles.*

THE CARPET BAZAAR
220 Westbourne Grove
London W11 2RH
Tel: (01) 229 8907
*Cleaning and repair of Oriental and tribal
carpets and rugs. Will work in situ if carpet
too big to move.*

ROBERT FRANSES AND SON
5 Nugent Terrace
London NW8
Tel: (01) 286 6913
Restoration of carpets and rugs.

KENNEDY CARPETS AND KELIMS
9A Vigo Street,
London W1.
Tel: (01) 439 8873
Restoration of carpets and kelims.

JOSEPH LAVIAN
53–79 Highgate Road
London NW5
Tel: (01) 485 7955 and 346 3140 (Home)
Restoration of carpets, rugs and kelims.

M. AND M. ORIENTAL GALLERY LTD
14 Hallswell Parade
Finchley Road
London NW11 ODL
Tel: (01) 455 4392
*Restoration and cleaning of old and antique
Oriental carpets and rugs.*

MAYFAIR CARPETS GALLERY
8 Old Bond Street
London W1
Tel: (01) 493 0126/0127
*Cleaning and repair of antique Persian
carpets.*

NISSIM AND COMPANY LTD
23 Charlotte Road
London EC2A 3PB
Tel: (01) 739 5051
*Restoration, repair and cleaning of all carpets
including Oriental, Chenilles and Aubusson,
including replacement of worn fringe.*

*Above and right: "Before" and "After" photos
showing a 19th c. Ersari Turkmen Engsi
carpet, as restored by David Black Oriental
Carpets.*

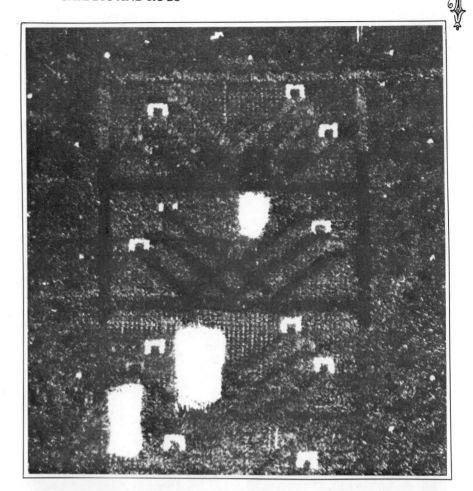

LONDON (CON'T)

THE ORIENTAL CARPET CLINIC
7 Portman Square
London W1
Tel: (01) 486 3770 and 486 9314
Hand cleaning and restoration, carried out at the clinic or in situ. Long established firm.

S. POYASTRO
5 Kirstein Mansions
Assam Street
London E1
Tel: (01) 247 7707
Restoration of all hand-made rugs.

VIGO CARPET GALLERY
6a Vigo Street
London W1
Tel: (01) 439 6971
Restoration and cleaning of carpets, rugs and tapestries.

M.L. WAROUJIAN
110–112 Hammersmith Road
London W6
Tel: (01) 748 7509
Cleaning and repair of Persian and Oriental carpets and rugs.

SOUTH AND SOUTHEAST ENGLAND

MASTERCLEAN
1 Collins Way
Leigh-on-Sea, Essex
Tel: (0702) 354567/528584
Persian and orientals undertaken, or steam-cleaned in situ.

AUDREY THURMAN
11 Ship Street
Brighton, Sussex
Tel: (0273) 733654
Restoration of old and antique rugs.

SOUTHWEST ENGLAND AND WALES

J.P.J. HOMER ORIENTAL RUGS
Stoneleigh
Parabola Road
Cheltenham, Glos GL50 3BD
Tel: (0242) 34243 (By appointment only)
Cleaning and repair of Oriental rugs.

ERIC PRIDE ORIENTAL RUGS
8 Imperial Square
Cheltenham, Glos GL50 1QB
Tel: (0242) 580 822
Cleaning and restoration of Oriental carpets and rugs.

NORTH OF ENGLAND AND SCOTLAND

WHYTOCK AND REID
Sunbury House
Belford Mews
Edinburgh, Scotland EH4 3DN
Tel: (031) 226 4911
Restoration of Eastern carpets and rugs.

CLOCK AND WATCH-MAKER.

LONDON

ASPREY AND COMPANY LTD
165–169 New Bond Street
London W1
Tel: (01) 493 6767
Restoration of clocks.

ROY BENNETT
5 Leeland Mansions
Leeland Road
London W13 9HE
Tel: (01) 567 7030
Complete restoration service to both case and movements. Will also make new cases for old movements to customer's specifications.

AUBREY BROCKLEHURST
123 Cromwell Road
London SW7 4ET
Tel: (01) 373 0319
Repair and restoration of any mechanical and electrical clocks.

H.W. BUCKINGHAM
86 Hatton Garden
London EC1
Tel: (01) 242 6746
Repair of antique and modern clocks and watches.

CAMERER CUSS AND COMPANY
54/56 New Oxford Street
London WC1
Tel: (01) 636 8968
Restoration of clocks and watches.

THE CLOCK CLINIC LTD
85 Lower Richmond Road
London SW15
Tel: (01) 788 1407
Restoration of clocks including dials and cases.

PEARL CROSS
35 St Martin's Court
London WC2
Tel: (01) 836 2814 and 240 0795
Restoration of clocks and watches.

DAEDALUS
43 The Village
Charlton
London SE7 8UG
Tel: (01) 858 2514
Clock and watch restoration including dial and case work, re-gilding, re-enamelling, verge reconversions, and manufacture of missing parts. Will also work in situ if required.

GARNER AND MARNEY LTD
41/43 Southgate Road
London N1
Tel: (01) 226 1535
Restoration and dial-making of brass clocks.

GARRARD AND COMPANY LTD
112 Regent Street,
London W1
Tel: (01) 734 7020
Restoration of clocks.

KEITH HARDING ANTIQUES
93 Hornsey Road
London N7
Tel: (01) 607 6181/2672
Restoration of clocks.

J.P. KIRWAN CLOCK AND WATCH REPAIRS
70 Fortune Green Road
London NW6
Tel: (01) 794 7468
Restoration of clocks and watches including replacement parts.

WILLIAM C. MANSELL
24 Connaught Street
London W2
Tel: (01) 723 4154
Repair of any mechanical and electrical clocks. Will travel anywhere.

L. NEWLAND
17 Picton Place,
London W1
Tel: (01) 935 2864
Restoration of clocks and watches.

NORTH LONDON CLOCK SHOP
72 Highbury Park
London N5 2XE
Tel: (01) 226 1609
Restoration of modern and antique clocks, and some watches.

PLEDGE AND ALDWORTH
Unit 157, First Floor
27 Clerkenwell Close
London EC1
Tel: (01) 251 0555
Restoration of clocks including dial work and engine turning, a 300 year old craft of engraving for cases, dials, boxes, and in preparation for enamelling. See ''Jewellery Restorers'' for illustration.

PUBLIC CLOCKS
1 Prideaux Place
Lloyd Square
London WC1X 9PR
Tel: (01) 837 4345
Specialists in tower or turret and house clock repair and renovation, including installation of automatic winding units where hand winding is a problem e.g. in church towers.

R.E. ROSE F.B.H.I.
731 Sidcup Road
London SE9
Tel: (01) 859 4754 and 464 2653 (Home)
Restoration of clocks including dial and case work involving Boulle or gilding.

A.R. AND J.S. ULLMANN LTD
10 Hatton Garden
London EC1N 8AH
Tel: (01) 405 1877
Restoration and repair of clocks and watches.

SOUTH AND SOUTHEAST ENGLAND

S.J. ALLEN
53 Stoke Road
Walton-on-Thames, Surrey KT12 3DD
Tel: (093 22) 41164
Restorer with facilities for replacement of parts.

A.E. BOOTH
9 High Street
Ewell
Epsom, Surrey KT17 1SG
Tel: (01) 393 5245
Restoration of clocks.

THE CLOCK SHOP
284 Wickham Road
Shirley, Surrey
Tel: (01) 656 2800
Repair of clocks.

EQUATIONS OF TIME
c/o John Exel
The Forge
105a High Street
Dorking, Surrey RH4 1AL
Tel: (0306) 887 559
Restoration and manufacture of clockcases.

LINCOLN HOUSE GALLERIES
587 London Road
Westcliff-on-Sea, Essex
Tel: (0702) 339106
Restoration of clocks.

GEOFFREY LUSCOMBE
26–28 East Street
Sittingbourne, Kent ME10 4RT
Tel: (0795) 23716
Restoration of clocks.

THE OLD MALTHOUSE
Hungerford, Berks
Tel: (048 86) 2209
Restoration of 18th and 19th c. clocks and barometers.

ONSLOW CLOCKS
36 Church Street
Twickenham, Middx
Tel: (01) 892 7632
Restoration of clocks including casework and movements.

C.F. SIMPSON
1 Station Buildings
Sherman Road
Bromley, Kent
Tel: (01) 460 7879
Restoration of clocks.

SMALLCOMBE CLOCKS
5 Grammavill Street
Grays, Essex
Tel: (0375) 77181
Restoration of clocks.

TAURUS ANTIQUES LTD
145 Masons Hill
Bromley, Kent BR2 9HY
Tel: (01) 464 8746
Restoration of clocks.

TELLING TIME ANTIQUES
42 Park Street
Thame, Oxon
Tel: (0844) 21 3007
Restoration of clocks and watches.

STEPHEN W. THOMAS
24 Walnut Way
Clacton-on-Sea, Essex CO15 2BT
Tel: (0255) 33476
Specialist in grandfather clock repairs.

D.O. THOROGOOD
38 Ninfield Road
Sidley
Bexhill-on-Sea, E Sussex TN39 5AE
Tel: (0424) 219957
Restoration of clocks.

M.V. TOOLEY O.M.B.H.I.
The Guildroom
The Lee
Great Missenden, Bucks
Tel: (024) 020 463
Repair of clocks and barometers as well as restoration of cases.

VINTAGE RESTORATIONS
The Old Bakery
Windmill Street
Tunbridge Wells, Kent
Tel: (0892) 25899
Specialists in ship and carriage clock restorations.

S. WARRENDER AND COMPANY
4 Cheam Road
Sutton, Surrey
Tel: (01) 643 4381
Restoration of quality clocks.

SOUTH WEST ENGLAND AND WALES

BELL PASSAGE ANTIQUES
38 High Street
Wickwar
Wotton-under-Edge, Glos GL12 8NP
Tel: (045 424) 251
Restoration of clocks.

LAWRENCE BRASS AND SON
93 and 95 Walcot Street
Bath, Avon
Tel: (0225) 64057
Restoration of clocks and case finishes.

J.R. CHISMAN
4 Station Road
St Blazey
Par, Cornwall PL24 2NF
Tel: (072681) 2309
Repair of clocks and watches.

GASTRELL HOUSE
33 Long Street
Tetbury, Glos GL8 8AA
Tel: (0666) 52228
Restoration of clocks.

C.T. GILMER LTD
Old Bond Street
Bath, Avon
Tel: (0225) 66754/64422
Repair of clocks in works or on site.

ARTHUR S. LEWIS
The Stables
Linkend House
Corselawn, Glos GH9 4LZ
Tel: (0452) 78 258
Restoration of all types of clocks.

TERENCE MORRISS
11–13 Patwell Street
Bruton, Somerset
Tel: (074 981) 3448
Restoration covering all finishes and replacing missing or damaged parts.

LESLIE STANTON
The Joiners Workshop
Ashbourne Road
Rocester, nr Uttoxeter, Staffs
Tel: (0889) 590186
Restoration of clocks and clockcase.

TIME RESTORED LTD
20 High Street
Pewsey, Wilts
Tel: (06726) 3544
All restoration including turret work, from fully qualified B.A.D.A. staff.

MIDLANDS AND EAST ANGLIA

LEONARD BALL
44 Market Street
Lutterworth, Leics
Tel: (045 55) 4942
Restoration of clocks and clockcases.

N. BYRAN-PEACH ANTIQUES
221a Derby Road
Loughborough, Leics
and
28 Far Street
Wymeswold, Leics
Tel: (0509) 880425 and (0509) 32026
Specialists in the restoration of English long case and bracket clocks, and French carriage clocks.

GAVINA EWART
37 Sheep Street
Stratford-upon-Avon, Warks
Tel: (0789) 293917
Repair of clocks and watches.

FEARNS ANTIQUES
9 Coleshill Street
Fazeley, nr Tamworth, Staffs
Tel: (0827) 54233
Restoration of antique clocks.

BERNARD HARBOURN
Croft Cottage
High Street
Sloley, Norwich, Norfolk
Tel: (069 260) 753
Specialist restoration of clocks, watches and barometers.

G.B.E. AND E. GOODING
12 Arden Buildings
Dorridge, Solihull, W Midlands
Tel: (056 45) 3040
Restoration of clocks including works and cases.

LOCKES
The Buttercross
Ludlow, Shropshire
Tel: (0584) 2061
Restoration and repair of clocks and pocket watches.

WHERRY HOUSE ANTIQUES
The Street
Sutton, Norfolk NR12 9RF
Tel: (0692) 81487 (By appointment only)
Restoration of clocks.

NORTH OF ENGLAND AND SCOTLAND

ADAMS ANTIQUES
65 Waterloo Row
Chester, Cheshire CH1 2LE
Tel: (0244) 319421
Restoration and repair of clocks.

PETER AUSTIN, C.M.B.H.I.
340 Bakewell Road
Darley Dale
Matlock, Derbs DE4 3EF
Tel: (0629) 55582
Specialist restoration of antique watches – dials restored, ultrasonic cleaning, electronic timing, and special parts handmade if required.

J. BRADLEY
84a High Street
Felling
Gateshead, Tyne & Wear
Tel: (0632) 698542
Specialist in watch restoration.

CUMBRIAN CLOCKS
Leeville, Boarbank Lane
Allithwaite
Grange-over-Sands, Cumbria LA11 7QR
Tel: (044 84) 3900
*Restoration and maintenance including
making necessary replacement components
Will work in situ.*

J.R. GELSTHORPE
Pebble Cottage
Barmston
Driffield, E Yorkshire
Tel: (026 286) 376
*Specialist restoration of cases for grandfather
clocks.*

ALAN S. HAMSHERE
Balcanquhal Farmhouse
Gateside, Strathmiglo
Cupar, Fife KY14 7SS, Scotland
Tel: (033 76) 325
*Specialist restorer who will also make parts
and movements to order.*

JOCELYN ANTIQUES
161 West George Street
Glasgow G2 2JJ, Scotland
Tel: (041) 248 3024
*Complete clock repair and restoration service
including dials and cases.*

JOHN PEARSON
Church Cottage
Birstwith
Harrogate, N Yorkshire
Tel: (0423) 770828
Specialist in long case clocks and painted dials.

C. REYNOLDS
The Spindles
Tonge, Melbourne, Derbs
Tel: (03316) 2609
*Specialist in the fitting of antique watch
glasses.*

CHRISTOPHER RYCROFT F.B.H.I.
Scarr House
Stainland
Halifax, W Yorkshire HX4 9PN
Tel: (0422) 74255
*Restoration of clocks including the
manufacture and fitting of ornate pierced
hands, engraved dials, chapter rings, date
rings, wheels and pinions.*

*Above: A plain backplate which has been
engraved and an escapement converted to
verge, as completed by Christopher Rycroft.*

E.H. SOUTHAM
Ancell's Clocks
3 Roundway
Rossall, Fleetwood, Lancs FY7 8JD
Tel: (039 17) 3898
Restoration of clocks.

PETER SNART
Willowbog Farm
Wark, Hexham, Northld
Tel: (043 481) 217
Specialists in clockcase restoration.

NORTHERN IRELAND

K. AND M. NESBITT
21 Tobermore Road
Magherafelt, Co. Derry BT45 5HB
Northern Ireland
Tel: (0648) 32713
*Restoration and repair of clocks and watches.
Willing to travel within Ireland and work in
situ.*

LONDON

YESTERDAY CHILD
24 The Mall
Camden Passage
London N1
Tel: (01) 354 1601 and (0908) 583403
Restoration of dolls.

SOUTH AND SOUTHEAST ENGLAND

MRS D. CHRISTOPHERS
86a St James Street
Brighton BN2 1TP, E Sussex
Tel: (0273) 695247
Conservation by museum historian who will tackle dolls made from any material. Will clean, replace limbs and wigs but repair mechanical movements.

MRS MARGARET GLOVER
42 Hartham Road
Isleworth, Middx
Tel: (01) 568 4662
Restoration and conservation of wax dolls including replacement of missing hair and repair or replacement of doll's clothing.

SOUTHWEST ENGLAND AND WALES

LILIAN MIDDLETON
Tudor House
Sheep Street
Stow-on-the-Wold, Glos
Tel: (0451) 30381
Restoration of dolls including re-stringing, re-dressing and the manufacture of new bodies and limbs.

TREWITHEN COTTAGE DOLLS
Trewithen Cottage
Fore Street
Grampound, Truro, Cornwall
Tel: (0726) 882692
Restoration of dolls.

MIDLANDS AND EAST ANGLIA

MERIDIAN HOUSE ANTIQUES
Meridian House
Market Street
Stourbridge, W Midlands
Tel: (038 43) 5384
Restoration of dolls and dolls clothing.

Below: "Before", "During" and "After" steps during the restoration of a wax doll's head, courtesy of Mrs Margaret Glover.

Above: Lillian Middleton fitting the bisque head of an "Armand Marseilles" doll to its composition body.

NORTH OF ENGLAND AND SCOTLAND

GILLIE DOLLS
69 Babylon Lame
Anderton, Nr Chorley, Lancs
Tel: (0257) 482074
Restoration of wax and bisque dolls, to museum standard, upon request.

DON MADDOX
47 Church Street
Ribchester, nr Preston
Lancs PR3 3YE
Tel: (025 484) 512
Doll's furniture made or reproduced to any scale.

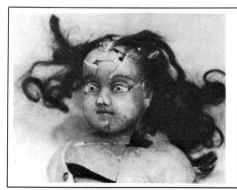

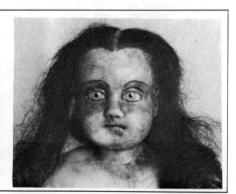

Above: Two similar stoves, on the right, before restoration; on the left, fully restored to working order, courtesy of the Stove Shop.

LONDON

AMAZING GRATES
153 Highgate Road
London N5
Tel: (01) 485 0496
Restoration of cast-iron fireplaces.

EATON-GAZE LTD
86 Teesdale Street
London E2 6PU
Tel: (01) 739 7272/3
Fibrous plasterwork restorations including mantelpieces. For illustration see entry under "Architecture".

PAUL FERGUSON
Workshop 5, First Floor
38 Mount Pleasant
London WC1
Tel: (01) 806 7799
Restoration of cast-iron fireplaces and most metal accessories.

INFOURNEAUX
65 Mill Lane
London NW6 1NB
Tel: (01) 794 1511
Restoration of Continental and British stoves, and Victorian, Edwardian, and Art Nouveau fireplaces and mantles.

STOVE SHOP
Camden Lock
Chalk Farm Road
London NW1
Tel: (01) 969 9531
Restoration of stoves and cooking ranges including replacement of materials and flues and installation.

MR WANDLE'S WORKSHOP
200–202 Garratt Lane
London SW18 4ED
Tel: (01) 870 5873
Restoration of cast iron fireplaces including shot-blasting and polishing. For illustration, see entry under "Specialist Dealers– Fireplaces".

SOUTH AND SOUTHEAST ENGLAND

J. BRINKMAN
13 Pall Mall
Leigh-on-Sea, Essex
Tel: (0702) 74661
Restoration of cast-iron fireplaces, including repairing, polishing and lacquering.

JOHN FORD
Old School View
Main Street
Grove, nr Wantage, Oxon OX12 7LQ
Tel: (023 57) 2201
Restoration of fireplaces, especially inglenook and Victorian styles.

RICHARD QUINNELL LTD
Rowhurst Forge
Oxshott Road
Leatherhead, Surrey
Tel: (0372) 375148
Restoration of all metals including cast iron fireplaces and brass or copper accessories.

MICHAEL STRAY
The Old White Horse
Hockliffe
Leighton Buzzard, Beds
Tel: (0525) 210372
Restoration of stone and brick fireplaces, by specialist property restorer.

MIDLANDS AND EAST ANGLIA

KINGFISHER RESTORATION
2 Westgate Terrace
Long Melford, Suffolk
Tel: (0787) 310 677
Sand-blasting of metal off-site.

NORTH OF ENGLAND AND SCOTLAND

COLIN BLAKEY GALLERIES LTD
61 Scotland Road
Nelson, Lancs
Tel: (0282) 64941
Restoration of fireplaces, specialising in marble and metal.

JOHN HENDERSON LTD
Inglis Lane
Castleblair
Dunfermline, Fife, Scotland
Tel: (0383) 21123/23714
Restoration of cast-iron metalwork, including fireplaces.

STOVE-MAKER.

LONDON

AND SO TO BED LTD
638/640 Kings Road
London SW6
Tel: (01) 731 3593/4/5
and
7 New Kings Road
London SW6
Tel: (01) 731 3593
Restoration of brass bedsteads.

AND SO TO BED LTD
96b Camden High Street
London NW1
Tel: (01) 388 0364/5
Restoration of brass bedsteads.

ANTIQUE RESTORATIONS
311 Westbourne Park Road
London W11
Tel: (01) 727 0467
Restoration of furniture. Speciality: gilded and painted pieces.

ANTIQUES LTD
18 Parson Street
London NW4
Tel: (01) 203 1194
Restoration of furniture.

ASHBY AND HORNER
32 Earl Street
London EC2A 2JD
Tel: (01) 377 0266
Decoration of furniture including glazing and period finishes.

ASHLEY STOCKS LTD
13 Crescent Place
London SW3
Tel: (01) 589 0044
Restoration including re-decoration, re-upholstery and French polishing.

ASPREY AND CO LTD
165–169 New Bond Street
London W1
Tel: (01) 493 6767
Restoration of furniture.

GUY F. BAGSHAW
96 Webber Street
London SE1
Tel: (01) 928 3624
Restoration of furniture including French and wax polishing, leather lining, cabinet-making, gilding, re-upholstery and veneering.

RAYMOND BENARDOUT LTD
4 William Street
London SW1X 9HL
Tel: (01) 235 9588
Restoration of furniture.

A.J. BRETT AND COMPANY LTD
168c Marlborough Road
London N19 4NP
Tel: (01) 272 8462
Restoration of furniture including French polishing, marquetry and Boulle work, and re-upholstery and cabinet-making.

AUBREY BROCKLEHURST
124 Cromwell Road
London SW7 4ET
Tel: (01) 373 0319
Restoration of furniture. Speciality: clocks. See page 00 for illustration.

JOHN CHAMBERS
4 Nugent Terrace
London NW8 9QB
Tel: (01) 289 1393
Speciality: restoration of 18th c. English furniture, including veneering.

CHAPMAN RESTORATIONS
10 Theberton Street
London N1 0QX
Tel: (01) 226 5565
Restoration of furniture including French polishing, leather lining, and replacement of hand-coloured hide upholstery, specialising in Arts and Crafts furniture, Gothic Revival and Art Deco pieces.

SIMON COLEMAN ANTIQUES
51 High Street
London SW13
Tel: (01) 878 5037
Restoration of furniture.

CSAKY'S ANTIQUES
133 Putney Bridge Road
London SW15
Tel: (01) 870 1525
Pine dealers offering a pine-stripping service.

TONY ELLIS ANTIQUES
90, 96 and 110 Highbury Park
London N5
and
2b Southerby Road
London N5
Tel: (01) 226 7551 and 272 0651 (Home)
Restoration of furniture including re-upholstery.

PAUL FERGUSON WOOD CARVERS
Unit 20
21 Wren Street
London WC1
Tel: (01) 278 8759
Woodcarving and gilding of frames or furniture. Speciality: watergilding and distressed finishes.

MICHAEL FOSTER
118 Fulham Road
London SW3 6HU
Tel: (01) 373 3636
Restoration of furniture including re-upholstery, specialising in 18th and early 19th c. pieces.

FURNITURE FAIR
22 Church Street
London NW8
Tel: (01) 262 1338
Restoration of furniture. Speciality: Victoriana.

THE FURNITURE HOSPITAL
14a Ravenscourt Avenue
London W6
Tel: (01) 741 0940
General restoration service.

G. GARBE
23 Charlotte Street
London W1P 1HB
Tel: (01) 636 1268
Restoration of furniture to museum standards.

GERANIUM PINE FURNITURE
121 Upper Street
London N1
Tel: (01) 359 4281
Specialists in stripping and repair of pine furniture.

IAN GOSS
De Beauvoir Workshops
52 De Beauvoir Road
London N1
General restoration of furniture. Speciality: walnut.

MARION GRAY
33 Crouch Hill
London N4
Tel: (01) 272 0372
Furniture restoration including re-upholstery.

D.Z. HAGI
91 Troutbeck
Albany Street
London NW1
Tel: (01) 388 1716
Gilding of antique carved wood and gesso furniture. Applied decorative or lacquer work can be arranged.

Below: Victorian kneehole desk as restored by Just Desks.

HATFIELD'S
42a St Michael's Street
London W2 1QP
Tel: (01) 723 8265
Restoration of furniture.

GERARD HESKIN
52 Princedale Road
London W11 4NL
Tel: (01) 221 5968
Repair, strengthening, colouring, waxing and French polishing of chairs.

HUDSON AND WILLIAMS
14 Crawford Street
London W1
Tel: (01) 935 7627
Restoration of furniture.

R. ISAACS
94/95 Troutbeck
Albany Street
London NW1
Tel: (01) 387 6950
Restorers with over 70 years experience, specialising in French polishing and stripping. Will work in situ.

S. AND H. JEWELL
26 Parker Street
London WC2B 5PH
Tel: (01) 405 8520
Restoration of furniture including French polishing, carving, gilding, leather lining and re-upholstery.

JUST DESKS
20 Church Street
London NW8
Tel: (01) 723 7976
Specialists in desk restoration, including relining leather tops.

CHRISTOPHER J. LEWIS
The Furniture Cave
533 Kings Road
London SW10
Tel: (01) 351 3870
Restoration including Boulle, carving and converting.

LOTT 32
32 Camden Road
London NW1
Tel: (01) 267 5828
Pine-stripping service.

N.M. MKHIZE
90 Lots Road
London SW10
Tel: (01) 352 9876 and 870 2118 (Home)
Restoration of furniture specialising in marquetry work and French polishing.

OAKWOODS JOINERY
Chambers Wharf
Chambers Street
London SE16
Tel: (01) 231 3161
General restoration service.

ORIGINAL FURNITURE CRAFT LTD
105 Boundary Road
London NW8
Tel: (01) 624 7671 and (01) 455 8420
Restoration of furniture including French polishing and cabinet-making.

RELCY ANTIQUES
9 Nelson Road
London SE10
Tel: (01) 858 2812
Restoration of furniture.

F.J. RUTTER AND A. FAGIANI
28–30 Wagner Street
London SE15
Tel: (01) 732 7188
Restoration of furniture including French polishing.

S. SANDLER LTD
5 Peary Place
Roman Road
London E2 0QW
Tel: (01) 980 1972
Repair and renovation of furniture including re-upholstery and French polishing.

SCALLYWAG
Wren Road
Camberwell Green
London SE5
Tel: (01) 701 5353
Pine stripping and restoration.

SENSATION LTD
66 Fulham High Street
London SW6 3LQ
Tel: (01) 736 4135
Restoration of furniture including re-upholstery.

SPREAD EAGLE ANTIQUES
22 and 23 Nelson Road
and
8 Nevada Street
London SE10
Tel: (01) 692 1618/858 9713
Restoration of furniture.

DAVID SUMMERS ANTIQUES
18 Theberton Street
London N1
Tel: (01) 226 8402 and 249 7520 (Home)
Restoration of furniture, especially mahogany, and including French polishing.

TERRY ANTIQUES
175 Junction Road
and
2b Monnery Road
London N19 5QA
Tel: (01) 263 1219
Restoration of furniture including re-upholstery.

CLIFFORD J. TRACY
6–40 Durnford Street
Seven Sisters Road
London N15 5NQ
Tel: (01) 800 4773
Restoration of furniture including marquetry, carving, turning, French polishing, re-upholstery and reproduction.

E. AND A. WATES LTD
82–84 Mitcham Lane
London SW16 6NR
Tel: (01) 769 2205
Restoration of furniture including re-upholstery.

J. WOLFF AND SON LTD
1 Chester Court
Albany Street
London NW1 4BU
Tel: (01) 935 3636
Restoration of furniture including parquetry, marquetry, carving, Boulle and gilding.

SOUTH AND SOUTHEAST ENGLAND

ABBEY ANTIQUES AND ARTS
97 High Street
Hemel Hempstead, Herts
Tel: (0442) 64667
Restoration of furniture.

CHRISTOPHER COLIN ALEXANDER
7 Albert Street
Fleet, Aldershot
Hants GU3 9RL
Tel: (025 14) 21520
Restoration of furniture and cabinet-making.

ALPHA ANTIQUE RESTORATIONS
c/o Graham Childs
High Street
Compton, Berks
Tel: (0635) 22 245
General restoration including marquetry and other fine inlays.

ASHLEY ANTIQUES AND RESTORATION
129 High Street
Hungerford, Berks
Tel: (0488) 82771
Restoration of furniture.

Left: Extremely ornate, inlaid, serpentine-shaped hardwood credenza with hand-chased ormolu mounts, circa 1860, as restored by J. Wolff and Son Ltd.

Above: Chairmaker working on the detailed carving of a Chippendale chairback, part of a special order, courtesy of Browns of West Wycombe.

ASHWOOD LTD
143 High Street
Rickmansworth, Herts
Tel: Rickmansworth 70194
Reproduction and restoration of furniture including hand-carving, French polishing and upholstery.

J. BARRINGTON-REYNOLDS
14/15 Charnham Street
Hungerford, Berks
Tel: (0488) 2532/3150
Restoration and reproduction of furniture including wood-carving and wood-turning.

K.A. BEALES AND W.R. PARR
28 Thompsons Lane
Cambridge, Cambs
Tel: (0223) 357263
Repair and restoration of furniture including cabinet-making and reproduction work.

MICHAEL BEAUMONT ANTIQUES
Hempstead Hall
Hempstead
Nr Saffron Walden, Essex CB10 2PR
Tel: (044 084) 239
Restoration of oak and mahogany furniture.

A.E. BOOTH
9 High Street
Ewell, Epsom, Surrey KT17 1SG

A.E. BOOTH (CON'T)
Tel: (01) 393 5245
Restoration of furniture including re-upholstery, gilding, and carving.

BOWDEN WOODCRAFT
Viables Centre
Harrow Way
Basingstoke, Hants
Tel: (0256) 21200/52847
Restoration of furniture including wood-turning and reproduction service.

CLIVE T. BRISTOW
32 Waltham Avenue
Stoughton
Guildford, Surrey GU2 6 QF
Restoration including French polishing.

ANTOINETTE DE BROMHEAD
Westmoor Farm
Burnt Chimney Drive
Littleport, Ely, Cambs
Tel: (0353) 860 651 and (01) 935 8946
Restoration of gilding, particularly mirrors and small furniture.

MOREN BROWN
The Green South
Warnborough, Oxford
Oxon OX9 8DR
Tel: (086 732) 8354
Restoration of furniture including marquetry, carving, turning and cabinet-making.

BROWNS OF WEST WYCOMBE
Church Lane
West Wycombe
High Wycombe, Bucks HP14 3AH
Tel: (0494) 24537
Restoration of furniture including a reproduction service.

RONALD A. BURGESS
17 Friday Street
Leighton Buzzard, Beds
Tel: (0525) 374664
Restoration of furniture.

DAVID BURKINSHAW
66 High Street
Lindfield, W Sussex
Tel: (044 47) 2826
Restoration of furniture. Speciality: Georgian and Queen Anne.

CAROUSEL
12 Springfield Road
Harrow, Middx
Tel: (01) 863 9455
Pine-stripping service.

BRIAN EDWIN CAUDELL
55 Stowe Road
Orpington, Kent
Tel: Orpington 73631
Restoration including French polishing veneering, polishing, turning, lacquering and re-caning.

CENTRE OF RESTORATION AND ARTS
20 Folly Lane
St Albans, Herts
Tel: (0727) 51555
Restoration of furniture including re-upholstery and re-caning.

CHURCH LANE RESTORATIONS
1 Church Lane
Teddington, Middx
Tel: (01) 977 2526
Restoration of furniture including French polishing, carving and inlay work. Speciality: pre-Victorian walnut.

COALBROOK HOUSE
76–78 High Street
Berkhamsted, Herts HP4 2BW
Tel: (04427) 5081
*Restoration of furniture including
re-upholstery and cabinet-making.*

ROBERT COLEMAN
Pauls, Water Lane
Hawkhurst, Kent
Tel: (058 05) 3351
*Restoration, re-polishing and re-upholstery of
furniture.*

RON COLEMAN
Pennyblack Cottage
Church Street
Brill, nr Aylesbury, Bucks
Tel: (0844) 237752
*Restorations of woodwork especially staircases
and other work in situ.*

DEACON AND SANDYS
Waterloo Road Depository
Cranbrook, Kent
Tel: (0580) 713775
Restoration of country furniture.

THE DESK SHOP
41 St Clements
Oxford, Oxon OX4 4AG
Tel: (0865) 45524
*Complete restoration service for desks
including relining leather tops and veneering.*

S.R. DIBBLE
22 Mitre Street
Buckingham, Bucks
Tel: (028 02) 3268
*Restoration of furniture including carving,
gilding, re-veneering and French polishing.*

*Opposite below: Chippendale-style chair in
mahogany, made to match an original set,
courtesy of Coalbrook House.*

*Below: Philip Freedman in his workshop
repairing a brass fitting.*

*Above: Half-round Sheraton-style marquetry
table made with a solid mahogany frame,
veneered in curled mahogany with inlays of
boxwood and dyed sycamore, as reproduced by
A. Dunn and Son, from a pair of originals.*

A. DUNN AND SON
The White House
8 Wharf Road
Chelmsford, Essex CM2 6LU
Tel: (092 575) 5177
*Restoration of furniture including brass and
semi-precious inlays.*

*Has restored a marquetry floor at Buckingham
Palace and panelling and doors of the
reinstated Orient Express. Reproduction work
also undertaken.*

EQUATIONS OF TIME
c/o John Exel
The Forge
105A High Street
Dorking, Surrey RH4 1AL
Tel: (0306) 887559
*Restoration of furniture specialising in
clockcases.*

G.E. EVERITT AND J. ROGERS
Dawsnest Workshop
Grove Road
Tiptree, Essex
Tel: (0621) 816508
*Complete restoration service including French
polishing.*

PAUL FEWINGS LTD
38 South Street
Titchfield, Nr Fareham, Hants
Tel: (0329) 43952
Pine-stripping service.

PHILLIP FREEDMAN
54 Osborne Road
Hornchurch, Essex RM11 1HE
Tel: (040 24) 42166
*Complete restoration service for over 50 years,
covering all small items made from 1600 to
1830.*

GRAY ANTIQUES
6 Shirley Grove
Rusthall
Tunbridge Wells, Kent
Tel: (0892) 20288
*Restoration of furniture including French
polishing and leather re-lining.*

LAURIE J. GRAYER
53 Church Street
Bloxham, Banbury, Oxon OX15 4ET
Tel: (0295) 721535
*Restoration of furniture, specialising in 18th
c. mahogany.*

GREAT GROOMS ANTIQUES LTD
Parbrook
Billingshurst, Sussex
Tel: (040 381) 2263
Restoration of furniture.

G.E. GRIFFIN
6 Laud Street
Croydon, Surrey CRO 1ST
Tel: (01) 688 3130
*Restoration of furniture and cabinet-making.
Family business established over 100 years.*

VICTOR M. GUNN LTD
14 Clifton Hill
Brighton, Sussex BN1 3HQ
Tel: (0273) 24659
Restoration of furniture including polishing.

HAGEN RESTORATIONS
Bakehouse Cottage
Northwood End
Haynes, Beds
Tel: (023 066) 424
Restoration and repair of furniture.

J.R. HARRIS
Old Forge Workshops
Church Road
Wheatley, Oxford, Oxon
Tel: (086 77) 3279
Restoration of furniture

Above: "Before" and "After" views of one of the doors of a Louis XIV Boulle armoire. Almost the entire surface had to be removed and then relaid, including the cutting of much "new" brass, courtesy of Hamilton Havers.

HAMILTON HAVERS
58 Conisboro Avenue
Caversham, Reading, Berks
Tel: (0734) 473379
Restoration of French and English furniture, especially those pieces involving inlay of brass, ivory, tortoise-shell, pewter, horn, mother-of-pearl and various woods. Has completed work for the Victoria and Albert Museum.

MICHAEL HEDGECOE
Rowan House
21 Burrow Hill Green
Chobham
Woking, Surrey GU24 8QS
Tel: (099 05) 8206
Restoration of furniture including marquetry, gilding, re-upholstery and chair copying.

A. HENNING
48 Walton Street
Walton-on-the-Hill
Tadworth, Surrey KT20 7RZ
Tel: ((073 781) 3337
Restoration of furniture.

G.A. HILL AND SONS
18 West End Street
High Wycombe, Bucks HP11 2QE
Tel: (0494) 27789
Restoration of furniture but no Boulle work. See opposite for illustration.

HORNDEAN ANTIQUES
69 London Road
Horndean, Hants
Tel: (0705) 592989
Restoration of furniture and cabinet-making.

THOMAS HUDSON
The Barn
117 High Street
Odell, Bedford, Beds
Tel: (0234) 721133
General restoration including woodwork and panelling in situ.

ROBIN S. JOHNSON
71 Hillside Gardens
Brockham, Betchworth, Surrey
Tel: Betchworth 2612
Restoration and conservation of furniture including inlay, tortoise-shell and lacquer.

PAUL JONES ANTIQUES
10 Market Place
Chalfont St Peter, Bucks SL9 9LA
Tel: Gerrards Cross 83367
Restoration of furniture including pine-stripping.

LINCOLN HOUSE GALLERIES
587 London Road
Westcliff-on-Sea, Essex
Tel: (0702) 339106
Restoration of furniture.

Below: Worm-eaten chair fully restored and re-upholstered by Michael Hedgecoe.

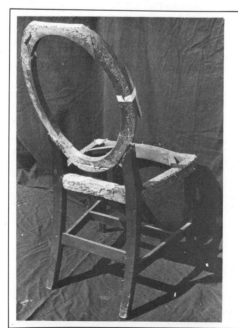

MARKET PLACE ANTIQUES
35 Market Place
Henley-on-Thames, Oxon RG9 2AA
Tel: (04912) 2387
Restoration of furniture specialising in country pieces.

J. MOWATT
Southdown House Antiques
Easole Street
Nonington, nr Dover, Kent CT15 4HE
Tel: (0304) 840987
Restoration of period upholstered furniture. See opposite for illustration.

MUNDAY AND GARNER
The Moncrieff Barn
(Off Lower Street)
Pulborough, W Sussex
Tel: (079 82) 3610
Restoration of furniture specialising in veneering, wood-carving and turning, plus cabinet work.

R.F. NEALE
Rowley Farmhouse
Lowfield Heath, Sussex
Tel: (0293) 21875
Restoration of furniture and French polishing.

BERTRAM NOLLER
14A London Road
Reigate, Surrey RH1 5RY
Tel: (073 72) 42548
Restoration of furniture including French polishing.

THE OLD MALTHOUSE
Hungerford, Berks
Tel: (048 86) 2209
Restoration of 18th and early 19th c. furniture, especially Queen Anne walnut.

RANDAL J. PAKEMAN
63 Gloucester Street
Faringdon, Oxon
Tel: (0367) 21423
Restoration and reproduction of furniture.

PAMELA AND BARRY ANTIQUES
216 Sandridge Road
St Albans, Herts
Tel: (0727) 51109
Restoration of furniture including French polishing, veneering, and wood-turning.

W.R. PARR
28 Thompsons Lane
Cambridge, Cambs CB5 8AQ
Tel: (0223) 357263
Restoring firm with over 50 years' experience.

J.C.D. PATTERSON
Forge Studio Workshops
Stour Street
Manningtree, nr Colchester
Essex CO11 1BE
Tel: (020 639) 6222
*Restoration of fine furniture from all periods
with experience in musuem work.*

A.R. PENFOLD LTD
17 Osprey Close
Lordswood, Southampton, Hants
Tel: (0703) 737432
*Restoration of furniture including French
polishing. Will work in situ.*

PENTON HOUSE
64 High Street
Harrow on the Hill, Middx
Tel: (01) 864 2234
Restoration of furniture and cabinet-making.

NOEL PEPPERALL
Dairy Lane Cottage
Walberton
Arundel, W Sussex
Tel: (0243) 551282
Restoration of furniture and cabinet-making.

PERIOD FURNITURE RESTORATION LTD
186 Main Road
Gidea Park, nr Romford, Essex
Tel: (01) 550 9540
Restoration of Victorian furniture.

PHELPS LTD
129/135 St Margarets Road
Twickenham, Middx
Tel: (01) 892 1778/7129
*Restoration of furniture including
re-upholstery.*

R. AND M. PUTNAM ANTIQUES
60 Downing Street
Farnham, Surrey
Tel: (0252) 715769
*Restoration of furniture including
reproductions using old wood.*

A. ROBINS AND SONS LTD
Fairfield
Farnham, Surrey
Tel: (0252) 714233
*Restoration of furniture including French
polishing, veneering, re-upholstery and
cabinet-making.*

J.T. RUTHERFORD AND SON
55 Sandgate High Street
Folkestone, Kent
Tel: (0303) 39515
Restoration of furniture.

J.M. SELLORS ANTIQUES
28 St James Road
Croydon, Surrey
Tel: (01) 689 1004/647 1768
*Restoration of pine furniture including
stripping and polishing.*

SKILLCRAFTS
5 Park Street
Thaxted, Essex CM6 2ND
Tel: (0371) 830162
*Restoration of furniture including
re-upholstery.*

*Above: Empire-style chair from a nine-piece
suite upholstered by J. Mowatt.*

D.J. SMITH
34 Silchester Road
Pamber Heath
Nr Basingstoke, Hants RG2 6EF
Tel: (0734) 700595
Restoration of carving, specialising in 18th c.

*Below: "Before" and "After" photos showing
a badly damaged walnut chest, courtesy of
G.A. Hill and Sons.*

A.J. SWABY
Great Grooms Antiques
Billingshurst, Sussex
Tel: (040 381) 2263
Restoration of furniture.

DAVID TAYLOR
No 4 The Arches
Ropetackle
Shoreham-by-Sea, Sussex
Tel: (079 17) 63829
*Restoration of furniture including veneering,
wood-carving, marquetry and cabinet-making.*

T.L. TURNER
Woodside Timber
131 Manor Road
Claddington, Luton, Beds
Tel: (0582) 414246
*Restoration of furniture including French
polishing.*

TURNER SERVICES LTD
Rear of 551 Newmarket Road
Cambridge, Cambs
Tel: (022 05) 3227
Restoration and reproduction of furniture.

THE TANKERDALE WORKSHOP
Tankerdale Farm
Steep Marsh
Petersfield, Hants GU32 2BH
Tel: (0730 82) 3839
*Restoration and conservation of English
furniture and interior woodwork.*

TAURUS ANTIQUES LTD
145 Masons Hill
Bromley, Kent BR2 9HY
Tel: (01) 464 8746
Dealers who also restore furniture.

W.G. UNDRILL LTD
103/111 Catherine Street
Cambridge, Cambs CB1 3AP
Tel: (0223) 47470
*Restoration of interior woodwork, polishing,
joinery and reproduction, in situ if necessary.*

VAN BROEK ANTIQUES
101 Station Road
Hampton, Middx
Tel: (01) 979 2089
Pine-stripping service.

JOHN D. WALTERS
10 Heather Drive
St Michaels
Tenterden, Kent
Tel: (058 06) 3079
*Restoration of furniture specialising in oak,
walnut and mahogany.*

PAUL WEAVER RESTORATIONS
18 Cavendish Mews
Grosvenor Road
Aldershot, Hants
Tel: (0252) 310174
*Restoration of furniture including French
polishing and desk-top leather lining.*

J. WESTON
Finches Lane
Twyford, Winchester, Hants
Tel: (0962) 713162
*Restoration of furniture including gilding,
carving, French polishing, and reproduction.*

R.F. WHEELER
59 Queens Road
Thame, Oxon OX9 3NF
Tel: (084 421) 2606
Restoration and reproduction of furniture.

*Above: Early 19th c. corner cupboard in oak,
crossbanded with mahogany, with original
brass knobs, as restored by Antique
Restorations.*

PETER WILDER
Glaslyn, Wycombe Road
Stokenchurch
High Wycombe, Bucks HP14 3RS
Tel: (024 026) 3455
Restoration and reproduction of furniture.

SOUTHWEST ENGLAND AND WALES

ANTIQUE RESTORATIONS
1 Severn Road
Gloucester, Glos
Tel: (0452) 29716
Restoration of furniture.

NEIL BATCHELOR
44 Querns Lane
Cirencester, Glos.
Tel: (0285) 68406
Restoration of furniture.

BELL PASSAGE ANTIQUES
38 High Street
Wickwar, Wotton-under-Edge
Glos GL12 8NP
Tel: (045) 424 251
*Restoration of furniture especially 18th and
19th c.*

LAWRENCE BRASS AND SON
93/95 Walcot Street
Bath, Avon
Tel: (0225) 64057
*Restoration of furniture, specialising in 16th
and 18th c. oak and walnut.*

J. COLLINS AND SON
63 and 28 High Street
Bideford, N Devon
Tel: (023 72) 3103
*Restoration of furniture (no reproduction work
undertaken).*

E.J. COOK AND SON
Seven Road
Gloucester, Glos GL1 2LE
Tel: (0452) 29716
Restoration and reproduction of furniture.

**COUNTRY ANTIQUES
RESTORATIONS**
Castle Mill
The Bridge
Kidwelly, Dyfed, Wales
Tel: (0554) 890534
*Restoration of furniture and pine-stripping
service.*

JOHN CRANE
11 Commercial Road
Shepton Mallet, Somerset
Tel: (0749) 4356
General restoration service.

CRICKLEPITT MILL
Commercial Road
Exeter, Devon EX2 4AE
Tel: (0272) 59692
*Restoration and stripping of furniture and
interior woodwork.*

J. EDWARD-COLLINS
Trevean, Trevenning
St Tudy, Bodmin, Cornwall
Tel: (0208) 850502
*Speciality: restoration of small articles of
furniture and chairs.*

FINE PINE LTD
Woodland Road
Harbertonford, Devon
and 85 High Street
Totnes, Devon
Tel: (080 423) 465
*Restoration of country furniture including a
pine-stripping service.*

R.H. FYSON
Manor Farm
Kencot, Lechlade, Glos
Tel: (037 786) 223
*Restoration of furniture including
hand-carving, turnery and gilding. Will work
in situ.*

GASTRELL HOUSE
33 Long Street
Tetbury, Glos GL8 8AA
Tel: (0666) 52228
Restoration of furniture.

JONATHAN GLUCK
Maes Y Glydfa
Llanfair Caereinion
Nr Welshpool, Powys, Wales
Tel: (0938) 810384
*Restoration of furniture; pine-stripping
service included.*

GUERNSEY WOODCARVERS
Les Issues
St Saviours, Guernsey, C.I.
Tel: (0481) 65373
*Antique restoration specialising in wood
carving and turning. See opposite for
illustration.*

ROGER LESLIE HARDY
10 Heol Hyfrydle
Coedpoeth

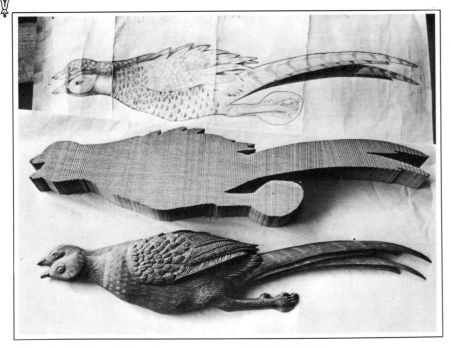

Above: Double pheasant in three stages, courtesy of Guernsey Woodcarvers.

ROGER HARDY (CON'T)
Nr Wrexham, Clwyd LL11 3NL, Wales
Tel: Not Available
Specialist duplication of wooden mouldings, pillars, turnings and carvings, large or small.

K. HOLME
Trescowe Vean
Trescowe,
Penzance, Cornwall TR20 9RN
Tel: (073 676) 3497
Restoration of furniture including replacing inlays and veneers, French polishing, and leather tabletop linings.

DONALD A. HOLLYOAK
153 Kinsman Street
Bodmin, Cornwall PL13 1PH
Tel: (0208) 5310
Restoration of furniture including French polishing, wood-turning, veneering and inlay.

M. MARKS
27 Larksleaze Road
Longwell Green
Bristol, Avon
Tel: (027 588) 3483
General restoration including work in situ.

GEORGE ARTHUR MATTHEWS
The Cottage Workshop
The Camp Site
Dudsey, Wimborne, Dorset
Tel: (020 16) 2665
Restoration and re-polishing of furniture.

OLD BARN ANTIQUES COMPANY
The Abbey Antique Shop
Half Moon Street
Sherborne, Dorset
Tel: (093 581) 2068
Restoration of furniture including made-to-order service.

CHRIS PASCOE
Court Cottage
Porthpean Village
St Austell, Cornwall PL26 6AY
Tel: (0726) 5653
Fifth-generation restorer and furniture maker.

JOHN PAYNTER
River View
Renrhin
St Dogmaels, Cardigan, Wales
Tel: (0239) 2815
Specialist in relief carving and French polishing.

PEPPERS PERIOD PIECES
29 Guildhall Street
Bury St Edmunds, Suffolk
Tel: (0284) 68786
Furniture repair, restoration and re-upholstery.

A.J. PONSFORD
51–53 Dollar Street
Cirencester, Glos
Tel: (0285) 2355
Restoration with specialist reproduction of oak refectory tables and chairs.

Below: "Before" and "After" of a Regency armchair in beechwood, simulated to look like rosewood, as restored by Tristan Salazar Restorations.

PRIORY ANTIQUES
37 East Street
Blandford, Dorset
Tel: (0258) 53472
Restoration of furniture.

TRISTAN SALAZAR RESTORATIONS
41 Market Place
Cirencester, Glos GL7 2NX
Tel: (0285) 68010
Restoration of furniture specialising in oak, and including repairs to marquetry and raised-ground japanning.

K.G. SERCOMBE
Moorview Antiques
Whiddon Down, nr Okehampton, Devon
Tel: (064 723) 201
Restoration of furniture.

TAMAR ANTIQUES RESTORATION
Tutwell House
Tutwell, Stoke Climsland
Callington, Cornwall
Tel: (057 97) 629
Restoration of furniture including French polishing and cabinet-making.

WOOD WORKSHOP
Penwerris Yard
Penwerris Lane
Falmouth, Cornwall
Tel: (0326) 315910
Restoration and reproduction of furniture including gilding, carving, turning and marquetry.

W.T. SERVICES
44B Fore Street and 13 The Walronds
Tiverton, Devon EX16 6LD
Tel: (08842) 3820
Restoration of furniture including re-upholstery, plus reproduction service.

MIDLANDS AND EAST ANGLIA

DAVID ACKROYD
Bleathwood Manor Farm
Bleathwood
Ludlow, Shropshire
Tel: (0584) 810726
Restoration of furniture and cabinet-making.

DAVID MARK AKROYD
Hellens, Much Marcle
Ledbury, Heref and Worcs
Tel: (053 184) 618
Restoration of furniture and cabinet-making.
Experience in working with exotic woods. Also
work in situ.

ALMA ANTIQUE RESTORERS
The Old Gospel Hall
Dereham Road
Norwich, Norfolk
Tel: (0603) 613184
Restoration of furniture including veneering,
marquetry, reproductions and re-upholstery.

ANGLIA ANTIQUE EXPORTERS
33 New Holt Street
Holt, Norfolk
Tel: (026 371) 3530
Restoration of furniture including French
polishing and leather lining.

ALEC ANNESS
3 Approach Cottages
Withersfield
Haverhill, Suffolk
Tel: (0440) 5895
Restoration of furniture including French
polishing, hand-carving and wood-turning.

LEONARD BALL
44 Market Street
Lutterworth, Leics
Tel: (045 55) 4942
Restoration of furniture.

Below: Walnut underframe designed and
made for the restored top by T.S. Barrows and
Son.

T.S. BARROWS AND SON
Hamlyn Lodge Station Road
Ollerton, Newark, Notts
Tel: (0623) 823600
Restoration of furniture including French
polishing.

JOHN BERRY
48 Longdale Lane
Ravenshead
Nottingham, Notts
Tel: (062 34) 2317
Restoration and reproduction of furniture.

BROCKDISH ANTIQUES
Commerce House
Brockdish, Diss, Norfolk
Tel: (037 975) 498
Restoration of furniture including
re-upholstery.

SIMON CARTER GALLERY
23 Market Hill
Woodbridge, Suffolk
Tel: (03943) 2242
Dealers who also restore early furniture.

EDMUND CZAJKOWSKI AND SON
96 Tor-O-Moor Road
Woodhall Spa, Lincs LN10 6SB
Tel: (0526) 52895
Restoration of furniture and cabinet-making
including Boulle, marquetry, carving and
gilding. For illustration see opposite.

D.J. AND COMPANY ANTIQUE
FURNITURE RESTORERS
34 Beach Road
Sutton Coldfield, W Midlands
Tel: (021 354) 5937
Restoration of furniture and cabinet-making.

J.D. FINN
Old Co-op Stores
Ellesmere Road
St Martins, Owestry, Shropshire
Tel: (0691) 772782
Restoration of furniture including wood
carving, turning and gilding. See entry under
"Specialist Restorers, Gilding" for
illustration.

FISHER RESTORATIONS
The Old Rectory
Aston Somerville
Broadway, Heref & Worcs
Tel: (0386) 852466
Restoration including veneering and svecial
colouring.

FLEETWOOD ANTIQUE
RESTORATION
10 Hewell Road
Barnt Green
Birmingham, W Midlands B45 8LT
Tel: (021) 445 2212
Restoration and reproduction services,
including mother-of-pearl and ivory inlays.

H.R. FOXALL
42a Underhill Street
Bridgnorth, Shropshire
Tel: (07462) 2437
Restoration of Victorian and Edwardian
furniture, including mirrors.

D.G. GRABHAM
The White House
Swan Lane
Westerfield
Ipswich, Suffolk
Tel: (0473) 58021
Restoration of furniture and cabinet-making.

Right: Edmund Czajkowski putting final touches to a fine Genoese commode circa 1760.

FRANCOIS GRECO
40 Vineyard Road
Newport, Shropshire
Tel: (0952) 813806
Restorers with over 40 years' experience. Service includes special finishes and colourings, veneering and marquetry,

BRIAN GREEN ANTIQUES
26 Evington Road
Leicester, Leics
Tel: (0533) 543444
Restoration and reproduction of furniture specialising in upholstered pieces.

A.D. JEFFERSON
23 High Street
Droitwich, Heref & Worcs
Tel: (0905) 778479
Restoration of furniture including marquetry and French polishing, cabinet-making. Will work in situ.

N.J.W. JOYCE
Alscot Estate Yard
Atherstone-on-Stour
Nr Stratford-on-Avon, Warks
Tel: (082 77) 345
Restoration of furniture, specialising in colouring and polishing.

KINGFISHER RESTORATION
2 Westgate Terrace
Long Melford, Suffolk
Tel: (0787) 310677
Paint stripping on site plus sand-blasting or non-abrasive methods off site. Collection service.

CHARLES LOWE AND SONS LTD
40 Church Gate
Loughborough, Leics
Tel: (0509) 217876
Restoration of furniture including French polishing, re-upholstery and chair-making. See overleaf for illustration.

MALVERN STUDIOS
56 Cowleigh Road
N Malvern, Heref & Worcs
Tel: (068 45) 4913
Restoration of furniture including carving, gilding, marquetry, polishing and special painted finishes.

WILLIAM KURT NEILSON
48 School Road
Moseley
Birmingham, W. Midlands
Tel: (021) 449 3633
Restorer with 32 years' experience specialising in inlay and polishing.

C.J. PRITCHARD
143A Belle Vue Road
Shrewsbury, Shropshire SY3 7NN
Tel: (0743) 62854
Restoration and repair of furniture.

RED LION RESTORATIONS
The Olde Red Lion
Bedingfield, Eye, Suffolk
Tel: (072 876) 491
Restoration of early furniture specialising in oak and mahogany and including wood carving and painted decoration

SPADESBOURNE ANTIQUES AND REPRODUCTIONS
Herring House
98 High Street

SPADESBOURNE ANTIQUES AND REPRODUCTIONS (CON'T)
Henley-in-Arden
Solihull, Warks
Tel: (056 42) 3560
Restoration of furniture including French polishing, turning and re-upholstery. Cabinet-making specialising in oak refectory tables and four-poster beds.

LESLIE STANTON
The Joiners Workshop
Ashbourne Road
Rocester, Nr Uttoxeter, Staffs
Tel: (0889) 590186
Restoration and reproduction of furniture.

PATRICK TAYLOR ANTIQUES
First Floor Under Arch
13 St Peter's Street
Ipswich, Suffolk IPL IXF
Tel: (0473) 50774/328351 (by appointment only)
Restoration of furniture.

TREEDALE FURNITURE
Garden Cottage
Little Dalby
Nr Melton Mowbray, Leics
Tel: (066 477) 535
Restoration of furniture and cabinet-making.

PERCY F. WALE LTD
32 and 34 Regent Street
Leamington Spa, Warks CV32 5EG
Tel: (0926) 21288
Restoration of furniture including re-upholstery.

TERENCE C.J. WALSH
Melbourne House
Whichford
Shipston-on-Stour, Warks
Tel: (060 884) 664
Restoration of furniture including marquetry, veneering, French and wax-polishing plus cabinet-making.

JACK WHITTLE
47 Peacocks Close
Cavendish
Sudbury, Suffolk CO10 8DA
Tel: (0787) 280652
General restoration including Cape Dutch and Continental furniture.

WOOD END RESTORERS
Wood End
Old Wood
Skellington, Lincs
Tel: (0522) 687302
Restoration and reproduction of furniture.

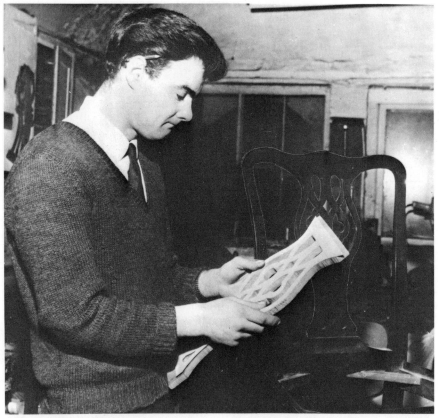

Above: Matching a country Chippendale chair back, in order to make up an incomplete set, courtesy of Charles Lowe and Sons Ltd.

WOODLAND FURNITURE COMPANY
3 King Street
Rugby, Warks
Tel: (0788) 61644/62541
Restoration of furniture and reproduction services.

PAUL R. WREFORD
19 Norbury Road
Ipswich, Suffolk 1PA 4RQ
Tel: (0473) 72639
Restoration of furniture.

NORTH OF ENGLAND AND SCOTLAND

ROBERT AAGAARD LTD
Frogmire House
Stockwell Road
Knaresborough, N Yorkshire HG5 OJP
Tel: (0423) 864805
Restoration of furniture.

ABERFORD ANTIQUES LTD
Hicklam House
Aberford
Nr Leeds, W Yorkshire
Tel: (0532) 813209
Pine-stripping service offered by dealers.

ADAMS ANTIQUES
65 Waterloo Row
Chester, Cheshire CH1 2LE
Tel: (0244) 319421
Restoration and repair of furniture

A. ALLEN ANTIQUE RESTORERS
Arden Street
Newmills
Stockport, Cheshire
Tel: (0663) 45274 or 42985 (Home)
Comprehensive restoration service.

ANDERSON AND SLATER ANTIQUES
8 King Street
Knutsford, Cheshire WA16 6DL
Tel: (0565) 2917
Restoration of furniture.

AND SO TO BED LTD
60 West Street
Sowerby Bridge
Halifax, W Yorkshire
Tel: (0422) 39759
and
133 Deansgate
Bolton, Lancs
Tel: (0204) 392386
and
65 Whitley Road
Whitley Bay
Tyne & Wear
Tel: (0632) 524611
Restoration of brass bedsteads.

A. AUEN ANTIQUE RESTORERS
Arden Street
New Mills, Stockport, Cheshire
Tel: New Mills 45274/42985
Restoration of furniture including inlaid and Boulle items. Also work in situ.

ADRIAN BLACK
36A Freeman Street
Grimsby, S Humberside
Tel: (0472) 55668
Restoration of furniture and interior woodwork and work in situ.

BOULEVARD REPRODUCTIONS
369 Skircoat Green Road
Skircoat Green
Halifax, W Yorkshire
Tel: (0422) 68628
General restoration including French polishing.

DEREK CASEMENT
Slack Lane Works
Slack Lane, Pendlebury
Swinton, Manchester
Gt Manchester M27 2QT
Tel: (061) 794 1610
Restoration and reproduction of furniture. Will work in situ.

J.H. COOPER AND SON LTD
33 Church Street
Ilkley, W Yorkshire
Tel: (0943) 608020
Restoration of furniture including made-to-order service.

M.H.P. CORKILL LTD
Mostyn
Lezayre Road
Ramsey, Isle of Man
Tel: (0624) 813356
Restoration of furniture.

J.K. CROOKS
842 Ecclesall Road
Sheffield, S Yorkshire
Tel: (0742) 686600
Restoration of furniture and cabinet-making.

FELTON PARK ANTIQUES
Felton Park
Felton, Northld NE65 9HN
Tel: (067 087) 319/652
Furniture restoration by BADA-trained restorer. Speciality: oak, walnut and mahogany. See opposite for illustration.

Below: French country cabinet, restored by Derek Casement.

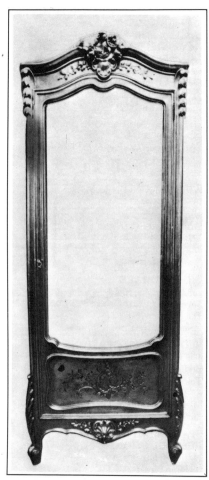

Right: Workshop at Felton Park Antiques.

GLYNN INTERIORS
92 King Street
Knutsford, Cheshire
Tel: (0565) 4418
Restoration of furniture from 1780–1910.

G.B. AND E. GOODING
12 Arden Buildings
Dorridge, Solihull, W Midlands
Tel: (056 45) 3040
Restoration of furniture including woodcarving, veneering, inlay, hand waxing, re-upholstery and replacing leather table tops.

ALAN GRICE
106 Aughton Street
Ormskirk, Lancs
Tel: (0695) 72007
Restoration of antique furniture including upholstered pieces.

DEREK HAINSWORTH
Lake House
Welham, Norton
Malton, N Yorkshire
Tel: (0653) 2609
Restoration of furniture including French polishing, marquetry, gilding, leatherwork and upholstery.

HANDSWORTH RESTORATIONS
47a Handsworth Road
North Shore
Blackpool, Lancs
Tel: (0253) 24994
Second-generation restorers specialising in Renaissance and Baroque furniture as well as similarly ornate interior woodwork.

J.A. AND T. HEDLEY
3 St Marys Chare
Hexham, Northld
Tel: (0434) 602317
Restoration of furniture including French polishing. Restorers to the National Trust and established over 150 years.

WILLIAM HOPEWELL-RYAN
Melbourne Street Garage
63 Melbourne Street
Derby, Derbs
Tel: (0332) 47858
Wood-turning service.

Below: "Before" view of a George III oak Welsh cupboard/dresser, circa 1800. See overleaf for "After" view, as restored by Paul Hopwell Antiques.

PAUL HOPWELL ANTIQUES
30 High Street
West Haddon, Northants
Tel: (078 887) 636
Restoration of 17th and 18th c. furniture. See overleaf for illustration.

JALNA ANTIQUES AND RESTORATION
Coley Lane, Little Haywood
Stafford, Staffs ST18 0UP
Tel: (0889) 881381
Restoration of furniture including re-upholstery.

JOCELYN ANTIQUES
161 West George Street
Glasgow G2 2JJ, Scotland
Tel: (041) 248 3024
Restoration of furniture including French polishing.

THE LITTLE ANTIQUE SHOP
167 Stone Road, Hanford
Stoke-on-Trent, Staffs
Tel: (0782) 657674
Restoration of furniture. Speciality: inlaid furniture from Georgian to Sheraton revival, circa 1880. Will also French polish and re-upholster.

DAVID LYON WORKSHOP
57 Hull Road
Withernsea, E Yorkshire
Tel: (3280) 09642
Restoration of furniture including marquetry and carving plus cabinet-making service.

DON MADDOX
47 Church Street
Ribchester, nr Preston
Lancs PR3 3YE
Tel: (025 484) 512
Restoration including wood-carving and reproduction including miniature furniture.

MARTIN ANTIQUES
36 St Stephen Street
Edinburgh EH3 5AL, Scotland
Tel: (031) 556 3527
Restoration of furniture including reproduction, specialising in pieces by Charles Rennie Mackintosh. See overleaf for illustration.

DAVID OFFLEY AND COMPANY
7 Shipley Common Lane
Ilkeston, Derbs DE7 8TR
Tel: (0602) 321653
Restoration including wood-turning and carving, as well as reproduction service for ladderback and spindleback chairs.

Above: "After" view of George III oak Welsh cupboard, as restored by Paul Hopwell Antiques.

PATINEX LTD
Unit 3, County Industrial Estate
County Road
Ormskirk, Lancs
Tel: (0695) 78766
Furniture stripping using "Patinex" system, a non caustic acid solution which does not affect the colour of the wood surface.

ELAINE PHILLIPS ANTIQUES LTD
2 Royal Parade
Harrogate, N Yorkshire
Tel: (0423) 69745
Restoration of 17th and 18th c. oak furniture.

PINDER BRIDGE ANTIQUES
38 Keighley Road
Skipton, N Yorkshire BD23 2NB
Tel: (0756) 4617
Restoration of furniture.

RHODELANDS CRAFT
528 Duffield Road
Allestree, Derby, Derbs DE3 2DL
Tel: (0332) 558754
Reproduction and restoration of furniture specialising in Welsh dressers, cabinets and chests.

GERALD SHAW RESTORATIONS
Jansville Quarry Lane
New Park
Harrogate, N Yorkshire HG1 3HR
Tel: (0423) 503590
Restoration and reproduction service.

JOHN SMITH OF ALNWICK LTD
West Cawledge Park
Alnwick, Northld NE66 2HJ
Tel: (0665) 604363
Restoration of furniture specialising in mahogany, oak, walnut, fruitwoods and buhl.

PETER SNART
Willowbog Farm
Wark, Hexham, Northld
Tel: (043 481) 217
Restoration of furniture including French polishing and specialising in clockcase repairs.

H. TEBB AND SON
77–81 Corporation Street
Merseyside WA10 1SX
Tel: (0744) 23074
Furniture restoration including French polishing, cabinet-making, and upholstery.

R. UDALL
Howgill Lane
Sedbergh, Cumbria
Tel: (0587) 20301 and 20719 (home)
Restorers for over 50 years, with work for the Victoria and Albert Museum to their credit.

ROBIN WARDROP
Ardess, Bridgend
Callander, Central, Scotland
Tel: (0877) 30446
Restoration of furniture and cabinet-making.

WHYTOCK AND REID
Sunbury House
Belford Mews
Edinburgh EH4 3DN, Scotland
Tel: (031) 226 4911
Restoration of furniture, including cabinet-making and re-upholstery.

NORTHERN IRELAND

FIONA CHICHESTER-CLARK
Moyola Park
Castledawson, N Ireland
Tel: (064 885) 606
Reproduction and restoration of furniture including marquetry, Boulle and French polishing. Also pine-stripping.

DUNLUCE ANTIQUES
33 Ballytober Road
Bushmills, Co Antrim BT57 8UU
N Ireland
Tel: (02657) 31140
Restoration of furniture.

HENRY PRICE
18 Shore Road
Holywood, Co Down, N Ireland
Tel: (023 17) 2643
Restoration of furniture including French polishing and re-upholstery.

Below: Argyll dining chair in oak, courtesy of Martin Antiques.

LONDON

ANTIQUE RESTORATIONS
311 Westbourne Park Road
London W11
Tel: (01) 727 0467
Restoration of gilded mirrors and furniture.

GUY F. BAGSHAW
96 Webber Street
London SE1
Tel: (01) 928 3624
Restoration of gilded furniture.

BLACKMAN HARVEY LTD
29 Earlham Street
London WC2H 9LE
Tel: (01) 836 1904
Regilding of picture frames.

BOSTOCK AND GERRISH
London NW1
Tel: (01) 723 9912 (By appointment only)
Restoration of gilding including water gilding.

A.J. BRETT AND COMPANY LTD
168c Marlborough Road
London N19 4NP
Tel: (01) 272 8462
Restoration of gilding.

CORK STREET FRAMING COMPANY LTD
5–6 Cork Street
London W1
Tel: (01) 734 9179
Restoration of gilded picture frames.

N. DAVIGHI
117 Shepherds Bush Road
London W6
Tel: (01) 603 5357
Restoration of gilding.

DENBIGH GALLERIES
3 Denbigh Road
London W11
Tel: (01) 229 6765
Regilding of 18th and 19th c. picture frames.

THOMAS DUGGAN
585 Kings Road
London SW6
Tel: (01) 736 7799 & 731 0905
Repair, restoration and cleaning of gilding.

PAUL FERGUSON WOOD CARVERS
Unit 20
21 Wren Street
London WC1
Tel: (01) 278 8759
Woodcarvers and gilders of picture frames, specialising in water gilding and distressed finishes.

GREEN AND STONE OF CHELSEA
259 Kings Road
London SW3
Tel: (01) 352 6521
Agents for restorers of carving and gilding.

DAVID HAGI
91 Troutbeck, Albany Street
London NW1
Tel: (01) 338 1716
Gilder of carved and gesso furniture, who also undertakes dry stripping to the original gilding.

P.L. JAMES
211 Westbourne Park Road
London W11
Tel: (01) 727 0467
Restoration of gilding, including carved surfaces.

S. AND H. JEWELL
26 Parker Street
London WC2B 5PH
Tel: (01) 405 8520
Restoration of gilded furniture.

ALEXANDRE KIDD
67 Castlebar Road
London W5
Tel: (01) 997 3896/8316
Gilding including water gilding in 22ct, oil gilding, and gilding in imitation gold leaf.

JILL SAUNDERS
91/93 Lots Road
London SW10
Tel: (01) 352 1365
Restoration of gilded furniture.

W. STITCH AND COMPANY LTD
48 Berwick Street
London W1
Tel: (01) 437 3776
Regilding of metalware

JOHN TANOUS
115 Harwood Road
London SW6
Tel: (01) 736 7999
Restoration of gilded and carved surfaces.

VERDIGRIS ART METALWORK RESTORERS
c/o Gerald Bacon
Clerkenwell Workshops
Unit E18
31 Clerkenwell Close
London EC1R OAT
Tel: (01) 253 7788
Regilding of metal.

Below: Preparing carved pieces for gilding, courtesy of Paul Ferguson Wood Carvers.

Above: Victorian butcher's shop sign with coat-of-arms used for royal appointments as restored by J.D. Finn.

J. WOLFF AND SON LTD
1 Chester Court
Albany Street
London NW1 4BU
Tel: (01) 935 3636
Complete restoration service including carving and gilding.

SOUTH AND SOUTHEAST ENGLAND

BRIAN BEELLEN
14 Hoath Hill
Mountfield
Nr Robertsfield, E Sussex
Tel: (0580) 880754 and (04246) 2270
Specialist in painted effects and restoration of same including gilding.

A.E. BOOTH
9 High Street
Ewell
Epsom, Surrey KT17 1SG
Tel: (01) 393 5245
Restoration of carving and gilding.

ANTOINETTE DE BROMHEAD
Westmoor Farm
Burnt Chimney Drive
Littleport, Ely, Cambs
Tel: (0353) 860 651 and (01) 935 8946
Regilding of picture and mirror frames.

MOREN BROWN
The Green South
Warborough, Oxford, Oxon OX9 8DR
Tel: (086 732) 8354
Restoration of gilding.

MICHAEL HEDGECOE
Roman House
Burrow Hall Green
Chobham, Woking, Surrey
Tel: (099 05) 8206
Restoration including gilded furniture.

D.J. SMITH
34 Silchester Road
Pamber Heath
Nr Basingstoke, Hants RG2 6EF
Tel: (0734) 700595
Restoration of gilded and/or carved mirrors and frames, specialising in water gilding.

JACQUELINE TABER
Jaggers, Fingringhow
Colchester, Essex
Tel: (0206) 28334
Restoration and regilding of picture frames.

SOUTH WEST ENGLAND AND WALES

LAWRENCE BRASS AND SON
93/95 Walcot Street
Bath, Avon
Tel: (0255) 64057
Restoration of gilding.

RAYMOND ARTHUR FINN
23 Bridge Street
Llangollen, Clywd, Wales
Tel: (0978) 860969
Restoration of gilded and carved surfaces.

A.J. PONSFORD
51–53 Dollar Street
Cirencester, Glos GL7 2AS
Tel: (0285) 23555
Restoration of gilt frames and gold leafing.

MIDLANDS AND EAST ANGLIA

EDMUND CZAJKOWSKI AND SON
96 Tor-O-Moor Road
Woodhall Spa, Lincs LN10 6SB
Tel: (0526) 52895
Restoration of gilding.

J.D. FINN
Old Co-op Stores
Ellesmere Road
St Martins, Oswestry, Shropshire
Tel: (0691) 772782
Regilding of picture frames and furniture.

MALVERN STUDIOS
56 Cowleigh Road
N Malvern, Heref & Worcs
Tel: (068 45) 4913
Restoration of gilding.

E.W. WENDT
Sudbury Picture Frames
21a Goal Lane
Sudbury, Suffolk
Tel: Not Available
Regilding of picture frames and panels.

NORTH OF ENGLAND AND SCOTLAND

DEREK HAINSWORTH
Lake House
Welham, Norton
Malton, N Yorkshire
Tel: (0653) 2609
Restoration of furniture including regilding.

Below: Carved and gilded Louis XV period wall mirror and console, circa 1740, restored in matt and burnished water gilding, by J. Wolff and Son Ltd.

*PLEASE NOTE THAT THERE IS NO
SUBSTITUTE FOR GLASS SO
ACTUAL HOLES CANNOT BE
FILLED. HOWEVER, BREAKS CAN BE
MENDED PROVIDING ALL PIECES
ARE AVAILABLE.*

LONDON

F.W. ALDRIDGE
Elizabethan Works
2 Ivy Road
London E17
Tel: (01) 539 3717
*Repairs to table glass including removal of
chips and scratches and, with decanters, silver
tops fitted. Can also supply blue glass linings
for silver tableware from stock of 1500 styles,
or will make them to order. Additionally have
various bottle stoppers for decanters.*

THE ARCHITECTURAL ANTIQUE
MARKET
4–8 Highgate High Street
London N6
Tel: (01) 341 3761/348 4846/340 8476/359
4330 and 830 5256
Restoration of stained glass panels.

DAVID ASHTON-BOSTOCK
21 Charlwood Street
London SW1V 2EA
Tel: (01) 828 3656
Restoration of glassware.

BLUE-CRYSTAL GLASS
Unit 8
21 Wren Street
London WC1X OHF
Tel: (01) 278 0142
*Restoration of glass including a selection of
Bristol blue glass linings, and silver collaring
of chipped crystal, plus a reproduction service
of antique glass in ruby, green or amber, and
re-silvering of mirrors.*

W.G.T. BURNE LTD
11 Elystan Street
London SW3 3NT
Tel: (01) 589 6074
*Dealer who will also repair and restore most
glassware, including chandeliers.*

CERAMIC RESTORATIONS
14 Theberton Street
London N1
Tel: (01) 359 5240
Repair of glassware.

GEORGE AND PETER COHN
112 Crawford Street
London W1
Tel: (01) 935 3518
Restoration of crystal chandeliers.

GARBE RESTORERS
23 Charlotte Street
London W1
Tel: (01) 636 1268
Restoration of glass.

HALL BROTHERS LTD
73 Kenton Street
London WC1
Tel: (01) 837 5151
*Repairs to glass including re-cutting of wine
glasses and tumblers.*

WHITEWAY AND WALDRON LTD
305 Munster Road
London SW6
Tel: (01) 381 3195
*Restoration of stained glass. For illustration
see entry under "Architectural" dealers.*

*Above: "Pietà", a stained glass panel
reconstructed from fragments and now installed
in St Mary Magdalene, Chewton Mendip,
Somerset, courtesy of Jasper and Molly
Kettlewell.*

R. WILKINSON AND SON
43/45 Wastdale Road
Forest Hill
London SE23 IHN
Tel: (01) 699 4420
*Restoration and repair of glass and glass
chandeliers, including a reproduction service.*

SOUTH AND SOUTHEAST
ENGLAND

ANTOINETTE DE BROMHEAD
Westmoor Farm
Burnt Chimney Drive
Littleport, Ely, Cambs
Tel: (0353) 860 651 and (01) 935 8946
Restoration of etched glass.

JASPER AND MOLLY KETTLEWELL
The Courtyard
Capel Manor
Horsmonden, Kent TN12 8BG
Tel: (089 272) 2769
*Restoration of stained and leaded glass as well
as glass mosaics.*

H. SARGEANT
21 The Green
Westerham, Kent TN16 1AY
Tel: (0959) 62130
Repairs to glass chandeliers and candelabra.

SOUTH WEST OF ENGLAND AND
WALES

LAWRENCE BRASS AND SON
93/95 Walcot Street
Bath, Avon
Tel: (0255) 64057
*General restoration service including
re-silvering mirrors.*

TY GWYDRAID STUDIO
Abercych, Boncath
Dyfed, Wales
Tel: (023 974) 421
*Restoration of stained glass windows, leaded
lights, Tiffany lampshades and mirrors.*

PLEASE NOTE THAT MOST JEWELLERS CAN DO SIMPLE REPAIRS, ALTHOUGH ALTERATIONS TO PRECIOUS MATERIALS AND STONES SHOULD BE CARRIED OUT BY A SPECIALIST.

LONDON

CARLTON C. ALLEN
3 Priory Gardens
Barnes
London SW13
Tel: (01) 878 6429
Restoration of jewellery.

ASPREY AND COMPANY LTD
165–169 New Bond Street,
London W1
Tel: (01) 493 6767
Restoration of jewellery.

CAMEO CORNER AT LIBERTY'S
Regent Street
London W1
Tel: (01) 734 1234
Restoration of jewellery

PEARL CROSS
35 St Martin's Court
London WC2
Tel: (01) 836 2814 and 240 0795
Restoration of jewellery.

DAEDALUS
43 The Village
London SE7 8UG
Tel: (01) 858 2514
Restoration of jewellery.

A.R. DOUCH
28 Conduit Street
London W1
Tel: (01) 493 9413
Repairs of jewellery.

Above: An engraved Easter egg, in silver with gold mounts, as restored by engine turning, courtesy of Pledge and Aldworth.

G. GARBE
23 Charlotte Street
London W1P 1HB
Tel: (01) 636 1268
Restoration of jewellery to museum standards.

THE GOLDEN PAST
6 Brook Street
London W1
Tel: (01) 493 6422
Restoration of jewellery.

J. GORDON PARKS AND PARTNER
193 Wardour Street
London W1
Tel: (01) 439 2347/8/9
Repairs, re-stringing, engraving, and plating as well as supplying stones and chain.

HANCOCKS AND COMPANY (JEWELLERS) LTD
1 Burlington Gardens
London W1
Tel: (01) 493 8904/5
Restoration of jewellery.

HARVEY AND GORE LTD
4 Burlington Gardens
London W1
Tel: (01) 493 2714
Restoration of jewellery.

HENNELL LTD
1 Davies Street
Berkeley Square
London W1
Tel: (01) 499 3011
Restoration of jewellery.

JOHNSON WALKER AND TOLHURST LTD
64 Burlington Arcade
London W1
Tel: (01) 629 2615
Restoration of jewellery, specialising in pearl-stringing.

L. NEWLAND
17 Picton Place
London W1
Tel: (01) 935 2864
Restoration and repair of jewellery, plus testing of precious metals and gem stones.

PLEDGE AND ALDWORTH
Unit 157, First Floor
27 Clerkenwell Close
London EC1
Tel: (01) 251 0555
Undertake engine turning, a 300 year old craft of engraving for cases, dials, boxes and in preparation for enamelling.

A.R. AND J.S. ULLMANN LTD
10 Hatton Garden
London EC1N 8AH
Tel: (01) 405 1877
Restoration and repair of jewellery.

SOUTH AND SOUTHEAST ENGLAND

THE CLOCK SHOP
284 Wickham Road
Shirley, Surrey
Tel: (01) 656 2800
Repair of jewellery

PHILIP NORMAN JEWELLERY
275 Watling Street
Radlett, Herts
Tel: Radlett 2798
Specialists in diamond re-mounting.

MICHAEL J. PAGE
Berwick
The Avenue
Claygate, Surrey KT10 ORY
Tel: (0372) 65724
Restoration and remodelling of old jewellery.

C.F. SIMPSON
1 Station Buildings
Sherman Road
Bromley, Kent
Tel: (01) 460 7879
Engraving of silver and gold.

SUSSEX JEWELLERY CENTRE
91 London Road
Brighton, Sussex
Tel: (0273) 696105
Repair and restyling of jewellery.

D.O. THOROGOOD
38 Ninfield Road
Sidley
Bexhill-on-Sea, E Sussex TN39 5AE
Tel: (0424) 219957
Repair of jewellery.

S. WARRENDER AND COMPANY
4 Cheam Road
Sutton, Surrey
Tel: (01) 643 4381
Restoration of jewellery.

JEWELLERY/LACQUER AND PAINTED FINISHES

WHICHCRAFT JEWELLERS
54/56 The Green
Writtle, Chelmsford, Essex
Tel: (0245) 420183
Repair and restoration of gold and silver jewellery.

SOUTH-WEST ENGLAND AND WALES

BOND STREET JEWELLERS LTD
8 Le Pollet
St Peter Port, Guernsey, C1
and
51 Victoria Street, Alderney, C1
Tel: (0481) 27613 and (0482) 2628
Repairs to gold, silver, brass or copper.

J.R. CHISMAN
4 Station Road
St Blazey
Par, Cornwall PL24 2NF
Tel: (072 681) 2309
Repair of jewellery.

G.M.S. ANTIQUES
36 High Street
Wickwar
Wotton-under-Edge, Glos GL12 8NP
Tel: (0454 24) 251
Repair of jewellery.

MIDLANDS AND EAST ANGLIA

B.J. BATEMAN
11 Key Hill Drive
Birmingham, W Midlands B18 5NY
Tel: (021 532) 7856
Specialists in the repair and restoration of signet rings and seals, including engraving stones and gold.

GEORGE ALAN LADELL
40 St Johns Hill
Shrewsbury, Shropshire
Tel: (0743) 4416
Repair and restyling of jewellery.

Below: A team of jewellery restorers courtesy of G.L. Cooper, N.A.G.

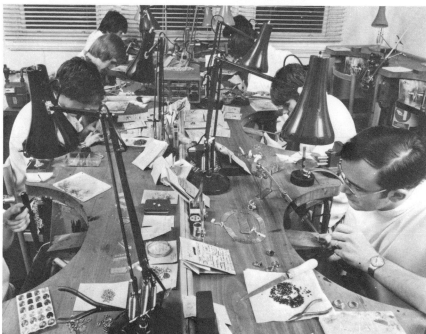

TOM PAYNE AND PETER TRIGGS
Priory Walk
Upper Castle Street
Hinkley, Leics LE10 1DD
Re-designing new pieces from worn or discarded jewels, as well as general repairs.

J.I. SUTTON
First Floor
3 Brook Square
Rugely, Staffs
Tel: (08994) 5064
Restoration of jewellery.

NORTH OF ENGLAND AND SCOTLAND

G.L. COOPER N.A.G.
Cleveland Buildings
94–100 Market Street
Manchester, Gt Manchester M1 1PF
Tel: (061 834) 0527
Restoration and repair of jewellery including stone setting, ultrasonic cleaning and rhodium, gold or silver plating.

A. HILL LTD
Hepworth Chambers
4 Church Street
Liverpool, Merseyside L1 3BG
Tel: (051) 708 7009
Repairs to jewellery and machine engraving.

K.G. SHEPHERD
7 Teesdale Road, Startforth
Barnard Castle, Co Durham DL12 9AT
Tel: (0833) 37754
Restoration and repair of gold, silver and platinum jewellery and small silver objects, as well as the supply and setting of gemstones.

TOPKAPI
11 Dundas Street
Redcar, Cleveland TS10 3AE
Tel: (0642) 472017
Jet and gemstones cut and polished as well as general restoration and repair.

JOHN DOUGLAS VAUGHAN
215 Freeman Street
Grimsby, Humberside
Tel: (0472) 52907
Repairs of jewellery.

PAINTER.

LONDON

ANTIQUE RESTORATIONS
311 Westbourne Park road
London W11
Tel: (01) 727 0467
Dealers who also restore lacquered and gilded furniture.

BOSTOCK AND GERRISH
London NW1
Tel: (01) 723 9912 (By appointment only)
Restoration of lacquer.

A.J. BRETT AND COMPANY LTD
168c Marlborough Road
London N19 4NP
Tel: (01) 272 8462
Restoration of lacquer including gilded decoration.

P.L. JAMES
211 Westbourne Park Road
London W11
Tel: (01) 727 0467
Restoration of lacquer, japanning and papier mâché, including gilded accents.

ALEXANDRE KIDD
67 Castlebar Road
London W5
Tel: (01) 997 3896/8316
Restoration of Oriental and European lacquer and papier mâché.

JILL SAUNDERS
91/93 Lots Road
London SW10
Tel: (01) 352 1365
Restoration of painted finishes including gilding and lacquering.

SOUTH AND SOUTH EAST ENGLAND

BRIAN BEELLEN
14 Hoath Hill
Mountfield
Nr Robertsbridge, E Sussex
Tel: (0580) 880754 and (04246) 2270
Specialist in painted effects including lacquering and gilding.

ANTOINETTE DE BROMHEAD
Westmoor Farm
Burnt Chimney Drive
Littleport, Ely, Cambs
Tel: (0353) 860 651 and (01) 935 8946
Restoration of lacquer and gilding.

BRIAN EDWIN CAUDELL
55 Stowe Road
Orpington, Kent
Tel: Orpington 73631
Restoration of lacquer.

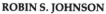

ROBIN S. JOHNSON
71 Hillside Gardens
Brockham, Betchworth, Surrey
Tel: Betchworth 2612
Restoration of lacquer.

MUNDAY AND GARNER
The Moncrieff Barn
(off Lower Street)
Pulborough, W Sussex
Tel: (079 82) 3610
General restoration including lacquer-work.

R. WARNER
11b Salisbury Avenue
Barking, Essex
Tel: Barking 6481
*Stripping and repolishing, specialising in
American and Continental colours and
finishes.*

SOUTHWEST ENGLAND AND WALES

LAWRENCE BRASS AND SON
93 and 95 Walcot Street
Bath, Avon
Tel: (0225) 64057
Restoration of lacquer.

MIDLANDS AND EAST ANGLIA

FRANCOIS GRECO
40 Vineyard Road
Newport, Shropshire
Tel: (0952) 813806
*Restoration with special emphasis on
unusual finishes including Vernis Martin and
French lacquer.*

MALVERN STUDIOS
56 Cowleigh Road
N Malvern, Heref & Worcs
Tel: (068 45) 4913
Restoration of special painted finishes.

RED LION RESTORATIONS
The Olde Red Lion
Bedingfield Eye, Suffolk
Tel: Worlingworth 491
Restoration of early hand-painted furniture.

LONDON

GUY F. BAGSHAW
96 Webber Street
London SE1
Tel: (01) 928 3624
Leather lining service.

CHAPMAN RESTORATIONS
10 Theberton Street
London N1 0QX
Tel: (01) 226 5565
*Restoration of leather linings and
hand-coloured hide upholstery.*

**CONNOLLY BROTHERS (CURRIERS)
LTD**
Wandle Bank
London SW19 1DW
Tel: (01) 542 5251 and 543 4611
*Leather renovation including the re-lining of
desk and table tops.*

MICHAEL FOSTER
118 Fulham Road
London SW3
Tel: (01) 373 3636
*Leather restoration and re-lining of desk and
table tops.*

S. AND H. JEWELL
26 Parker Street
London WC2B 5PH
Tel: (01) 405 8520
*Restoration of furniture including leather
lining.*

JUST DESKS
20 Church Street
London NW8
Tel: (01) 723 7976
Leather lining service.

SOUTH AND SOUTH EAST ENGLAND

GRAY ANTIQUES
6 Shirley Grove
Rusthall
Tunbridge Wells, Kent
Tel: (0892) 20288
Re-lining of leather desk and table tops.

SOUTH WEST ENGLAND AND WALES

JUDY CUNNINGHAM-SMITH
19 Camperdown Terrace
Exmouth, Devon
Tel: (03952) 77424
*Repair of saddlery and harnesses, as well as
restoration of fire bellows. Hand sewing also a
speciality.*

A.J. PONSFORD
51–53 Dollar Street
Cirencester, Glos GL7 2AS
Tel: (0285) 2355
Restoration of gold-tooled leather desk tops.

MIDLANDS AND EAST ANGLIA

ANGLIA ANTIQUE EXPORTERS
33 New Holt Street
Holt, Norfolk
Tel: (026 371) 3530
Leather lining service.

JUDITH DORE
Castle Lodge
Sandown Road,
Deal, Kent
Tel: (03045) 3684
*Restoration of leather costume accessories such
as shoes and handbags.*

G.B. AND E. GOODING
12 Arden Buildings
Dorridge, Solihull, W Midlands
Tel: (056 45) 3040
Re-lining leather table tops.

NORTH OF ENGLAND AND SCOTLAND

DEREK CASEMENT
Slack Lane Works
Slack Lane, Pendlebury
Swinton, Manchester, Gt Manchester
M27 2QT
Tel: (061) 794 1610
Replacement of gold-tooled leather inserts.

LONDON

W.G.T. BURNE LTD
11 Elystan Street
London SW3 3NT
Tel: (01) 589 6074
Glassware dealers who will restore chandeliers.

GEORGE AND PETER COHN
112 Crawford Street
London W1
Tel: (01) 935 3518
Restoration of crystal chandeliers.

CRAVEN ANTIQUES
17 Garson House
Gloucester Terrace
London W1
Tel: (01) 262 4176 (By appointment only)
Specialists in converting vases to lamp bases, including re-wiring.

N. DAVIGHI
117 Shepherds Bush Road
London W6
Tel: (01) 603 5357
Restoration of antique light fittings, including the repair of chandeliers.

GODDARD AND FARMER
8 Thackeray Street
London W8
Tel: (01) 937 4917
Renovation of old lampshades, including reproducing them if necessary.

THE LAMP SHOP
24 Bedfordbury
London WC2
Tel: (01) 836 3852 and (01) 402 4337 (Home)
Polishing and rewiring of lighting fixtures.

PETER METCALFE
2 Parsifal Road
London NW6 1UH
Tel: (01) 435 5025 (By appointment only)
Restoration of lamps as well as conversion from vases and manufacture of silk lampshades.

BRONSON SHAW DESIGN
Granary
61 Marychurch Street
London SE16
Tel: (01) 994 3212
Restoration of leaded and stained glass lighting as well as papua shell lampshades.

Below: Restored 18th c. Swiss stained glass panels being inserted into new diamond-shaped leaded window, courtesy of Bronson Shaw Design.

LAMP-MAKER.

W. SITCH AND COMPANY LTD
48 Berwick Street
London W1
Tel: (01) 437 3776
Repairs to lighting including rewiring, and conversion of vases to lamps plus restoring, colouring and lacquering metalwork. Have restored the chandeliers at Burlington House as well as most of the lighting fixtures at the Ritz Hotel.

Below: "Before" photo showing a twelve light glass chandelier as restored by R. Wilkinson and Son. See overleaf for "After" view.

R. WILKINSON AND SON
43/45 Wastdale Road
Forest Hill
London SE23 1HN
Tel: (01) 699 4420
Restoration of glass chandeliers.

CHRISTOPHER WRAY'S LIGHTING EMPORIUM
600 Kings Road
London SW6
Tel: (01) 736 8434
Restoration of oil, gas and early electric lamps of the 1900s. Replacement parts including wicks, chimneys and galleries.

See also entry under "Specialist Products".

SOUTH AND SOUTH EAST ENGLAND

DAVID FILEMAN
Squirrels Bayards
Horsham Road
Steyning, W Sussex
Tel: (0903) 813229
Restoration of chandeliers and table lights, especially those in glass.

Right: "After" photo showing a twelve light glass chandelier as restored by R. Wilkinson and Son.

H. SARGEANT
21 The Green
Westerham, Kent TN16 1AY
Tel: (0959) 62130
Repairs to glass chandeliers, candelabra, wall lights.

D.W. WINDSOR LTD
Netherfield Lane
Standstead Abbots
Ware, Herts
Tel: (0920) 870567
Specialists in restoration of antique lanterns for public, commercial and private use.

NORTH OF ENGLAND AND SCOTLAND

KELLY'S OF KNARESBOROUGH
96 High Street
Knaresborough, N Yorkshire
Tel: (0423) 862041
Restoration of lighting fixtures including glass, ormolu and brass.

TY GWYFED STUDIO
Abercych, Boncath
Dyfed, Wales
Tel: (023 974) 421
Restoration of glass and leaded lighting such as Tiffany lampshades. See illustration under "Glass"

Below right: Glass chandelier made from old glass pieces, as restored by H. Sargeant.

LONDON

BRIONY ADAMS
Gainsborough Studios
4 Gainsborough Road
London W4
Tel: (01) 995 8626
Restoration and repair of any metal.

AMAZING GRATES
153 Highgate Road
London N5
Tel: (01) 485 0496
Repair of cast iron metalwork, specialising in fireplaces and accessories.

THE ART BRONZE FOUNDRY LTD
1 Michael Road
London SW6
Tel: (01) 736 7292
Repairs and repatination to bronze statuary.

GUY F. BAGSHAW
96 Webber Street
London SE1
Tel: (01) 928 3624
Brass casting.

B.C. METALCRAFTS LTD
51 Dorset Street
London W1
Tel: (01) 935 9646
Restoration of metalware.

G.M. BETSER AND COMPANY LTD
22 Albemarle Street
London W1
Tel: (01) 493 2641/2/3
Specialists since 1902 in hand-engraving ivory and precious and semi-precious metals.

Below: Bronze lanterns after the style of the original hexagonal gas lights in London, for the Royal Palace at Jeddah, courtesy of Henwood Decorative Metal Studios.

BLUE-CRYSTAL GLASS
Unit 8, 21 Wren Street
London WC1X OHF
Tel: (01) 278 0412
Gilding and hand-engraving of non-ferrous metal.

N. DAVIGHI
117 Shepherds Bush Road
London W6
Tel: (01) 603 5357
Brass polishing.

G. GARBE
23 Charlotte Street
London W1P 1HB
Tel: (01) 636 1268
Restoration of bronzes.

HATFIELD'S
42a St Michael's Street
London W2 1QP
Tel: (01) 723 8265
Restoration of bronzes.

FELIX HILTON
45 St John's Wood High Street
London NW8
Tel: (01) 722 7634
Restoration of all non-ferrous metals, especially pewter.

PLEDGE AND ALDWORTH
Unit 157, 27 Clerkenwell Close
London EC1
Tel: (01) 251 0555
Engraving on silver or gold as well as engraving for enamelling. See "Jewellery Restorers" for illustration.

N.W.B. PORTLOCK
22 Iffey Road
London W6 OPA
Restoration of brass and copper including hand-turning and metal spinning.

W. SITCH AND COMPANY LTD
48 Berwick Street
London W1
Tel: (01) 437 3776
Restoration of metalwork, especially as applied to lighting fixtures and including gold lacquering, gilding, silverplating, brazing and lacquering.

TWENTY ONE ANTIQUES
21 Chalk Farm Road
London NW1
Tel: (01) 485 1239
Brass, copper and iron cleaning, polishing and sand blasting.

VERDIGRIS ART METALWORK RESTORERS
Clerkenwell Workshops
Unit B18
31 Clerkenwell Close
London EC1R OAT
Tel: (01) 253 7788
Repair of bronze and pewter, as well as special patinas, plus lamp conversions, polishing, lacquering, gilding, silverplating and casting.

MR WANDLE'S WORKSHOP
200–202 Garratt Lane
London SW18 4ED
Tel: (01) 870 5873
Restoration of Victorian metalwork and castings specialising in fireplaces.

R. WILKINSON AND SON
43–45 Wastdale Road
Forest Hill
London SE23 1HN
Tel: (01) 699 4420
Restoration and repair of metalwork (especially brass) and including casting, turning, polishing, plating, plus silverplating and regilding.

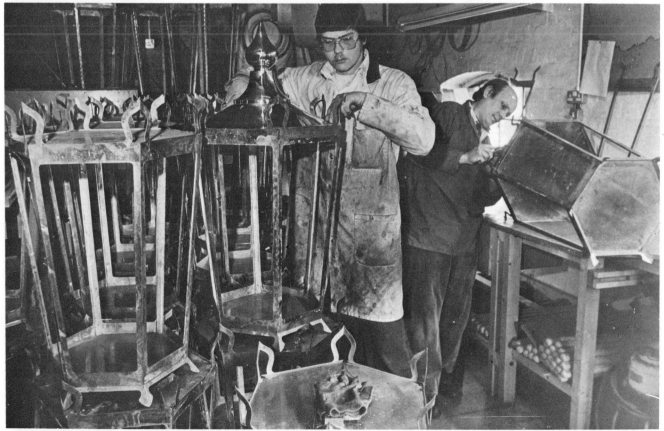

METALWARE

SOUTH AND SOUTHEAST ENGLAND

ANTIQUE METALWARE RESTORATION
9 Courtenay Road
Wantage, Oxon
Tel: (023 57) 4564
Repair and replacement of copper, brass and steelware. Special services include brass casting, silver brazing and shot blasting.

A.E. BOOTH
9 High Street
Ewell
Epsom, Surrey KT17 1SG
Tel: (01) 393 5245
Restoration of brassware.

J. BRINKMAN
13 Pall Mall
Leigh-on-Sea, Essex
Tel: (0702) 74661
Repair, restoration and replacement service including welding, brazing, soldering, polishing, lacquering, casting and shot blasting. Also fireplace renovation.

MOREN BROWN
The Green South
Warborough, Oxford
Oxon OX9 8DR
Tel: (086 732) 8354
Brass handle and escutcheon copying service.

THE ELSTREE FORGE
21 High Street
Elstree, Herts WD6 3EZ
Tel: (01) 953 2553
Manufacture and restoration of wrought metalwork.

HAGEN RESTORATIONS
Bakehouse Cottage
Northwood End
Haynes, Beds
Tel: (023 066) 424
Restoration and repair of craft tools.

HENWOOD DECORATIVE METAL STUDIOS LTD
The Bayle
Folkstone, Kent CT20 1SQ
Tel: (0303) 50911
Restoration of precious and non-precious metals, including a plating service capable of simulating special finishes such as silver, BMA, and gold. See previous page for illustration.

B. & A. MARKS
London House, 4 Market Square
Westerham, Kent
Tel: (0959) 64479
Repair of metalwork.

RICHARD QUINNELL LTD
Rowhurst Forge
Oxshott Road
Leatherhead, Surrey
Tel: (0372) 375148
Restoration of all metals including brass, copper, bronze, wrought and cast ironwork.

C.F. SIMPSON
1 Station Buildings
Sherman Road
Bromley, Kent
Tel: (01) 460 7879
Engraving of silver and gold.

Right: "Before" and "After" view of Multi-reed, semi-broad rim charger by Nicholas Kelk, circa 1670, as restored by P.G. Kydd.

SKILLCRAFTS
5 Park Street
Thaxted, Essex CM6 2ND
Tel: (0371) 830162
Restoration of brass and copper.

W.H. WELLER AND SON
12 Worth Street
Eastbourne, E Sussex
Tel: (0323) 23592
Restoration of brass and copper.

J. WILSON ENGINEERING
High Road
Wisbech St Mary, nr Wisbech
Cambs
Tel: (094 581) 238/377
Repair of any wrought metalwork.

SOUTHWEST ENGLAND AND WALES

LAWRENCE BRASS AND SON
93/95 Walcot Street
Bath, Avon
Tel: (0225) 64057
Brass and bronze casting.

L.G. AND K.L. DISNEY
The Forge
Kewstoke Road
Worle, Weston-super-Mare, Avon
Tel: (0934) 512423
Restoration of ornamental ironwork

THE FLINTLOCK
17a High Street
Glastonbury, Somerset
Tel: (0458) 31525
Restoration of metalwork, specialising in the unusual.

P.G. KYDD
Cannon Antiques
70 Colston Street
Bristol, Avon BS1 5AZ
Tel: (0272) 299265
Restoration of base metalware including brass, copper, iron, silver and plate.

TAMAR ANTIQUES RESTORATION
Tutwell House
Tutwell, Stoke Climsland
Callington, Cornwall
Tel: (057 97) 629
Repair and polishing of metalwork.

WING AND STAPLES
The Forge, Motcombe
Shaftesbury, Dorset SP7 9PE
Tel: (0747) 3104
Restoration of hand-wrought metalwork.

Above: Brass engraving of Herman de Werthere as executed by Alan Roberts.

R.T. VAUGHAN-JOHNSON
The Shoreline
Trevelyan Road
Seaton, Devon EX12 2NN
Tel: (0297) 22723
Manufacture and restoration of hand-wrought metalwork.

MIDLANDS AND EAST ANGLIA

BORDER POLISHING COMPANY
c/o Richard Osbourne
95 Old Street
Ludlow, Shropshire
Tel: (0584) 5110
Repair, restoration and repolishing service including stripping items that have been chromed, plated or anodised.

J.C. ELLIS
18 Humbleyard
Cloverhill, Bow Thorpe
Norwich, Norfolk
Tel: (0603) 745899
Restorer for over 30 years, specialising in brass, copper, silver and pewter.

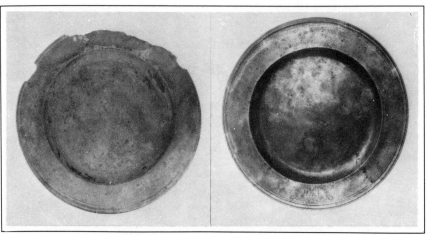

Above: "Before" and "After" of lead cherub with a bow, as restored by Andrew Naylor.

KINGFISHER RESTORATION
2 Westgate Terrace
Long Melford, Suffolk
Tel: (0787) 310 677
Sand-blasting of metal off-site.

H.B. MOORE
The Forge
Bradeston
Woodbridge, Suffolk
Tel: (072 882) 354
Restoration of wrought metalwork.

ANDREW NAYLOR
Unit H3
Halesfield 19
Telford, Shropshire
Tel: (0952) 583116
Conservation and restoration of metalwork, specialising in lead garden sculpture and architectural ornament.

NORTH OF ENGLAND AND SCOTLAND

C.P. BRAMLEY
Outgang Works, Outgang Road
Pickering, N Yorkshire YO18 7JA
Tel: (0751) 73493
Specialist in repair and fabrication of copper and brass.

JOHN HENDERSON LTD
Inglis Lane
Castleblair
Dunfermline, Fife, Scotland
Tel: (0383) 21123/23714
Established in 1890 for fabrication and restoration of wrought and cast iron metalwork. Architectural work carried out in situ.

KENCOLL CRAFTS LTD
c/o Maurice Collinge
Bollin Works
9b Mill Lane
Heatley Heath
Lymm, Cheshire WA13 9SD
Tel: (092 575) 5177
Restoration and reproduction of metalwork, specialising in copper and including replacements ports.

NORTHUMBRIA GUILD OF WROUGHT IRON CRAFTSMEN
Hallgarth House
Hallgarth Street
Durham, Co Durham
Tel: (0385) 3511
Restoration of wrought iron.

ALAN ROBERTS
39a Knight Street
Liverpool L1 9DT, Merseyside
Tel: (051) 709 3404
Hand-engraving of brass plates.

COPPERSMITH.

BLACKSMITH.

TINSMITH.

SOUTH AND SOUTHEAST OF ENGLAND

SUPERSCALE LTD
Bentalls
Basildon, Essex SS14 3DD
Tel: (0268) 3535/24824
Construction and restoration of engineering and architectural scale models.

SOUTHWEST ENGLAND AND WALES

RAYMOND CARTWRIGHT
23 Valletort Road
Millbridge
Plymouth, Devon PL1 5PH
Tel: (0752) 50217
Restoration and construction of model ships to quarter-inch scale.

MUSICAL INSTRUMENTS

LONDON

FAGIN'S PHONOGRAPH EMPORIUM
189 Blackstock Road
London N5
Tel: (01) 359 4793
Restoration of phonograph equipment and replacement parts.

KEITH HARDING ANTIQUES
93 Hornsey Road
London N7
Tel: (01) 607 6181/2672
Restoration of music boxes.

N.P. MANDER LTD
St Peter's Organ Works
London E2
Tel: Not Available
Restoration of pipe organs.

N.M. MKHIZE
90 Lots Road
London SW10
Tel: (01) 352 9876 and 870 2118 (Home)
Reconditioning and tuning of pianos.

SOUTH AND SOUTHEAST ENGLAND

ABC MUSIC COMPANY
85 High Street
Esher, Surrey KT10 9QA
Reconditioning and tuning of pianos.

PETER FREEMAN
67 Cromwell Road
Cambridge, Cambs CB1 3EB
Tel: (0223) 42672
Repair of woodwind instruments, especially clarinets, flutes, oboes and piccolos.

KEYBOARD HOUSE
41a Church Street
St Martin's Centre
Caversham, Reading, Berks
Tel: (0734) 476831
Major renovations plus in situ tuning and minor repairs to all pianos.

BRIAN D. PARKINSON
20 South Hill Grove
Sudbury Hill
Harrow, Middx HA1 3PR
Tel: (01) 422 7073
Restoration of violins, violas, and violoncellos.

Above: Voicing a harpsichord, courtesy of Malcolm Rose.

MALCOLM ROSE
1 The Mount
Rotherfield Lane
Mayfield, Sussex
Tel: (0435) 872268
Restoration and conservation of keyboard instruments and those in the lute and guitar families.

J.C.D. PATTERSON
Forge Studio Workshops
Stour Street
Manningtree, nr Colchester
Essex CO11 1BE
Tel: (020 639) 6222
Restoration of antique keyboard instruments, with experience in museum work.

SOUTHWEST ENGLAND AND WALES

CROFTON MILLIER
84 Norton Road
Bournemouth, Dorset BH9 2PZ
Tel: (0202) 529437
Restoration and maintenance of pianos.

ARTHUR S. LEWIS
The Stables, Linkend House
Corselawn, Glos GH9 4LZ
Tel: (0452) 78 258
Restoration of cylinder and disc music boxes.

SAN DOMENICO STRINGED INSTRUMENTS
177 Kings Road
Cardiff, S Glamorgan CF1 9DF, Wales
Tel: (0222) 35881
Restoration of the violin family, specialising in bow repairs.

TIME RESTORED
20 High Street
Pewsey, Wilts
Tel: (06726) 3544
Restoration of music boxes.

KENNETH H. WEBB
36 Roath Court Road
Roath, Cardiff
S Glamorgan, Wales
Tel: (0222) 495104
Tuning and repair of pianos.

MIDLANDS AND EAST ANGLIA

JOHN W. ROBINSON
Tile Hall
Wickhambrook
Newmarket, Suffolk CB8 8PX
Tel: (044 082) 394
Restoration of pianos including re-stringing, re-felting, regulating and tuning.

GEORGE WORSWICK
108/110 Station Road
Bardney, Lincoln
Lincs LN3 5UF
Tel: (0526) 398352
Restoration of cylinder-type music box mechanisms, plus tuning of otherwise good mechanisms.

NORTH OF ENGLAND AND SCOTLAND

JOHN BROWN
23 Renny Crescent
Montrose, Tayside DD10 9BW
Scotland
Tuning and repair of pianos.

CLIFF HEPPELL
17 Ewbank Avenue
Newcastle-upon-Tyne
Tyne & Wear NE4 9NY
Tel: (0632) 736762
Tuning and restoration of pianos including re-stringing and re-covering keys.

GEOFFREY WINTER
The Old Forge
Britway Road
Dinas Powys, S Glamorgan, Wales
Tel: (0222) 512394
Restoration, rebuilding and maintenance of pianos, pianolas and harmoniums.

NORTHERN IRELAND

WELLS-KENNEDDY PARTNERSHIP LTD
85–87 Gregg Street
Lisburn, Co Antrim BT27 5AW
N Ireland
Tel: (084 62) 4257
Restoration of old pipe organs.

LONDON

AGNEW RESTORATION SERVICES
43 Old Bond Street
London W1X 4BA
Tel: (01) 629 6176
Restoration of oil paintings, watercolours, drawings and prints carried out in situ, if required.

ANTIQUES LTD
18 Parson Street
London NW4
Tel: (01) 203 1194
Restoration of paintings.

BLACKMAN HARVEY LTD
29 Earlham Street
London WC2H 9LE
Tel: (01) 836 1904
Restoration of oil paintings including revarnishing.

JAMES BOURLET FRAMES LTD
26a Conduit Street
London W1
Tel: (01) 493 0621/2
Restoration of oil paintings.

K.F. CHANCE
14 Addison Avenue
London W11
Tel: (01) 602 5474
Restoration of pre-19th c. oil paintings.

ANTHONY DALLAS AND SONS LTD
9 Old Bond Street
London W1
Tel: (01) 491 8662
Restoration of oil paintings and watercolours.

Below: "Before" and "After" of "Still Life" by Luis Mendez, completely restored by Paul Mitchell.

JOHN DENHAM
The Gallery
114 Fortune Green Road
London NW6
Tel: (01) 794 2635
Restoration of oil paintings.

SEBASTIAN D'ORSAI LTD
39 Theobalds Road
London WC1
Tel: (01) 405 6663
Restoration of paintings and prints.

FORES GALLERY LTD
15 Sicilian Avenue
Southampton Row
London WC1
Tel: (01) 404 3063

G. GARBE
23 Charlotte Street
London W1P 1HB
Tel: (01) 636 1268
Restoration of works on canvas or paper to museum standards.

GREEN AND STONE OF CHELSEA
259 Kings Road
London SW3
Tel: (01) 352 6521
Restoration of any media.

MALCOLM INNES GALLERY
172 Walton Street
London SW3
Tel: (01) 584 0575
Dealers who also restore oil paintings.

ALAN JACOBS GALLERY
8 Duke Street
London SW1Y 6EN
Tel: (01) 930 3709
Restoration of oil paintings, specialising in Dutch and Flemish Old Masters.

LIMNER ANTIQUES
Stand 25/26
Bond Street Antique Centre
124 New Bond Street
London W1
Tel: (01) 629 5314 and (01) 493 6115 (home)
Restoration of miniatures.

MANGATE GALLERY
3 Chiswick Lane
London W4 2LR
Tel: (01) 995 9867 (by appointment only)
Restoration and cleaning of watercolours.

PAUL MASON GALLERY
149 Sloane Street
London SW1X 9BZ
Tel: (01) 730 3683
Dealer who also restores oil paintings, watercolours and prints.

JOHN MITCHELL AND SON
8 New Bond Street
First Floor
London W1
Tel: (01) 493 7567
Restoration of oil paintings and works on paper.

PAUL MITCHELL
99 New Bond Street
London W1Y 9LF
Tel: (01) 493 8732/0860
Cleaning and restoration of oil paintings on canvas or panel.

JOHN MITCHELL AND SONS
99 New Bond Street
London W1Y 9LF
Tel: (01) 493 8732
Cleanning, re-lining, and restoration of oil paintings.

THE OLD DRURY
187 Drury Lane
London WC2
Tel: (01) 242 4939
Restoration of oil paintings, watercolours and prints.

RELCY ANTIQUES
9 Nelson Road
London SE10
Tel: (01) 858 2812
Restoration of oil paintings and watercolours.

ELIZABETH SOBCZYNSKI
106 St George's Square
London SW1 3QY
Tel: (01) 821 8566
and
36c Borough Road
London SE1
Tel: (01) 928 6094
Conservation of works on paper and parchment including drawings and watercolours.

SPREAD EAGLE ANTIQUES
22 and 23 Nelson Road
and
8 Nevada Street
London SE10
Tel: (01) 692 1618 and (01) 858 9713
Restoration of oil paintings and watercolours.

LAURI STEWART ANTIQUES
36 Church Lane
London N2
Tel: (01) 883 7719
Restoration of watercolours.

JOHN TANOUS LTD
115 Harwood Road
London SW6
Tel: (01) 736 1422
Cleaners and restorers of oil paintings and watercolours.

WARWICK LEADLAY GALLERY
5 Nelson Road
London SE10 9JB
Tel: (01) 858 0317
Cleaning and re-colouring of maps and prints.

WATTS AND COMPANY LTD
7 Tufton Street
London SW1 3QE
Tel: (01) 222 2893/7169
Restoration of wallpaper. See opposite for illustration.

SUSANNAH WATTS-RUSSELL
9 Bolton Studios
17b Gilston Road
London SW10
Tel: (01) 352 0207
Cleaning, re-lining and restoration of oil and tempera paintings. Will work in situ if necessary.

SOUTH AND SOUTHEAST ENGLAND

ABBEY ANTIQUES AND ARTS
97 High Street
Hemel Hempstead, Herts
Tel: (0442) 64667
Restoration of oil paintings and watercolours.

Above: "Before" and "After" versions of "Aeneas and the Arms of Mezentius," tempera on paper by Sir Peter Paul Rubens (1577–1640), as restored for the National Museum, Cardiff, by Elizabeth Sobczynski.

APOLLO GALLERIES
61, 64 and 67 South End
Croydon, Surrey
Tel: (01) 681 3727 and (01) 680 1968
Restoration of paintings.

LIEUT. COL. R.V. FRENCH BLAKE
Midgham Park Farm
Woolhampton, nr Reading, Berks
Tel: (073 521) 3104
Restoration of oil paintings.

CAMBRIDGE FINE ART LTD
68 Trumpington Street
Cambridge CB2 1RJ
Tel: (0223) 68488
Restoration of oil paintings.

COLLECTOR'S TREASURES LTD
Hogarth House
High Street
Wendover, Bucks HP22 6DU
Tel: (0296) 624402
Restoration of maps and engravings including colouring.

EASTBOURNE FINE ART
47 South Street
Eastbourne, Sussex
Tel: (0323) 25634 or 23769
Cleaning and renovation of oil paintings and watercolours including the re-lining of oils and de-foxing of watercolours. See opposite for illustration.

Above and right: Wallpaper panel drawn up and reproduced to match the original scrap discovered during the restoration of the Landmark Trust Headquarters in Westminster, courtesy of Watts and Company Ltd.

THE HAMPTON HILL GALLERY LTD
203 & 205 High Street
Hampton Hill, Middx TW12 1NP
Tel: (01) 977 5273
Cleaning, restoration, mounting and framing of watercolours, drawings and prints.

HASTINGS ANTIQUES
59–61 Norman Road
St Leonards on Sea, E Sussex
Tel: (0424) 428561
Restoration of oil paintings, water-colours, prints and paintings on silk.

HUGHENDEN HOUSE GALLERY
35 Park Road
Teddington, Middx
Tel: (01) 977 4660
Cleaning and conservation of oil paintings.

PHILIP LAMBERT STUDIOS
115 Bournemouth Road
Chandler's Ford
Eastleigh, Hants
Tel: (042 15) 2839
Cleaning and restoration of oil paintings, watercolours and prints including a re-lining service.

ANTHONY J. LESTER
The Dower House
Hithercroft, nr Wallingford, Oxon
Tel: (0491) 36683
Cleaning, restoration and relining of paintings.

JAMES MACINTYRE
98 Western Avenue
Herne Bay, Kent CT6 8UF
Tel: (02 273) 61537
Restorer specialising in Victorian paintings.

THE OAKLEIGH GALLERY
5 High Street
Potters Bar, Herts EN6 5AJ
Tel: (0707) 43989
Cleaning and restoration of oil paintings, watercolours and prints.

THE NEW ASHGATE GALLERY
Wagon Yard
Farnham, Surrey GU9 7JR
Tel: (0252) 713208
Cleaning and restoration of oil paintings, watercolours and prints.

Below: This vacuum relining table is of interest because it cuts the cost of relining and remounting old canvases on to new backings, thus extending the life of the picture. The table is one of the few in the U.K.; courtesy of Eastbourne Fine Art.

PERIWINKLE PRESS
Chequers Hill
Doddington
Sittingbourne, Kent ME9 OBN
Tel: (079 586) 246
Restoration of prints and paintings.

STOTFOLD ANTIQUES
21 High Street
Westerham, Kent
Tel: (0959) 63055
Restoration of 19th c. oil paintings.

JACQUELINE TABER
Jaggers, Fingringhoe
Colchester, Essex
Tel: (0206) 28334
Restoration of oil and tempera paintings on wood or canvas. Will work in situ if necessary.

ROBERT TREHERNE
Herons Folly
Mayfield, Sussex
Tel: (0435) 2394
Restoration and cleaning of oil paintings.

H.S. WELLBY
The Malt House
Church End
Haddenham, Bucks
Tel: (0844) 290036
Restoration of 18th and 19th c. oil paintings.

ROBERT WILLIAMS
9a South Street
Eastbourne, E Sussex
Tel: (0323) 25337
Restoration of oils, watercolours and prints.

SOUTHWEST ENGLAND AND WALES

LAWRENCE BRASS AND SON
93 and 95 Walcot Street
Bath, Avon
Tel: (0225) 64057
Restoration of paintings.

C.S. STUDIOS
45 Abbey Road
Torquay, Devon TQ2 5NQ
Tel: (0803) 27144
Restorer specialising in 19th c. oil paintings.

Below: Painting showing "patches" of test-cleaning areas; courtesy of Jacqueline Taber.

COTSWOLD GALLERIES
High Street
Moreton-in-Marsh, Glos
Tel: (0608) 50601
Restoration and cleaning of oil paintings and watercolours, plus re-lining of canvases.

GASTRELL HOUSE
33 Long Street
Tetbury, Glos GL8 8AA
Tel: (0666) 52228
Restoration of oil paintings.

HAMPSHIRE GALLERY
18 Lansdowne Road
Bournemouth, Dorset BH1 1SD
Tel: (0202) 21211
Restoration of oil paintings and watercolours.

Above: "Before" and "After" photos showing a cleaned Old Master oil painting as restored by Robert Treherne.

LYNN MITCHELL
The Old Vicarage
Slad, Stroud, Glos
Tel: (0452) 813887
Restoration of works of art on paper

REGENT GALLERY
10 Montpelier Arcade
Cheltenham, Glos GL50 1SU
Tel: (0242) 512826
Dealers who also restore maps and prints.

TAMAR GALLERY
5 Church Street
Launceston, Cornwall
Tel: (0566) 4233
Restoration and cleaning of watercolours.

THE TUDOR GALLERY
c/o Leonard Smith A.B.P.A.
93 Sidwell Street
Exeter, Devon
Tel: (0392) 77659
Restoration and cleaning of oil paintings.

MIDLANDS AND EAST ANGLIA

BROBURY HOUSE GALLERY
Brobury, nr Hay-on-Wye
Heref & Worcs
Tel: (0497) 229
Restoration of works on paper.

MRS A. BURTON
5 Church Street
Clifton-upon-Dunsmore
Rugby, Warks
Tel: (0788) 78495
Restoration of oil paintings.

BURTON FINE ART
30 Main Street
Clifton-upon Dunsmore
Nr Rugby, Warks
Tel: (0788) 78495
Restoration of oil paintings.

SIMON CARTER GALLERY
23 Market Hill
Woodbridge, Suffolk
Tel: (03943) 2242
Dealers who also restore oil paintings.

KESTREL HOUSE
72 Gravelly Hill
North Erdington
Birmingham, W Midlands B23 6BB
Tel: (021) 373 2375
Cleaning and restoration of oil paintings.

LOWER NUP-END GALLERY LTD
Cradley
Nr Malvern, Worcs
Tel: (088 684) 334 (by appointment only)
Dealers who also clean and restore oil paintings.

EUGENE OKARMA
Brobury House Gallery
Brobury, Heref & Worcs
Tel: (0497) 09817
Restoration of oils, watercolours and prints. Thermo-vacuum wax re-lining of damaged canvases.

JOHN PROBERT STUDIO
1 Wootton Hall
Wootton Wawen, Warks
Tel: (056 42) 3467
Cleaning and restoration to museum standards of oil paintings and watercolours, including the re-lining of oils.

E.W. WENDT
Sudbury Picture Frames
21a Goal Lane
Sudbury, Suffolk
Tel: (0787) 76014
Restoration of oils and pastels.

NORTH OF ENGLAND AND SCOTLAND

ADAMS ANTIQUES
65 Waterloo Row
Chester, Cheshire CH1 2LE
Tel: (0244) 319421
Restoration of oil paintings.

DYSON'S ARTISTS LTD
87 Scotland Road
Nelson, Lancs
Tel: (0282) 65468
Cleaning and restoration of oil paintings.

ALAN S. HAMSHERE
Balcanquhal Farmhouse
Gateside, Strathmiglo
Cupar, Fife KY14 7SS, Scotland
Tel: (033 76) 325
Restoration of watercolours and oils.

AUSTIN HAYES GALLERIES
44 The Shambles
York, N Yorkshire
Tel: (0904) 22885
Restoration of oils paintings, watercolours, and engravings.

MALCOLM INNES GALLERY
67 George Street
Edinburgh, Scotland
Tel: (031) 226 4151
Dealers who also restore oil paintings.

RONALD AND MARY TILLEY
Banna
Bewcastle, Carlisle, Cumbria CA6 6PS
Tel: (0228) 78 338
Restoration of oil paintings and watercolours.

Below and left: "Before" and "After" photos showing a still life, as cleaned and restored by Leonard Smith of The Tudor Gallery.

LONDON

BLACKMAN HARVEY LTD
29 Earlham Street
London WC2H 9LE
Tel: (01) 836 1904
Restoration of any type of frame including regilding and remounting.

CORK STREET FRAMING COMPANY LTD
5–6 Cork Street
London W1
Tel: (01) 734 9179
Restoration of picture frames including gilding.

DENBIGH GALLERIES
3 Denbigh Road
London W11
Tel: (01) 229 6765
Restoration of frames, especially those from 18th and 19th c.

PAUL FERGUSON WOOD CARVERS
Unit 20
21 Wren Street
London WC1
Tel: (01) 278 8759
Regilding and recarving of picture frames, specialising in water gilding.

GREEN AND STONE OF CHELSEA
259 Kings Road
London SW3
Tel: (01) 352 6521
Restoration of carved or plaster picture frames.

JOHN MITCHELL AND SONS
99 New Bond Street
London W1Y 9LF
Tel: (01) 493 8732
Restoration of picture frames.

JOHN TANOUS LTD
115 Harwood Road
London SW6
Tel: (01) 736 1422
Restoration of mirrors and picture frames, including gilded items.

SOUTH AND SOUTHEAST ENGLAND

EASTBOURNE FINE ART
47 South Street
Eastbourne, Sussex
Tel: (0323) 25634 or 23769
Picture framing service. Washline mounts also supplied.

D.J. SMITH
34 Silchester Road
Pamber Heath
Nr Basingstoke, Hants RG2 6EF
Tel: (0734) 700595
Regilding and recarving of picture frames, specialising in water-gilding.

JACQUELINE TABER
Jaggers, Fingringhoe
Colchester, Essex
Tel: (0206) 28334
Picture restorer who also repairs and regilds picture frames.

ROBERT WILLIAMS
9a South Street
Eastbourne, Sussex
Tel: (0323) 25337
Regilding of picture frames.

SEE ALSO RESTORERS OF GILDING

SOUTHWEST ENGLAND AND WALES

RAYMOND ARTHUR FINN
23 Bridge Street
Llangollen, Clwyd, Wales
Tel: (0978) 860969
Gesso and gold leaf restoration, as well as carving and turning where required.

TRISTAN SALAZAR RESTORTIONS
41 Market Place
Cirencester, Glos GL7 2NX
Tel: (0285) 68010
Restoration of gesso, carved, and composition gilded picture and mirror frames.

MIDLANDS AND EAST ANGLIA

J.D. FINN
Old Co-op Stores
Ellesmere Road
St Martins, Oswestry, Shropshire
Tel: (0691) 772782
Gilded and gesso picture frame restoration. See entry under "Specialist Restorers, Furniture" for illustration.

MALVERN STUDIOS
56 Cowleigh Road
N Malvern, Heref & Worcs
Tel: (068 45) 4913
Restoration of special painted finishes.

JOHN PROBERT STUDIO
1 Wootton Hall
Wootton Wawen, Warks
Tel: (056 42) 3467
Restoration of picture frame.

E.W. WENDT
Sudbury Picture Frames
21a Goal Lane, Sudbury, Suffolk
Tel: (0787) 76014
Specialist in gilding and restoration of Continental frames and panels.

LONDON

DAVID ASHTON-BOSTOCK
21 Charlwood Street
London SW1V 2EA
Tel: (01) 828 3656
Restoration of pottery, porcelain and enamels. China restoration of two types: full restoration involving refiring and reglazing, an expensive process which takes about six months but renders repairs invisible; and the ordinary mending process which is much cheaper but perfectly adequate for everyday pieces.

AUBYN ANTIQUES
1 Wandon Road, London SW6 2JE
Tel: (01) 736 1196
Restoration of pottery and porcelain.

CERAMIC RESTORATIONS
14 Theberton Street, London N1
Tel: (01) 359 5240
Repair of Art Nouveau and Art Deco, including tiles.

CHINAMEND LTD
54 Walton Street, London SW3
Tel: (01) 589 1182
General restoration of modern and antique pottery and porcelain.

CHINA REPAIRERS LTD
64 Charles Lane, London NW8
Tel: (01) 722 8407
Repair of English and Continental pottery and porcelain, including figurines.

G. GARBE
23 Charlotte Street
London W1P 1HB
Tel: (01) 636 1268
Restoration of pottery and porcelain to museum standards.

HALL BROTHERS
73 Kenton Street
London WC1
Tel: (01) 837 5151
Restoration and repair of pottery and porcelain, modern and antique.

HATFIELD
42 and 42a St Michael Street
London W2 1OP
Tel: (01) 723 8265
Restoration of porcelain.

ROBIN HOOD'S WORKSHOP
18 Bourne Street
London SW1
Tel: (01) 730 0425
Specialists in the restoration of Oriental pottery, including small marble pieces.

BELINDA JOHNS
Studio 9
Dovedale Studios
465 Battersea Park Road
London SW11
Tel: (01) 288 3155
Restoration of Oriental and European pottery and porcelain of every period, up to and including Art Deco.

T. KAROLAK
4 Harcourt Street,
London W1
Tel: (01) 723 5075, (01) 828 6807 and (043 53) 2988 (home)
Restoration of porcelain.

SANDA LIPTON
The Knightsbridge Pavilion
112 Brompton Road
London SW1
Tel: (01) 581 2794 and (01) 407 0278
Restoration of porcelain specialising in early figurines, terracotta and Staffordshire pottery.

RELCY ANTIQUES
9 Nelson Road
London SE10
Tel: (01) 858 2812
Restoration of porcelain.

LAURI STEWART ANTIQUES
36 Church Lane
London N2
Tel: (01) 883 7719
Restoration of porcelain.

STUDIO 1D
Kensington Church Walk
London W8
Tel: (01) 937 7583
Restoration of pottery and porcelain.

STUDIO NINE PORCELAIN RESTORERS
465 Battersea Park Road
London SW11
Tel: (01) 228 3155
Restoration of antique and modern pottery and porcelain.

WATERBYRN LTD
11 St John's Wood High Street
London NW8
Tel: (01) 722 7058
Restoration of porcelain.

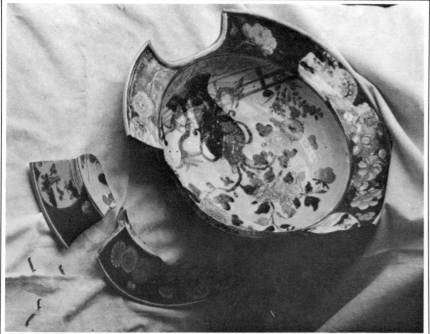

Above: Damaged early Imari barber's bowl, to be restored by Wenduine Copley and typical of the work she undertakes.

SOUTH AND SOUTHEAST ENGLAND

BERKSHIRE CHINA SURGERY
The Studio
Westbury Farm
Purley, nr Reading, Berks
Tel: (073 57) 3667/3123
Restoration of porcelain, specialising in early figurines, terracotta and Staffordshire pottery.

WENDUINE COPLEY
Tudor House, Dymchurch
Romney Marsh, Kent
Tel: (030 382) 3392
Restoration of pottery and porcelain; will reproduce, seal and/or cure invisibly.

GREAT GROOMS ANTIQUES LTD
Parbrook
Billingshurst, Sussex
Tel: (040 381) 2263
Restoration of porcelain.

MARIANNE MORRISH
The Studio
Westbury Farm, Westbury Lane
Purley, nr Reading, Berks
Tel: (07357) 3667
Specialist figurine restorer who also teaches her craft.

SHEILA SOUTHWELL
7 West Street
Burgess Hill, Sussex
Tel: (044 46) 44307
Specialist hand-painter who will match old china, porcelain and fireplace tiles.

BASIA WATSON GANDY
Squirrel Court Hare Lane
Little Kingshill
Great Missenden, Bucks HP16 OEF
Tel: (024 06) 5441
China painter who can duplicate any pattern so that missing pieces can be replaced.

SOUTHWEST ENGLAND AND WALES

MRS BERYL M. BYRNE
Ty Croes
Brynsiencyn, Anglesey, Gwynedd
N Wales
Tel: (024) 873 412
Restoration of ceramics specialising in figurines.

MARY ROSE PULVERTAFT
Tucketts
Trusham, nr Newton Abbot, Devon
Tel: (0626) 852288
Restoration of pottery and porcelain.

TAMAR ANTIQUES RESTORATION
Tutwell House
Tutwell, Stoke Climsland
Callington, Cornwall
Tel: (057 97) 629
Repair of pottery and porcelain.

MIDLANDS AND EAST ANGLIA

PATRICK TAYLOR ANTIQUES
First Floor Under Arch
13 St Peter's Street
Ipswich, Suffolk 1PI 1XF
Tel: (0473) 50774/328351 (by appointment only)
Restoration of porcelain.

KEITH WHITEHOUSE
Bodiam, Fentonhouse Lane
Wheaton Aston, Staffs
Tel: (0785) 840112
Restoration of English, Continental, and Oriental pottery and porcelain.

NORTH OF ENGLAND AND SCOTLAND

ADAMS ANTIQUES
65 Waterloo Row
Chester, Cheshire CH1 2LE
Tel: (0244) 319421
Restoration of porcelain.

L. AND M. LEWIS
8 Central Drive
Wingerworth
Chesterfield, Derbs S42 6QL
Tel: (0246) 34578
Dealers who restore pottery and porcelain, including figurines.

JOHN DOUGLAS VAUGHAN
215 Freeman Street
Grimsby, Humberside
Tel: (0472) 52907
Restoration of pottery and porcelain.

NORTHERN IRELAND

DUNLUCE ANTIQUES
33 Ballytober Road
Bushmills, Co Antrim BT57 8UU
N Ireland
Tel: (02657) 31140
Restoration of porcelain.

Below: "Before" and "After" of Capo di Monte figure restored by Sheila Southwell.

SCIENTIFIC INSTRUMENTS / SEMI-PRECIOUS MATERIALS

LONDON

AUBREY BROCKLEHURST
124 Cromwell Road
London SW7
Tel: (01) 373 0319
Restoration and repair of barometers.

NORTH LONDON CLOCK SHOP
72 Highbury Park
London N5 2XE
Tel: (01) 226 1609
Restoration of barometers.

RELCY ANTIQUES
9 Nelson Road
London SE10
Tel: (01) 858 2812
Restoration of scientific and maritime instruments.

R.E. ROSE F.B.H.I.
731 Sidcup Road
London SE9
Tel: (01) 859 4754 and 464 2653 (Home)
Restoration of barometers.

T. WHEELER LTD
Cline Road, Bounds Green
London N11 2LY
Tel: (01) 368 4422
Restoration and manufacture of aneroid barometers and barographs.

SOUTH AND SOUTHEAST ENGLAND

A.E. BOOTH
9 High Street
Ewell
Epsom, Surrey KT17 1SG
Tel: (01) 393 5245
Restoration of barometers.

COURT HOUSE ANTIQUES
19 Market Place
Brentford, Middx
Tel: (01) 560 7074 and Walton-on-Thames 27186
Restoration of barometers.

B. AND A. MARKS
London House
4 Market Square
Westerham, Kent
Tel: (0959) 64479
Repair of barometers.

VINTAGE RESTORATIONS
The Old Bakery
Windmill Street
Tunbridge Wells, Kent TN2 4DD
Tel: (0892) 25899
Restoration as well as duplication of parts for vintage cars, specialising in chronometers. See entry under "Specialist Restorers, Vehicles" for illustration.

SOUTHWEST ENGLAND AND WALES

LAWRENCE BRASS AND SON
93 and 95 Walcot Street
Bath, Avon
Tel: (0225) 64057
Restoration of barometers.

DEREK RAYMENT ANTIQUES
42 Alyn Drive
Rossett, Wrexham
Clwyd, N Wales
Tel: (0244) 570 869
Restoration and repair of barometers.

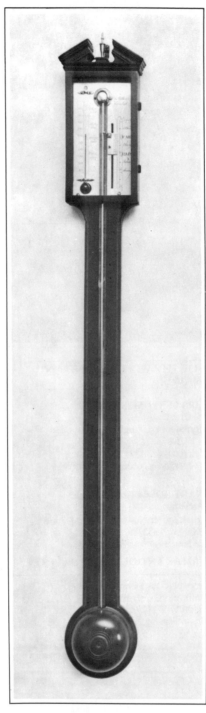

Above: A late Georgian "Door Stick Barometer", mahogany with silvered engraved dial, by Dolland of London, circa 1820, as restored by Derek Rayment Antiques

MIDLANDS AND EAST ANGLIA

LEONARD BALL
44 Market Street
Lutterworth, Leics
Tel: (045 55) 4942
Restoration of barometers.

GAVINA EWART
37 Sheep Street
Stratford-upon-Avon, Warks
Tel: (0789) 293917
Restoration of barometers.

FEARNS ANTIQUES
9 Coleshill Street
Fazeley, nr Tamworth, Staffs
Tel: (0827) 54233
Repair of aneroid and mercury barometers.

FLEETWOOD ANTIQUE RESTORATION
10 Hewell Road
Barnt Green
Birmingham, W Midlands B45 8LT
Tel: (021) 445 2212
Restoration of barometers.

JOHN D. LOCKE
Raven Lane
Ludlow, Shropshire
Tel: (0584) 4303
Restoration of barometers.

NORTH OF ENGLAND AND SCOTLAND

JOCELYN ANTIQUES
161 West George Street
Glasgow G2 2JJ, Scotland
Tel: (041) 248 3024
Restoration of barometers.

SEMI PRECIOUS MATERIALS

LONDON

DAVID ASHTON-BOSTOCK
21 Charlwood Street
London SW1V 2EA
Tel: (01) 828 3656
Repair of ivory and jade.

G.M. BETSER AND COMPANY LTD
22 Albemarle Street
London W1
Tel: (01) 493 2641/2/3
Engraving of ivory by hand.

A.J. BRETT AND COMPANY LTD
168c Marlborough Road
London N19 4NP
Tel: (01) 272 8462
Restoration of ivory, tortoise-shell and brass inlay.

G. GARBE
23 Charlotte Street
London W1P 1HB
Tel: (01) 636 1268
Restoration of ivory, enamel, jade, and tortoise-shell to museum standards.

SOUTH AND SOUTHEAST ENGLAND

A. DUNN AND SON
The White House
8 Wharf Road
Chelmsford, Essex CM2 6LU
Tel: (092 575) 5177
Restoration of semi-precious materials including ivory and tortoise-shell

ROBIN S. JOHNSON
71 Hillside Gardens
Brockham, Betchworth, Surrey
Tel: Betchworth 2612
Restoration of tortoise-shell and lacquer.

LONDON

BRIONY ADAMS
Gainsborough Studios
4 Gainsborough Road
London W4
Tel: (01) 995 8628
Restoration and repair of silver.

F.W. ALDRIDGE
Elizabethan Works
2 Ivy Road
London E17
Tel: (01) 539 3717
Silver plating and polishing. Suppliers of blue glass linings from stock of over 1500 moulds, or will make to order. Handles, finials and insulators can also be supplied and fitted to tea and coffee pots.

DAVID ASHTON-BOSTOCK
21 Charlwood Street
London SW1V 2EA
Tel: (01) 828 3656
Repair of silver.

ASPREY AND COMPANY LTD
165–169 New Bond Street
London W1
Tel: (01) 493 6767
Restoration of silver.

G.M. BETSER AND COMPANY LTD
22 Albemarle Street
London W1X 3HA
Tel: (01) 493 2641/2/3
Repair of silver and gold including plating and hand engraving in the traditional manner.

BLUE-CRYSTAL GLASS
Unit 8
21 Wren Street
London WC1X OHF
Tel: (01) 278 0142
Repair of silver including replating plus replacing rosewood, black fibre or metal handles.

BRICK SILVER LTD
14a Clerkenwell Green
London EC1
Tel: (01) 253 8602
Repair of silver and silver plate.

PEARL CROSS
35 St Martins Court
London WC2
Tel: (01) 836 2814 and (01) 240 0795
Restoration of silver.

G. GARBE
23 Charlotte Street
London W1P 1HB
Tel: (01) 636 1268
Restoration of silver to museum standards.

GARRARD AND COMPANY LTD
112 Regent Street
London W1
Tel: (01) 734 7020
Restoration of antique silver.

SIMON GRIFFIN ANTIQUES
3 Royal Arcade
28 Old Bond Street
London W1
Tel: (01) 491 7367 and (0525 220) 256 (home)
Restoration of silver and silver plate.

HANCOCKS AND COMPANY LTD
1 Burlington Gardens
London W1
Tel: (01) 493 8904/5
Restoration of silver.

HARVEY AND GORE (ANTIQUES) LTD
4 Burlington Gardens
London W1
Tel: (01) 493 2714
Restoration of silver.

HENNELL LTD
1 Davies Street
Berkeley Square
London W1
Tel: (01) 499 3011
Restoration of silver.

JOHN LAURIE
352 Upper Street
London N1
Tel: (01) 226 0913
Restoration of silver and silver plate.

RICHARD LAWTON LTD
33 Greville Street
Hatton Garden
London EC1
Tel: (01) 242 1894
Repair of silver and silver plate including repolishing, replating, gilding, re-handling, reblading and rebristling. Also willing to find missing items, or make to order. Trade only.

SIMON KAYE LTD
1½ Albemarle Street
Piccadilly, London W1
Tel: (01) 493 7658
Restoration of silver.

J. GORDON PARKS AND PARTNER
193 Wardour Street
London W1
Tel: (01) 439 2347/8
Restoration of all precious metals, specialising in silver, gold and platinum.

PIERS RANKIN
Grays Mews
1–7 Davies Mews
London W1
Tel: (01) 629 1184
Restoration of silver.

S.J. SHRUBSOLE LTD
43 Museum Street
London WC1A 1LY
Tel: (01) 405 2712
Repair of silver and Sheffield plate.

TWENTY ONE ANTIQUES
21 Chalk Farm Road
London NW1
Tel: (01) 485 1239
Repair of silver including replating.

A.R. AND J.S. ULLMANN LTD
10 Hatton Garden
London EC1N 8AH
Tel: (01) 406 1877
Restoration and repair of silver.

VERDIGRIS ART METALWORK RESTORERS
Gerald Bacon
c/o Clerkenwell Workshops
Unit B18
31 Clerkenwell Close
London EC1R OAT
Tel: (01) 253 7788
Restoration and repair of all metals including replating and regilding.

R. WILKINSON AND SON
43–45 Wastdale Road
Forest Hill
London SE23 1HN
Replating and gilding service.

SOUTH AND SOUTHEAST ENGLAND

RICHARD BULL SILVERSMITHING
68a Hayes Place
Marlow, Bucks
Tel: (062 84) 73206
Repair and restoration of fine contemporary and antique silverware.

B.N. BUTTON
6 Saffron Close
Shoreham-by-Sea, Sussex
Tel: (0273) 591 752
Restoration of silver and gold by small workshop with 20 years experience. As well as cleaning and polishing, will supply new fibre handles and ivory insulators.

GOLD CONNECTION ANTIQUES
40/44 St George's Walk
Croydon, Surrey
Tel: (01) 642 3772
Repairs to silver flatware.

HENWOOD DECORATIVE METAL STUDIOS LTD
The Bayle
Folkstone, Kent CT20 1SQ
Tel: (0303) 50911
Restoration of precious and non-precious metals, including a plating service capable of simulating special finishes such as BMA and gold.

S. WARRENDER AND COMPANY
4 Cheam Road
Sutton, Surrey
Tel: (01) 643 4381
Restoration of silver.

RICHARD WHITEHOUSE
Ardleigh Craft Workshop
Ardleigh, Colchester CO7 7RH
Essex
Tel: (0206) 230117
Manufacture and repair of silver, specialising in Victorian and Georgian, but excepting pieces made from Britannia metal.

SOUTHWEST ENGLAND AND WALES

G.M.S. ANTIQUES
36 High Street
Wickwar
Wotton-under-Edge, Glos GL12 8NP
Tel: (0454 24) 251
Repair and replating of silver.

MIDLANDS AND EAST ANGLIA

GEORGE ALAN LADELL
40 St Johns Hill
Shrewsbury, Shropshire
Tel: (0743) 4416
Repair and restoration of silver plate.

PATRICK TAYLOR ANTIQUES
First Floor Under Arch
13 St Peter's Street
Ipswich, Suffolk 1PI 1XF
Tel: (043) 50774/328351 (by appointment only)
Restoration of silver.

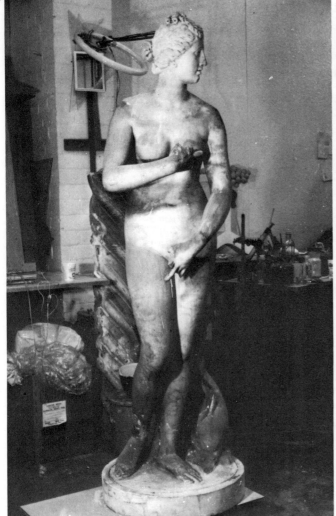

Above: "Before" and "After" views of "Medici Venus" in marble by Jean-Jacques Clerion (1639–1714), as restored by Voitek Sobczynski.

NORTH OF ENGLAND AND SCOTLAND

A. HILL LTD
Hepworth Chambers
4 Church Street
Liverpool, Merseyside L1 3BG
Tel: (051) 708 7009
Repair of silver and silver plate.

K.G. SHEPHERD
7 Teesdale Road
Startforth
Barnard Castle, Co Durham DL12 9AT
Tel: (0833) 37764
Repair of silver tableware.

R. THOMPSON
Beehive Works
Milton Street
Sheffield, S Yorkshire S3 7WF
Repair and restoration of any silver, silver plate and old Sheffield plate.

JOHN DOUGLAS VAUGHAN
215 Freeman Street
Grimsby, Humberside
Tel: (0472) 52907
Repair of silver and silver plate.

STONE

LONDON

SEE ALSO ARCHITECTURAL RESTORATION LISTINGS

IAN CLAYTON LTD
277 Grays Inn Road
London WC1X 8PF
Tel: (01) 278 0281
Statuary and monument consolidation, including cleaning and preservation, to international museum standards.

MICHAEL FOSTER
118 Fulham Road
London SW3
Tel: (01) 373 3636
Restoration of marble table tops.

ROBIN HOOD'S WORKSHOP
18 Bourne Street
London SW1
Tel: (01) 730 0425
Specialists in the restoration of Oriental pottery, including small marble pieces.

KEN NEGUS LTD
44 South Side
Clapham Common
London SW4 9BU
Tel: (01) 720 2938
Restoration of marble, both indoor and external.

H.W. POULTER AND SON
279 Fulham Road
London SW10
Tel: (01) 352 7268
Restoration and repair of marble and stoneware.

VOITEK SOBCZYNSKI
106 St George's Square
London SW1 V3QY
Tel: (01) 821 8566
and
36c Borough Road
London SE1
Tel: (01) 928 6094
Conservation of sculpture, including works of art in marble, stone, terracotta and wood.

MIDLANDS AND EAST ANGLIA

MEN OF THE STONES
The Rutland Studio
Tinwell, Stamford, Lincs PE9 3UD
Tel: (0780) 3372
Advice on conservation of stonework; supply list of local stonemasons and quarries.

Opposite right: Embroidered panel "Before" showing perished silk, circa 1900, and restored panel "After" matching the original in colour and design, courtesy of Watts and Company Ltd.

LONDON

RAYMOND BENARDOUT
5 William Street
London SW1X 9HL
Tel: (01) 235 3360
*Cleaning and restoration of Oriental tapestries
and textiles.*

BOHUN AND BUSBRIDGE
8 Clarendon Road
London W11
Tel: (01) 229 7825
Repair and cleaning of all types of textiles.

MICHEL DUMEZ-ONOF
109 Mount Street
London W1
Tel: (01) 499 6648
Restoration of needlework.

ROYAL SCHOOL OF NEEDLEWORK
25 Princes Gate
London SW7 1QE
Tel: (01) 589 0077
Repair of embroideries and lace.

**THE PATCHWORK DOG AND THE
CALICO CAT LTD**
21 Chalk Farm Road
London NW1
Tel: (01) 485 1239
*Restoration of patchwork quilts, using fabrics
from the same period as the original.*

WATTS AND COMPANY LTD
7 Tufton Street
London SW1 3QE
Tel: (01) 222 2893/7169
Restoration of textiles.

SOUTH AND SOUTHEAST
ENGLAND

JUDITH DORE
Castle Lodge
271 Sandown Road
Deal, Kent
Tel: (03045) 3684
*Conservation of embroidered, printed and
woven textiles, costumes and costume
accessories such as parasols and fans.*

*Above right: Coronation robes of King George
IV purchased by Madame Tussaud's, vendor
unknown. The robes were lost in 1938 and
only found in a cupboard in 1965. Repairs by
the Royal School of Needlework.*

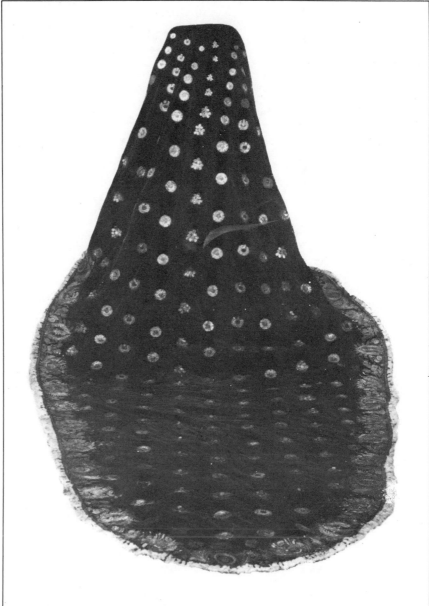

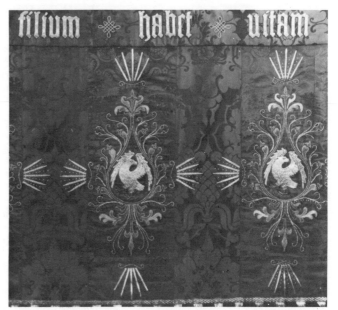

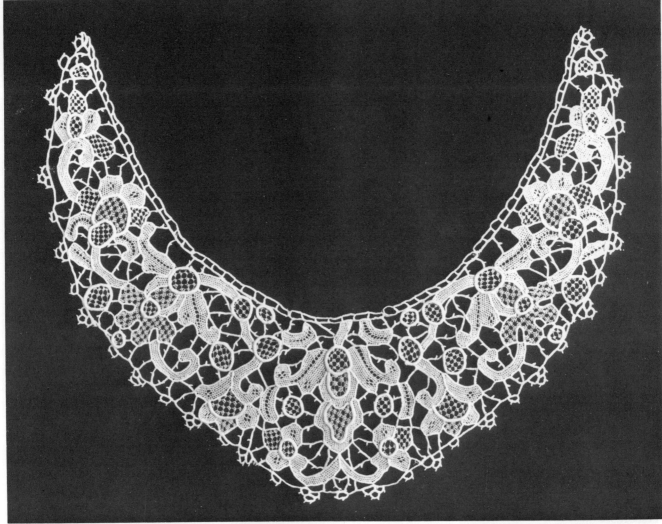

Above: Needlepoint lace collar showing variety of stitches, as restored by Nenia Lovesey.

HASTINGS ANTIQUES
59–61 Norman Road
St Leonards-on-Sea, E Sussex
Tel: (0424) 428561
Restoration of painting on silk.

NENIA LOVESEY
16 Woodrow Drive
Wokingham, Berks RG11 1RS
Tel: (0734) 787043
Restoration of needlepoint lace.

**THE TEXTILE CONSERVATION
CENTRE LTD**
Apt 22, Hampton Court Palace
East Molsey, Surrey KT8 9AU
Tel: (01) 977 4943
Conservation of historic textiles.

MIDLANDS AND EAST ANGLIA

MRS FRANCES COLLECOTT-DOE
Berrymans Dip
Ingham, Norwich
Norfolk NR12 9TB
Tel: (0692) 81926
Cleaning and repair of woven and embroidered textiles.

UPHOLSTERY

LONDON

**ALLABOUT ANTIQUES AND
INTERIOR DESIGN**
68 Marylebone High Street, London W1
Tel: (01) 935 5859
Restoration of upholstery.

GUY F. BAGSHAW
96 Webber Street
London SE1 OQN
Tel: (01) 928 3624
Re-upholstery service.

CHAPMAN RESTORATIONS
10 Theberton Street
London N1 OQX
Tel: (01) 226 5565
Furniture restoration including hand-coloured hide upholstery.

TONY ELLIS ANTIQUES
90, 96 and 110 Highbury Park and 2b
Southerby Road
London N5
Tel: (01) 226 7551 and 272 0651 (Home)
Restoration of furniture including re-upholstery.

MARION GRAY
33 Crouch Hill
London N4
Tel: (01) 272 0372
Restoration of furniture including re-upholstery.

S. AND H. JEWELL
26 Parker Street
London WC2B 5PH
Tel: (01) 405 8520
Restoration of furniture including re-upholstery.

S. SANDLER LTD
5 Peary Place, Roman Road
London E2 OQW
Tel: (01) 980 1972
Furniture repairs, specialising in re-upholstery.

JILL SAUNDERS
91/93 Lots Road
London SW10
Tel: (01) 352 1365
Re-upholstery service including loose covering.

PATRICK SCAIFE
108a Fortune Green Road
London NW6
Tel: (01) 794 3048
Traditional upholstery service including deep buttoning, hand springing and hand stuffing. See opposite for illustration.

Above: "Before" and "After" views of an upholstered chair, as restored by Patrick Scaife.

ASHLEY STOCKS LTD
13 Crescent Place
London SW3
Tel: (01) 589 0044
Re-upholstery service.

E. AND A. WATES LTD
82–84 Mitcham Lane
London SW16 6NR
Tel: (01) 769 2205
Re-upholstery and loose covers.

SOUTH AND SOUTHEAST ENGLAND

A.E. BOOTH
9 High Street
Ewell
Epsom, Surrey KT17 1SG
Tel: (01) 393 5245
Restoration of upholstery including leather.

MOREN BROWN
The Green South
Warnborough, Oxford
Oxon OX9 8DR
Tel: (086 732) 8354
General restoration including re-upholstery.

RONALD A. BURGESS
17 Friday Street
Leighton Buzzard, Beds
Tel: (0525) 374664
Specialists in deep buttoning.

ANGELA BURGIN
87 Miswell Lane
Tring, Herts
Tel: (044) 282 3151
Restoration of exposed wooden frames as well as period upholstery, including deep-buttoning.

CENTRE OF RESTORTION AND ARTS
20 Folly Lane
St Albans, Herts
Tel: (0727) 51555
Furniture restoration including re-upholstery.

MICHAEL HEDGECOE
Roman House
Burrow Hall Green
Chobham, Woking, Surrey
Tel: (099 05) 8206
Restoration of furniture including re-upholstery.

DONALD MOWATT
Southdown House
Nonington, nr Dover, Kent CT15 4HE
Tel: (0304) 840987
Restoration of furniture as well as upholstery.

NADJ'S ANTIQUES
36 Crown Road
Twickenham, Middx
Tel: (01) 892 6965
Re-upholstery service.

PAMELA AND BARRY ANTIQUES
216 Sandridge Road
St Albans, Herts
Tel: (0727) 51109
Furniture restoration including traditional upholstery.

PHELPS LTD
129/135 St Margarets Road
Twickenham, Middx
Tel: (01) 892 1778/7129
Restoration of furniture including re-upholstery.

A. ROBINS AND SONS LTD
Fairfield
Farnham, Surrey
Tel: (0252) 714233
Re-upholstery, loose cushion and curtain making service.

JOHN SMALL FURNISHINGS
88 Dean Road
Bitterne, Southampton, Hants SO2 5AT
Tel: (04218) 2225
Re-upholstery, renovation and re-covering service.

VINE COTTAGE ANTIQUES
High Street
Streatley
Reading, Berks RG8 9JD
Tel: (0491) 872425
Re-upholstery service.

W.G. UNDRILL LTD
103/111 Catherine Street
Cambridge, Cambs CB1 3AP
Tel: (0223) 47470
Re-upholstery service.

SOUTHWEST ENGLAND AND WALES

LAWRENCE BRASS AND SON
93 and 95 Walcot Street
Bath, Avon
Tel: (0225) 64057
Furniture restoration including re-upholstery.

W.T. SERVICES
44b Fore Street
Tiverton, Devon EX16 6LD
Tel: (08842) 3820
Specialists in deep buttoning.

MIDLANDS AND EAST ANGLIA

ALMA ANTIQUE RESTORERS
The Old Gospel Hall
Dereham Road
Norwich, Norfolk
Tel: (0603) 613184
General restoration including re-upholstery.

BROCKDISH ANTIQUES
Commerce House
Brockdish, Diss, Norfolk
Tel: (037 975) 498
Furniture restoration including re-upholstery using traditional methods.

FLEETWOOD ANTIQUE RESTORATION
10 Hewell Road
Barnt Green
Birmingham, W Midlands B45 8LT
Tel: (021) 445 2212
Restoration of upholstery using traditional methods.

BRIAN GREEN
26 Evington Road
Leicester, Leics
Tel: (0533) 543444
Refurbishment to all period upholstery

JALNA ANTIQUES AND RESTORATION
Coley Lane
Little Haywood
Stafford, Staffs ST18 OUP
Tel: (0889) 881381
Restoration of furniture including re-upholstery.

CHARLES LOWE AND SONS LTD
40 Church Gate
Loughborough, Leics
Tel: (0509) 217876
Specialists in restoration of traditional upholstery using horsehair and correct period coverings.

SPADESBOURNE ANTIQUES AND REPRODUCTIONS
Herring House
98 High Street
Henley-in-Arden
Solihull, Warks
Tel: (056 42) 3560
Re-upholstery and reproduction service.

PERCY F. WALE LTD
32 and 34 Regent Street
Leamington Spa, Warks CV32 5EG
Tel: (0926) 21288
Furniture restoration including re-upholstery.

NORTH OF ENGLAND AND SCOTLAND

ALAN GRICE
106 Aughton Street
Ormskirk, Lancs
Tel: (0695) 72007
Restoration of antique furniture including upholstery.

DEREK HAINSWORTH
Lake House
Welham, Norton
Malton, N Yorkshire
Tel: (0653) 2609
General restoration of furniture including upholstery.

JOSEPH ANTIQUES
Corney Square
Penrith, Cumbria CA11 7PX
Tel: (0768) 62065
Re-upholstery service.

S AND G UPHOLSTERY
73–75 Doncaster Road
Wakefield, W Yorkshire WF1 5DX
Tel: (0924) 74266
Re-upholstery service.

TAMESIDE ANTIQUES
85 Cavendish Street
Cavendish Mill
Ashton-under-Lyne, Gt Manchester
Tel: (061) 344 5477
Re-upholstery service.

NORTHERN IRELAND

HENRY PRICE
18 Shore Road
Holywood, Co Down, N Ireland
Tel: (023 17) 2643
Re-upholstery service.

SMITH OF SMITHFIELD
Unit 18, Smithfield Market
Belfast 1, Co Antrim, N Ireland
Tel: (0232) 747004
Re-upholstery service.

SOUTH AND SOUTHEAST ENGLAND

ADAMS AND OLIVER LTD
Ramsey Road
Warboys, Huntington, Cambs
Tel: (0487) 822488
Restoration of motor vehicles, particularly Rolls Royces and Bentleys.

BASKETMAKERS ASSOCIATION
Mrs Olivia Elton Barratt
Millfield Cottage
Little Hadham, Herts
Tel: (0279) 51497
Restoration of cane, close cane, willow skeining and rush work on furniture or antique vehicles.

CRAILVILLE MOTORS
Canal Yard
Hayes Road
Southall, Middx
Tel: (01) 571 4291
Specialists in hand-crafted bodywork, including aluminium coachwork.

FORSEWELD FABRICATIONS
Unit A6
Station Road, Industrial Estate
Hailsham, E Sussex
Tel: (0323) 840 283
Restoration and rebuilding of vintage cars, space frames and old chassis.

VINTAGE RESTORATIONS
The Old Bakery
Windmill Street
Tunbridge Wells, Kent
Tel: (0892) 25899
Specialists in vintage vehicle instrument restoration, including clocks and chronometers.

Above: "Before" and "After" of 1934 Alvis Silver Eagle instruments and panel, as restored by Vintage Restorations

---

SOUTHWEST ENGLAND AND WALES

ASHTON KEYNES VINTAGE RESTORATIONS
c/o Keith Bowley
Church Farm
Ashton Keynes, nr Swindon, Wilts
Tel: (0285) 861 288
Restoration of coachwork in original style using ashwood frames and aluminum or steel panelling as well as paintwork lining and cellulose spraying.

AUTO BODY CENTRE
2 Biltor Road
Ippleton, Newton Abbot, Devon
Tel: (0803) 812579
Renovation of corroded metalwork on classic car bodies.

IAN R.W. HAMILTON
The Old Grammar School
Church Street
Ruabon, Clwyd, Wales
Tel: (0978) 822038
Wheelwright and carriage builder who undertakes commissions and restorations.

RUABON LOCKSMITH AND WHEELWRIGHT
The Old Grammar School
Church Street
Ruabon, nr Wrexham
Clwyd, N Wales
Tel: (0978) 822038
Specialist wheelwright for horse-drawn vehicles.

NEIL VENTIN
27 Rockhouse Estate
Letterston, Dyfed, Wales
Tel: (034) 84 726
Wagon building, wheelwrighting and woodturning.

MIDLANDS AND EAST ANGLIA

G.S. WILLIAMSON AND SONS
Industrial Estate
Weston Road
Honeybourne, Evesham, Heref & Worcs
Tel: (0386) 840062
Specialists in restoration of upholstery in horse-drawn and motorised vehicles, including hoods and tonneau covers.

Above: Horse-drawn wagon restored including the hubs, some spokes on the wheels and several parts of the bodywork, courtesy of Neil Ventin.

VEHICLES

NORTH OF ENGLAND AND SCOTLAND

ALTECH SERVICES
c/o Ron Field
Langley Park Industrial Estate
Witton, Gilbert, Co Durham
Tel: (0385) 730491
Mechanical repairs to vintage vehicles.

MISCELLANEOUS

LONDON

BLUE-CRYSTAL GLASS
Unit 8
21 Wren Street
London WC1X OHF
Tel: (01) 278 0412
Rebristling of clothes and hand brushes.

CAVENDISH CLASSIC CARS
c/o Ronald Pountain
Derby Road
Doveridge, Derbs
Tel: Doveridge 5740
Restoration of vintage cars to concourse standards.

JOHN HENDERSON LTD
Ingis Lane
Castleblair, Dunfermline
Fife KY12 9DP, Scotland
Tel: (0383) 21123/23714
Restoration of motor-driven and horse-drawn vehicles.

FAGIN'S PHONOGRAPH EMPORIUM
189 Blackstock Road
London N5
Tel: (01) 359 4793
Restoration of phonograph equipment and replacement parts.

GAME ADVICE
1 Holmes Road
London NW5
Tel: (01) 485 2188/4226
Restoration of 18th and 19th c. games, chess pieces and toys.

P.C. WAITE
15 Clifton Street
Trawden Forest
Nr Colne, Lancs BB8 8AL
Tel: Not Available.
Restoration of industrial archaeology including steam locomotives, traction engines, road rollers and waterwheels. Also steel fabrication of missing parts and ornate metalwork and woodwork duplication. Will work in situ.

GET STUFFED
105 Essex Road
London N1
Tel: (01) 226 1364
Restoration of stuffed and mounted animals.

SOUTH AND SOUTHEAST ENGLAND

HAGEN RESTORATIONS
Bakehouse Cottage
Northwood End
Haynes, Beds
Tel: (023 066) 424
Restoration and repair of craft tools.

COURSES ON RESTORATION

LONDON

CHISWICK CERAMICS
31 Bollo Lane
London W4
Tel: (01) 995 6290
Day and evening sessions in china painting.

CITY AND GUILDS OF LONDON ART SCHOOL
c/o The Secretary
124 Kennington Park Road
London SE11
Tel: (01) 735 2306
Two year certificate course in woodcarving and gilding; two year diploma course in restoration, carving and polychrome (T.E.C.); and three year diploma course in restoration of wood, stone and polychrome. Non-diploma and part-time day classes also.

COURTAULD INSTITUTE OF ART
20 Portman Square
London W1H OBE
Tel: (01) 935 9292–5
Post-graduate three year diploma course in the conservation of paintings.

ROBIN HOOD'S WORKSHOP
18 Bourne Street
Sloane Square, London SW1
Tel: (01) 730 0425
Courses in restoration of pottery and porcelain.

RAVEN ANTIQUES
(Mrs Irene Williams)
256 Lee High Road
London SE13
Tel: (01) 852 5066
Courses in restoration of pottery and porcelain.

STUDIO NINE PORCELAIN RESTORERS
465 Battersea Park Road
London SW11
Tel: (01) 228 3155
Porcelain restoration course.

STUDIO ONE "D"
Kensington Church Walk
London W8
Tel: (01) 937 7583
Intensive one week course in pottery and porcelain restoration.

PETER WOLFE AND GUDDE JANE SKYRME WORKSHOPS
84 Camden Mews
London NW1
Tel: (01) 267 4979
Courses arranged at any venue throughout the year in cloisonné foundations and painting, plus plique à jour enamelling.

SOUTH AND SOUTHEAST OF ENGLAND

BERKSHIRE CHINA SURGERY
c/o Marianne Morrish
The Studio
Westbury Farm
Purley, nr Reading, Berks
Tel: (073 57) 3667/3123
Three-week courses from March to October.

CENTRE FOR RENAISSANCE STUDIES
Stained Glass Studio
St Michaels' Hall
31 Queen Street
Oxford, Oxon
Tel: (0865) 41071
Residential or day, evening and summer classes in stained glass.

THE EARNLEY CONCOURSE
Earnley
Nr Chichester, Sussex PO20 7JL
Tel: (0243) 670326/670392
Residential and non-residential courses; two-level weekly courses in upholstery, furniture, canework and china restoration. Some facilities for the disabled.

ELMBRIDGE ADULT EDUCATION CENTRE
19 The Green
Esher, Surrey
Tel: Esher 65374
Residential and non-residential courses all year for mothers and children in canework, basketry, china restoration, stained glass.

FLATFORD MILL FIELD CENTRE
East Bergholt
Colchester, Essex
Tel: (0206) 298283
Residential and non-residential stained glass course from February to November.

HAGEN RESTORATIONS
Bakehouse Cottage
Northwood End
Haynes, Beds
Tel: (023 066) 424
Courses in furniture restoration.

MISSENDEN ABBEY ADULT EDUCATION CENTRE
Missenden Abbey
Great Missenden, Bucks
Tel: (02406) 2328
Residential and non-residential year-long courses in woodcarving, plus weekly and bi-weekly summer courses in basket and cane work, bookbinding, china painting, furniture and upholstery restoration and porcelain restoration. Also weekly and bi-weekly courses in August on furniture restoration, cane and basket weaving, china painting, bookbinding, and upholstery renovation.

THE OLD RECTORY
Fittleworth
Pulborough, Sussex
Tel: (079 882) 306
Residential and non-residential courses all year in bookbinding, china painting, stained glass and furniture restoration.

THE ORTON TRUST
82 The Walk
Potters Bar, Herts
Tel: Potters Bar 42716
Residential course in gilding and restoration of furniture.

PORCELAIN ART GALLERY
Brook Street
Bishops Waltham, Southampton, Hants
Tel: (048 93) 5409
China painting course.

SCHOOL OF PRINTING
Colchester Institute
Sheepen Road
Colchester, Essex CO3 3LL
Tel: (0206) 70271
Two-year course in book conservation.

WEST DEAN COLLEGE
West Dean
Nr Chichester, Sussex
Tel: (024 363) 301
One and two year Advanced Diploma courses for experienced craftspeople in the conservation and restoration of furniture, clocks and ceramics, run in conjunction with the British Antique Dealer's Association.

Below: The furniture restoration class, courtesy of the Earnley Concourse.

SOUTHWEST ENGLAND AND WALES

MRS BERYL BYRNE
Ty Croes
Brynsiencyn
Anglesey, Gwynedd, Wales
Tel: (024) 873 412
Private tuition in china restoration by arrangement.

DEVON CENTRE FOR FURTHUR EDUCATION
Dartington Hall
Totnes, Devon
Tel: (0803) 862 267
Residential and non-residential woodturning course.

DILLINGTON HOUSE COLLEGE
Ilminster, Somerset
Tel: (046 05) 2427
Residential and non-residential courses all year in china restoration.

THE ENGLISH LACE SCHOOL
c/o The Principal
Tiverton, Devon
Tel: Not Available
Short residential courses in care and preservation of lace, plus lace-making.

JANA STUART JONES
Old School
Stawell
Bridgwater, Somerset
Tel: (0278) 722023
One or two week courses in china restoration, with subsequent follow-up days for assessment purposes.

THE LONGHOUSE
Maxworthy Cross
North Petherwin
Launceston, Cornwall
Tel: (056 685) 322
Residential woodturning course.

NINA SKINNER
Lower Ford
Shebbear
Beaworthy, Devon
Tel: (040 928) 218
Residential canework courses from April to September.

STAFFORD HOUSE HOTEL
5 Cornhill
Ottery St Mary, Devon
Tel: (040 481) 2025
Residential, open-plan courses in woodturning and woodcarving.

TRI THY CRAFT CENTRE
Coed Talon
Nr Mold, Clwyd, Wales
Tel: (0352) 80359
Residential day and evening classes all year in canework.

MIDLANDS AND EAST ANGLIA

BELSTEAD HOUSE RESIDENTIAL CENTRE
Sprites Lane
Ipswich, Suffolk
Tel: (0473) 686321
Residential and non-residential courses all year in china painting.

FOR A MAP OF THE BRITISH ISLES, SEE PAGE 7.

HORNCASTLE RESIDENTIAL COLLEGE
Mareham Road
Horncastle, Lincs
Tel: (06582) 2449
Residential course in woodcarving.

LINCOLNSHIRE COLLEGE OF ART
Lindum Road
Lincoln, Lincs
Tel: (0522) 23268
Vocational two-year course in conservation and restoration with areas of specializations including bookbinding, paper restoration, gilding, lace- and replica-making.

MALVERN HILLS COLLEGE
Albert Road North
Great Malvern, Heref & Worcs
Tel: (068 45) 65351
Non-residential courses all year in bookbinding, canework, basketry.

SUSAN NOEL
The Studio
Hopton Hall
Gt Yarmouth, Norfolk
Tel: (0502) 730576
Courses in restoration of pottery and porcelain.

THE ORTON TRUST
High Street
Brigstock
Kettering, Northants
Tel: (053 673) 253
National centre for the training of stonemasons with weekend courses in restoration, maintenance, monumental carving and gilding.

NORTH OF ENGLAND AND SCOTLAND

BURTON MANOR COLLEGE
Burton
South Wirral, Cheshire
Tel: (051 331) 2262
Residential and non-residential course in china painting.

CRAFT SUPPLIES
The Mill
Millers Dale
Buxton, Derbs
Tel: (0298) 871636
Residential woodturning course.

LEEDS POLYTECHNIC
Becket Park
Leeds, Yorkshire
Tel: Not Available
Residential summer courses in canework and basketry.

Please note that although the manufacturers and suppliers in this section are scattered around the country, most have a mail order service.

LONDON

ARDENBRITE PRODUCTS LTD
57 Farringdon Road
London EC1M 3JH
Tel: (01) 405 2487
Manufacturers of ARDENBRITE metallic paints in fourteen shiny or matte shades including Pewter Grey, Gun Metal, Light and Dark Copper. Often used where the cost of gold or silver leaf is prohibitive, e.g. on large architectural restorations or where the surface of an object is badly corroded or damaged. The paints should not be used where the monetary value of an object would be reduced.

Below: New plaster cast for an original Victorian bust, painted with "Antique Gold", courtesy of Ardenbrite Products Ltd.

J.T. BATCHELOR
146 Fleet Road
London NW3 2RH
Tel: (01) 267 0593
Reputedly Europe's largest brass buckle wholesalers, they also supply leatherworking tools such as stamps, cutters and gouges, plus a leather stainer – "Fiebings Antique Finish" and four other finishers plus carnauba cream, a restorative. Also supply leather including vegetable-tanned cowhides, reject sides, dark green upholstery hide, and aniline leather dyes in 10 shades. Mail order.

J. D. BEARDMORE AND COMPANY
3/5 Percy Street
London W1P OEJ
Tel: (01) 637 7041
Retailers with enormous well-displayed selection of cabinet fittings, mostly in solid brass.

DISTINCTIVE TRIMMINGS COMPANY LTD
17 Kensington Church Street
London W8 4LF
Tel: (01) 937 6174
and
11 Marylebone Lane
London W1M 5FE
Tel: (01) 486 6456
Specialist suppliers of furnishing trimmings including upholstery in 27 shades, tiffany or trellis-headed fringes, key and bolster tassels, gimps, braids and ruches. Will send samples upon receipt of a fabric cutting, an idea of the type of trimming required and S.A.E.

THE EATON BAG COMPANY LTD
16 Manette Street
London W1V 5LB
Tel: (01) 437 9391
Selection of whole and split canes, natural grass, raffia, palm and woven cane matting, various diameters of bamboo. S.A.E. for information and samples.

THE ENAMEL SHOP
Craft O'Hans
21 Macklin Street
London WC2
Tel: (01) 242 7053
Distributors of German, American and British equipment and materials for enamelling including enamels in dozens of colours and textures. Mail order.

GARNER AND MARNEY LTD
41/43 Southgate Road
London N1
Tel: (01) 226 1535
Replacement parts for longcase, lantern, bracket and skeleton clocks and clock faces plus part of mercurial and aneroid barometers. Mail order.

A.S. HANDOVER LTD
Angel Yard
Highgate High Street
London N6 5JU
Tel: (01) 340 0665
Brush manufacturers with unusual selection such as lacquer brushes, French polisher's mops, gilder's tips and sable artist's brushes, as well as gold leaf. Mail order. See overleaf for illustration.

HEIRLOOM EMBROIDERY
9 Burnley Road
London NW10 1DY
Tel: (01) 452 0091/2

Below: A selection of trimmings, courtesy of Distinctive Trimmings Company Ltd.

HEIRLOOM EMBROIDERY (CON'T)
Sole distributors of the Danish Handicraft Guild products including pure cotton thread dyed to match vegetable and plant shades, even-weave linen thread 18 to 30 threads to the inch, and Swedish linen threads and lace yarns. Mail order.

LEAD AND LIGHT
15 Camden Lock
Commercial Place
London NW1 8AF
Tel: (01) 485 4568
Suppliers of materials for the manufacture or restoration of stained glass including tools, fittings, fluxes, lead canes and six types of opal, cathedral and semi-antique tint glass. Mail order.

THE PATCHWORK DOG AND THE CALICO CAT LTD
21 Chalk Farm Road
London NW1
Tel: (01) 485 1239
Patchwork and quilting supplies including templates, fabrics, wadding, hoops, frames, thread, needles, patterns and reference books. Mail order.

PICREATOR ENTERPRISES LTD
44 Park View Gardens
London NW4 2PN
Tel: (01) 202 8972
Manufacturers of micro-crystalline RENAISSANCE wax polish, produced by special authority of the British Musem. Its advantage is that it is acid free and will therefore remain neutral. May be used on wood, metal, marble, onyx, shell, stone, ivory leather, paper and even plastics. It neither stains nor discolours and has high moisture resistance. The firm also makes GROOMSTICK, a non-abrasive, non-staining paper cleaner, a leather reviver and several other conservation and restoration chemicals and supplies. Mail order.

R.E. ROSE F.B.H.I.
731 Sidcup Road
London SE9
Tel: (01) 859 4754
Material and supplies for restoration of clocks and barometers, including silvering powder, brass castings and lacquers. Mail order.

Below: Selection of picture frames, courtesy of John Tanous Ltd.

JOHN TANOUS LTD
115 Harwood Road
London SW6
Tel: (01) 736 1142
Specialists in reproduction picture frames with over 250 patterns in stock. Will also mould to match client's damaged frame.

TAYLOR AND COMPANY LTD
54 Old Street
London EC1V 9AL
Tel: (01) 253 2592/3319
Manufacturer of rolls and stamps for gold leaf leather tooling with 193 designs for centre and corner tools, and 141 designs for edging rules, plus special finishing tools with wood handles for amateurs. Mail order.

TURNBRIDGES LTD
72 Longley Road
London SW17
Tel: (01) 672 6581
Manufacturers of JOY paint products including heatproof stove black, flat black for wrought iron, French polish, gold size, knotting compound, furniture scratch dressing, raw and boiled linseed oils, teak oil, metal lacquer, shellac, terebine, 18 enamel paints and "Plastic Wood", as well as "Plastic Metal".

Below: A selection of designs for decorative gold-tooled borders, courtesy of Taylor and Company Ltd.

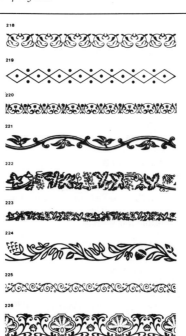

Above: Gilder's tip of 100% finest pure badger, courtesy of A.S. Handover Ltd.

CHRISTOPHER WRAY'S LIGHTING EMPORIUM
600 King's Road
London SW6
Tel: (01) 736 8434
Replacement parts for oil, gas and electric lamps including wicks, chimneys, galleries and over 500 different glass lamp shades.

SOUTH AND SOUTHEAST ENGLAND

ART NEEDLEWORK INDUSTRIES LTD
7 St Michael's Mansions
Ship Street
Oxford, Oxon OX1 3DG
Tel: Not Available
Authentic shades in crewel wool for rug and tapestry restoration plus cottons, linens and cotonperle. Mail order.

Below: A ramose, facsimile of the prototype of the Virgin's Veil from Cairo, 1405 BC., courtesy of Art Needlework Industries.

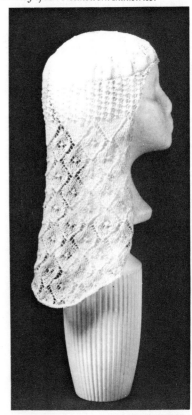

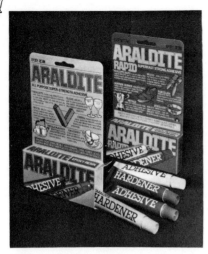

Above: ARALDITE standard or rapid epoxy resin adhesives, courtesy of Ciba-Geigy Plastics and Additives Company.

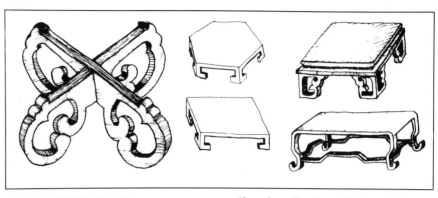

J.W. BOLLOM AND COMPANY LTD
P.O. Box 78
Beckenham, Kent BR3 4BL
Tel: (01) 658 2299
Manufacturers of dozens of special products for restoration purposes including button polish, piano polish, seven spray polishes and a spray lacquer, four sealers, nineteen spirit varnishes including two true shellacs, nine oil varnishes plus beeswax, paraffin wax, carnauba wax and a dewaxing solution. In addition, they also have three commercial wax polishes – "Briwax" in clear and six other shades specifically for pine and oak; "Sheradale" in dark and light shades; and "Harracks" a general purpose wax in light, medium or dark. For amateur French polishers, there's "Mr Flack's French Polishing Kit" which is a comprehensive kit plus a 40 page booklet on the care of antique furniture.

Below: "Liquid Sander" (left) and WOODPLAN range (right), courtesy of International Building Paints.

BOWDEN WOODCRAFT
Viables Centre
Harrow Way
Basingstoke, Hants
Tel: (0256) 21200/52847
Wood veneers and veneering supplies.

CIBA-GEIGY PLASTICS AND ADDITIVES COMPANY
Duxford, Cambridge, Cambs CB2 4QA
Tel: (0223) 832121
Manufacturers of ARALDITE epoxy resin, two-part adhesive for the repair of pottery, porcelain, glass and most rigid plastics. Joints made with ARALDITE will resist heat, corrosion and water.

D. FARMILOE
15 Kent Close
Bexhill-on-Sea, Sussex TN40 2LD
Tel: (0424) 214943
Manufacturers of TOUCH AND GO furniture refinishing kit containing 6 different shades of colour, a French polish, and shades of wax stopping for filling deep scratches and dents.

HENRY FLACK LTD
Borough Works
Croydon Road
Beckenham, Kent BR3 4BL
Tel: (01) 650 9171/6
and London showroom at
13 Theobalds Road
London WC1
Tel: (01) 242 0313
and Northern showroom at
40 Port Street
Manchester, Gt Manchester
Tel: (061) 236 7715

Above: Carved bowl stand (left), two display tables (right) and two brass article stands (centre), courtesy of the Lenham Import and Export Company. See overleaf.

HENRY FLACK LTD (CON'T)
Manufacturer of numerous refinishing products including 8 lacquers, 3 waxes and a dewaxing solution, "Harracks" wax polish, solvents, 19 spirit varnishes, 7 spray polishes, 9 oil varnishes including gold size, plus "Briwax", a furniture and woodwork wax in 5 shades.

LAURENCE J. GRAYER
Easter Cottage
Church Street
Bloxham, Banbury, Oxon
Tel: (0295) 720912
Restoration specialist with shop for related supplies on premises.

INTERNATIONAL BUILDING PAINTS
24/30 Canute Road
Southampton, Hants SO9 3AS
Tel: (0703) 37838
"Liquid Sander" for use on gloss-painted surfaces. Cleans off grease and keys old surface for repainting. WOODPLAN range has a timber preserver/protector, and 7 wood stains — pine, mahogany, teak, dark oak, mid oak, light oak and pine green, plus 2 varnishes — satin and gloss. For high-wear areas like floors, there is a two-part varnish and a yacht varnish. "Golden Wood Dressing" highlights the grain of lighter woods and dries to a durable finish, ideal for recently stripped furniture.

JACOBS, YOUNG AND WESTBURY LTD
Bridge Road
Haywards Heath, Sussex RH16 1TZ
Tel: (0444) 412411
Importers and suppliers of chair rushes, twisted seagrass cord and rattan canes for seating repairs. Additionally, hollow bamboo poles in all sizes and lengths.

THE LENHAM IMPORT AND EXPORT COMPANY
Ashdown House
16 Ashdown Avenue
Rottingdean, Sussex BN2 8AH
Tel: (0273) 33351
Hand-carved display stands for plates, saucers, cups, vases, eggs, bowls and fans in natural rosewood or a black finish. Also some brass, acrylic and metal article stands. Mail order catalogue sent on receipt of S.A.E. See previous page for illustration.

THE ROPE SHOP
26 High Street
Emsworth, Hants PO10 7AW
Tel: (024 34) 2642
Suppliers of natural ropes, cords and threads in sisal, hemp, jute, manila, coir, cotton and flax. Mail order.

TAMAR ANTIQUES RESTORATION
Tutwell House
Tutwell, Stoke Climsland
Callington, Cornwall
Tel: (057 97) 629
Mail order cabinet fittings and leather-lining supplies.

WEAVES AND WAXES
53 Church Street
Bloxham, Banbury, Oxon OX15 4ET
Tel: (0295) 721535
Shop and mail order service with very comprehensive range of chemicals and products for the professional conservation and restoration of furniture including specialist brushes, touch-up filler sticks, green baize, garnet paper, leather skivers in 6 shades, several polishes and waxes plus veneers, inlay bandings, stringings, upholstery supplies and chair canes in 6 weights. Also supplies brass polished handles in 30 styles, most in several sizes. Fittings can also be made to order.

Below: Brass cabinet handles in six styles, part of a larger selection courtesy of Weaves and Waxes.

Above: A selection of cabinet handles and pulls in the ANTIQUE range, courtesy of B. Lilly and Sons Ltd.

SOUTHWEST ENGLAND AND WALES

CUPRINOL LTD
Adderwell
Frome, Somerset BA11 1NL
Tel: (0373) 5151
Manufacturers of CUPRINOL products including a wood preserver in clear, light or dark oak finishes, a woodworm killer and "Transcolour" preservative stain in 14 shades.

GASTRELL HOUSE
33 Long Street
Tetbury, Glos GL8 8AA
Brass cabinet fittings.

E. PARSONS AND SON LTD
Blackfriars Road
Nailsea, Bristol, Avon BS19 2BU
Tel: (027 55) 4911
Manufacturers of primers for wood and metal, four varnishes including copal and yacht, five French polishes, black spirit enamel for stove renovation plus wood dye in ten shades — Light Oak, Medium Oak, Dark Oak, Mahogany, Walnut, Teak, Dark Jacobean, Spanish Mahogany and English Oak and Cedar. Information sheets on many of the products also available.

MIDLANDS AND EAST ANGLIA
THE ART VENEERS COMPANY LTD
Industrial Estate
Mildenhall, Suffolk IP28 7AY
Tel: (0638) 712550
Mail order veneer specialist with 60 different cabinet and marquetry veneers, including curled and burred woods, plus inlay bandings, motifs and stringing, brass cabinet fittings, marquetry and veneering tools, and gold-tooled cowhide for table top lining. Mail order samples of veneers available.

LEONARD BALL
44 Market Street
Lutterworth, Leics
Tel: (045 55) 4942
Suppliers and cast brass bezels, handmade clock hands, wooden frets and wooden mouldings in oak, pine, Brazilian mahogany and African walnut for cabinet fittings and restoration materials, including hard-to-find items like beeswax and pumice power and the old-fashioned "scumbles" oil stain.

A. BELL AND COMPANY LTD
Kingsthorpe
Northampton, Northants
Tel: (0604) 712505
Manufacturers of a cleaner, polish and sealer for marble and stone, plus a touch-up kit.

BOSTIK LTD
Consumer Products Division
Ulverscroft Road
Leicester, Leics LE4 6BW
Tel: (0533) 50015
Manufacturers of "8" woodworking adhesive, water soluble while wet but dries clear.

I. AND J. BROWN
58 Commercial Road
Hereford, Heref & Worcs HE1 2BP
Tel: (0432) 58895
Restorers of rushed seating who will also supply rushes.

G.K. HADFIELD
Black Brook Hill House
Ticklow Lane
Shepshed, Longborough, Leics
Tel: (050 95) 3014
English-made parts for restoration of clocks including bells, keys, springs, pins, chains, lines, pendulums, rods, bobs, suspensions, barometer parts, spandrels, dials, wooden finials, hands, tools, cleaning preparations, weights, and Vienna case ornaments. Mail order catalogue available.

HARRISON BEACON LTD
Bradford Street
Birmingham, W Midlands B12 OPE
Tel: (021) 773 1111
Manufacturers of brass cabinet fittings including hinges, card frames, drugget and upholstery pins.

B. LILLY AND SONS LTD
Baltimore Road
Birmingham, W Midlands B42 1DJ
Tel: (021) 357 1761
Manufacturers of reproduction ANTIQUE range of cabinet fittings in polished and relief brass finishes.

NORTH HEIGHAM SAWMILLS
Paddock Street
Norwich, Norfolk NR2 4TW
Tel: (0603) 22978
Air- and kiln-dried beech, box, cedar, ebony, kingwood, laburnum, mahogany, lime, maple,

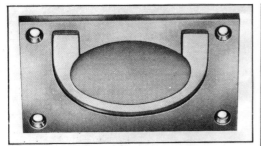

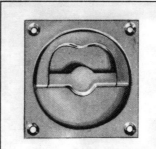

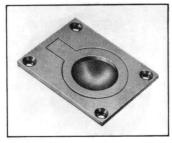

Above: Four styles of flush handles, courtesy of Perkins and Powell Ltd.

Above: A selection of products courtesy of Horological Solvents Ltd.

NORTH HEIGHAM SAWMILLS
oak, olivewood, reosewood, satinwood, tulip wood, walnut and yew.

PERKINS AND POWELL LTD
Cobden Works
Leopold Street
Birmingham, W Midlands B12 OUJ
Tel: (021) 772 2306
Manufacturers of builder's and marine brassware, including fittings ideal for campaign chest restoration such as the flush handles in four styles and in four finishes including traditional polished brass. Also useful is the strap hinge in three sizes.

SILKEN STRANDS
33 Linksway
Gatley, Cheadle, Cheshire SK8 4LA
Tel: (061 428) 9018
Rayon threads and cords in hundreds of colours, linen and cotton natural-textured yarns, 20 types of metallic threads and cords, plus extra fine wire, snake skins, gold and silver kidskin, natural and dyed feathers, gold, silver, pearl and tinted glass beads, and 5 types of sequins. Mail order list and samples available.

K.J. TRAYLER
Fir Close
Frostenden
Wangford, Suffolk
Tel: (050 278) 261
Suppliers of canes, sea grass and rushes.

NORTH OF ENGLAND AND SCOTLAND

JOHN BODDY AND SON LTD
Riverside Sawmills
Boroughbridge, N Yorkshire YO5 9LJ
Tel: (09012) 2370
Kiln-dried, air-dried and fresh sawn prime British hardwoods; specialising in oak, ash, sycamore, beech, sweet chestnut, lime, yew, cherry and walnut, plus oak or elm beams up to 30 ft.

JAMES BRIGGS AND SONS LTD
Lion Works
Old Market Street
Manchester, Gt Manchester M9 3DU
Tel:(061) 795 8410
Manufacturers of ANTIQUAX products including a furniture polish in wax or aerosol form, a wood food for new or untreated wood surfaces and for use under the furniture wax; a teak oil, a furniture cleaner for removing the build-up of grease and old polish plus a neutral leather food, a leather cream for hide and vinyl, a simulated chamois from 100% cotton for cleaning silver and glass, silver and copper or brass polishes, a silver mitt for facilitating silver polishing, an anti-tarnish lacquer for metals once the desired lustre has been achieved and a glass cleaner for porcelain, glass and mirrors.

CONSTRUCTION AND ENGINEERING COMPANY LTD
Faraway House
Pygons Hill Lane
Lydiate, Merseyside L31 4AE
Tel: (051 531) 9490
Manufacturers of "Patinex" wood-stripping system, a non-caustic and harmless solution which does not affect the colour of the wood surface.

HOROLOGICAL SOLVENTS LTD
Proctor Street
Bury, Lancs
Tel: (061) 764 2741
Retail and mail order suppliers with full range of products for cabinet-makers, and furniture restorers, but specialising in chemicals for the clock restorer.

KASHA CRAFT
37 Armroyd Lane
Elsecar, Barnsley, S Yorkshire
Tel: (0226) 747424
Suppliers of cathedral and opalescent glass plus bevels and glass-working tools. Mail order and deliver throughout the U.K.

Right: Plate stand in black and clear plastic (top); spoon rack in darkwood finish (centre); and cup and saucer stand in black or clear plastic (bottom), courtesy of the Leeds Display Stand Company Ltd.

THE LEEDS DISPLAY STAND COMPANY LTD
David Street
Leeds, Yorks LS11 9AQ
Tel: (0532) 458067
Comprehensive range of display stands for the dealer or collector in clear or black plastic for plates, cups and saucers, bowls and figurines. Additionally plate wires in four sizes for wall mounting and three display cabinets in darkwood or pine finish for miniatures, spoons or thimbles.

GRAHAM OXLEY TRADE TOOLS LTD
London Works
Bridge Street
Sheffield, S Yorkshire S3 8NT
Tel: (0742) 24659
Manufacturers of carpenter's and cabinet-maker's tools including a large selection of chisels, gouges, and gauges.

STANLEY TOOLS LTD

Woodside,
Sheffield, S Yorkshire S3 9PD
Tel: (0742) 78678
Comprehensive range of carpenter's and cabinet-maker's tools and spare parts.

STERLING RONCRAFT

Chapeltown
Sheffield, S Yorkshire S30 4YP
Tel: Ecclesfield 3171
RONSEAL wood preservatives in four wood colours (honey brown, nut brown, dark brown, and charcoal) and a clear finish. Designed for preservation and protection of wooden garden furniture and ornaments, containing a biocide, resins and waxes.

KURUST metal treatment products of two types: Double-Action which kills rust and primes ready for painting and Kurust jelly which dissolves rust on chrome and bare metal.

COLRON refinishing range designed for amateur use including a restorer and cleaner for removing old finishes, a wood reviver which nourishes the wood, a liquid wax in three shades for light, medium and dark woods and a finishing wax from beeswax and carnauba wax.

To remove layers of paint or varnish in one application, there is ''Peel-Off Ronstrip'', a powder which is mixed with water for easy removal of painted finishes. Not recommended for oak, hemlock or iroko.

UNIVERSAL STAINER is suitable for tinting all types of paints including varnishes and wood stains, except gloss emulsions, and is ideal for achieving the perfect shade when applying a textured painted finish.

Available in yellow, orange, red, blue, black, ochre, burnt sienna, burnt umber, green and purple.

COLRON WOOD DYES in 9 natural wood shades: Georgian medium oak, English light oak, Peruvian mahogany, Canadian cedar, American walnut, Burmese teak, Jacobean dark oak, Tudor black oak and Indian rosewood.

VANDERVILLES LEATHER LINING

47 High Street
Nantwich, Cheshire
Tel: (0270) 65996
Supplies goatskin skivers or liners for desk and table tops in a wide choice of colours, with optional gold tooling, and button polishing.

Above: COLRON refinishing range comprising four products, courtesy of Sterling Roncraft.

WOODFIT LTD

Whittle Low Mill
Chorley, Lancs PR6 7HB
Tel: (025 72) 66421
Extremely comprehensive selection of cabinet and furniture fittings including brass or nickel piano hinges up to 33" (84cm), brass snake hinges, table hinges, beech dowels in 4 sizes, mirror fittings, antique bronzed handles, gold-plated handles, and 5 styles of wooden knobs. Mail order catalogue available.

EARNEST WRIGHT AND SON LTD

Kutrite Works
Smithfield, Sheffield S Yorkshire S3 7AR
Tel: (0742) 21915/21620
Manufacturers of specialist tools, including lampwick scissors, carpet scissors, palette knives, shavehook and cabinet-maker's tools.

REPUBLIC OF IRELAND

ECOTECH LTD

Crocodile Crafts
Lodge Road
Westport, Mayo, Rep of Ireland
Tel: Westport 548
Leather-matching service upon receipt of sample swatch plus suppliers of upholstery leather and table top inlays. Also, embossing tools and gold foil and upholsterer's tools as well as unusual supplies such as crocodile sealer and wax polish.

VALLI AND COLOMBO LTD

Cookstown Industrial Estate
Belgard Road
Tallaght, Co Dublin, Ireland
Tel: (01) 514633
From a comprehensive and beautiful range of cabinet fittings, six in brass suitable for antiques: ''Castiglia'', Louis XV, Louis XVI, Lorena, Medicea and Gaudia.

Below: Three wardrobehooks in ''gilt'' brass, from the Castiglia range, courtesy of Valli and Colombo Ltd.

Below: Selection of solid brass handles (left) and ''antique'' bronze handles (right), courtesy of Woodfit Ltd.

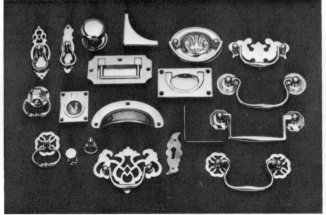

ARMS, ARMOUR AND MILITARIA

Please note that while we hope to have included most of the major specialist collections in museums, galleries and a few National Trust or privately-owned properties, for reasons of space we have not included all the houses open to the public. For further information, the reader is referred to the current National Trust handbook available from the Trust at 42 Queen Anne's Gate, London SW1; and ''Historic Houses, Castles and Gardens'', from ABC Publications, World Timetable Centre, Church Street, Dunstable, Beds. When referring to opening times, the reader is advised to phone beforehand for confirmation, as cuts in the national arts budget have forced some museums and collections to adopt shorter working hours.

LONDON

THE ARMOURIES
H.M. Tower of London
London EC3
Tel: (01) 709 0765
Open Mar 1-Oct 31, Mon–Sat 9.30–5; Mar 2-Oct 26, Sun 2–5; Nov 1-Feb 28, Mon–Sat 9.30–4.

Outstanding collection of arms and armour.

ARTILLERY MUSEUM
The Rotunda
Repository Road
Woolwich, London SE18
Tel: (01) 856 5533 and 854 2424
Open summer Mon–Fri 12–5, Sat, Sun 1–5; winter closes at 4.

Well-arranged, comprehensive display of armaments and munitions from 14th c. to present day.

IMPERIAL WAR MUSEUM
Lambeth Road
London SE1
Tel: (01) 735 8922
Open Mon–Sat 10–5.50, Sun 2–5.50; closed Dec 24, 25, 26, Jan 1, Good Fri.

Models, tanks and armaments plus vast archive material.

NATIONAL ARMY MUSEUM
Royal Hospital Road
London SW3
Tel: (01) 730 0717
Open Mon–Sat 10–5.30, Sun 2–5.30; closed Dec 24, 25, 26, Jan 1, Good Fri.

Outstanding collection of medals; also archives and study centre.

NATIONAL MARITIME MUSEUM
Romney Road
Greenwich, London SE10
Tel: (01) 858 4422
Open summer Mon–Sat 10–6, Sun 2.30–6; winter Mon–Fri 10–5, Sun 2.30–6; closed Dec 24, 25, 26, Jan 1, Good Fri.

Superb display of British maritime history including medals, paintings, navigational instruments, Nelson's uniforms and Cutty Sark nearby.

SOUTH AND SOUTHEAST ENGLAND

GURKHA BRIGADE MUSEUM
Queen Elizabeth Barracks
Church Crookham, Aldershot, Hants
Tel: (02514) 3541, ext 63
Open Mon–Fri 9.45–4.30.

Gurkha weapons and medals from 1818 onwards.

Above: Suit of armour made for Henry VIII in the Royal Workshops at Greenwich in 1540, courtesy of The Armouries at H.M. Tower of London.

MUSEUM OF THE ROYAL SUSSEX REGIMENT, CHICHESTER DISTRICT MUSEUM
29 Little London
Chichester, W Sussex
Tel: (0243) 784683
Open Apr 1–Sep 30, Tue–Sat 10–6; Oct 1–Mar 31, Tue–Sat 10–5.

Regiment's decorations and battle honours.

PORTSMOUTH ROYAL NAVAL MUSEUM
H.M. Naval Base
Portsmouth, Hants
Tel: (0705) 22351, ext 23868
Open Mar–Oct, Mon–Sat 10.30–5.30, Sun 1–5; Nov–Feb, Mon–Sat 10.30–4.30, Sun 1–4.30; closed Dec 25, 26, Jan 1.

Nelson memorabilia, ship models, tools and figureheads.

SOUTHSEA CASTLE
Clarence Esplanade
Southsea, Portsmouth, Hants
Tel: (0705) 24584
Open daily 10.30–5.30.

Portsmouth's naval and military history; also exhibit of salvage and preservation of ''Mary Rose'', Henry VIII's flagship.

SUSSEX COMBINED SERVICES MUSEUM
The Redoubt
Royal Parade
Eastbourne, E Sussex
Tel: (0323) 35809
Open Easter–Oct 15, daily 10–5.

Sussex military history since Romans.

WARNHAM WAR MUSEUM
Durfold Hill
Warnham, nr Horsham, W Sussex
Tel: (0403) 65607
Open daily Mar 2–Sep 30 10–6; Oct 1–Mar 1 10–4.30.

Large collection of World War I weapons, uniforms and medals.

SOUTHWEST ENGLAND AND WALES

COTEHELE
Calstock, Cornwall
Tel: (0579) 50434
Open daily Apr 1–Oct 31 on 11–6.

Collection of armour and other items in mediaeval manor house (National Trust).

SNOWSHILL MANOR
Broadway, Glos
Tel: (0386) 852410
Open Apr and Oct Sat, Sun and Bank Hol Mon 11–1, 2–6; closed Good Fri; May-end Sep, Wed–Sun and Bank Hol Mon 11–1, 2–6.

Good collection of Japanese armour.

NORTH OF ENGLAND AND SCOTLAND

DURHAM LIGHT INFANTRY MUSEUM
Aykley Heads
Durham, Co Durham
Tel: (0385) 2214
Open Tue–Sat 10–5, Sun 2–5.
Treasures of Durham Light Infantry from 18th c. to 1968.

ARGYLL AND SUTHERLAND HIGHLANDERS MUSEUM
Stirling Castle
Stirling, Central, Scotland
Tel: (0786 2356)
Open Apr–Sept, Mon–Fri, 10–5.30.
Relics from Indian Mutiny and Battle of Balaclava.

BRITISH IN INDIA MUSEUM
Sun Street
Colne, Lancs
Tel: (0282) 63129
Open May 1–Sep 30, Sat & Sun, 2–5.
Medals and belt-buckles among exhibits from the Raj's last days.

Below: Front view of the museum showing the 15-inch guns from the battleships ''Ramillies'' and ''Resolution'', courtesy of the Imperial War Museum.

CLOCKS AND WATCHES

LONDON

BRITISH MUSEUM
Great Russell Street
London WC1
Tel: (01) 636 1555
*Open Mon–Sat 10–5, Sun 2.30–6; closed
Dec 24, 25, 26, Jan 1, Good Fri.*
*History of mechanical time-keeping in
specially-designed gallery.*

NATIONAL MARITIME MUSEUM
(also in Royal Observatory)
Romney Road
London SE10
Tel: (01) 858 4422
*Open summer Mon–Sat 10–6, Sun 2.30–6;
winter Mon–Fri 10–5, Sun 2.30–6, Sat
10–6; closed Dec 23, 24, 25, Jan 1, Good Fri.*
*Precision time-keeping equipment and
comprehensive collection of navigational
instruments, including John Harrison's early
chronometers.*

SCIENCE MUSEUM
Exhibition Road
London SW7
Tel: (01) 589 3456
*Open Mon–Sat 10–6; Sun 2.30–6; closed
Dec 24, 25, 26, Jan 1, Good Fri, May 5.*
*Record of technical aspects of time-keeping up
to atomic clock.*

VICTORIA AND ALBERT MUSEUM
Cromwell Road
London SW7
Tel: (01) 589 6371
*Open Mon–Thur, Sat 10–5.50; Sun
2.30–5.50; closed Fri, Jan 1, May 1, Dec 24,
25, 26.*
*Fine collection chosen for decorative appeal as
well as historical value.*

WALLACE COLLECTION
Manchester square
London W1
Tel: (01) 935 0687
*Open Mon–Sat 10–5, Sun 2–5; closed Jan 1,
Good Fri, Dec 24, 25, 26.*
Intricately-veneered French clocks.

SOUTH AND SOUTHEAST ENGLAND

FITZWILLIAM MUSEUM
Trumpington Street
Cambridge, Cambs
Tel: (0223) 69501
*Open Tue–Sat, Lower Galleries 10–2, Upper
Galleries 2–5, Sun 2.15–5; open Bank Hol
Mons; closed Dec 24–Jan 1, Good Fri.
Advisable to check in advance that appropriate
gallery is open.*
*Fine clocks and highly decorative early
watches.*

MINORIES ART GALLERY
Colchester, Essex
Tel: (0206) 77067
Open Tue–Sat 11–5, Sun 2–6.
18th c. Colchester clocks.

**MUSEUM OF THE HISTORY OF
SCIENCE**
Broad Street
Oxford, Oxon
Tel: (0865) 43997
*Open Mon–Fri 10.30–1, 2.30–4; closed
Bank Hols and Christmas and Easter weeks.
Locally-made clocks and watches; magnificent
astrolabes.*

*Above: Keyless pocket watch made by the
Lancashire Watch Company, Prescot in 1904,
courtesy of the Prescot Museum of Clock- and
Watchmaking.*

WILLIS MUSEUM
New Street
Basingstoke, Hants
Tel: (0256) 65902
Open Tue–Sat 10–5; closed Sun, Mon.
*Local watchmaker's collection of 18th and 19th
c. watches and tools.*

SOUTHWEST ENGLAND AND WALES

**RED HOUSE MUSEUM AND ART
GALLERY**
Quay Road
Christchurch, Dorset
Tel: (0202) 482860
Open Tue–Sat 10–1, 2–5, Sun 2–5.
*Exhibit shows local industry making fusee
chain used in Verge watch movements'
mechanism.*

VICTORIA ART GALLERY
Bridge Street
Bath, Avon
Tel: (0225) 61111, ext 327/418
*Open Mon–Fri 10–6, Sat 10–5; closed Sun,
Bank Hols.*
Collection of clocks and watches.

MIDLANDS AND EAST ANGLIA

**BRIDEWELL MUSEUM OF LOCAL
INDUSTRIES AND LOCAL CRAFTS**
Bridewell Alley
Norwich, Norfolk
Tel: (0603) 611277
Open Mon–Sat 10–5.
*Exhibits illustrate clock-making as a local
industry.*

**JOHN GERSHOM-PARKINGTON
MEMORIAL COLLECTION**
Angel Corner
Bury St Edmunds, Suffolk
Tel: (0284) 63233
*Open daily Mar–Oct 10–1, 2–5; Nov–Feb
10–1, 2–4.*
*Outstanding collection with clocks by Quare,
Tompion, Knibb, Vulliamy et al. Also
watches, pocket sundials, etc.*

NEWARKE HOUSES MUSEUM
The Newarke
Leicester, Leics
Tel: (0533) 554100
*Open Mon–Sat 10–5.30, Sun 2–5.30; open
Bank Hols.*
*Interesting lantern and long-case clocks.
Reconstructed workshops of a local clockmaker
at nearby Castle View.*

USHER MUSEUM
Lindum Road
Lincoln, Lincs
Tel: (0522) 27980
Open Mon–Sat 10–5.30, Sun 2–5.
*Exquisite French and English watches, mostly
18th c.*

NORTH OF ENGLAND AND SCOTLAND

BOWES MUSEUM
Barnard Castle
Co Durham
Tel: (0833) 37139
*Open Mon–Sat 10–5.30 summer; 10–5 Oct,
Mar, Apr; 10–4 Nov–Feb; Sun 2–5 summer;
2–4 winter; closed Dec 25, 26, Jan 1.*
Watches feature among other objets d'art.

MERSEYSIDE COUNTY MUSEUMS
William Brown Street
Liverpool, Merseyside
Tel: (051) 207 0001
*Open Mon–Sat 10–5, Sun 2–5; closed Dec
24, 25, 26, Jan 1, Good Fri.*
*Gallery on "Time" displays tools and a
reconstructed workshop as well as timepieces.*

**PRESCOT MUSEUM OF CLOCK- AND
WATCHMAKING**
34 Church Street
Prescot
Liverpool, Merseyside
Tel: (051) 430 7787
*Open Tue–Sat 10–5, Sun 2–5; closed Mon,
Dec 24, 25, 26, Jan 1, Good Fri.*
*Museum devoted to S. Lancs clock- and
watchmaking industries.*

LONDON

BRITISH MUSEUM
Great Russell Street
London WC1
Tel: (01) 636 1555
Open Mon–Sat 10–5, Sun 2.30–6; closed Dec 24, 25, 26, Jan 1, May Day Bank Hol, Good Fri.

Vast collection of rare and valuable British and foreign coins.

SOUTH AND SOUTHEAST ENGLAND

ASHMOLEAN MUSEUM
Beaumont Street
Oxford, Oxon
Tel: (0865) 512651
Open Mon–Sat 10–4, Sun 2–4; closed Dec 24, 25, 26, Jan 1, Good Fri-Easter Sun, Mon and Tue after first Sun after Sep 2.

The Heberden coin room has largest and most important British collection after the British Museum's.

COLCHESTER AND ESSEX MUSEUM
The Castle
Colchester, Essex
Tel: (0206) 77457/76071
Open Mon–Sat 10–5 (Oct–Apr closes at 4 on Sat); Apr–Sep Sun 2.30–5.

Roman coins accompanied by information on people they portray.

FITZWILLIAM MUSEUM
Trumpington Street
Cambridge, Cambs
Tel: (0223) 69501
Open Tue–Sat, Lower Galleries 10–2, Upper Galleries 2–5, Sun 2.15–5; open Bank Hol Mons; closed Dec 24–Jan 1, Good Fri. Advisable to check in advance that appropriate gallery is open.

Important coin collection.

MIDLANDS AND EAST ANGLIA

ASSAY OFFICE
Birmingham, W Midlands
Tel: (021) 236 6951
Open by appointment only

18th and 19th c. coins, medals and tokens.

BIRMINGHAM MUSEUM AND ART GALLERY
Chamberlain Square
Birmingham, W Midlands
Tel: (021) 235 2834
Open Mon–Sat 10–5.30, Sun 2–5.30; closed Good Fri, Dec 24, 25, 26, Jan 1.

Department of Archaelogy and Ethnography collections of ancient and mediaeval coins, specialising in those struck locally.

USHER GALLERY
Lindum Road
Lincoln, Lincs
Tel: (0522) 27980
Open Mon–Sat 10–5.30, Sun 2–5.

Large collection of coins and medals.

NORTH OF ENGLAND AND SCOTLAND

MANCHESTER MUSEUM
University of Manchester
Oxford Road
Manchester, Gt Manchester
Tel: (061) 273 3333
Open Mon–Wed, Fri, Sat 10–5; Thur 10–9; closed Dec 24, 25, 26, Jan 1, Good Fri, May Day Bank hol.

Major collection of coins and medals.

HUNTERIAN MUSEUM
Glasgow University
Glasgow, Strathclyde, Scotland
Tel: (041) 339 8855, ext 221
Open Mon–Fri 9–5, Sat 9–12.

Important collection in Coin Cabinet.

COINS AND MEDALS

LONDON

MUSEUM OF LONDON
London Wall
London EC2
Tel: (01) 600 3699
Open Tue-Sat 10–6, Sun 2–6.

Unique Spence glove collection in costume galleries.

SOUTH AND SOUTHEAST ENGLAND

CECIL HIGGINS ART GALLERY
Castle Close
Bedford, Beds
Tel: (0234) 211222
Open Tue–Fri 12.30–5, Sat 11–5, Sun 2–5; Bank Hols 12.30–5.

Costume and lace collection.

LUTON MUSEUM AND ART GALLERY
Wardown Park
Luton, Beds
Tel: (0582) 36941/2
Open Mon–Sat 10–6, Sun 2–6; closes at 5, Oct 1–Mar 31; closed Dec 25, 26, Jan 1, Sun in Dec and Jan.

Costume and needlework accessories; the local straw hat and pillow lace industries are illustrated; reconstructed lacemaker's workroom.

WORTHING MUSEUM AND ART GALLERY
Chapel Road
Worthing, Sussex
Tel: (0903) 204226
Open Mon–Sat 10–7; Oct–Mar, 10–5.

Costume from 1740–1940.

SOUTHWEST ENGLAND AND WALES

THE AMERICAN MUSEUM
Claverton Manor
Bath, Avon
Tel: (0225) 63538/60503
Open Apr–Oct, Tue–Sun 2–5; Bank Hol Mons and preceding Suns 11–5; Nov–Mar by appointment; closed Jan.

Large collection of patchwork quilts is particularly interesting.

ARLINGTON COURT
Arlington
Nr Barnstaple, Devon
Tel: (0271) 82296
Open Apr 1–Oct 31, Tue–Sun 11–6.

Large collection of Victorian dresses.

BANGOR ART GALLERY AND MUSEUM OF WELSH ANTIQUITIES
Ffordd Gwynedd
Bangor, Gwynedd, Wales
Tel: (0248) 51151
Open Mon–Sat 10.30–4.30.

Costumes and samplers; also displays relating to textile manufacture.

BATH MUSEUM OF COSTUME
Assembly Rooms
Bennett Street
Bath, Avon
Tel: (0225) 61111
Open Apr 1–Sep 30, Mon–Sat 9.30–6, Sun 10–6; Oct 1–Mar 31, Mon–Sat 10–5, Sun 11–5.

Dress and accessories from 17 c. on.

BLAISE CASTLE HOUSE MUSEUM
Henbury
Bristol, Avon
Tel: (0272) 506789
Open Mon–Sat 2–5.

Costume figures in context; also changing exhibits on clothing.

KILLERTON HOUSE
Broadclyst
Nr Exeter, Devon
Tel: (039 288) 345
Open daily Apr–end Oct, 11–6.

The Paulise de Bush Collection of Costumes from 18 c. on, displayed in rooms furnished in period style.

FOR MAP OF THE BRITISH ISLES, SEE PAGE 7.

Left: Prosperous man's, woman's and child's fashions from 1830–1840, courtesy of the Museum of Costume, Bath.

COSTUME AND TEXTILES

ROYAL ALBERT MEMORIAL MUSEUM
Queen Street
Exeter, Devon
Tel: (0392) 56724
Open Tue–Sat 10–5.30.

Costumes and superb lace exhibits.

WELSH FOLK MUSEUM
St Fagans
Cardiff, S Glamorgan, Wales
Tel: (0222) 561357
Open Apr 1–Sep 30, Mon–Sat 10–6, Sun 2.30–6; Oct 1–Mar 31, Mon–Sat 10–5, Sun 2.30–5; closed Dec 24, 25, 26, Jan 1, May 5.

Major costume gallery.

MIDLANDS AND EAST ANGLIA

CENTRAL MUSEUM AND ART GALLERY
Guildhall Road
Northampton, Northants
Tel: (0604) 34881
Open Mon–Sat 10–6.

All kinds of footwear from the 17th c. onwards including Nijinsky's ballet slippers and Queen Victoria's wedding slippers.

MUSEUM OF COSTUME AND TEXTILES
51 Castlegate
Nottingham, Notts
Tel: (0602) 411881
Open daily 10–5; closed Dec 25.

17th c. costume embroidery; tapestries, lace, accessories and underwear from 1756–1950; Victorian costume in period rooms.

NOTTINGHAM MUSEUM OF COSTUME AND TEXTILES
Castlegate
Nottingham, Notts
Tel: (0602) 411881
Open daily 10–5.

Costumes and textiles, particularly lace; lace-making techniques through the ages; Middleton collection of rare 16th and 17th clothing.

STRANGERS HALL MUSEUM
Charing Cross
Norwich, Norfolk
Tel: (0603) 22233
Open Mon–Sat 10–5

Various themes from sporting gear to local shawls.

WYGSTON'S HOUSE MUSEUM OF COSTUME
25 St Nicholas Circle
Leicester, Leics
Tel: (0533) 554100
Open Mon–Sat 10–5.30, Sun 2–5.30; closed Dec 25, 26, Good Fri.
Costumes and three fascinating, reconstructed shop interiors from the 1920's.

NORTH OF ENGLAND AND SCOTLAND

BANKFIELD MUSEUM
Akroyd Park
Halifax, W Yorkshire
Tel: (0422) 54823
Open Mon–Sat 12–5, Sun 2.30–5.
British court costume and Royal robes from various countries.

THE BOWES MUSEUM
Barnard Castle
Co Durham
Tel: (0833) 37139
Open Mon–Sat 10–5.30 summer, 10–5 Oct, Mar, Apr; 10–4 Nov–Feb; Sun 2–5 summer, 2–4 winter; closed Dec 25, 26, Jan 1.

Servants' uniforms.

CASTLE HOWARD COSTUME GALLERIES
Castle Howard
York, N Yorkshire
Tel: (065 384) 333
Open daily Mar 25–Oct 31.

Domestic, military, ecclesiastical and theatrical costume from early 18th to early 20th c. including Diaghilev ballet costumes and Coronation robes.

CLIFFE CASTLE ART GALLERY AND MUSEUM
Keighley, W Yorkshire
Tel: (0535) 64184
Open daily 10–5; closed Dec 25, 26, Good Fri.

Costume displays and reconstructed workshops of a weaver and a shoemaker.

GALLERY OF ENGLISH COSTUME
Platt Hall
Platt Fields
Rusholme, Gt Manchester
Tel: (061) 224 5217
Open Mar–Oct, Mon–Sat 10–6, Sun 2–6; May–Aug, Sun 12–6; Nov–Feb, Mon–Sat 10–4, Sun 2–4.

Largest source of costumes outside London, with wide-ranging changing exhibits.

NATIONAL MUSEUM OF ANTIQUITIES
Queen Street
Edinburgh, Lothian, Scotland
Tel: (031) 556 8921
Open Mon–Sat 10–5, Sun 2–5.

Displays include history of knitting and tartans.

Below: Interior of Edwardian draper's shop with typically dressed "customers", courtesy of the Castle Howard Costume Galleries.

PAISLEY MUSEUM AND ART GALLERY
High Street
Paisley, Strathclyde, Scotland
Tel: (041 889) 3151
Open Mon–Fri 10–5, except Tue 10–8; Sat 10–6.
Finest collection of Paisley shawls in world; also looms, tools and design patterns.

ROCHDALE MUSEUM
Sparrow Hill
Rochdale, Gt Manchester
Tel: (0706) 47474
Open Tue–Sat 10.30–5.

Well-displayed costumes.

ROYAL SCOTTISH MUSEUM
Chambers Street
Edinburgh, Lothian, Scotland
Tel: (031) 225 7534
Open Mon–Sat 10–5, Sun 2–5.

Pre-20th c. clothes, with outstanding Chinese display.

THE WEST HIGHLAND MUSEUM
Cameron Square
Fort William, Highland, Scotland
Tel: (0397) 2169
Open mid–June to mid–Sep, Mon–Sat 9.30–9; rest of year Mon–Sat 9.30–1, 2–5.

Highland dress and history of the kilt.

WHITWORTH ART GALLERY
University of Manchester
Whitworth Park
Manchester, Gt Manchester
Tel: (061) 273 4865
Open Mon–Sat 10–5, Thur 10–9; closed Good Fri, May 5.

Outstanding textile collections from all over the world.

NORTHERN IRELAND

COMBINED IRISH CAVALRY REGIMENT'S MUSEUM
Carrickfergus Castle
Carrickfergus
Co Antrim, N Ireland
Tel: (023 83) 62273
Open weekdays 10–1, 2–6; winter closes 4.

Uniforms from Waterloo on.

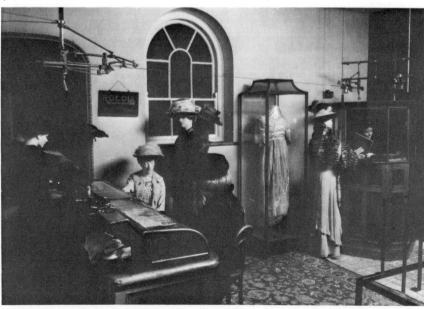

LONDON

BETHNAL GREEN MUSEUM OF CHILDHOOD
Cambridge Heath Road
London E2
Tel: (01) 980 2415
Open Mon–Thur 10–6, Sun 2.30–6; closed Fri, Dec 24, 25, 26, Jan 1, May 1, Good Fri.

Finest British collection of dolls and toys plus puppets, children's games, books and clothes.

LONDON TOY AND MODEL MUSEUM
October House
23 Craven Hill
London W2
Tel: (01) 262 7905
Open Mon–Fri 10–6, Sat 10–5, Sun 2–6.

Private museum devoted to railway models and mechanical toys, mainly pre-1914.

POLLOCK'S TOY MUSEUM
1 Scala Street
London W1
Tel: (01) 636 3452
Open Mon–Sat 10–5; closed Bank Hols.

Huge variety of toys from all over the world, from board games to teddy bears. Toy theatres a speciality.

SOUTH AND SOUTHEAST ENGLAND

THE HOLLY TREES
High Street
Colchester, Essex
Tel: (0206) 76071, ext 345
Open weekdays 10–1, 2–5; closes at 4 on Sat, Oct 1–Mar 1.

Room of cradles and toys in social history museum.

PRECINCT TOY COLLECTION
38 Harnet Street
Sandwich, Kent
Open Easter–end Sep, Mon–Sat 10–5, Sun 2–5; Oct, Sat, Sun only 2–5.

Doll's houses, Noah's Arks, dolls, clockwork toys, etc.

THE ROTUNDA
Grove House
44 Iffley Turn
Oxford, Oxon
Open Sun only May to mid-Sep 2.15–5.15; parties at other times by arrangement.

Early doll's houses and their contents.

UPPARK
South Harting, Petersfield
Hants
Tel: (073 085) 317/458
Open Apr 1–Sep 30, Wed, Thur, Sun, Bank Hol Mon 2–6.

Remarkable Queen Anne doll's house in 18th c. National Trust country house.

SOUTHWEST ENGLAND AND WALES

BURROWS TOY MUSEUM
York Street
Bath, Avon
Tel: (0225) 61819
Open daily 10–5.30 (ex Dec 25, 26).

Well displayed playthings including dolls, doll's houses, toys and games from 18th c. onwards.

MUSEUM OF CHILDHOOD
Water Street
Menai Bridge, Anglesey,
Gwynedd, Wales
Tel: (0248) 712001
Open Easter–Oct 31, Mon–Sat 10–5.30, Sun 1–5.

Impressive collection of toys and pastimes including dolls, clockwork toys, trains, cars, money boxes and magic lanterns.

PENRHYN CASTLE
Bangor
Gwynedd, Wales
Tel: (0248) 53084
Open daily Apr, May, Oct, 2–5; June–Sep 11–5.

Dolls from many countries.

FOR MAP OF THE BRITISH ISLES, SEE PAGE 7.

SOMERSET COUNTY MUSEUM
Taunton Castle
Castle Green
Taunton, Somerset
Tel: (0823) 3451, ext 286
Open Apr 1–Sep 30, Mon–Sat 10–5; Oct 1–Mar 31, Tue–Sat 10–5.

Museum with good collection of dolls.

MIDLANDS AND EAST ANGLIA

HEREFORD AND WORCESTER COUNTY MUSEUM
Hartlebury Castle
Hartlebury, nr Kidderminster
Heref & Worcs
Tel: (0299) 250416
Open Feb 1–Nov 30, Mon–Thur 10–5, Sat–Sun 2–5.
Children's gallery with Edwardian toys and dolls.

MUSEUM OF CHILDHOOD AND GILLOW MUSEUM
Judges' Lodgings
Church Street
Lancaster, Lancs
Tel: (0524) 2808
Open Apr–Oct, Mon–Fri 2–5; May–end June, Mon–Sat 2–5; July–end Sep, Mon–Fri 10–1, Sat 2–5.

Exhibits showing different aspects of children's life in the past; excellent doll collection.

PLAYTHINGS PAST MUSEUM
Beaconwood
Beacon Lane, Rednal,
Nr Birmingham, W Midlands
Tel: (021 453) 2006
Open by appointment.

Splendid collection of clockwork toys and also non-mechanical items.

NORTH OF ENGLAND AND SCOTLAND

CLIFFE CASTLE ART GALLERY AND MUSEUM
Keighley, W Yorkshire
Tel: (0535) 64184
Open daily 10–5 (ex Dec 25, 26, Good Fri).

Toy displays, well laid out for children.

MUSEUM OF CHILDHOOD
38 High Street
Edinburgh, Scotland
Tel: (031) 556 5447
Open Mon–Sat, June–Sept, 10–6; Oct–May 10–5.

Toys and dolls from many countries and periods, including unusual Lovett collection of toys from London slums.

SUDBURY HALL MUSEUM
Sudbury, Derbs
Tel: (028 378) 305
Open Apr 1–Oct 31, Wed–Sun 1–5.30.

Interesting exhibition showing life in Edwardian nursery.

Left: "Darktown Battery", a mechanical money box baseball game, made in 1888. The pitcher throws the coin, the batter raises his bat, and the money disappears into the crouching catcher, courtesy of the Museum of Childhood, Menai, Anglesey.

FURNITURE

LONDON

GEFFRYE MUSEUM
Kingsland Road
Shoreditch
London E2
Tel: (01) 739 8368
Open Tue–Sat 10–5, Sun 2–5; closed Mon (except Bank Hols), Dec 25, 26, Good Fri.

Display of period rooms showing development of English home from 1600 to 1930.

KENWOOD, THE IVEAGH BEQUEST
Hampstead Lane
London NW3
Tel: (01) 348 1286/7
Open daily 10–5 or dusk; closed Dec 24, 25, Good Fri.

Mainly 18th c. furniture.

LEIGHTON HOUSE ART GALLERY AND MUSEUM
12 Holland Park Road
London W14
Tel: (01) 602 3316
Open Mon–Sat 11–5; closed Dec 25, 26, Bank Hols.

Home of the Victorian painter, Lord Leighton, with period rooms of Victorian furniture.

LINLEY SAMBOURNE HOUSE
18 Stafford Terrace
London W8
Phone for appointment: The Victorian Society (01) 994 1019
Open by appointment Wed 10–4, Sun 2–5.

Unique late Victorian interior.

VICTORIA AND ALBERT MUSEUM
Cromwell Road
London SW7
Tel: (01) 589 6371
Open Mon–Thur, Sat 10–5.50, Sun 2.30–5.50; closed Fri, Dec 24, 25, 26, Jan 1, Good Fri, May Day Bank Hol.

Fine furniture of every period.

Below: The dining room with walls covered with William Morris wallpaper; the frieze is imitation gilt leather, the ceiling hung with stamped gilt paper, while the collection of blue-and-white porcelain and photographs occupy the remaining space, courtesy of The Victorian Society, Linley Sambourne House.

Above: Gilded armchair carved with dolphins from a set of six armchairs and six sidechairs, all with their original silk covers, circa 1670, from Ham House, courtesy of the Victoria and Albert Museum.

WALLACE COLLECTION
Hertford House
Manchester Square
London W1
Tel: (01) 936 0687
Open Mon–Sat 10–5, Sun 2–5; closed Dec 24, 25, 26, Jan 1, Good Fri, May Day Bank Hol.

Fine French furniture and objets d'art.

SOUTH AND SOUTHEAST ENGLAND

BRIGHTON MUSEUM AND ART GALLERY
Church Street
Brighton, E Sussex
Tel: (0273) 603005
Open Tue–Sat 10–5.45, Sun 2–5 (summer 2–6); closed Mon, Dec 25, 26, Good Fri.

17th to 19th c. furniture, but noted for its outstanding exhibits of Art Nouveau and Art Deco.

BUSCOT PARK
Nr Faringdon, Oxon
Open Apr–Sep, Wed, Thur, Fri 2–6; 2nd and 4th weekends in month 2–6.

Faringdon collection of fine furniture in 18th c. house.

FITZWILLIAM MUSEUM
Trumpington Street
Cambridge, Cambs
Tel: (0223) 69501
Open Tue–Sat, Lower Galleries 10–2, Upper Galleries 2–5, Sun 2.15–5; open Bank Hol Mons; closed Dec 24–Jan 1, Good Fri. Advisable to check in advance that appropriate gallery is open.

Fine furniture displayed principally on first floor but also throughout the picture galleries.

Right: Wall bracket in wrought iron, with glass shade made by Daum, designed by Edgar Brandt, circa 1928, courtesy of the Brighton Museum and Art Gallery.

HAM HOUSE
Richmond, Surrey
Tel: (01) 940 1950
Open Apr–Sept, Tue–Sun 2–6, Oct–Mar 12–4, Bank Hol Mons except May Day Bank Hol.

Superb Charles II and early Georgian furnishings.

HATFIELD HOUSE
Hatfield, Herts
Tel: Hatfield 62823/65159
Open end Mar–end Oct, Tue–Sat 12–5, Sun 2–5.30; open Bank Hols 11–5.

Staterooms with fine furniture and tapestries.

CECIL HIGGINS ART GALLERY
Castle Close
Bedford, Beds
Tel: (0234) 211222
Open Tue–Fri 12.30–5, Sat 11–5, Sun 2–5, Bank Hols 12.30–5.

Selections from Handley-Read collection of furniture and decorative arts in appropriate room settings in 19th c. house. Fine examples of Art Nouveau and Art Deco.

KNOLE
Sevenoaks, Kent
Tel: (0732) 53006
Open Apr–Sep, Wed–Sat, Bank Hol Mons, Good Fri 11–5, Sun 2–5; Oct–Nov, Wed–Sat 11–4; closed Dec–Mar.

17th and 18th c. furniture.

OSTERLEY PARK HOUSE
Isleworth, Middx
Tel: (01) 560 3918
Open Apr–Sep, Tue–Sun, Bank Hols 2–6; Oct–Mar 12–4; closed May Day Bank Hol.

Robert Adam house with original furniture and decorations.

PALLANT HOUSE GALLERY
9 North Pallant
Chichester, W Sussex
Tel: (0243) 784683
Open Tue–Sat 10–6 (Oct–Mar, 10–5); closed Sun and Mon.

Queen Anne residence furnished in period style.

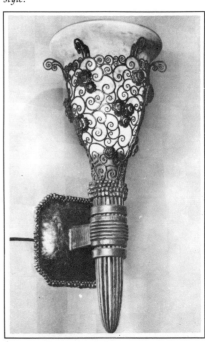

PENSHURST PLACE
Tunbridge Wells, Kent
Tel: (0892) 870307
*Open Apr–Oct, Tue–Sun 1–5.30, also Good
Fri and Bank Hol Mons.*
Outstanding furniture in state rooms.

THE ROYAL PAVILION
Brighton, E Sussex
Tel: (0273) 603005
*Open daily 10–5 (July–Sep 10–6.30); closed
Dec 25, 26 and one day prior to Regency
Exhibition.*
*Superb Georgian-Chinoiserie decor and
furniture.*

THOMAS STANFORD MUSEUM
Preston Manor
Preston Park
Brighton, E Sussex
Tel: (0273) 552101
*Open Wed–Sat 10–5, Sun 2–5; closed Dec
24, 25, 26, 27, Jan 1, Good Fri.*
*Opulent Edwardian country house with period
furnishings.*

UPTON HOUSE
Edge Hill
Nr Banbury, Oxon
Tel: (029 587) 266
*Open Apr–Sep, Mon–Thur 2–6; some
weekends in May and Aug.*
18th c. furniture and tapestries.

WADDESDON MANOR
Nr Aylesbury, Bucks
Tel: (0296) 651282
*Open end Mar–end Oct, Wed–Sun 2–6,
Bank Hol Mons 11–6; closed Wed after Bank
Hols. Note: Children under 12 not admitted to
house.*
*Superb 17th and 18th c. decorative art,
including Royal furniture.*

WOBURN ABBEY
Woburn, Beds
Tel: (052) 525 666
*Open daily Feb 1–Easter, Nov 1–30 1–4.45;
Good Fri–Oct 31, Mon–Sat 11–5.45, Sun
11–6.15.*
18th c. English and French furniture.

**WYCOMBE CHAIR AND LOCAL
HISTORY MUSEUM**
Castle Hill
High Wycombe, Bucks
Tel: (0494) 23879
Open Mon, Tue, Thur, Fri, Sat 10–1, 2–5.
*Chairs of most periods but main emphasis on
the Windsor chair.*

SOUTHWEST ENGLAND AND
WALES

**THE AMERICAN MUSEUM IN
BRITAIN**
Claverton Manor
Bath, Avon
Tel: (0225) 63538
*Open end Mar–beginning Nov daily (ex
Mon) 2–5; Bank Hol Mons and preceding
Suns 11–5; winter by appointment only.*
*Furnished rooms illustrating 17th to mid-19th
c. American life.*

**BANGOR ART GALLERY AND
MUSEUM OF WELSH ANTIQUITIES**
Ffordd Gwynedd
Bangor, Gwynedd, Wales
Tel: (0248) 51151
Open Mon–Sat 10.30–4.30; closed Sun.
Fine collection of Welsh furniture.

**CHELTENHAM ART GALLERY AND
MUSEUM**
Clarence Street
Cheltenham, Glos
Tel: (0242) 37431
Open Mon–Sat 10–5.30; closed Sun.
*Large furniture collection, including work by
Cotswold craftsmen.*

COTEHELE
Calstock, Cornwall
Tel: (0579) 50434
Open Apr–end Oct daily 11–6.
*Mediaeval and Tudor house with original
furniture and tapestries.*

ELIZABETHAN HOUSE
32 New Street
Plymouth, Devon
*Open Mon–Sat 10–1, 2.15–6 (closes 4.30 in
winter); Sun (summer only) 3–5.*
Period furnishings in 16th c. house.

THE ELIZABETHAN HOUSE
70 Fore Street
Totnes, Devon
Tel: (0803) 863821
Open Mar–Oct, Mon–Sat 10.30–1, 2–5.30.
Period furniture.

ERDDIG
Wrexham, Clwyd, Wales
Tel: (0978) 55314
*Open daily Apr–Sep except Fri (but open
Good Fri) 12–5.30; Oct daily except Fri
12–4.30; Chinese and tapestry rooms open
Wed and Sat only.*
*Many original furnishings in beautifully
restored 17th c. house (National Trust).*

GAINSBOROUGH HOUSE
46 Gainsborough Street
Sudbury, Suffolk
Tel: (0787) 72958
Open Tue–Sat 10–12.30, 2–5, Sun 2–5.
18th c. furniture.

THE GEORGIAN HOUSE
7 Great George Street
Bristol, Avon
Tel: (0272) 299771, ext 237
Open Mon–Sat 10–5.
*Period furnishings illustrating lifestyle of a
prosperous family in house built 1791.*

HOLBURNE OF MENSTRIE MUSEUM
Great Pulteney Street
Bath, Avon
Tel: (0225) 66669
Open Mon–Sat 11–5, Sun 2.30–6.
18th c. furniture in elegant setting.

MONTACUTE HOUSE
Montacute
Nr Yeovil, Somerset
Tel: (0935 82) 3289
Open Apr–Oct daily (ex Tue), 12.30–6.
*Magnificent Elizabethan mansion with period
furnishings.*

THE RED LODGE
Park Row
Bristol, Avon
Tel: (0272) 299771
Open Mon–Sat 2–5.
*Elizabethan house with 18th c. additions and
alterations; furniture from both periods.*

*FOR MAP OF THE BRITISH ISLES,
SEE PAGE 7.*

No 1, ROYAL CRESCENT
Bath, Avon
Tel: (0225) 28126
*Open Mar–end Oct, Tue–Sat 11–5, Sun
2–5.*
*Restored Georgian house furnished in period
style.*

SALTRAM HOUSE
Plymouth, Devon
Tel: (0752) 336 546
*Open Apr–end Oct, Tue–Sun 12.30–6;
closed Mon except Bank Hols.*
Fully furnished late 18th c. reception rooms.

MIDLANDS AND EAST ANGLIA

ASTON HALL
Trinity Road
Aston
Birmingham, W Midlands
Tel: (021) 472 7775
*Open Apr–Oct, Mon–Sat 10–1, 2–5, Sun
2–5; closed Nov–Mar, Good Fri.*
17th c. house with 17th to 19th c. furnishings.

BELGRAVE HALL
Thurcaston Road
Leicester, Leics
Tel: (0533) 554100
*Open Mon–Sat 10–5.30, Sun 2–5.30; closed
Dec 25, 26, Good Fri.*
Furnished Queen Anne house.

ELIZABETHAN HOUSE MUSEUM
4 South Quay
Great Yarmouth, Norfolk
Tel: (0493) 55746
*Open June 1–Sep 30, Sun–Fri 10–1,
2–5.30; Oct 1–May 31, Mon–Fri 10–1,
2–5.30.*
*Merchant's house of 1596 furnished in period
style.*

**HERBERT ART GALLERY AND
MUSEUM**
Jordan Well
Coventry, W Midlands
Tel: (0203) 25555, ext 2662
*Open Mon–Sat 10–6, Sun 2–5; closed
part of Christmas period and Good Fri.*
*Frederick R. Poke collection of English
furniture.*

THE OLD HOUSE
High Town
Hereford, Heref & Worcs
Tel: (0432) 68121, ext 207
*Open Apr–Sep, Mon–Sat 10–1, 2–5.30;
Oct–Mar, Mon 10–1, Tue–Fri 10–1,
2–5.30.*
*Jacobean house with appropriate 17th c.
furnishings.*

RAGLEY HALL
Alcester
Nr Stratford-upon-Avon, Warks
Tel: (0789) 762090/762455
*Open Apr–Oct, Tue–Thur 1.30–5.30; open
Bank Hols.*
*Fine Palladian mansion with 18th c. English
and French furniture.*

STAFFORDSHIRE COUNTY MUSEUM
Shugborough
Nr Stafford, Staffs
Tel: (0889) 881388
*Mansion open mid-Mar–mid-Oct, Tue–Fri,
Bank Hol Mons 10.30–5.30; Sat, Sun
2–5.30.*
Fine French furniture and other objets d'art.

STRANGERS' HALL MUSEUM
Charing Cross
Norwich, Norfolk
Tel: (0603) 611277, ext 275
Open Mon–Sat 10–5.
*Late mediaeval mansion furnished as museum
of domestic life.*

NORTH OF ENGLAND AND SCOTLAND

ABBOT HALL ART GALLERY
Kendal, Cumbria
Tel: (0539) 22464
*Open Mon–Fri 10.30–5.30, Sat, Sun 2–5;
closed 2 weeks Christmas–New Year and
Good Fri.*
18th c. furnished rooms.

BOLLING HALL MUSEUM
Bolling Hall Road
Bradford, W Yorkshire
Tel: (0274) 23057
*Open Apr 1–Sep 30, Mon, Wed–Fri 10–6,
Tue, Sat, Sun 10–8; Oct 1–Mar 31 daily
10–5; closed Dec 25, 26, Good Fri.*
*Fine collection including old oak and
farmhouse furniture and Chinese
Chippendale.*

BOWES MUSEUM
Barnard Castle, Co Durham
Tel: (0833) 37139
*Open Oct, Mar, Apr, Mon–Sat 10–5,
May–Sep, 10–5.30; Nov–Feb, 10–4; Sun
2–5 (winter 2–4).*
Fine collection of European furniture.

*Below: Oak chair with floral inlay of box and
bog oak, probably made in the
Yorkshire/Lancashire area, circa 1610,
courtesy of the Bolling Hall Museum.*

*Above: Panel from the "Warwick Cabinet"
from the Warwick Castle collection, made in
England about 1780 and incorporating
extremely fine French marquetry of the late
17th c., courtesy of the Bowes Museum,
Barnard Castle.*

CANNON HALL MUSEUM
Cawthorne
Barnsley, S. Yorkshire
Tel: (0226) 790270
Open Mon–Sat 10.30–5, Sun 2.30–5.
*Furniture and accessories displayed in period
rooms in 18th c. house.*

CASTLE HOWARD
York, N Yorkshire
Tel: (065 384) 333
Open daily Mar 25–Oct 31, 11.30–5.
*Fine furniture in magnificent Vanbrugh
mansion.*

CHATSWORTH
Bakewell, Derbs
Tel: (024 688) 2204
Open daily end Mar–end Oct 11.30–4.30.
*Magnificent home of the Dukes of Devonshire
with rooms of fine furniture.*

CRAGSIDE
Rothbury, North'ld
Tel: (0669) 20333
*Open Apr–end Sep daily except Mon (but
open Bank Hol Mons) 1–6; Oct, Wed, Sat,
Sun 2–5.*
*Late Victorian house designed by Shaw with
much of the original furniture.*

THE GEORGIAN HOUSE
7 Charlotte Square
Edinburgh, Scotland
Tel: (031) 225 2160
*Open Apr 1–Oct 31, Mon–Sat 10–5, Sun
2–5; Nov 1–Dec 12, Sat 10–4.30 and Sun
2–4.30 only.*
*Part of Georgian House furnished as in time of
first owners.*

GLASGOW MUSEUM AND ART GALLERY
Kelvingrove
Glasgow, Strathclyde, Scotland
Tel: (041) 334 1134
*Open Mon–Sat 10–5, Sun 2–5; closed Dec
25, Good Fri.*
*18th and 19th c. tapestries and furniture in
Burrell Collection.*

HAREWOOD HOUSE
Leeds, W Yorkshire
Tel: (0532) 886225
*Open Apr–end Oct daily from 11; Nov, Feb &
Mar, Sun, Tue–Thur.*
Chippendale furniture.

HEATON HALL
Heaton Park
Prestwick
Manchester, Gt Manchester
Tel: (061) 773 1231
*Open Apr–Sept, Mon–Sat 10–6, Sun 2–6
(May–Aug 12–6); closed Oct–Mar.*
*Sumptuously decorated interiors in 18th c.
house built by James Samuel and Lewis Wyatt
for the First Earl of Wilton.*

HOPETOUN HOUSE AND STABLES MUSEUM
Hopetoun House
South Queensferry, Lothian, Scotland
Tel: (031) 331 2451
*Open Easter weekend, then May–end Sep
daily 11–5.30.*
Fine Chippendale furniture.

HUNTERIAN MUSEUM
Glasgow University
Glasgow, Strathclyde, Scotland
Tel: (041) 339 8855
Open Mon–Fri 9–5, Sat 9–12.
*Collection of work by Charles Rennie
Mackintosh of particular interest.*

JUDGES' LODGINGS
Church Street
Lancaster, Lancs
Tel: (0524) 2808
*Open Apr and Oct, Mon–Fri 2–5; May–end
June, Mon–Sat 2–5; July–end Sep,
Mon–Fri 10–1, 2–5, Sat 2–5.*
*Town house with collection of furniture by
Gillow of Lancaster.*

Above: Reconstructed dining room at the Mackintosh House after the designer/architect Charles Rennie Mackintosh, courtesy of the Hunterian Art Gallery.

LOTHERTON HALL
Aberford
Leeds, W Yorkshire
Tel: (097) 332 259
Open Tue–Sun, Bank Hols 10.30–6.15 (or dusk if earlier); May 1–Sep 30, also Thur until 8.30.

Victorian and Edwardian (and other 20 c.) furniture and decorative items.

MANCHESTER CITY ART GALLERY
Mosley Street
Manchester, Gt Manchester
Tel: (061) 236 9422, ext 226
Open Mon–Sat 10–6, Sun 2.30–6; closed Dec 25, Good Fri.

Some important Pre-Raphaelite furniture, plus work by William Burges.

NORMANBY HALL
Normanby Country Park
Scunthorpe, S Humberside
Tel: (0724) 720215
Open Apr 1–Oct 31, Mon, Wed, Sat 10–12.30, 2–5.30, Sun 2–5.30; Nov 1–Mar 31, Mon–Fri 10–12.30, Sun 2–5.

Early 19th c. mansion furnished in period style (with paintings and costumes included).

POLLOK HOUSE
2060 Pollokshaws Road
Pollok Park
Glasgow, Strathclyde, Scotland
Tel: (041) 632 0274
Open Mon–Sat 10–5, Sun 2–5.

House by William Adam built in 1752 and furnished with pieces from 1750–1820.

PROVOST SKENE'S HOUSE
Guestrow (off Broad Street)
Aberdeen, Grampian, Scotland
Tel: (0225) 25788
Open Mon–Sat 10–5.

17th c. furnished house with period rooms illustrating domestic life.

SPEKE HALL
Nr Liverpool, Merseyside
Tel: (051) 427 7231
Open Mon–Sat 10–5, Sun Apr–Sep 2–7 (Oct–Mar 2–5); closed Dec 24, 25, 25, Jan 1, Good Fri.

Fully furnished 16th c. half-timbered house.

TATTON PARK
Knutsford, Cheshire
Tel: (0565) 3155
Open Easter–Oct 31, Tue–Sat 1–4, Sun and Bank Hols 1–5.

Beautifully furnished Georgian house with collection of Gillow furniture.

TEMPLE NEWSAM HOUSE
Leeds, W Yorkshire
Tel: (0532) 647321/641358
Open Tue–Sun, Bank Hols 10.30–6.15 (or dusk if earlier); May 1–Sep 30, also Thur, until 8.30.

Early 17th c. museum house with 17th–18th c. English furniture.

TURTON TOWER
Turton
Blackburn, Lancs
Tel: (0254) 667130
Open Sat–Wed 12–6; closed Thur, Fri, Dec 25, 26, Jan 1.

Mediaeval tower and 16th c. farmhouse with period furniture.

WILBERFORCE HOUSE AND GEORGIAN HOUSES
23–25 High Street
Hull, Humberside
Tel: (0482) 223111, ext 2737
Open Mon–Sat 10–5, Sun 2.30–4.30.

17th and 18th c. merchants' houses with collections of furniture.

WYTHENSHAWE HALL
Wythenshawe Park
Northenden
Manchester, Gt Manchester
Tel: (061) 998 2331
Opening times must be confirmed by telephone, as it has been closed for repairs.

17th c. oak, walnut and inlaid furniture.

GLASS

LONDON

BRITISH MUSEUM
Great Russell Street
London WC1
Tel: (01) 636 1555
Open Mon–Sat 10–5, Sun 2.30–6; closed Dec 24, 25, 26, Jan 1, Good Fri, May Day Bank Hol.

Excellent general collection.

FOR MAP OF LONDON'S POSTAL DISTRICTS, SEE PAGE 61.

MUSEUM OF LONDON
London Wall
London EC2
Tel: (01) 600 3699
Open Tue–Sat 10–6, Sun 2–6; closed Mon, Dec 25, 26, Jan 1.
Lead crystal, early bottles and some ancient glass.

VICTORIA AND ALBERT MUSEUM
Cromwell Road
London SW7
Tel: (01) 589 6371
Open Mon–Thur, Sat 10–5.50, Sun 2.30–5.50; closed Fri, Dec 24, 25, 26, Jan 1, May Day Bank Hol.
Glass from ancient to modern times.

SOUTH AND SOUTHEAST ENGLAND

BRIGHTON MUSEUM AND ART GALLERY
Church Street
Brighton, E Sussex
Tel: (0273) 603005
Open Tue–Sat 10–5.45, Sun 2–5 (summer 2–6); closed Mon, Dec 25, 26, Good Fri.

Outstanding Art Deco and Art Nouveau displays including Lalique.

FOR MAP OF THE BRITISH ISLES, SEE PAGE 7.

CECIL HIGGINS ART GALLERY
Castle Close
Bedford, Beds
Tel: (0234) 211222
*Open Tue–Fri 12.30–5, Sat 11–5, Sun 2–5;
closed Mon and Christmas.
One of the finest collections of English and
European glass in Britain.*

ROYAL MUSEUM AND ART GALLERY
The Beaney
High Street
Canterbury, Kent
Tel: (0227) 52747
*Open Mon–Sat 10–5.
Good examples from Roman and Anglo-Saxon
sites plus English mediaeval glass and
fragments.*

THE STAINED GLASS MUSEUM
Ely Cathedral,
Ely, Cambs
Tel: (0353) 2078
*Open Mon–Sat 11–4.30, Sun 12–3, Bank
Hols 11–5.
Small, well-displayed collection of 14th to
20th c. stained glass and exhibits showing its
fabrication.*

SOUTHWEST ENGLAND AND WALES

BRISTOL CITY MUSEUM AND ART GALLERY
Queens Road,
Clifton, Bristol, Avon
Tel: (0272) 299771
*Open Mon-Sat 10–5; closed Dec 25, 26, Jan
1, Good Fri.
This glass-making city shows fine exhibits,
including the Bomford collection of glass
containers. Local coloured glass and lead
crystal.*

FOLK MUSEUM
99–103 Westgate Street
Gloucester, Glos
Tel: (0452) 26467
*Open Mon–Sat 10–5, Suns in August 2–5.
English glass from all periods.*

*Above: A Venetian tazza, circa 1500,
courtesy of the Cecil Higgins Art Galery.*

GLYNN VIVIAN ART GALLERY AND MUSEUM
Alexandra Road
Swansea, Glamorgan, Wales
Tel: (0792) 55006/51738
*Open Mon–Sat 10.30–5.30; closed Dec 25,
26, Jan 1.
Famous collection of paperweights from
Baccarat, St Louis and Clichy.*

HARVEY'S WINE MUSEUM
12 Denmark Street
Bristol, Avon
Tel: (0272) 298011
*Open by appointment only.
Outstanding collection of 18th c. drinking
glasses in museum devoted to the history of
sherry.*

MOMPESSON HOUSE
The Close
Salisbury, Wilts
Tel: (0722) 5659
*Open Apr–end Oct, Mon–Wed, Sat, Sun
12.30–6.
Turnbull collection of 18th c. English drinking
glasses.*

NATIONAL MUSEUM OF WALES
Cathays Parks,
Cardiff, S Glamorgan, Wales
Tel: (0222) 397951
*Open Mon–Sat 10–5, Sun 2.30–5; closed
Dec 24, 25, 26, Jan 1, Good Fri.
Fine collection of 20th c. work by Maurice
Marinot. Also 18th c. bottles, silver-mounted
lead crystal and fragments from Welsh
Romano-British sites.*

ROYAL ALBERT MEMORIAL MUSEUM AND ART GALLERY
Queen Street
Exeter, Devon
Tel: (0392) 56724
*Open Tue–Sat 10–5.15.
Henry Hamilton Clarke collection of English
glass.*

*Left: 18th c. English drinking glass,
stipple engraved by David Wolff, courtesy of
Harvey's Wine Museum.*

RUSSELL-COTES ART GALLERY AND MUSEUM
Eastcliff
Bournemouth, Dorset
Tel: (0202) 21009
Open Mon–Sat 10.30–5.

Lead crystal and other glass.

SOMERSET COUNTY MUSEUM
Taunton Castle
Castle Green
Taunton, Somerset
Tel: (0823) 73451, ex 286
*Open summer Mon–Sat 10–5, Oct onwards
Mon–Fri 10–5; closed Bank Hols.*

Collection of Nailsea glass.

VICTORIA ART GALLERY
Bridge Street
Bath, Avon
Tel: (0225) 61111, ext 418
*Open Mon–Fri 10–6, Sat 10–5; closed Sun,
Bank Hols.*

Early English and 19th c. Venetian glass.

*Below: Cameo glass copy of the Portland
vase, engraved by F. Zach, circa 1880,
courtesy of the Royal Albert Memorial
Museum.*

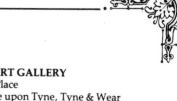

MIDLANDS AND EAST ANGLIA

BIRMINGHAM CITY MUSEUM AND ART GALLERY
Chamberlain Square
Birmingham, W Midlands
Tel: (021) 235 2834
Open Mon–Sat 10–5.30, Sun 2–5.30; closed Dec 25, 26, Jan 1, Good Fri.
Stained glass; Roman, Murano and Venetian glass and lead crystal.

BROADFIELD HOUSE GLASS MUSEUM
Compton Drive
Kingswinford, W Midlands
Tel: (038 44) 3011
Open Tue–Fri 2–6, Sat 10–1, 2–5, Sun 2–5; closed Mon except Bank Hols; closed Dec 25, 26, Jan 1.
One of Britain's best collections concentrating on Victorian and Edwardian pieces including fine Stourbridge glass and cameo glass.

CHRISTCHURCH MANSION
Christchurch Park
Ipswich, Suffolk
Tel: (0473) 53246
Open Mon–Sat 10–5, Sun 2.30–4.30; closed at dusk in winter.
The Tibbenham collection of Old English drinking glasses; good small collection of mediaeval glass and other fragments.

MOYSE'S HALL MUSEUM
Cornhill
Bury St Edmunds, Suffolk
Tel: (0284) 63233, ext 236
Open Mon–Sat 10–1, 2–5 (closes at 4 in winter).
Early glass of local interest and some 18th c. glass.

NORTH OF ENGLAND AND SCOTLAND

ABERDEEN ART GALLERY
Schoolhill
Aberdeen, Grampian, Scotland
Tel: (0224) 26333
Open Mon–Sat 10–5 (Thur 10–8), Sun 2–5.
European glass.

FOR MAP OF THE BRITISH ISLES, SEE PAGE 7.

Above: A selection of twenty scent bottles from all periods, courtesy of the Harris Museum and Art Gallery.

ART GALLERY AND MUSEUM
Kelvingrove
Glasgow, Strathclyde, Scotland
Tel: (041) 334 1134/5/6
Open Mon–Sat 10–5, Sun 2–5.
Syrian, Venetian and Spanish glass; some German glass and stained glass; loan collection of lead crystal.

ART GALLERY AND MUSEUM
Union Street
Oldham, Gt Manchester
Tel: (061) 624 0505
Open Mon, Wed, Thur, Fri 10–7, Tue 10–1, Sat 10–4; closed Sun.
Part of Francis Buckley collection of old glass (mainly North Country.).

BOLLING HALL MUSEUM
Bradford, W Yorkshire
Tel: (0274) 23057
Open Tue–Sun 10–5; closed Mon, except Bank Hols, Dec 25, 26, Good Fri.
Lead crystal and other glass especially of Yorkshire manufacture, plus bottles.

BUXTON MUSEUM AND ART GALLERY
Terrace Road
Buxton, Derbs
Tel: (0928) 4658
Open Tue–Fri 9.30–5.30, Sat 9.30–5.
Lead crystal and coloured glass.

HARRIS MUSEUM AND ART GALLERY
Market Square
Preston, Lancs
Tel: (0772) 582 4819
Open Mon–Sat 10–5; closed Bank Hols.
2,500 beautiful scent bottles and large collection of drinking glasses.

HAWARTH ART GALLERY
Hawarth Park
Accrington, Lancs
Tel: (0254) 33782
Open Mon–Thur, Sat, Sun, 2–5; closed Dec 25, 26, Jan 1, Good Fir.
Best collection of Tiffany glass in Europe.

LAING ART GALLERY
Higham Place
Newcastle upon Tyne, Tyne & Wear
Tel: (0632) 327734
Open Mon–Sat 10–6, Sun 2.30–5.30, Bank Hols 10–6.
18th and 19th c. North Country, Newcastle and Gateshead glass plus some lead crystal.

MERSEYSIDE COUNTY MUSEUMS
William Brown Street
Liverpool, Merseyside
Tel: (051) 207 0001
Open Mon–Sat 10–5, Sun 2–5; closed Dec 24, 25, 26, Jan 1, Good Fri.
Ancient glass plus examples of post-Renaissance European glass, including Bristol, façon de Venise and German.

PILKINGTON MUSEUM OF GLASS
Prescot Road
St Helens, Merseyside
Tel: (0744) 28882
Open Mon–Fri 10–5 (Mar–Oct, Wed 10–9), Sat, Sun and Bank Hols 2–4.30; closed Dec 25, Jan 1.
Evolution of glass-making shown plus collection of glass through the ages.

ROYAL SCOTTISH MUSEUM
Chambers Street
Edinburgh, Scotland
Tel: (031) 225 7534
Open Mon–Sat 10–5, Sun 2–5.
English, Venetian, Persian, Arabian, Greek, Roman and Chinese glass.

Below: Rare Mughal Hukka base in clear glass encased in pale blue glass with raised parts in gilt, circa 1700, courtesy of the Pilkington Glass Museum.

LONDON

BRITISH MUSEUM
Great Russell Street
London WC1
Tel: (01) 636 1555
*Open Mon–Sat 10–5, Sun 2.30–6; closed
Dec 24, 25, 26, Jan 1, May Day Bank Hol,
Good Fri.*
Unique antique and mediaeval jewellery.

MUSEUM OF LONDON
London Wall
London EC2
Tel: (01) 600 3699
Open Tue–Sat 10–6, Sun 2–6.
*Most of the amazing Cheapside hoard
displayed – mainly Elizabethan jewellery, but
also Italianate and Byzantine pieces.*

VICTORIA AND ALBERT MUSEUM
Cromwell Road
London SW7
Tel: (01) 589 6371
*Open Mon–Thur–Sat 10–5.50, Sun
2.30–5.50; closed Fri, Dec 24, 25, 26, Jan 1,
May Day Bank Hol, Good Fri.*
Fine jewellery from all periods.

SOUTH AND SOUTHEAST ENGLAND

CECIL HIGGINS ART GALLERY
Castle Close
Bedford, Beds
Tel: (0234) 211222
*Open Tue–Fri, 12.30–5, Sat 11–5, Sun
2–5, closed Dec 24, 25.*
*Jewellery among other Victorian and
Edwardian exhibits.*

COLCHESTER AND ESSEX MUSEUM
The Castle
Colchester, Essex
Tel: (0206) 77475/76071
*Open Mon–Sat 10–5 (Oct–Apr, closes at 4
on Sat); Apr–Sep, Sun 2.30–5*
Fine Roman jewellery.

LUTON HOO
Luton, Beds
Tel: (0582) 22955
*Open Apr–Oct, Mon, Wed, Thur, Sat, Good
Fri 11–5.45, Sun 2–5.45.*
*Only collection of Carl Fabergé's work on
permanent display.*

MIDLANDS AND EAST ANGLIA

THE CASTLE MUSEUM
Norwich, Norfolk
Tel: (0603) 22233
*Open Mon–Sat 10–5, Sun 2–5; closed Dec,
24, 25, Jan 1, Good Fri.*
*Superb examples from Hull-Grundy
collection; torcs from Snettisham treasure.*

NORTH OF ENGLAND AND SCOTLAND

BOWES MUSEUM
Barnard Castle, Co Durham
Tel: (0833) 37139
*Open Oct–Apr Mon–Sat 10–5.30, Sun 2–5;
Nov–Feb, 10–4, 2–4.*
*Small high quality exhibit of jewellery (also
minatures and snuff boxes).*

THE CASTLE MUSEUM
Tower Street
York, N Yorkshire
Tel: (0904) 53611
*Open Apr–Sep, Mon–Sat 9.30–6, Sun
10–6; Oct–Mar, Mon–Sat 9.30–4.30, Sun
10–4.30*
Excellent general jewellery collection.

WHITBY MUSEUM
Pannett Park
Whitby, N Yorkshire
Tel: (0947) 2908
*Open May–Sep, Mon–Sat 9.30–5.30, Sun
2–5; Oct–Apr, Mon, Tue, Thur, Fri
10.30–1, Wed, Sat 10.30–4, Sun 2–4; closed
Dec 25, 26, Jan 1.*
*Victorian jewellery and ornaments made in
heyday of Whitby jet.*

MUSICAL INSTRUMENTS

LONDON

FENTON HOUSE
Hampstead Grove
London NW3
Tel: (01) 435 3471
*Open Feb, Mar and Nov, Sat 11–5, Sun 2–5
(or sunset if earlier); Apr–end Oct,
Mon–Wed, Sat, Bank Hols 11–5, Sun 2–5;
closed Jan, Dec, Good Fri.*
*The Benton-Fletcher collection of early
instruments – spinets, virginals,
harpsichords.*

HORNIMAN MUSEUM
London Road
Forest Hill
London SE23
Tel: (01) 699 2339/1872/4911
*Open Mon–Sat 10.30–6, Sun 2–6; open
Good Fri, closed Dec 24, 25.*
*Large collection of instruments from all over
world.*

RANGERS HOUSE
Chesterfield Walk
Blackheath
London SE10
Tel: (01) 853 0035
*Open daily 10–5 (Nov–Jan closes at 4); closed
Good Fri, Dec 24, 25*
Collection of musical instruments.

*Right: Stradivarius violin, ''Le Messie'',
made in Cremona in 1716, arguably the most
famous violin in the world, courtesy of the
Ashmolean Museum.*

ROYAL COLLEGE OF MUSIC
Prince Consort Road
South Kensington
London SW7
Tel: (01) 589 3643
*Open to public Mon and Wed 10.30–4.30
during termtime by previous appointment
with Curator.*
*Donaldson Collection of instruments;
extensive library of printed music and original
manuscripts.*

VICTORIA AND ALBERT MUSEUM
Cromwell Road,
London SW7
Tel: (01) 589 6371
*Open Mon–Thur, Sat 10–5.50; Sun
2.30–5.50; closed Fri, Dec 24, 25, 26, Jan 1,
May Day Bank Hol, Good Fri.*
*Keyboard, string and wind instruments,
many notable for their decorative value.*

SOUTH AND SOUTHEAST ENGLAND

ASHMOLEAN MUSEUM OF ART AND ARCHAEOLOGY
Beaumont Street
Oxford, Oxon
Tel: (0865) 512651
*Open Mon–Sat 10–4, Sun 2–4; closed Dec
24, 25 26, Jan 1, Good Fri–Easter Sun, Mon
and Tue after first Sun after Sep 2.*
*The Hill collection, including a famous
Stradivarius.*

CARISBROOKE CASTLE MUSEUM
Newport
Isle of Wight
Tel: (0983) 523112
*Open Mar and Oct, Mon–Sat 9.30–5.30,
Sun 2–5.30; Apr daily, 9.30–5.30;
May–Sep daily, 9.30–7; Nov–Feb,
Mon–Sat 9.30–4, Sun 2–4; closed Dec 24,
25, 26, Jan 1, Maundy Thur, Good Fri.*
A rare still-playable 17th c. organ.

FINCHCOCKS
Goudhurst, Kent
Tel: (0580) 211702
*Open May–end Jul, Sun 2–6, end Jul–end
Aug, Wed–Sun 2–6.*
Magnificent collection of early pianos.

THE NATIONAL MUSICAL MUSEUM
368 High Street
Brentford, Middx
Tel: (01) 560 8108
Open Apr–Oct, Sat, Sun 2–5.
*Huge number of keyboard instruments,
pianolas, automatic pianos, theatre organs and
music boxes. Lectures and demonstrations.*

PITT RIVERS MUSEUM
(Entrance through University Museum)
Parks Road
Oxford, Oxon
Tel: (0865) 512541
*Open Mon–Sat 2–4; closed Easter and
Christmas weeks.*
*Musical instrument collection in mainly
ethnological museum.*

*FOR MAP OF THE BRITISH ISLES,
SEE PAGE 7.*

*FOR MAP OF LONDON'S POSTAL
DISTRICTS, SEE PAGE 61.*

*Below: Goat and Tree (Rain in a Thicket), Ur
Iraq, from Western Asiatic Antiquities,
courtesy of the British Museum.*

*Above: Single pedestal harpsichord, patented
in 1771, and made in 1777 by Thomas Haxby
of York, courtesy of the Castle Museum.*

MIDLANDS AND EAST ANGLIA

THE THURSFORD COLLECTION
Thursford Green
Fakenham, Norfolk
Tel: (0328) 3839
*Open Easter–end Oct, Sun–Sat 2–5.30;
Nov–Easter, Sun only 2–5.30.*

*Theatre organs; demonstrations on the
Wurlitzer on Tuesday evenings,
June–September.*

ORIENTAL ART

LONDON

BRITISH MUSEUM
Great Russell Street
London WC1
Tel: (01) 636 1555
*Open Mon–Sat 10–5, Sun 2.30–6; closed
Dec 24, 25, 26, Jan 1, Good Fri, May Day
Bank Hol.*
*Magnificent Oriental antiquities: Buddhist
art, Chinese bronzes and porcelain; fine
Japanese prints in Prints and Drawings
department (student's ticket required, but
some are periodically displayed).*

PERCIVAL DAVID FOUNDATION OF
CHINESE ART
53 Gordon Square
London WC1
Tel: (01) 387 3909
*Open Mon 2–5, Tue–Fri 10.30–5, Sat
10.30–1; closed Bank Hols.*
*Part of London University, this outstanding
collection of mainly 10th to 18th c. Chinese art
reflects Imperial taste.*

VICTORIA AND ALBERT MUSEUM
Cromwell Road
London SW7
Tel: (01) 589 6371
*Open Mon–Thur, Sat 10–5.50; Sun
2.30–5.50; closed Fri, Dec 24, 25, 26, Jan 1,
May Day Bank Hol, Good Fri.*
*Chinese ceramics, Oriental rugs and carpets
and Indian miniatures, among many other
fine exhibits.*

NORTH OF ENGLAND AND
SCOTLAND

THE BAGPIPE MUSEUM
The Black Gate
St Nicholas Street
Newcastle upon Tyne, Tyne & Wear
*Open Wed, Thur, Fri 12–4, Sat 10–2
(Jun–Aug 10–4); closed Sun–Tue, Dec 25,
26, Jan 1, Good Fri.*
Comprehensive bagpipe collection.

CASTLE MUSEUM
Tower Street
York, N Yorkshire
Tel: (0904) 53611
*Open Apr–Sep, Mon–Sat 9.30–6, Sun
10–6; Oct–Mar, Mon–Sat 9.30–4.30, Sun
10–4.30.*
*Ancient instruments such as the serpent and
ophicleide, virginals and spinets; also harps
and wind instruments.*

DEAN CASTLE
Dean Road
Kilmarnock, Strathclyde, Scotland
Tel: (0563) 26401
Open daily mid–May to mid–Sep, 2–5.
200 lutes, viols and clavichords in upper hall.

THE RUSSELL COLLECTION
St Cecilia's Hall, Niddry Street, Cowgate
Edinburgh, Scotland
Tel: (031) 667 1011, ext 4414/5
*Open Sat 2–5 throughout year; daily
mornings during Festival (Aug).*
*Harpsichords and clavichords, spinets,
virginals and other early keyboard
instruments.*

SOUTH AND SOUTHEAST
ENGLAND

ASCOTT
Wing, Bucks
Tel: (029 668) 242
*Open Apr–Sept, Wed, Thur 2–6; also Sats in
Aug and Sep 2–6.*
*Rothschild collection of exceptional Oriental
porcelain.*

*Below: Famille rose flask, circa 1725,
presented to the first British ambassador to
Japan by the last Tokugawa Shogun of Japan
in 1868, courtesy of the Percival David
Foundation.*

Above: Pilgrim bottle, Ch'ing dynasty from the Colthurst Collection, courtesy of the Somerset County Museum.

ASHMOLEAN MUSEUM
Beaumont Street
Oxford, Oxon
Tel: (0865) 512651
Open Mon–Sat 10–4, Sun 2–4; closed Dec 24, 25, 26, Jan 1, Good Fri–Easter Sun, Mon and Tue after first Sun after Sept 2.
Chinese porcelain including celadon ware.

BARLOW COLLECTION
University of Sussex
Falmer
Nr Brighton, Sussex
Tel: (0273) 606755
Open Tue and Thur 10–12, 2–4; closed University Hols.
Early (mainly pre-15th c.) Chinese pottery and porcelain; Korean celadon; fine T'ang period jade.

SOUTHWEST ENGLAND AND WALES

SOMERSET COUNTY MUSEUM
Taunton Castle
Castle Green
Taunton, Somerset
Tel: (0823) 73451, ext 286
Open Apr 1–Sep 30, Mon–Sat 10–5; Oct 1–Mar 31, Tue–Sat 10–5.
Chinese ceramics.

NORTH OF ENGLAND AND SCOTLAND

BAGSHAW MUSEUM
Wilton Park
Batley, Kirklies, W Yorkshire
Tel: (0924) 472514
Open Apr–Oct, Tue–Sat 10–6, Sun 1–5; Nov–Mar, Tue–Sat 10–5.
Hilditch collection of Oriental art.

HEATON HALL
Heaton Park
Prestwick
Manchester, Gt Manchester
Tel: (061) 773 1231
Open Apr–Sept, Mon–Sat 10–6, Sun 2–6, (May–Aug 12–6); closed Oct–Mar.
Oriental collections with Chinese porcelain from Han to Qing dynasties, Japanese arms and armour, ivories and prints.

GULBENKIAN MUSEUM OF ORIENTAL ART
School of Oriental Studies
The University
Elvet Hill
Durham, Co Durham
Tel: (0385) 66711
Open Mon–Fri 9.30–1, 2.15–5, Sat 9.30–12, 2.15–5, Sun 2.15–5; closed weekends between Christmas and Easter.
Tibetan and Nepalese Buddhist art; high quality Chinese porcelain from Neolithic period to 19th c.

Above: Double gourd vase in porcelain painted in underglaze blue with landscape scenes and animals from the Jiajing period, Ming dynasty (1522–66), courtesy of Heaton Hall.

LAING ART GALLERY
Higham Place
Newcastle upon Tyne, Tyne & Wear
Tel: (0632) 27734/269891
Open Mon, Wed, Fri, Sat 10–6, Tue, Thur 10–8, Sun 2.30–5.30, Bank Hols 10–6.

Outstanding Japanese woodblock prints.

FOR MAP OF THE BRITISH ISLES, SEE PAGE 7.

LONDON

THOMAS CORAM FOUNDATION FOR CHILDREN (FOUNDLING HOSPITAL ART TREASURES)
40 Brunswick Square
London WC1
Tel: (01) 278 2424
Open Mon–Fri 2–4; closed weekends and Bank Hols (advisable to check rooms are open).
Paintings and prints, including Hogarth, Gainsborough and Reynold.

COURTAULD INSTITUTE GALLERIES
Woburn Square
London WC1
Tel: (01) 636 2095
Open Mon–Sat 10–5, Sun 2–5.
One of Britain's finest collections. Gambier-Parry and Princes Gate collections of Old Master paintings and drawings plus magnificent Impressionist and post-Impressionist works.

Right: "The Flower Girl", oil painting by Bartolome Esteban Murillo (1617–1682), courtesy of the Dulwich Picture Gallery.

DULWICH PICTURE GALLERY
College Road
London SE21
Tel: (01) 693 5254
Open Tue–Sat 10–5, Sun 2–5; closed Mon.
Old Masters: Rembrandt, Rubens, Poussin, Gainsborough and good Dutch collection.

IMPERIAL WAR MUSEUM
Lambeth Road
London SE1
Tel: (01) 735 8922
Open Mon–Sat 10–5.50, Sun 2–5.50; closed Dec 24, 25, 26, Jan 1, Good Fri, May Day Bank Hol.
Important drawings and paintings by war artists.

KENWOOD, THE IVEAGH BEQUEST
Hampstead Lane
London NW3
Tel: (01) 348 1286/7
Open daily 10–5 or dusk; closed Dec 24, 25, Good Fri.
Old Masters, including Rembrandt, Vermeer, Van Dyck, Gainsborough etc.

LEIGHTON HOUSE ART GALLERY AND MUSEUM
12 Holland Park Road
London W14
Tel: (01) 602 3316
Open Mon–Sat 11–5.
High Victorian art by Leighton, Burne-Jones, Watts, Millais, etc.

PAINTINGS, DRAWINGS AND PRINTS

*Above: "Over the Top" by John Northcote
Nash, oil on canvas painted at Marcoing, Dec
30, 1917, courtesy of the Imperial War
Museum.*

WILLIAM MORRIS GALLERY
Water House
Lloyd Park, Forest Road
Walthamstow, London E17
Tel: (01) 527 5544, ext 390
*Opening times under review; telephone for
details.*

Frank Brangwyn 19th c. collection.

NATIONAL GALLERY
Trafalgar Square
London WC2
Tel: (01) 839 3321
*Open Mon–Sat 10–6, Sun 2–6; closed Dec
24, 25, 26, Jan 1, Good Fri, May Day Bank
Hol.*
*Magnificent national collection of
international masters. Also English painting
from Hogarth to Turner.*

NATIONAL MARITIME MUSEUM
Romney Road
Greenwich
London SE10
Tel: (01) 858 4422
*Open Mon–Sat 10–6 (10–5 winter); Sun
2–5.30; closed Mon (except Bank Hol Mons,
when closed following Tue), Dec 24, 25, 26,
Jan 1, Good Fri, May Day Bank Hol.*

*Paintings and prints relating to maritime
history.*

NATIONAL PORTRAIT GALLERY
St Martin's Place
Trafalgar Square
London WC2
Tel: (01) 930 1552
*Open Mon–Fri 10–5, Sat 10–6, Sun 2–6;
closed Dec 24, 25, 26, Jan 1, Good Fri, May
Day Bank Hol.*

Historic portraits from Tudor times on.

*Right: "Dante in Exile", by Frederic Lord
Leighton P.R.A., circa 1864, courtesy of the
Leighton House Museum.*

RANGERS HOUSE
Chesterfield Walk
Blackheath
London SE10
Tel: (01) 853 0035
*Open daily Feb 1–Oct 31, 10–5; Nov 1–Jan
31, 10–4; closed Dec 24, 25, Good Fri.*
*Suffolk collection of Tudor, Stuart and 18th c.
portraits.*

TATE GALLERY
Millbank
London SW1
Tel: (01) 821 7128
*Open Mon–Sat 10–6, Sun 2–6; closed Dec
24, 25, 26, Jan 1, Good Fri, May Day Bank
Hol.*
*National collections of British painting to
1900, and 20th c. British and European
painting; also Turner, Blake and
pre-Raphaelite collections.*

VICTORIA AND ALBERT MUSEUM
Cromwell Road
London SW7
Tel: (01) 589 6371

VICTORIA AND ALBERT MUSEUM (CON'T)
*Open Mon–Thur, Sat 10–5.50, Sun 2.30–
5.50; closed Fri, Dec 24, 25, 26, Jan 1, Good
Fri, May Day Bank Hol.*
*Fine paintings, prints and drawings,
including Raphael cartoons, Constable
collection and English miniatures.*

SOUTH AND SOUTHEAST ENGLAND

ASHMOLEAN MUSEUM
Beaumont Street
Oxford, Oxon
Tel: (0865) 512651
*Open Mon–Sat 10–4, Sun 2–4; closed Dec
24, 25, 26, Jan 1, Good Fri–Easter Sun, Mon
and Tue after first Sun after Sep 2.*
*Fine Italian, Dutch, Flemish, French and
English works including miniatures.*

BRIGHTON MUSEUM AND ART GALLERY
Church Street
Brighton, E Sussex
Tel: (0273) 603005
*Open Tue–Sat 10–5.45, Sun 2–5 (summer
2–6); closed Mon, Dec 25, 26, Good Fri.*

17th to 19th c. pictures plus Art Nouveau.

CHRIST CHURCH PICTURE GALLERY
Christ Church (college)
Oxford, Oxon
Tel: (0865) 42102
*Open daily 10.30–1, 2–4.30; closed Dec
24–Jan 1 and 1 week after Easter weekend.*

Old Master paintings and drawings.

CITY MUSEUM AND ART GALLERY
Museum Road
Old Portsmouth, Hants
Tel: (0705) 827261
Open daily 10.30–5.30; closed Dec 25, 26.

Paintings and prints from 16th c. on.

FIRLE PLACE
Firle, Nr Lewes, E Sussex
Tel: (0323) 843902
*Open June–Sep, Wed, Thur, Sun 2.15–5.30;
also Easter and Bank Hol Suns and Mons.*

European and British Old Masters.

FITZWILLIAM MUSEUM

Trumpington Street
Cambridge, Cambs
Tel: (0223) 69501

Open Tue–Sat, Lower Galleries 10–2, Upper Galleries 2–5, Sun 2.15–5; open Bank Hol Mons; closed Dec 24–Jan 1, Good Fri. Avisable to check in advance that appropriate gallery is open.

17th to early 20th c. paintings, drawings and prints.

CECIL HIGGINS ART GALLERY

Castle Close,
Bedford, Beds
Tel: (0234) 211222

Open Tue–Fri 12.30–5, Sat 11–5, Sun 2–5, Bank Hols 12.30–5.

English watercolours including Turner, and European prints.

SOUTHAMPTON ART GALLERY

Civic Centre
Southampton, Hants
Tel: (0703) 23855, ext 769

Open Tue–Sat 11–5.45, Sun 2–5; closed Mon.

Old Masters, Impressionists and Post-Impressionists, specialising in early 20th c. British works.

WADDESDON MANOR

Waddesdon
Nr Aylesbury, Bucks
Tel: (029 665) 211/282

Open end Mar–end Oct, Wed–Sun 2–6; Good Fri and Bank Hol Mons 11–6.

Rothschild art collection of French, Italian, Dutch and Flemish paintings plus portraits by Gainsborough, Reynolds and Romney.

SOUTHWEST ENGLAND AND WALES

CHELTENHAM ART GALLERY AND MUSEUM

Clarence Street
Cheltenham, Glos
Tel: (0242) 37431

Open Mon–Sat 10–5.30.

European paintings, especially 17th Dutch artists.

CITY MUSEUM AND ART GALLERY

Queen's Road
Bristol, Avon
Tel: (0272) 299771

Open Mon–Sat 10–5.

Old Masters plus 19th and early 20th c. paintings including English watercolours.

CITY MUSEUM AND ART GALLERY

Drake Circus
Plymouth, Devon
Tel: (0752) 6688000, ext 4378

Open Mon–Sat 10–6.

Old Master drawings and family portraits by Joshua Reynolds.

CORSHAM COURT

Chippenham, Wilts
Tel: (0249) 712 214

Open mid Jan–mid Dec, Tue, Wed, Thur, Sat, Sun and Bank Hol Mons 2–4, except Summer Bank Hol 2–6.

British, Spanish, Italian and Flemish Old Masters.

GALLERY OF TUDOR AND JACOBEAN PORTRAITS

Montacute House
Montacute
Nr Yeovil, Somerset
Tel: (093 582) 3289

Open Apr–end Oct daily (except Tue) 12.30–6; other times by written appointment

Period portraits from National Portrait Gallery loan.

HOLBURNE OF MENSTRIE MUSEUM

Great Pulteney Street
Bath, Avon
Tel: (0225) 66669

Open Mon–Sat 11–5, Sun 2.30–6.

Old Masters, including Stubbs and Gainsborough.

NEWLYN ORION GALLERY

Newlyn, Cornwall
Tel: (0736) 3715

Open Mon–Sat 10–5.

Paintings of the Newlyn school (late 19th– early 20th c).

ROYAL ALBERT MEMORIAL MUSEUM

Queen Street
Exeter, Devon
Tel: (0392) 56724

Open Tue–Sat 10–5.30.

18th and 19th c. English paintings and watercolours.

RUSSELL-COTES ART GALLERY AND MUSEUM

East Cliff
Bournemouth, Dorset
Tel: (0202) 21009

Open Mon–Sat 10.30–5.

17th–early 20th c. European paintings.

SALTRAM HOUSE

Nr Plympton, Devon
Tel: (0752) 336546

Open daily Apr–end Oct except Mon (but open Bank Hol Mons) 12.30–6.

Picture collection which Sir Joshua Reynolds helped form.

Above: "A First-Rate Taking in Stores", watercolour by J.M.W. Turner, painted in 1818, courtesy of the Cecil Higgins Art Gallery.

SUDELEY CASTLE

Winchcombe, Glos
Tel: (0242) 602308

Open Mar–Oct daily 12–5.30.

Fine paintings including Rubens, Constable and Van Dyck.

WILTON HOUSE

Salisbury, Wilts
Tel: (072 274) 3641

Open Apr–Oct, Tue–Sat and Bank Hol Mons 11–6, Sun 1–6.

Famous Old Master paintings.

MIDLANDS AND EAST ANGLIA

BIRMINGHAM MUSEUM AND ART GALLERY

Chamberlain Square
Birmingham, W Midlands
Tel: (021) 235 3890

Open Mon–Sat 10–5.30, Sun 2–5.30; closed Dec 25, 26, Jan 1, Good Fri.

Old Masters, 17th c. Italian paintings, English watercolours and famous Pre-Raphaelite works.

CENTRAL ART GALLERY

Lichfield Street
Wolverhampton, W Midlands
Tel: (0902) 24549

Open Mon–Sat 10–6.

English paintings and watercolours by Gainsborough, Turner, Zoffany, Bonington and others; Victorian genre paintings.

CENTRAL MUSEUM AND ART GALLERY

Guildhall Road
Northampton, Northants
Tel: (0604) 34881

Open Mon–Sat 10–6.

Old Masters.

PAINTINGS, DRAWINGS AND PRINTS

CHRISTCHURCH MANSION AND WOLSEY ART GALLERY
Christchurch Park
Ipswich, Suffolk
Tel: (0473) 53246
Open Mon–Sat 10–5, Sun 2.30–4.30 (closed at dusk in winter).
Works by Gainsborough, Constable and other Suffolk artists.

CITY MUSEUM AND ART GALLERY
Broad Street
Hanley
Stoke-on-Trent, Staffs
Tel: (0782) 29611
Open Mon, Tue, Thur–Sat 10.30–5, Wed 10.30–8.
Mainly British 18th–20th c. works.

GAINSBOROUGH'S HOUSE
46 Gainsborough Street
Sudbury, Suffolk
Tel: (0787) 72958
Open Tue–Sat 10–12.30, 2–5, Sun 2–5.
Artist's paintings displayed in his birthplace.

LEICESTERSHIRE MUSEUM AND ART GALLERY
New Walk
Leicester, Leics
Tel: (0533) 554100
Open Mon–Sat 10–5.30, Sun 2–5.30; closed Fri.
Old Masters plus 18th to early 20th c. British paintings, drawings and watercolours.

NORWICH CASTLE MUSEUM
Norwich, Norfolk
Tel: (0603) 611277, ext 279
Open Mon–Sat 10–5, Sun 2–5.
Important collection with works by Norwich school painters (Cotman, Crome etc).

SAINSBURY CENTRE FOR THE VISUAL ARTS
University of East Anglia
Norwich, Norfolk
Tel: (0603) 56060
Open Tue–Sun 12–5; closed Mon and Bank Hols and Dec 24–Jan 10.
Anderson Collection of Art Nouveau.

UPTON HOUSE
Edge Hill
Nr Banbury, Warks
Tel: (029 587) 266
Open Apr–Sep Mon–Thur 2–6; some weekends in May and Aug.
Very fine collection of British, French, Dutch, Flemish, German, Italian and Spanish paintings.

USHER GALLERY
Lindum Road
Lincoln, Lincs
Tel: (0522) 27980
Open Mon–Sat 10–5.30, Sun 2–5.
Outstanding gallery with watercolours by Peter de Wint, miniatures, local paintings and drawings.

WALSALL MUSEUM AND ART GALLERY
Lichfield Street
Walsall, W Midlands
Tel: (0922) 21244 ext 3124
Open Mon–Fri 10–6, Sat 10–4.45.
Graham-Ryan collection of European art including works by Blake, Degas, Van Gogh.

WARWICK CASTLE
Warwick, Warks
Tel: (0926) 495421
Open daily Mar 1–Oct 31, 10–5.30; Nov–end Feb, 10–4.30; closed Dec 25.

Fine paintings including Rubens and Van Dyck.

WIGHTWICK MANOR
Nr Wolverhampton, W Midlands
Tel: Not Available
Open Thur, Sat, Bank Hol Suns and Mons (Wed, May–Sep only) 2.30–5.30; closed Feb, Dec 25, 26, Jan 1, 2.

Pre-Raphaelite paintings and William Morris tapestries.

NORTH OF ENGLAND AND SCOTLAND

ART GALLERY AND MUSEUM
Union Street
Oldham, Gt Manchester
Tel: (061) 624 0505
Open Mon, Wed, Thur, Fri 10–7, Tue 10–1, Sat 10–4; closed Sun.

Early English watercolours; 19th and early 20th c. British paintings.

ASTLEY CHEETHAM ART GALLERY
Trinity Street
Stalybridge, Gt Manchester
Tel: (061) 338 2708
Open Tue–Fri 1–8, Sat 9–4; closed Sun, Mon.

Mediaeval, early Renaissance, 18th and 19th c. paintings.

BENINGBROUGH HALL
Shipton, N Yorkshire
Tel: (0904) 470715
Open Apr–Oct, Tue, Wed, Thur, Sat, Sun and Bank Hol Mons 12–6.

Portraits from 1688–1760. (National Portrait Gallery loan).

BOWES MUSEUM
Barnard Castle, Co. Durham
Tel: (0833) 37139
Open Oct, Mar, Apr Mon–Sat 10–5; May–Sep, 10–5.30; Nov–Feb, 10–4; Sun (summer) 2–5, (winter) 2–4.

Important art collection with Tiepolo, Goya, Boucher etc.

BRADFORD ART GALLERY AND MUSEUM
Cartwright Hall
Lister Park
Bradford, W Yorkshire
Tel: (0274) 493313
Open daily 10–5; closed Dec 25, 26, Good Fri.

British art from 17th c. on.

BUXTON MUSEUM AND ART GALLERY
Terrace Road
Buxton, Derbs
Tel: (0928) 4658
Open Tue–Fri 9.30–5.30, Sat 9.30–5.

19th and early 20th c. oils and watercolours.

CANNON HALL MUSEUM
Cawthorne
Barnsley, S Yorkshire
Tel: (0226) 790270
Open Mon–Sat 10.30–5, Sun 2.30–5.

Fine paintings, mainly Dutch and Flemish.

CHATSWORTH
Bakewell, Derbs
Tel: (024 688) 2204
Open end Mar–end Oct daily 11.30–4.30.

17th to 19th c. paintings and drawings.

CITY ART GALLERY
Mosley Street
Manchester, Gt Manchester
Tel: (061) 236 9422, ext 226
Open Mon–Sat 10–6, Sun 2.30–6.

Pre-1900 Old Masters plus Gainsborough, Stubbs, Turner, Impressionists.

DERBY MUSEUMS AND ART GALLERY
The Strand
Derby, Derbs
Tel: (0332) 311111, ext 781
Open Tue–Fri 10–5, Sat 10–4.45.

Pictures of local and topographical interest, including industrial scenes by Joseph Wright.

FERENS ART GALLERY
Queen Victoria Square
Hull, Humberside
Tel: (0482) 223111, ext 2750
Open Tue–Fri 10–1, 2–5, Sat 10–1, 2–4.30; closed Mon, Sun and Bank Hols.

Old Masters, including Dutch School (Hals) and Italians (Canaletto); local marine painting.

GRAVES ART GALLERY
Surrey Street
Sheffield, S Yorkshire
Tel: (0742) 734781
Open Mon–Sat 10–8, Sun 2–5.

British portraits and watercolours, also Continental painting, (mainly French and Spanish).

GRAY ART GALLERY AND MUSEUM
Hartlepool, Cleveland
Tel: (0429) 68916
Open Mon–Sat 10–5.30, Sun 3–5; closed Dec 25, 26, Jan 1, Good Fri.

19th and early 20th c. paintings.

Left: "Tattershall Castle" by Peter de Wint (1784–1849), courtesy of the Usher Gallery, Lincolnshire Museums.

PAINTINGS, DRAWINGS AND PRINTS

HARRIS MUSEUM AND ART GALLERY
Market Square
Preston, Lancs
Tel: (051) 645 3623
Open Mon–Sat 10–5, Sun 2–5.

18th c. paintings by the Devis family and part of the Newsham bequest.

HATTON GALLERY
The Quadrangle
University of Newcastle upon Tyne
Tyne & Wear
Tel: (0632) 22359
Open Mon–Fri 10–5.30, Sat during term 10–5.

Painting and drawing from 14th c. on.

HAWORTH ART GALLERY
Haworth Park
Accrington, Lancs
Tel: (0254) 33782
Open daily except Fri 2–5.

Early English watercolours.

HOPETOUN HOUSE
South Queensferry
Nr Edinburgh, Lothian, Scotland
Tel: (031) 331 2451
Open Easter weekend, then May–Sep daily 11–5.30.

Magnificent interiors with fine picture collection.

HUNTERIAN MUSEUM
Glasgow University
Glasgow, Strathclyde, Scotland
Tel: (041) 339 8855, ext 221
Open Mon–Fri 9–5, Sat 9–12.

French, Dutch, Flemish, Italian and British 17th and 18th c. paintings. British 18th c. portraits; late 19th and early 20th c. Scottish paintings.

LAING ART GALLERY
Higham Place
Newcastle upon Tyne
Tyne & Wear
Tel: (0632) 327734
Open Mon–Sat 10–6, Sun 2.30–5.30, Bank Hols 10–6.

High quality British drawing and painting from 17th c.

Below: "Francis Vincent and Family", oil painting by Arthur Devis (1711–1787), courtesy of the Harris Museum and Art Gallery.

LADY LEVER ART GALLERY
Port Sunlight
Wirral, Merseyside
Tel: (051) 645 3623
Open Mon–Sat 10–5, Sun 2–5.
Victorian paintings by Frith, Leighton, Alma-Tadema etc. Also fine 18th c. English portraits.

MAPPIN ART GALLERY
Weston Park
Sheffield, S Yorkshire
Tel: (0742) 26281
Open June 1–Aug 31, Mon–Sat 10–8, Sun 2–5; Sep 1–May 31, Mon–Sat 10–5, Sun 2–5.
Mainly 18th to early 20th c. English paintings including Gainsborough, Turner, Constable and Pre-Raphaelites.

NATIONAL GALLERY OF SCOTLAND
The Mound
Edinburgh, Scotland
Tel: (031) 556 8921
Open Mon–Sat 10–5, Sun 2–5; during Edinburgh Festival Mon–Sat 10–6, Sun 11–6; print room Mon–Fri 10–12.30, 2–4.30.
Scotland's national collection of 14th–19th c. European art; Scottish art up to 1900.

PANNETT ART GALLERY AND MUSEUM
Pannett Park
Whitby, N Yorkshire
Tel: (0947) 602908
Open May–Sep, Mon–Sat 9.30–5.30, Sun 2–5; Oct–Apr, Mon, Tue, Thur, Fri 10.30–1, Wed, Sat 10.30–4, Sun 2–4.
Early English watercolours and oils including works by Turner, Bonington and Cox.

POLLOK HOUSE
2060 Pollokshaws Road
Pollok Park
Glasgow, Strathclyde, Scotland
Tel: (041) 632 0274
Open Mon–Sat 10–5, Sun 2–5.
Stirling Maxwell collection of European paintings, with works by El Greco, Murillo and Goya.

ROCHDALE ART GALLERY
Esplanade
Rochdale, Gt Manchester
Tel: (0706) 47474, ext 764
Open Mon–Sat 10–5, Sun 2.30–5.
Many British paintings from 18th c. on.

SALFORD MUSEUM AND ART GALLERY
Peel Park
Salford, Gt Manchester
Tel: (061) 736 2649
Open Mon–Sat 10–5, Sun 2–5.
Local artists' work including many paintings by Lowry.

SUDLEY ART GALLERY AND MUSEUM
Mossley Hill Road
Liverpool, Merseyside
Tel: (051) 724 3425
Open Mon–Sat 10–5, Sun 2–5.
18th and 19th c. paintings including Turner, Gainsborough and many Pre-Raphaelites.

Right: "Monsignor Agucchi" painted in 1623 by Domenichino, courtesy of the City of York Art Gallery.

TATTON PARK
Knutsford, Cheshire
Tel: (0565) 3155
Open Easter–mid-May and Sep, Mon–Sat 1–4, Sun, Bank Hol Mons 1–5; mid-May–Aug, 1–5, Sun 1–4; Oct–Easter closed except Sun, Bank Hols in Nov, Mar.
Fine paintings including Canaletto and Van Dyck.

UNIVERSITY OF LIVERPOOL ART GALLERY
3 Abercromby Square
Liverpool, Merseyside
Tel: (051) 709 6022
Open Wed, Fri (except public hols) 12–4.
University collection of paintings, including Turner's watercolours.

WALKER ART GALLERY
William Brown Street
Liverpool, Merseyside
Tel: (051) 227 5234
Open Mon–Sat 10–5, Sun 2–5.
Famous collection of early Italian and Flemish paintings; later European and English schools (Rubens, Rembrandt, Hogarth, Stubbs etc); Pre-Raphaelites.

WHITWORTH ART GALLERY
Oxford Road
Manchester, Gt Manchester
Tel: (061) 273 4865
Open Mon–Sat 10–5, except Thur 10–9; closed Dec 24, Jan 1, Good Fri.
Outstanding collections of Old Masters, English watercolours, Post-Impressionist and early 20th c. drawings and prints.

WILLIAMSON ART GALLERY AND MUSEUM
Slatey Road
Birkenhead
Wirral, Merseyside
Tel: (051) 652 4177
Open Mon–Wed, Fri, Sat 10–5, Thur 10–9, Sun 2–5; closed Bank Hols.
Very important watercolour collection.

YORK CITY ART GALLERY
Exhibition Square
York, N Yorkshire
Tel: (0904) 23839
Open Mon–Sat 10–5, Sun 2.30–5.
European and British paintings from 14th c. on. Also Yorkshire-based works.

PHOTOGRAPHICA AND CINEMATOGRAPHICA
POTTERY AND PORCELAIN

LONDON

NATIONAL FILM ARCHIVE
81 Dean Street
London W1
Tel: (01) 437 4355
Open daily 10–6 by appointment only.
Collection of films and television programmes, film stills and posters.

NATIONAL PORTRAIT GALLERY
St Martin's Place
Trafalgar Square
London WC2
Tel: (01) 930.1552
Open Mon–Fri 10–5, Sat 10–6, Sun 2–6; closed Dec 24, 25, 26, Jan 1, Good Fri, May Day Bank Hol.

Many interesting early photographs.

SOUTH AND SOUTHEAST ENGLAND

KINGSTON-UPON THAMES MUSEUM AND ART GALLERY
Fairfield West
Kingston-upon-Thames, Surrey
Tel: (01) 546 5386
Open Mon–Sat 10–5.
Interesting for the historically important Zoopraxiscope of Eadward Muybridge.

THE KODAK MUSEUM
Headstone Drive
Harrow, Middx
Tel: (01) 863 0534
Open Mon–Fri 9.30–4.30; Sat, Sun, Bank Hols 2–6.
Over 8,000 items of apparatus, optical toys magic lanterns and accessories, photographs; historical exhibition; changing photographic exhibition.

MUSEUM OF THE HISTORY OF SCIENCE
Old Ashmolean Building, Broad Street
Oxford, Oxon
Tel: (0865) 43997
Open Mon–Fri 10.30–1, 2.30–4; closed Bank Hols and 1 week at Christmas and Easter.
Photographic apparatus and records.

NEWBURY MUSEUM
Wharf Street
Newbury, Berks
Tel: (0635) 30511
Open Apr–Sep, Mon–Sat (ex Wed afternoon) 10–5; Oct–Mar, 10–4; closed Sun, Bank Hols.
Camera collection.

SOUTHWEST ENGLAND AND WALES

BARNES MUSEUM OF CINEMATOGRAPHY
44 Fore Street
St Ives, Cornwall
Open daily Apr–Sep 11–1, 2.30–5.

History of moving pictures and the photographic image.

FOX TALBOT MUSEUM
Lacock Abbey
Lacock, Wilts
Tel: (024 973) 459
Open daily Mar–Oct 11–6; closed Good Fri.

Home of William Henry Fox, the pioneer of photography. History of early days displayed in converted barn near the abbey.

THE ROYAL PHOTOGRAPHIC SOCIETY NATIONAL CENTRE OF PHOTOGRAPHY
The Octagon
Milsom Street
Bath, Avon
Tel: (0225) 62841
Open Mon–Sat 10–4.45; Sun (Easter and school summer hols only), Bank Hol Mons 11–4; closed Xmas.

History of photography including Leica collection and rare photographs.

NORTH OF ENGLAND AND SCOTLAND

NORTH WESTERN MUSEUM OF SCIENCE AND INDUSTRY
97 Grosvenor Street
Manchester, Gt Manchester
Tel: (061) 273 6636
Open Mon–Sat 10–5; closed Dec 25, 26, Good Fri.

Fine collection of early photographic equipment.

WELHOLME GALLERIES
Welholme Road
Great Grimsby, Humberside
Tel: (0472) 59161
Open Tue–Sat 10–5.

Hallgarth collection of Lincolnshire photographs.

POTTERY AND PORCELAIN

LONDON

FENTON HOUSE
Hampstead Grove
London NW3
Tel: (01) 435 3471
Open Feb, Mar, Nov, Sat 11–5, Sun 2–5 (or dusk if earlier); Apr–end Oct, Mon, Tue, Wed, Sat, Bank Hols 11–5, Sun 2–5 (or dusk).
Binning collection of porcelain.

MUSEUM OF LONDON
London Wall
London EC2
Tel: (01) 600 3699
Open Tue–Sat 10–6, Sun 2–6.
Chelsea and Bow porcelain plus mediaeval pottery.

VICTORIA AND ALBERT MUSEUM
Cromwell Road
London SW7
Tel: (01) 589 6371
Open Mon–Thur, Sat 10–5.50, Sun 2.30–5.50; closed Fri, Jan 1, May 1, Dec 24, 25, 26.
Magnificent ceramics collection, outstanding for Chelsea, Meissen and Sevres.

Right: Majolica dish from the Isabella d'Erte service, made in Urbino, Italy, circa 1525, courtesy of the Fitzwilliam Museum.

SOUTH AND SOUTH EAST ENGLAND

ASHMOLEAN MUSEUM OF ART AND ARCHAEOLOGY
Beaumont Street
Oxford, Oxon
Tel: (0865) 57522
Open Mon–Sat 10–4, Sun 2–4; closed Good Fri–Easter Sun, Mon and Tue after first Sun after Sep 2, Dec 24, 25, 26, Jan 1.

Superb exhibits include fine Marshall collection of early Worcester.

BRIGHTON MUSEUM AND ART GALLERY
Church Street
Brighton, E Sussex
Tel: (0273) 603005
Open Tue–Sat 10–5.45, Sun 2–5 (summer 2–6); closed Dec 25, 26 Good Fri.

Outstanding Willett collection of pottery and porcelain formed in late 19th to illustrate social themes.

FITZWILLIAM MUSEUM
Trumpington Street
Cambridge, Cambs
Tel: (0223) 69501
Open Tue–Sat, Lower Galleries 10–2, Upper Galleries 2–5, Sun (Lower or Upper open alternate weeks) 2.15–5; open Bank Hol Mon; closed Dec 24–Jan 1, Good Fri.

Fine pottery and porcelain display room.

HOVE MUSEUM OF ART
19 New Church Road
Hove, Sussex BN3 4AB
Tel: (0273) 779410
Open Mon–Fri 11–1, 2–4.30, Sat 11–1, 2–5; closed Bank Hols.

General ceramics collection including local Sussex ware and studio pottery. See overleaf for illustration.

FOR MAP OF THE BRITISH ISLES, SEE PAGE 7.

Above: Bow figurine decorated by James Giles, circa 1760, courtesy of the Borough of Hove Museum of Art.

LUTON HOO
Luton, Beds
Tel: (0582) 22955
Open Apr–Oct, Mon, Wed, Thur, Sat, Good Fri 11–5.45, Sun 2–5.45.

Ceramics collection, including Chelsea, Worcester, Staffordshire, Derby, Bristol, Liverpool, Swansea, Rockingham and Limoges.

SOUTHAMPTON ART GALLERY
Civic Centre
Southampton, Hants
Tel: (0703) 23855
Open Tue–Sat 11–5.45, Sun 2–5.

Post–1930s studio pottery. (Based on Milner-White bequest.)

WOBURN ABBEY
Woburn, Beds
Tel: (052 525) 666
Open daily Feb–Nov; Feb 1–Easter, Nov 1–30, 1–4.45; Good Fri–Oct 31, 11–5.45, Sun 11–6.15.

Magnificent Sèvres dinner service presented to 4th Duke of Bedford by Louis XV.

SOUTHWEST ENGLAND AND WALES

BATH MUSEUMS
Victoria Art Gallery
Bridge Street
Bath, Avon
Tel: (0225) 61111
Open: Mon–Fri 10–6, Sat 10–5, closed Sun and Bank Hols.

Important English Delftware collection.

CHELTENHAM ART GALLERY AND MUSEUM
Clarence Street
Cheltenham, Glos
Tel: (0242) 37431
Open Mon–Sat 10–5.30.

Pottery and porcelain, including Chinese ceramics.

CORNWALL COUNTY MUSEUM
River Street
Truro, Cornwall
Tel: (0872) 2205
Open Mon–Sat 9–1, 2–5; closed Bank Hols.
English ceramics of many periods, including local products.

ROYAL SOUTH WALES MUSEUM
Victoria Road
Swansea, Glamorgan, Wales
Tel: (0792) 53763
Open Mon–Sat 10–4.30; closed Dec 24–Jan 1, Good Fri.
Excellent ceramics collections, with displays from Cambrian Pottery, also Swansea and Nantgarw porcelain and Ynysmedw pottery.

SOMERSET COUNTY MUSEUM
Taunton Castle
Taunton, Somerset TA1 4AA
Tel: (0823) 73451
Open Apr 1–Sept 30, Mon–Sat 10–5; Oct 1–Mar 31, Tue–Sat 10–5.
Collection of Elton ware

Left: Mid-18 c. Bristol Delftware plate, courtesy of the Bath Musuems, Victoria Art Gallery.

MIDLANDS AND EAST ANGLIA

CLIVE HOUSE MUSEUM
College Hill
Shrewsbury, Shropshire
Tel: (0743) 54811
Open Mon 12–6, Tue–Sat 10–6 (winter 10–4.30).

Collection of local pottery including Caughley and Coalport.

DYSON PERRINS MUSEUM TRUST
Severn Street
Worcester, Heref & Worcs
Tel: (0905) 20272
Open Mon–Fri 10–1, 2–5; Sat, Apr–Sep, 10–1, 2–5; closed Bank Hols.

Finest collection of Worcester existing catalogued and displayed in highly scholarly fashion.

GLADSTONE POTTERY MUSEUM
Uttoxeter Road
Longton, Stoke-on-Trent, Staffs
Tel: (0782) 311378/319232
Open Mon–Sat 10.30–5.30 (ex Mon, Oct–Mar), Sun and Bank Hols 2–6: closed Dec 25.

History of Staffordshire potteries with displays of local products and techniques.

MINTON FACTORY MUSEUM
Stoke-on Trent, Staffs
Tel: (0782) 49171
Open Mon–Fri 9.30–12.30, 2–4.30; closed Bank Hols.

Representative Minton pieces, including Parian ware and Majolica.

Below: The first piece of porcelain made at the Worcester Porcelain Company in 1751, the "Wigornia" creamboat. Moulded with raised patterns and painted in enamel colours in the quaint mixture of English silver shapes and Chinese porcelain that was typical of the period, courtesy of the Dyson Perrins Museum.

Above: One of a pair of plaques, freely painted in enamels by William Stephen Coleman, studio manager at the Minton Art Pottery Studio, South Kensington, (1871–1875), circa 1871, courtesy of the Minton Museum Royal Doulton Tableware Ltd.

NOTTINGHAM CASTLE MUSEUM
The Castle
Nottingham, Notts
Tel: (0602) 411881
Open daily Apr 1–Sep 30, 10–10.45; Oct 1–Mar 31, 10–4.45; closed Dec 25.

Large collection of British and European ceramics.

SPODE MUSEUM
Spode Works
Stoke-on-Trent, Staffs
Tel: (0782) 46011
Open by appointment

Huge collection of Spode and Copeland from 1780's onwards.

Below: Queen's Ware plate from the famous "Frog Service" made for Catherine the Great Russia in 1773/4, with scene of Castle Acre Castle in Norfolk, bordered with oak leaves and the frog emblem of La Grenouillière (the froggery) – the site of the palace for which the service was intended, courtesy of the Wedgwood Museum.

WALLINGTON
Cambo, Northld
Tel: (067074) 283
Open Tue–Fri 2–5, Sat 9–1.
Fine porcelain collection.

WEDGWOOD MUSEUM
Barlaston
Stoke-on-Trent, Staffs
Tel: (078 139) 4141
Open Mon–Fri 9–5; closed Dec 25.
Wedgwood products including 18th c. pieces; also demonstration display.

NORTH OF ENGLAND AND SCOTLAND

CARLISLE MUSEUM AND ART GALLERY
Castle Street
Carlisle, Cumbria
Tel: (0228) 34781
Open Apr–Sep, Mon–Fri 9–7, Sat 9–5; Sep–Mar, Mon–Sat 9–5; June–Aug, Sun 2.30–5; closed Bank Hols.
Williamson collection of fine English porcelain, mostly 18th c., including Chelsea, Derby, Worcester, Bow, Spode, Rockingham.

CLIFTON PARK MUSEUM
Clifton Park
Rotherham, S Yorkshire
Tel: (0709) 2121, ext 3569/3519
Open Apr–Sep, Mon–Thur, Sat 10–6, Sun 2.30–5 (closed Fri); Oct–Mar, Mon–Thur, Sat 10–5, Sun 2.30–4.30 (closed Fri).
British ceramics, including large collection of Rockingham.

DERBY MUSEUMS AND ART GALLERY
The Strand
Derby, Derbs
Tel: (0332) 311111
Open Tue–Fri 10–5, Sat 10–4.45.
Collection of local Derby porcelain in Gallery.

MANCHESTER CITY ART GALLERY
Mosley Street
Manchester, Gt Manchester
Tel: (061) 236 9422,
Open Mon–Sat 10–6, Sun 2.30–6; closed Dec 25, Good Fri.
Recently-bequeathed Lacks collection of European porcelain, including fine 18th c. pieces from German and English factories.

ROYAL CROWN DERBY WORKS MUSEUM
Osmaston Road
Derby, Derbs DE3 8JZ
Tel: (0332) 47051/2/3
Open first Tue in month 10–4.
Recently-founded museum with collection of 18th and 19th c. Derby porcelain; identification service offered.

SUNDERLAND MUSEUM
Borough Road
Sunderland, Tyne & Wear
Tel: (0783) 41235
Open Mon–Fri 9.30–6, Sat 9.30–4, Sun 2–5; Bank Hols 10–5; closed Dec 25, 26, Jan 1, Good Fri.
Local lustre ware.

Above: "Figure of a Harlequin", Derby, circa 1765, from the Lacks collection, courtesy of the Manchester City Art Gallery.

WILLIAMSON ART GALLERY AND MUSEUM
Slatey Road
Birkenhead, Wirral, Merseyside
Tel: (051 652) 4177
Open Mon–Wed, Fri, Sat 10–5, Thur 10–9, Sun 2–5; closed Bank Hols.
Birkenhead Della Robbia ware and Liverpool pottery.

Below: The celebrated Kedlestone vase, circa 1790, courtesy of the Royal Crown Derby Works Museum.

LONDON

BRITISH DENTAL ASSOCIATION MUSEUM
63–64 Wimpole Street
London W1
Tel: (01) 935 0875
Open by appointment only.

History of dental surgery plus early instruments.

MICHAEL FARADAY'S LABORATORY AND MUSEUM
The Royal Institution of Great Britain
21 Albemarle Street
London W1
Tel: (01) 409 2992
Open Tue, Thur 1–4.

Laboratory restored to original state; also collection of Faraday's original apparatus.

NATIONAL MARITIME MUSEUM
Romney Road
London SE10
Tel: (01) 858 4422
Open Tue–Sat 10–6 (10–5 in winter) Bank Hols, Sun 2–5.30; closed Mon, Dec 24, 25, 26, Jan 1, Good Fri, May Day Bank Hol, Tue following Mon Bank Hol.

Navigational instruments, history of astronomy. (See also Old Royal Observatory.)

THE OLD ROYAL OBSERVATORY
Greenwich Park
London SE10
Tel: (01) 885 1167
Open summer Mon–Sat 10–6, Sun 2.30–6; winter Mon–Fri 10–5, Sat 10–6, Sun 2.30–6; closed Dec 24, 25, 26, Jan 1, Good Fri, May Day Bank Hol.

Many unique early astronomical instruments, such as Halley's telescopes and quadrants.

PHARMACEUTICAL SOCIETY'S MUSEUM
1 Lambeth High Street
London SE1
Tel: (01) 735 9141
Open by appointment.

History of pharmacy, with early dispensing apparatus.

SCIENCE MUSEUM
Exhibition Road
London SW7
Tel: (01) 589 3456
Open Mon–Sat 10–6, Sun 2.30–6; closed Dec 24, 25, 26, Jan 1, May Day Bank Hol.

Unrivalled collections relating to all branches of the sciences including historic astronomical instruments and Wellcome Collection of the History of Medicine, with over 1,500 microscopes and many rare instruments from all over the world.

SOUTH AND SOUTHEAST ENGLAND

BRITISH TYPEWRITER MUSEUM
Rothesay Museum
8 Bath Road
Bournemouth, Hants
Tel: (0202) 21009
Open Mon–Sat 10.30–5.30; closed Dec 25, 26, Jan 1, Good Fri.

World's largest collection of antique typewriters on public display.

Above: Selection of some of the Coakbrookdale and other cast iron objects, courtesy of the Coalbrookdale Museum of Iron, Ironbridge Gorge Museum.

MUSEUM OF THE HISTORY OF SCIENCE
Old Ashmolean Building
Broad Street
Oxford, Oxon
Tel: (0865) 43997
Open Mon–Fri 10.30–1, 2.30–4; closed Bank Hols, one week at Christmas and Easter. Valuable early instruments (astrolabes, sundials, microscopes, medical and chemical apparatus); library and manuscripts.

WHIPPLE MUSEUM OF THE HISTORY OF SCIENCE
Free School Lane
Cambridge, Cambs
Tel: (0223) 358381
Open Mon–Fri 2–4; closed during vacations except by special appointment.
Mainly 16th to 18th c. historic scientific instruments.

SOUTHWEST ENGLAND AND WALES

JENNER MUSEUM
Church Lane
Berkeley, Glos
Tel: (0453 810) 631
Open Apr–Sep, Tue–Sun 2.30–6.
Displays relating to Jenner's early experiments in vaccination.

MIDLANDS AND EAST ANGLIA

AVERY HISTORICAL MUSEUM
Smethwick
Warley, W Midlands
Tel: (021) 558 1112
Open during factory hours by appointment.
Machines and weights relating to history of weighing.

COALBROOKDALE MUSEUM OF IRON (IRONBRIDGE GORGE MUSEUM)
Ironbridge
Telford, Shropshire
Tel: (095 245) 3522
Open daily Apr–Oct 10–6; Nov–Mar 10–5.
Large museum complex of industrial archaeology including Coalbrookdale Museum of Iron beside the site of Abraham Darby's blast furnace.

HALL'S CROFT
Old Town
Stratford-upon-Avon, Warks
Tel: (0789) 2107
Open Apr–Oct, Mon–Sat 9–6, Sun 2–6, Nov–Mar, Mon–Sat 9–12.45, 2–4.

Displays relating to Tudor medicine in Shakespeare's father-in-law's home.

HEREFORD AND WORCESTER COUNTY MUSEUM
Hartlebury Castle
Hartlebury, nr Kidderminster
Heref & Worcs
Tel: (0299) 250416
Social history exhibits including horse-drawn vehicles. See overleaf for illustration.

MUSEUM OF SCIENCE AND INDUSTRY
Newhall Street
Birmingham, W Midlands
Tel: (021) 236 1022
Open Mon–Fri 10–5 (first Fri in month 10–9), Sat 10–5.30, Sun 2–5.30; closed Dec 25, 26, Good Fri.

Reflecting city's importance in engineering, museum has steam engines, machine tools and scientific instruments.

MUSEUM OF TECHNOLOGY
Abbey Pumping Station
Abbey Lane
Leicester, Leics
Tel: (0533) 61330
Open Mon–Sat 10–5.30, Sun 2–5.30.

Beam engines and display of knitting machinery.

NORTH OF ENGLAND AND SCOTLAND

NORTH WESTERN MUSEUM OF SCIENCE AND INDUSTRY
97 Grosvenor Street
Manchester, Gt Manchester
Tel: (061) 273 6636
Open Mon–Sat 10–5; closed Dec 25, 26, Good Fri.

Early textile machinery; development of steam power; apparatus and notebooks of Joule, founder of science of thermodynamics; exhibits relating to Dalton's atomic theory; many other displays of development of technology.

ROYAL SCOTTISH MUSEUM
Chambers Street
Edinburgh, Scotland
Tel: (031) 225 7534
Open Mon–Sat 10–5, Sun 2–5.

National collections of science and technology; Frank collection of microscopes and Playfair collection of rare 18th c. chemical glassware.

NORTHERN IRELAND

ULSTER MUSEUM
Botanic Gardens
Belfast, N Ireland
Tel: (0232) 668251
Open Mon–Sat 10–5, Sun 2.30–5.30.

Well-displayed exhibits on industry and technology.

LONDON

VICTORIA AND ALBERT MUSEUM
Cromwell Road
London SW7
Tel: (01) 589 6371
*Open Mon–Thur, Sat 10–5.50, Sun
2.30–5.50; closed Fri, Dec 24, 25, 26, Jan 1,
Good Fri, May Day Bank Hol.*
*Unrivalled collection of English domestic plate
from 14th c. to Victorian era.*

WALLACE COLLECTION
Hertford House
Manchester Square
London W1
Tel: (01) 935 0687
*Open Mon–Sat 10–5, Sun 2–5; closed Dec
24, 25, 26, Jan 1, Good Fri, May Day Bank
Hol.*
Goldsmiths' work.

SOUTH AND SOUTHEAST ENGLAND

FORTY HALL
Forty Hill
Enfield, Middx
Tel: (01) 363 8196
*Open Easter–Sep, Tue–Fri 10–6, Sat, Sun
10–8; Oct–Easter, Tue–Sun 10–5.*
Collection of silver plate.

ASHMOLEAN MUSEUM
Beaumont Street
Oxford, Oxon
Tel: (0865) 512651
*Open Mon–Sat 10–4, Sun 2–4; closed Dec
24, 25, 26, Jan 1, Good Fri–Easter Sun, Mon
and Tue after first Sun after Sep 2.*
*Outstanding collection of Huguenot silver,
including work by Paul de Lamerie.*

LUTON HOO
Luton, Beds
Tel: (0582) 22955
*Open Apr–Oct, Mon, Wed, Thur, Sat; Good
Fri 11–5.45, Sun 2–5.45.*
Fine quality silver-gilt.

THOMAS-STANFORD MUSEUM
Preston Manor
Preston Park
Brighton, E Sussex
Tel: (0273) 552101
*Open Wed–Sat 10–5, Sun 2–5; closed Mon,
Tue, Dec 25, 26, Good Fri.*
*Outstanding collection, including English,
Portuguese and Scandinavian work; Russian
silver niello snuff boxes.*

WOBURN ABBEY
Woburn, Beds
Tel: (052 525) 666
*Open daily Feb–Nov; Feb 1–Easter, Nov
1–30, 1–4.45; Good Fri–Oct 31 11–5.45,
Sun 11–6.15.*
Fine 18th c. silver.

SOUTHWEST ENGLAND AND WALES

BERKELEY CASTLE
Nr Bristol, Glos
Tel: (0453) 810332
*Open Apr, Tue, Sun 2–5; May–Aug,
Tue–Sat 11–5, Sun 2–5; Sep, Tue–Sun
2–5; Oct, Sun only 2–4.30; Bank Hol Mons
11–5.*
World-famous Berkeley silver.

*Above: Silver tea kettle by John Elston of
Exeter, assayed in 1713, courtesy of the Royal
Albert Memorial Museum.*

CITY MUSEUM AND ART GALLERY
Brunswick Road
Gloucester, Glos
Tel: (0452) 24131
Open Mon–Sat 10–5; Suns in Aug 2–5.

English silver from all periods.

CITY MUSEUM AND ART GALLERY
Drake Circus
Plymouth, Devon
Tel: (9752) 68000, ext 4378
Open Mon–Sat 10–6.

*Small collection of fine silver including the
Drake Cup and the Eddystone Salt.*

GUILDHALL
High Street
Exeter, Devon
Tel: Not Available
*Open Mon–Sat 10–5.30, subject to civic
functions.*

City regalia and silver.

HOLBURNE OF MENSTRIE MUSEUM
Great Pulteney Street
Bath, Avon
Tel: (0225) 66669
Open Mon–Sat 11–5, Sun 2.30–6

Fine silver in elegant 18th c. building.

NATIONAL MUSEUM OF WALES
Cathays Park
Cardiff, S Glamorgan, Wales
Tel: (0222) 397951–9
*Open Mon–Sat 10–5, Sun 2.30–5; closed
Dec 24, 25, 26, Jan 1, Good Fri.*

*Fine silver from the Jackson collection,
including an impressive table centrepiece by
Paul Storr; church plate and silver-gilt.*

*FOR MAP OF THE BRITISH ISLES,
SEE PAGE 7.*

ROYAL ALBERT MEMORIAL MUSEUM AND ART GALLERY
Queen Street
Exeter, Devon
Tel: (0392) 56724
Open Tue–Sat 10–5.15.

Collections of Exeter silver.

MIDLANDS AND EAST ANGLIA

ASSAY OFFICE
Birmingham, W Midlands
Tel: (021) 236 6951
Open by appointment only

*18th and 19th c. silverware made in
Birmingham.*

HERBERT ART GALLERY AND MUSEUM
Jordan Well
Coventry, W Midlands
Tel: (0203) 25555, ext 2662
*Open Mon–Sat 10–6, Sun 2–5; closed Good
Fri and Xmas period*

Frederick R. Poke collection of fine silver.

ICKWORTH
Nr Bury St Edmunds
Suffolk
Tel: (028 488) 270
*Open Apr–end Oct, Tue, Wed, Thur, Sat,
Sun, Bank Hol Mons 2–6.*

Magnificent silver collection.

LINCOLN CATHEDRAL TREASURY
Lincon, Lincs
Tel: (0522) 30320
Open Mon–Sat 2.30–4.30.

Gold and silver plate.

NORWICH CASTLE MUSEUM
Norwich, Norfolk
Tel: (0603) 611277
Open Mon–Sat 10–5, Sun 2–5.

Local silver.

NOTTINGHAM CASTLE MUSEUM
Nottingham, Notts
Tel: (0602) 411881
*Open daily Apr–Sep, 10–5.45; Oct–Mar
10–4.45.*

Fine collection of silver.

WESTON PARK
Nr Shifnal, Shropshire
Tel: (095 276) 207/385
*Open Apr, May, Sep, Sat, Sun 10–5; June,
July, Aug, Tue, Wed, Thur, Sat, Sun, Bank
Hols 10–5; closed Oct–Mar.*

Some fine 17th c. silver.

NORTH OF ENGLAND AND SCOTLAND

CANNON HALL ART GALLERY AND MUSEUM
Barnsley, S Yorkshire
Tel: (0226) 790270
*Open Mon–Sat 10.30–5, Sun 2.30–5; closed
Dec 25, 26, 27, Good Fri.*

*18th c. country house museum with silver
displayed in period rooms.*

CLIFTON PARK MUSEUM
Clifton Park
Rotherham, S Yorkshire
Tel: (0709) 2121, ext 3569/3519
*Open Apr–Sep, Mon–Thur, Sat 10–6, Sun
2.30–5; Oct–Mar, Mon–Thur, Sat 10–5,
Sun 2.30–4.30; closed Fri.*

Display of church silver.

SHEFFIELD CITY MUSEUM
Weston Park
Sheffield, S Yorkshire
Tel: (0742) 27226
*Open June, July, Aug, Mon–Sat 10–8, Sun
11–8; Sep–May, Mon–Sat 10–5, Sun 11–5;
closed Dec 24, 25, 26.*

*Vast collection of local plate and gallery of
cutlery.*

TEMPLE NEWSAM
Nr Leeds, W Yorkshire
Tel: (0532) 647321/641358
*Open Tue–Sun, Bank Hols 10.30–6.15 (or
dusk if earlier); Wed from May 1–Sep 30,
open until 8.30.*

17th and 18th c. English silver.

WAKEFIELD MUSEUM
Wood Street
Wakefield, W Yorkshire
Tel: (0924) 70211, ext 7190
*Open Mon–Sat 12.30–5.30, Sun 2.30–5.30;
closed public hols.*

Displays of silver.

WILBERFORCE HOUSE AND
GEORGIAN HOUSES
23–25 High Street
Hull, Humberside
Tel: (0482) 223111, ext 2737
Open Mon–Sat 10–5, Sun 2.30–4.30.

*17th and 18th c. merchants' houses with large
silver collections.*

HUNTLEY HOUSE
142 Canongate
Edinburgh, Scotland
Tel: (031) 225 1131
Open Mon–Sat 10–5 (10–6 June–Sep)

Important collection of Edinburgh silver.

MERSEYSIDE COUNTY MUSEUMS
Liverpool, Merseyside
Tel: (051) 207 0001
*Open Mon–Sat 10–5, Sun 2–5; closed Dec
24, 25, 26, Jan 1, Good Fri.*

Fine collection of English silver.

SUNDERLAND MUSEUM AND ART
GALLERY
Borough Road
Sunderland, Tyne & Wear
Tel: (0783) 41235
*Open Mon–Fri 9.30–6, Sat 9.30–4, Sun
2–5; Easter, Spring, Summer Bank Hols
10–5.*

*Mid-16th to mid-19th c. English silver, plus
local church silver.*

*Above: Pair of castors, made by Alice Sheene,
London 1703; cream jug (left) by George
Smith, London 1722; cream jug (right) maker
unknown, London 1771; and two-handled cup
(centre) by John Langlands, Newcastle 1757,
courtesy of the Sunderland Museum, Tyne
and Wear Council Museums.*

NORTHERN IRELAND

COMBINED IRISH CAVALRY
REGIMENTS MUSEUM
Carrickfergus Castle
Carrickfergus
Co Antrim, N Ireland
Tel: (023 83) 62273
Open weekdays 10–1, 2–6; winter closes at 4.

Napoleonic silver and trophies.

STAMPS

LONDON

BRUCE CASTLE MUSEUM
Lordship Lane
London N17
Tel: (01) 808 8772
*Open Mon–Fri, (ex Wed) 10–5, Sat
10–12.30, 1.30–5; closed Wed, Sun.*

Postal history.

NATIONAL POSTAL MUSEUM
King Edward Building
King Edward Street
London EC1
Tel: (01) 432 3851
Open Mon–Thur 10–4.30, Fri 10–4.

*British postage stamps and world collection
since 1878 plus philatelic archives of De La
Rue and Company, 1855–1965.*

SOUTHWEST ENGLAND AND
WALES

BATH POSTAL MUSEUM
51 Great Pulteney Street
Bath, Avon
Tel: (0225) 63073

*Well-documented postal history with
reproduction travelling post office of 1870's.
1870's.*

ANTIQUE DEALERS AND COLLECTORS SERVICE
Freepost
Andover, Hants SP10 3BR
Tel: Not Available
Computerized contact service, open to both dealers and private collectors, £2.00 enrolment fee, £4.00 annual subscription.

ASSOCIATION OF BRITISH CRAFTSMEN
c/o Gerry Richardson
57 Coombe Bridge Avenue
Stoke Bishop, Bristol
Tel: Not Available
Full membership by invitation only, open to craftsmen and women with high level of skill and sound design experience, rather than formal qualifications.

ASSOCIATION OF BRITISH LAUNDERERS AND CLEANERS LTD
Lancaster Gate House
319 Pinner Road
Harrow, Middx
Tel: (01) 863 7755
Will recommend specialist cleaners.

ASSOCIATION OF BRITISH PEWTER CRAFTSMEN
c/o P.W. Adams
Heathcote House
136 Hagley Road
Edgbaston, Birmingham
Tel: Not Available
Professionals only, with fee based on amount of pewter used every year.

ASSOCIATION OF MASTER UPHOLSTERERS
Dormar House, Mitre Bridge
Scrubs Lane
London NW10 6QX
Tel: (01) 205 0465
Will investigate complaints of any work undertaken by a member.

THE BRITISH ANTIQUE DEALERS ASSOCIATION LTD (BADA)
20 Rutland Gate
London SW7 1BD
Tel: (01) 589 4128/2102
See page 8

BRITISH DOLL ARTISTS ASSOCIATION
c/o June Gale
49 Cromwell Road
Beckenham, Kent
Tel: Not Available
Membership open to professionals only.

BRITISH HOROLOGICAL INSTITUTE
Upton Hall
Upton, Newark, Notts
Tel: (0636) 813795

THE CARPET CLEANERS ASSOCIATION
97 Knighton Fields Road West
Leicester LE2 6LH
Tel: (0533) 836065
Authority on all aspects of carpet cleaning and maintenance.

CONSERVATION BUREAU
Conservation Officer
Scottish Development Agency
102 Telford Road
Edinburgh EH4 2NP
Tel: (031) 343 1911/6
Hold lists of conservation specialists in Scotland.

COTSWOLD ANTIQUE DEALER'S ASSOCIATION
c/o The Secretary
High Street
Blockley, Glos
Tel: (0386) 700280

THE CRAFTS COUNCIL CONSERVATION SECTION
12 Waterloo Place
London SW1
Tel: (01) 930 4811
Hold lists of conservation specialists all over England.

THE EMBROIDER'S GUILD
c/o Ann Joyce
Apt 41A, Hampton Court Palace
East Molesey, Surrey
Tel: (01) 943 1229
Open to professionals and amateurs.

GUILD OF GLASS ENGRAVERS
c/o Margaret Methven
19 Portland Place
London W1
Tel: (01) 580 6952
Open to professionals and amateurs.

THE GUILD OF MASTER CRAFTSMEN LTD
170 High Street
Lewes, East Sussex BN7 1YE
Tel: (079 16) 77374
Membership open to professionals only.

GUILD OF WOODWORKERS
P.O. Box 35
Hemel Hempstead HP1 1EE, Herts
Tel: Not Available
Open to professionals and amateurs.

THE HOME MINIATURIST ASSOCIATION
c/o Mary Churchill
Foxwarren, 18 Calvert Road
Dorking, Surrey
Tel: (0306) 81673
Open to collectors's of doll's house furniture.

LONDON AND PROVINCIAL ANTIQUE DEALERS ASSOCIATION (LAPADA)
112 Brompton Road
London SW3 1JJ
Tel: (01) 584 7911
See page 8. Over 700 member dealers nationwide.

THE LOCAL ENTERPRISE DEVELOPMENT UNIT
Lamont House, Purdy's Lane
Newtown, Breda, Belfast BT8 4TB
Tel: (0232) 691031
Hold lists of conservation specialists in Northern Ireland.

MONUMENTAL BRASS SOCIETY
c/o Society of Antiquaries
Burlington House
Piccadilly
London W1V OHS
Tel: Not Available
Devoted to study, care and repair of monumental brasses with a tri-annual bulletin.

MUSICAL BOX SOCIETY OF GREAT BRITIAN
The Secretary
40 Station Approach
Hayes, Bromley, Kent
Tel: Not Available
Devoted to the study of all aspects of mechanical music.

THE QUILTERS GUILD
c/o Margaret Petit
Clarendon, 56 Wilcot Road
Pewsey, Wilts
Tel: Not Available
Open to anyone collecting, studying or making quilts.

THE SOCIETY OF ORNAMENTAL TURNERS
c/o W.A. Bourne
2 Parry Drive
Rustington, Sussex
Tel: Not Available
Membership open to amateurs only.

SOCIETY FOR PROTECTION OF ANCIENT BUILDINGS
55 Great Ormond Street
London WC1
Tel: (01) 405 2646
Publishes information on the history and care of old houses plus maintains an index of houses threatened with demolition and provides potential purchasers with relevant information.

THE WRITING EQUIPMENT SOCIETY
4 Greystones Grange Crescent
Sheffield S11 7JL
Tel: (0742) 667140
Society of collectors who publish a bi-annual journal.

LONDON

Most of the firms listed below will pack and ship goods anywhere in the world, and also provide insurance and customs advice. When considering transportation of goods, it is recommended that a few quotations are obtained.

ANGLO OVERSEAS TRANSPORT COMPANY LTD
16 New Street
London EC2
Tel: (01) 283 7121

CHARLES BARTLETT LTD
Mercantile House
All Saints Street
London N1
Tel: (01) 278 2366

BEAULIEU FREIGHT SERVICES LTD
223 Dartmouth Road
London SE26
Tel: (01) 291 1331

BLYTH HASEL LTD
65 Glasshill Street
London SE1
Tel: (01) 928 7745

BRINKS-MAT LTD
P.O. Box 251
36–41 Holywell Lane
London EC2
Tel: (01) 247 9481

CAZALY, MILLS AND COMPANY LTD
Cazaly House
Devonshire Row
Bishopsgate, London EC2
Tel: (01) 247 6993/4/5/6/7

THOMAS COOK FREIGHT LTD
70–77 Cowcross Street
London EC1
Tel: (01) 252 3011

CPS (CONTAINER & PACKING SERVICES)
Old World Shipping Company Ltd
867–869 Fulham Road
London SW6
Tel: (01) 731 4708/0658

DAVIES TURNER REMOVALS
334 Queenstown Road
Battersea, London SW8
Tel: (01) 622 4393

EMBASSY FREIGHT SERVICES LTD
207 Great Portland Street
London W1
Tel: (01) 637 2333

EUROCRAT TRANSPORT INTERNATIONAL LTD
The Clergy House
Mark Street
London EC2
Tel: (01) 739 8094/5707

EVAN COOK LTD
134 Queens Road
London SE15
Tel: (01) 639 0224

FARON LTD
68 Willow Walk
London SE1
Tel: (01) 237 6666

FEATHERSTONE TRANSPORT
274 Queenstown Road
London SW8
Tel: (01) 720 0422

C.R. FENTON AND COMPANY LTD
Beachy Road
Old Ford, London E3
Tel: (01) 985 6504
and
Maidstone House
25–27 Berners Street
London W1
Tel: (01) 637 4811

GANDER AND WHITE SHIPPING LTD
Empress Place
Lillie Road
London SW6 1TT
Tel: (01) 381 0571
or
14 Mason's Yard
Duke Street
London SW1
Tel: (01) 930 5383

GLOBE PACKING AND SHIPPING LTD
35–37 Alfred Place
Store Street
London WC1
Tel: (01) 636 5495

HEDLEYS HUMPERS
Orpheus Street
London SE5
Tel: (01) 701 6471/2/3

HERNU, PERON AND STOCKWELL LTD
Forwarding House
70–77 Cowcross Street
London EC1
Tel: Not Available

SIMON JONES SUPERFREIGHT LTD
591 King's Road
London SW6
Tel: (01) 731 4700

J. LEETE AND SON (OVERSEAS) LTD
179/181 Bermondsey Street
London SE1
Tel: (01) 407 4354

LEP PACKING LTD
Corney Road
London W4
Tel: (01) 995 1300

LOCKSON SERVICES LTD
29 Bromfield Street
London E14
Tel: (01) 515 8600

MASTERPACK
Albion House
860 Coronation Road
London NW10
Tel: (01) 961 1222
and
Robert House
6–15 Florfield Road
London E8
Tel: (01) 986 7404

MAT TRANSPORT INTERNATIONAL GROUP LTD
Arnold House
36–41 Holywell Lane
London EC2
Tel: (01) 247 6500

THOMAS MEADOWS AND COMPANY LTD
36 Grosvenor Gardens
London SW1
Tel: (01) 730 0266

STEPHEN MORRIS SHIPPING
89 Upper Street
London N1
Tel: (01) 359 3159

MULLER BATAVIER LTD
78 Broadway
Strafford, London E15
Tel: (01) 534 5555

NEALE AND WILKINSON
78 The Broadway
London E15
Tel: (01) 519 3232

VIC PEARSON AND COMPANY LTD
11–13 Macklin Street
London WC2
Tel: (01) 831 6696/6700

PENNANT SHIPPING AND FORWARDING LTD
110 Three Colt Street
London E14
Tel: (01) 987 4131/6

JOHN B. PHILLIPS
22 Hampstead Gardens
London NW11
Tel: (01) 458 6253

PITT AND SCOTT LTD
20–24 Eden Grove
London N7
Tel: (01) 607 7321

L.J. ROBERTON LTD
98–122 Green Street
London E7
Tel: (01) 552 1132

T. ROGERS AND COMPANY (PACKERS) LTD
la Broughton Street
London SW8
Tel: (01) 622 9151

SETH-SMITH BROS LTD
The Pantechnicon
Heathfield Terrace
London W4
Tel: (01) 995 1101

SMITH AND HERBERT LTD
122–124 Golden Lane
London EC1
Tel: (01) 251 1633

STANLEYS FINE ART CARRIERS
7 Webb Road
London SW11
Tel: (01) 228 7673

G. THOMPSON LTD
63 Gray's Inn Road
London WC1
Tel: (01) 405 4836

TRANSBEND TRANSPORT LTD
10 Malton Road
London W10
Tel: (01) 969 6766

TREEFLOW LTD
4 Creswick Road
London W3
Tel: (01) 992 9373/993 1978

W. WINGATE AND JOHNSTONE (FINE ART) LTD
78 Broadway
London E15
Tel: (01) 555 8123

SOUTH AND SOUTHEAST ENGLAND

AIR EXPRESS INTERNATIONAL AGENCY INC
International House
Central Trading Estate
Staines, Middx
Tel: Staines 57831

ALLTRANSPORT INTERNATIONAL GROUP LTD
FINE ART DEPT
Unitair Centre
Great South West Road
Feltham, Middx
Tel: (01) 890 1444

JAMES BOURLET AND SONS LTD
3 Space Waye
Feltham, Middx
Tel: (01) 751 1155

BRITISH ANTIQUE EXPORTERS LTD
206 London Road
Burgess Hill, W Sussex
Tel: (044 46) 45577

GEORGE COPSEY AND COMPANY LTD
Danes Road
Romford, Essex
Tel: Romford 24213

MICHAEL DAVIS SHIPPING LTD
111 Mortlake Road
Richmond, Surrey TW9 4AY
Tel: (01) 876 0434 or Freephone 2304 for quotation

EXPRESS UNITED FREIGHT LTD
90a Longbridge Road
Barking, Essex
Tel: (01) 591 5900

GILTSPUR SHIPPING LTD
Elstree Way
Boreham Wood, Herts
Tel: (01) 953 1661

HARRISON, LENNON AND HOY
147 Masons Hill
Bromley, Kent
Tel: (01) 460 8535

HOWARTH ANTIQUES
31 High Street
Wingham, Kent
Tel: (022 772) 318

KERBY SHIPPING LTD
363 Rayleigh Road
Leigh-on-Sea
Essex
Tel: (0702) 524020

LONDON AND SOUTHERN SHIPPING LTD
14 Clifton Hill
Brighton, Sussex
Tel: (0273) 202989/203151

MARTELL'S OF SUTTON LTD
71–74 Westmead Road
Sutton, Surrey
Tel: (01) 642 9551

THE OLD HOUSE (SEAFORD) LTD
15–17 High Street
Seaford, E Sussex
Tel: (0323) 892091

PICKFORDS REMOVALS LTD
400 Great Cambridge Road
Enfield, Middx
Tel: (01) 366 1211

SEMUS LEWIS CONTAINERS LTD
69–77 North Street
Portslade
Sussex
Tel: Portslade 420154

SKENE INTERNATIONAL LTD
Abbey Mill, Abbey Mill Lane
St Albans, Herts AL1 4HP
Tel: (0727) 33121

TELEFREIGHT LTD
Charterhouse Road
Godalming, Surrey
Tel: (048 68) 4897

WAKEMAN BROS
78 Brighton Road
Redhill, Surrey
Tel: Redhill 895

WOBURN ABBEY ANTIQUES CENTRE
Woburn Abbey
Woburn, Beds
Tel: (052 525) 350

T.N. WINTER
Supply Stores
Fritham
Lyndhurst, Hants
Tel: (042 127) 2353/2114

SOUTHWEST ENGLAND AND WALES

COTTERELL CONTINENTAL REMOVAL SERVICES
29 Newfoundland Street
Bristol 2, Avon
Tel: (0272) 46522

GROSVENOR GALLERIES
Wynnstay Road
Ruthin, Clwyd, Wales
Tel: (082 42) 3126

MIDLANDS AND EAST ANGLIA

BLYTH HASEL LTD
London Road
Brandon, Suffolk
Tel: (0842) 822333

INTERPATCH
High Street, Stake Ferry
Kings Lynn
Norfolk
Tel: (0366) 466

KNIGHT AND RILEY LTD
P.O. Box 11
Berry Hill, Fenton
Stoke-on-Trent, Staffs
Tel: (0782) 24724

NORTH OF ENGLAND AND SCOTLAND

DAWSONS LTD
107 Mauchline Street
Glasgow G5, Scotland
Tel: (041) 429 5341

JOCELYN SERVICE AGENCIES
161 West George Street
Glasgow G2, Scotland
Tel: (041) 248 3024

LAWRENCE AND HALL LTD
Princes Buildings
Princes Square
Harrogate, N Yorkshire
Tel: (0423) 67261

JOHN H. LUNN LTD
6 Hopetoun Crescent
Edinburgh, Lothian, Scotland
Tel: (031) 556 6666

JOHN MASON
127 High Street
Liverpool 15, Merseyside
Tel: (051) 722 3158

PINDER BRIDGE ANTIQUES
38 Keighley Road
Skipton, N Yorkshire BD23 2NB
Tel: (0756) 4617

SCOTPAC, P & O INTERNATIONAL REMOVALS
Kilsyth Road
Kirkintilloch
Glasgow G66, Scotland
Tel: (041) 776 5194

S.K. REMOVERS
54 Cecil Street
Hillhead
Glasgow G12, Scotland
Tel: (041) 221 0489

S. AND R. SMYTH (REMOVERS) LTD
94 Aigburth Road
Liverpool 17, Merseyside
Tel: (051) 727 2331

TAMESIDE ANTIQUES
85 Cavendish Street
Cavendish Mill
Ashton-U-Lyne, Gt Manchester
Tel: (061 344) 5477

TURNBULLS (REMOVERS) LTD
287 Roundhay Road
Leeds LS8, W Yorkshire
Tel: (0532) 495828

WILLIAM WHITTLE LTD
River Street
Bolton, Gt Manchester
Tel: (0204) 21965/31896

REPUBLIC OF IRELAND

BEVERLEY SMYTH AND SONS LTD
30 South Street
Dublin, Rep of Ireland
Tel: (0001) 773087/67493/64652